Modern Canadian Plays

third edition

volume one

MODERN
CANADIAN
PLAYS

third edition
volume one

edited by Jerry Wasserman

TALONBOOKS   •   VANCOUVER   •   1993

Copyright © 1993 Talon Books Ltd.

Published with assistance from the Canada Council

Talonbooks
201 - 1019 East Cordova
Vancouver, British Columbia
Canada V6A 1M8

This book was typeset in Optima by Pièce de Résistance Ltée., and printed in Canada by Hignell Printing Ltd.

Third Edition, Second Printing: January 1996

The Ecstasy of Rita Joe by George Ryga, © 1970, published by Talon Books Ltd.
Fortune and Men's Eyes by John Herbert, © 1967, published by Grove Press.
Les Belles-Soeurs by Michel Tremblay, © 1992, published by Talon Books Ltd.
Creeps by David Freeman, © 1971, published by University of Toronto Press.
Leaving Home by David French, © 1985, published by Stoddart.
1837: The Farmers' Revolt by Rick Salutin and Theatre Passe Muraille, © 1976, published by James Lorimer & Company.
Walsh by Sharon Pollock, © 1973, published by Talon Books Ltd.
The St. Nicholas Hotel, Wm Donnelly, Prop. (The Donnellys, Part Two) by James Reaney, © 1976, published in *The Donnellys* by Press Porcépic.
Jacob's Wake by Michael Cook, © 1975, published by Talon Books Ltd.
Automatic Pilot by Erika Ritter, © 1980, published by Playwrights Canada.

Canadian Cataloguing in Publication Data

> Main entry under title:
>
> Modern Canadian plays, volume I
>
>> Includes bibliographical references.
>> ISBN 0-88922-340-8 (v. 2). — ISBN 0-88922-343-2 (set)
>
>> 1. Canadian drama (English)—20th century.*
> I. Wasserman, Jerry, 1945-
> PS8315.M63 1993   C812'.5408   C93-091739-1
> PR9196.6.M63 1993

CONTENTS

PREFACE

When Talonbooks first published *Modern Canadian Plays* in 1985, the need for an afford-able collection of representative plays from the modern Canadian theatre seemed imperative to me. College and university courses in Canadian drama were proliferating, yet no suitable anthology existed to serve them or the drama surveys and Canadian Literature courses that increasingly incorporated Canadian plays. Individual playtexts were becoming too expensive for students to buy in any numbers for these courses. Moreover, no single critical or historical study existed to help define the field of modern Canadian drama which, while a relatively recent phenomenon, was nevertheless a high growth and high quality enterprise that deserved, I felt, a correspondingly high profile. I expressed the hope then that *Modern Canadian Plays* would be a useful textbook for surveys as well as specialized drama courses, and that outside the classroom it would be the book that anyone interested in an overview of Canadian drama in English would turn to for a sense of its highlights since 1967.

Eight years later I still feel the same way. For while some things have changed, the need for a text like this has not. Individual scripts have become even more expensive. And although other credible anthologies have now become available, the big difference is that no single volume of twelve or fifteen plays can any longer hope to represent modern Canadian drama, even provi-sionally. As our drama continues to flourish, both in theatres and in classrooms, a greater num-ber of plays and playwrights needs to be included. Teachers, students and the playreading pub-lic demand a more varied, extensive, and up to date sampling of the work. The lively debate over the issue of canonization during the past few years has also focused attention on the desir-ability of ensuring that any definitions or limitations of the field, such that anthologies implicitly create, be as dynamic and flexible as possible. This new version of *Modern Canadian Plays* aims to accommodate these changing needs while at the same time including plays and play-wrights that have been of obvious significance in the evolving repertoire. My final criterion is highly subjective. These are all plays that I like—a lot.

The ten plays in Volume One date from 1967 to 1980 and include most of the contents of the original *Modern Canadian Plays*. The new additions are notable: *Les Belles Soeurs* and *Leaving Home* both played key roles in the development of modern Canadian drama and remain in active production today. Anthology rights for neither play were available in 1985, and I am excited finally to be able to offer these genuine classics alongside the other plays that first brought Canadian drama to prominence. Michel Tremblay's agreement to allow *Les Belles Soeurs* to be anthologized is especially welcome. As the central figure in Quebec theatre, the Canadian playwright most celebrated internationally, and the *québécois* writer whose plays, in translation, have had the greatest impact on English-Canadian theatre, Tremblay's presence is essential. Missing from this volume are David French's *Jitters*, replaced by *Leaving Home*, and three plays from the late 1970s which have been moved to Volume Two: George F. Walker's *Zastrozzi*, David Fennario's *Balconville*, and John Gray's *Billy Bishop Goes to War*.

Volume Two covers the period 1977-1990 and reflects the continued importance of Walker, Fennario and Gray, as well as three key phenomena of that era: the emergence of a substantial body of work by a number of very fine women playwrights, perhaps most notably Judith Thompson; the development of a Native playwriting network led by Tomson Highway; and the appearance of a new international superstar from Quebec whose work has crossed over into English Canada, Robert Lepage. Hence, rounding out the volume are Sharon Pollock's *Doc*, Wendy Lill's *The Occupation of Heather Rose*, Joan MacLeod's *Toronto, Mississippi*, Sally Clark's *Moo*, Thompson's *I Am Yours*, Lepage's *Polygraph* (written with Marie Brassard), and

Highway's *Dry Lips Oughta Move to Kapuskasing.* Like the original *Modern Canadian Plays,* each volume contains a general introduction, individual introductions to each playwright and play, as well as an updated and expanded three-part Selective Bibliography of Source Material—general surveys and studies of modern Canadian drama and its backgrounds, critical and biographical material specific to each playwright, and selected reviews of each play.

I would like to re-acknowledge everyone who made *Modern Canadian Plays* possible from the beginning: my family, students, and colleagues, the writers themselves and the theatre people who keep the work alive. Special thanks to Karl Siegler and the whole gang at Talonbooks, and to Sue, Kelsey and Brodie for their love and patience. I wish to re-dedicate *Modern Canadian Plays* to the memory of two people who, in different ways, first inspired it: Susan Wood and George Ryga.

INTRODUCTION

Theatrical activity in Canada has a long and fascinating history. Canadian plays go back as far as 1606 when Marc Lescarbot wrote *Le Théâtre de Neptune en la Nouvelle-France* and staged it in Indian war canoes to honour the arrival of French dignitaries at Port Royal. Playwriting in Canada in English dates back to the eighteenth century, and in the nineteenth century Canadian playhouses sprang up in substantial numbers, though mainly to accommodate American and British touring companies. The first half of the twentieth century saw the development of a thriving amateur theatre movement and the best radio drama on the continent, as well as the emergence of a handful of playwrights of distinction. But as late as 1945 there were no Canadian professional theatre companies. As late as 1959 the foremost theatre critic in the country could write, "there is not in Canada a single person who earns a living as a playwright, or who has any practical hope of doing so."[1] Even as late as 1965 a report on "Trends in Canadian Theatre" could omit any mention of the role of Canadian plays or playwrights.[2]

The remarkable fact is that Canadian theatre as an indigenous professional institution dates only as far back as the end of World War II. And English-Canadian *drama*, in the sense of a body of dramatic work by Canadian playwrights written for performance in professional theatres, is a more recent development still. Modern drama in Quebec had its inception with Gratien Gélinas' *Tit-Coq* in 1948. For English Canada the key date was 1967: Centennial Year, the year of Expo and of the first (and last) all-Canadian Dominion Drama Festival. With due respect to Robertson Davies and James Reaney whose plays highlighted theatre in English Canada from the late 1940s through the mid-60s, 1967 was also the year that English-Canadian drama began to achieve legitimacy.

Over the course of that year amateur companies presented sixty-two Canadian plays in French and English in the Dominion Drama Festival competitions, twenty-nine of which were performed for the first time. (Not surprisingly, a play from the already more mature Quebec theatre, Robert Gurik's *Le Pendu*, took home all the major awards.)[3] More important was the success of the new plays given professional productions literally from coast to coast as part of the Centennial celebrations: Gélinas' *Yesterday the Children Were Dancing* in English translation at the Charlottetown Festival, Reaney's *Colours in the Dark* at Stratford, Ann Henry's *Lulu Street* in Winnipeg, John Coulter's *The Trial of Louis Riel* in Regina, George Ryga's *The Ecstasy of Rita Joe* in Vancouver. Right across the country audiences and critics, buoyed by a new national self-consciousness and pride, were taking note of this latest cultural phenomenon—plays, good plays, written by Canadian playwrights, performed by Canadian actors in Canadian theatres. And in New York, Toronto's John Herbert had a major hit with *Fortune and Men's Eyes*.

These events and the subsequent explosion of Canadian drama over the next decade seem in retrospect products of a particular historical moment, like the new European theatre that appeared in the 1870s, the new American theatre of the 1920s and the British theatrical renaissance of the mid-1950s. Yet all these movements were culminations of social and cultural forces that had been gathering momentum for many years. In the case of Canadian theatre the revolution of 1967 was rooted in an evolutionary process that began to take shape clearly around the time of the First World War.

I.

Inspired by the vogue of European art theatres at the turn of the century—especially the Irish Abbey Theatre which would be cited time and again as a positive model for Canadians—amateur groups such as Toronto's Arts and Letters Club Players devoted themselves to performing contemporary works from the world repertoire as an alternative to the predictable fare, commercialism and imported talent offered by the circuit theatres. (Three of the same complaints would help give rise to a second wave of Canadian alternative theatres in the early 1970s.) One thing that became clear in the midst of these first stirrings was that a genuine Canadian theatre would need its own dramatists. "There are no signs as yet upon our literary horizon of the arrival of our dramatist," a writer for *The Canadian Magazine* concluded poignantly in 1914, "but we are waiting expectantly, for we feel that he should soon come now."[4] At about the same time theatre pioneer Vincent Massey realized that "if we are to have a Canadian drama we must have a Canadian theatre in which to produce it."[5]

Under Massey's auspices both these ideals began to take form with the founding of Hart House Theatre in 1919. This was a well-equipped building as well as a company of the most talented actors, designers and directors in Toronto, dedicated to doing plays which would otherwise have gone unproduced in that city, including plays written by Canadians. Encouraged by this policy dramatists did arrive, enough to fill two modest volumes of *Canadian Plays from Hart House Theatre* by 1927. The most interesting was Merrill Denison. His Hart House successes, especially the satirical comedy "Brothers in Arms," and his 1923 published collection, *The Unheroic North*, established him as Canada's first playwright of note. Unable to make a living writing for the stage in Canada, Denison eventually moved to the United States in 1931 to write for American radio. But Hart House remained a focal point of the developing Canadian theatre for many more years.

Throughout the 1920s and into the '30s amateur theatre flourished under the umbrella of the Little Theatre movement, a burgeoning of homegrown playmaking in large and small communities on both sides of the Canada-U.S. border. Some Canadian commentators, ever on the lookout for the theatrical messiah, saw these companies as the route to deliverance "because they build the foundation for more mature creative theatres and develop an audience for the Ultimate National Canadian theatre."[6] That hazy ideal of a National Theatre (always capitalized) seemed to move a large step closer to realization with the establishment in 1932 of the Dominion Drama Festival, a nationwide competition organized by the new Governor General, Lord Bessborough, and chaired by Vincent Massey. The Festival was to consist of an annual series of regional playoffs climaxing in a final (held in a different city each year) at which various awards would be given for production and performance. Community theatres, school and university drama groups and such established amateur companies as Hart House would all be eligible, and adjudicators would provide helpful comments as well as determining the winners. The aim of the Festival was to showcase theatre in Canada and at the same time upgrade the quality of Canada's theatrical arts and crafts through competition and cross-fertilization.

During the years of its existence (1933-70, with a hiatus from 1940-46 due to the war), the DDF helped institutionalize amateur theatre in Canada. Whether it accomplished much more than that has been a matter of some debate. It certainly provided a proving ground for Canadian talent which often went on to New York, London, Hollywood, or by the 1950s to Stratford or other areas of the nascent Canadian professional theatre. Through special trophies and cash prizes the DDF also encouraged the writing and production of Canadian plays, an encouragement which proved at least statistically impressive. In 1934 the Festival organizers could come up with just nine Canadian titles for inclusion on its list of suggested plays sent out to participating groups; by 1966 the list contained 240 Canadian titles in English alone. But the quality and adventurousness of the work the Festival inspired were often questionable. Even as late as 1967, the DDF would refuse to allow Michel Tremblay's contentious *Les Belles Soeurs* to be produced as part of its all-Canadian celebrations.

An earlier indictment of the limitations of the DDF was its inability to contend with the multi-media expressionism of Herman Voaden's plays, which consistently failed to advance beyond regional competitions in the 1930s because the adjudicators did not know what to make of them.[7] Voaden was an ardent nationalist and theatrical innovator who desired a Canadian dramatic art as distinctive as the paintings of the Group of Seven. To that end he sponsored a playwriting competition in Toronto in 1929 which required that each play be set in the Canadian North and suggested that the play's subject or mood be based on the writer's favourite Canadian painting. Voaden himself combined an obsession with the Canadian landscape and such disparate theatrical influences as modern dance, Wagnerian opera and symbolist drama to create a synaesthetic form he called "symphonic expressionism" in plays with titles like *Rocks, Earth Song* and *Hill-Land*. The Play Workshop he ran from 1934 to 1936 with the aim of encouraging Canadian playwriting and an indigenous theatrical style resulted in the production of twenty-five new works as well as continued experiments in total theatre. For all his eccentric and sometimes brilliant work as playwright, producer, director and educator, Voaden probably made his greatest impact on the development of Canadian drama as a persistent lobbyist for increased government support for the theatre, leading to his election as the first president of the new Canadian Arts Council in 1945.

The Play Workshop and Hart House were not the only centres of Canadian playwriting activity. A group of women journalists organized the Playwrights' Studio Group in Toronto in 1932 and by the end of the decade they had produced more than fifty new plays, mainly society comedies. At the other end of the spectrum were the Progressive Arts Clubs in Toronto, Montreal, Winnipeg and Vancouver, leftist workers' theatre groups that created and performed agitprop and social protest plays throughout the Depression years. Meanwhile in Alberta the Banff School of the Theatre was founded in 1933, later evolving into the Banff School of Fine Arts which is still an important centre for theatre training and workshop production. Associated with Banff from the beginning was Gwen Pharis Ringwood, whose stark prairie tragedies "Still Stands the House" and *Dark Harvest* were among the strongest Canadian plays of the 1930s and '40s. (Later she would teach playwriting at Banff to George Ryga among others.) Ringwood remained a prolific and popular dramatist (in amateur circles) until her death in 1984, but her residence in northern B.C. left her out of the mainstream of the new Canadian professional theatre that grew up during the last thirty years of her life.

Probably the most significant development of the 1930s and '40s in terms of the creation of a genuine Canadian drama was the rise of radio. The CBC had been established in 1932, and in 1936 it began broadcasting radio plays for which it actually paid writers, producers, directors, actors, musicians and technicians. What came to be known as "The Golden Age" of Canadian radio began when Andrew Allan became Supervisor of Drama for CBC and producer of its weekly *Stage* series. Under Allan from 1944 to 1955 *Stage* and *Wednesday Night* created consistently bold and imaginative drama that maintained high standards of excellence while proving broadly popular—at one time only *Hockey Night in Canada* drew more listeners than *Stage*. The stable of writers and actors that Allan assembled was "far and away the most exciting repertory group that can be heard," *The New York Times* proclaimed in 1946,[8] and it became Canada's equivalent of a national professional theatre. Hundreds of original scripts by Allan's house writers such as Lister Sinclair and Len Peterson were produced for broadcast. Even though radio's golden age faded with the coming of television in the '50s, CBC radio drama still pays the bills for a lot of Canadian playwrights who wouldn't otherwise be able to afford the luxury of writing for the chronically impecunious live stage.

In spite of the varied successes of the DDF and CBC, neither amateur theatricals nor radio drama amounted to a real Canadian theatre. John Coulter, who quickly became an award-winning DDF playwright and one of the most frequently produced CBC dramatists after emigrating to Canada from Ireland in 1936, was a vocal critic of the Canadian theatre scene. In "Canadian Theatre and the Irish Exemplar," an article published in 1938, he passionately held up Dublin's Abbey Theatre as a model for Canadians, a theatre "showing the Irish to themselves . . . Irish mugs in Irish mirrors." Canadians too, he argued, could find dramatic subject matter in indigenous situations: "in prairie droughts and crop failures, in mining disasters, in the poverty of slum dwellers of city streets or country shacks" (a catalogue of the kinds of naturalistic subjects that have in fact occupied a good many Canadian plays ever since). "But if there were a great Canadian play," he concluded, "would Canadians bother to stage it? Till someday Americans or British do it and tell them not to be ashamed."[9] After a series of plays set in Ireland, Coulter took his own advice and turned to Canadian history (about which he had already written for radio), achieving his greatest success with a trilogy of stage plays about Louis Riel. First produced in 1950, *Riel* would serve as a paradigm for the history plays of James Reaney and the Theatre Passe Muraille dramatists of the 1970s: revisionist Canadian history with the rebel or underdog as hero, presented as a synthesis of documentary and myth.

Coulter was fortunate that by the time *Riel* was ready for production there was a professional company to do it: the New Play Society, founded by Dora Mavor Moore in 1946. From 1950 it also included a drama school, one of whose students would be John Herbert (who later went on to act, design and stage manage for the company). Though the New Play Society remained active until 1971, its glory years were 1946-50 when its full seasons of plays in the Royal Ontario Museum Theatre proved to many skeptics the viability of a professional Canadian stage. Its most substantial success was *Spring Thaw*, a musical revue satirizing all things topical in the Great White North, first staged in 1948 and remounted with increased popularity annually for the next twenty years. The ice was broken; Canada finally had a home-grown professional theatre.

In 1954 Toronto found itself with a second, the Crest, which soon superceded the New Play Society in importance, presenting quality theatre in continuous repertory for thirteen seasons until its demise in 1966. The major Canadian playwright associated with the Crest was Robertson Davies, whose *A Jig for the Gypsy* and *Hunting Stuart* premiered there in 1954-55. Davies had already become English Canada's foremost playwright on the amateur circuit with "Eros at Breakfast," "Overlaid" and *Fortune, My Foe* in 1948-49, satires of Canadian philistinism and the national disease, "emotional understimulation." Like the Crest itself, Davies remained a significant force in Canadian theatre until the mid-60s when his playwriting career gave way to his work as a novelist.

Aside from his playwriting, Davies' journalism made a strong contribution to the developing Canadian theatre in the 1940s and '50s. Both in his own name and under the pseudonym of Samuel Marchbanks, he raised his voice in continual protest like Voaden and Coulter against the conditions under which would-be Canadian theatre professionals had to labour—what he called in 1952 "the seedy amateurism which has afflicted the arts here for so long."[10] No wonder then that he reacted with enthusiasm to the idea of a world-class Shakespeare festival theatre in Stratford, Ontario. Davies, along with Dora Mavor Moore and Festival organizer Tom Patterson, was instrumental in arranging for the innovative British producer-director Tyrone Guthrie to head the venture, which held its first season of two plays under a tent in the summer of 1953. Guthrie imported Alec Guinness and Irene Worth to play the leads and fleshed out the rest of the company with Canadian actors, a policy that by and large became standard for Stratford. Reviewing that first season, Davies concluded that it had given Canadians "a new vision of the theatre":

This cannot help but have its effect on work everywhere in the country. For one thing, many of our best Canadian actors are working at Stratford . . . . Are these actors, who have tasted the wine of true theatre, ever again to be satisfied with the sour slops of under-rehearsed, under-dressed, under-mounted, under-paid, and frequently ill-considered and ill-financed theatre projects? . . . The Stratford Festival is an artistic bombshell, exploded just at the time when Canadian theatre is most ready for a break with the dead past and a leap into the future.[11]

There is no doubt that the Stratford Festival did have an enormous impact on theatre and the *idea* of theatre in Canada. It became an event of international importance and influence (its new non-proscenium thrust stage designed by Guthrie and Tanya Moisiewitsch made waves in theatres world-wide). Thus it raised the profile of theatre in Canada as nothing else had been able to do and served as a focus of national cultural pride. Stratford also became a training ground for many of the best actors who emerged in Canada over the next three decades, making stars of Christopher Plummer, Frances Hyland and others. Moreover, it was argued,

Stratford created a model for indigenous Canadian theatre: a non-profit organization, unconcerned with the values of New York, unashamedly using imported personnel where Canadian expertise was lacking, equally unashamedly welcoming subsidy support in return for placing its destiny—at a policy-making level—in the hands of a volunteer citizen Board of Governors, and representatives of the community in which it found itself.[12]

But Stratford did little to effect or support the development of Canadian playwriting. Writers like Herbert and Reaney would receive workshop and small-scale public performances of their plays there in the late '60s, and in 1971 a Third Stage was added, in part to produce Canadian work. But by that time Stratford was no longer an adequate model. With its huge financial operation it became in many eyes a cultural dinosaur, devouring large subsidies at the expense of the smaller theatres whose productions of Canadian plays, often on shoestring budgets, were perceived as being more central to an emerging national drama than a theatre devoted to Shakespeare. Ironically, while Stratford feasted, Canadian drama came of age in the early '70s as a kind of poor theatre nourished on just those "sour slops" that Davies had complained of in 1953.

In any case by 1956 there was good reason for the feeling that "the Canadian theatre . . . like the stock market, is bullish these days . . . ."[13] The success of Stratford and the other new professional theatres was being augmented by CBC television, which from its inception in 1952 gave starts to a number of important dramatists who would later go on to write for the stage, including George Ryga, David French and Michel Tremblay. On the horizon as well was the Canada Council, whose founding in 1957 would change the nature of theatre in Canada more than any other single development, providing a sudden massive influx of government funding for buildings, companies and individuals engaged in the arts.

The Canada Council was the most concrete manifestation of the Royal Commission on National Development in the Arts, Letters and Sciences appointed by Prime Minister St. Laurent in 1949 with Vincent Massey as chairman. Its mandate was to examine how government could contribute to the development of those areas of endeavour "which express national feeling, promote common understanding and add to the variety and richness of Canadian life."[14] The Massey Commission's Report in 1951 proved a tremendous national consciousness-raiser. It found that Canadian culture was being stifled by the omnipresence of American influences and the lack of support and facilities for artists in Canada. Its major recommendation was the formation of the Canada Council for the Encouragement of the Arts, Letters, Humanities and Social

Sciences to support Canadian culture at home and abroad. From an initial outlay of $2.6 million in arts grants in 1957, the Council's investment in individuals and groups totalled more than $60 million by 1970, a quantum leap in the funds available to fuel the engine of Canadian cultural nationalism.

Money wasn't the only catalyst for change, though. In 1958 in Winnipeg, with virtually no capital but their missionary commitment to convert a whole province to the ideal of a regional professional theatre, Tom Hendry and John Hirsch merged their amateur Theatre 77 with the Winnipeg Little Theatre to create the Manitoba Theatre Centre, with Hirsch as its first artistic director. From the start the MTC "was meant to be more than a theatre, something that could in fact become a focus for all theatrical energy and resources in one community."[15] Combining mainstage productions in Winnipeg with a touring company, children's theatre, and a school, the MTC succeeded so well in galvanizing the support and resources of its constituency that it became the basis for a new concept: a Canadian national theatre that would be decentralized and regional, like the nation itself—a professional theatre version of the Canadian mosaic. With support and encouragement from the Canada Council a network of regional theatres spread across the country: Vancouver's Playhouse and Halifax's Neptune in 1963, Edmonton's Citadel in 1965 and Regina's Globe in 1966. By 1970 Montreal, Calgary, Fredericton and Toronto also had theatres catering in principle to regional communities.

Canada, it seemed, had indeed become bullish on theatre. The building boom didn't stop with the regionals, either. To train and supply actors for the new national theatre network, the National Theatre School was opened in Montreal in 1960 with separate French and English programs. At Niagara-on-the-Lake the Shaw Festival began operation in 1962, and P.E.I.'s Charlottetown Festival was inaugurated in 1964 specializing in Canadian musical theatre. St. John's got its Arts and Culture Centre in 1967. Finally, in 1969-70 the completion of three major Centennial construction projects—Ottawa's National Arts Centre, Toronto's St. Lawrence Centre, and a new building for the MTC—rounded out a decade of extraordinary growth for the Canadian theatre.

II.

With the superstructure finally intact the question now was, where were the plays? In particular where was *the play* that might crystallize the new drama in English Canada, implanting it at the heart of the nation's cultural life the way John Osborne's *Look Back in Anger* had done in Britain and Gélinas' *Tit-Coq* in Quebec (and the way Tremblay's *Les Belles Soeurs* would do again in Quebec, in a different way, in 1968). Those plays had had in common vernacular speech, anti-establishment anger, and characters, settings and situations that were definitively of their own time and place. So too had the play that finally touched the nerve of English Canada. *The Ecstasy of Rita Joe* premiered at the Vancouver Playhouse on November 23,1967, in a landmark production that was remounted for the opening of the National Arts Centre in 1969. That year the play was also broadcast on CBC-TV and produced in a French translation by Gratien Gélinas in Montreal, as *Rita Joe* reverberated through the nation's collective consciousness. In a review of a later production, Jamie Portman recalled that "*Rita Joe* happened during Centennial year when Canadians were anxious to look at themselves. But the look that this play provided was an unsettling one. It punctured the euphoria and the smug complacency of Canada's birthday celebrations and declared unequivocally that all was not well with this country and its institutions." Its implications for Canadian playwriting were equally dramatic:

> This was an indigenous Canadian drama that surfaced and succeeded at a time
> when indigenous Canadian drama was generally considered to be an aberration. It

was a play of merit, worthy of production in any Canadian theatre. It prompted an awareness of the existence of other plays potentially worthy of production. It provided resounding evidence that it was not necessary for any Canadian theatre to rely solely on imported fare. With the arrival of *The Ecstasy of Rita Joe*, Canadian plays ceased to be a rarity in English-speaking Canada. Companies dedicated to the production of new Canadian drama sprang up, and in so doing nurtured the further growth of playwriting activity. Canada's regional theatres—some of them grudgingly—found themselves forced to take the Canadian playwright seriously for the first time.[16]

Yet the battle for credibility was not quite so easily won. Just how grudgingly the theatre establishment came to accept the Canadian playwright was vividly registered by a 1971 study that found that in the previous year, the seven major regional theatres had produced the work of a total of two Canadian dramatists, and paid them less than $5000 out of combined budgets of more than $2 million.[17] Consider the case of the once pioneering Manitoba Theatre Centre. Despite its success with Winnipeg writer Ann Henry's *Lulu Street*, more than a decade would pass before the MTC presented another new play by a local playwright. The flurry of Canadian play production in 1967 had obviously been in some respects no more than Centennial Year tokenism.

The stage history of John Herbert's *Fortune and Men's Eyes* is especially revealing of the difficulties faced by Canadian playwrights. *Fortune* had been workshopped at Stratford in 1965. But denied a full production there or anywhere else in Canada, the play opened in New York in 1967 and ran for a year off-Broadway. By the end of 1968 it had had a long run in London and become a full-scale international hit. By 1969 it was already being revived in New York. The play's impact on other Canadian dramatists was immediate and inspirational: "the ice-breaker in the channel," George Ryga called it.[18] But for all that, professional productions of *Fortune and Men's Eyes* in Canada to 1970 consisted of a week at the Vancouver Playhouse's "experimental" Stage 2 and a brief run in the MTC's Studio Theatre. There was not a mainstage production to be seen. Herbert's hometown of Toronto would have to wait until 1975 to see the play at all.

What had gone wrong? The expectations and struggles of a half-century had resulted in a Canadian theatre that by the late 1960s had already become entrenched and conservative. Rather than living up to the original promise of the regionals to create new models adapted to the distinctive needs of their communities, which surely should have meant presenting plays written about those communities from within them, the large subsidized theatres mostly tried to emulate Broadway and the West End. When artistic directors were asked about Canadian plays and playwrights, their responses were often remarkably similar:

> I don't see how a play can be Canadian.
> I don't think there are any plays that you could call strictly Canadian.
> But if you start to define what is a Canadian and what is a Canadian playwright, what do you end up with?
> What does the phrase mean?[19]

With few exceptions the regionals served up homogenized theatre: safe, commercial seasons of British and American hits plus a smattering of world classics. Moreover, it was theatre as Cultural Event, like the opera or the symphony, the kind of thing you got dressed up for.

But in the late '60s, the Age of Aquarius and the Generation Gap, many theatre artists and much of the potential audience were evolving in a different direction. The Canadian Centennial just happened to coincide with the most radical cultural upheaval of the century in the Western world. There was a sexual revolution, a musical revolution, a drug revolution; long hair, peace marches and a Summer of Love. By 1968 in Chicago, Paris and Prague the revolution would spill over into the streets. Canada wasn't immune to theses forces nor could its theatre be, no matter how stubbornly it tried to remain middle-aged and middle-class.

That the most significant Canadian plays of the decade should have appeared in 1967-68 was not coincidental. *The Ecstasy of Rita Joe, Fortune and Men's Eyes* and *Les Belles Soeurs* are plays very much of their age, marked by strong social consciousness and critical, anti-establishment perspectives. The playwrights too, by virtue of their alienation from the main-stream, were in sync with the temper of the times. Herbert and Tremblay were gay men. Ryga and Herbert were outspoken and uncompromising in their social, artistic and political views. It was characteristic of their outsider status that neither was initially allowed entry into the United States to see his own play in production; characteristic that Herbert refused the DDF's Massey Award (and its $1000 cash prize) for Best Play for *Fortune* in 1968; characteristic that the politics of Ryga's 1970 play *Captives of the Faceless Drummer* would so enrage the Board of the Vancouver Playhouse, which had commissioned it, that they would refuse it production. It was ironic but perhaps also inevitable that the two writers whose plays brought modern English-Canadian drama into existence would eventually find themselves virtually unproduced by the major Canadian theatres.

Modern Canadian drama was born out of an amalgam of the new consciousness of the age—social, political and aesthetic—with the new Canadian self-consciousness. Since the larger theatres were generally unsympathetic and unaccommodating to both these forces, an even newer Canadian theatre had to be invented, an alternate theatre. One of its prime movers in Toronto was Martin Kinch, who describes those first heady days as having little to do with nationalism:

> The real influences were Fritz Perls and Timothy Leary, Peter Brook and Jerzy Grotowski, Tom O'Horgan, Cafe La Mama, Julian Beck, Judith Malina, and the ensemble of the Living Theatre; in short, a host of European and American artists, most of them primarily dedicated to the ethic and the aesthetic of "doing your own thing." . . . It was an exciting time, a time of experiment and exploration . . . expressionism, hallucination, confrontation, and audience participation flourished. Perhaps most important, however, there existed a definite bond between the theatres and their audience; an audience that was characterized by long hair, beards, bells, and babies in the front rows of the most outrageous plays. Its concerns were the concerns of "the sixties": the breaking of sexual taboo, the problems of individual freedom, and the yearning for community.[20]

In 1969 Kinch became a co-director of Toronto's Theatre Passe Muraille, founded the previous year by Jim Garrard. As its name suggests, Passe Muraille was to be a theatre without walls: neither the traditional fourth wall between actors and audience nor necessarily even the walls of a theatre building. Garrard envisioned "a guerilla theatre": "Theatre in the subways, get a truck and do theatre in small towns, real circuses, grab people in the streets . . . . I'd like to make theatre as popular as bowling."[21] A milestone for the new alternate theatre movement was Passe Muraille's production of Rochelle Owen's *Futz* in February 1969. An American play about a man in love with a pig (!), in both style and content it established the parameters of the alternate theatre's self-conscious anti-conventionality. The sex, obscenity and nudity it featured would become almost obligatory. When the show was closed by the morality squad, and the company charged and subsequently acquitted, the new movement had its red badge of courage.

By the summer of 1970 alternate theatre in Toronto had developed to the point where it could celebrate itself with a Festival of Underground Theatre. When the smoke from the festival cleared, the emphasis of the alternates could be seen to have undergone something of a shift from sensationalism to nationalism. Central to the new emphasis were Ken Gass and his Factory Theatre Lab, and the new artistic director of Theatre Passe Muraille, Paul Thompson.

Gass, who had been helping run John Herbert's tiny Garret Theatre, set out to prove that there was no lack of Canadian playwrights; they were just waiting to be discovered and encouraged. His theatre would be both a factory and a laboratory, presenting polished new works as well as works-in-progress, fragments, staged ideas. Most importantly it would be "The Home of the Canadian Playwright." His concept paid off almost immediately with a string of notable new plays: David Freeman's *Creeps*, Herschel Hardin's *Esker Mike and His Wife, Agiluk* and George Walker's *Prince of Naples* all in 1971; most of Walker's other plays over the next dozen years; and exciting (though not necessarily enduring) work by Hrant Alianak, Larry Fineberg, Bryan Wade and Gass himself.

Paul Thompson came to Passe Muraille after working in France with Roger Planchon, whose process-oriented, political brand of theatre was in direct contrast with Thompson's experiences during a brief apprenticeship at Stratford. Rejecting the Stratford model, Thompson steered his company towards a focus on local subject matter and collective creation, involving his actors in first-hand research, improvisation and continual revision, and utilizing their particular skills as key elements in the play wherever possible. When Thompson took over Passe Muraille there was already a precedent for this kind of theatre in Toronto. George Luscombe had been involved with Joan Littlewood's Theatre Workshops in England in the mid-50s and had put together Toronto Workshop Productions in 1959 based on Littlewood's political and stylistic principles: left-wing politics and an eclectic style that integrated improvs, documentary, *commedia* and often collective scripting. In the late '60s and early '70s TWP was creating potent socio-political theatre with agitprop pieces like *Mister Bones* and *Chicago '70* on race and politics in America, and its bittersweet evocation of the Canadian Depression, *Ten Lost Years*. In 1984, the partnership of Luscombe and Toronto Workshop Productions celebrated its twenty-fifth year, still very much a going concern.

Nevertheless it was Passe Muraille under Paul Thompson's stewardship that became the most important theatre in Canada in the early '70s. Creations like *Doukhobors, The Farm Show* (first performed in a Clinton, Ontario barn), *Under the Greywacke* and *The Adventures of an Immigrant* (performed in Toronto streetcars among other venues) made often stirring theatrical poetry out of material that was sometimes mundane and always local. Docudrama with a high degree of theatricality became the Passe Muraille trademark: a small company of actors using little but their own bodies and voices to create ingenious stage metaphors. They inspired countless imitators across the country, though in less talented hands the deceptively rigorous demands of collective scripting and Passe Muraille's presentational style sometimes had unfortunate results. Among the best of their offshoots was Twenty-Fifth Street House Theatre in Saskatoon, whose *Paper Wheat* was in the finest Passe Muraille tradition, and Newfoundland's CODCO. In addition the company specialized in resurrecting, popularizing, dramatizing and often mythicizing Canadian history in collective scripts or in conjunction with a writer. *Buffalo Jump* with Carol Bolt, *1837: The Farmers' Revolt* with Rick Salutin, *Them Donnellys* with Frank MacEnany and *Far as the Eye Can See* with Rudy Wiebe were some of the best of the collaborations. Later in the decade two Passe Muraille alumni would create *Billy Bishop Goes to War*, and Linda Griffiths (with Paul Thompson) would let loose *Maggie & Pierre* upon the country. Perhaps the most exciting Canadian playwright to emerge in the 1980s, Judith Thompson, also came out of Passe Muraille with her extraordinary first play, *The Crackwalker*.

Not everything was happening in Toronto. In Vancouver, where Sidney Risk had pioneered post-war professional touring with his Everyman Theatre (1946-53), and where John Juliani's experimental Savage God project had been operating since 1966, John Gray, Larry Lillo and a group of other UBC graduates formed Tamahnous Theatre in 1971, a collective that would remain Vancouver's most original and progressive company for the next ten years. Its most enduring legacy may prove to be the special brand of small-cast musical best represented by Gray's *Billy Bishop* and Morris Panych's "post-nuclear cabaret," *Last Call!* Meanwhile the New Play Centre had come into being in 1970 dedicated to developing new scripts by local writers with production as only a secondary priority. Under the direction of Pamela Hawthorn from 1972 until 1989, the New Play Centre had a hand in most of the drama to come out of B.C., including the work of Margaret Hollingsworth, Tom Walmsley, Ted Galay, John Lazarus, Sheldon Rosen, Betty Lambert, Eric Nicol and Sherman Snukal.

Seeded by government grants from Local Initiatives Programs (LIP) and Opportunities for Youth (OFY), new companies doing indigenous theatre sprouted everywhere in 1971-72: Edmonton's Theatre 3, Calgary's Alberta Theatre Projects, Pier One in Halifax, the Mummers Troupe in St. John's. Lennoxville, Quebec even provided a kind of "alternate" festival theatre. Festival Lennoxville presented all-Canadian summer seasons of plays by the likes of Michael Cook, Herschel Hardin and Sharon Pollock from 1972 until its demise in 1982, a victim of poor demographics and Parti Québécois cultural policy.

Toronto, though, was where most of the action was, and nothing did more to cement its position at the centre of the new movement than Tarragon Theatre. Founded in 1971 by Bill Glassco, who had directed *Creeps* at the Factory Lab earlier in the year, Tarragon opened with a revised version of *Creeps* that proved even more successful than the original. The first Tarragon season ended with a new work which was to become probably the single most influential Canadian play of the 1970s, David French's *Leaving Home*. Its story of generational conflict and a singularly Canadian form of immigrant alienation (ex-Newfoundlanders spiritually adrift in Toronto) elicited strong audience identification, and its straightforward, accessible style had a broad appeal. *Leaving Home* created a vogue for domestic realism that some have argued was a debilitating counterforce to the more adventurous directions that Canadian drama seemed to be taking at the time. Tarragon soon became identified with that particular style, especially in light of Glassco's productions of subsequent plays by Freeman and French that were stylistically tame. But it wasn't really a fair reputation. Tarragon also introduced English Canada to the plays of Michel Tremblay with Glassco as director and co-translator—plays that are domestic in setting but hardly realistic in style. Moreover, from 1973-75 Tarragon produced James Reaney's Donnelly trilogy, which is about as far removed from stylistic realism or naturalism as plays can get. Unlike the great majority of companies devoted to Canadian works, Tarragon managed both to combine artistic and commercial success and to sustain it over a number of years. More than any other theatre it succeeded in bringing Canadian drama into the mainstream.

The great wave of new alternate theatres in Toronto crested in 1972 with the founding of Toronto Free Theatre by Tom Hendry, Martin Kinch and John Palmer. Subsidized by LIP grants, performances were literally free until 1974 when the impossible economics of that policy led to gradually increasing admissions. But Toronto Free's cultivation of an excellent ensemble of actors and a distinctive taste for the psychologically bizarre in plays and production remained constant until (and even after) its merger with Centrestage in 1988 to create the Canadian Stage Company. Many of its early successes were plays by its in-house triumvirate—especially Hendry and Palmer—along with Carol Bolt. George Walker and Erika Ritter were among the most noteworthy later additions to Toronto Free's playwriting corps.

Notwithstanding the dynamism of the alternate theatres, drama in Canada in the early '70s was in danger of falling victim to an insidious form of ghettoization. Canadian plays were relegated to small, low-budget theatres that lacked the financial and technical resources available to the heavily subsidized festivals and regionals. While non-Canadian works had access to lush productions, large casts and relatively highly paid actors, Canadian plays were doomed to what George Ryga called "beggars theatre."[22] Concurrently, of course, Canadian playwrights were denied the financial opportunities that might allow them to actually make a living by practicing their craft. In an attempt to remedy this situation a group of playwrights met in the summer of 1971 to consider "The Dilemma of the Playwright in Canada." What ensued was a series of strongly worded recommendations, the most contentious of which called for a 50% Canadian content quota for all theatres receiving government funding. Most artistic directors and editorialists were predictably outraged. ("If it ever happened, then critics should also get Canada Council grants for sitting through the plays," was one wit's response.[23]) Though no formal quota system was ever adopted, the controversy led to a full public airing of the situation and, more importantly, to an informal policy decision by the Canada Council to "appeal" to its client theatres to do more Canadian plays. The results were startling. By the 1972-73 season nearly 50% of the plays produced by subsidized theatres were in fact Canadian.

Among the most tangible consequences of this new policy was a return to one of the original precepts of the "regional" ideal, the commissioning of new plays by regional theatres from playwrights with local roots and interests. These arrangements proved mutually fruitful for playwrights and theatres alike, especially Sharon Pollock's work for the Vancouver Playhouse and Theatre Calgary, John Murrell and W.O. Mitchell also at Theatre Calgary, Ken Mitchell and especially Rex Deverell with Regina's Globe, and David Fennario with the Centaur in Montreal. The Blyth and Kawartha Summer Festivals, in their cultivation of Anne Chislett, proved the value of a homegrown product even in the traditionally more commercial milieu of summer theatre. In each of these cases plays written with very specific associations for local audiences made their way into theatres across the country with no lack of success. Maybe Canada had achieved its long-elusive "national theatre" after all.

Following the tremendous expansion of the Canadian theatre in the first half of the 1970s, a certain amount of retrenchment was inevitable. Tougher economic times and a general trend towards conservatism put additional strains on an endeavour that is economically marginal even under the best conditions. Theatres as widely divergent as Stratford and Twenty-Fifth Street House had to weather financial and artistic crises that threatened their survival. Some went under: Vancouver's Westcoast Actors, Edmonton's Theatre 3, Montreal's Saidye Bronfman. Robin Phillips' ambitious Grand Theatre Company in London, Ontario, couldn't survive its first season. Facing new audience expectations and a changing ideological climate, the major "alternate" theatres (the term is no longer really accurate) in Toronto and Vancouver all underwent structural reorganization and found new artistic directors.

But at the end of the decade Passe Muraille, Tarragon, Factory Lab, Toronto Free and Tamahnous were still very much in operation, still providing a springboard for Canadian plays along with the resurgent regionals and theatres like Vancouver's Arts Club that successfully occupied the middle ground. And a new generation of neo-alternates arose to take the place of those that fell by the wayside or entered the mainstream, companies like Theatre Network in Edmonton, Touchstone in Vancouver, Prairie Theatre Exchange in Winnipeg, and Toronto's Actor's Lab, Necessary Angel and Buddies in Bad Times. The Toronto International Theatre Festival in 1981 showcased Canadian plays and productions alongside some of the best theatre companies in the world, and no one had to apologize for the quality of the domestic product. The early '80s would see, too, the establishment of a series of new awards. Joining the prestigious Chalmers Award (given by the Toronto Drama Bench since 1972 for best Canadian play produced each year in Toronto) were the Governor General's Award in Drama for the best new

Canadian play in publication, and Vancouver and Toronto's equivalents to New York's Tony Awards, the Doras in Toronto (after Dora Mavor Moore) and the Jessies in Vancouver (after Jessie Richardson). More than just self-congratulations, these plaudits signified that Canadian drama and theatre were a *fait accompli*, occupying at last a prominent place in the nation's cultural profile. And the prognosis for the future seemed very good, the Canadian play even threatening to become an exportable commodity. "The next ten years," the dramaturge of New York's Public Theater predicted in 1979, "are going to be the decade of the Canadian playwright."[24]

III.

Hyperbole aside, Canadian theatre since 1967 has brought forth a substantial body of plays worthy of continued attention both as scripts to be performed and texts to be read and studied. This first volume of *Modern Canadian Plays* presents many of the highlights of modern Canadian drama up to 1980. Volume Two continues the saga through the next decade. *Rita Joe* and *Fortune and Men's Eyes* set it all in motion in 1967 and became its first true classics. *Les Belles Soeurs* revolutionized francophone theatre in Quebec, and helped establish Tremblay's work as an essential component of the English-Canadian repertoire. *Creeps* and *Leaving Home* helped launch the Factory Lab and Tarragon theatres, and defined the naturalism that characterized a good deal of Canadian theatre through the first half of the '70s, just as *1837: The Farmers' Revolt* epitomized Passe Muraille's influential collective, quasi-documentary style. The history play took new directions in the prairies with *Walsh* and in Ontario with the brilliant theatricality of the Donnelly trilogy. *Jacob's Wake* was a family play with a powerful Newfoundland accent, and *Automatic Pilot* blazed a bright comic path of urban sophistication.

The plays in these two volumes are also, in a variety of ways, representative of the primary patterns into which modern Canadian drama has shaped itself. Probably the strongest impression made by Canadian plays through the mid-1970s was of a theatre of the underdog and the outsider. This is not entirely surprising in the context of Canadian literature generally, which shows many of the same impulses. Although Margaret Atwood paid virtually no attention to plays in her thematic study of Canadian literature, *Survival* (1972), her arguments concerning the characteristic "victim-positions" of Canadian protagonists apply equally well to the drama, especially pre-1980. In *Rita Joe*, *Fortune* and *Creeps*, and nearly everything written for the stage by Fennario and Tremblay, the victimization is played out in the mode of social protest within a contemporary landscape. But even when the perspective is historical, as in *1837*, *Walsh* and the Donnelly plays, the dramatic focus is on the losers rather than the winners, the victims (or the process of victimization) rather than the victors. From *Riel* onwards there have been few exceptions to this rule.

The alienated Outsider is the central figure not just in modern Canadian plays, of course, but in modern literature as a whole, and particularly in the post-war drama. Gélinas' bastard hero Tit-Coq, the British "angry young men" and the American rebels without a cause of the 1950s are the true spiritual ancestors of Rita Joe, Fennario's workers, Tom Walmsley's outlaws and even some the playwrights themselves. (David French tells a good story in *Stage Voices* about going to his first acting class dressed like James Dean.) New dramatic movements seem in fact to thrive on the outsider status of their plays' characters: witness Ibsen's artists and social rebels and O'Neill's early protagonists. Perhaps the dramatist's own position in the vanguard of a new movement, himself alienated from the establishment and challenging its order, demands his sympathy for the outsider.

In that regard it is useful to consider the autobiographical nature of much of the new Canadian drama. Writing about *Fortune and Men's Eyes* in 1968, Nathan Cohen attributed the play's success to its origins in Herbert's own experience, and he noted critically "how seldom the [Canadian playwright] bases himself on his own involvements and observations, or how rarely he takes for his point of artistic departure the social tensions of life in his own back-yard."[25] But all that changed very quickly. Many of the best plays of the era were autobiographi-cally based (*Creeps, Lulu Street, Leaving Home*) or at least drawn from immediate personal observation (*Rita Joe, Les Belles Soeurs*). A favourite theme was the experience of coming of age (French's *Of the Fields, Lately* and *Leaving Home*, Tom Hendry's *Fifteen Miles of Broken Glass*) with its attendant disillusionment and revisionism. Considering that even the history plays shared those attitudes, and that the Centennial experience was something like a national coming of age, it is possible to see the Canadian drama of this period as embodying a kind of collective national autobiography. (In James Reaney's *Colours in the Dark* the autobiographical impulse surges beyond the personal and national into the archetypal) In the best dramatic tradition the playwrights insisted on holding up a mirror before their audiences so that Canadians might see themselves, no matter how flawed or unflattering the reflection.

But what were the images being reflected? Frequently they were Indians or Newfound-landers, criminals, the handicapped or homosexuals; the socially marginal and disenfranchised took centre stage. Outsiders became insiders as the revolutionary impulses of the late '60s and early '70s counterculture inverted the traditional aesthetic order. Cultural militancy in the Third World and among Black Americans also helped to awaken a new awareness of and among Canadian minorities. All this worked to accelerate a process noted by Northrop Frye in his analysis of the "garrison mentality" in Canadian literature:

> As the centre of Canadian life moves from the fortress to the metropolis, the garrison mentality changes correspondingly. It begins as an expression of the moral values generally accepted in the group as a whole, and then, as society gets more compli-cated and more in control of its environment, it becomes more of a revolutionary garrison within a metropolitan society . . . . It changes from a defence to an attack on what society accepts as conventional standards . . . .[26]

The courtroom (and even the city itself) from which Rita Joe can't escape, the prison in *Fortune and Men's Eyes*, the kitchen in *Les Belles Soeurs*, the sheltered workshop in *Creeps*, the shipping room in Fennario's *On the Job*—these are all more than just physical settings. They are metaphors of a repressive System which paradoxically keeps its outsiders shut up inside, creating garrisons with revolutionary potential. As Canadian history and history plays tell us, however, from 1837 to Riel to the FLQ, Canadian revolutions don't succeed. At best all these plays celebrate moral victories, preservations of integrity, possibilities of escape.

Perhaps because the Canadian mosaic and our domestic geopolitics make nearly *everyone* here feel like something of an outsider, the family looms large in Canadian drama. Those who don't have one (Tit-Coq, *Lulu Street*'s Elly) idealize it as the locus of security and identity. At its best, as in the Donnelly plays, it really is that and more—the source of all strength. The family provides the ultimate garrison for the Donnellys and others who feel themselves surrounded by hostility or stranded in an alien environment, like the elder Mercers in David French's plays. But for young Ben Mercer who has set his sights wider, the family is a trap, stifling and devouring where it purports to nourish and protect. Modern drama from Strindberg through O'Neill to Miller and Pinter has more often than not portrayed the family as a battleground on which primal wars are fought, and so it is too in Canadian plays as different as *Leaving Home*, *Jacob's Wake*, Pollock's *Blood Relations*, Margaret Hollingsworth's *War Baby*, Timothy Findley's *Can You See Me Yet?* and Tremblay's *Forever Yours, Marie-Lou*. In the latter play Carmen, like Ben Mercer, fights to become a creative outsider, to escape the terrible grip of what her mother calls with bitter irony "the family cell": the garrison become prison. Ironically, such plays present the family as a microcosm of the larger society of which it is a part. The convicts in *Fortune and Men's Eyes* construct a surrogate family every bit as corrupt and self-destructive as those they grew up in on the outside.

Surrogate families don't have to be destructive. The "family" of theatre people in French's *Jitters* manages, in spite of its tensions, to achieve a delicate equilibrium that gets them through the toughest times. The same is true of the tenement-dwellers in Fennario's *Balconville*. A different kind of surrogate family is constituted in plays like Sheldon Rosen's *Ned and Jack* and Tremblay's *Hosanna* which investigate the way relationships between people of the same sex can grow into a mutuality like the family at its best (or degenerate into a parody of family role-playing at its very worst). With the decline of the nuclear family and the advent of gay liberation and the women's movement has come a testing of new sexual attitudes and domestic arrangements. This has found popular expression in comedies of manners like *Automatic Pilot*, Anne Chislett's *The Tomorrow Box* and Sherman Snukal's *Talking Dirty*, and in the reconstituted families of 1980s plays like Joan MacLeod's *Toronto, Mississippi*, Sally Clark's *Moo* and Tomson Highway's *The Rez Sisters*.

Because the rise of Canadian drama coincided with a surge of nationalism and national self-awareness, the history play has had a prominent place in the developing repertoire. Canadian plays about non-Canadian history have been relatively rare, but perhaps not surprisingly they have tended to concern themselves almost exclusively with revolutionaries. (Carol Bolt's *Red Emma*, Ryga's *Paracelsus*, Michael Cook's *The Gayden Chronicles* and Ken Mitchell's *The Great Cultural Revolution* are typical examples.) Plays about Canadian history have a slightly more complex range of concerns. For a time their primary purpose seemed to be to make Canadians aware that they *had* a history and that it was actually interesting (both assumptions about which many Canadians remain skeptical). Beyond that, there were a number of different messages: that Canadian history hadn't always happened the way it was taught in school, if it had been taught at all; that it had sometimes been shameful; and that it was full of genuine Canadian heroes, some of them relatively unknown and most extremely unlikely.

The harshest dramatic treatments have been reserved for various acts of genocide committed against native Indians in Canada—*Walsh*, Cook's *On the Rim of the Curve*, Herschel Hardin's *The Great Wave of Civilization*, Wendy Lill's *Sisters*—and similar expressions of racism (Pollock's *The Komagata Maru Incident*). In a lighter vein politicians have made ripe pickings for critical portraits, Mackenzie King in particular (in Reaney's *The Dismissal* and Alan Stratton's *Rexy!*). But on the whole, Canadian playwrights have been more interested in accentuating the historically positive. Coulter and Reaney resurrect Louis Riel and the Black Donnellys, polish up their badly tarnished reputations and turn them from villains into heroes. William Lyon Mackenzie in *1837*, Dr. Norman Bethune in Rod Langley's *Bethune* and Ken Mitchell's *Gone the Burning Sun*, and Billy Bishop are all reintroduced as legitimate Canadian heroes, even if contentious men. *1837* also celebrates a *collective* hero—it is after all *The Farmers' Revolt*—using agitprop techniques borrowed from the political theatre of the 1930s. The collective struggles of Saskatchewan farmers (*Paper Wheat*), unemployed workers (Bolt's *Buffalo Jump*) and coal miners (Rex Deverell's *Black Powder*) have been chronicled and lionized in similar ways.

"Chronicled" is not really the right word. Canadian history plays often take the form of "docudrama," combining the truthfulness of documentary with the imaginative freedom of drama. But what proportions of fact and fiction are necessary to ensure that Canadian history turns out, in the eyes of the playwright, satisfactorily? How does one mitigate the fact that the good guys have rarely won? In a comment on his own pseudo-history play, *The Boy Bishop*, Ken Gass proposes that "the only important thing about history is that it needs to be transcended. We should lie about our history or make one up if we don't like the one we have."[27] Other playwrights prefer less radical terminology. In his preface to *The Crime of Louis Riel*, John Coulter refers to his Riel as a "legendary hero." Both Rick Salutin (referring to his *Les Canadiens*) and Carol Bolt use the term "myth" to describe their plays. "Myth is more appealing than fact," says Bolt. "It postulates that heroism is possible, that people can be noble and effective and change things."[28]

But is there an identifiable *Canadian* myth that runs through the plays in this collection, a "distinctive mythology which reflects . . . who we are and how we got that way"?[29] If there is, maybe it is the awareness implicit in many of them that, though winning might be nice, the quality of experience is more important than the final score. This is true in plays as different as *Fortune and Men's Eyes, Les Belles Soeurs* and *Automatic Pilot*; as varied as *Zastrozzi, Billy Bishop Goes to War* and *Doc*. Victory is always somehow tainted, if not pyrrhic; a cause for melancholy as much as celebration. "You're a typical Canadian, / You're modesty itself," Lady St. Helier sings to Billy Bishop. That too is part of the Canadian myth. But is it true? What is undoubtedly true, as these plays confirm, is that theatre at its best always brings us closer to ourselves.

NOTES

[1]Nathan Cohen, "Theatre Today: English Canada," *Tamarack Review*, 13 (Autumn 1959), 28.

[2]Thomas B. Hendry, "Trends in Canadian Theatre," *Tulane Drama Review*, 10 (Fall 1965), 62-70. That same year Michael Tait concluded his survey of "the grey wastes of Canadian drama" from 1920-60 by noting "perhaps the most depressing feature of theatre in Canada: the lack of any vital and continuing relationship between theatrical activity and the work of the Canadian playwright." See "Drama and Theatre," *Literary History of Canada*, ed. Carl F. Klinck, 2nd ed. (Toronto: Univ. of Toronto Press, 1976), II, 159, 167.

[3]Betty Lee, *Love and Whiskey: The Story of the Dominion Drama Festival* (Toronto: McClelland and Stewart, 1973), 296.

[4]Fred Jacobs, "Waiting for a Dramatist," *The Canadian Magazine*, 43 (June 1914), 146.

[5]Vincent Massey, "The Prospects of a Canadian Drama," *Queen's Quarterly*, 30 (October 1922), 200.

[6]Rupert Caplan, "The Ultimate National Theatre," *Canadian Forum*, 9 (January 1929), 143-44.

[7]See Anton Wagner, "The Developing Mosaic: English Canadian Drama to Mid-Century," in *Canada's Lost Plays, Volume Three*, ed. Anton Wagner (Toronto: CTR Productions, 1980), 19-21.

[8]Jack Gould, "Canada Shows Us How," *New York Times*, 1 Sept. 1946, Sec. II, 7.

[9]John Coulter in *Stage Voices*, ed. Geraldine Anthony (Toronto: Doubleday, 1978), 19-20.

[10]Robertson Davis, *The Well-Tempered Critic: One Man's View of Theatre and Letters in Canada*, ed. Judith Skelton Grant (Toronto: McClelland and Stewart, 1981), 66.

[11]Davies, 74.

[12]Hendry, "Trends in Canadian Theatre," 64-65.

[13]Mavor Moore, "A Theatre for Canada," *University of Toronto Quarterly*, 26 (October 1956), 2.

[14]Quoted in Don Rubin, "Creeping Toward a Culture: The Theatre in English Canada Since 1945," *Canadian Theatre Review*, 1 (Winter 1974), 8.

[15]Tom Hendry, "MTC: A View from the Beginning," *Canadian Theatre Review*, 4 (Fall 1974), 16.

[16]Jamie Portman, "*Ecstasy of Rita Joe* Still Manages to Shock and Scourge," *Vancouver Province*, 12 April 1976, 10. Cf. Neil Carson, "Towards a Popular Theatre in English Canada," *Canadian Literature*, 85 (Summer 1980), 64-65.

[17]David Gustafson, "Let's Really Hear It for Canadian Theatre," *Maclean's*, 84 (October 1971), 84.

[18]George Ryga, "Contemporary Theatre and Its Language," *Canadian Theatre Review*, 14 (Spring 1977), 8.

[19]Quoted verbatim from a series of interviews with artistic directors of regional theatres in *The Stage in Canada*: Edward Gilbert (MTC), 3 (May 1967), 14; Robert Glenn (Citadel), 3 (June 1967), 7; Joy Coghill (Playhouse), 3 (Sept. 1967), 10; Kurt Reis (MTC), 5 (Nov. 1969), 13.

[20]Martin Kinch, "The Canadian Theatre: In for the Long Haul," *This Magazine*, 10 (Nov.-Dec. 1976), 4-5.

[21]Quoted in Robert Wallace, "Growing Pains: Toronto Theatre in the 1970s," *Canadian Literature*, 85 (Summer 1980), 77.

[22]George Ryga, "Theatre in Canada: A Viewpoint on Its Development and Future," *Canadian Theatre Review*, 1 (Winter 1974), 30.

[23]Bill Thomas in the *Victoria Colonist*, quoted in "Playwrights," *The Stage in Canada*, 6 (January 1972), 17.

[24]John Bentley Mays, "Taking It on the Road," *Maclean's*, 92 (4 June 1979), 60.

[25]Nathan Cohen, "John Herbert," in *Canadian Writing Today*, ed. Mordecai Richler (Harmondsworth: Penguin, 1970), 212.

[26]Northrop Frye, "Conclusion," *Literary History of Canada*, II, 346.

[27]"Postscript: Interview with Ken Gass," *Canadian Theatre Review*, 12 (Fall 1976), 123.

[28]*Playwrights in Profile: Carol Bolt* (Toronto: Playwrights Co-op, 1976), 8.

[29]George Ryga, "The Need for a Mythology," *Canadian Theatre Review*, 16 (Fall 1977), 5.

GEORGE RYGA (1932-1987)

"Playwright George Ryga Thursday night peeled a cicatrice off Canadian society and showed the bleeding flesh beneath." Jack Richards, reviewing the first performance of *The Ecstasy of Rita Joe* for the *Vancouver Sun* in 1967, identified an essential quality of Ryga's work that proved to be one of his major strengths and most serious difficulties. With stubborn integrity and singlemindedness Ryga made a career of tearing at sensitive wounds, stirring up controversy and sometimes making himself unpopular in the process. Outspoken, abrasive and always fiercely committed to social justice and the defense of human dignity, he created a body of dramatic work that is among the most impressive and least well known in Canada.

Ryga gave warning of his uncompromising political views soon after leaving the Ukrainian community in northern Alberta where he had grown up. At the Banff School of Arts in 1950 he lost a scholarship for writing a poem critical of the Korean War. Four years later he was forced to resign his job as a radio producer in Edmonton because of his public protests against the Rosenberg trial. When in 1962 after a decade of writing poetry and fiction Ryga turned his hand to drama, the imprint of his convictions was immediately clear.

His first play, *Indian*, written for television, is an austere, powerful work that announced a remarkable dramatic talent. The nameless Indian of the title is initially seen as a stereotype but gradually reveals a desperate humanity in whose light his white employer and the complacent government agent (a recurrent character type in Ryga's work) seem bloodless ciphers. The abrupt plunges into memory that punctuate the naturalism of *Indian* look forward to the more sophisticated stylization of Ryga's stage plays, just as the play's tone of anger combined with deep sadness would mark the best of Ryga's work to come.

In 1963 Ryga settled permanently in Summerland, B.C. After publishing two novels about the harshness of prairie life, *Hungry Hills* (1963) and *Ballad of a Stonepicker* (1966), he was commissioned to write a Centennial play for the Vancouver Playhouse. *The Ecstasy of Rita Joe* was the result. He followed it with a huge box office hit, *Grass and Wild Strawberries* (1969), a multi-media exploration of the conflict between '60s youth culture and the adult establishment. When his third commission from the Playhouse coincided with the October Crisis in 1970, Ryga reshaped his work-in-progress into a confrontation between a government mandarin and the terrorist holding him hostage. Upset by the politics of the script, the theatre's board refused to produce it. Months of bitter public controversy ensued and for a short time *Captives of the Faceless Drummer* became a *cause célèbre*. But long after the play was forgotten the bitterness lingered and Ryga became increasingly alienated from the mainstream of Canadian theatre.

Ryga's subsequent plays were produced in the relative obscurity of Banff (*Sunrise on Sarah* and *Portrait of Angelica*), Edmonton's Theatre Network (*Seven Hours to Sundown*), Western Canada Theatre Company in Kamloops (*Ploughmen of the Glacier*), Kam Theatre Lab of North Bay, Ontario (the excellent *Letter to My Son*), and Vancouver's Firehall (*One More for the Road*). Few of the larger theatres have ever done any of his work except *Rita Joe*. One of his most interesting and ambitious plays, *Paracelsus*, first published in 1974, didn't receive a professional production until 1986. Ryga wrote two more novels, *Night Desk* (1976) and *In the Shadow of the Vulture* (1985), and a book about his trip to China, *Beyond the Crimson Morning* (1979). Two volumes of his uncollected writings were published after his death in 1987. *The Athabasca Ryga* (1990) and *Summerland* (1992) include stories, essays, TV and radio plays, and his last poem.

Ryga's work remains extremely popular in Europe where it is regularly produced on radio and stage, winning awards and setting attendance records. This may be in part attributable to the European sensibility in his writing, especially *The Ecstasy of Rita Joe*. The quality of Rita's suffering, her passivity and sense of spiritual homelessness are evocative of Dostoevsky (whom Ryga claimed to have read in full). The nightmarishness of Rita's experience, her feelings of entrapment and unaccountable guilt have roots that go back through Kafka to early expressionist drama—to Büchner's *Woyzeck* and, in America, O'Neill's *The Hairy Ape*. Rita takes her place in that tradition: the outsider perceived as a sort of freak, struggling to preserve her integrity in the face of a system socially and politically designed to frustrate her every attempt to make sense of her life; struggling to avoid internalizing the guilt imposed by a world that grows increasingly monstrous until it completes its inevitable process of destruction.

Central to Rita's torment is the cultural and epistemological schism between whites and Indians, represented in its extreme form by the contrast between the mechanical, life-denying pseudo-rationalism of the Magistrate and the humane, intuitive impressionism of David Joe. These ways of seeing and understanding the world are so fundamentally different that the results of their clashes are sometimes comical. When Rita claims to have seen God in the sky she's told to call the Air Force. When Jaimie Paul sees a TV commercial that shows a knife "cutting up good shoes like they were potatoes," he reacts with comic bewilderment (edged with the bitter irony that he and Rita have nothing to eat). But Rita's inability to assimilate is also the real crime of which the white Witnesses along with the Teacher and Priest, the Magistrate and Mr. Homer take turns accusing her. In court, while the Magistrate rambles on about "the process of legal argument," Rita asks him if she can bum a cigarette; in the stage direction the Policeman "smiles and exits"—he rests his case. Later the Magistrate tells Rita, "the obstacles to your life are here . . . in your thoughts . . . possibly even in your culture," and he suggests that she fix her hair, tame her accent, "perhaps even change your name."

But Rita won't be helped and can't be saved. She certainly gets no help from the hollow paternalism of the Priest, the Magistrate or the ironically named Mr. Homer. Nor can Rita be aided by her own father. For all the sympathy Ryga invests in him, David Joe is impotent to save his people, just as Jaimie Paul says. And when he comes to take Rita home to the reserve from the city, she refuses to go. Rita is trapped. The rural past, though pastoral in her memory, she knows is a dead-end. The urban present holds only degradation and the promise of an early death. And what about the future? The circular ramp that comprises the set traces Rita's futile journey through the play; the shadowy Murderers who appear and reappear symbolize her doom, immanent from the start; the Brechtian Singer who sings of the fate of Rita and Jaimie forecloses any hope of salvation. The one rich fantasy she and Jaimie indulge turns quickly sour: their dream of having children in the city collides with the ugly fact that Clara Hill has had to give hers away. The scene that begins with the implied promise of lovemaking in Jaimie's room ends in frustration, disgust and despair.

Is Rita Joe tragic? Does she retain her selfhood with a stubborn persistence that transforms her death from a sordid ritual of rape and murder into the "ecstasy" of a martyr? Or is she a passive victim doomed by birth, culture and her own feeble resignation? The play's articulation of these questions is complicated by the problems inherent in a white male writer's depiction of a Native woman's experience—a character represented onstage in the original production by a classically trained white actress. Not until 1981 would a production of the play use Native performers in all the Native roles. By the mid-1980s an increasingly strong contingent of Native actors and playwrights would begin telling us their theatrical stories themselves. But George Ryga's probing of this terrible wound near the heart of Canadian society, radical in 1967, continues to resonate with its own dark truths.

The *Ecstasy of Rita Joe* opened at the Playhouse Theatre Centre, Vancouver, on November 23, 1967, with the following cast:

RITA JOE	Frances Hyland
JAIMIE PAUL	August Schellenberg
DAVID JOE	Chief Dan George
MAGISTRATE	Henry Ramer
MR. HOMER	Walter Marsh
PRIEST	Robert Clothier
EILEEN JOE	Patricia Gage
OLD INDIAN WOMAN	Rae Brown
TEACHER	Claudine Melgrave
POLICEMAN	Bill Clarkson
WITNESS; MURDERER	Merv Campone
WITNESS; MURDERER	Alex Bruhanski
WITNESS	Jack Leaf
MURDERER	Jack Buttrey
YOUNG INDIAN MEN	Leonard George, Robert Hall, Frank Lewis, Paul Stanley
GUITARIST	Willy Dunn
SINGER	Ann Mortifee

Directed by George Bloomfield
Set and Lighting Design by Charles Evans
Costume Design by Margaret Ryan
Music by Willy Dunn and Ann Mortifee
Lyrics by George Ryga
Choreography by Norbert Vesak

THE ECSTASY OF RITA JOE

CHARACTERS

RITA JOE
JAIMIE PAUL
DAVID JOE, *Rita's father*
MAGISTRATE
MR. HOMER
FATHER ANDREW, *a priest*
EILEEN JOE, *Rita's sister*
OLD INDIAN WOMAN
MISS DONOHUE, *a teacher*
POLICEMAN
WITNESSES
MURDERERS
YOUNG INDIAN MEN
SINGER

SET

A circular ramp beginning at floor level stage left and continuing downward below floor level at stage front, then rising and sweeping along stage back at two-foot elevation to disappear in the wings of stage left. This ramp dominates the stage by wrapping the central and forward playing area. A short approach ramp, meeting with the main ramp at stage right, expedites entrances from the wings of stage right. The MAGISTRATE's chair and representation of court desk are situated at stage right, enclosed within the sweep of the ramp. At the foot of the desk is a lip on stage right side.

The SINGER sits here, turned away from the focus of the play. Her songs and accompaniment appear almost accidental. She has all the reactions of a white liberal folklorist with a limited concern and understanding of an ethnic dilemma which she touches in the course of her research and work in compiling and writing folk songs. She serves too as an alter ego to RITA JOE.

No curtain is used during the play. At the opening, intermission and conclusion of the play, the curtain remains up. The onus for isolating scenes from the past and present in RITA JOE's life falls on highlight lighting.

Backstage, there is a mountain cyclorama. In front of the cyclorama there is a darker maze curtain to suggest gloom and confusion, and a cityscape.

ACT ONE

The house lights and stage work lights remain on. Backstage, cyclorama, and maze curtains are up, revealing wall back of stage, exit doors, etc.

CAST and SINGER enter offstage singly and in pairs from the wings, the exit doors at the back of the theatre, and from the auditorium side doors. The entrances are workmanlike and untheatrical. When all the CAST is on stage, they turn to face the audience momentarily. The house lights dim.

The cyclorama is lowered into place. The maze curtain follows. This creates a sense of compression of stage into the auditorium. Recorded voices are heard in a jumble of mutterings and throat clearings. The MAGISTRATE enters as the CLERK begins.

CLERK: *(recorded)* This court is in session. All present will rise . . . .

The shuffling and scraping of furniture is heard. The CAST repeat "Rita Joe, Rita Joe." A POLICEMAN brings on RITA JOE.

MAGISTRATE: Who is she? Can she speak English?

POLICEMAN: Yes.

MAGISTRATE: Then let her speak for herself!

He speaks to the audience firmly and with reason.

MAGISTRATE: To understand life in a given society, one must understand laws of that society. All relationships . . .

CLERK: *(recorded)* Man to man . . . man to woman . . . man to property . . . man to the state . . .

MAGISTRATE: . . . are determined and enriched by laws that have grown out of social realities. The quality of the law under which you live and function determines the real quality of the freedom that was yours today.

The rest of the CAST slowly move out.

MAGISTRATE: Your home and your well-being were protected. The roads of the city are open to us. So are the galleries, libraries, the administrative and public buildings. There are buses, trains . . . going in and coming out. Nobody is a prisoner here.

RITA: (*with humour, almost a sad sigh*) The first time I tried to go home I was picked up by some men who gave me five dollars. An' then they arrested me.

The POLICEMAN retreats into the shadows. The SINGER crosses down.

MAGISTRATE: Thousands leave and enter the city every day . . .

RITA: It wasn't true what they said, but nobody'd believe me . . .

SINGER: (*singing a recitivo searching for a melody*)
Will the winds not blow
My words to her
Like the seeds
Of the dandelion?

MAGISTRATE: (*smiling, as at a private joke*) Once . . . I saw a little girl in the Cariboo country. It was summer then and she wore only a blouse and skirt. I wondered what she wore in winter?

The MURDERERS hover in the background on the upper ramp. One whistles and one lights a cigarette—an action which will be repeated at the end of the play.

RITA: (*moving to him, but hesitating*) You look like a good man. Tell them to let me go, please!

The MAGISTRATE goes to his podium.

MAGISTRATE: Our nation is on an economic par with the state of Arkansas . . . . We are a developing country, but a buoyant one. Still . . . the summer report of the Economic Council of Canada predicts a reduction in the gross national product unless we utilize our manpower for greater efficiency. Employed, happy people make for a prosperous, happy nation . . . .

RITA: (*exultantly*) I worked at some jobs, mister!

The MAGISTRATE turns to face RITA JOE. The MURDERERS have gone.

MAGISTRATE: Gainful employment. Obedience to the law . . .

RITA: (*to the MAGISTRATE*) Once I had a job . . .

He does not relate to her. She is troubled. She talks to the audience.

RITA: Once I had a job in a tire store . . . an' I'd worry about what time my boss would come . . . . He was always late . . . and so was everybody. Sometimes I got to thinkin' what would happen if he'd not come. And nobody else would come. And I'd be all day in this big room with no lights on an' the telephone ringing an' people asking for other people that weren't there . . . . What would happen?

As she relates her concern, she laughs. Towards the end of her monologue she is so amused by the absurdity of it all that she can hardly contain herself.

Lights fade on the MAGISTRATE who broods in his chair as he examines his court papers.

Lights up on JAIMIE PAUL approaching on the backstage ramp from stage left. He is jubilant, his laughter blending with her laughter. At the sound of his voice, RITA JOE runs to him, to the memory of him.

JAIMIE: I seen the city today and I seen things today I never knew was there, Rita Joe!

RITA: (*happily*) I seen them too, Jaimie Paul!

He pauses above her, his mood light and childlike.

JAIMIE: I see a guy on top of a bridge, talkin' to himself . . . an' lots of people on the beach watchin' harbour seals . . . . Kids feed popcorn to seagulls . . . an' I think to myself . . . boy! Pigeons eat pretty good here!

RITA: In the morning, Jaimie Paul . . . very early in the morning . . . the air is cold like at home . . . .

JAIMIE: Pretty soon I seen a little woman walkin' a big black dog on a rope . . . . Dog is mad . . . . Dog wants a man!

JAIMIE PAUL moves to RITA JOE. They embrace.

RITA: Clouds are red over the city in the morning. Clara Hill says to me if you're real happy . . . the clouds make you forget you're not home . . . .

They laugh together. JAIMIE PAUL breaks from her. He punctuates his story with wide, sweeping gestures.

JAIMIE: I start singin' and some hotel windows open. I wave to them, but nobody waves back!

They're watchin' me, like I was a harbour seal! (*He laughs.*) So I stopped singin'!

RITA: I remember colours, but I've forgot faces already . . . .

JAIMIE PAUL looks at her as her mood changes. Faint light on the MAGISTRATE brightens.

RITA: A train whistle is white, with black lines . . . . A sick man talkin' is brown like an overcoat with pockets torn an' string showin' . . . . A sad woman is a room with the curtains shut . . . .

MAGISTRATE: Rita Joe?

She becomes sobered, but JAIMIE PAUL continues laughing. She nods to the MAGISTRATE, then turns to JAIMIE PAUL.

RITA: Them bastards put me in jail. They're gonna do it again, they said . . . . Them bastards!

JAIMIE: Guys who sell newspapers don't see nothin' . . .

RITA: They drive by me, lookin' . . .

JAIMIE: I'm gonna be a carpenter!

RITA: I walk like a stick, tryin' to keep my ass from showin' because I know what they're thinkin' . . . . Them bastards!

JAIMIE: I got myself boots an' a new shirt . . . . See!

RITA: (*worried now*) I thought their jail was on fire . . . . I thought it was burning.

JAIMIE: Room I got costs me seven bucks a week . . . .

RITA: I can't leave town. Every time I try, they put me in jail.

A POLICEMAN enters with a file folder.

JAIMIE: They say it's a pretty good room for seven bucks a week . . . .

JAIMIE PAUL begins to retreat backwards from her, along the ramp to the wings of stage left. She is isolated in a pool of light away from the MAGISTRATE. The light isolation between her and JAIMIE PAUL deepens, as the scene turns into the courtroom again.

MAGISTRATE: Vagrancy . . . . You are charged with vagrancy.

JAIMIE: (*with enthusiasm, boyishly*) First hundred bucks I make, Rita Joe . . . I'm gonna buy a car so I can take you every place!

RITA: (*moving after him*) Jaimie!

He retreats, dreamlike, into the wings. The spell of memory between them is broken. Pools of light between her and the MAGISTRATE spread and fuse into a single light area. She turns to the MAGISTRATE, worried and confused.

MAGISTRATE: (*reading the documents in his hand*) The charge against you this morning is vagrancy . . . .

The MAGISTRATE continues studying the papers he holds. She looks up at him and shakes her head helplessly, then blurts out to him.

RITA: I had to spend last night in jail . . . . Did you know?

MAGISTRATE: Yes. You were arrested.

RITA: I didn't know when morning came . . . there was no windows . . . . The jail stinks! People in jail stink!

MAGISTRATE: (*indulgently*) Are you surprised?

RITA: I didn't know anybody there . . . . People in jail stink like paper that's been in the rain too long. But a jail stinks worse. It stinks of rust . . . an' old hair . . . .

The MAGISTRATE looks down at her for the first time.

MAGISTRATE: You . . . are Rita Joe?

She nods quickly. A faint concern shows in his face. He watches her for a long moment.

MAGISTRATE: I know your face . . . yet . . . it wasn't in this courtroom. Or was it?

RITA: I don't know . . .

MAGISTRATE: (*pondering*) Have you appeared before me in the past year?

RITA: (*turning away from him, shrugging*) I don't know. I can't remember . . . .

The MAGISTRATE throws his head back and laughs. The POLICEMAN joins in.

MAGISTRATE: You can't remember? Come now . . . .

RITA: (*laughing with him and looking to the POLICEMAN*) I can't remember . . . .

MAGISTRATE: Then I take it you haven't appeared before me. Certainly you and I would remember if you had.

RITA: (*smiling*) I don't remember . . . .

The MAGISTRATE makes some hurried notes, but he is watching RITA JOE, formulating his next thought.

RITA: (*naively*) My sister hitchhiked home an' she had no trouble like I . . .

MAGISTRATE: You'll need witnesses, Rita Joe. I'm only giving you eight hours to find witnesses for yourself . . . .

RITA: Jaimie knows . . .

She turns to where JAIMIE PAUL had been, but the back of the stage is in darkness. The POLICE-MAN exits suddenly.

RITA: Jaimie knew . . .

Her voice trails off pathetically. The MAGIS-TRATE shrugs and returns to studying his notes. RITA JOE chafes during the silence which follows. She craves communion with people, with the MAGISTRATE.

RITA: My sister was a dressmaker, mister! But she only worked two weeks in the city . . . . An' then she got sick and went back to the reserve to help my father catch fish an' cut pulpwood. (*smiling*) She's not coming back . . . that's for sure!

MAGISTRATE: (*with interest*) Should I know your sister? What was her name?

RITA: Eileen Joe.

EILEEN JOE appears spotlit behind, a memory crowding in.

MAGISTRATE: Eileen . . . that's a soft, undulating name.

RITA: Two weeks, and not one white woman came to her to leave an order or old clothes for her to fix. No work at all for two weeks, an' her money ran out . . . . Isn't that funny?

The MAGISTRATE again studies RITA JOE, his mind elsewhere.

MAGISTRATE: Hmmmmm . . . .

EILEEN JOE disappears.

RITA: So she went back to the reserve to catch fish an' cut pulpwood!

MAGISTRATE: I do know your face . . . yes! And yet . . . .

RITA: Can I sit someplace?

MAGISTRATE: (*excited*) I remember now . . . . Yes! I was on holidays three summers back in the Cariboo country . . . driving over this road with not a house or field in sight . . . just barren land, wild and wind-blown. And then I saw this child beside the road, dressed in a blouse and skirt, barefooted . . .

RITA: (*looking around*) I don't feel so good, mister.

MAGISTRATE: My God, she wasn't more than three or four years old . . . walking towards me beside the road. When I'd passed her, I stopped my car and then turned around and drove back to where I'd seen her, for I wondered what she could possibly be doing in such a lonely country at that age without her father or mother walking with her . . . . Yet when I got back to where I'd seen her, she had disappeared. She was nowhere to be seen. Yet the land was flat for over a mile in every direction . . . . I had to see her. But I couldn't . . . .

He stares down at RITA JOE for a long moment.

MAGISTRATE: You see, what I was going to say was that this child had your face! Isn't that strange?

RITA: (*with disinterest*) Sure, if you think so, mister . . .

MAGISTRATE: Could she have been . . . your daughter?

RITA: What difference does it make?

MAGISTRATE: Children cannot be left like that . . . . It takes money to raise children in the woods as in the cities . . . . There are institutions and people with more money than you who could . . .

RITA: Nobody would get my child, mister!

She is distracted by EILEEN JOE's voice in her memory. EILEEN's voice begins in darkness, but as she speaks, a spotlight isolates her in front of the ramp, stage left. EILEEN is on her hands and knees, two buckets beside her. She is picking berries in mime.

EILEEN: First was the strawberries an' then the blueberries. After the frost . . . we picked the cranberries . . .

She laughs with delight.

RITA: (*pleading with the MAGISTRATE, but her attention on EILEEN*) Let me go, mister . . .

MAGISTRATE: I can't let you go. I don't think that would be of any use in the circumstances. Would you like a lawyer?

Even as he speaks, RITA JOE has entered the scene with EILEEN picking berries. The MAGISTRATE's light fades on his podium.

RITA: You ate the strawberries an' blueberries because you were always a hungry kid!

EILEEN: But not cranberries! They made my stomach hurt.

RITA JOE goes down on her knees with EILEEN.

RITA: Let me pick . . . . You rest. (*holding out the bucket to EILEEN*) Mine's full already . . . . Let's change. You rest . . . .

During the exchange of buckets, EILEEN notices her hands are larger than RITA JOE's. She is both delighted and surprised by this.

EILEEN: My hands are bigger than yours, Rita . . . . Look! (*taking RITA JOE's hands in hers*) When did my hands grow so big?

RITA: (*wisely and sadly*) You've worked so hard . . . . I'm older than you, Leenie . . . . I will always be older.

The two sisters are thoughtful for a moment, each watching the other in silence. Then RITA JOE becomes animated and resumes her mime of picking berries in the woods.

RITA: We picked lots of wild berries when we were kids, Leenie!

They turn away from their work and lie down alongside each other, facing the front of the stage. The light on them becomes summery, warm.

RITA: In the summer, it was hot an' flies hummed so loud you'd go to sleep if you sat down an' just listened.

EILEEN: The leaves on the poplars used to turn black an' curl together with the heat . . .

RITA: One day you and I were pickin' blueberries and a big storm came . . . .

A sudden crash of thunder and a lightning flash. The lights turn cold and blue. The three MURDERERS stand in silhouette on a riser behind them. EILEEN cringes in fear, afraid of the storm, aware of the presence of the MURDERERS behind them. RITA JOE springs to her feet, her being attached to the wildness of the atmosphere. Lightning continues to flash and flicker.

EILEEN: Oh, no!

RITA: (*shouting*) It got cold and the rain an' hail came . . . the sky falling!

EILEEN: (*crying in fear*) Rita!

RITA: (*laughing, shouting*) Stay there!

A high flash of lightning, silhouetting the MURDERERS harshly. They take a step forward on the lightning flash. EILEEN dashes into the arms of RITA JOE. She screams and drags RITA JOE down with her. RITA JOE struggles against EILEEN.

RITA: Let me go! What in hell's wrong with you? Let me go!

MAGISTRATE: I can't let you go.

The lightning dies, but the thunder rumbles off into the distance. EILEEN subsides, and pressing herself into the arms of RITA JOE as a small child to her mother, she sobs quietly.

RITA: There, there . . . . (*with infinite tenderness*) You said to me, "What would happen if the storm hurt us an' we can't find our way home, but are lost together so far away in the bush?"

EILEEN looks up, brushing away her tears and smiling at RITA JOE.

RITA and EILEEN: (*in unison*) Would you be my mother then?

RITA: Would I be your mother?

RITA JOE releases EILEEN who looks back fearfully to where the MURDERERS had stood. They are gone. She rises and, collecting the buckets, moves hesitantly to where they had been. Confident now, she laughs softly and nervously to herself and leaves the stage. RITA JOE rises and talks to EILEEN as she departs.

RITA: We walked home through the mud an' icy puddles among the trees. At first you cried, Leenie . . . and then you wanted to sleep. But I held you up an' when we got home you said you were sure you would've died in the bush if it hadn't been for us being together like that.

EILEEN disappears from the stage. The MAGISTRATE's light comes up. RITA JOE shakes her head sadly at the memory, then comes forward to the apron of the stage. She is proud of her sister and her next speech reveals this pride.

RITA: She made a blouse for me that I wore every day for one year, an' it never ripped at the armpits like the blouse I buy in the store does the first time I stretch. (*She stretches languidly.*) I like to stretch when I'm happy! It makes all the happiness go through me like warm water . . . .

The PRIEST, the TEACHER, and a YOUNG INDIAN MAN cross the stage directly behind her. The PRIEST wears a Roman collar and a checked bush-jacket of a worker-priest. He pauses before passing RITA JOE and goes to meet her.

PRIEST: Rita Joe? When did you get back? How's life?

RITA JOE shrugs noncommittally.

RITA: You know me, Father Andrew . . . could be better, could be worse . . . .

PRIEST: Are you still working?

RITA JOE is still noncommittal. She smiles at him. Her gestures are not definite.

RITA: I live.

PRIEST: (*serious and concerned*) It's not easy, is it?

RITA: Not always.

The TEACHER and the YOUNG INDIAN MAN exit.

PRIEST: A lot of things are different in the city. It's easier here on the reserve . . . life is simpler. You can be yourself. That's important to remember.

RITA: Yes, Father . . . .

The PRIEST wants to ask and say more, but he cannot. An awkward moment between them and he reaches out to touch her shoulder gently.

PRIEST: Well . . . be a good girl, Rita Joe . . . .

RITA: (*without turning after him*) Goodbye, Father.

MAGISTRATE: (*more insistently*) Do you want a lawyer?

The PRIEST leaves stage right. As he leaves, cross light to where a happy JAIMIE PAUL enters from stage left. JAIMIE PAUL comes down to join RITA JOE.

JAIMIE: This guy asked me how much education I got, an' I says to him, "Grade six. How much education a man need for such a job?" . . . An' the bum, he says it's not good enough! I should take night school. But I got the job, an' I start next Friday . . . like this . . . .

JAIMIE PAUL does a mock sweeping routine as if he was cleaning a vast office building. He and RITA JOE are both laughing.

JAIMIE: Pretty good, eh?

RITA: Pretty good.

JAIMIE: Cleaning the floors an' desks in the building . . . . But it's a government job, and that's good for life. Work hard, then the government give me a raise . . . . I never had a job like that before . . . .

RITA: When I sleep happy, I dream of blueberries an' sun an' all the nice things when I was a little kid, Jaimie Paul.

The sound of an airplane is heard. JAIMIE PAUL looks up. RITA JOE also stares into the sky of her memory. JAIMIE PAUL's face is touched with pain and recollection. The TEACHER, RITA JOE's FATHER, an OLD WOMAN, four YOUNG INDIAN MEN and EILEEN JOE come into the background quietly, as if at a wharf watching the airplane leave the village. They stand looking up until the noise of the aircraft begins to diminish.

JAIMIE: That airplane . . . a Cessna . . . .

He continues watching the aircraft and turns, following its flight path.

JAIMIE: She said to me, maybe I never see you again, Jaimie Paul.

There is a faint light on the MAGISTRATE in his chair. He is thoughtful, looking down at his hands.

MAGISTRATE: Do you want a lawyer?

RITA: (*to JAIMIE PAUL*) Who?

JAIMIE: Your mother . . . . I said to her, they'll fix you up good in the hospital. Better than before . . . . It was a Cessna that landed on the river an' took her away . . . . Maybe I never see you again, Jaimie, she says to me. She knew she was gonna die, but I was a kid and so were you . . . . What the hell did we know? I'll never forget . . . .

JAIMIE PAUL joins the village group on the upper level.

SINGER: (*singing an indefinite melody developing into a square-dance tune*)
There was a man in a beat-up hat
Who runs a house in the middle of town,
An' round his stove-pipe chimney house
The magpies sat, just a-lookin' round.

The Indian village people remain in the back of the stage, still watching the airplane which has vanished. JAIMIE PAUL, on his way, passes MR. HOMER, a white citizen who has the hurried but fulfilled appearance of the socially responsible man. MR. HOMER comes to the front of the stage beside RITA JOE. He talks directly to the audience.

MR. HOMER: Sure, we do a lot of things for our Indians here in the city at the Centre . . . . Bring 'em in from the cold an' give them food . . . . The rest . . . well, the rest kinda take care of itself.

RITA JOE lowers her head and looks away from him. MR. HOMER moves to her and places his hand on her shoulders possessively.

MR. HOMER: When your mother got sick we flew her out . . . . You remember that, Rita Joe?

RITA: (*nodding, looking down*) Yes, Mr. Homer . . . . Thank you.

MR. HOMER: And we sent her body back for the funeral . . . . Right, Rita Joe?

The people of the village leave except for the YOUNG INDIAN MEN who remain and mime drinking.

MR. HOMER: And then sometimes a man drinks it up an' leaves his wife an' kids and the poor dears come here for help. We give them food an' a place to sleep . . . . Right, Rita?

RITA: Yes.

MR. HOMER: Clothes too . . . . White people leave clothes here for the Indians to take if they need 'em. Used to have them all up on racks over there . . . just like in a store . . . . (*pointing*) But now we got them all on a heap on a table in the basement.

He laughs and RITA JOE nods with him.

MR. HOMER: Indian people . . . 'specially the women . . . get more of a kick diggin' through stuff that's piled up like that . . . .

MR. HOMER chuckles and shakes his head. There is a pale light on the MAGISTRATE, who is still looking down at his hands.

MAGISTRATE: There are institutions to help you . . . .

MR. HOMER again speaks to the audience, but now he is angry over some personal beef.

MR. HOMER: So you see, the Centre serves a need that's real for Indians who come to the city. (*wagging his finger at the audience angrily*) It's the do-gooders burn my ass, you know! They come in from television or the newspaper . . . hang around just long enough to see a drunken Indian . . . an' bingo!

JAIMIE: Bingo!

MR. HOMER: That's their story! Next thing, they're seeing some kind of Red Power . . .

The YOUNG INDIAN MEN laugh and RITA JOE gets up to join them.

MR. HOMER: . . . or beatin' the government over the head! Let them live an' work among the Indians for a few months . . . then they'd know what it's really like . . . .

The music comes up sharply.

SINGER:
Round and round the cenotaph,
The clumsy seagulls play.
Fed by funny men with hats
Who watch them night and day.

The four YOUNG INDIAN MEN join with RITA JOE and dance. Leading the group is JAIMIE PAUL. He is drunk, dishevelled. Light spreads before them as they advance onstage. They are laughing rowdily. RITA JOE moves to them.

RITA: Jaimie Paul?

MR. HOMER leaves. JAIMIE PAUL is overtaken by two of his companions who take him by the arms, but he pushes them roughly away.

JAIMIE: Get the hell outa my way! . . . I'm as good a man as him any time . . . .

JAIMIE PAUL crosses downstage to confront a member of the audience.

JAIMIE: You know me? . . . You think I'm a dirty Indian, eh? Get outa my way!

He puts his hands over his head and continues staggering away.

JAIMIE: Goddamnit, I wanna sleep . . . .

The YOUNG INDIAN MEN and JAIMIE PAUL exit. RITA JOE follows after JAIMIE PAUL, reaching out to touch him, but the SINGER stands in her way and drives her back, singing . . . . Music up tempo and volume.

SINGER:
Oh, can't you see that train roll on,
Its hot black wheels keep comin' on?
A Kamloops Indian died today.
Train didn't hit him, he just fell.
Busy train with wheels on fire!

The music dies. A POLICEMAN enters.

POLICEMAN: Rita Joe!

He repeats her name many times. The TEACHER enters ringing the school handbell and crosses through.

TEACHER: (*calling*) Rita Joe! Rita Joe! Didn't you hear the bell ring? The class is waiting . . . . The class is always waiting for you.

The TEACHER exits.

MAGISTRATE and POLICEMAN: (*sharply, in unison*) Rita Joe!

The POLICEMAN grabs and shakes RITA JOE to snap her out of her reverie.

Light up on the MAGISTRATE who sits erect, with authority.

MAGISTRATE: I ask you for the last, time, Rita Joe . . . . Do you want a lawyer?

RITA: (*defiantly*) What for? . . . I can take care of myself.

MAGISTRATE: The charge against you this morning is prostitution. Why did you not return to your people as you said you would?

The light on the backstage dies. RITA JOE stands before the MAGISTRATE and the POLICEMAN. She is contained in a pool of light before them.

RITA: (*nervous, with despair*) I tried . . . . I tried . . . .

The MAGISTRATE settles back into his chair and takes a folder from his desk, which he opens and studies.

MAGISTRATE: Special Constable Eric Wilson has submitted a statement to the effect that on June 18th he and Special Constable Schneider approached you on Fourth Avenue at nine-forty in the evening . . .

POLICEMAN: We were impersonating two deck-hands newly arrived in the city . . .

MAGISTRATE: You were arrested an hour later on charges of prostitution.

The MAGISTRATE holds the folder threateningly and looks down at her. RITA JOE is defiant.

RITA: That's a goddamned lie!

MAGISTRATE: (*sternly, gesturing to the POLICE-MAN*) This is a police statement. Surely you don't think a mistake was made?

RITA: (*peering into the light above her, shuddering*) Everything in this room is like ice . . . . How can you stay alive working here? . . . I'm so hungry I want to throw up . . .

MAGISTRATE: You have heard the statement, Rita Joe . . . . Do you deny it?

RITA: I was going home, trying to find the highway . . . . I knew those two were cops, the moment I saw them . . . I told them to go f . . . fly a kite! They got sore then an' started pushing me around . . . .

MAGISTRATE: (*patiently now, waving down the objections of the POLICEMAN*) Go on.

RITA: They followed me around until a third cop drove up. An' then they arrested me.

MAGISTRATE: Arrested you . . . . Nothing else?

RITA: They stuffed five dollar bills in my pockets when they had me in the car . . . . I ask you, mister, when are they gonna charge cops like that with contributing to . . .

POLICEMAN: Your worship . . .

MAGISTRATE: (*irritably, indicating the folder on the table before him*) Now it's your word against this! You need references . . . people who know you . . . who will come to court to substantiate what you say . . . today! That is the process of legal argument!

RITA: Can I bum a cigarette someplace?

MAGISTRATE: No. You can't smoke in court.

The POLICEMAN smiles and exits.

RITA: Then give me a bed to sleep on, or is the sun gonna rise an' rise until it burns a hole in my head?

Guitar music cues softly in the background.

MAGISTRATE: Tell me about the child.

RITA: What child?

MAGISTRATE: The little girl I once saw beside the road!

RITA: I don't know any girl, mister! When do I eat? Why does an Indian wait even when he's there first thing in the morning?

The pool of light tightens around the MAGISTRATE and RITA JOE.

MAGISTRATE: I have children . . . two sons . . .

RITA: (*nodding*) Sure. That's good.

The MAGISTRATE gropes for words to express a message that is very precious to him.

MAGISTRATE: My sons can go in any direction they wish . . . into trades or university . . . . But if I had a daughter, I would be more concerned . . . .

RITA: What's so special about a girl?

MAGISTRATE: I would wish . . . well, I'd be concerned about her choices . . . her choices of living, school . . . friends . . . . These things don't come as lightly for a girl. For boys it's different . . . . But I would worry if I had a daughter . . . . Don't hide your child! Someone else can be found to raise her if you can't!

RITA JOE shakes her head, a strange smile on her face.

MAGISTRATE: Why not? There are people who would love to take care of it.

RITA: Nobody would get my child . . . . I would sooner kill it an' bury it first! I am not a kind woman, mister judge!

MAGISTRATE: (*at a loss*) I see . . . .

RITA: (*a cry*) I want to go home . . . .

Quick up tempo music is heard. Suddenly, the lights change.

JAIMIE PAUL and the YOUNG INDIAN MEN sweep over the backstage ramp, the light widening for them. RITA JOE moves into this railway station crowd. She turns from one man to another until she sees JAIMIE PAUL.

EILEEN JOE and an OLD WOMAN enter.

RITA: Jaimie!

EILEEN: (*happily, running to him*) Jaimie Paul! God's sakes . . . . When did you get back from the north? . . . I thought you said you wasn't coming until breakup . . . .

JAIMIE: (*turning to EILEEN*) I was comin' home on the train . . . had a bit to drink and was feeling pretty good . . . . Lots of women sleeping in their seats on the train . . . . I'd lift their hats an' say, "Excuse me, lady . . . I'm lookin' for a wife!" (*turning to the OLD WOMAN*) One fat lady got mad, an' I says to her, "That's alright, lady . . . . You got no worries . . . . You keep sleepin'!"

Laughter.

JAIMIE PAUL and the OLD WOMAN move away. EILEEN sees RITA JOE who is standing watching.

EILEEN: Rita! . . . Tom an' I broke up . . . did I tell you?

RITA: No, Leenie . . . you didn't tell me!

EILEEN: He was no good . . . . He stopped comin' to see me when he said he would. I kept waiting, but he didn't come . . . .

RITA: I sent you a pillow for your wedding!

EILEEN: I gave it away . . . . I gave it to Clara Hill.

RITA: (*laughing bawdily and miming pregnancy*) Clara Hill don't need no pillow now!

JAIMIE: (*smiling, crossing to her and exiting*) I always came to see you, Rita Joe . . . .

RITA JOE looks bewildered.

OLD WOMAN: (*exiting*) I made two Saskatoon pies, Rita . . . . You said next time you came home you wanted Saskatoon pie with lots of sugar . . . .

EILEEN and the OLD WOMAN drift away. JAIMIE PAUL moves on to the shadows. The THREE MURDERERS enter in silhouette; one whistles. RITA JOE rushes to the YOUNG INDIAN MEN downstage.

RITA: This is me, Rita Joe, God's sakes . . . . We went to the same school together . . . . Don't you know me now, Johnny? You remember how tough you was when you was a boy? . . . We tied you up in the Rainbow Creek and forgot you was there after recess . . . . An' after school was out, somebody remembered. (*laughing*) And you was blue when we got to you. Your clothes was wet to the chin, an' you said, "That's a pretty good knot . . . . I almost gave up trying to untie it!"

The music continues. RITA JOE steps among the YOUNG INDIAN MEN and they mime being piled in a car at a drive-in.

Steve Laporte? . . . You remember us goin' to the drive-in and the cold rain comin' down the car windows so we couldn't see the picture show anyhow?

She sits beside STEVE LAPORTE. They mime the windshield wipers.

A cold white light comes up on the playing area directly in front of the MAGISTRATE's chair. A MALE WITNESS of dishevelled, dirty appearance steps into the light and delivers testimony in a whining, defensive voice. He is one of the MURDERERS, but apart from the other three, he is nervous.

FIRST WITNESS: I gave her three bucks . . . an' once I got her goin' she started yellin' like hell! Called me a dog, pig . . . some filthy kind of animal . . . . So I slapped her around a bit . . . . Guys said she was a funny kind of bim . . . would do it for them standing up, but not for me she wouldn't . . . . So I slapped her around . . . .

The MAGISTRATE nods and makes a notation. The light on the FIRST WITNESS dies. RITA JOE speaks with urgency and growing fear to STEVE LAPORTE.

RITA: Then you shut the wipers off an' we were just sitting there, not knowing what to do . . . . I wish . . . we could go back again there an' start livin' from that day on . . . . Jaimie!

RITA JOE looks at STEVE LAPORTE as at a stranger. She stands and draws away from him. JAIMIE PAUL enters behind RITA JOE.

There is a cold light before the MAGISTRATE again and another MALE WITNESS moves into the light, replacing the FIRST WITNESS. He too is one of the MURDERERS. This SECOND WITNESS testifies with full gusto.

SECOND WITNESS: Gave her a job in my tire store . . . took her over to my place after work once . . . . She was scared when I tried a trick, but I'm easy on broads that get scared, providin' they keep their voices down . . . . After that, I slipped her a fiver . . . . Well, sir, she took the money, then she stood in front of the window, her head high an' her naked shoulders shakin' like she was cold. Well, sir, she cried a little an' then she says, "Goddamnit, but I wish I was a school teacher . . . . "

He laughs and everyone onstage joins in the laughter. The light dies out on the SECOND WITNESS. JAIMIE PAUL enters and crosses to RITA JOE. They lie down and embrace.

RITA: You always came to see me, Jaimie Paul . . . . The night we were in the cemetery . . . you remember, Jaimie Paul? I turned my face from yours until I saw the ground . . . an' I knew that below us . . . they were like us once, and now they lie below the ground, their eyes gone, the bones showin' . . . . They must've spoke and touched each other here . . . like you're touching me, Jaimie Paul . . . an' now there was nothing over them, except us . . . an' wind in the grass an' a barbwire fence creaking. An' behind that, a hundred acres of barley.

JAIMIE PAUL stands.

RITA: That's something to remember, when you're lovin', eh?

The sound of a train whistle is heard. JAIMIE PAUL goes and the lights onstage fade. The music comes up and the SINGER sings. As JAIMIE PAUL passes her, the SINGER pursues him up the ramp, and RITA JOE runs after them.

SINGER:
Oh, can't you see that train roll on,
Gonna kill a man, before it's gone?
Jaimie Paul fell and died.
He had it comin', so it's alright.
Silver train with wheels on fire!

The music dies instantly. RITA JOE's words come on the heels of the music as a bitter extension of the song. She stands before the MAGISTRATE, again in the court, but looks back to where JAIMIE PAUL had been in the gloom. The POLICEMAN enters where JAIMIE PAUL has exited, replacing him, for the fourth trial scene.

RITA: Jaimie, why am I here? . . . Is it . . . because people are talkin' about me and all them men . . . . Is that why? I never wanted to cut cord-wood for a living . . . . (*with great bitterness*) Never once I thought . . . it'd be like this . . . .

MAGISTRATE: What are we going to do about you, Rita Joe? This is the seventh charge against you in one year . . . . Laws are not made to be violated in this way . . . . Why did you steal?

RITA: I was hungry. I had no money.

MAGISTRATE: Yet you must have known you would be caught?

RITA: Yes.

MAGISTRATE: Are you not afraid of what is happening to you?

RITA: I am afraid of a lot of things. Put me in jail. I don't care . . . .

MAGISTRATE: (*with forced authority*) Law is a procedure. The procedure must be respected. It took hundreds of years to develop this process of law.

RITA: I stole a sweater . . . . They caught me in five minutes!

She smiles whimsically at this. The MAGISTRATE is leafing through the documents before him. The POLICEMAN stands to one side of him.

MAGISTRATE: The prosecutor's office has submitted some of the past history of Rita Joe . . . .

POLICEMAN: She was born and raised on a reservation. Then came a brief period in a public school off the reservation . . . at which time Rita Joe established herself as something of a disruptive influence . . .

RITA What's that mean?

MAGISTRATE: (*turning to her, smiling*) A trouble maker!

RITA JOE becomes animated, aware of the trap around her closing even at moments such as this.

RITA: Maybe it was about the horse, huh?

She looks up at the MAGISTRATE who is still smiling, offering her no help.

RITA: There was this accident with a horse . . . . It happened like this . . . I was riding a horse to school an' some of the boys shot a rifle an' my horse bucked an' I fell off. I fell in the bush an' got scratched . . . . The boys caught the horse by the school and tried to ride him, but the horse bucked an' pinned a boy against a tree, breaking his leg in two places . . . .

She indicates the place the leg got broken.

RITA: They said . . . an' he said I'd rode the horse over him on purpose!

MAGISTRATE: Well . . . did you?

RITA: It wasn't that way at all, I tell you! They lied!

The POLICEMAN and the SINGER laugh.

MAGISTRATE: Why should they lie, and Rita Joe alone tell the truth? . . . Or are you a child enough to believe the civilization of which we are a part . . .

He indicates the audience as inclusive of civilization from his point of view.

MAGISTRATE: . . . does not understand Rita Joe?

RITA: I don't know what you're saying.

MAGISTRATE: (*with a touch of compassion*) Look at you, woman! Each time you come before me you are older. The lines in your face are those of . . .

RITA: I'm tired an' I want to eat mister! I haven't had grub since day before yesterday . . . . This room is like a boat on water . . . . I'm so dizzy . . . . What the hell kind of place is this won't let me go lie down on grass?

She doubles over to choke back her nausea.

MAGISTRATE: This is not the reservation, Rita Joe. This is another place, another time . . . .

RITA: (*straining to remember, to herself*) I was once in Whitecourt, Alberta. The cops are fatter there than here. I had to get out of Whitecourt, Alberta . . .

MAGISTRATE: Don't blame the police, Rita Joe! The obstacles to your life are here . . . (*He touches his forefinger to his temples.*) . . . in your thoughts . . . possibly even in your culture . . . .

RITA JOE turns away from him, searching the darkness behind her.

MAGISTRATE: What's the matter?

RITA: I want to go home!

MAGISTRATE: But you can't go now. You've broken a law for which you will have to pay a fine or go to prison . . . .

RITA: I have no money.

MAGISTRATE: (*with exasperation*) Rita Joe . . . . It is against the law to solicit men on the street. You have to wash . . . .

RITA JOE begins to move away from him, crossing the front of the stage along the apron, her walk cocky. The light spreads and follows her.

MAGISTRATE: You can't walk around in old clothes and running shoes made of canvas . . . . You have to have some money in your pockets and an address where you live. You should fix your hair . . . perhaps even change your name.

And try to tame that accent that sounds like you have a mouthful of sawdust . . . . There is no peace in being extraordinary!

The light dies on the MAGISTRATE and the POLICEMAN.

RITA JOE is transported into another memory. JAIMIE PAUL enters and slides along the floor, left of centre stage. He is drunk, counting the fingers on his outstretched hands. MR. HOMER has entered with a wagon carrying hot soup and mugs. Four YOUNG INDIAN MEN come in out of the cold. MR. HOMER speaks to the audience in a matter-of-fact informative way.

MR. HOMER: (*dispensing soup to the YOUNG INDIAN MEN*) The do-gooders make something special of the Indian . . . . There's nothing special here . . . . At the centre here the quick cure is a bowl of stew under the belt and a good night's sleep.

JAIMIE: Hey, Mister Homer! How come I got so many fingers? Heh?

He laughs. MR. HOMER ignores JAIMIE PAUL and continues talking to the audience.

MR. HOMER: I wouldn't say they were brothers or sisters to me . . . no sir! But if you're . . .

JAIMIE PAUL gets up and embraces RITA JOE.

JAIMIE: I got two hands an' one neck . . . . I can kill more than I can eat . . . . If I had more fingers I would need mittens big as pie plates . . . . Yeh?

MR. HOMER: (*to JAIMIE PAUL*) Lie down, Jaimie Paul, an' have some more sleep. When you feel better, I'll get you some soup.

RITA JOE laughs. JAIMIE PAUL weaves his way uncertainly to where MR. HOMER stands.

JAIMIE: (*laughing*) I spit in your soup! You know what I say? . . . I say I spit in your soup, Mister Homer . . . .

He comes to MR. HOMER and seems about to do just what he threatens.

MR. HOMER: (*pushing him away with good humour*) I'll spit in your eyeball if you don't shut up!

JAIMIE: (*breaking away from MR. HOMER, taunting*) You . . . are not Mister Homer!

MR. HOMER: I'm not what?

JAIMIE: You're not Mister Homer . . . . You're somebody wearing his pants an' shirt . . . (*stumbling away*) But you're not Mister Homer . . . . Mister Homer never gets mad . . . . No sir, not Mister Homer!

MR. HOMER: I'm not mad . . . . What're you talkin' about?

JAIMIE PAUL turns and approaches the YOUNG INDIAN MEN. He threatens to fall off the apron of the stage.

JAIMIE: No . . . not Mister Homer! An' I got ten fingers . . . . How's that?

MR. HOMER: For Chris' sake, Jaimie . . . go to sleep.

JAIMIE PAUL stops and scowls, then grins knowingly. He begins to mime a clumsy paddler paddling a boat.

JAIMIE: (*laughing again*) I know you . . . . Hey? I know you! . . . I seen you up Rainbow Creek one time . . . I seen you paddling!

He breaks up with laughter.

MR. HOMER: (*amused, tolerant*) Oh, come on . . . I've never been to Rainbow Creek.

JAIMIE: (*controlling his laughter*) Sure you been to Rainbow Creek . . . . (*He begins to mime paddling again.*) Next time you need a good paddler, you see me. I have a governmen' job, but screw that. I'm gonna paddle! I seen you paddle . . . .

Again he breaks up in laughter as he once more demonstrates the quality of paddling he once saw. RITA JOE is fully enjoying the spectacle. So are the YOUNG INDIAN MEN. MR. HOMER is also amused by the absurdity of the situation. JAIMIE PAUL turns, but chokes up with laughter after saying . . .

JAIMIE: I have seen some paddlers . . . but you!

JAIMIE PAUL turns and waves his hand derisively, laughing.

MR. HOMER: It must've been somebody else . . . . I've never been to Rainbow Creek.

JAIMIE: Like hell, you say!

JAIMIE PAUL paddles the soup wagon out. Guitar music comes in with an upbeat tempo. RITA JOE and the YOUNG INDIAN MEN dance to the beat. The YOUNG INDIAN MEN then drift after MR. HOMER.

The light fades slowly on centre stage and the music changes.

RITA JOE, happy in her memory, does a circling butch walk in the fading light to the song of the SINGER. At the conclusion of the song, she is on the apron, stage right, in a wash of light that includes the MAGISTRATE and the SINGER.

SINGER:
I woke up at six o'clock
Stumbled out of bed,
Crash of cans an' diesel trucks
Damned near killed me dead.

Sleepless hours, heavy nights,
Dream your dreams so pretty.
God was gonna have a laugh
An' gave me a job in the city!

RITA JOE is still elated at her memory of JAIMIE PAUL and his story. With unusual candour, she turns girlishly before the MAGISTRATE, and in mild imitation of her own moment of drunkenness, begins telling him a story. Faint guitar music in the background continues.

RITA: One night I drank a little bit of wine, an' I was outside lookin' at the stars . . . thinking . . . when I was a little girl how much bigger the trees were . . . no clouds, but suddenly there was a light that made the whole sky look like day . . .

Guitar out.

RITA: . . . just for a moment . . . an' before I got used to the night . . . I saw animals, moving across the sky . . . two white horses . . . . A man was takin' them by the halters, and I knew the man was my grandfather . . . .

She stares at the MAGISTRATE, unsure of herself now.

MAGISTRATE: Yes! Is that all?

RITA: No . . . . But I never seen my grandfather alive, and I got so sad thinkin' about it I wanted to cry. I wasn't sure it was him, even . . . . (*She begins to laugh.*) I went an' telephoned the police and asked for the chief, but the chief was home and a guy asks what I want.

MAGISTRATE: (*mildly amused*) You . . . called the police?

RITA: I told the guy I'd seen God, and he says, "Yeh? What would you like us to do about it?" An' I said, "Pray! Laugh! Shout!"

MAGISTRATE: Go on . . . .

RITA: He . . . asked where I'd seen God, an' I told him in the sky. He says you better call this number . . . . It's the Air Force. They'll take care of it!

She laughs and the MAGISTRATE smiles.

RITA: I called the number the guy gave me, but it was nighttime and there was no answer! If God was to come at night, after office hours, then . . . .

A terrible awkwardness sets in. There is a harsh light on her. She turns away, aware that she is in captivity. The MAGISTRATE stirs with discomfort.

RITA: (*with great fear*) How long will this be? Will I never be able to . . .

MAGISTRATE: (*annoyed at himself, at her*) There is nothing here but a record of your convictions . . . nothing to speak for you and provide me with any reason to moderate your sentence! What the hell am I supposed to do? Violate the law myself because I feel that somehow . . . I've known and felt . . . . No! (*turning from her*) You give me no alternative . . . no alternative at all!

The MAGISTRATE packs up his books.

RITA: I'll go home . . . jus' let me go home. I can't get out of jail to find the highway . . . or some kind of job!

MAGISTRATE: (*standing*) Prison and fines are not the only thing . . . . Have you, for instance, considered that you might be an incurable carrier? There are people like that . . . . They cannot come into contact with others without infecting them. They cannot eat from dishes others may use . . . . They cannot prepare or touch food others will eat . . . . The same with clothes, cars, hospital beds!

The MAGISTRATE exits. RITA JOE shakes her head with disbelief. The idea of perpetual condemnation is beyond her comprehension. She falls to the floor. Guitar music is heard in the background.

She turns away from the MAGISTRATE and the light comes up over the ramp at the back of the stage. Another light comes up on centre stage left. Here, EILEEN JOE and the OLD WOMAN are miming clothes washing using a scrubbing board and placing the wash into woven baskets. The woman and the girl are on their knees, facing each other.

On the ramp above them, JAIMIE PAUL is struggling with a POLICEMAN who is scolding him softly for being drunk, abusive and noisy. JAIMIE PAUL is jocular; the POLICEMAN, harassed and worried. They slowly cross the ramp from stage left.

SINGER:
Four o'clock in the morning,
The sailor rides the ship
An' I ride the wind!

Eight o'clock in the morning,
My honey's scoldin' the sleepyheads
An' I'm scoldin' him.

JAIMIE: (*to the POLICEMAN*) On the Smoky River . . . four o'clock in the morning . . . hey? There was nobody . . . just me . . . . You know that?

POLICEMAN: No, I don't. Come on. Let's get you home.

JAIMIE PAUL moves forward and embraces the POLICEMAN.

JAIMIE: You wanna see something?

JAIMIE PAUL takes out a coin to do a trick.

OLD WOMAN: (*to EILEEN*) Your father's been very sick.

EILEEN: He won't eat nothing . . . .

OLD WOMAN: Jus' sits and worries . . . . That's no good.

JAIMIE PAUL: (*finishing his coin trick*) You like that one? Hey, we both work for the government, eh?

They exit laughing.

JAIMIE PAUL: Watch the rough stuff . . . . Just don't make me mad.

OLD WOMAN: If Rita Joe was to come and see him . . . maybe say goodbye to him . . . .

RITA: (*calling from her world to the world of her strongest fears*) But he's not dying! I saw him not so long ago . . . .

The women in her memory do not hear her. They continue discussing her father.

OLD WOMAN: He loved her an' always worried . . . .

RITA: I didn't know he was sick!

OLD WOMAN: You were smart to come back, Eileen Joe.

RITA: (*again calling over the distance of her soul*) Nobody told me!

SINGER:
Nine o'clock in the evening,
Moon is high in the blueberry sky
An' I'm lovin' you.

JAIMIE: (*now passing along the apron beside RITA JOE, talking to the POLICEMAN*) You seen where I live? Big house with a mongolia in front . . . . Fancy place! You wanna see the room I got?

POLICEMAN: (*gruffly, aware that JAIMIE PAUL can become angry quickly*) When I get holidays, we'll take a tour of everything you've got . . . but I don't get holidays until September!

From the apron they cross upstage diagonally, between the OLD WOMAN with EILEEN, and RITA JOE.

JAIMIE: You're a good man . . . good for a laugh. I'm a good man . . . you know me!

POLICEMAN: Sure, you're first class when you're sober!

JAIMIE: I got a cousin in the city. He got his wife a stove an' washing machine! He's a good man . . . . You know my cousin maybe?

Fading off. They leave the stage.

The OLD WOMAN has risen from her knees and wearily collected one basket of clothes. She climbs the ramp and moves to the wings, stage right. EILEEN is thoughtful and slower, but she also prepares her clothes wash and follows.

OLD WOMAN: Nothing in the city I can see . . . only if you're lucky. A good man who don't drink or play cards . . . that's all.

EILEEN: And if he's bad?

OLD WOMAN: Then leave him. I'm older than you, Eileen . . . . I know what's best.

The OLD WOMAN exits. The guitar music dies out. JAIMIE PAUL's laughter and voice is heard offstage.

JAIMIE: (*offstage, loud, boisterous*) We both work for the gov'ment! We're buddies, no? . . . You think we're both the same?

Laughter. The lights on the ramp and centre stage die.

RITA: (*following JAIMIE PAUL's laughter*) Good or bad, what difference? So long as he's a livin' man!

RITA JOE and EILEEN giggle. The light spreads around her into pale infinity.

The TEACHER enters on the ramp. She rings a handbell and stops a short distance from the wings to peer around. She is a shy, inadequate woman who moves and behaves jerkily, the product of incomplete education and poor job placement.

TEACHER: (*in a scolding voice*) Rita! Rita Joe!

The bell rings.

TEACHER: The class is waiting for you. The class is always waiting.

RITA JOE is startled to hear the bell and see the woman. She comes to her feet, now a child before the TEACHER, and runs to join EILEEN. JAIMIE PAUL and YOUNG INDIAN MEN have entered with the bell and sit cross-legged on the floor as school children.

RITA: The sun is in my skin, Miss Donohue. The leaves is red and orange, and the wind stopped blowin' an hour ago.

The TEACHER has stopped to listen to this. RITA JOE and EILEEN, late again, slip into class and sit on the floor with the others.

TEACHER: Rita! What is a noun?

No answer. The kids poke RITA JOE to stand up.

TEACHER: Did you hear what I asked?

RITA: (*uncertain*) No . . . yes?

TEACHER: There's a lot you don't know . . . . That kind of behaviour is exhibitionism! We are a melting pot!

RITA: A melting pot?

TEACHER: A melting pot! Do you know what a melting pot is?

RITA: It's . . . (She shrugs.) . . . a melting pot!

The class laughs.

TEACHER: Precisely! You put copper and tin into a melting pot and out comes bronze . . . It's the same with people!

RITA: Yes, Miss Donohue . . . out comes bronze . . . .

Laughter again. The TEACHER calls RITA JOE over to her. The light fades on the other children.

TEACHER: Rita, what was it I said to you this morning?

RITA: You said . . . wash my neck, clean my fingernails . . . .

TEACHER: (*cagey*) No, it wasn't, Rita!

RITA: I can't remember. It was long ago.

TEACHER: Try to remember, Rita.

RITA: I don't remember, Miss Donohue! I was thinkin' about you last night, thinkin' if you knew some . . .

TEACHER: You are straying off the topic! Never stray off the topic!

RITA: It was a dream, but now I'm scared, Miss Donohue. I've been a long time moving about . . . trying to find something! . . . I must've lost . . .

TEACHER: No, Rita. That is not important.

RITA: Not important?

TEACHER: No, Rita . . . . Now you repeat after me like I said or I'm going to have to pass you by again. Say after me . . .

RITA: Sure. Say after you . . .

TEACHER: Say after me . . . "A book of verse underneath the spreading bough . . . "

RITA: "A book of verse underneath the spreading bough . . . "

TEACHER: "A jug of wine, a loaf of bread and thou beside me . . . singing in the wilderness."

RITA: (*the child spell broken, she laughs bawdily*) Jaimie said, "To heck with the wine an' loaf . . . . Let's have some more of this here thou!"

Her laughter dies. She wipes her lips, as if trying to erase some stain there.

TEACHER: (*peevish*) Alright, Rita . . . . Alright, let's have none of that!

RITA: (*plaintively*) I'm sorry, Miss Donohue . . . . I'm sure sorry!

TEACHER: That's alright.

RITA: I'm sorry!

TEACHER: Alright . . . .

RITA: Sorry . . .

TEACHER: You will never make bronze! Coming from nowhere and going no place! Who am I to change that?

RITA JOE grips the edge of the desk with both hands, holding on tightly.

RITA: No! They said for me to stay here, to learn something!

TEACHER: (*with exasperation*) I tried to teach you, but your head was in the clouds, and as for your body . . . Well! I wouldn't even think what I know you do!

The TEACHER crosses amongst the other children.

RITA: I'm sorry . . . please! Let me say it after you again . . . (*blurting it out*) "A book of verse underneath the spreading . . . "

TEACHER: Arguing . . . always trying to upset me . . . and in grade four . . . I saw it then . . . pawing the ground for men like a bitch in heat!

RITA: (*dismayed*) It . . . isn't so!

TEACHER: You think I don't know? I'm not blind . . . I can see out of the windows.

The TEACHER marches off into the wings and the class runs after her leaving RITA JOE alone onstage.

RITA: That's a lie! For God's sake, tell the judge I have a good character . . . . I am clean an' honest . . . . Everything you said is right, I'm never gonna argue again . . . . I believe in God . . . an' I'm from the country and lost like hell! Tell him!

She shakes her head sadly, knowing the extent of her betrayal.

RITA: They only give me eight hours to find somebody who knows me . . . . An' seven and a half hours is gone already!

The light on the scene dies.

SINGER: (*recitivo*)
Things that were . . .
Life that might have been . . .

A pale backlight on the back of the ramp comes up. Recorded sounds of crickets and the distant sound of a train whistle are heard.

RITA JOE's FATHER and JAIMIE PAUL enter on the ramp from stage left. The FATHER leads the way. JAIMIE PAUL is behind, rolling a cigarette. They walk slowly, thoughtfully, following the ramp across and downstage. RITA JOE stands separate, watching.

SINGER:
The blue evening of the first
Warm day
Is the last evening.
There'll not be another
Like it.

JAIMIE: No more handouts, David Joe . . . . We can pick an' can the berries ourselves.

FATHER: We need money to start a cooperative like that.

JAIMIE: Then some other way!

The old man listens, standing still, to the sounds of the train and the night.

FATHER: You're a young man, Jaimie Paul . . . young an' angry. It's not good to be that angry.

JAIMIE: We're gonna work an' live like people . . . not be afraid all the time . . . stop listening to an old priest an' Indian Department guys who're working for a pension!

FATHER: You're a young man, Jaimie Paul . . . .

JAIMIE: I say stop listening, David Joe! . . . In the city they never learned my name. It was "Hey, fella" . . . or "You, boy" . . . that kind of stuff.

Pause. The sound of the train whistle is heard.

FATHER: A beautiful night, Jaimie Paul.

JAIMIE: We can make some money. The berries are good this year!

JAIMIE PAUL is restless, edgy, particularly on the train whistle sound.

FATHER: Sometimes . . . children . . . you remember every day with them . . . . Never forget you are alive with children.

JAIMIE PAUL turns away and begins to retrace his steps.

JAIMIE: You want us all to leave an' go to the city? Is that what you want?

The FATHER shakes his head. He does not wish for this, but the generation spread between them is great now. JAIMIE PAUL walks away with a gesture of contempt.

The sounds die. The light dies and isolates the FATHER and RITA JOE.

RITA: You were sick, an' now you're well.

FATHER: (*in measured speech, turning away from RITA JOE, as if carefully recalling something of great importance*) You left your father, Rita Joe . . . never wrote Eileen a letter that time . . . . Your father was pretty sick man that time . . . pretty sick man . . . . June ninth he got the cold, an' on June twenty he . . .

RITA: But you're alive! I had such crazy dreams I'd wake up laughing at myself!

FATHER: I have dreams too . . . .

RITA JOE moves forward to him. She stops talking to him, as if communicating thoughts rather than words. He remains standing where he is, facing away from her.

RITA: I was in a big city . . . so many streets I'd get lost like nothin' . . . . When you got sick I was on a job . . .

FATHER: June ninth I got the cold . . .

RITA: Good job in a tire store . . . Jaimie Paul's got a job with the government, you know?

FATHER: Pretty sick man, that time . . .

RITA: A good job in a tire store. They was gonna teach me how to file statements after I learned the telephone. Bus ticket home was twenty dollars . . . . But I got drunk all the same when I heard an' I went in and tried to work that day . . . (smiling and shaking her head) Boy, I tried to work! Some day that was!

FATHER: I have dreams . . . . Sometimes I'm scared . . . .

They finally look at each other.

RITA: (shuddering) I'm so cold . . . .

FATHER: Long dreams . . . I dream about Rita Joe . . . . (sadly) Have to get better. I've lived longer, but I know nothing . . . nothing at all. Only the old stories.

RITA JOE moves sideways to him. She is smiling happily.

RITA: When I was little, a man came out of the bush to see you. Tell me why again!

The FATHER hesitates, shaking his head, but he is also smiling. The light of their separate yearnings fades out and the front of the stage is lit with the two of them together. The FATHER turns and comes forward to meet her.

FATHER: You don't want to hear that story again.

He sits on the slight elevation of the stage apron. RITA JOE sits down in front of him and snuggles between his knees. He leans forward over her.

RITA: It's the best story I ever heard!

FATHER: You were a little girl . . . four years old already . . . an' Eileen was getting big inside your mother. One day it was hot . . . sure was hot. Too hot to try an' fish in the lake, because the fish was down deep where the water was cold.

RITA: The dog started to bark . . .

FATHER: The dog started to bark . . . . How!

FATHER and RITA: (in unison) How! How! How!

FATHER: Barking to beat hell an' I says to myself why . . . on such a hot day? Then I see the bushes

moving . . . somebody was coming to see us. Your mother said from inside the house, "What's the matter with that dog?" An' I says to her, "Somebody coming to see me." It was big Sandy Collins, who ran the sawmill back of the reserve. Business was bad for big Sandy then . . . but he comes out of that bush like he was being chased . . . his clothes all wet an' stickin' to him . . . his cap in his hands, an' his face black with the heat and dirt from hard work . . . . He says to me, "My little Millie got a cough last night an' today she's dead." . . . "She's dead," big Sandy says to me. I says to him, "I'm sorry to hear that, Sandy. Millie is the same age as my Rita." And he says to me, "David Joe . . . look, you got another kid coming . . . won't make much difference to you . . . . Sell me Rita Joe like she is for a thousand dollars!"

RITA JOE giggles. The FATHER raises his hand to silence her.

FATHER: "A thousand dollars is a lot of money, Sandy," I says to him . . . "Lots of money. You got to cut a lot of timber for a thousand dollars." Then he says to me, "Not a thousand cash at once, David Joe. First I give you two hundred fifty dollars . . . . When Rita Joe comes ten years old and she's still alright, I give you the next two hundred fifty . . . . An' if she don't die by fifteen, I guarantee you five hundred dollars cash at once!"

RITA JOE and the FATHER break into laughter. He reaches around her throat and draws her close.

FATHER: So you see, Rita Joe, you lose me one thousand dollars from big Sandy Collins!

They continue laughing. A harsh light on the MAGISTRATE, who enters and stands on his podium.

MAGISTRATE: Rita Joe, when was the last time you had dental treatment?

RITA JOE covers her ears, refusing to surrender this moment of security in the arms of her FATHER.

RITA: I can't hear you!

MAGISTRATE: (loudly) You had your teeth fixed ever?

RITA: (coming to her feet and turning on him) Leave me alone!

MAGISTRATE: Have you had your lungs X-rayed recently?

RITA: I was hungry, that's all!

MAGISTRATE: (*becoming staccato, machine-like in his questions*) When was your last Wasserman taken?

RITA: What's that?

RITA JOE hears the TEACHER's voice. She turns to see the approaching TEACHER give the MAGISTRATE testimony. The stage is lit in a cold blue light now.

TEACHER: (*crisply to the MAGISTRATE as she approaches, her monologue a reading*) Dear Sir . . . . In reply to your letter of the twelfth, I cannot in all sincerity provide a reference of good character for one Rita Joe . . .

The WITNESSES do not see her and the testimony takes on the air of a nightmare for RITA JOE. She is baffled and afraid. The TEACHER continues to quietly repeat her testimony. RITA JOE appeals to the MAGISTRATE.

RITA: Why am I here? What've I done?

MAGISTRATE: You are charged with prostitution.

Her FATHER stands and crosses upstage to the ramp to observe. He is joined by EILEEN JOE, the OLD WOMAN and the PRIEST. MR. HOMER approaches briskly from stage left.

MR. HOMER: She'd been drinking when she comes into the centre . . . . Nothing wrong in that I could see, 'specially on a Friday night. So I give her some soup an' a sandwich. Then all of a sudden in the middle of a silly argument, she goes haywire . . . an' I see her comin' at me . . . . I'll tell you, I was scared! I don't know Indian women that well!

MAGISTRATE: Assault!

RITA JOE retreats from him. The TEACHER and MR. HOMER now stand before the MAGISTRATE as if they were frozen. MR. HOMER repeats his testimony under the main dialogue. JAIMIE PAUL staggers in from stage right, over the ramp, heading to the wings of lower stage left.

JAIMIE: (*to himself*) What the hell are they doing?

RITA: (*running to him*) Say a good word for me, Jaimie!

JAIMIE: They fired me yesterday . . . . What the hell's the use of living?

JAIMIE PAUL leaves the stage as the SCHOOL BOARD CLERK enters to offer further testimony to the MAGISTRATE.

SCHOOL BOARD CLERK: I recommended in a letter that she take school after grade five through correspondence courses from the Department of Education . . . but she never replied to the form letter the school division sent her . . . .

RITA: (*defending herself to the MAGISTRATE*) That drunken bastard Mahoney used it to light fire in his store . . . . He'd never tell Indians when mail came for us!

SCHOOL BOARD CLERK: I repeat . . . I wish our position understood most clearly . . . . No reply was ever received in this office to the letter we sent Rita Joe!

RITA: One letter . . . one letter for a lifetime?

TEACHER: Say after me! "I wandered lonely as a cloud, that floats on high o'er vales and hills . . . . When all at once I saw a crowd . . . a melting pot . . . "

A POLICEMAN and a MALE WITNESS enter. The PRIEST crosses downstage. The testimonies are becoming a nightmare babble. RITA JOE is stung, stumbling backward from all of them as they face the MAGISTRATE with their condemnations.

POLICEMAN: We were impersonating two deck-hands . . . .

The PRIEST is passing by RITA JOE. He makes the sign of the cross and offers comfort in a thin voice, lost in the noise.

PRIEST: Be patient, Rita . . . . The young are always stormy, but in time, your understanding will deepen . . . . There is an end to all things.

WITNESS: I gave her a job, but she was kind of slow . . . . I can't wait around, there's lots of white people goin' lookin' for work . . . so I figure, to hell with this noise . . .

MAGISTRATE: (*loudly over the voices*) Have your ears ached?

RITA: No!

MAGISTRATE: Have you any boils on your back? Any discharge? When did you bathe last?

The MURDERERS appear and circle RITA JOE.

MAGISTRATE: Answer me! Drunkenness! Shoplifting! Assault! Prostitution, prostitution, prostitution, prostitution!

RITA: (*her voice shrill, cutting over the babble*) I don't know what happened . . . but you got to listen to me and believe me, mister!

The babble ceases abruptly. RITA JOE pleads with them as best she knows.

RITA: You got rules here that was made before I was born . . . . I was hungry when I stole something . . . an' I was hollerin' I was so lonely when I started whoring . . . .

The MURDERERS come closer.

MAGISTRATE: Rita Joe . . . has a doctor examined you? . . . I mean, really examined you? Rita Joe . . . you might be carrying and transmitting some disease and not aware of it!

RITA: (*breaking away from the MURDERERS*) Bastards! (*to the MAGISTRATE*) Put me in jail . . . I don't care . . . I'll sign anything. I'm so goddamn hungry I'm sick . . . . Whatever it is, I'm guilty!

She clutches her head and goes down in a squat of defeat.

MAGISTRATE: Are you free of venereal disease?

RITA: I don't know. I'm not sick that way.

MAGISTRATE: How can you tell?

RITA: (*lifting her face to him*) I know . . . . A woman knows them things . . . .

Pause.

MAGISTRATE: Thirty days!

The POLICEMAN leads RITA JOE off and the house lights come up. The ACTORS and the SINGER walk off the stage, leaving emptiness as at the opening of the act.

ACT TWO

The house lights dim. A POLICEMAN brings RITA JOE in downstage centre. She curls up in her jail cell and sleeps. RITA JOE's FATHER enters on the ramp and crosses down to the audience. The stage worklights die down. Lights isolate RITA JOE's FATHER. Another light with prison bar shadows isolates RITA JOE in her area of the stage.

FATHER: (*looking down on RITA JOE*) I see no way . . . no way . . . . It's not clear like trees against snow . . . not clear at all . . . .

To the audience.

FATHER: But when I was fifteen years old, I leave the reserve to work on a threshing crew. They pay a dollar a day for a good man . . . an' I was a good strong man. The first time I got work there was a girl about as old as I . . . . She'd come out in the yard an' watch the men working at the threshing machine. She had eyes that were the biggest I ever seen . . . like fifty-cent pieces . . . an' there was always a flock of geese around her. Whenever I see her I feel good. She used to stand an' watch me, an' the geese made a helluva lot of noise. One time I got off my rick an' went to get a drink of water . . . but I walked close to where she was watching me. She backed away, and then ran from me with the geese chasin' after her, their wings out an' their feet no longer touching the ground . . . . They were white geese . . . . The last time Rita Joe come home to see us . . . the last time she ever come home . . . I watched her leave . . . and I seen geese running after Rita Joe the same way . . . white geese . . . with their wings out an' their feet no longer touching the ground. And I remembered it all, an' my heart got so heavy I wanted to cry . . . .

The light fades to darkness on the FATHER, as he exits up the ramp and off. RITA JOE wakes from her dream, cold, shaking, desperate.

SINGER:
The blue evening of the
First warm day
Is the last evening.
There'll not be another
Like it.

The PRIEST enters from darkness with the POLICEMAN. He is dressed in a dark suit which needs pressing. He stops in half shadow outside RITA JOE's prison light. The scene between them is played out in the manner of two country people meeting in a time of crisis. Their thoughts come slowly, incompletely. There is both fear and helplessness in both characters.

PRIEST: I came twice before they'd let me see you . . . .

RITA JOE jumps to her feet. She smiles at him.

RITA: Oh, Father Andrew!

PRIEST: Even so, I had to wait an hour.

A long pause. He clumsily takes out a package of cigarettes and matches from his pocket and hands them to her, aware that he is possibly breaking a prison regulation.

PRIEST: I'm sorry about this, Rita.

RITA JOE tears the package open greedily and lights a cigarette. She draws on it with animal satisfaction.

RITA: I don't know what's happening, Father Andrew.

PRIEST: They're not . . . hurting you here?

RITA: No.

PRIEST: I could make an appointment with the warden if there was something . . .

RITA: What's it like outside? . . . Is it a nice day outside? I heard it raining last night . . . . Was it raining?

PRIEST: It rains a lot here . . .

RITA: When I was a kid, there was leaves an' a river . . . . Jaimie Paul told me once that maybe we never see those things again.

A long pause. The PRIEST struggles with himself.

PRIEST: I've never been inside a jail before . . . . They told me there was a chapel . . . .

He points indefinitely back.

RITA: What's gonna happen to me? . . . That judge sure got sore . . . .

She laughs.

PRIEST: (*with disgust, yet unsure of himself*) Prostitution this time?

RITA: I guess so . . . .

PRIEST: You know how I feel . . . . City is no place for you . . . nor for me . . . . I've spent my life in the same surroundings as your father!

RITA: Sure . . . but you had God on your side!

She smiles mischievously. The PRIEST angers.

PRIEST: Rita, try to understand . . . . Our Lord Jesus once met a woman such as you beside the well . . . . He forgave her!

RITA: I don't think God hears me here . . . . Nobody hears me now, nobody except cops an' pimps an' bootleggers!

PRIEST: I'm here. I was there when you were born.

RITA: You've told me lots of times . . . . I was thinkin' about my mother last night . . . . She died young . . . . I'm older than she was . . . .

PRIEST: Your mother was a good, hard-working woman. She was happy . . . .

A pause between them.

RITA: There was frost on the street at five o'clock Tuesday morning when they arrested me . . . . Last night I remembered things flyin' and kids runnin' past me trying to catch a chocolate wrapper that's blowin' in the wind . . . . (*She presses her hands against her bosom.*) It hurts me here to think about them things!

PRIEST: I worry about you . . . . Your father worries too . . . . I baptized you . . . . I watched you and Leenie grow into women!

RITA: Yes . . . I seen God in what you said . . . in your clothes! In your hair!

PRIEST: But you're not the woman I expected you to be . . . . Your pride, Rita . . . your pride . . . may bar you from heaven.

RITA: (*mocking him*) They got rules there too . . . in heaven?

PRIEST: (*angry*) Rita! . . . I'm not blind . . . I can see! I'm not deaf . . . I know all about you! So does God!

RITA: My uncle was Dan Joe . . . . He was dyin' and he said to me, "Long ago the white man come with Bibles to talk to my people, who had the land. They talk for hundred years . . . then we had all the Bibles, an' the white man had our land . . . . "

PRIEST: Don't blame the Church! We are trying to help . . .

RITA: (*with passion*) How? I'm looking for the door . . . .

PRIEST: (*tortured now*) I . . . will hear your confession . . .

RITA: But I want to be free!

PRIEST: (*stiffly*) We learn through suffering, Rita Joe . . . . We will only be free if we become humble again. (*Pause.*) Will you confess, Rita Joe? (*A long pause.*) I'm going back on the four o'clock bus. (*He begins walking away into the gloom.*) I'll tell your father I saw you, and you looked well.

He is suddenly relieved.

RITA: (*after him as he leaves*) You go to hell!

The PRIEST turns sharply.

RITA: Go tell your God . . . when you see him . . . tell him about Rita Joe an' what they done to her! Tell him about yourself too! . . . That you were not good enough for me, but that didn't stop you tryin'! Tell him that!

The PRIEST hurries away. Guitar in. RITA JOE sits down, brooding.

SINGER:
I will give you the wind and a sense of wonder
As the child by the river, the reedy river.
I will give you the sky wounded by thunder
And a leaf on the river, the silver river.

A light comes up on the ramp where JAIMIE PAUL appears, smiling and waving to her.

JAIMIE: (*shouting*) Rita Joe! I'm gonna take you dancing after work Friday . . . . That job's gonna be alright!

RITA JOE springs to her feet, elated.

RITA: Put me back in jail so I can be free on Friday!

A sudden burst of dance music. The stage lights up and JAIMIE PAUL approaches her. They dance together, remaining close downstage centre.

SINGER:
Round an' round the cenotaph,
The clumsy seagulls play.
Fed by funny men with hats
Who watch them night and day.

Sleepless hours, heavy nights,
Dream your dreams so pretty.
God was gonna have a laugh
An' gave me a job in the city!

The music continues for the interlude.

Some YOUNG INDIAN MEN run onto the stage along the ramp and join JAIMIE PAUL and RITA JOE in their dance. The MURDERERS enter and elbow into the group, their attention specifically menacing towards JAIMIE PAUL and RITA JOE. A street brawl begins as a POLICEMAN passes through on his beat. The MURDERERS leave hastily.

I woke up at six o'clock,
Stumbled out of bed.
Crash of steel and diesel trucks
Damned near killed me dead.

Sleepless hours, heavy nights,
Dream your dreams so pretty.
God was gonna have a laugh
An' gave me a job in the city!

Musical interlude. RITA JOE and JAIMIE PAUL continue dancing languidly. The YOUNG INDI-AN MEN exit.

I've polished floors an' cut the trees,
Fished and stooked the wheat.
Now "Hallelujah, Praise the Lord,"
I sing before I eat!

Sleepless hours, heavy nights,
Dream your dreams so pretty.
God was gonna have a laugh
An' gave me a job in the city!

Musical interlude.

The music dies as the YOUNG INDIAN MEN wheel in a brass bed, circle it around and exit. The stage darkens except for a pool of light where RITA JOE and JAIMIE PAUL stand, embracing. JAIMIE PAUL takes her hand and leads her away.

JAIMIE: Come on, Rita Joe . . . you're slow.

RITA: (*happy in her memories, not wishing to forget too soon, hesitating*) How much rent . . . for a place where you can keep babies?

JAIMIE: I don't know . . . maybe eighty dollars a month.

RITA: That's a lot of money.

JAIMIE: It costs a buck to go dancin' even . . . .

They walk slowly along the apron to stage left, as if following a street to JAIMIE PAUL's rooming house.

JAIMIE: It's a good place . . . . I got a sink in the room. Costs seven bucks a week, that's all!

RITA: That's good . . . . I only got a bed in my place . . . .

JAIMIE: I seen Mickey an' Steve Laporte last night.

RITA: How are they?

JAIMIE: Good . . . . We're goin' to a beer parlour Monday night when I get paid . . . the same beer parlour they threw Steve out of! Only now there's three of us goin' in!

They arrive at and enter his room. A spot illuminates the bed near the wings of stage left. It is old, dilapidated. JAIMIE PAUL and RITA JOE enter the area of light around the bed. He is aware that the room is more drab than he would wish it.

JAIMIE: How do you like it . . . I like it!

RITA: *(examining room critically)* It's . . . smaller than my place.

JAIMIE: Sit down.

She sits on the edge of the bed and falls backward into a springless hollow. He laughs nervously. He is awkward and confused. The ease they shared walking to his place is now constricted.

JAIMIE: I was gonna get some grub today, but I was busy . . . . Here . . . .

He takes a chocolate bar out of his shirt pocket and offers it to her. She opens it, breaks off a small piece, and gives the remainder to him. He closes the wrapper and replaces the bar in his pocket. She eats ravenously. He walks around the bed nervously.

JAIMIE: No fat d.p.'s gonna throw me or the boys out of that beer parlour or he's gonna get this!

He holds up a fist in a gesture that is both poignant and futile. She laughs and he glowers at her.

JAIMIE: I'm tellin' you!

RITA: If they want to throw you out, they'll throw you out.

JAIMIE: Well, this is one Indian guy they're not pushing around no more!

RITA: God helps them who help themselves.

JAIMIE: That's right! *(laughing)* I was lookin' at the white shirts in Eaton's and this bugger comes an' says to me, you gonna buy or you gonna look all day?

RITA: *(looking around her)* It's a nice room for a guy, I guess . . .

JAIMIE: It's a lousy room!

RITA JOE lies back lengthwise in the bed. JAIMIE PAUL sits on the bed beside her.

RITA: You need a good job to have babies in the city . . . . Clara Hill gave both her kids away they say . . . .

JAIMIE: Where do kids like that go?

RITA: Foster homes, I guess.

JAIMIE: If somebody don't like the kid, back they go to another foster home?

RITA: I guess so . . . . Clara Hill don't know where her kids are now.

JAIMIE: *(twisting sharply in his anger)* Goddamn it!

RITA: My father says . . .

JAIMIE PAUL rises, crosses round the bed to the other side.

JAIMIE: *(harshly)* I don't want to hear what your father got to say! He's like . . . like the kind of Indian a white man likes! He's gonna look wise and wait forever . . . for what? For the kids they take away to come back?

RITA: He's scared . . . I'm scared . . . . We're all scared, Jaimie Paul.

JAIMIE PAUL lies face down and mimes a gun through the bars.

JAIMIE: Sometimes I feel like takin' a gun and just . . . .

He waves his hand as if to liquidate his environment and all that bedevils him. He turns over on his back and lies beside RITA JOE.

JAIMIE: I don't know . . . . Goddamnit, I don't know what to do. I get mad an' then I don't know what I'm doing or thinkin' . . . . I get scared sometimes, Rita Joe.

RITA: (*tenderly*) We're scared . . . everybody . . . .

JAIMIE: I'm scared of dyin' . . . in the city. They don't care for one another here . . . . You got to be smart or have a good job to live like that.

RITA: Clara Hill's gonna have another baby . . .

JAIMIE: I can't live like that . . . . A man don't count for much here . . . . Women can do as much as a man . . . . There's no difference between men and women. I can't live like that.

RITA: You got to stop worrying, Jaimie Paul. You're gonna get sick worryin'.

JAIMIE: You can't live like that, can you?

RITA: No.

JAIMIE: I can't figure out what the hell they want from us!

RITA: (*laughing*) Last time I was in trouble, the judge was asking me what I wanted from him! I could've told him, but I didn't!

They both laugh. JAIMIE PAUL becomes playful and happy.

JAIMIE: Last night I seen television in a store window. I seen a guy on television showing this knife that cuts everything it's so sharp . . . . He was cutting up good shoes like they were potatoes . . . . That was sure funny to see!

Again they laugh in merriment at the idea of such a demonstration. JAIMIE PAUL continues with his story, gesturing with his hands.

JAIMIE: Chop . . . chop . . . chop . . . . A potful of shoes in no time! What's a guy gonna do with a potful of shoes? Cook them?

They continue laughing and lie together again. Then JAIMIE PAUL sobers. He rises from the bed and walks around it. He offers his hand to RITA JOE, who also rises.

JAIMIE: (*drily*) Come on. This is a lousy room!

SINGER: (*reprise*)
God was gonna have a laugh,
And gave me a job in the city!

The light goes down on RITA JOE and JAIMIE PAUL. The YOUNG INDIAN MEN clear the bed. Cross fade to the rear ramp of the stage. RITA JOE's FATHER and the PRIEST enter and cross the stage.

PRIEST: She got out yesterday, but she wouldn't let me see her. I stayed an extra day, but she wouldn't see me.

FATHER: (*sadly*) I must go once more to the city . . . . I must go to see them.

PRIEST: You're an old man . . . . I wish I could persuade you not to go.

FATHER: You wouldn't say that if you had children, Andrew . . . .

The lights go down on them. The lights come up downstage centre. Three YOUNG INDIAN MEN precede MR. HOMER, carrying a table between them. MR. HOMER follows with a hamper of clothes under his arm.

MR. HOMER: Yeh . . . right about there is fine, boys. Got to get the clutter out of the basement . . . . There's mice coming in to beat hell.

MR. HOMER empties the clothes hamper on the table. The YOUNG INDIAN MEN step aside and converse in an undertone. On the ramp, a YOUNG INDIAN MAN weaves his way from stage left and down to centre stage where the others have brought the table. He is followed by JAIMIE PAUL and RITA JOE, who mime his intoxicated progress.

MR. HOMER: (*speaking to the audience*) The Society for Aid to the Indians sent a guy over to see if I could recommend someone who'd been . . . well, through the mill, like they say . . . an' then smartened up an' taken rehabilitation. The guy said they just wanted a rehabilitated Indian to show up at their annual dinner. No speeches or fancy stuff . . . just be there.

The YOUNG INDIAN MAN lies down carefully to one side of MR. HOMER.

MR. HOMER: Hi, Louie. Not that I would cross the street for the Society . . . . They're nothing but a pack of do-gooders out to get their name in the papers . . . .

The YOUNG INDIAN MAN begins to sing a tuneless song, trailing off into silence.

MR. HOMER: Keep it down, eh, Louie? I couldn't think of anybody to suggest to this guy . . . so he went away pretty sore . . . .

RITA JOE begins to rummage through the clothes on the table. She looks at sweaters and holds a red one thoughtfully in her hands. JAIMIE PAUL is in conversation with the YOUNG INDIAN MEN to one side of the table. MR. HOMER turns from the audience to see RITA JOE holding the sweater.

MR. HOMER: Try it on, Rita Joe . . . . That's what the stuff's here for.

JAIMIE PAUL turns. He is in a provocative mood, seething with rebellion that makes the humour he triggers both biting and deceptively innocent. The YOUNG INDIAN MEN respond to him with strong laughter. JAIMIE PAUL takes a play punch at one of them.

JAIMIE: Whoops! Scared you, eh?

He glances back at MR. HOMER, as if talking to him.

JAIMIE: Can't take it, eh? The priest can't take it. Indian Department guys can't take it . . . . Why listen to them? Listen to the radio if you want to hear something.

The YOUNG INDIAN MEN laugh.

JAIMIE: Or listen to me! You think I'm smart?

YOUNG INDIAN MAN: You're a smart man, Jaimie Paul.

JAIMIE: Naw . . . I'm not smart . . . (*pointing to another YOUNG INDIAN MAN*) This guy here . . . calls himself squaw-humper . . . he's smart! . . . Him . . . he buys extra big shirts . . . more cloth for the same money . . . . That's smart! (*Laughter.*) I'm not smart. (*seriously*) You figure we can start a business an' be our own boss?

YOUNG INDIAN MAN: I don't know about that . . . .

JAIMIE PAUL leaves them and goes to lean over the YOUNG INDIAN MAN who is now asleep on the floor.

JAIMIE: Buy a taxi . . . be our own boss . . . .

He shakes the sleeping YOUNG INDIAN MAN, who immediately begins his tuneless song.

JAIMIE: Aw, he's drunk . . . .

JAIMIE PAUL goes over to the table and stares at the YOUNG INDIAN MAN beyond the table.

JAIMIE: (*soberly*) Buy everything we need . . . . Don't be bums! Bums need grub an' clothes . . . . Bums is bad for the country, right Mr. Homer?

MR. HOMER: (*nodding*) I guess so . . . . (*to RITA JOE who is now wearing the old sweater*) Red looks good on you, Rita Joe . . . . Take it!

JAIMIE PAUL goes over and embraces RITA JOE, then pushes her gently away.

JAIMIE: She looks better in yellow. I never seen a red dandelion before.

He and the YOUNG INDIAN MEN laugh, but the laughter is hollow.

MR. HOMER: Come on, Jaimie! Leave the girl alone. That's what it's here for . . . . Are you working?

JAIMIE: (*evasive, needling*) Yeh! . . . No! . . . "Can you drive?" the guy says to me. "Sure, I can drive," I says to him. "Okay," he says, "then drive this broom until the warehouse is clean."

They all laugh.

MR. HOMER: That's a good one . . . Jaimie, you're a card . . . . Well, time to get some food for you lot . . . .

MR. HOMER leaves. RITA JOE feels better about the sweater. She looks to one of the YOUNG INDIAN MEN for approval. JAIMIE PAUL becomes grim-faced.

RITA: Do you like it?

YOUNG INDIAN MAN: Sure. It's a nice sweater . . . . Take it.

JAIMIE: Take it where? Take it to hell . . . . Be men! (*pointing after MR. HOMER*) He's got no kids . . . . Guys like that get mean when they got no kids . . . . We're his kids an' he means to keep it that way! Well, I'm a big boy now! (*to RITA JOE*) I go to the employment office. I want work an' I want it now. "I'm not a goddamned cripple," I says to him. An' he says he can only take my name! If work comes he'll call me! "What the hell is this," I says to him. "I'll never get work like that . . . . There's no telephone in the house where I got a room!"

MR. HOMER returns pushing a wheeled tray on which he has some food for sandwiches, a loaf of bread and a large cutting knife. He begins to make some sandwiches.

RITA: (*scolding JAIMIE PAUL*) You won't get work talking that way, Jaimie Paul!

JAIMIE: Why not? I'm not scared. He gets mad at me an' I say to him . . . "You think I'm some stupid Indian you're talkin' to? Heh? You think that?"

JAIMIE PAUL struts and swaggers to demonstrate how he faced his opponent at the employment office.

MR. HOMER: (*cutting bread*) You're a tough man to cross, Jaimie Paul.

JAIMIE: (*ignoring MR. HOMER, to the YOUNG INDIAN MEN*) Boy, I showed that bastard who he was talkin' to!

RITA: Did you get the job?

JAIMIE: (*turning to her, laughing boyishly*) No! He called the cops an' they threw me out!

They all laugh. The YOUNG INDIAN MEN go to the table now and rummage through the clothes.

MR. HOMER: Take whatever you want, boys . . . there's more clothes comin' tomorrow.

JAIMIE PAUL impulsively moves to the table where the YOUNG INDIAN MEN are fingering the clothes. He pushes them aside and shoves the clothes in a heap leaving a small corner of the table clean. He takes out two coins from his pockets and spits in his hands.

JAIMIE: I got a new trick . . . . Come on, Mister Homer . . . I'll show you! See this!

He shows the coins, then slams his hands palms down on the table.

JAIMIE: Which hand got the coins?

MR. HOMER: Why . . . one under each hand . . . .

JAIMIE: Right! (*turning up his hands*) Again? (*He collects the coins and slaps his hands down again.*) Where are the coins now? Come on, guess!

MR. HOMER is confident now, and points to the right hand with his cutting knife. JAIMIE PAUL laughs and lifts his hands. The coins are under his left hand.

MR. HOMER: Son of a gun.

JAIMIE: You're a smart man.

He puts the coins in his pockets and, laughing, turns to RITA JOE who stands uncertainly, dressed in the red sweater. She likes the garment, but she is aware JAIMIE PAUL might resent her taking it. The YOUNG INDIAN MEN again move to the table, and MR. HOMER returns to making sandwiches.

MR. HOMER: There's a good pair of socks might come in handy for one of you guys!

A YOUNG INDIAN MAN pokes his thumbs through the holes in the socks, and laughs.

JAIMIE: Sure . . . take the socks! Take the table!

He slaps the table with his hands and laughs.

JAIMIE: Take Mister Homer cutting bread! Take everything!

MR. HOMER: Hey, Jaimie!

JAIMIE: Why not? There's more comin' tomorrow, you said!

RITA: Jaimie!

MR. HOMER: You're sure in a smart-assed mood today, aren't you?

JAIMIE: (*pointing to the YOUNG INDIAN MAN with the socks, but talking to MR. HOMER*) Mister, friend Steve over there laughs lots . . . . He figures . . . the way to get along an' live is to grab his guts an' laugh at anything anybody says. You see him laughing all the time. A dog barks at him an' he laughs . . . . (*Laughter from the YOUNG INDIAN MAN.*) Laughs at a fence post fallin' . . . . (*Laughter.*) Kids with funny eyes make him go haywire . . . . (*Laughter.*) Can of meat an' no can opener . . . .

MR. HOMER *watches the* YOUNG INDIAN MEN *and grins at* JAIMIE PAUL.

MR. HOMER: Yeh . . . he laughs quite a bit . . . .

JAIMIE: He laughs at a rusty nail . . . . Nice guy . . . . laughs all the time.

MR. HOMER: (*to* JAIMIE PAUL, *holding the knife*) You wanted mustard on your bread or just plain?

JAIMIE: I seen him cut his hand and start laughin' . . . . Isn't that funny?

The YOUNG INDIAN MEN *laugh, but with less humour now.*

MR. HOMER: (*to* JAIMIE PAUL) You want mustard? . . . I'm talkin' to you!

JAIMIE: I'm not hungry.

The YOUNG INDIAN MEN *stop laughing altogether. They become tense and suspicious of* JAIMIE PAUL, *who is watching them severely.*

MR. HOMER: Suit yourself. Rita?

She shakes her head slowly, her gaze on JAIMIE PAUL's *face.*

RITA: I'm not hungry.

MR. HOMER *looks from* RITA JOE *to* JAIMIE PAUL, *then to the* YOUNG INDIAN MEN. *His manner stiffens.*

MR. HOMER: I see . . . .

JAIMIE PAUL *and* RITA JOE *touch hands and come forward to sit on the apron of the stage, front. A pale light is on the two of them. The stage lights behind them fade. A low light that is diffused and shadowy remains on the table where* MR. HOMER *has prepared the food. The* YOUNG INDIAN MEN *move slowly to the table and begin eating the sandwiches* MR. HOMER *offers to them. The light on the table fades very low.* JAIMIE PAUL *hands a cigarette to* RITA JOE *and they smoke.*

Light comes up over the rear ramp. RITA JOE's *FATHER enters onto the ramp from the wings of stage right. His step is resolute. The* PRIEST *follows behind him a few paces. They have been arguing. Both are dressed in work clothes: heavy trousers and windbreakers.*

JAIMIE: When I'm laughing, I got friends.

RITA: I know, Jaimie Paul . . . .

PRIEST: That was the way I found her, that was the way I left her.

JAIMIE: (*bitterly*) When I'm laughing, I'm a joker . . . a funny boy!

FATHER: If I was young . . . I wouldn't sleep. I would talk to people . . . let them all know!

JAIMIE: I'm not dangerous when I'm laughing . . . .

PRIEST: You could lose the reserve and have nowhere to go!

FATHER: I have lost more than that! Young people die . . . young people don't believe me . . . .

JAIMIE: That's alright . . . that's alright . . . .

The light dies out on JAIMIE PAUL *and* RITA JOE. *The light also dies out on* MR. HOMER *and the* YOUNG INDIAN MEN.

PRIEST: You think they believe that hot-headed . . . that troublemaker?

FATHER: (*turning to face the* PRIEST) Jaimie Paul is a good boy!

PRIEST: David Joe . . . you and I have lived through a lot. We need peace now, and time to consider what to do next.

FATHER: Eileen said to me last night . . . she wants to go to the city. I worry all night . . . . What can I do?

PRIEST: I'll talk to her, if you wish.

FATHER: (*angry*) And tell her what? . . . Of the animals there . . . (*gesturing to the audience*) who sleep with sore stomachs because . . . they eat too much?

PRIEST: We mustn't lose the reserve and the old life, David Joe . . . . Would you . . . give up being chief on the reserve?

FATHER: Yes!

PRIEST: To Jaimie Paul?

FATHER: No . . . to someone who's been to school . . . maybe university . . . who knows more.

PRIEST: (*relieved by this, but not reassured*) The people here need your wisdom and stability, David Joe. There is no man here who knows as much about hunting and fishing and guiding. You can survive . . . . What does a youngster who's been away to school know of this?

FATHER: (*sadly*) If we only fish an' hunt an' cut pulpwood . . . pick strawberries in the bush . . . for a hundred years more, we are dead. I know this, here . . . . (*He touches his breast.*)

The light dies on the ramp. A light rises on stage front, on JAIMIE PAUL and RITA JOE sitting at the apron of the stage. MR. HOMER is still cutting bread for sandwiches. The three YOUNG INDIAN MEN have eaten and appear restless to leave. The fourth YOUNG INDIAN MAN is still asleep on the floor. RITA JOE has taken off the red sweater, but continues to hold it in her hand.

JAIMIE: (*to MR. HOMER*) One time I was on a trapline five days without grub. I ate snow an' I walked until I got back. You think you can take it like me?

MR. HOMER approaches JAIMIE PAUL and holds out a sandwich to him.

MR. HOMER: Here . . . have a sandwich now.

JAIMIE PAUL ignores his hand.

RITA: Mister Homer don't know what happened, Jaimie Paul.

MR. HOMER shrugs and walks away to his sandwich table.

JAIMIE: Then he's got to learn . . . . Sure he knows! (*to MR. HOMER*) Sure he knows! He's feedin' sandwiches to Indian bums . . . . He knows. He's the worst kind!

The YOUNG INDIAN MEN freeze and MR. HOMER stops.

MR. HOMER: (*coldly*) I've never yet asked a man to leave this building.

RITA JOE and JAIMIE PAUL rise to their feet. RITA JOE goes to the clothes table and throws the red sweater back on the pile of clothes. JAIMIE PAUL laughs sardonically.

MR. HOMER: (*to RITA JOE*) Hey, not you, girl . . . . You take it!

She shakes her head and moves to leave.

RITA: I think we better go, boys.

The sleeping YOUNG INDIAN MAN slowly raises his head, senses there is something wrong, and is about to be helped up when . . .

JAIMIE: After five days without grub, the first meal I threw up . . . stomach couldn't take it . . . But after it was alright . . . (*to MR. HOMER, with intensity*) I don't believe nobody . . . no priest nor government . . . They don't know what it's like to . . . to want an' not have . . . to stand in line an' nobody sees you!

MR. HOMER: If you want food, eat! You need clothes, take them. That's all . . . But I'm runnin' this centre my way, and I mean it!

JAIMIE: I come to say no to you . . . That's all . . . that's all!

He throws out his arms in a gesture that is both defiant and childlike. The gesture disarms some of MR. HOMER's growing hostility.

MR. HOMER: You've got that right . . . no problems. There's others come through here day an' night . . . . No problems.

JAIMIE: I don't want no others to come. I don't want them to eat here! (*indicating his friends*) If we got to take it from behind a store window, then we break the window an' wait for the cops. It's better than . . . than this!

He gestures with contempt at the food and the clothes on the table.

MR. HOMER: Rita Joe . . . where'd you pick up this . . . this loudmouth anyway?

RITA: (*slowly, firmly*) I think . . . Jaimie Paul's . . . right.

MR. HOMER looks from face to face. The three YOUNG INDIAN MEN are passive, staring into the distance. The fourth is trying hard to clear his head. JAIMIE PAUL is cold, hostile. RITA JOE is determined.

MR. HOMER: (*decisively*) Alright! You've eaten . . . looked over the clothes . . . . Now clear out so others get a chance to come in! Move!

He tries to herd everyone out and the four YOUNG INDIAN MEN begin to move away. JAIMIE PAUL mimics the gestures of MR. HOMER and steps in front of the YOUNG INDIAN MEN herding them back in.

JAIMIE: Run, boys, run! Or Mister Homer gonna beat us up!

RITA JOE takes JAIMIE PAUL's hand and tries to pull him away to leave.

RITA: Jaimie Paul . . . you said to me no trouble!

JAIMIE PAUL pulls his hand free and jumps back of the clothes table. MR. HOMER comes for him, unknowingly still carrying the slicing knife in his hand. An absurd chase begins around the table. One of the YOUNG INDIAN MEN laughs, and stepping forward, catches hold of MR. HOMER's hand with the knife in it.

YOUNG INDIAN MAN: Hey! Don't play with a knife, Mister Homer!

He gently takes the knife away from MR. HOMER and drops it on the food table behind. MR. HOMER looks at his hand, an expression of shock on his face. JAIMIE PAUL gives him no time to think about the knife and what it must have appeared like to the YOUNG INDIAN MEN. He pulls a large brassiere from the clothes table and mockingly holds it over his breasts, which he sticks out enticingly at MR. HOMER. The YOUNG INDIAN MEN laugh. MR. HOMER is exasperated and furious. RITA JOE is frightened.

RITA: It's not funny, Jaimie!

JAIMIE: It's funny as hell, Rita Joe. Even funnier this way!

JAIMIE PAUL puts the brassiere over his head, with the cups down over his ears and the straps under his chin. The YOUNG INDIAN MEN are all laughing now and moving close to the table. MR. HOMER makes a futile attempt at driving them off.

Suddenly JAIMIE PAUL's expression turns to one of hatred. He throws the brassiere on the table and gripping its edge, throws the table and clothes over, scattering the clothes. He kicks at them. The YOUNG INDIAN MEN all jump in and, picking up the clothes, hurl them over the ramp.

RITA JOE runs in to try and stop them. She grips the table and tries lifting it up again.

MR. HOMER: (*to JAIMIE PAUL*) Cut that out, you sonofabitch!

JAIMIE PAUL stands watching him. MR. HOMER is in a fury. He sees RITA JOE struggling to right the table. He moves to her and pushes her hard.

MR. HOMER: You slut! . . . You breed whore!

RITA JOE recoils. With a shriek of frustration, she attacks MR. HOMER, tearing at him. He backs away, then turns and runs. JAIMIE PAUL overturns the table again. The others join in the melee with the clothes. A POLICEMAN enters and grabs JAIMIE PAUL. RITA JOE and the four YOUNG INDIAN MEN exit, clearing away the tables and remaining clothes.

A sharp, tiny spotlight comes up on the face and upper torso of JAIMIE PAUL. He is wild with rebellion as the POLICEMAN forces him, in an arm lock, down towards the audience.

JAIMIE: (*screaming defiance at the audience*) Not jus' a box of cornflakes! When I go in I want the whole store! That's right . . . the whole goddamned store!

Another sharp light on the MAGISTRATE standing on his podium looking down at JAIMIE PAUL.

MAGISTRATE: Thirty days!

JAIMIE: (*held by POLICEMEN*) Sure, sure . . . . Anything else you know?

MAGISTRATE: Thirty days!

JAIMIE: Gimme back my truth!

MAGISTRATE: We'll get larger prisons and more police in every town and city across the country!

JAIMIE: Teach me who I really am! You've taken that away! Give me back the real me so I can live like a man!

MAGISTRATE: There is room for dialogue. There is room for disagreement and there is room for social change . . . but within the framework of institutions and traditions in existence for that purpose!

JAIMIE: (*spitting*) Go to hell! . . . I can die an' you got nothing to tell me!

MAGISTRATE: (*in a cold fury*) Thirty days! And after that, it will be six months! And after that . . . God help you!

The MAGISTRATE marches off his platform and offstage. JAIMIE PAUL is led off briskly in the other direction offstage.

The lights change. RITA JOE enters, crossing the stage, exchanging a look with the SINGER.

SINGER:
Sleepless hours, heavy nights,
Dream your dreams so pretty.
God was gonna have a laugh
An' gave me a job in the city!

RITA JOE walks the street. She is smoking a ciga-rette. She is dispirited.

The light broadens across the stage. RITA JOE's FATHER and JAIMIE PAUL enter the stage from the wings of centre stage left. They walk slowly towards where RITA JOE stands. At the sight of her FATHER, RITA JOE moans softly and hurriedly stamps out her cigarette. She visibly straightens and waits for the approaching men, her expression one of fear and joy.

FATHER: I got a ride on Miller's truck . . . took me two days . . . .

JAIMIE: It's a long way, David Joe.

The FATHER stops a pace short of RITA JOE and looks at her with great tenderness and concern.

FATHER: (*softly*) I come . . . to get Rita Joe.

RITA: Oh . . . I don't know . . . .

She looks to JAIMIE PAUL for help in deciding what to do, but he is sullen and uncommunicative.

FATHER: I come to take Rita Joe home . . . . We got a house an' some work sometime . . . .

JAIMIE: She's with me now, David Joe.

RITA: (*very torn*) I don't know . . . .

JAIMIE: You don't have to go back, Rita Joe.

RITA JOE looks away from her FATHER with humility. The FATHER turns to JAIMIE PAUL. He stands ancient and heroic.

FATHER: I live . . . an' I am afraid. Because . . . I have not done everything. When I have done everything . . . know that my children are safe . . . then . . . it will be alright. Not before.

JAIMIE: (*to RITA JOE*) You don't have to go. This is an old man now . . . . He has nothing to give . . . nothin' to say!

RITA JOE reacts to both men, her conflict deepening.

FATHER: (*turning away from JAIMIE PAUL to RITA JOE*) For a long time . . . a very long time . . . she was in my hands . . . like that! (*He cups his hands into the shape of a bowl.*) Sweet . . . tiny . . . lovin' all the time and wanting love . . . (*He shakes his head sadly.*)

JAIMIE: (*angrily*) Go tell it to the white men! They're lookin' for Indians that stay proud even when they hurt . . . just so long's they don't ask for their rights!

The FATHER turns slowly, with great dignity, to JAIMIE PAUL. His gestures show JAIMIE PAUL to be wrong; the old man's spirit was never broken. JAIMIE PAUL understands and looks away.

FATHER: You're a good boy, Jaimie Paul . . . a good boy . . . . (*to RITA JOE, talking slowly, painfully*) I once seen a dragonfly breakin' its shell to get its wings . . . . It floated on water an' crawled up on a log where I was sitting . . . . It dug its feet into the log an' then it pulled until the shell bust over its neck. Then it pulled some more . . . an' slowly its wings slipped out of the shell . . . like that!

He shows with his hands how the dragonfly got his freedom.

JAIMIE: (*angered and deeply moved by the FATHER*) Where you gonna be when they start bustin' our heads open an' throwing us into jails right across the goddamned country?

FATHER: Such wings I never seen before . . . folded like an accordion so fine, like thin glass an' white in the morning sun . . . .

JAIMIE: We're gonna have to fight to win . . . there's no other way! They're not listenin' to you, old man! Or to me.

FATHER: It spread its wings . . . so slowly . . . an' then the wings opened an' began to flutter . . . just like that . . . see! Hesitant at first . . . then stronger . . . an' then the wings beatin' like that made the dragonfly's body quiver until the shell on its back falls off . . .

JAIMIE: Stop kiddin' yourself! We're gonna say no pretty soon to all the crap that makes us soft an' easy to push this way . . . that way!

FATHER: . . . An' the dragonfly . . . flew up . . . up . . . up . . . into the white sun . . . to the green sky . . . to the sun . . . faster an' faster . . . . Higher . . . higher!

The FATHER reaches up with his hands, releasing the imaginary dragonfly into the sun, his final words torn out of his heart. RITA JOE springs to her feet and rushes against JAIMIE PAUL, striking at him with her fists.

RITA: (*savagely*) For Chris' sakes, I'm not goin' back! . . . Leave him alone . . . . He's everything we got left now!

JAIMIE PAUL stands, frozen by his emotion which he can barely control. The FATHER turns. RITA JOE goes to him. The FATHER speaks privately to RITA JOE in Indian dialect. They embrace. He pauses for a long moment to embrace and forgive her everything. Then he goes slowly offstage into the wings of stage left without looking back.

FATHER: Goodbye, Rita Joe . . . . Goodbye, Jaimie Paul . . . .

RITA: Goodbye, Father.

JAIMIE PAUL watches RITA JOE who moves away from him to the front of the stage.

JAIMIE: (*to her*) You comin'?

She shakes her head to indicate no, she is staying. Suddenly JAIMIE PAUL runs away from her diagonally across to the wings upstage. As he nears the wings, the four YOUNG INDIAN MEN emerge, happily on their way to a party. They stop him at his approach. He runs into them, directing them back, his voice breaking with feelings of love and hatred intermingling.

JAIMIE: (*shouting at them*) Next time . . . in a beer parlour or any place like that . . . I'll go myself or you guys take me home . . . . No more white buggers pushin' us out the door or he gets this!

He raises his fist. The group of YOUNG INDIAN MEN, elated by their newly-found determination, surround JAIMIE PAUL and exit into the wings of the stage. The light dies in back and at stage left.

The MAGISTRATE enters. There is a light on RITA JOE where she stands. There is also a light around the MAGISTRATE. The MAGISTRATE's voice and purpose are leaden. He has given up on RITA JOE. He is merely performing the formality of condemning her and dismissing her from his conscience.

MAGISTRATE: I sentence you to thirty days in prison.

RITA: (*angry, defiant*) Sure, sure . . . . Anything else you know?

MAGISTRATE: I sentence you to thirty days in prison, with a recommendation you be examined medically and given all necessary treatment at the prison clinic. There is nothing . . . there is nothing I can do now.

RITA: (*stoically*) Thank you. Is that right? To thank you?

MAGISTRATE: You'll be back . . . always be back . . . growing older, tougher . . . filthier . . . looking more like stone and prison bars . . . the lines in your face will tell everyone who sees you about prison windows and prison food.

RITA: No child on the road would remember you, mister!

The MAGISTRATE comes down to stand before her. He has the rambling confidence of detached authority.

MAGISTRATE: What do you expect? We provide schools for you and you won't attend them because they're out of the way and that little extra effort is too much for you! We came up as a civilization having to . . . yes, claw upwards at times . . . . There's nothing wrong with that . . . . We give you X-ray chest clinics . . . .

He turns away from her and goes to the apron of the stage and speaks directly to the audience.

MAGISTRATE: We give them X-ray chest clinics and three-quarters of them won't show up . . . . Those that do frequently get medical attention at one of the hospitals . . .

RITA: (*interjecting*) My mother died!

MAGISTRATE: (*not hearing her*) But as soon as they're released they forget they're chronically ill and end up on a drinking party and a long walk home through the snow . . . . Next thing . . . they're dead!

RITA: (*quietly*) Oh, put me in jail an' then let me go.

MAGISTRATE: (*turning to her*) Some of you get jobs . . . . There are jobs, good jobs, if you'd only look around a bit . . . and stick with them when you get them. But no . . . you get a job and promise to stay with it and learn, and two weeks later you're gone for three, four days without explanation . . . . Your reliability record is ruined and an employer has to regard you as lazy, undependable . . . . What do you expect?

RITA: I'm not scared of you now, bastard!

MAGISTRATE: You have a mind . . . you have a heart. The cities are open to you to come and go as you wish, yet you gravitate to the slums and skid rows and the shanty-town fringes. You become a whore, drunkard, user of narcotics . . . . At best, dying of illness or malnutrition . . . . At worst, kicked or beaten to death by some angry white scum who finds in you something lower than himself to pound his frustrations out on! What's to be done? You Indians seem to be incapable of taking action to help yourselves. Someone must care for you . . . . Who? For how long?

RITA: You don't know nothin'!

MAGISTRATE: I know . . . I know . . . . It's a struggle just to stay alive. I know . . . I understand. That struggle is mine, as well as yours, Rita Joe! The jungle of the executive has as many savage teeth ready to go for the throat as the rundown hotel on the waterfront . . . . Your days and hours are numbered, Rita Joe . . . . I worry for the child I once saw . . . . I have already forgotten the woman!

He turns away from her and exits into the wings of stage right.

The lights on RITA JOE fade. Lights of cold, eerie blue wash the backdrop of the stage faintly. RITA JOE stands in silhouette for a long moment.

Slowly, ominously, the three MURDERERS appear on the ramp backstage, one coming from the wings of stage right; one from the wings of stage left; and one rising from the back of the ramp, climbing it. One of the MURDERERS is whistling, a soft nervous noise throughout their scene onstage.

RITA JOE whimpers in fear, and as the MURDERERS loom above her, she runs along the apron to stage left. Here she bumps into JAIMIE PAUL who enters. She screams in fear.

JAIMIE: Rita Joe!

RITA: (*terrorized*) Jaimie! They're comin'. I seen them comin'!

JAIMIE: Who's coming? What's the matter, Rita Joe?

RITA: Men I once dreamed about . . . . I seen it all happen once before . . . an' it was like this . . . .

JAIMIE PAUL laughs and pats her shoulders reassuringly. He takes her hand and tries to lead her forward to the apron of the stage, but RITA JOE is dead, her steps wooden.

JAIMIE: Don't worry . . . I can take care of myself!

A faint light on the two of them.

RITA: You been in jail now too, Jaimie Paul . . . .

JAIMIE: So what? Guys in jail was saying that they got to put a man behind bars or the judge don't get paid for being in court to make the trial . . . . Funny world, eh, Rita Joe?

RITA: (*nodding*) Funny world.

The light dies on them. They come forward slowly.

JAIMIE: I got a room with a hot plate . . . . We can have a couple of eggs and some tea before we go to the movie.

RITA: What was it like for you in jail?

JAIMIE: So so . . . .

JAIMIE PAUL motions for RITA JOE to follow him and moves forward from her. The distant sound of a train approaching is heard. She is wooden, coming slowly after him.

RITA: It was different where the women were . . . . It's different to be a woman . . . . Some women was wild . . . and they shouted they were riding black horses into a fire I couldn't see . . . . There was no fire there, Jaimie!

JAIMIE: (*turning to her, taking her arm*) Don't worry . . . we're goin' to eat and then see a movie . . . . Come on, Rita Joe!

She looks back and sees the MURDERERS rise and slowly approach from the gloom. Her speech becomes thick and unsteady as she follows JAIMIE PAUL to the front of the ramp.

RITA: One time I couldn't find the street where I had a room to sleep in . . . forgot my handbag . . . had no money . . . . An old man with a dog said hello, but I couldn't say hello back because I was worried an' my mouth was so sticky I couldn't speak to him . . . .

JAIMIE: Are you comin'?

RITA: When you're tired an' sick, Jaimie, the city starts to dance . . . .

JAIMIE: (taking her hand, pulling her gently along) Come on, Rita Joe.

RITA: The street lights start rollin' like wheels an' cement walls feel like they was made of blanket cloth . . . .

The sound of the train is closer now. The lights of its lamps flicker in back of the stage. RITA JOE turns to face the MURDERERS, one of whom is whistling ominously. She whimpers in fear and presses herself against JAIMIE PAUL. JAIMIE PAUL turns and sees the MURDERERS hovering near them.

JAIMIE: Don't be scared . . . . Nothing to be scared of, Rita Joe . . . . (to the MURDERERS) What the hell do you want?

One of the MURDERERS laughs. JAIMIE PAUL pushes RITA JOE back behind himself. He moves towards the MURDERERS, taunting them.

JAIMIE: You think I can't take care of myself?

With deceptive casualness, the MURDERERS approach him. One of them makes a sudden lurch at JAIMIE PAUL as if to draw him into their circle. JAIMIE PAUL anticipates the trap and takes a flying kick at the MURDERER, knocking him down.

They close around JAIMIE PAUL with precision, then attack. JAIMIE PAUL leaps, but is caught mid-air by the other two. They bring him down and put the boots to him. RITA JOE screams and runs to him. The train sound is loud and immediate now.

One of the MURDERERS has grabbed RITA JOE. The remaining two raise JAIMIE PAUL to his feet and one knees him viciously in the groin. JAIMIE PAUL screams and doubles over. The lights of the train are upon them. The MURDERERS leap off the ramp leaving JAIMIE PAUL in the path of the approaching train. JAIMIE PAUL's death cry becomes the sound of the train horn. As the train sound roars by, the MURDERERS return to close in around RITA JOE. One MURDERER springs forward and grabs RITA JOE. The other two help to hold her, with nervous fear and lust. RITA JOE breaks free of them and runs to the front of the stage. The three MURDERERS come after her, panting hard. They close in on her leisurely now,

playing with her, knowing that they have her trapped.

Recorded and overlapping voices.

CLERK: The court calls Rita Joe . . .

MAGISTRATE: Who is she? . . . Let her speak for herself . . .

RITA: In the summer it was hot, an' flies hummed . . .

TEACHER: A book of verse, a melting pot . . .

MAGISTRATE: Thirty days!

FATHER: Barkin' to beat hell . . . . How! How!

JAIMIE: (laughing, defiant, taunting) You go to hell!

PRIEST: A confession, Rita Joe . . .

Over the voices she hears, the MURDERERS attack. Dragging her down backwards, they pull her legs open and one MURDERER lowers himself on her.

RITA: Jaimie! Jaimie! Jaimie!

RITA JOE's head lolls over sideways. The MURDERERS stare at her and pull back slightly.

MURDERER: (thickly, rising off her twisted, broken body) Shit . . . she's dead . . . . We hardly touched her.

He hesitates for a moment, then runs, joined by the SECOND MURDERER.

SECOND MURDERER: Let's get out of here!

They run up onto the ramp and watch as the THIRD MURDERER piteously climbs onto the dead RITA JOE.

Sounds of a funeral chant. MOURNERS appear on riser backstage. RITA JOE's FATHER enters from the wings of stage left, chanting an ancient Indian funeral chant, carrying the body of JAIMIE PAUL. The MURDERER hesitates in his necrophilic rape and then runs away.

The YOUNG INDIAN MEN bring the body of JAIMIE PAUL over the ramp and approach. The body is placed down on the podium, beside RITA JOE's. All the Indians, young and old, kneel around the two bodies. The FATHER continues *his death chant. The PRIEST enters from the wings of stage right reciting a prayer. The TEACHER, SINGER, POLICEMAN and MURDERERS come with him forming the outside perimeter around the Indian funeral.*

PRIEST: Hail Mary, Mother of God . . . pray for us sinners now and at the hour of our death.

Repeated until finally EILEEN JOE slowly rises to her feet and, turning to the PRIEST and WHITE MOURNERS, says softly . . .

EILEEN: (over the sounds of chanting and praying) No! . . . No! . . . No more!

The YOUNG INDIAN MEN rise one after another facing the outer circle defiantly, and the CAST freezes on stage, except for the SINGER.

SINGER:
Oh, the singing bird
Has found its wings
And it's soaring!

My God, what a sight!
On the cold fresh wind of morning! . . .

During the song, EILEEN JOE steps forward to the audience and as the song ends, says . . .

EILEEN: When Rita Joe first come to the city, she told me . . . the cement made her feet hurt.

END

JOHN HERBERT (b. 1926)

Although John Herbert Brundage was a prime mover in the creation of Toronto's alternate theatre in the 1960s—"the single most important figure of the decade," according to Bill Glassco—his success as a playwright, to a much greater extent even than George Ryga's, has happened outside of Canada. And more so than Ryga's it rests on a single play. At last count *Fortune and Men's Eyes* had been performed in over a hundred countries in at least forty different translations. It has sold, in an American edition, more copies than any other published Canadian play. It even led to the founding of the Fortune Society, an organization devoted to prison reform in the United States. Yet *Fortune* was an established international success for nearly eight years before Herbert got to see a professional production in his home and native city, "cold, bitter, suspicious Toronto," as he entitled a 1971 *Saturday Night* article.

Herbert's bitterness about Toronto stems in part from an incident in 1946 when, as he tells it, he was beaten and robbed by a street gang. Instead of laying charges against his assailants, the police charged Herbert with having sexually propositioned them and he was convicted of gross indecency. The six months he spent in Guelph reformatory would later become the basis for *Fortune and Men's Eyes*. The vivid third-person description of his time in prison that Herbert contributed to Geraldine Anthony's *Stage Voices* makes clear that the characters of both Mona and Queenie in *Fortune* are projections of his own experience behind bars.

Herbert's theatrical career began in 1955 when he enrolled in the New Play Society School of Drama, studying acting, directing and production for three years followed by two years of dance training at the National Ballet school. In 1960 he founded Adventure Theatre in Toronto and from 1962-1965 was artistic director of the New Venture Players with whom he produced and directed his own early plays "Private Club," "A Household God" and an adaptation from Dumas, "A Lady of Camelias." In 1965 he opened a fifty-seat theatre over a pizzeria on Yonge Street. The Garret Theatre ran off and on until 1970, subsidized by Herbert's labours as a waiter. Among its productions were his plays "Closer to Cleveland" and "World of Woyzeck," adapted from Büchner.

Meanwhile Herbert had written *Fortune and Men's Eyes* in 1964, and while serving drinks at the University Club he had mentioned it to Robertson Davies who suggested submitting the play to a summer workshop at Stratford. *Toronto Star* critic Nathan Cohen got wind of the 1965 workshop production, read the script and sent it to New York producer David Rothenberg. *Fortune and Men's Eyes* opened off-Broadway in 1967, and within a few years it was making its way around the world.

The international success of *Fortune* did little, however, for Herbert's fortunes in Canada. Unable to get a major Canadian production of the play and with the Garret devouring his foreign royalties, Herbert closed the theatre permanently in 1970 (deeding its equipment to Ken Gass who promptly set up the Factory Lab) and left in frustration to live in England. But two years later he was back in Toronto to stay, trying again to establish his presence in the Canadian theatre. Between 1972 and 1974 he staged two ambitious new plays, *Born of Medusa's Blood* and *Omphale and the Hero*, and four one-acts under the title *Some Angry Summer Songs*, but no one seemed to be listening. By 1975, when *Fortune* won the Chalmers Award for its first professional production in Toronto, Herbert had pretty well retired from the theatre. He has since written a novel (*The House That Jack Built*), taught drama and creative writing, worked as an art and theatre critic, and served as Associate Editor of *Onion*, a Toronto arts newsletter.

All Herbert's full-length plays and many of his one-acts concern relationships characterized by selfishness and betrayal usually resulting in destruction. At the centre of both *Born of Medusa's Blood* and *Omphale and the Hero* are female figures of redemption (who both happen to be whores) destroyed by perverse machismo and a corrupt social order. *Fortune and Men's Eyes* uses the same formula but in a much more dramatically compelling way. The prison environment enforces a distinctive kind of garrison mentality among its inhabitants whose struggle for survival involves not just their physical well-being but their ethical and sexual identities as well.

Fortune and Men's Eyes (originally titled *The Christmas Concert*) has the structure of a morality play. Smitty, as his name suggests, is the Everyman character. He enters the prison world an innocent and is immediately confronted by a distorted value system which demands from him a series of unpalatable choices. As represented by his three cellmates, his choices are to accept, reject or accommodate himself to the prison's values. Rocky has clearly adopted those values as his own. His authoritarianism and racism, his blackmail of the guard and manipulation of Catso show him to be completely at home in the prison system, the jungle in which he calls himself king. At the other extreme is Mona who transcends "her" surroundings by separating body and spirit, preserving—only at a terrible price—an essentially feminine gentleness and sensitivity inimical to the perverted masculinity of the prison that expresses itself through homosexual gang rapes and brutal beatings. In between these two is Queenie. He knows the prison game even better than Rocky and can be just as vicious; yet like Mona he has not entirely lost himself to the system. His outrageous drag routines are a personal signature marking his distance from the prison's drab conformity (and making him the play's most entertaining character). But behind the personae of the clown and the helpful "mother" that Queenie plays in the prison's travesty of domestic order is just one more sad, damaged boy.

"I feel like I'm in another country," Smitty says when he first enters the cellblock. But it's not long before he's forced to adopt native customs, and by Scene Two he's already speaking the language. He comes under the influence first of Rocky, then of Queenie, learning the rules of the game so well that by the end he is almost too far gone to embrace the possibility of salvation held out by Mona and amplified in the Shakespeare sonnet from which the play's title comes. After their moment of communion is shattered by the brutality of the others and the prison's injustice, Smitty shows that he has become another Rocky: cruel, desensitized, irrevocably lost.

Although *Fortune and Men's Eyes* is certainly an exposé of the brutalizing effects of prison life, environment is not the only operative factor in the play. Herbert's naturalism also encompasses the other traditional element, heredity. In his study *Modern Tragedy*, Raymond Williams describes how "in Ibsen, the hero defines an opposing world, full of lies and compromises and dead positions, only to find, as he struggles against it, that as a man he belongs to this world and has its destructive inheritance in himself." Smitty too carries within him a destructive inheritance. Like his father, the practical businessman who turns out to be a "hardhearted bastard," Smitty reveals a coldblooded pragmatism that leaves him emotionally crippled. He no sooner complains that his father treats his mother like a prostitute than he offers Mona the same treatment. Just as Rocky is an inevitable product and victim of his criminal family, Queenie of his mother's abandonment, and Mona of an effeminate physical appearance, Smitty is doomed by a condition more devastating than anything symbolized by the final clang of the jail door.

Fortune and Men's Eyes opened at the Actors Playhouse in New York on February 23, 1967.

ROCKY	Victor Arnold
MONA	Robert Christian
QUEENIE	Bill Moor
GUARD	Clifford Pellow
SMITTY	Terry Kiser

Directed by Mitchell Nestor
Setting by C. Murawski
Costumes by Jan
Music and Sound Effects by Terry Ross

FORTUNE AND MEN'S EYES

CHARACTERS

SMITTY, a good-looking, clean-cut youth of clear intelligence, aged seventeen years. He has the look of a collegiate athlete. The face is strong and masculine with enough sensitivity in feature and expression to soften the sharp outline. He is of a type that everyone seems to like, almost on sight.

ROCKY, a youth of nineteen years who seems older and harder than his age should allow, though there is an emotional immaturity that reveals itself constantly. He has a nature, driven by fear, that uses hatred aggressively to protect itself, taking pride in harbouring no soft or gentle feelings. He lives like a cornered rat, vicious, dangerous and unpredictable. He is handsome in a lean, cold, dark, razor-featured way.

QUEENIE, a large, heavy-bodied youth of nineteen or twenty with the strength of a wrestler but the soft white skin of a very blond person. Physical appearance is a strange combination of softness and hulking strength. For a large person he moves with definite grace and fine precision, almost feminine in exactness, but in no way frivolous or fluttery. Movements, when exaggerated purposely, are big, showy and extravagant. The face is dainty in features as a "cupie-doll's"— plump-cheeked and small-nosed. The mouth has a pouting, self-indulgent look, but the eyes are hard, cold, and pale blue like ice. The hair is fair, fine, and curly, like a baby's. One looks at him and thinks of a madam in a brothel . . . coarse, cruel, tough and voluptuously pretty.

MONA, a youth of eighteen or nineteen years, of a physical appearance that arouses resentment at once in many people, men and women. He seems to hang suspended between the sexes, neither boy nor woman. He is slender, narrow-shouldered, long-necked, long-legged, but never gauche or ungainly. He moves gracefully, but not self-consciously. His nature seems almost more feminine than effeminate because it is not mannerism that calls attention to an absence of masculinity so much as the sum of his appearance, lightness of movement, and gentleness of action. His effeminacy is not aggressive . . . just exists. The face is responsible for his nickname of "Mona Lisa." Features are madonna-like, straight-nosed, patrician-mouthed and sad-eyed. Facial contour is oval and the expression enigmatic. If he had been a woman, some would have described him as having a certain ethereal beauty.

GUARD, a rugged-faced man of about forty-five to fifty, who looks like an ex-army officer. He has a rigid military bearing, a look of order and long acquaintance with discipline. He presents an impressive exterior of uniformed law enforcement, but one senses behind the unsmiling features some nagging doubt or worry, as if something of his past returned occasionally to haunt him, when he would prefer it forgotten. At these moments, his actions are uneasy and he does not seem so impressive, in spite of his uniform. He has a stomach ulcer that causes him much physical discomfort, manifesting itself in loud belching.

SCENE

A Canadian reformatory, prep school for the penitentiary. The inmates are usually young, but there are often older prisoners, as indicated by the dialogue in places. We are primarily concerned here with four who are young, though they tell us others exist. The overwhelming majority of prisoners in a reformatory are in the late teens and early twenties. Those who are older have been convicted of offenses that do not carry a sentence large enough to warrant sending them to a penitentiary.

SET

The setting is a dormitory with four beds and two doorways. One door leads to the corridor, but we do not see it. There is a stone alcove, angled so that we get the impression of a short hall. We hear the guard's key open this unseen door whenever he or the four inmates enter or exit. The whole upstage wall is barred so that we look into the corridor where the guard and inmates pass in entrance and exit. Another doorway leads to the toilet and shower room.

ACT ONE

Scene One

Mid-October, evening.

Overture: 3 songs—"Alouette" (sung by Group of Boys' Voices); "Down in the Valley" (One Male Voice); "Jesus Loves Me" (sung by Group of Boys' Voices).

ROCKY is stretched on his bed like a prince at rest; QUEENIE sits on his own bed upstage; MONA leans against the wall of bars, upstage of QUEENIE. In the distance we hear the clang of metal doors, and a gruff voice issuing orders. MONA turns at the sounds, and looks along the hall.

Just before lights come up, after curtain has opened, a BOY'S VOICE is heard singing, at a distance—as if farther along a corridor.

BOY'S VOICE: *(singing)*
Oh, if I had the wings of an angel
Over these prison walls would I fly—

Sound of metal doors clanging open and shut. And sound of heavy boots marching along corridor.

VOICE: *(English accent)* Halt! Attention! Straighten that line! Guard! Take this one down and put him in Observation!

GUARD: Yes sir! Smith! Step out—and smartly!

Lights come up.

BOY'S VOICE: *(singing)* Oh, if I had the wings of—

QUEENIE: *(on stage)*
Oh, if I had the wings of an angel
And the ass of a big buffalo,
I would fly to the heavens above me,
And crap on the people below.

VOICE: *(English accent; raised now, the voice is not only gruff as before but high and shrill in overtone, like Hitler's recorded speech)* And you, Canary-Bird—shut that bloody row, or I shall cut off your seed supply.

Repeated sound of metal doors, and of boots marching away.

QUEENIE: Oh, oh! That's Bad Bess. The Royal Sergeant don't come this close to the common folk, except when they're bringin' in a batch o' fish.

ROCKY: What's the action out there, Queenie?

MONA: *(standing nearest the bars)* It's the new arrivals.

ROCKY: Anybody ask you to open your mouth, fruity?

QUEENIE: Oh, lay off the Mona Lisa, for Christ sake, Rocky.

ROCKY: Always getting her jollies looking out that hole.

QUEENIE: Does Macy's bother Gimbel's?

ROCKY: They got their own corners.

QUEENIE: Well she ain't in yours, so dummy up!

ROCKY: Don't mess with the bull, Queenie!

QUEENIE: Your horn ain't long enough to reach me, Ferdinand.

ROCKY: You might feel it yet.

QUEENIE: Worst offer I've had today, but it's early.

ROCKY: Screw off! *(turning toward MONA)* Look at the queer watchin' the fish! See anything you can catch, Rosie?

QUEENIE: How's the new stock, Mona? Anything worth shakin' it for?

MONA: They're all so young.

QUEENIE: That'll suit Rocky. If he could coop a new chicken in his yard, he might not be so salty.

ROCKY: Where'd you get all that mouth . . . from your mother?

QUEENIE: The better to gobble you up with, Little Red Riding Wolf!

ROCKY: Tell it to your old man.

QUEENIE: Which one? Remember me? I'm my own P.I.

ROCKY: You got a choice?

QUEENIE: I don't mean pimp, like you, I mean political influence, like me!

ROCKY: So you got a coupla wheels in the office! Big deal!

QUEENIE: I like it that way . . . makes it so I don't have to take no crap from a would-be hippy like you.

MONA: They're coming this way.

QUEENIE: Hell! And I didn't set my hair in toilet-paper curls last night. Oh well! I'll try to look seductive.

ROCKY: You better turn around then.

QUEENIE: Well, my backside looks better than your face, if that's what you wanta say.

ROCKY: *(with disdain)* Queers!

Enter GUARD with a youth who is about seventeen.

ROCKY: Hi, screw! What's that . . . your new baby?

GUARD: You planning a return trip to the tower, smart boy?

ROCKY: Just bein' friendly, Captain! I like to make the kids feel at home.

GUARD: So I've noticed. *(to the new boy)* Okay, Smith, this is your dormitory for now. Try to get along with the others and keep your nose clean. Do as you're told, keep your bunk tidy, and no talking after lights out. You'll be assigned your work tomorrow. Meanwhile, follow the others to washup and meals. Pick up the routine and don't spend too much time in the craphouse, or you'll end up in an isolation cell.

ROCKY: He means Gunsel's Alley. Too bad all the queers don't make it there.

QUEENIE: *(to the GUARD)* Now he wants a private room. Take him away, Nurse!

GUARD: Okay you two! Turn off the vaudeville. You'll get your chance to do your number at the Christmas concert.

He exits.

QUEENIE: The Dolly Sisters! After you got your royal uniform, in the delousing room, did Bad Bess challenge you to a duel?

SMITTY: Who?

QUEENIE: Little Sergeant Gritt—that chalk-faced, pea-eyed squirt in the rimless goggles! He's always goin' on about the "Days of Empire" and "God and Country" and all suchlike Bronco Bullcrap.

SMITTY: Oh, yes! He did most of the talking.

QUEENIE: That's our Cockney cunt—never closes her hole. Didn't he want you to square off for fisticuffs, old chap? Sporting chance an' all that stale roast beef an' Yorkshire pudding?

SMITTY: Well, he did say he'd been boxing champion at some school in England, and that, if any of us thought we were tough, this was our chance to prove it—man to man, with no interference.

QUEENIE: Yeah—that's his usual pitch. Corny, ain't it? It makes him feel harder than those stone lions out front o' Buckingham Palace. Yellow-bellied little rat! When he's outa that uniform, he's scared to death o' any eleven-year-old kid he meets on the street. Did his Lordship get any challengers?

SMITTY: Well, no! I wasn't surprised at that. I felt sure it was just a way of letting the prisoners know who's boss.

QUEENIE: I must say—you ain't exactly a idiot.

ROCKY: One o' these farty Fridays, he's gonna get it good, from some guy faster'n that goddam Indian.

QUEENIE: How stupid kin a Iroquois be? Imagine this jerky Indian from Timmins, takin' that fish-faced little potato chip at his word. The only one ever took the chance—far as I know.

SMITTY: He'd have to have a lot of guts.

QUEENIE: Oh yeah—and they showed them to him fast. He was a brave brave all right—an' stupid as a dead buffalo. The second he an' Bad Bess squared off at each other, two guards jumped Big Chief Running Blood, an' the three British bully boys beat the roaring piss outa him. Heroes all!

ROCKY: What a mess they made o' that squaw-banger!

QUEENIE: You couldn't exactly put that profile on a coin no more—not even a cheap little copper. Oh, well—let's look on the bright side o' the penny; he's in pretty good shape for the shape he's in. After all, he got a free nose-bob an' can pass for a pale nigger now. A darkie can get a better job 'n a redskin any day.

ROCKY: Whoever heard of a Indian what worked? They git government relief.

QUEENIE: Howdya think he got here, Moronia? He was one o' them featherheads from Matachewan Reservation, tryin' t' get a job in the mines. There was this great big ol' riot, an' the cowboys won again. Pocahontas' husband is up here because he tried t' scalp some Timmins cop. An', believe you me, that's the wrong way to get yourself a wig in that tin town.

ROCKY: An' you believe that crap, like he tells you his stories about how some stinkin' bird got its name? Jeez! Maybe you should git yerself a blanket an' become a squaw—you dig these tepee tales so much.

QUEENIE: I dig all kinds o' tail, pale-ass—except yours.

ROCKY: All Indians is screwin' finks an' stoolies, an' I woulden trust 'em with a bottle o' cheap shavin' lotion; and that Blackfeet bum probably slugged some ol' fairy in a public crapper, t' git a bottle o' wine.

QUEENIE: Always judgin' everybody by yourself! Tch! Tch! That's the sign of a slow con man, Sweetie.

MONA: *(to new boy)* What's your name? I'm Jan.

SMITTY: Smith.

QUEENIE: But you can call her Mona, and I'm Queenie.

ROCKY: Look at the girls givin' the new boy a fast cruise. Give him time to take his pants off, Queenie.

QUEENIE: So you can get into them, Daddy-O? Don't let him bug you, Smitty. He thinks he's the big rooster here.

ROCKY: You know it too. Welcome home, punk!

SMITTY: This is my first time.

ROCKY: Braggin' or complainin'?

SMITTY: Neither. It's just a fact.

ROCKY: Well, that's nice. You shouldn't be here at all I guess. Got a bum beef?

SMITTY: A . . . a what?

ROCKY: Crap! A beef! A rap! Whose cookies did you boost . . . your mother's?

QUEENIE: What the judge wants to know, honey, is what special talent brought you this vacation . . . are you a store-counter booster or like myself do you make all your house calls when nobody's home?

SMITTY: Neither!

QUEENIE: Rolled a drunk . . . autographed somebody's cheques . . . raped the girl next door?

SMITTY: No, and I . . . I don't want to talk about it.

QUEENIE: You might as well spill it, kid. I can't stand suspense. Ask Mona . . . she screwed all around the mulberry bush until I finally had to go find out in the office.

ROCKY: I coulda saved you the trouble and told you she reached for the wrong joy stick. Did you ever get one you didn't like, Mona?

MONA: *(to SMITTY)* I've learned it doesn't matter what you've done. If you don't say, everyone assumes it's something far worse, so you might as well get it over with.

SMITTY: I just can't.

QUEENIE: OKAY Smitty . . . skip it! I'll find out on the Q.T., but I won't spill it.

ROCKY: Ottawa's First Lady! How did you do it, Ladybird?

QUEENIE: Well . . . I lifted my left leg and then my right, and between the two of them, I rose right to the top.

ROCKY: Of a pile of bull!

MONA: How long is your sentence?

SMITTY: Six months.

MONA: Same as mine. I have a few to go.

SMITTY: Does . . . does it seem as long as . . . as . . . .

MONA: Not after a while. You get used to the routine, and there are diversions.

ROCKY: That's an invitation to the crapper.

MONA: Do you like to read?

SMITTY: I never did . . . much.

MONA: Well, this is a good place to acquire the habit.

ROCKY: Yeah! Let Mona the fruit teach you her habits, then you can go and make yourself an extra pack of weed a week.

QUEENIE: She don't go as cheap as you, Rocky. We're tailor-made cigarette girls or nothin'.

ROCKY: I get what I want without bending over.

QUEENIE: Sure! You can always con some stupid chicken into doing it for you. How many left in your harem now, Valentino?

ROCKY: My kids wouldn't spit on the best part of you.

QUEENIE: Who's interested in a lot of little worn-out punks? I've seen them all hustling their skinny asses in the Corner Cafeteria, and if it wasn't for the old aunties who feel them up in the show and take them for a meal, they'd starve to death. Did you tell them before they left that you'd provide them with a whole bus terminal to sleep in when you get out?

ROCKY: After I smarten them up, they don't have to flop in your hunting grounds. They go where the action is and cruise around in Cadillacs.

QUEENIE: Yours, of course?

ROCKY: What I *take*, you can call *mine*.

QUEENIE: What a pity you couldn't get a judge to see it the same way.

ROCKY: You're cruisin' for a bruisin', bitch!

QUEENIE: Thanks awfully, but I'm no maso-sissy, sad-ass. I always kick for the balls when attacked.

He sings to the tune of "Habanera" from Carmen:

My name is Carmen,
I am a whore,
And I go knocking
From door to door.

ROCKY: I'll meet you in front of the city hall next Christmas.

QUEENIE: Lovely, but don't ask me for a quarter, like last time.

ROCKY: Since when did you walk on the street with more than a dime?

QUEENIE: After I stopped letting bums like you roost at my place overnight.

ROCKY: Cripes! You'll never forget you played Sally Ann to me once. When you sobered up and felt like a little fun, did you miss me?

QUEENIE: Yeah—also my marble clock, my garnet ring, and eleven dollars.

ROCKY: *(laughing)* Oh jeez, I wish I coulda seen your face. Was your mascara running?

QUEENIE: He's having such a good time, I hate to tell him I like Bob Hope better. So where did you come from Smitty . . . the big corner?

MONA: That means the city . . . it's a slang term. You'll get used to them.

SMITTY: I feel like I'm in another country.

ROCKY: What's your ambition, kid? You wanna be a Square John . . . a brown nose?

QUEENIE: Ignore the ignoramus. He loves to play the wise guy.

SMITTY: I'm willing to catch on.

QUEENIE: You will, but you gotta watch yourself . . . play it cool and listen to the politicians.

SMITTY: Politicians?

QUEENIE: The hep guys . . . hippos, who are smart enough to make it into the office. They get the best of it . . . good grub, new shirts and jeans, lightweight booties and special privileges . . . extra gym, movie shows, and sometimes even tailor-made cigarettes. Like to get in on that?

SMITTY: I don't smoke.

QUEENIE: Well for cripes' sake don't tell them. Take your deck of weed and give it to your mother.

SMITTY: My . . .

QUEENIE: Me, honey! Who else!

SMITTY: Oh! Okay!

MONA: Tailor-made cigarettes are contraband, but your package of tobacco is handed out with a folder of cigarette papers and a razor blade when you go for clothing change once a week . . . it's sort of a payday!

ROCKY: Listen to our little working girl. She works in the gash-house sewing pants together for the guys to wear. Her only complaint is there's nothing in 'em when they're finished.

SMITTY: Is that what I'll be doing . . . ?

QUEENIE: No baby, you won't. The tailor shop and the laundry are especially for us girls. They can make sure, that way, we don't stray behind a bush. But I like the laundry since they made me forelady. It's a sweet act of fate because it's the only place in the joint where I can get Javex—to keep myself a natural blonde.

ROCKY: And it's easier to show your ass bending over a tub than under a sewing machine or a wheelbarrow.

QUEENIE: You've got a one-track mind, and it's all dirt.

ROCKY: My shovel's clean.

QUEENIE: I don't know how. Every time you get in a shower, you've got it in somebody's ditch.

ROCKY: Don't be jealous. I'll get around to shovelling in yours.

QUEENIE: Be sure you can fill it with diamonds when you come callin'.

ROCKY: You'd be happy with a fistful of chocolates.

QUEENIE: Feed the Lauras to your chickens at jug-up, eh Smitty?

SMITTY: Jug-up?

QUEENIE: Meals! Didn't they yell jug-up at you before you ate today?

SMITTY: I wasn't hungry. I thought the food would be the same as at the city jail, and it always made me sick after.

QUEENIE: Don't remind me of that sewage dump on the River. I think they bought that bloody old baloney and those withered wieners once a year . . . and you could put up wallpaper forever with that goddam porridge. Don't worry . . . the pigs they keep here are fed better than that.

MONA: Yes, the meals are good, Smitty. This place has its own farm, so the animals and vegetables are all raised by the prisoners.

SMITTY: I once worked on a farm, between school terms. I wouldn't mind if they put me on that . . . the time would go fast.

QUEENIE: That's the idea, honey! I'll try to wangle you a good go so you don't hafta do hard time. I got some pull in the office.

ROCKY: You'll have to serve a little keester to the politicians who wanna put you in the barn.

SMITTY: What?

ROCKY: But I guess you been in the hay before. Queenie's all for fixin' you up with an old man. You're ripe for tomato season.

QUEENIE: One thing about it, Rockhead. It'll be a hippy who's got it made, and no crap disturber like you that picks him off my vine.

SMITTY: I don't want to hurt anybody's feelings, but I'm not . . . queer. I've got a girl friend: she even came to court.

ROCKY: You shoulda brought her with you. I'da shared my bunk with her.

SMITTY: You don't understand, she's not that kind of . . .

MONA: It's all right, Smitty; he's just teasing you. Life inside is different, but you still don't have to do anything you don't want to, not if you—

QUEENIE: I'm tryin' to smarten him up, Mona, and you try to queer the play. Has sittin' outside the fence got you anything? At jug-up some punk's always grabbin' the meat off your plate and you're scared to say boo.

MONA: I get enough to eat. If anybody's that hungry, I don't begrudge it.

QUEENIE: And look at your goddam rags. They give you that junk on purpose, to make a bloody clown outa you. You ain't had a garment that fits since you come in.

MONA: I can fix them to look better at the shop when the guard's not looking.

QUEENIE: Well I like everything new. I can't feel sexy in rags.

MONA: I don't really care what I look like here.

QUEENIE: (sigh of despair) See, Smitty! I try to sharpen the girls I like and she don't listen to a screwin' word I say. I coulda got her a real good old man, but she told him she liked her "independence" if you can picture it.

SMITTY: I can understand that.

QUEENIE: Yeah? So what happens? One day in the gym a bunch of hippos con her into the storeroom to get something for the game, and teach her another one instead. They make up the team, but she's the only basket. They all took a whack, now she's public property. You can't say no around here unless you got somebody behind you. Take it from your mother . . . I know the score.

SMITTY: I'll have to think about it.

QUEENIE: Well don't wait until they give you a gang splash in the storeroom. Mona had to hold onto the wall to walk, for a week.

MONA: They won't do it to him. He doesn't look gay, and he's probably not here on a sex charge. They felt I had no rights.

SMITTY: That doesn't seem fair.

MONA: I didn't think so either. It takes a while to get used to the rules of the game, and I've made a few concessions since . . . just to make life bearable. One thing, Smitty; don't depend on protection from the guards, and don't ever go to them. You have to solve your own problems.

ROCKY: And Mona'll show you her scars to prove it . . . fink! Squealed to a goddam screw! Cut you up pretty good after that, didn't we, bitch?

SMITTY: But how could they get away with it?

QUEENIE: The usual way . . . it was an "accident."

SMITTY: Jan?

MONA: Everyone agreed it was an accident . . . including me. Be careful, Smitty!

QUEENIE: Now Mona's givin' you some smart news. There's only two kinds of guards: the ones you can use like Holy Face who brought you in— and the fink screws that go straight to the General.

When you see one comin' give six so we can play it safe.

SMITTY: Six?

QUEENIE: Say "six" instead of "nix" . . . a warning!

SMITTY: Oh, I get it.

QUEENIE: It's no game, Honey! They got a nice cold tower here with no blankets or mattresses on the iron bunks and a diet of bread and water to tame you. If that don't work, there's a little machine that fastens your hips and ankles, while some sad-ass screw that's got a rod on for you bangs you across the ass with a leather belt fulla holes, and some other son of a bitch holds your arms over your head, twisted in your shirt. They can make you scream for God and your mother before they let you go.

SMITTY: (aghast) It sounds like the late late show.

QUEENIE: It's no Hollywood horror-vision. Ask Mona; she was in a fog for a month after.

SMITTY: Mona? . . . Jan?

MONA: I don't want to talk about that, Smitty.

ROCKY: No. She'd rather dream about it.

QUEENIE: She wakes the whole place in the middle of the night with those bloody awful screams—"Mother! Mother!" Crap!

SMITTY: (petrified) You're only trying to scare me . . . all of you.

MONA: (gently) No, we're not, Smitty . . . someone's always waiting for you to make a misstep. Please be careful.

SMITTY: I've heard of lashes, but I thought it was only in very special cases.

MONA: (bitterly) They don't keep those little goodies because they have to but because they want to. Learn to look into their eyes before you stick out a hand.

SMITTY: Thanks, Mona. I'll remember.

QUEENIE: Well, now we're gettin' someplace. You see what a wise girl Mona's gettin' to be? She'll know the ropes better than me next time around.

SMITTY: Same thing happen to you?

QUEENIE: Well not exactly, but then I handle myself a little different. Mona's a girl who's gotta learn the hard way. I always see the trap before it springs. But then I have the advantage of early training. I was a Children's Aid ward, and shuffled around from foster homes to farms, to God knows what. I been locked in closets so my foster mother could drink and play cards unseen; I had farmers treat me worse'n their dogs, and I learned before I was twelve that nobody gives a crap about you in this cruddy world. So I decided to do something about it. Queenie looks after Queenie, and pretty good too let me tellya.

SMITTY: Sounds like you've had a rough time.

QUEENIE: Skip it! I wouldn't trade places with any soft son of a bitch who needs a goddam mother to tell it what to do and a lousy house in some phony suburb with home-baked pies, and a lot of chitchat around a kitchen table. I've seen what that does to people, and I hate them gutless bastards who go to work eight hours a day, to parties and shows the rest of the time, and walk around with their noses in the air like their own crap don't stink.

MONA: Queenie's never been able to find her mother. The Children's Aid wouldn't give the address because of her criminal record.

QUEENIE: Who wants it anyway? She's probably a pukin' prostitute somewhere, walkin' around the street with a gutful of gin. What dirty bitch would leave a kid before its eyes was open to be pushed around by a buncha bastards who only want some sucker to do the housework for them? I bailed myself outa that crap when I was lucky thirteen and found out somebody liked my body. I been renting it out ever since.

ROCKY: But the offers are gettin' fewer and the rates are gettin' lower. Next year you'll be dishwasher at the corner lunch.

QUEENIE: Listen, asshole, as long as there's houses fulla jewelry an' furs, this girl's hands will help to keep the insurance companies in business, and don't you forget it. It's you stinkin' pimps who better move fast an' get it made before your hair an' teeth rot out on the sidewalk. I'll wave at your bench as I ride past the park in my limousine.

MONA: *(seeing the GUARD approach)* Six!

Enter the GUARD called "Holy Face."

GUARD: Book-up! Okay Curlylocks, it's your turn to wheel the library around, I'm advised from the office, so try not to spend too much time visiting your friends en route . . . everybody's entitled to a book, too. Your pram's in the corridor.

QUEENIE: Thanks Daddy-O, I'll save you a Baby Bunting book.

QUEENIE combs his hair in preparation for the excursion.

GUARD: We have another nice little detail in the V.D. ward. A new patient just puked all over his cell, but he's too weak to mop it up.

MONA: The poor kid!

GUARD: Okay, beautiful. I figure even you might be trusted up there.

QUEENIE: Always the little mother, but don't go giving any kisses till he's had his shots, Nurse.

QUEENIE exits into the corridor wheeling the library cart.

QUEENIE: Cigars, cigarettes, vaseline! Everything for the home!

ROCKY: Thanks, Captain! I was just about to bash their heads together when you made the scene. You saved me a trip to the tower.

GUARD: It's temporary, believe me. You've been getting closer to it every day. Don't start brooding, Smith . . . that doesn't help in here. Get yourself a book or something before lights out.

SMITTY: Yes sir.

ROCKY: My, my! What a polite little chap. Isn't he sweet, Officer?

GUARD: Lay off him Tibber, or I'll have you moved to a stricter dormitory. Can't you get along anywhere?

ROCKY: Sure, outside!

GUARD: Is that why we're honoured by your presence so often?

ROCKY: Well the law don't like to see a smart guy get ahead. They want suckers who'll take a few cents a week, a row of brass buttons, and call it a living.

GUARD: But we can walk home when the work's done without an armed escort. Think about that, big shot!

ROCKY: I'm thinkin'.

He gives the GUARD a look that seems to make the GUARD uneasy.

ROCKY: You wanta stay nice an' honest—and keep it that way. Like, I mean next year ya kin take off wit' yer pension, ain't it? That is—if nothing don't go wrong.

GUARD: Lights out at eight o'clock, Smith! Be ready for bed by then.

SMITTY: Eight?

GUARD: That's right. You're up at six. It won't seem so early when you get used to the idea that, in the evening, there's no place to go.

SMITTY: I guess so.

GUARD: Okay, Florence Nightingale—on the double!

He exits with MONA.

ROCKY: Oh boy! That sucker's ulcer's gonna kill'im afore he gits the chance t'sit at home in a rockin' chair.

SMITTY: He sure did look sick when he went out.

ROCKY: He's sick an' he makes me sick. You ain't smart, ya know, Smitty!

SMITTY: How come?

ROCKY: Fruits always get ya in the deep crap.

SMITTY: I don't know; I never knew any before.

ROCKY: You ain't been around.

SMITTY: No, I guess not.

ROCKY: They'll screw you up every time.

SMITTY: How?

ROCKY: 'Cause they're all phonies . . . gutless; they're all finks.

SMITTY: You sound like you've had experience with them.

ROCKY: An overdose! But no more! I gotta get me one when I get outa the joint. I'm gonna break both her legs . . . then I'm gonna put a

coupla sharp chicks out on the hustle for me. That's the real dough.

SMITTY: You mean . . . women?

ROCKY: Let me tell ya! They were fallin' all over Rocky for me to be their boy, but I latched on to this one homo first to make a fast buck. Took him for everything he had . . . almost!

SMITTY: The homo?

ROCKY: Fag!

SMITTY: Oh—queer.

ROCKY: More money than bloody brains! Crazy about me! Old man's a big shot millionaire—stock exchange, race horses—the whole bit, but his one son was real fruit. It took some connin', but I got in solid . . . weekly allowance, swell apartment, lotsa booze and company and a Cadillac convertible.

SMITTY: All yours?

ROCKY: Except the heap! That's how she got me. I was browned off with the freak and split. Sold the works . . . television set, cut-glass decanters and whisky glasses, paintin's and statoos . . . all that crap! I split in the Caddy with a roll would choke an elephant an' had me a ball . . . hotel rooms an' motels from Montreal to Windsor . . . . Forty-two Street, Frisco . . . dames, cards, booze! Man, was I livin' high!

SMITTY: Money run out?

ROCKY: Hell no! When ya got it, ya can always make it, but that fruit had the brass to call the bulls and get me picked up for takin' the Caddy.

SMITTY: Because it wasn't yours?

ROCKY: What I take is mine—that's my motto. But these queers always like one string to keep ya in line. This bastard kept the car in her name so she could screw me up when the time came.

SMITTY: So he . . . she laid a charge?

ROCKY: Hell, no! She wanted me back, that's all! We agreed on a story to cover all the crap stirred up, but her old man and the bulls stepped in anyways and fixed me good. They tried to throw the book at me. Now, I'm gonna fix her, an' when I'm finished she won't be able to cruise no more little boys for about a year, except out a window or on a stretcher!

SMITTY: If you do that, maybe they'll send you back again.

ROCKY: You sure are dumb. After you do a job, like I'm gonna, on somebody, they're scared crapless . . . glad to give ya both sides o' the street. Never let a fruit scare ya . . . the cops don't like them either, so underneath they're yellow as a broken egg. Don't ever forget that.

SMITTY: I'll remember.

ROCKY: Ya know, I could make a real sharp guy outa you. Ya got a head an' ya don't shoot your mouth too much.

SMITTY: I don't know too much.

ROCKY: You'll learn, kid! You'll learn. Listen to old Rocky an' you'll get to sit on the sunny side of the yard. See . . . I'm in this dormitory because I raise hell a bit. That's why they put me with these two fruits—to watch me. But there's bigger an' better dorms with more guys, an' that's where I'll be goin' back to . . . an' so could you, if you play along with Rocky.

SMITTY: How do you mean?

ROCKY: Well ya gotta have a buddy, see? Ya can't get chummy with the whole joint, an' specially no fruits. If ya get that name, your ass is cooked when you get to a good dorm. Why d'ya think I give 'em a hard time here? If you're smart, you'll do the same thing. There's real guys in some corridors, so ya wanna keep your nose clean.

SMITTY: I sure don't want anybody to think I'm queer.

ROCKY: Good! That's what I like t'hear.

SMITTY: Why would they put me in this particular dormitory, I wonder? To watch me, too?

ROCKY: Ya musta done somethin' goofy before your bit here . . . took a poke at a copper or somethin' like that. They won't leave ya here if Rocky can swing somethin' for us. The other blocks are probably filled up, but we'll be movin' soon. Would you go for that, kid?

SMITTY: Maybe it would be better.

ROCKY: Stick with the Rock an' you'll be looked up at. That ain't easy in the joint. Every jerk's lookin' for your jelly-spot. I didn't get the name I got by takin' it off these goons. Even the screws step easy on me. See how I talk to Holy Face? His blood turns to crap around Rocky.

SMITTY: He doesn't seem to stop you too much.

ROCKY: Nobody stops this boy. Besides I got somethin' on Holy Face. I'll tell you if you make up your mind who your buddy's gonna be. Remember what happened to Mona. You're sittin' duck for a gang splash if ya ain't got a old man. I'm offerin' to be your old man, kid, an' if you're wise you'll think fast. Whadda ya say?

SMITTY: Would it keep me from . . . what happened to Mona . . . in the storeroom?

ROCKY: Ya wouldn't want all those goons to pile on ya, would ya now?

SMITTY: No . . . for God's sake, no!

ROCKY: Am I your old man then?

SMITTY: Like . . . a buddy, you mean?

ROCKY: Sure, that's the score. I'll kill any son of a bitch lays a hand on ya.

SMITTY: Okay . . . and . . . thanks!

ROCKY: (tossing SMITTY his cigarette lighter) Here's a firebox for ya, kid. Keep it! We're gonna get along good, Smitty. Ya wanna know what I got on Holy Face?

SMITTY: Well, sure!

ROCKY: He took a pigeon outa the joint for a pal o' mine, so I know all about it, an' he knows I got the goods on him. I throw him a hint every once in a while when he thinks he's gonna push me around.

SMITTY: A pigeon?

ROCKY: A letter . . . a message! Jailbird lingo for stuff that ain't allowed—(with a confiding wink) like a punk kid is a chicken an' if he gives ya a kiss, that's a bluebird. Everythin' you write's gotta go through a censor in the office, but if ya got somethin' goin' for ya, ya can allays buy some screw. One o' my buddies gave Holy Face fifty bucks t' get a pigeon out for him. That's about as much dough as a lousy screw makes in a week, an' Holy Face ain't so holy as he acts when it comes to makin' hisself a buck.

SMITTY: But there's no money in here. They kept mine at the office.

ROCKY: You're green, kid. There's all kinds of lines goin' around the joint.

SMITTY: But how?

ROCKY: Easy! Some relative calls in for a Sunday visit, slips Holy Face the dough, an' next chance he's got, he divvies up, takes out his half-C note and posts your pigeon.

SMITTY: Why not get the relatives to take a message for nothing?

ROCKY: There's things some relatives won't do. This was a junk deal . . . dope . . . big-time stuff!

SMITTY: What kind of excuse could you give to ask fifty dollars from a relative . . . here?

ROCKY: Plenty! Tell 'em the meals are crap an' cash could get ya candy, magazines, or nice face soap . . . some story like that. Say ya can only get stuff through a good-hearted screw who's takin' a chance for ya. Play it hearts and flowers . . . works good on most relatives.

SMITTY: I guess so.

ROCKY: So come on, baby, let's me and you take a shower before bedtime.

SMITTY: A shower?

ROCKY: Sure! I like one every night before lights out!

SMITTY: Go ahead! I had one this afternoon when they brought me in and gave me a uniform.

ROCKY: It ain't gonna kill ya t'take another. I like company.

SMITTY: Tomorrow, Rocky.

ROCKY: Right now!

SMITTY: No . . . thanks!

ROCKY: I like my kids clean.

SMITTY: I'm clean.

ROCKY: Get up!

SMITTY: What . . .

ROCKY: Get movin' . . . into that shower room.

SMITTY: Rocky, you're not . . .

ROCKY: I said *move*, boy!

SMITTY: No! I changed my mind. I don't want an old man.

ROCKY: You got a old man, an' that's better than the storeroom, buddy boy!

SMITTY: I'll take a chance.

ROCKY: I'll make sure it's no chance. It's me or a gang splash. Now move your ass fast. I'm not used to punks tellin' me what they want.

He grabs SMITTY's arm, twisting it behind the boy's back. SMITTY gives a small cry of pain, but ROCKY throws a hand over his mouth, pushing him toward the shower room. SMITTY pulls his face free.

SMITTY: Rocky . . . please . . . if you like me . . .

ROCKY: I like you . . . an' you're gonna like me!

Blackout.

Scene Two

Three weeks later, evening.

As the scene opens, SMITTY and MONA are lying or sitting on their own cots, each reading his own book. ROCKY can be heard offstage, singing in the shower room. QUEENIE and the GUARD are both absent.

ROCKY: *(singing)* Oh, they call me The Jungle King, The Jungle King . . . *(shouting)* Hey-y Smitty!

SMITTY: Yeah?

He continues reading.

ROCKY: *(offstage)* Hey Smitty!

SMITTY: Yeah, Rocky.

ROCKY: *(offstage)* Roll me some smokes!

SMITTY: Okay, okay.

He moves, still reading, to ROCKY's cot, where he finds packages of tobacco, but no papers.

ROCKY: *(still offstage and singing)* Oh, the Lion and the Monkey . . .

SMITTY: What you got there, Jan? You must have had thirty takeouts in three weeks.

MONA: It's a book of poems.

SMITTY: Any good?

MONA: Yes, but it's not exactly what I wanted.

SMITTY: I've got something better; well, more useful, anyway. Come here; have a look.

MONA: (after crossing to join SMITTY on ROCKY's bed) "Advanced Automobile Mechanics." Very practical!

SMITTY: I'm a practical guy. You see, I figure I might not be able to get a job in an office, because—well—bonding, and all that. You know what I mean. Anyway, I worked evenings after school and all day Saturday in my fath—in a garage. I learned a lot about car motors, so I might as well put it to use. Mechanics are paid pretty good, you know.

MONA: That's wonderful, Smitty. This way, your time won't be wasted. You can make your six months really tell, and then after . . .

ROCKY: (entering singing and combing his hair) The Jungle King, the Jungle King . . . . Say-y! Whadya call this here scene—squatters' rights? Let me tellya somethin'—quick! In good ol' Cabbage-town, there's a li'l joint where me gang hangs out; it's called the Kay Won Cafe. Guess who runs it?

SMITTY: A Chinaman?

ROCKY: Wrong! Charlie owns it, but Rocky runs it. A pretty-boy comes in there 'n' I don't like his face much—me boys wait fer 'im outside, an' grab aholt his arms 'n' legs, an' Rock, who's welterweight champ 'round there, changes the smart guy's kisser a li'l.

SMITTY: You don't like your punching bag to swing too free. Your toughs have to hold him, eh?

ROCKY: I do things *my* way. There's another spot, on the roughest corner in town, called Eddie's Poolroom. Now—guess who runs it?

SMITTY: Eddie?

ROCKY: Oh boy, do you learn slow! Same story. Eddie owns the shack, but ya kin bet yer sweet billiard cue The Rock says who's behin' the eight ball 'round there.

MONA: (rising from ROCKY's bed) All right, Rocky—I get the point.

ROCKY: Ya better see it, Pinhead—or I'll give ya a fat eye t' wear. Now beat it!

SMITTY: Leave him alone.

ROCKY: Oh, you ain't talkin' t' me.

SMITTY: Just don't touch him.

ROCKY: Whadya think he is—precious or somethin'?

SMITTY: Lay off, that's all.

ROCKY: How come ya talk t' me like that? Ain't I good t'ya kid? Don't I getya cookies outa the kitchen? An' rubber t' chew, off Holy Face?

SMITTY: You're so good to me—and I'm so sick of it all.

ROCKY: Now, now! That ain't a nice way t' talk, when I just bin fixin' it up with Baldy t' git us in "D" Dorm. Ain't that whatya wanted all along?

SMITTY: Let's not overdo this "togetherness."

ROCKY: Sad—sad—sad! We-ell—I guess I'll just hafta 'range us a li'l extra gym, so's ya don't feel too neglected. The boys'll wanna meet ya before we move inta their Big Dorm. Tomorrow afternoon, Smitty? Get together wit de gang—just like at Eddie's or the Kay Won?

SMITTY: No, Rocky—no!

ROCKY: No what? No ketchup or no applesauce?

SMITTY: No—no extra gym.

MONA: Please, Rocky—we were only . . .

ROCKY: Shut up, ya wall-eyed whore!

MONA: I only . . .

QUEENIE is heard singing, approaching in corridor.

SMITTY: Six! Six! Forget it!

QUEENIE: (offstage, singing)
I'm a big girl now,
I wanna be handled like a big girl now;
I'm tired a stayin' home each evenin' after dark,
Tired a bein' dynamite without a spark . . .

Let me in. *(stamping his feet)* Let me in this cell!

QUEENIE and the GUARD called Holy Face enter, QUEENIE carrying a small, white, cone-shaped Dixie cup. He continues singing.

QUEENIE: I wanna learn what homos do in old Queen's Park . . . .

GUARD: I wanna learn what you do up in that hospital so often.

QUEENIE: I show the surgeon my stretch marks.

GUARD: I know it can't be only for that coneful of cold cream. I'll bet if I gave you a frisk, I'd find scissors or a scalpel tucked in the seam of your shirt. I oughta search you every time out.

QUEENIE: *(throwing open his arms)* Oh do, Daddy-O! I just can't wait t' feel your big callous hands on m' satin-smooth bod-ee!

GUARD: I'd as soon have syphilis.

QUEENIE: Who's she? Any relation to Gonorita?

GUARD: Cut it! Let's have a little common decency.

QUEENIE: What's that—somethin' ya eat? Ya know, you're not well at all; the way you been belchin' and turnin' green around here lately. Maybe that ulcer of yours has soured into cancer, an' you'll never make that first pension cheque.

GUARD: I'll live to collect it all, and my stomach will sweeten considerably next winter, when I'm down in Florida—away from you bunch of bums.

GUARD belches loudly.

QUEENIE: Pardon *you!* Will the rest be up in a minute? Maybe if the Doc finds out you ain't fit to work, they'll fire ya. Part-pension won't pay the shot for Palm Beach.

GUARD: One thing—I'm going to find out what you do with all those gobs of goo from the dispensary. I suspect it's got somethin' to do with the backside of decency.

GUARD exits to shower room.

QUEENIE: How gross of you, Gertrude. No secret at all! I mix the cold cream with coal dust off the window sills, an' sell it to the screws for mascara. Helen Roobenbitch ain't got nothin' on me.

He exits to shower room. Sound of a slap.

QUEENIE: *(offstage)* Brutality! Brutality!

GUARD: *(entering)* Next stop for that one is the bug wing. It might as well wear its jacket the same way it does everything else—backwards!

ROCKY: Take it an' tie it up an' don't never ever bring it back no more.

GUARD: Okay. Book-up time. Anybody want a trip to the library?

ROCKY: Yeah! I'll take a book of matches—t' the works.

GUARD: Pyromania would become you, Tibber; you got all the other bugs.

ROCKY: It bugs me sometimes watchin' noses stuck into sheets o' paper day 'n' night. Ain't that right, Smitty?

GUARD: Keep right on reading, Smith! There's no safer pastime around here. Tibber never got past Super-Rat. Well—if that's it, I'll head for a smoke in the lock—

MONA: I'd like to go to the library.

GUARD: Again? You're there every time the doors open. Can't you wait for the cart to come around?

MONA: It won't have what I'm looking for.

GUARD: Cripes! If there wasn't bars on that book room, you'd be breakin' in.

MONA: Mr. Benson said that I could find some-thing to do for the Christmas concert.

He shows GUARD a library pass-card.

GUARD: I thought Benson ran the orchestra. Why don't he get you to play the skin flute?

ROCKY: Yah! Yah! The Minnie-Lousy could give him lessons.

MONA: Mr. Benson's in charge of drama for the concert, too. I'm going to do something like that.

GUARD: Why don't you do "I'm a Big Girl Now"? Sassy-face in there could teach you the words.

MONA: I don't sing.

GUARD: Oh, hell! Come on, Hortense; your carriage awaits without.

MONA: Thank you.

SMITTY: See you after, Jan.

MONA: See you, Smitty.

GUARD and MONA exit.

ROCKY: *(singing introduction to "I'm a Big Girl Now")*
Me 'n' my chilehood sweetheart
Ha' come t' de partin' o' de ways . . .

SMITTY: Oh, you're really funny.

QUEENIE: *(entering from shower room singing)*
He still treats me like he did
In our bab-ee days,
But I'm a little bit older
And a little bit bolder
Since both of us were three . . .

ROCKY: Put down that bloody book, kid!

SMITTY does so, and sits looking at ROCKY.

QUEENIE: *(still singing)*
I'm a little more padded
Somethin' new has been added . . .

ROCKY: I got best bunk in this joint; can see everything comin' at us down the hall. I wantya t' know I'm real particular who uses it. That thing don't sit on my bunk no more.

SMITTY: *(rising)* That'll make two of us . . .

ROCKY: *(pushing him back)* What's mine is yours, kid.

QUEENIE: An' what's urine is my-un.

SMITTY: Keep it! I only want what's mine.

He gets up again and goes to lie face down on his own cot.

ROCKY: Come again on them mashed potatoes.

SMITTY: You heard me.

ROCKY: Watchit! I warned ya 'bout the tomato sauce. Be a good kid now, an' roll me a smoke.

SMITTY casually rolls a cigarette, as though it is second nature to do so for ROCKY.

QUEENIE: And when you've done that, Cinderella—mop the floor, wash the windows, shake the rugs and . . .

SMITTY: Aw, cut it, Queenie!

ROCKY: Smitty likes to keep the old man happy, don't you, kid?

SMITTY: Sure!

QUEENIE: *(singing to the tune of "Old Man River")*
Far far be it from me to free the slaves;
I'm not honest, and my name ain't Abe.
He just keeps rollin'—rollin' those ciggie-boos.

ROCKY: Yer name'll be mud if you keep that up.

QUEENIE: Queen Mud to you, peasant!

ROCKY: I think she's jealous, Smitty.

QUEENIE: Of what, for crap's sake?

ROCKY: 'Cause me an' Smitty is such good buddies. Bugs you, don't it?

QUEENIE: I don't give a damn if you legalize it in church-up next Sunday, and have fourteen babies. It ain't green you see in my eye, it's red, 'cause I hate to see a guy who could be a hippo playin' bumboy to a haywire loony who'll get him an assbeat or a trip to the tower before his time's up.

ROCKY: You're really askin' for it, ain't ya?

QUEENIE: I'd like nothin' better than for you to take a swing at me, rockhead. Then we'll see who's gonna be called mud!

ROCKY: I'll find a better way, and you can believe it.

QUEENIE: It'll have to be while I'm asleep, 'cause I can see your next move like you drew me a map.

ROCKY: How come you're so smart . . . for a queer?

QUEENIE: 'Cause I get to bed bright an' early, and I'm up with the jailbirds—fresh as a pansy! We can't all be as dumb as you, Dora; it makes for bad publicity.

ROCKY: When you find me underneath, class me with you. For now you call me Mister!

QUEENIE: How'd you like to say hello to your dear old friend Baldy in the office? He tells me he knows you from your first semester here, when you were chicken, like Smitty. I believe he gave your coming out party, and made you debutante of the year.

ROCKY: I ain't interested in no old fairy's tales.

QUEENIE: May I quote you, or don't you want Baldy to pick you out a nice private room, where you can count your belly button and say your prayers, to pass the time?

ROCKY: Shoot off your mouth any way you want. Baldy an' me get along just fine.

QUEENIE: Yeah, he's got a soft spot in his head for you . . . except when he sees Smitty. Your sonny outshines you, it seems.

ROCKY: If he likes me, he's gotta like my buddy too.

QUEENIE: He does. Oh yes indeedy, *how* he does!

SMITTY: Why don't you two turn it off? What am I anyways, a piece of goods on the bargain counter?

QUEENIE: That's up to you, honey. If you smartened up, you could be as high-priced as you want.

SMITTY: I just don't want to be bugged, that's all. Let me do my time the easy way.

QUEENIE: Like the Mona Lisa?

SMITTY: What's Mona Lisa got to do with it?

QUEENIE: Well, she don't believe in wheelin' and dealin' either, and you see what she gets. You gotta hustle inside too, you know, or you could end up like a chippy-ass, wipin' up some-body's puke.

SMITTY: I thought you were Mona's friend.

QUEENIE: I am, and I guess I like her 'cause she's different from me. But that don't mean a comer like you has to settle for the crappy end of the stick. You could have it all your own way . . . by just reachin' for it. You can't park your keester in a corner 'round here.

SMITTY: I'm satisfied to sit it out.

QUEENIE: Okay. Play it safe, but don't be sorry later. Nobody'll bother you while you got a old man, but you'll be anybody's baby when he drops you for a new chicken.

ROCKY sings first two lines of "Jalousie"

QUEENIE: It's Catso-Ratso, your old gearbox buddy who's got the greenies. That Wop's gonna get you good.

ROCKY: No macaroni scares me, sister!

Sound of metal door opening and closing at a distance.

VOICE: *(at distance along corridor)* Tower up!

SECOND VOICE: Tower screw!

THIRD VOICE: *(closer)* Hack from Tower!

FOURTH VOICE: Holy Face with hack!

FIFTH VOICE: *(nearby)* Who they after?

SIXTH VOICE: *(next cell)* They're still comin'. Must be after Rocky! *(same)* Hey Rocky! What'd ya do now?

GUARD: *(offstage)* Shut those goddam traps!

VOICE: *(at distance)* Holy Face is a stinkin' lush.

On-stage cell inmates pick it up.

ROCKY: Beats his wife an' bangs his daughter.

QUEENIE: Not our Holy Face! He does it on his dear ol' granny.

GUARD: *(offstage)* Who in hell said that?

A short silence.

VOICE: *(at distance)* It was me, Sir—GAWD! Ain't you ashamed o' yerself?

General laughter from all voices along corridor and on stage.

GUARD: *(to unseen tower guard)* Jenkins! Go get those bastards!

Sound of a heavy stick banging on metal doors, fading into distance—then silence. GUARD appears.

ROCKY: (singing old hymn)
Rock of ages, cleft for me-ee
Let me hide meself in thee-hee—

GUARD: (entering cell) That's just lovely—
Tibber! I can hardly wait to hear the rest at the
Christmas concert.

ROCKY: Thanks, Cap! Bring the wife and kids.
They deserve a treat for living with you all year.

GUARD: I'd as soon see them into a monkey
cage at the zoo.

ROCKY: Fine sense of loyalty to your students,
professor! Tch-tch . . . You hurt my feelin's.

QUEENIE: How do you think the monkeys must
feel? Speakin' of monkeys, where in hell's the
Mona Lisa?

GUARD: I took it over to the library. It's trying to
find some book it needs for a number in the
Christmas concert.

QUEENIE: I don't need no book for my act!
What's she gonna do . . . read "Alice in
Wonderland"?

GUARD: I believe it's hunting on the Shakespeare
shelf.

QUEENIE: Oh no, who does she think she is . . .
Bette Davis?

GUARD: As long as it doesn't ask me to play
Romeo, I couldn't care less.

QUEENIE: "But soft, what balcony from yonder
Juliet breaks . . . "

SMITTY: Mona shouldn't try to do Shakespeare
here. They'd probably laugh, and . . .

QUEENIE: And what? Don't you think we could
use a good laugh around this dump? Let her do it
if she's fool enough. She'd be worse tryin' to do
my act.

SMITTY: But they might hurt her feelings . . .

QUEENIE: Yeah? Maybe you should play
Romeo. What do you think, Captain?

GUARD: I suppose a little Shakespeare's all
right. We've never had the classics before. Maybe
it'll start a whole new trend in Christmas concerts.

QUEENIE: Well, I'll stick to song and dance and
a few bumps and grinds.

SMITTY: (thinking aloud) But why?

QUEENIE: Why bumps and grinds?

SMITTY: Huh? No . . . no I was thinking of something else.

GUARD: Come on Tibber . . . on your feet! They
want you in the big office.

ROCKY: What in hell for?

GUARD: Well, I'm reasonably sure it's not to
give you the Nobel Peace Prize.

ROCKY: I ain't done nothin'.

GUARD: I wouldn't know. I got a few dozen
other characters to watch besides you. Make it
fast. I've got to bring the Shakespearean actress
back before lights out.

ROCKY: Crap! Roll me some smokes for later,
Smitty!

SMITTY: Yeah! I'll try to keep busy so I don't
miss you.

ROCKY and GUARD exit.

QUEENIE: (singing first three lines of "I'll See
You Again" after them) You don't smoke, an' you
spend half your time rollin' smokes for that
haywire goon. What's the matter with you?

SMITTY: (dryly) We're "buddies."

QUEENIE: I'd like to know how he got you to
make a mistake like that! I had an idea when I
first saw you that you're the kind of guy who'd
like to be on top.

SMITTY: Of what?

QUEENIE: Of everything. You're no lolliflier—
you don't have to play it the way I do. Whatever
you're gonna be here . . . you gotta be it in a big
way. My way, I'm happy. The hippos know I'm a
mean bitch, so I got no questions to answer. But
I'm nobody's punk, and you shouldn't be either.

SMITTY: So what am I supposed to do . . . let
you pick me an old man? How the hell would
that make any difference?

QUEENIE: You don't need a old man, you could
be a hippo, if you play your cards right.

SMITTY: So deal me a hand, and see if it comes
up a winner.

QUEENIE: Okay. Here's a straight. Rocky's nowhere near top dog in this joint . . . just a hard crap disturber who gets a wide berth from everybody. He ain't in at all, and as long as you're with him, you ain't either. If you get out from under Rocky, and I spread the news you're boss in this block, they'll listen.

SMITTY: So how do I do it? Give him to some sucker for Christmas?

QUEENIE: Who'd take him as a gift? You could wrap him up, just the same.

SMITTY: I'm tempted. What would I use, crap paper?

QUEENIE: You ain't scared of Rocky?

SMITTY: Hell, no! I just figured he helped to keep me out of the storeroom. He said if I was asked to that party, I wouldn't be guest, and I didn't like the idea of providing entertainment for anybody's wolf pack.

QUEENIE: So that's how he caught you . . . the cagey bastard.

SMITTY: You going to sound off about that?

QUEENIE: Not on your life! It wouldn't do me any good to broadcast how Rocky conned you into his nest. When I tipped you off to the storeroom gang splash, it was a cue to get next to the politicians who can do you some good. You shouldn't have give in so soon, or so easy.

SMITTY: Were you here?

QUEENIE: No, damn it!

SMITTY: Well, let me tell you, it wasn't so easy.

QUEENIE: Yeah? Can you go?

SMITTY: You think I didn't fight?

QUEENIE: So how come Rocky won?

SMITTY: With his mouth! Every time he said storeroom, I remembered about Mona, and my fists melted like candy floss.

QUEENIE: (excited) You takin' a shower tonight?

SMITTY: I don't know. I try to make them few and far between. If I had a choice, I'd be dirty as a craphouse rat before taking a shower with Rocky.

QUEENIE: Take one tonight, and I'll give six. One thing about Rocky, he don't squeal.

SMITTY: What did you say?

QUEENIE: I'll . . . give . . . six!

SMITTY: Well! How do you think I should play it?

QUEENIE: You want to be on top, don't ya? I ain't interested in no stars can't live up to their billing. If I put it out that you're telling me an' Rocky what to do, I gotta believe half of it.

SMITTY: I begin to read you. You want me to punch his head in. Right?

QUEENIE: Have you got what it takes?

SMITTY: All stored up!

QUEENIE: Then let it go.

SMITTY: In the crapper?

QUEENIE: I'll give you six in case Holy Face is hangin' around, but try and make it fast. Turn on a coupla showers to cover the slammin'.

SMITTY: You're on! Oh! Oh! Hold it a minute! What about after?

QLUEENIE: What about it?

SMITTY: What will I owe you? You're not doing this out of sweet charity.

QUEENIE: Am I so hard to be nice to?

SMITTY: That depends . . .

QUEENIE: I mean . . . when you want and how you want—I'm nobody's old man, if you know what I mean.

SMITTY: It'd be a change, anyway.

QUEENIE: Whatever you want. You'll be top dog in this corner.

SMITTY: Six!

Sound of key in corridor door . . . enter GUARD and ROCKY.

GUARD: Slipped out of that one like a snake, didn't you, Tibber?

ROCKY: Sure! I don't let no finks hang me on the hook.

GUARD: You'll get caught one day, and when you do, I want to be there.

ROCKY: And here I thought you was my true friend.

GUARD: You make no friends, Tibber!

ROCKY: I got Smitty. I tell him everything . . . but everything, screw.

GUARD: That's his business.

ROCKY: Now, don't ya wish ya hadn't slapped me across the mouth three years ago, Mr. Screw?

GUARD: If I had to worry about every mouth I slapped around here, I'd be better off working as a wet nurse.

ROCKY: Well, maybe ya slug so many, ya forgot, but I ain't. It was my first day in the joint, an' I didn't call you "sir."

GUARD: You always were a nervy little brat.

ROCKY: So you said, an' ya smashed me across the jaw wit' both sides o' your big mitt, an' when I says, "Ain't y'afraid I'll tell the Warden?" ya says, why should ya be; twenty years ago ya smacked me father in the mouth, an' he was a thief an' a pimp just like me. Ain't that so, Hack?

GUARD: Yeah, that's it all right.

ROCKY: So-o, how's it feel t' have yer own arse roastin' over the pit—an' fer a little fifty-buck boo-boo?

GUARD: You bastard!

He exits.

ROCKY: Oh, how sweet it is. *(laughing)* See how I shake 'em up, Smitty old kid? *(stretching out on his bed)* Say, where's my weeds, pal?

SMITTY: Roll your own—pal.

ROCKY rolls a cigarette without taking his eyes from SMITTY's face.

ROCKY: Gimme a light, kid!

SMITTY: *(tossing a lighter to ROCKY)* Light on your ass!

ROCKY: *(carefully)* You two take a shower while The Rock was out on business?

QUEENIE: *(coyly)* I should be so lucky.

ROCKY: Smitty, come here. I'm gonna to tell you what happens to jokers what try to give Rocky the dirty end.

SMITTY: I can hear you.

ROCKY: That phony Wop, Catsolini, finked to a shop screw on me, an' now he's all wrapped up in the General's office . . . wishin' he'd kept his hole closed.

QUEENIE: I thought good old Catso was your machine-shop buddy.

ROCKY: Think again. He mouthed off to the machine-shop screw I lifted his lousy firebox, so they hauled me up to the General, give me a quick frisk, an' when they couldn't find nothin', put the pressure on me. I took it good for you, Smitty.

SMITTY: For me?

ROCKY: Sure! Where d'ya think you got your screwin' firebox—from Ronson's?

SMITTY: But I didn't want the bloody lighter. All I used it for was to light your crappin' smokes when you ask me to come on like your butler.

ROCKY: Alla same, I took it good so's they wouldn't put you on the spot, kid.

QUEENIE: My hero! They make medals for people like you and Saint Joan.

ROCKY: Can it! One thing about it, old Catso's headed for the tower as sure as Christ made little apples an' his mother's ass. His Wop temper got riled up when the screws started shovin' him, and he gave old Sad-Ass Shriker a punch in the mouth. He sure picked the wrong target. Shriker's had a rod-on for that Wop a mile long. Shriker don't like no sissies, Micks, Wops, or Kikes, an' when he gets ahold of one, he's just gotta get 'em into the butcher shop so he can have his jollies.

QUEENIE: That's Mona's dearest boy friend . . . the one who slapped her little keester for her. I think she still dreams about him.

SMITTY: That's not funny, Queenie.

QUEENIE: Who says so? It gives me a laugh.

ROCKY: Six!

Sound of key in the door. Enter GUARD and MONA.

GUARD: Make way for the great Sarah Bernhardt . . . or is it Heartburn?

He exits.

QUEENIE: Don't stand up; she's just passing through. No autographs, no interviews, no pictures, and please desist from climbing up on her balcony. Cripes! Look at the expression. She's takin' this tragic stuff serious. Pardon me, madam . . . do we perchance breathe the same air?

SMITTY: Leave her alone, Queenie. You look upset, Mona, what's eating you?

MONA: *(trembling)* I . . . I saw something awful as I passed the hospital door.

QUEENIE: Don't tell me one of the boys was havin' a baby?

MONA: Tony . . .

QUEENIE: *(quickly interested)* Catsolino?

MONA: Yes, he . . .

ROCKY: Cripes! Those screws musta really marked him up. That circus troupe he calls his family'll be cut off from Sunday visits while old Catso's walkin' around lookin' like a road map.

MONA: It wasn't just that.

SMITTY: What then, for God's sake?

MONA: The doctor was holding a stethoscope to his heart.

ROCKY: Maybe they wanted t' see if Wops has got one.

QUEENIE: I know what she means, an' so do you, rat. Some buddy you are to let him get it. See where Rocky takes his pals, Smitty?

SMITTY: What? Let me in on it.

QUEENIE: You wouldn't know of course. The butcher always tests your heart before he lets 'em cut you up in the kitchen.

SMITTY: What are you blowing about?

QUEENIE: There's a little room off the kitchen where they keep a machine an' a coupla long pieces of cowhide . . . only that torture chamber ain't for the dumb animals.

SMITTY: They're not going to . . .

QUEENIE: You're goddam right they are. You don't slug a screw in the chops an' get off light. Catso's going to get the cat-o'-nine-tails.

SMITTY: God help him.

QUEENIE: Shall we pray?

ROCKY: The only time you get on your knees, bitch, it ain't to pray.

SMITTY: Over a lousy little firebox . . .

QUEENIE: Ease off Smitty. It ain't your beef.

SMITTY: The lighter was lifted for me.

ROCKY: That ain't what he's getting a ass-beat for. I got no sympathy for a bloody fink. All squealers oughta be shot.

SMITTY: Because of me . . .

ROCKY: You're buggy . . .

SMITTY: *(to MONA)* What are you doing that for?

MONA is standing close to the upstage bars at the extreme end of the wall, near the exit hall, poised in a position of straining to hear some sound from a great distance away. He seems completely occupied with the effort, unaware of the others in the room.

QUEENIE: She's listening for the screams. Sometimes the screws leave the kitchen door open, an' you can just hear from that corner. Once I even heard the bloody slaps of the belt. Musta been old Shriker swingin'.

MONA: Oh-h-h . . .

He does not seem to hear or see SMITTY.

QUEENIE: Oh, let her get 'er kicks. I think she's a goddam masochist.

SMITTY crosses to pull MONA from the bars almost brutally, but the boy does not seem to care; he only covers his ears with both hands, as though to shut out some sound.

SMITTY: *(voice shaking)* What do you want to do that for? You trying to bug me? Make me feel guilty?

MONA: *(dazed)* I'm sorry . . . I'm sorry.

He sits in a trance on his bed.

ROCKY: I'm sick of this crap. Come on, Smitty, let's take a shower. For some reason I feel real good tonight.

SMITTY: Glad to hear it!

ROCKY: Jesus! Don't tell me you're actual gettin' co-operative?

SMITTY: I am . . . tonight.

ROCKY: We-ll, it's about time! Give us six, Mona, if you can come outa that stupor.

QUEENIE: Don't bug her! I'll give you six tonight.

ROCKY: When did you get so friendly? I had the impression you didn't exactly like us leavin' you alone, Mother dear.

QUEENIE: *(sweetly)* Tonight I like it. I'll baby-sit.

ROCKY: I smell a sardine, or two.

QUEENIE: What are ya worried about, Rocky? You must have a guilty conscience!

ROCKY: I got no conscience an' no fat fruit worries me either. Come on, buddy boy.

SMITTY: You can call me Smith.

ROCKY: I don't care what I call you as long as y' do like you're told. Now move your ass.

SMITTY walks into the shower room. ROCKY turns a questioning look on QUEENIE who smiles in reply like the Cheshire cat. ROCKY goes out to shower room and QUEENIE crosses to stand near door to corridor, without looking toward shower-room door.

MONA: *(starting)* Something's wrong in there. What's that?

QUEENIE: Mind your own screwin' business.

MONA: But Smitty . . .

QUEENIE: Can take care of himself. He's my boy now, and don't you forget it.

MONA: But Rocky . . .

QUEENIE: Is getting a lesson he's needed for a long time.

MONA: How do you . . . ?

QUEENIE: Because I can pick 'em real good, honey. I know a born hippo when I see one. I ain't spent time around these joints since I was fourteen for nothing. Smitty's got everythin' it takes to run his own show, but he needs me t' help him. I'm big-hearted that way.

MONA: There's no sound now . . .

QUEENIE: I said make it fast. You give me six. I'm gonna check the damage.

QUEENIE goes to shower room, returning almost at once.

QUEENIE: You still got that alcohol an' bandages I give you t' hide under your mattress?

MONA: You planned this—to get Smitty.

QUEENIE: Right where I can see him—like I got all the other suckers on this street.

MONA: He could have been caught—or killed. You're not even on his side.

QUEENIE: If he's got a side! Shut your nellie jaw, before I blind you, bitch—an' get me that goddam medicine bag.

MONA: Yes—I'll get it. *(He does so.)*

QUEENIE: An' get ready to bow low, Miss Shakespeare. This block had a good queen; all it needed was a king.

He exits triumphantly, leaving MONA looking lost and alone.

Curtain.

ACT TWO

Christmas Eve.

At the end of the dormitory, ROCKY lies smoking on his bed; at the other end, SMITTY is propped up on his with a book, reading; the GUARD, Holy Face, sits on a high stool upstage, and a portable record player is going, the music filling the dormitory with something of a night-club atmosphere.

ROCKY: Crap, Captain! The Christmas stunt is lousy enough, without havin' t' watch stinkin' rehearsals.

GUARD: We could always arrange to reserve you a private room, Mr. Tibber. There's a vacancy right now in Gunsel's Alley . . .

ROCKY: Screw off!

GUARD: If you think this is any treat for me, guess again. I got a television when I want to be entertained. The tumblers and acrobats and what-have-you are using up the stage and gym floor, so the leading ladies will just have to practise here at home, with the family. You are what might be described as a captive audience. *(walking toward shower room door)* Move it, girls . . . you're on! These critics of yours will be asleep before you get into those costumes.

QUEENIE: *(calling from shower room)* Thank you, Mr. Sullivan. A little cruisin' music, please, while I remove my jock. I'll take it from the top . . . as we used to say at the Casino.

The GUARD crosses to reset the record, and QUEENIE enters, looking like a combination of Gorgeous George, Sophie Tucker and Mae West. He wears a platinum-blond wig, spangled sequin dress, long black gloves, large rhinestone jewelry on ears, neck and wrists, heavy make-up, and is carrying a large feather fan. There is no self-consciousness or lack of confidence: movements are large, controlled, voluptuous and sure. He throws open the fan, as ROCKY, SMITTY and the GUARD watch, bending his knees in a slow dip, so the tight gown pulls across his heavy, rounded body, giving the look of an overweight strip teaser beginning the act; slowly he undulates the hips forward and upward in a series of professionally controlled bumps and grinds, the meat and muscle of burlesque dancing. As the record plays the opening to a song, an old night-club favorite, QUEENIE prepares the way with these bold, sex-conscious movements.

SMITTY: Holy mother of . . . you look as sexy as hell. Look what we had here, and didn't know it.

QUEENIE: It's all yours, honey—every precious pound.

He picks up the melody from the recording, a parody of "A Good Man Is Hard to Find."

Here is a story, without morals
An' all you fags better pay some mind
'Cause if ya find a man worth keepin'
Be satisfied—and treat him kind.

A hard man is good to find
I always get the other kind
Just when I think that he's my pal
I turn around an' find him actin' like somebody's gal
And then I rave; I even crave
To see him lyin' dead in his grave.
So if your hippo's nice
Take my advice
Hug him in the shower, kiss him every night
Give him plenty oompah, treat him right
'Cause a hard man nowadays is good to find.

There is spontaneous applause, from even ROCKY and the GUARD, for there is an all-embracing extrovert quality to QUEENIE's performance that is somehow contagious, partly because of a warmth generated by a feeling that QUEENIE seems completely happy with himself and his surroundings.

ROCKY: Come on, Queenie . . . give us another one . . . real lowdown and dirty.

SMITTY: Yeah, Queenie . . . sing it for Daddy, and don't forget I like the wiggle accompaniment.

QUEENIE: *(like a famous star)* Sorry, boys . . . that's gotta wait for the show. Get your tickets early, before the front seats are sold out. I wouldn't wantya t' miss anything headed your way.

SMITTY: Throw it here, kid; I don't need a catcher's mitt.

ROCKY: Turn that stuff on again, Queenie; I might get in the mood.

QUEENIE: Put your gloves on, boys. We ain't got that much time before the show starts, an' this is more or less a costume an' make-up rehearsal. We got our numbers down already, but they didn't get these Christmas decorations in till today. Ain't this gown a flip?

SMITTY: Fits like a second skin. What did you do . . . grow into it?

QUEENIE: I hadda get Mona to shove me with a shoehorn.

SMITTY: What you hiding under there?

QUEENIE: Nothing, baby—but your Christmas box.

ROCKY: I'll look after the diamonds for ya.

QUEENIE: They musta took a chandelier apart to get all this glass. Feels good, but you couldn't hock it for a plate o' beans.

ROCKY: Looks like they shot a ostrich for ya, too.

QUEENIE: (waving the fan) I hope it ain't moulting season in Africa.

SMITTY: You sprung those curls awful fast.

QUEENIE: My teeth an' my ass are my own, Honey!

GUARD: (caught in the mood) If my wife could see me now, she'd start divorce proceedings.

QUEENIE: Never mind, baby; think of the beautiful music you an' me could make while she's in Mexico.

ROCKY: As long as you're spreadin' it around, Queenie . . . my pad's over here. Holy Face ain't got anythin' I can't better.

QUEENIE: (enjoying every moment) What am I bid? Line up the Cadillacs on stage left an' the mink coats on the right. What's your offer, Smitty?

SMITTY: All I got is this book on auto mechanics.

QUEENIE: (with a wink) Oh, that ain't all you got, Honey.

SMITTY: (laughing) You've been peeking again.

ROCKY: Turn on the walkin' music, Queenie, an' give us a the strip you did at the last Christmas concert.

QUEENIE: Are you kidding? I did a week in the tower for that surprise performance. I could hear the boys still whistlin', when they turned the key on your mother. Oh well, the bread an' water was good for my figure. I started the New Year lookin' like a cover off Vogue!

GUARD: No more surprises like that one, Queenie, or your concert days will be over. The conveners of this one had a hell of a time getting the General to trust you again.

QUEENIE: Oh, I told them how to fix that up.

GUARD: That's news to me. What did you do?

QUEENIE: I promised the General a little bit.

ROCKY, SMITTY and the GUARD laugh uproariously. At this moment, MONA enters, wearing a makeshift costume for Portia's court scene in The Merchant of Venice. It is a converted red velvet curtain and becomes him somewhat, but contrast between the graceful, almost classic costume and Queenie's glittering ensemble seems incongruous.

ROCKY: Flyin' crap! What's that supposed to be? Your bathrobe an' nightcap? What're you gonna do . . . "The Night Before Christmas"?

QUEENIE: (in impresario fashion) Ladies and gentlemen, I want you all to meet Tillie—The Birdwoman, God's gift to the Tree People.

ROCKY, SMITTY and GUARD howl at the announcement, but MONA remains as enigmatic in expression as the painting he is named for.

QUEENIE: What kinda music do you want, Tillie . . . a slow waltz or a minuet? You'll never get those window drapes off the ground.

MONA: I won't need music.

QUEENIE: Well, you need something. (proffering the fan) How about these feathers? If you wave 'em hard enough, they might lift you up on your toes; you could call it "The Dying Duck" ballet.

ROCKY: Maybe she oughta have a window to hang herself in.

QUEENIE: You better not do a strip, 'cause you'd hafta have red flannel underwear to go with that smock.

MONA: It's from The Merchant of Venice.

QUEENIE: Well, I'd take it back to him, dearie; you got gypped, whatever you paid.

MONA: This costume is for the courtroom scene . . .

QUEENIE: Oh, I get it. You're gonna play a judge. That should go over big in this joint.

MONA: It's Portia . . .

QUEENIE: It's poor something.

SMITTY: (sober and fierce suddenly) Cut it, Queenie!

QUEENIE: What's biting your backside, big boy? She oughta be able to take a little fun.

SMITTY: You go past the point where it's funny.

QUEENIE: When I want you to tell me what to laugh at, I'll write you a certificate of authority.

GUARD: *(standing)* Okay, children . . . cool it! Or we cut the run-through right here.

QUEENIE: Let's have Miss Shakespeare's number. I'm sure Rocky and the other boys will just love it, especially the ones who write poems on the wall of the crapper.

SMITTY: I know the scene, Mona; we took it in high-school English. It's where Portia goes to court for her boyfriend. Isn't that the part?

MONA: *(attention on SMITTY only)* Yes . . . it is the plea she makes in the name of human charity and . . .

SMITTY: *(gently)* Mercy?

MONA: Yes.

SMITTY: I'd like to hear it again. Will you say it for me?

QUEENIE: Oh mercy my me.

The others move into the background, sitting on beds; the GUARD returns to his stool. They watch, as though at some amusing spectacle where one should not laugh but cannot resist. QUEENIE pokes ROCKY in the ribs with his elbow, then opens the fan over his face, holding it as a shield. ROCKY casually lights a cigarette and the GUARD yawns with indifference. Only SMITTY moves to hear MONA, looking into the serious, sad face.

MONA begins very hesitantly, stuttering (with comic pathos and badly spoken)—as the others giggle and roll eyes, etc.

QUEENIE and ROCKY interrupt MONA's speech throughout.

MONA: The quality of mercy is not strained,
It droppeth, as the gentle rain from heaven
Upon the place beneath: it is twice blessed;
It blesseth him that gives, and him that takes:
'Tis mightiest in the mightiest; it becomes
The throned monarch better than his crown;
His sceptre shows the force of temporal power
The attribute to awe and majesty,

Wherein doth sit the dread and fear of kings;
But mercy is above this sceptred sway,
It is enthroned in the hearts of kings,
It is an attribute of God himself;
And earthly power doth then show likest God's,
When mercy seasons justice.

QUEENIE: *(to SMITTY, standing)* Down in front.

SMITTY sits and MONA strives to continue.

QUEENIE: *(with finality)* Thank you!

MONA continues.

ROCKY: Take it off.

QUEENIE: Put it on.

ROCKY: Ya dropped yer lunch.

QUEENIE: Encore!

ROCKY: Turn off the lights.

QUEENIE: Gee, you're pretty, lady!

ROCKY: Pretty ugly.

QUEENIE: Would you mind terribly—coming out of a cake?

MONA falters and seems unable to continue.

QUEENIE: Oh, she doesn't know it by heart.

SMITTY: *(turning to the GUARD)* Will you make them shut up?

GUARD: Okay. Good enough! The guys are waitin' and they won't know them words any better 'n you do. Let's go, Christmas dolls! Come on, Shirley, Dimples—and you too, Raggedy Ann!

QUEENIE: *(grabbing MONA away from SMITTY)* Laws has muhcy, Miss Melanie—de Yankees is hyeah. Ain't you skeered dey gonna find yoah sissy brudder in dat closet? *(propelling MONA toward corridor and concert)* Run foh yoah life; all Atlanta am on fiyah!

They exit.

GUARD: *(to ROCKY and SMITTY)* You bums get busy with a boot brush, and button up those shirt fronts. The General's wife and the Salvation Army are out there tonight.

He exits

ROCKY: *(shouting after him)* Yeah! I'll wear me best tie—de one wit' stripes. Queenie's browned off with you, Smitty.

SMITTY: Who gives a screw?

ROCKY: Mona . . . maybe?

SMITTY: How come Mona bothers you so much? You got a rod-on for her?

ROCKY: I got something I'd like t' give all fruits, but it ain't what they're looking for.

SMITTY: Seems to me that Mona doesn't know you're alive.

ROCKY: Oh, the Mona knows I'm here all right, only it's too lily-livered to look.

SMITTY: For a joker who claims he doesn't go in that direction, it looks to me like you ride the train awful hard.

ROCKY: You tryin' t' prove somethin', wise guy?

SMITTY: I don't have to. You prove the point every time you open your trap . . . it snaps shut on what you are.

ROCKY: Don't ever get the idea I'm a pansy, punker!

SMITTY: Watch your words there, Rocky. I'm nobody's punker these days, or have you forgotten what the floor of the crapper smells like . . . up close?

ROCKY: I ain't forgot.

SMITTY: Don't make me remind you too often.

ROCKY: Y'use yer meat hooks pretty good, but that don't make you big time, Mister. Queenie tells me you're doing a lousy little joy-ride rap. That's kid stuff.

SMITTY: It's big enough for me.

ROCKY: Ya didn't know yer ass from a hole in the ground before ya hit this joint here. It took me and Queenie t' smarten y' up.

SMITTY: I'm not interested in getting smart like you or Queenie. Did you get a chance to keep any of the stuff you got knocked off for? I guess not. And it must have taken a lot of Queenie's guts to smash a little old lady over the head for a closetful of diamonds and furs.

ROCKY: I'da got away clean if the lousy heap didn't run outa stinkin' gas, but Queenie screwed herself . . . she hadda play the actress before sluggin' some old bitch, by standin' in the hall singin' Happy Birthday to cover up the screams. Too bad the next-door neighbour knew it wasn't the old dame's birthday, and called the cops. Crap! I'da gave my right eye to a' seen Queenie's face when they put the arm on her with that load of mink coats and diamonds. I'll bet she was plannin' to wear 'em, like Queen Elizabeth, on Halloween.

SMITTY: So today she's wearing a neckload of cheap glass and singing her songs to a gymnasium full of pickpockets and petty boosters.

ROCKY: Well, I ain't in that class. When my bit's up here, my real old man'll be outta Kingston, and me and him's gonna hit the big time together. I guess a pun . . . *(thinking better of using the term)* . . . a joy-rider like you don't know who Tiger Tibber is.

SMITTY: Sure . . . I've read about your father . . . the high priest of pipe dreams.

ROCKY: But you wouldn't know what kind of cash a guy gets, dealin' out the junk.

SMITTY: Look Rocky. I don't give a crap what you and your old man do to get back here or someplace else. Queenie's always telling me what a big thing it is to pry open somebody's door or window, and you want to impress me by telling me your father peddles dope and your mother sells bingo to wine-hounds. Well, it cuts no ice with me. If I was to choose a racket it wouldn't be lousy drugs and cheap booze.

ROCKY: Well, ya better find somethin', buddy boy, cause y'ain't gonna be able t' git a decent job no more—maybe not even a half-assed one. Lookit Queenie! She was workin' the counter o' a Chinatown restaurant, after her first bit here. She wuzn't there two weeks when Seven-Foot Tiny o' the Morality Squad steps inta the kitchen t' scoff a free cuppa coffee. He catches sight o' sweet Queenie playin' tea maid t' all them tourists n' square Chinks, so sends down t' the cash register for the manager. He asks him does he know he's got a queer an' a thief workin' fer 'im. Dear Queenie, who planned on gittin' fat that winter, wuz out in the alley wit' the rest o' the cats— before Big Tiny finishes his bummy cuppa coffee.

SMITTY: So? Queenie made a try, anyway. It was probably better than selling bingo to wine-hounds. You pick your form of animal life; I'll find mine.

ROCKY: You keep my old lady outa it. When she was a big-time bootlegger she use'ta eat little boys like you for breakfast.

SMITTY: I can believe it!

ROCKY: And she still rakes in more dough in a day than you seen in a year.

SMITTY: I hope she saves it to pay her fines. They must love her at City Hall.

ROCKY: Can it.

SMITTY: You started this bomb rolling, big mouth.

ROCKY: That's what I get for tryin' to level withya about Queenie! She's bugged by you playin' nursemaid to Mona.

SMITTY: I don't like to see somebody shoved around by a couple of yellow-bellied crapheads.

ROCKY: You tangled with Queenie yet?

SMITTY: I'm ready when it comes!

ROCKY: I got news for you. Queenie's in solid with the politicians. She keeps old Baldy fixed up with punkers, and he pays by takin' the jokers she fingers, and locking 'em up in Gunsel's Alley.

SMITTY: I'm worried sick; notice how my nails are chewed to the elbow.

ROCKY: You ain't done hard time till they make you sit it out in Gunsel's Alley. Y'eat, crap, wash, jerk an' flop . . . all in a lonely little six-by-six. It's real cozy if ya don't go haywire the first month. A couple of goons smashed their own heads on the brick wall . . . wide open like eggs. They figgered they was better off in the hospital than locked up alone in a cage, like a screwin' canary.

SMITTY: I'd sing all day long, if I thought I wouldn't have to look at your ugly map for the rest of my time.

ROCKY: Yeah? Well they don't let little Mona drop in for visits, y'know.

SMITTY: Let's take a shower, Rocky!

ROCKY: I'm nice and clean right now, thanks.

SMITTY: Well don't rub any more of your dirt on me, 'cause I'll get the urge to clean it off . . . on you. Dig me, punk?

GUARD: (entering with MONA) Okay Hans and Fritz! Patch it up and come on to the Christmas concert. They've got a bag of candies and an orange waiting for you at the door.

SMITTY: Why aren't you backstage, Mona? It's about time to start.

MONA: They decided I shouldn't do any Shakespeare.

SMITTY: Who decided?

MONA: Mr. Benson said they would only laugh at me and make life more unpleasant afterwards.

SMITTY: Well come on and watch with me, then.

GUARD: No, leave it here! Whenever that one gets into an assembly, there's trouble. Last time it was at church-up . . . somebody split its pants down the back with a razor blade.

SMITTY: You wouldn't call that his fault.

GUARD: Look, Junior! If you had a bunch of hunters waving rifles around, you wouldn't throw a bird in the air, and expect nobody to shoot, would ya? It stays here.

SMITTY: This is Christmas!

GUARD: I don't care if it's the day of the Second Coming, the target stays here. Anyhow, it's got the whole corridor to roam around in tonight. The cell doors are all open, an' silly-bitch can go sniffin' around the empty beds for entertainment.

SMITTY: Isn't there a rule that says everybody attends the Christmas concert?

GUARD: You ask too many questions, Smith.

SMITTY: I thought you went by all the rules.

GUARD: (uneasy, as sometimes with ROCKY'S words) Yeah! Come on, let's go.

SMITTY: I'll celebrate right here.

GUARD: Pick the kind of company you want, Smitty, but take my advice . . . don't get caught. Come on, Tibber.

ROCKY: Let's move! The concert can't be as corny as this act. So long, sweethearts.

GUARD and ROCKY exit.

In the distance, BOYS' voices can be heard singing a round of:

Row, row, row your boat,
Gently down the stream
Merrily, merrily, merrily, merrily,
Life is but a dream . . .

Sounds are from gathering in the auditorium.

SMITTY: I hate that son of a bitch, and I'm soon going to show him how much. Then, he'll know the shower of knuckles I gave him was only a baptism.

MONA: Rocky can destroy himself soon enough.

SMITTY: He ought to be squashed—like a bedbug.

MONA: What would you expect of him? Do you know that his father . . .

SMITTY: Hell, yes! He takes great pride in his parents—the famous dope-peddler and the fabulous bootlegger. He sure rounds out that family circle.

MONA: Before he came here, this time, his mother was sent to jail. She's been convicted so many times, the court wouldn't accept another fine.

SMITTY: My heart beats for the dear, lost lady and her deprived offspring. Who'll make the pancakes now and run the still?

MONA: Rocky's sixteen-year-old brother took over the bootlegging and began, besides, to sell his teenage girl-friends to anybody who has five dollars.

SMITTY: Say! Outside, did you live near that slum?

MONA: No, I probably wouldn't have lived this long, or, at least, my nose would be a different shape.

SMITTY: How come you know so much about the rockhead?

MONA: I listen to him and read between the lines.

SMITTY: What a waste of time! That's their mess—not ours. I'm interested in you and me. You make excuses for them, but you keep your secrets, like Greta Garbo—under a hat.

MONA: You haven't said much about your life outside.

SMITTY: I'm forgetting, that's why—I'm going to spend the rest of my life forgetting my father. He put me here. To hell with him! Who put you in?

MONA: No one—really! It just—happened.

SMITTY: Happened? How can a thing like getting here just happen?

MONA: My life—like that from the start; I expect what comes.

SMITTY: That tells me a lot.

MONA: It's just that I can't . . .

SMITTY: So shove it, then!

MONA: A gang—of guys—in the neighbourhood—that night—pushed me around. My payday—had it on me—they knew. Next thing—I'm on the ground—kicking me—kicking. I look up—all those legs, but there's a big cop. Thank God! Thank God! Bleeding—numb—on my feet at last! Then—he looked at me, and I saw his sympathy shift—to the gang. Forgot my money—excited, asked were they mixed up with me—sexually. Smitty?

SMITTY: Don't get off the damn pot! Crap it out!

MONA: A—a huddle—like a football game—formation; all came out, laid charges—said I made passes. Four gave witness in court. Only voice for me—my poor, shocked mother, and sitting out there, trying to smile at me —eyes dark, afraid—God help her—my younger sister!

SMITTY: But you should have had a lawyer.

MONA: Oh, I had one—or did I? Yeah—too late, after he got his money—we saw he didn't care— to tarnish his reputation. No real defense. A deal. Magistrates's court is like trial in a police station—all pals, lawyers and cops together! Threw me on the mercy of the court. Oh Christ—that judge, with his hurry-up face, heard the neat police evidence and my lawyer's silly, sugar-sweet plea. So half-hearted—I wanted to shout, "Let me speak; leave me some damn dignity!" The fat, white-haired frown looked down on me—"Go to jail for six months!"—like I'd dirtied his hands, and that would wipe them clean. Six months! Six thousand would have sounded the same.

SMITTY: Well, things are going to be a lot different by next month. There's a brand new year on the way.

MONA: How—"different"?

SMITTY: I mean, you're not going to be pushed around by anybody—goons, like Rocky and Queenie. They taught me more than was good for them. I'm on my way to being a politician, and I don't plan to do anymore hard time because of anybody. We've had it rough lately, but I'm about to even the score.

MONA: I don't know how that can be done.

SMITTY: Hell, kid! What I'm saying is we're going to wear the best of everything—new shirts, fresh from the tailor shop, and lightweight boots. We'll get extra grub—candy and fresh fruit—everything good that's going around. What do you say to that?

MONA: What do you expect me to say—about those things?

SMITTY: Well, for cripe's sake you might say "thanks." I'll have to. Or, "I like you, Smitty," or even—you might—

MONA: What's happened to you, Smitty?

SMITTY: I've discovered I'm human. You're not blind. Who's been acting like your old man lately?

MONA: I don't have any old man. I thought you understood that.

SMITTY: You only think you don't. Look, Jan, when I came to this joint, I didn't know up from down. I've made a few mistakes since the one that got me here, and that's the only one I'm not sorry for. I stole a car—to get my mother out of town, away from my drunken slob of a father. I had to—he had the keys. I was helping her to run away with Ben—Ben's a nice guy. They tried to get me out of this jackpot, together, but I slugged a cop when they were arresting me. My dear father got back at us all. He didn't have a good word for me in court. After all, he was the respectable married man, a substantial citizen with his own business—the hardhearted bastard! Hard is a good word for him. He likes hard women, hard liquor, and hard words. For all he wanted from my mother, he might as well have

hired a housekeeper and visited a prostitute regularly. Screw him! What I'm saying is you've got to work at it to make things go your way.

MONA: I can see you're not going to park your keester in a corner. Your father and Queenie have taught you well.

SMITTY: And I'm sick of that fat whore treating me like a piece of her property. I'll pick my own bedmate from here in. I shouldn't have to give you all this jazz, you know what I need. Haven't you any feelings after all?

MONA: Yes—some, but not the kind you're getting at—at least, not with you.

SMITTY: What did you say?

MONA: I said—not with you, Smitty.

SMITTY: Saving yourself for those dirty bastards in the gym? Is that what you enjoy—being forced into a corner?

MONA: It's better that way.

SMITTY: Better? Are you playing hard to get or something? Because I know different; anybody who grabs you, gets you.

MONA: Slicings—patterns—blind and empty release; sure, I'll go on being a party to it.

SMITTY: Do you like that? I thought you liked me.

MONA: I do, Smitty—a great deal.

SMITTY: I knew you put up with what you got because you had no choice; that you really went for me. You showed it in a hundred ways, so now, while we're alone—a chance—

MONA: Just a minute! How do you feel with Queenie—afterward?

SMITTY: I could spit on her.

MONA: It would be the same with me; it's not in your nature.

SMITTY: I came to you.

MONA: No! Just circumstance! You're looking for a girl—not for me.

SMITTY: Do I smell or something? What's wrong with *my* body?

MONA: Nothing—it's very—Smitty, don't ask me to.

SMITTY: Should I ask you to do it with somebody else? Keep on being public property? I guess you like change—a different one every day, for variety. What do you do? Make comparisons?

MONA: I—separate! Yes, that's right. I separate things in order to live with others and myself. What my body does and feels is one thing, and what I think and feel apart from that is something else.

SMITTY: You're crazy.

MONA: It's to the world I dream in you belong. It endures better. I won't let you move over, into the other, where I would become worthless to you—and myself. I have a right to save something.

SMITTY: I was afraid of everyone—everything—except you—until now. You're trying to shake me.

MONA: You're trying to kill me. You think I can be just used any old way—even by you.

SMITTY: To hell with me then!

MONA: No—listen! It's the sight of myself I can't stand— the way you throw it back.

SMITTY: Where do you get the goddam gall to tell me how I see you?

MONA: The right to say or be anything or everything or nothing to myself—and not a tame little fruit. Wasn't that it—soft, worshipping, harmless? Now you've flexed your muscles and found power, I'm an easy convenience. Not a Queenie! Oh no; I'd never turn on you. If I mattered, you'd be afraid of my feelings—not sure of them. You're offering me—indifference. Well, I don't want it.

SMITTY: Did you think I wanted your body? You make me sick. I wanted some kind of reaction to me, and only because I'm caught in this hellhole, you filthy fairy! You cocksucker!

MONA: You see? You see?

SMITTY: (running to the bars) Let me out of here! I'll go to the bloody concert—anywhere—where there's life—

He bangs wildly on the bars with his fists. MONA follows to stand behind SMITTY, puts out a hand gently, but not touching him, then with difficulty punches him on the shoulder. SMITTY reacts violently, turning on MONA.

MONA: No! Wait a minute!

He goes to SMITTY's bunk, picks up a book and holds it out.

MONA: Look—listen—you read it.

SMITTY goes slowly to sit beside MONA and begins to read, clumsily, haltingly. They laugh, embarrassed, and continue to read until they are in a slight hysteria of laughter that causes them to break up and fall against each other.

When in disgrace with fortune and men's eyes
I, all alone, beweep my outcast state,
And trouble deaf heaven with my bootless cries,
And look upon myself, and curse my fate,
Wishing me like to one more rich in hope,
Featur'd like him, like him with friends possess'd,
Desiring this man's art, and that's man's scope,
With what I most enjoy, contented least;
Yet in these thoughts myself almost despising,
Haply I think on thee, and then my soul
(Like to the lark at break of day arising,
From sullen earth) sings hymns at heaven's gate;
For thy sweet love remembered such wealth brings,
That then I scorn to share my state with kings.

SMITTY and MONA are laughing, heads close together, when QUEENIE and ROCKY enter.

QUEENIE: I'll give the bitch a bluebird!

He smashes his fist into MONA's cheek.

ROCKY: Give it to the dirty little fruit.

SMITTY has leaped up, fists ready to swing. He punches QUEENIE on the jaw.

SMITTY: Screw off, bastard!

QUEENIE (backing away, but preparing to fight) I'll take the punk, Rocky. Put your boots to the bitch.

SMITTY turns to take ROCKY, and QUEENIE uses the advantage to put a wrestling hold on SMITTY, pinning his arms behind his back.

QUEENIE: I got him. Go, Rocky! Go!

ROCKY: (shaking MONA as though he were a rag doll) I'm gonna smash your face, fairy.

He throws MONA to the floor, raising his foot to kick, but SMITTY breaks from QUEENIE, hurling the heavy blond to the floor, and kicks ROCKY in the groin. ROCKY screams, doubling over with pain. SMITTY then goes after QUEENIE just as the GUARD comes in, gun drawn.

GUARD: To the wall fast, or I cut your feet off.

All except MONA, who lies on the floor, move toward the wall.

Raise those mitts, children!

The three raise their hands.

Okay, crap-disturbers, what's the score here?

QUEENIE and ROCKY and SMITTY: *(together)* That dirty little bitch . . . . The goddam fruit . . . . These filthy bastards . . . .

GUARD: Cut it! One at a time! *(to QUEENIE)* You Goldilocks, what's your story?

QUEENIE: When me an' Rocky come in from the concert, that lolliflier on the floor was tryin' to make the kid here. *(wide-eyed)* We done it for his own good, Cap!

GUARD: Yeah! I can just imagine your motives. *(to ROCKY)* Okay, you now, Terrible Tibber! Let's hear your phony. Who were you saving?

ROCKY: Queenie gave it to you straight, Cap; an' I'm sticking with that story. The fruit was gropin' pretty good when we made the scene. We don't want that kinda stuff in here. You know how it is. Just turn your back an' that little queer's reachin' . . .

GUARD: Okay, turn it off, Tibber! Next thing you'll be telling me you want to go to church next Sunday to pray. *(to SMITTY)* All right, Romeo! Let's have your version of the balcony scene.

SMITTY: My name is Smith.

GUARD: Well, well! May I call you Mister Smith? Names don't mean a damned thing in here, sonny. Actions mean everything. Did that thing on the floor make a pass at you?

SMITTY: Nobody made a pass.

GUARD: Oh, now, this isn't your mother or a judge you're talking to, Smarty Smith. We know by now a pass was made. I'm not asking you if you liked it. I want to know who made a the pass.

SMITTY: Nobody made a pass at anybody.

GUARD: Real stubborn, aren't you?

SMITTY: You asked me. I can't help it that you don't believe me. We were talking when these haywire goons hit the block. They started the hey rube and I took over, since they seemed to want to play.

GUARD: You're not only getting too smart, Smith, you're becoming arrogant as well. Where do you think this attitude's going to lead you?

SMITTY: Into the office, where I can put an end to this crap.

GUARD: You're right . . . the General's office, where you'll need some much smarter answers.

SMITTY: I've got them.

GUARD: Your answers aren't worth much when you get hauled up on the big guy's carpet, kid.

SMITTY: Says you! Don't you think they might be worth about . . . fifty bucks?

The GUARD is stunned into silence. He steals a quick accusing look at ROCKY, who averts his eyes carefully.

GUARD: *(shakily)* I don't think you know what you're talking about. What is this . . . some kind of bluff?

SMITTY: I don't say anything I can't back up with the facts . . . like names, dates and letters. Dig me, screw?

GUARD: *(enraged but cornered)* You crapping fink! Learned it all, haven't you? Found a way to save your precious little hide? *(to ROCKY)* I ought to shoot you a second mouth, Tibber.

ROCKY just grins in reply, now enjoying the GUARD's discomfiture.

GUARD: There's one hide's not gonna get off so easy. *(pushing MONA with his foot)* Up off your ass, you little pansy! You know what you got the last time this happened, don't you?

He pushes MONA ahead of him, toward the corridor door.

GUARD: You can bend over all you want, in the kitchen.

MONA: *(realizing)* No! Oh, no, no, no, no . . .

His protests mount to screams offstage.

SMITTY: *(running to the bars)* Stop it! Stop it! I did it! I made the pass. *(shouting after them)* Do you hear? I made the pass . . . I made the . . .

QUEENIE and ROCKY begin to laugh in derision.

SMITTY: *(turning vicious)* Shut up you yellow bastards! I'll wipe the floor with your rotten guts. One more laugh out of your ugly kissers and I'll spray teeth from here to hell.

QUEENIE: We didn't mean anything, Smitty. What are you so hot about? That little . . .

SMITTY: Shut your filthy hole, you fat whore!

ROCKY: Jeez, Smitty, that thing ain't worth . . .

SMITTY: Listen to me, Rock-ass! Before I leave this stinking joint I'm going to demolish your mug so bad that no fruit will ever look at you again . . . let alone a woman. When will depend on you. Ask for it once and you've got it. This is my show from now on. I got that lousy screw over a barrel, and I'm going to keep him there. Also, Baldy's making me a politician . . . a wheel in the office. You see, Queenie, I wasn't hustling my little ass in the park at thirteen for peanuts. I went to school; I got typing and bookkeeping, so Baldy's put me where I can make things move my way. If you'd learned to write, maybe you'd be better off . . . but you'll swallow chicken crap when I make up the menu. And you, monkey; would you like to be my punchin' bag around here or should I ship you into Gunsel's Alley for safekeeping? Choose fast!

ROCKY: I . . . I'll take it off you.

SMITTY: Okay. You'll volunteer to be my sparring partner in the gym every time I want to box somebody, and sweetie, I'm gonna knock you senseless. Now get into that goddam crapper and stick your heads into a coupla bowls till I yell for you to come out. That'll be after lights out, cause I don't want to see your ugly maps again today.

ROCKY and QUEENIE look at each other, dazed.

SMITTY: You know who Baldy is? You know what he can do? Well, I'm his boy now.

QUEENIE: Ain't it the bitter truth? *(pulling ROCKY away)* Come on, Snake-Eyes; we rolled too low in the game—this time around.

SMITTY: So move, goddam it!

He takes a step toward them. In their haste to get out, the two bump into each other, ridiculous and clumsy in their new roles. SMITTY laughs loudly, revealing a cruelty that fills the room with its sound. Suddenly his head turns in another direction as though just recalling something. He steals a quick look toward the shower room, then stealthily and lithely as a cat, he moves to the corner of the dorm where MONA had listened to the sound of Catsolino's beating. From an attitude of strained listening, SMITTY suddenly contorts in pain as MONA had done before, but there is no sound from his distorted mouth. He seems to be whipped by unseen strokes of a lash, until he is spread-eagled across the upstage bars. When it seems he can bear no more he covers his ears with both hands, stumbling blindly downstage. Standing thus, head and shoulders down, he rises slowly out of the hunched position to full height, hands lowering. His face now seems to be carved of stone, the mouth narrow, cruel and grim, the eyes corresponding slits of hatred. He speaks in a hoarse, ugly whisper.

I'm going to pay them back.

He then walks, almost casually, down to ROCKY's bunk where cigarettes, which we have not seen him use before, and a lighter lie on the side table. He picks up a cigarette, lights it, then stretches out on ROCKY's bed, torso upright against the back of it. Looking coolly out to the audience with a slight, twisted smile that is somehow cold, sadistic and menacing, he speaks his last line.

I'll pay you all back.

Light fades to black, and there is heard a final slam of the jail door.

Curtain.

END

MICHEL TREMBLAY (b. 1942)

When Michel Tremblay saw his first play, *Le Train*,[1] televised in 1964, he realized he had written "a bad French play." As he recalls in *Stage Voices*, "When I began to write drama, I wrote bad *French* plays because what I had seen on TV were good *French* plays!" He resolved to write about the people he knew in ways that would reflect their lives and experience as Quebeckers, and in the language they really spoke—not French or even "French-Canadian," but *québécois*. With the tremendous success of *Les Belles Soeurs* in 1968 Tremblay changed the face of theatre in Quebec, becoming an icon of *québécois* nationalism and launching a career that would make him Quebec's—and Canada's—foremost dramatist.

The attempt to write modern Quebec onto the stage had really begun in 1948 with Gratien Gélinas' *Tit-Coq*, a well-made, sentimental melodrama that pitted an outsider (the "little rooster" of the title, a young soldier played by Gélinas himself) against the established order in the form of church and family. Tit-Coq's illegitimacy, his colloquial language, the realist backdrop of working-class Montreal—all these struck powerful chords in the Quebec audience and made the play an unprecedented success. Led by writers like Gélinas and Marcel Dubé, whose *Zone* (1953) depicted the tragedy of a teenage gang in the Montreal slums, indigenous theatre thrived in 1950s Quebec, aided by the popularity of television drama. But by the end of the decade Gélinas, Dubé and the other mainstays of the new theatre seemed to have abandoned *québécois* idioms for more standardized Parisian language and style, writing the "good French plays" Tremblay inadvertently took as his own early models. It remained for Tremblay to break the mold by grounding his plays in a radically localized, deromanticized Montreal milieu. Beginning with *Les Belles Soeurs*, his characters would speak not in "proper French" but, for the first time ever on the stage, entirely in *joual*, the bastardized local slang that was for some Quebeckers an embarrassing sign of their cultural degradation, but for others a symbol of their uniqueness as a people.

Tremblay wrote *Le Train* in 1959, his playwriting debut coinciding with the death of Premier Maurice Duplessis and the end of the deeply conservative political regime that had ruled Quebec through the entire post-war era. *Les Belles Soeurs* premiered the same year René Lévesque founded the nationalist Parti Québécois. The decade framed by these two plays saw the beginning of the period of social renaissance dubbed the Quiet Revolution, as well as the not so quiet revolutionary campaign for Quebec independence mounted by the FLQ, and French President Charles de Gaulle's famous "Vivre le Québec libre" speech in Montreal. As the redefinition of Quebec's political identity intensified, the articulation of its culture played an increasingly important role in the ferment of the times. Michel Tremblay was right in its midst.

He grew up in a working class neighborhood in east end Montreal, the Plateau Mont-Royal, raised by an extended family of women. Though a gifted student, Tremblay eventually left school to work as a printer, his father's profession, before turning to writing full time. In 1964 he met the young director André Brassard who became his lifelong collaborator and primary dramatic interpreter. The next year Brassard staged several short stories from what would be Tremblay's first published book, *Stories for Late Night Drinkers* (1966). Tremblay wrote *Les Belles Soeurs* in 1965, and during the three years it took to get produced, he revised and

---

[1]All titles are those of the published English translation unless the work has remained untranslated. Many of the plays have the same title in English and French. Dates in parentheses denote the first French-language production for a play or publication date for a book.

expanded some earlier one-acts into *En Pièces Détachées*, which opened in 1969 at Théâtre de Quat'Sous, the Montreal venue that has become most closely identified with his work. (All Tremblay's plays have premiered in Montreal or at Ottawa's National Arts Centre.)

By this time the parameters of Tremblay's dramatic world had been clearly laid out. The unhappy women of *Les Belles-Soeurs* and *En Pièces Détachées*, and the broken men of the latter play, live on a street very much like the rue Fabre on which Tremblay himself grew up, festering in what we would today call severely dysfunctional families, sexually and emotionally frustrated, and desperate to escape their alienation. Their fantasies of escape are often directed at another street: boulevard St. Laurent, or "The Main," a fringe society of clubs and bars, hookers and drag queens, where anything seems possible. But ultimately it proves to be a world of false glamour and shattered dreams. Eventually the "Cycle of Les Belles Soeurs" would comprise more than a dozen plays mapping the rich human territory around these two streets.

La Duchesse de Langeais (1969), the lengthy monologue of an ageing transvestite, provides Tremblay's first direct introduction to the world of The Main, elaborated again in the musical *Demain matin, Montréal m'attend* (1970), and *Hosanna* (1973), one of his most popular and enduring plays. The poignant story of a hairdresser *cum* drag queen with a biker lover and the burning desire to be Elizabeth Taylor in *Cleopatra*, the play had productions in Paris, New York and London between 1978 and 1981, and has been frequently revived in English Canada and Quebec. An engaging human drama, *Hosanna* also functions as cultural allegory. "We submitted to a foreign culture and this turned us into transvestites," Tremblay has said. "Finally, in the Sixties, we began taking off our foreign clothes and trying to rediscover the centre of our Quebec reality . . . "

The family plays, too, speak to Tremblay's sense of the broader *québécois* condition. *Forever Yours, Marie-Lou* (1971) is his most brutal portrait of the self-destructive family, an image of colonized Quebec with its internecine warfare and self-hatred. In the play two sisters, Carmen and Manon, live haunted by the ghosts of their dead parents, paralyzed by the dead hand of the past. Carmen flees to the clubs of The Main and becomes a country singer, returning in Tremblay's *Sainte Carmen of the Main* (1976) as a martyr to cultural authenticity. Manon (whom Tremblay has said he loves most of all his characters) becomes a religious fanatic, appearing again in *Damnée Manon, Sacrée Sandra* (1977) along with her alter ego, the transvestite Sandra, Hosanna's arch-rival. In 1991 the three plays appeared together in Montreal under the title *La Trilogie des Brassard*.

Forever Yours, Marie-Lou initiated the popularization of Tremblay's plays in English, premiering at Toronto's Tarragon Theatre in 1972, directed by Bill Glassco in a translation by Glassco and John Van Burek. Five years later it became his first play to get an English-language production in Quebec when the election of the Parti Québécois prompted Tremblay to lift his prohibition against such productions. By that time *En Pièces Détachées*, *Les Belles-Soeurs* and *Hosanna* had also entered the English-Canadian repertoire, as had *Bonjour, là, Bonjour* (1974), in which brother-sister incest and the ability of a son to say "I love you" to his father indicated Tremblay's more positive feelings about the possibilities of healing within both the micro- and macrocosms of modern Quebec. It quickly became one of his most popular plays, produced across the United States in the late 1970s and early 1980s.

After *Damnée Manon*, Tremblay felt he had temporarily said all he had to say in the drama and turned his attention to a semi-autobiographical cycle of novels set on the same rue Fabre in the 1940s and 50s. *The Fat Lady Next Door Is Pregnant* (1978)—the title character is Tremblay's mother, pregnant with him—*Thérèse and Pierette and the Little Hanging Angel* (1980), *La Duchesse et le Roturier* (1982), *Des nouvelles d'Edouard* (1984) and *Le Premier quartier de la lune* (1989) comprise the magic-realist "Chronicles of Plateau Mont-Royal." Another novel, *The Heart Laid Bare* (1986), is a gay love story.

But he was far from through with the stage. After a brief theatrical detour into the bourgeois drawing room of four sisters (whose discussions include the scandalous opening night of *Les Belles-Soeurs*) in *The Impromptu of Outremont* (1980), and an artsy gay couple in *Remember Me* (1981), he returned to the gritty emotional landscapes of his early plays with *Albertine in Five Times* (1984), in which five actresses simultaneously play the desperate Albertine at different decades in her life. In *The Real World?* (1987) Tremblay metatheatrically examines the ways he exploited his own family for his dramatic art, and *La Maison Suspendue* (1990) celebrates reconciliation and the imagination in a dreamy, sentimental weaving together of three generations from both the play and novel cycles. *Marcel poursuivi par les chiens* (1992), a prequel of sorts to *En Pièces Détachées*, once again finds the tawdry Main a beacon of hope for escape from the misery of family and neighborhood.

Tremblay's substantial opus also includes successful stage adaptations of plays by Aristophanes, Tennessee Williams, Paul Zindel, Dario Fo, Chekhov and Gogol. (The latter, *Les Gars de Québec* [1985], sets *The Inspector General* in rural Quebec during the Duplessis era.) He has written a *québécois* pop opera, *Nelligan* (1990); two autobiographical memoirs, *Les Vues animées* (1990) and *Douze coups de théâtre* (1992); and a number of films, including *Il était une fois dans l'est* (1974), an extension of his early dramatic material in collaboration with André Brassard. Tremblay's numerous honours include five Chalmers Awards for best Canadian play in Toronto, the Ontario Lieutenant Governor's Medal, and the Prix France-Québec (twice). In 1984 France named him Chevalier de l'Ordre des Arts et des Lettres, and he has since received honorary degrees from Concordia, McGill, and the University of Stirling in Scotland.

Les Belles-Soeurs remains his most celebrated work, both in French and in translation. From 1991-93 alone, it played in English at Stratford, in Spanish in Buenos Aires, in Yorkshire dialect in Sheffield, and in French, Yiddish and Scots in Montreal. As *The Guid Sisters* it has been one of Scotland's most widely produced and published plays since 1988. France's prestigious literary magazine *Lire* named *Les Belles-Soeurs* one of the 49 plays in its ideal repertoire of world theatre since antiquity. But initially it met with great resistance. Rejected by the Dominion Drama Festival for its 1967 all-Canadian showcase, the play finally gained public attention through a reading at Montreal's Centre d'Essai des Auteurs Dramatiques, the most important laboratory for new play development in Quebec since its founding in 1965.

The premiere of *Les Belles-Soeurs*, directed by André Brassard at the Théâtre du Rideau-Vert in August 1968, elicited howls of protest and torrents of praise. The protesters complained of the play's unflattering portrayal of *québécoise* womanhood, family and religion. But they focused their attacks on the use of *joual* with its crudity and vulgarity ("a filthy bathroom language," wrote one reviewer), its incorporation of English words and phrases, and its implications of Quebec's inferiority to the imperial French standard of language and culture. (The play itself anticipated these criticisms in the affected character of Lisette de Courval, gushing over how refined and polite Europeans are, and how beautifully everyone speaks in Paris: "There they talk *real* French . . . Not like here.") For Tremblay, the language established his characters' authenticity. It reflected the frustrations of their daily existence and emblemized Quebec's historical legacy of bitterness and defeat echoed at the end of the play in the ironic singing of "O Canada" ("an anthem of submission," in Tremblay's words).

In short order the play's champions overcame its critics. Following two popular revivals in Montreal, *Les Belles-Soeurs* had a triumphant production in Paris in 1973, and that same year Brassard directed its English-language debut at Toronto's St. Lawrence Centre to rave reviews. Seattle hosted the American premiere in 1979. The play's successes in English have come despite the severe difficulties of translating a language whose precise flavour and cultural particularities can only be roughly approximated.

Literally translated, "les belles-soeurs" means "the sisters-in-law." Like the creators of other well-known stage "sisters," Anton Chekhov and Tomson Highway, and like his favourite playwright, Samuel Beckett, Tremblay writes tragicomedy. He satirizes the manners and dissects the values of the female society gathered in Germaine Lauzon's kitchen on the rue Fabre—their philistine tastes, greed and envy, social and religious hypocrisy—through sharply comic character portraits and often hilarious ensembles like the "Ode to Bingo." But at the same time he details the fifteen women's painfully repressed desires and thwarted aspirations. They span three generations, but profound unhappiness and pessimism is their common lot. Lacking joy ("I've never laughed in my life"), desperate for affection ("I need . . . to love someone"), resigned to futility ("Do I look like someone who's ever won anything?"), they turn their bitterness to resentment. No one can be allowed to snatch a little happiness, not friend or sister, mother-in-law or daughter. The lives of the young—Linda, Lise and Ginette—promise only to repeat the patterns of the old. The clubs on the Main offer the illusion of hope but no long-term escape, as Pierrette's sad story reveals. Even Germaine's apparent good fortune only leads her down the classic tragic path through pride to a fall, complete with dramatic irony. No one ever gets to Moscow and Godot never comes.

Tremblay's admiration for the Greek tragic chorus is reflected in the play's choral interludes. In typical Tremblayan fashion the chorus lamenting "this stupid, rotten life" combines pain ("My husband bitches. The kids scream. We all fight") and comic painkiller ("But at night we watch TV"). But Tremblay suggests that this chorus has yet another function: "One woman saying she is unhappy with her life is pitiful, but five women saying at the same time that they are unhappy with their lives is the beginning of a revolution" (*Stage Voices*). The absence of men in the play (the image, in one sense, of a politically emasculated Quebec) and the kitchen setting provide the women a comfortably feminized space in which to voice their complaints and frustrations, many of them regarding sex or domestic oppression linked directly to gender. But they fail to find allies in each other. Their solo turns, when they come downstage to speak to the audience in monologue, occur far more frequently than choral solidarity. "They're women who should have rebelled but it was still too early in our history for that to happen," Tremblay told Donald Smith in 1986. "They know why they're unhappy and they'd like it to change, but they still don't have the means to do it. All they can do is give in and go on accepting it."

•

Les Belles-Soeurs was first produced at Le Théâtre du Rideau-Vert in Montreal on August 28, 1968, with the following cast:

GERMAINE LAUZON	Denise Proulx
LINDA LAUZON	Odette Gagnon
ROSE OUIMET	Denise Filiatrault
GABRIELLE JODOIN	Lucille Bélair
LISETTE DE COURVAL	Hélène Loiselle
MARIE-ANGE BROUILLETTE	Marthe Choquette
YVETTE LONGPRE	Sylvie Heppel
DES-NEIGES VERRETTE	Denise de Jaguère
THERESE DUBUC	Germaine Giroux
OLIVINE DUBUC	Nicole Leblanc
ANGELINE SAUVE	Anne-Marie Ducharme
RHEAUNA BIBEAU	Germaine Lemyre
LISE PAQUETTE	Rita Lafontaine
GINETTE MENARD	Josée Beauregard
PIERRETTE GUERIN	Luce Guilbeault

Directed and designed by André Brassard

Les Belles-Soeurs was first performed in English, translated by John Van Burek and Bill Glassco, at the St. Lawrence Centre in Toronto on April 3, 1973:

GERMAINE LAUZON	Candy Kane
LINDA LAUZON	Elva-May Hoover
ROSE OUIMET	Monique Mercure
GABRIELLE JODOIN	Araby Lockhart
LISETTE DE COURVAL	Mia Anderson
MARIE-ANGE BROUILLETTE	Deborah Packer
YVETTE LONGPRE	Louise Nichol
DES-NEIGES VERRETTE	Maureen Fitzgerald
THERESE DUBUC	Irene Hogan
OLIVINE DUBUC	Lilian Lewis
ANGELINE SAUVE	Patricia Hamilton
RHEAUNA BIBEAU	Nancy Kerr
LISE PAQUETTE	Trudy Young
GINETTE MENARD	Suzette Couture
PIERRETTE GUERIN	Melanie Morse

Directed and designed by André Brassard

LES BELLES-SOEURS

CHARACTERS

GERMAINE LAUZON
LINDA LAUZON, *Germaine's daughter*
ROSE OUIMET, *Germaine's sister*
GABRIELLE JODOIN, *another sister*
LISETTE DE COURVAL
MARIE-ANGE BROUILLETTE
YVETTE LONGPRE   } *neighbours*
DES-NEIGES VERRETTE
THERESE DUBUC, *Germaine's sister-in-law*
OLIVINE DUBUC, *Thérèse's mother-in-law*
ANGELINE SAUVE   } *neighbours*
RHEAUNA BIBEAU
LISE PAQUETTE   } *Linda's friends*
GINETTE MENARD
PIERRETTE GUERIN, *Germaine's youngest sister*

SCENE

The kitchen of a Montreal tenement, 1965. Four enormous boxes occupy centre stage.

ACT ONE

LINDA LAUZON enters. She sees four boxes in the middle of the kitchen.

LINDA: God, what's that? Ma!

GERMAINE: Is that you, Linda?

LINDA: Yeah! What are all these boxes in the kitchen?

GERMAINE: They're my stamps.

LINDA: Already? Jeez, that was fast.

GERMAINE LAUZON enters.

GERMAINE: Yeah, it surprised me too. They came this morning right after you left. The doorbell rang. I went to answer it and there's this big fellow standing there. Oh, you'd have liked him, Linda. Just your type. About twenty-two, twenty-three, dark curly hair. Nice little moustache. Real handsome. Anyway, he says to me, "Are you the lady of the house, Mme. Germaine Lauzon?" I said, "yes that's me." And he says, "Good, I've brought your stamps." Linda, I was so excited. I didn't know what to say. Next thing I knew, two guys are bringing in the boxes and the other one's giving me this speech. Linda, what a talker. And such manners. I'm sure you would have liked him.

LINDA: So, what did he say?

GERMAINE: I can't remember. I was so excited. He told me the company he works for was real happy I'd won the million stamps. That I was real lucky, ... Me, I was speechless. I wish your father had been here, he could have talked to him. I don't even know if I thanked him.

LINDA: That's a lot of stamps to glue. Four boxes! One million stamps, that's no joke!

GERMAINE: There's only three boxes. The other one's booklets. But I had an idea, Linda. We're not gonna do all this alone! You going out tonight?

LINDA: Yeah, Robert's supposed to call me . . .

GERMAINE: You can't put it off till tomorrow? Listen, I had an idea. I phoned my sisters, your father's sister and I went to see the neighbours. And I've invited them all to come and paste stamps with us tonight. I'm gonna give a stamp-pasting party. Isn't that a great idea? I bought some peanuts, and your little brother went out to get some Coke . . . .

LINDA: Ma, you know I always go out on Thursdays! It's our night out. We're gonna go to a show.

GERMAINE: You can't leave me alone on a night like this. I've got fifteen people coming . . .

LINDA: Are you crazy! You'll never get fifteen people in this kitchen! And you can't use the rest of the house. The painters are here. Jesus, Ma! Sometimes you're really dumb.

GERMAINE: Sure, that's right, put me down. Fine, you go out, do just as you like. That's all you ever do anyway. Nothing new. I never have any pleasure. Someone's always got to spoil it for me. Go ahead Linda, you go out tonight, go to your goddamned show. Jesus Christ Almighty, I'm so fed up.

LINDA: Come on, Ma, be reasonable . . . .

GERMAINE: I don't want to be reasonable, I don't want to hear about it! I kill myself for you and what do I get in return? Nothing! A big fat nothing! You can't even do me a little favour! I'm warning you, Linda, I'm getting sick of waiting on you, you and everyone else. I'm not your servant, you know. I've got a million stamps to paste and I'm not about to do it myself. Besides, those stamps are for the whole family, which means everybody's gotta do their share. Your father's working tonight but if we don't get done he says he'll help tomorrow. I'm not asking for the moon. Help me for a change, instead of wasting your time with that jerk.

LINDA: Robert is not a jerk.

GERMAINE: Sure, he's a genius! Boy, I knew you were stupid, but not that stupid. When are you going to realize your Robert is a bozo? He doesn't even make sixty bucks a week. All he can do is take you to the local movie house Thursday nights. Take a mother's advice, Linda, keep hanging around with that dope and you'll end up just like him. You want to marry a shoe-gluer and be a strapper all your life?

LINDA: Shut up, Ma! When you get sore, you don't know what you're saying. Anyway, forget it . . . . I'll stay home . . . Just stop screaming, okay? And by the way, Robert's due for a raise soon and he'll be making lots more. He's not as dumb as you think. Even the boss told me he might start making big money 'cause they'll put him in charge of something. You wait. Eighty bucks a week is nothing to laugh at. Anyway . . . I'm gonna go phone him and tell him I can't go to the show . . . Hey, why don't I tell him to come and glue stamps with us?

GERMAINE: Mother of God, I just told you I can't stand him and you want to bring him home tonight. Where the hell are your brains? What did I do to make God in heaven send me such idiots? Just this afternoon, I send your brother to get me a bag of onions and he comes home with a quart of milk. It's unbelievable! You have to repeat everything ten times around here. No wonder I lose my temper. I told you, Linda. The party's for girls. Just girls. Your Robert's not queer, is he?

LINDA: Okay Ma, okay, don't flip your wig. I'll tell him not to come. Jesus, you can't do a thing around here. You think I feel like gluing stamps after working all day. (She starts to dial a number.) Why don't you go dust in the living room, eh? You don't have to listen to what I'm going to say . . . . "Hello, may I speak to Robert? . . . . When do you expect him? . . . . Okay, will you tell him

Linda phoned? . . . Fine, Mme. Bergeron, and you? . . . That's good . . . Okay, thanks a lot. Bye." (She hangs up. The phone rings right away.) "Hello?" . . . Ma, it's for you.

GERMAINE: Twenty years old and you still can't say "One moment please" when you answer a phone.

LINDA: It's only Aunt Rose. Why should I be polite to her?

GERMAINE: (putting her hand over the receiver) Will you be quiet! What if she heard you?

LINDA: Who gives a shit?

GERMAINE: "Hello? Oh, it's you, Rose . . . Yeah, they're here . . . How 'bout that? A million of 'em! They're sitting right in front of me and I still can't believe it. One million! One million! I don't know how much that is, but who cares. A million's a million . . . . Sure, they sent a catalogue. I already had one but this one's for this year, so it's a lot better. The old one was falling apart . . . They've got the most beautiful stuff, wait till you see it. It's unbelievable! I think I'll be able to take everything they've got. I'll re-furnish the whole house. I'm gonna get a new stove, new fridge, new kitchen table and chairs. I think I'll take the red one with the gold stars. I don't think you've seen that one . . . . Oh, it's so beautiful, Rose. I'm getting new pots, new cutlery, a full set of dishes, salt and pepper shakers . . . Oh, and you know those glasses with the "caprice" design. Well, I'm taking a set of those, too. Mme. de Courval got a set last year and she paid a fortune for them, but mine will be free. She'll be mad as hell . . . What? . . . Yeah, she'll be here tonight. They've got those chrome tins for flour and sugar, coffee and stuff . . . . I'm taking it all. I'm getting a Colonial bedroom suite with full accessories. There's curtains, dresser-covers, one of those things you put on the floor beside the bed . . . No, dear, not that . . . New wallpaper . . . Not the floral, Henri can't sleep with flowers . . . I'm telling you Rose, it's gonna be one beautiful bedroom. And the living room! Wait till you hear this . . . . I've got a big TV with a built-in stereo, a synthetic nylon carpet, real paintings . . . You know those Chinese paintings I've always wanted, the ones with the velvet? . . . Aren't they though? Oh, now get a load of this . . . I'm gonna have the same crystal platters as your sister-in-law, Aline! I'm not sure, but I think mine are even nicer. There's ashtrays and lamps . . . I guess that's about it for the living room . . . there's an electric razor for Henri to shave with, shower curtains. So what? We'll put one in. It all comes with the stamps. There's a sunken bathtub, a new sink, bathing suits for everyone . . . No, Rose, I am not too fat. Don't get smart. Now listen, I'm gonna re-do the kid's room, completely. Have you seen what they've got for kids' bedrooms? Rose, it's fabulous! They've got Mickey Mouse all over everything. And for Linda's room . . . Okay, sure, you can just look at the catalogue. But come over right away, the others will be here any minute. I told them to come early. I mean it's gonna take forever to paste all those stamps."

MARIE-ANGE BROUILLETTE enters.

GERMAINE: "Okay, I've gotta go. Mme. Brouillette's just arrived. Okay, yeah . . . . Yeah . . . Bye!"

MARIE-ANGE: Mme. Lauzon, I just can't help it, I'm jealous.

GERMAINE: Well, I know what you mean. It's quite an event. But excuse me for a moment, Mme. Brouillette, I'm not quite ready. I was talking to my sister, Rose. We can see each other across the alley, it's handy.

MARIE-ANGE: Is she gonna be here?

GERMAINE: You bet! She wouldn't miss this for love nor money. Here, have a seat and while you're waiting look at the catalogue. You won't believe all the lovely things they've got. And I'm getting them all, Mme. Brouillette. The works! The whole catalogue. *(She goes into her bedroom.)*

MARIE-ANGE: You wouldn't catch me having luck like that. Fat chance. My life is shit and it always will be. A million stamps! A whole house. If I didn't bite my tongue, I'd scream. Typical. The ones with all the luck least deserve it. What did Mme. Lauzon do to deserve this, eh? Nothing. Absolutely nothing! She's no better looking than me. In fact, she's no better period. These contests shouldn't be allowed. The priest the other day was right. They ought to be abolished. Why should she win a million stamps and not me? Why? It's not fair. I work too, I've got kids, too, I have to wipe their asses, just like her. If anything, my kids are cleaner than hers. I work like a slave, it's no wonder I'm all skin and bones. Her, she's fat as a pig. And now, I'll have to live next door to her and the house she gets for free. It burns me up, I can't stand it. What's more, there'll be no end to her smart-assed comments 'cause it'll all go straight to her head. She's just the type, the loud-mouthed bitch. We'll be hearing about her goddamned stamps for years. I've a right to be

angry. I don't want to die in this shit while madame Fatso here goes swimming in velvet! It's not fair! I'm sick of knocking myself out for nothing! My life is nothing. A big fat zero. And I haven't a cent to my name. I'm fed up. I'm fed up with this stupid, rotten life.

During the monologue, GABRIELLE JODOIN, ROSE OUIMET, YVETTE LONGPRE and LISETTE DE COURVAL have entered. They take their places in the kitchen without paying attention to MARIE-ANGE. The five women get up and turn to the audience. The lighting changes.

THE FIVE WOMEN: *(together)* This stupid, rotten life! Monday!

LISETTE: When the sun with his rays starts caressing the little flowers in the fields and the little birdies open wide their little beaks to send forth their little cries to heaven . . .

THE OTHERS: I get up and I fix breakfast. Toast, coffee, bacon, eggs. I nearly go nuts trying to get the others out of bed. The kids leave for school, my husband goes to work.

MARIE-ANGE: Not mine, he's unemployed. He stays in bed.

THE FIVE WOMEN: Then I work. I work like a demon. I don't stop till noon. I wash . . . Dresses, shirts, stockings, sweaters, pants, underpants, bras. The works. I scrub it, wring it out, scrub it again, rinse it . . . My hands are chapped. My back is sore. I curse like hell. At noon, the kids come home. They eat like pigs, they wreck the house, they leave. In the afternoon I hang out the wash, the biggest pain of all. When that's finished, I start the supper. They all come home. They're tired and grumpy. We all fight. But at night, we watch TV. Tuesday.

LISETTE: When the sun with his rays . . .

THE OTHERS: I get up and I fix breakfast. The same goddamn thing. Toast, coffee, bacon, eggs. I drag the others out of bed and I shove them out the door. Then it's the ironing. I work, I work, I work and I work. It's noon before I know it and the kids are mad because lunch isn't ready. I make 'em baloney sandwiches. I work all afternoon. Suppertime comes, we all fight. But at night, we watch TV Wednesday . . . Shopping day. I walk all day, I break my back carrying parcels this big, I come back home exhausted. But I've still got to make supper. When the others get home I look like I'm dead. I am. My husband bitches, the kids scream. We all fight. But at night, we watch TV.

Thursday and Friday . . . Same thing . . . I work. I slave. I kill myself for my pack of morons. Then I spend the day Saturday tripping over the kids and we all fight. But at night, we watch TV. Sunday we go out, the whole family, we get on the bus and go for supper with the mother-in-law. I have to watch the kids like a hawk, laugh at the old man's jokes, eat the old lady's food, which everyone says is better than mine . . . At night, we watch TV. I'm fed up with this stupid, rotten life! This stupid, rotten life! This stupid, rotten life. This stup . . . .

The lights return to normal. They sit down suddenly.

LISETTE: On my last trip to Europe . . . .

ROSE: There she goes with her Europe again. We're in for it now. Once she gets started, there's no shutting her up!

DES-NEIGES VERRETTE comes in. Discreet little greetings are heard.

LISETTE: I only wished to say that in Europe they don't have stamps. I mean, they have stamps, but not like these ones. Only letter stamping stamps.

DES-NEIGES: That's no fun! So they don't get presents like us? Sounds pretty dull to me, Europe.

LISETTE: Oh no, it's very nice despite that . . .

MARIE-ANGE: Mind you, I've got nothing against stamps, they're useful. If it weren't for the stamps, I'd still be waiting for that thing to grind my meat with. What I don't like is the contests.

LISETTE: But why? They can make families happy.

MARIE-ANGE: Maybe, but they're a pain in the ass for the people next door.

LISETTE: Mme. Brouillette, your language! I speak properly, and I'm none the worse for it.

MARIE-ANGE: I talk the way I talk, and I say what I got to say. I never went to Europe, so I can't afford to talk like you.

ROSE: Hey, you two, cut it out! We didn't come here to fight. You keep it up, I'm crossing the alley and going home.

GABRIELLE: What's taking Germaine so long? Germaine!

GERMAINE: *(from the bedroom)* Be there in a minute. I'm having a hard time getting into my . . . Well, I'm having a hard time . . . Is Linda there?

GABRIELLE: Linda! Linda! No, she's not here.

MARIE-ANGE: I think I saw her go out a while ago.

GERMAINE: Don't tell me she's snuck out, the little bugger.

GABRIELLE: Can we start pasting stamps in the meantime?

GERMAINE: No wait! I'm going to tell you what to do. Don't start yet, wait till I get there. Chat for a bit.

GABRIELLE: "Chat for a bit?" What are we going to chat about . . .

The telephone rings.

ROSE: My God, that scared me! Hello . . . No, she's out, but if you want to wait I think she'll be back in a few minutes. *(She puts the receiver down, goes out on the balcony and shouts.)* Linda! Linda, telephone!

LISETTE: So, Mme. Longpré how does marriage agree with your daughter Claudette?

YVETTE: Oh, she loves it. She's having a ball. She told me about her honeymoon, you know.

GABRIELLE: Where did they go to?

YVETTE: Well, he won a trip to the Canary Islands, eh? So you see, they had to put the wedding ahead a bit . . . .

ROSE: *(laughing)* The Canary Islands! A honeymoon in bird shit, eh?

GABRIELLE: Come on, Rose!

ROSE: What?

DES-NEIGES: The Canary Islands, where's that?

LISETTE: We stopped by there, my husband and I, on our last trip to Europe. It's a real . . . It's a very pleasant country. The women only wear skirts.

ROSE: The perfect place for my husband!

LISETTE: And I'm afraid the natives are not very clean. Of course, in Europe, people don't wash.

DES-NEIGES: It shows, too. Look at those Italians next door to me. You wouldn't believe how that woman stinks.

They all burst out laughing.

LISETTE: *(insinuating)* Did you ever notice her clothesline, on Monday?

DES-NEIGES: No, why?

LISETTE: Well, all I know is this . . . . Those people don't have any underwear.

MARIE-ANGE: You're kidding!

ROSE: I don't believe it!

YVETTE: You gotta be joking!

LISETTE: It's the God's truth! Take a look for yourselves next Monday. You'll see.

YVETTE: No wonder they stink.

MARIE-ANGE: Maybe she's too modest to hang them outside.

The others laugh.

LISETTE: Modest! A European? They don't know what it means. Just look at their movies you see on TV. It's appalling. They stand right in the middle of the street and kiss. On the mouth, too! It's in their blood, you know. Take a look at that Italian's daughter when she brings her friends around . . . . Her boyfriends, that is . . . It's disgusting what she does, that girl. She has no shame! Which reminds me, Mme. Ouimet. I saw your Michel the other day . . .

ROSE: Not with that slut, I hope!

LISETTE: I'm afraid so.

ROSE: You must be mistaken. It couldn't have been him.

LISETTE: I beg your pardon, but the Italians are my neighbours, too. The two of them were on the front balcony . . . I suppose they thought no one could see them . . .

DES-NEIGES: It's true, Mme. Ouimet, I saw them myself. I tell you, they were necking like crazy.

ROSE: The little bastard! As if one pig in the family's not enough. By pig I mean my husband. Can't even watch a girl on TV without getting a . . . . Without getting worked up. Goddamn sex! They never get enough, those Ouimets. They're all alike, they . . .

GABRIELLE: Rose, you don't have to tell the whole world . . .

LISETTE: But we're very concerned . . .

DES-NEIGES and MARIE-ANGE: Yes, we are . . .

YVETTE: To get back to my daughter's honeymoon . . .

GERMAINE: *(entering)* Here I am, girls! *(Greetings, "how are you's," etc.)* So, what have you all been talking about?

ROSE: Oh, Mme. Longpré was telling us about her daughter Claudette's honeymoon . . . .

GERMAINE: Really? *(to YVETTE)* Hello, dear . . . *(to ROSE)* And what was she saying?

ROSE: Sounds like they had a great trip. They met all these people. They went on a boat. They were visiting islands, of course, The Canary Islands . . . They went fishing and they caught fish this big. They ran into some couples they knew . . . . Old friends of Claudette's. Then they came back together and, oh yes, they stopped over in New York. Mme. Longpré was giving us all the details . . .

YVETTE: Well . . .

ROSE: Eh, Mme. Longpré, isn't that right?

YVETTE: Well, as a matter of fact . . .

GERMAINE: You tell your daughter, Mme Longpré, that I wish her all the best. Of course, we weren't invited to the wedding, but we wish her well anyway.

There is an embarrassed silence.

GABRIELLE: Hey! It's almost seven! The rosary!

GERMAINE: Dear God, my novena for Ste.-Thérèse. I'll get Linda's radio. *(She goes out.)*

ROSE: What does she want with Ste.-Thérèse, especially after winning all that?

DES-NEIGES: Maybe she's having trouble with her kids . . . .

GABRIELLE: No, she would have told me . . . .

GERMAINE: *(from the bedroom)* Goddamn it! Where did she put that frigging radio?

ROSE: I don't know, Gaby. Our sister usually keeps things to herself.

GABRIELLE: Not with me. She tells me everything. You, you're such a blabbermouth . . . .

ROSE: You've got a lot of nerve! What do you mean, blabbermouth? Gabrielle Jodoin! My mouth's no bigger than yours.

GABRIELLE: Come off it, you know you can't keep a secret!

ROSE: Well, I never . . . If you think . . .

LISETTE: Wasn't it you, Mme. Ouimet, who just said we didn't come here to quarrel?

ROSE: Hey, you mind your own business. Besides, I didn't say "quarrel." I said "fight."

GERMAINE comes back in with a radio.

GERMAINE: What's going on? I can hear you at the other end of the house!

GABRIELLE: Nothing, it's our sister again . . .

GERMAINE: Settle down, Rose. You're supposed to be the life of the party . . . No fighting tonight.

ROSE: You see! In our family we say "fight."

GERMAINE turns on the radio. We hear a voice saying the rosary. All the women get down on their knees. After a few "Hail Marys" a great racket is heard outside. The women scream and run to the door.

GERMAINE: Oh my God! My sister-in-law Thérèse's mother-in-law just fell down three flights of stairs!

ROSE: Did you hurt yourself, Mme. Dubuc?

GABRIELLE: Rose, shut up! She's probably dead!

THERESE: *(from a distance)* Are you all right, Mme. Dubuc? *(A faint moan is heard.)* Wait a minute. Let me get the wheelchair off you. Is that better? Now I'm gonna help you get back in your chair. Come on, Mme. Dubuc, make a little effort. Don't be so limp! Ouch!

DES-NEIGES: Here, Mme. Dubuc. Let me give you a hand.

THERESE: Thanks Mlle. Verrette. You're so kind.

The other women come back into the room.

ROSE: Germaine, shut off the radio. I'm a nervous wreck!

GERMAINE: What about my novena?

ROSE: How far have you gotten?

GERMAINE: I'm only up to seven, but I promised to do nine.

ROSE: So, pick it up tomorrow and you'll be finished on Saturday.

GERMAINE: It's not for nine days, it's for nine weeks.

THERESE DUBUC and DES-NEIGES VERRETTE enter with OLIVINE DUBUC, who is in a wheelchair.

GERMAINE: My God, she wasn't hurt bad, I hope.

THERESE: No, no, she's used to it. She falls out of her chair ten times a day. Whew! I'm all out of breath. It's no joke, hauling this thing up three flights of stairs. You got something to drink, Germaine?

GERMAINE: Gaby, give Thérèse a glass of water. *(She approaches OLIVINE DUBUC.)* And how are you today, Mme. Dubuc?

THERESE: Don't get too close, Germaine. She's been biting lately.

In fact, OLIVINE DUBUC tries to bite GERMAINE's hand.

GERMAINE: My god, you're right! She's dangerous! How long has she been doing that?

THERESE: Shut off the radio, Germaine, it's getting on my nerves. I'm too upset after what's happened.

GERMAINE: *(reluctantly shuts off the radio)* It's alright, Thérèse, I understand.

THERESE: Honestly, you don't know what it's like, I'm at the end of my tether! You can't imagine my life since I got stuck with my mother-in-law. It's not that I don't love her, the poor woman, I pity her. But she's sick, and so temperamental. I've gotta watch her like a hawk!

DES-NEIGES: How come she's out of the hospital?

THERESE: Well, you see, Mlle. Verrette, three months ago my husband got a raise, so welfare stopped paying for his mother. If she'd stayed there, we would have had to pay all the bills ourselves.

MARIE-ANGE: My, my, my . . .

YVETTE: That's awful.

DES-NEIGES: Dreadful!

During THERESE's speech, GERMAINE opens the boxes and distributes the stamps and books.

THERESE: We had to bring her home. It's some cross to bear, believe me! Don't forget, that woman's ninety-three years old. It's like having a baby in the house. I have to dress her, undress her, wash her . . . .

DES-NEIGES: God forbid!

YVETTE: You poor thing.

THERESE: No, it's no fun. Why only this morning, I said to Paul . . . he's my youngest . . . "Maman's going shopping, so you stay here and take good care of Granny." Well, when I got home, Mme Dubuc had dumped a quart of molasses all over herself and was playing in it like a kid. Of course, Paul was nowhere to be seen. I had to clean the table, the floor, the wheelchair . . .

GERMAINE: What about Mme. Dubuc?

THERESE: I left her like that for the rest of the afternoon. That'll teach her. If she's gonna act like a baby, I'll treat her like one. Do you realize I have to spoon feed her?

GERMAINE: My poor Thérèse. How I feel for you.

DES-NEIGES: You're too good, Thérèse.

GABRIELLE: Much too good, I agree.

THERESE: What can you do, we all have our crosses to bear.

MARIE-ANGE: If you ask me, Thérèse, you've got a heavy one!

THERESE: Oh well, I don't complain. I just tell myself that our Lord is good and He's gonna help me get through.

LISETTE: I can't bear it, it makes me want to weep.

THERESE: Now, Mme. de Courval, don't overdo it.

DES-NEIGES: All I can say, Mme. Dubuc, is you're a real saint.

GERMAINE: Well, now that you've got stamps and booklets, I'll put a little water in some saucers and we can get started, eh? We don't want to spend the night yacking.

She fills a few saucers and passes them around. The women start pasting stamps in the books. GERMAINE goes out on the balcony.

GERMAINE: If Linda were here, she could help me! Linda! Linda! Richard, have you seen Linda? I don't believe it! She's got the nerve to sit and drink Coke while I'm slaving away! Be an angel, will you, and tell her to come home right away? Come see Mme. Lauzon tomorrow and she'll give you some peanuts and candy, if there's any left, okay? Go on, sweetie, and tell her to get home this minute! *(She comes back inside.)* The little bitch. She promised to stay home.

MARIE-ANGE: Kids are all the same.

THERESE: You can say that again! They got no respect.

GABRIELLE: You're telling me. At our house, it's unbearable. Ever since my Raymond started his *cours classique* he's changed something awful . . . We don't recognize him! He walks around with his nose in the air like he's too good for us. He speaks Latin, at the table! We have to listen to his awful music. Can you imagine, classical music in the middle of the afternoon? And when we don't want to watch his stupid TV concerts, he throws a fit. If there's one thing I hate it's classical music.

ROSE: Ah! You're not the only one.

THERESE: I agree. It drives me crazy. Clink! Clank! Bing, Bang, Bong!

GABRIELLE: Of course, Raymond says we don't understand it. As if there's something to understand! Just because he's learning all sorts of non-sense at school, he thinks he can treat us like dirt. I've got half a mind to yank him out and put him to work.

ALL THE WOMEN: Kids are so ungrateful! Kids are so ungrateful!

GERMAINE: Be sure to fill those books, eh, girls? Stamps on every page.

ROSE: Relax, Germaine, you'd think we'd never done it before.

YVETTE: Isn't it getting a little warm in here? Maybe we could open the window a bit . . .

GERMAINE: No, no, not with the stamps. It'll make a draft.

ROSE: Come on, Germaine, they're not birds. They won't fly away. Oh, speaking of birds, last Sunday I went to see Bernard, my oldest. Well, you've never seen so many birds in one house. The house is one big bird cage. And it's her doing, you know. She's nuts about birds! And she doesn't want to kill any. Too soft-hearted, but surely to God there's a limit. Listen to this, it's a scream.

Spotlight on ROSE OUIMET.

ROSE: I'm telling you the woman's nuts. I joke about it but really, it's not funny. Anyway, last Easter, Bernard picked up this bird cage for the two kids. Some guy at the tavern needed money, so he sold it to him cheap . . . . Well, the minute he got it in the house, she went bananas. Fell head over heels in love with his birds. No kidding. She took better care of them than she did her kids. Of course, in no time at all the females were laying eggs . . . And when they started to hatch, Manon thought they were so cute. She didn't have the heart to get rid of them. You've got to be crazy, eh? So she kept them! The whole flock! God knows how many she's got. I never tried to count 'em . . . But, believe me, every time I set foot in the place I nearly go out of my mind! But wait, you haven't heard anything yet. Every day around two, she opens up the cage and out come her stupid birds. What happens? They fly all over the house. They shit all over everything, including us, and we run after them cleaning it all up. Of course, when it's time to get them back in the cage, they don't want to go. They're having too much fun! So Manon starts screaming at the kids, "Catch Maman's little birdies, Maman's too tired." So the kids go charging after the birds and the place is a frigging circus. Me, I get the hell out! I go sit on the balcony and wait till they've all been caught. *(The women laugh.)* And those kids! God, what brats! Oh, I like them okay, they're my grandchildren. But Jesus, do they drive me nuts. Our kids weren't like that. Say what you like. Young people today, they don't know how to bring up their kids.

GERMAINE: You said it!

YVETTE: That's for sure.

ROSE: I mean, take the bathroom. Now we wouldn't have let our kids play in there. Well, you should have seen it on Sunday. The kids went in there like they were just going about their business and in no time flat they'd turned the place upside down. I didn't say a word! Manon always says I talk too much. But I could hear them alright and they were getting on my nerves. You know what they were doing? They took the toilet paper, and they unrolled the whole god-damn thing. Manon just yelled "Look, you kids, Maman's gonna get angry." A lot of good that did. They didn't pay any attention. They kept right on going. I would've skinned 'em alive, the little buggers. And were they having a ball! Bruno, the youngest . . . Can you imagine calling a kid "Bruno"? . . . Anyway, Bruno climbed into the bathtub fully dressed and all rolled up in toilet paper and turned on the water. Listen, he was laughing so hard he nearly drowned! He was making boats out of soggy paper and the water was running all over the place. A real flood! Well, I had to do something. I mean, enough is enough, so I gave them a licking and sent them off to bed.

YVETTE: That's exactly what they needed!

ROSE: Their mother raised a stink, of course, but I'll be damned if I was gonna let them carry on like that. Manon, the dim-wit, she just sits there peeling potatoes and listening to the radio. Oh, she's a winner, that one! But I guess she's happy. The only thing she worries about is her birds. Poor Bernard! At times I really feel sorry for him, being married to that. He should have stayed home with me. He was a lot better off . . . *(She bursts out laughing.)*

Lights return to normal.

YVETTE: Isn't she a riot! There's no stopping her.

GABRIELLE: Yeah, there's never a dull moment with Rose.

ROSE: I always say, when it's time to laugh, might as well have a good one. Every story has a funny side, you know? Even the sad ones . . . .

THERESE: You're damn lucky if you can say that, Mme. Ouimet. It's not everyone . . .

DES-NEIGES: We understand, dear. It must be hard for you to laugh with all your troubles. You're far too good, Mme. Dubuc! You're always thinking of others . . .

ROSE: That's right, you should think of yourself sometimes. You never go out.

THERESE: I don't have time! When would you have me go out? I have to take care of her . . . Ah! If only that was all . . .

GERMAINE: Thérèse, don't tell me there's more.

THERESE: If you only knew! Now that my husband's making some money the family thinks we're millionaires. Why only yesterday, a sister-in-law of my sister-in-law's came to the door with her hand out. Well, you know me. When she told me her story it just broke my heart. So I gave her some old clothes I didn't need anymore . . . Ah, she was so happy . . . . weeping with gratitude . . . she even kissed my hands.

DES-NEIGES: I'm not surprised. You deserve it!

MARIE-ANGE: Mme. Dubuc, I really admire you.

THERESE: Oh, don't say that . . . .

DES-NEIGES: No, no, no. You deserve it.

LISETTE: You certainly do, Mme. Dubuc. You deserve our admiration and I assure you, I shan't forget you in my prayers.

THERESE: Well, I always say, "If God put poor people on this earth, they gotta be encouraged."

GERMAINE: When you're through filling your books there, instead of piling them on the table, why don't we put them back in the box? . . . Rose, give me a hand. We'll take out the empty books and put in the full ones.

ROSE: Good idea. My God! Look at all these books. We gotta fill all them tonight?

GERMAINE: Sure, why not? Besides, everyone's not here yet, so we . . .

DES-NEIGES: Who else is coming, Mme. Lauzon?

GERMAINE: Rhéauna Bibeau and Angeline Sauvé are supposed to come by after the funeral parlour. One of Mlle. Bibeau's old girlfriends has a daughter whose husband died. His name was . . . Baril, I think . . .

YVETTE: Not Rosaire Baril.

GERMAINE: Yeah, I think that's it . . .

YVETTE: But I knew him well! I used to go out with him for Godsake. How do you like that! I'd have been a widow today.

GABRIELLE: Guess what, girls? I got the eight mistakes in last Saturday's paper. It's the first time I ever got 'em all and I've been trying for six months . . . I sent in the answer . . .

YVETTE: Did you win anything yet?

GABRIELLE: Do I look like someone who's ever won anything?

THERESE: Hey, Germaine, what are you going to do with all these stamps?

GERMAINE: Didn't I tell you? I'm going to re-decorate the whole house. Wait a minute . . . Where did I put the catalogue? . . . Ah, here it is. Look at that, Thérèse. I'm gonna have all that for nothing.

THERESE: For nothing! You mean it's not going to cost you a cent?

GERMAINE: Not a cent! Aren't these contests wonderful?

LISETTE: That's not what Mme. Brouillette said a while ago . . .

GERMAINE: What do you mean?

MARIE-ANGE: Mme. de Courval, really!

ROSE: Well, come on, Mme. Brouillette. Don't be afraid to say what you think. You said earlier you don't like these contests because only one family wins.

MARIE-ANGE: Well, it's true! All these lotteries and contests are unfair. I'm against them.

GERMAINE: Just because you never won anything.

MARIE-ANGE: Maybe, maybe, but they're still not fair.

GERMAINE: Not fair, my eye! You're jealous, that's all. You said so yourself the minute you walked in. Well, I don't like jealous people, Mme. Brouillette. I don't like them one bit! In fact, if you really want to know, I can't stand them!

MARIE-ANGE: Well! In that case, I'm leaving!

GERMAINE: No, no don't go! Look I'm sorry . . . I'm all nerves tonight, I don't know what I'm saying. We'll just forget it, okay? You have every right to your opinions. Every right. Just sit back down and keep pasting.

ROSE: Our sister's afraid of losing one of her workers.

GABRIELLE: Shut up, Rose! You're always sticking your nose where it don't belong.

ROSE: What's eating you? I can't even open my mouth?

MARIE-ANGE: Alright, I'll stay. But I still don't like them.

From this point on, MARIE-ANGE BROUILLETTE will steal all the books she fills. The others will see what she's doing right from the start, except for GERMAINE, obviously, and they will decide to follow suit.

LISETTE: Well, I figured out the mystery charade in last month's *Chatelaine*. It was very easy . . . My first syllable is a Persian king . . .

ROSE: Onassis?

LISETTE: No, a *Persian* king . . . It's a "shah" . . .

ROSE: That's a Persian?

LISETTE: Why, of course . . .

ROSE: *(laughing)* That's his tough luck!

LISETTE: My second is for killing bugs . . . No one? . . . Oh, well, "Raid" . . . .

ROSE: My husband's a worm, do you think it would work on him? . . . She's really nuts with all this stuff, eh?

LISETTE: And the whole thing is a social game . . .

ROSE: Spin the bottle!

GABRIELLE: Rose, will you shut up for Godsake! *(to LISETTE)* Scrabble?

LISETTE: Oh, come now, it's simple . . . Shah-raid . . . Charade!

YVETTE: Ah . . . What's a charade?

LISETTE: Of course, I figured it out in no time . . . It was so easy . . .

YVETTE: So, did you win anything?

LISETTE: Oh, I didn't bother to send it in. I just did it for the challenge . . . Besides, do I look like I need to win things?

ROSE: Well, I like mystery words, hidden words, crosswords, turned-around words, bilingual words. All that stuff with words. It's my specialty. I'm a champ, you know, I've broken all the records! Never miss a contest . . . Costs me two bucks a week just for stamps!

YVETTE: So did you win yet?

ROSE: *(looking at GERMAINE)* Do I look like somebody who's ever won anything?

THERESE: Mme. Dubuc, will you let go of my saucer? . . . There, now you've done it! You've spilled it! That's the last straw!

She socks her mother-in-law on the head and the latter settles down a little.

GABRIELLE: Wow! You don't fool around! Aren't you afraid you'll hurt her?

THERESE: No, no. She's used to it. It's the only way to shut her up. My husband figured it out. If you give her a good bash on the head, it seems to knock her out a while. That way she stays in her corner and we get some peace.

Blackout. Spotlight on YVETTE LONGPRE.

YVETTE: When my daughter Claudette got back from her honeymoon, she gave me the top part of her wedding cake. I was so proud! It's such a lovely piece. A miniature sanctuary all made of icing. It's got a red velvet stairway leading up to a platform and on top of the platform stand the bride and groom. Two little dolls all dressed up like newly-weds. There's even a priest to bless them and behind him there's an altar. It's all icing. I've never seen anything so beautiful. Of course, we paid a lot for the cake. After all, six levels! It wasn't all cake though. That would have cost a fortune. Just the first two levels were cake. The rest was wood. But it's amazing, eh? You'd never have guessed. Anyway, when my daughter gave me the top part, she had it put under this glass bell. It looked so pretty, but I was afraid it would spoil . . . you know, without air. So I took my husband's glass knife . . . He's got a special knife for cutting glass . . . And I cut a hole in the top of the bell. Now the air will stay fresh and the cake won't go bad.

Lights up.

DES-NEIGES: Me too. I took a stab at a contest a few weeks ago. You had to find a slogan for some bookstore . . . I think it was Hachette or something . . . Anyway, I gave it a try . . . I came up with "Hachette will chop the cost of your books." Not bad, eh?

YVETTE: Yeah, but did you win anything?

DES-NEIGES: Do I look like somebody who's ever won anything?

GERMAINE: By the way, Rose, I saw you cutting your grass this morning. You should buy a lawn-mower.

ROSE: What for? I get along fine with scissors. Besides it keeps me in shape.

GERMAINE: You were puffing away like a steam engine.

ROSE: I'm telling you, it's good for me. Anyway, I can't afford a lawn-mower. Even if I could, that's the last thing I'd buy.

GERMAINE: I'll be getting a lawn-mower with my stamps . . .

DES-NEIGES: Her and her stamps, she's starting to get on my nerves! *(She hides a booklet in her purse.)*

ROSE: What are you gonna do with a lawn-mower on the third floor?

GERMAINE: You never know, it might come in handy. And who knows, we might move someday.

DES-NEIGES: I suppose she's going to tell us she needs a new house for all the stuff she's gonna get with her lovely stamps.

GERMAINE: You know, we probably will need a bigger place for all the stuff I'm gonna get with my stamps.

DES-NEIGES VERRETTE, MARIE-ANGE BROUILLETTE and THERESE DUBUC all hide two or three books each.

GERMAINE: Rose, if you want, you can borrow my lawn-mower.

ROSE: No way! I might bust it. I'd be collecting stamps for the next two years just to pay you back.

The women laugh.

GERMAINE: Don't be smart.

MARIE-ANGE: Isn't she something! Can you beat that!

THERESE: Hey, I forgot to tell you. I guessed the mystery voice on the radio . . . It was Duplessis . . . My husband figured it out 'cause it was an old voice. I sent in twenty-five letters just to be sure they'd get it. And for extra luck, I signed my youngest boy's name, Paul Dubuc . . . .

YVETTE: Did you win anything yet?

THERESE: *(looking to GERMAINE)* Do I look like someone who's ever won anything?

GABRIELLE: Say, do you know what my husband's gonna get me for my birthday?

ROSE: Same as last year. Two pairs of nylons.

GABRIELLE: No sir-ee! A fur coat. Of course, it's not real fur, but who cares? I don't think real fur's worth buying anymore. The synthetics they make nowadays are just as nice. In fact, sometimes nicer.

LISETTE: Oh, I disagree . . .

ROSE: Sure, we all know who's got a fat mink stole!

LISETTE: Well, if you ask me, there's no substitute for authentic, genuine fur. Incidentally, I'll be getting a new stole in the autumn. The one I have now is three years old and it's starting to look . . . . Well, a bit ratty. Mind you, it's still mink, but . . . .

ROSE: Shut your mouth, you bloody liar! We know goddamn well your husband's up to his ass in debt because of your mink stoles and trips to

Europe! She's got no more money than the rest of us and she thinks her farts smell like perfume!

LISETTE: Mme. Jodoin, if your husband wants to buy my stole, I'll sell it to him cheap. Then you'll have real mink. After all, between friends . . . .

YVETTE: You know the inflated objects game in the paper, the one where you're supposed to guess what the objects are? Well, I guessed them. There was a screw, a screw-driver and some kind of bent up hook.

THE OTHERS: So . . .

YVETTE sits down.

GERMAINE: You know Daniel, Mme. Robitaille's little boy? He fell off the second floor balcony the other day. Not even a scratch! How 'bout that?

MARIE-ANGE: Don't forget he landed on Mme. Turgeon's hammock. And Monsieur Turgeon was in it at the time . . .

GERMAINE: That's right. He's in hospital for three months.

DES-NEIGES: Speaking of accidents, I heard a joke the other day . . .

ROSE: Well, aren't you gonna tell us?

DES-NEIGES: Oh, I couldn't. It's too racy . . .

ROSE: Come on, Mlle. Verrette! We know you've got a stack of them . . .

DES-NEIGES: No. I'm too embarrassed. I don't know why, but I am . . . .

GABRIELLE: Don't be such a tease, Mlle. Verrette. You know darn well you're gonna tell us anyway . . .

DES-NEIGES: Well . . . Alright . . . There was this nun who got raped in an alley . . .

ROSE: Sounds good!

DES-NEIGES: And the next morning they found her lying in the yard, a real mess, her habit pulled over her head, moaning away . . . so this reporter comes running over and he says to her, "Excuse me, Sister, but could you tell us something about this terrible thing that's happened to you?" Well, she opens her eyes, looks up at him and in a very small voice she says, "Again, please."

All the women burst out laughing except for LISETTE DE COURVAL who appears scandalized.

ROSE: Christ Almighty, that's hysterical! I haven't heard such a good one for ages. I'm gonna pee my pants! Mlle. Verrette, where in the world do you get them?

GABRIELLE: You know where, from her travelling salesman . . .

DES-NEIGES: Mme. Jodoin, please!

ROSE: That's right too. Her travelling salesman . . .

LISETTE: I don't understand.

GABRIELLE: Mlle. Verrette has a travelling salesman who comes to sell her brushes every month. I think she likes him more than his brushes.

DES-NEIGES: Mme. Jodoin, honestly!

ROSE: One thing's for sure, Mlle. Verrette has more brushes than anyone in the parish. Hey, I saw your boyfriend the other day . . . He was sitting in the restaurant . . . He must have been to see you, eh?

DES-NEIGES: Yes, he was—but I assure you, there's nothing between us.

ROSE: That's what they all say.

DES NEIGES: Really, Mme. Ouimet, you're always twisting things to make people look bad. Monsieur Simard is a very nice man.

ROSE: Yeah, but who's to say you're a nice lady? Now, now, Mlle. Verrette, don't get angry. I'm only pulling your leg.

DES-NEIGES: Then don't say things like that. Of course, I'm a nice lady, a thoroughly respectable one too. By the way, the last time he was over, Henri . . . 'er . . . Monsieur Simard was telling me about a project he has in mind . . . And he asked me to extend you all an invitation. He wants me to organize a demonstration next week . . . At my house. He chose me because he knows my house . . . It'd be for a week Sunday, right after the rosary. I need at least ten people if I'm gonna get my gift . . . You know, they give away those fancy cups to the one who holds the demonstration . . . Fantasy Chinaware . . . You should see them, they're gorgeous. They're souvenirs he brought back from Niagara Falls . . . They must have cost a fortune.

ROSE: You bet, we'll go, eh, girls? I love demonstrations! Any door prizes?

DES-NEIGES: I don't know. I suppose. Maybe . . . Anyway, I'll provide snacks . . .

ROSE: That's more than you get around here. We'll be lucky to see a glass of water!

OLIVINE DUBUC tries to bite her daughter-in-law.

THERESE: Mme. Dubuc, if you don't stop that I'm gonna lock you in the bathroom and you can stay there for the rest of the evening.

Blackout. Spotlight on DES-NEIGES VERRETTE.

DES-NEIGES: The first time I saw him I thought he was ugly . . . it's true. He's not good-looking. When I opened the door he took off his hat and said, "Would you be interested in buying some brushes, Madame?" I slammed the door in his face. I never let a man in the house! Who knows what might happen . . . . The only one who gets in is the paper boy. He's still too young to get any wrong ideas. Well, a month later my friend with the brushes came back. There was a terrible snowstorm outside, so I let him stand in the hall. Once he was in the house, I was frightened, but I told myself he didn't look dangerous, even if he wasn't good looking . . . He's always well-dressed . . . Not a hair out of place . . . He's a real gentleman . . . . And so polite! Well, he sold me a couple of brushes and then he showed me his catalogue. There was one that I wanted, but he didn't have it with him, so he said I could place an order. Ever since then, he's come back once a month. Sometimes I don't buy a thing. He just comes in and we chat for a while. He's such a nice man. When he speaks, you forget he's ugly. And he knows so many interesting things! The man must travel all over the province! I think . . . . I think I'm in love with him . . . I know it's crazy. I only see him once a month, but it's so nice when we're together. I'm so happy when he comes. I've never felt this way before. Never. Men never paid much attention to me. I've always been . . . unattached. But he tells me about his trips, and all kinds of stories . . . Sometimes they're a bit risqué, but honestly, they're so funny! I must admit, I've always liked stories that are a bit off-colour . . . And it's good for you to tell them sometimes. Not all his jokes are dirty, mind you. Lots of them are clean. And it's only lately that he's been telling me the spicy ones. Sometimes they're so dirty I blush! The last time he came he took my hand when I blushed. I nearly went out of my mind. My insides went all funny when he put his big hand on mine. I need him so badly! I don't want him to go away! Sometimes, just sometimes, I dream about him. I dream . . . that we're married. I need him to come and see me. He's the first man that ever cared about me. I don't want to lose him! I don't want to! If he goes away, I'll be all alone again, and I need . . . someone to love . . . *(She lowers her eyes and murmurs.)* I need a man.

The lights come on again. LINDA LAUZON, GINETTE MENARD and LISE PAQUETTE enter.

GERMAINE: Ah, there you are!

LINDA: I was at the restaurant.

GERMAINE: I know you were at the restaurant. You keep hanging around there, you're gonna end up like your Aunt Pierrette . . . In a whorehouse.

LINDA: Lay off, Ma! You're making a stink over nothing.

GERMAINE: I asked you to stay home . . .

LINDA: Look, I went to get cigarettes and I ran into Lise and Ginette . . .

GERMAINE: That's no excuse. You knew I was having company, why didn't you come right home. You do it on purpose, Linda. You do it just to make my blood boil. You want me to blow my stack in front of my friends? Is that it? You want me to swear in public? Well, Jesus Christ Almighty, you've succeeded! But don't think you're off the hook yet, Linda Lauzon. I'll take care of you later.

ROSE: This is no time to bawl her out, Germaine!

GABRIELLE: Rose, you mind your own business.

LINDA: So, I'm a little late, my God, it's not the end of the world!

LISE: It's our fault, Mme. Lauzon.

GINETTE: Yeah, it's our fault.

GERMAINE: I know it's your fault. And I've told Linda a hundred times not to run around with tramps. But you think she gives a damn? Sometimes I'd like to strangle her!

ROSE: Now, Germaine . . .

GABRIELLE: Rose, I told you, stay out of this! You got that? It's their business. It's nothing to do with you.

ROSE: Hey, get off my back! What's with you anyway? Linda's getting bawled out and she hasn't done a goddamn thing!

GABRIELLE: It's none of our business!

LINDA: Leave her alone, Aunt Gaby. She's only trying to defend me.

GABRIELLE: Don't you tell me what to do! I'm your Godmother!

GERMAINE: You see what she's like! Day in and day out! I never brought her up to act this way.

ROSE: Now that you mention it, how do you bring up your kids?

GERMAINE: Hah! You should talk! . . . . Your kids . . .

LINDA: Go on, Aunt Rose, tell her. You're the only one who can give it to her good.

GERMAINE: So, you're siding with your Aunt Rose now are you? You've forgotten what you said when she phoned a while ago, eh? You've forgotten about that? Come on, Linda, tell Aunt Rose what you said about her.

LINDA: That was different . . .

ROSE: Why, what did she say?

GERMAINE: Well, she answered the phone when you called, right? And she was too rude to say, "One moment, please," so I told her to be more polite with you . . . .

LINDA: Will you shut up, Ma! That has nothing to do with it.

ROSE: I want to know what you said, Linda.

LINDA: It's not important, I was mad at her.

GERMAINE: She said, "It's only Aunt Rose. Why should I be polite to her?"

ROSE: I don't believe it . . . You said that?

LINDA: I told you, I was mad at her!

ROSE: I never thought that of you, Linda. There, you've let me down. You've really let me down.

GABRIELLE: Let them fight it out themselves, Rose.

ROSE: You bet I'll let 'em fight. Go on, Germaine. Knock her silly, the little brat! You wanna know something, Linda? Your mother's right. If you're not careful, you'll end up like your Aunt Pierrette. I've got a good mind to slap your face!

GERMAINE: Just you try it! You don't lay a hand on my kids! If they need a beating, I'll do it. Nobody else!

THERESE: Will you please stop bickering, I'm tired!

DES-NEIGES: Lord, yes, you're wearing us out.

THERESE: You'll wake up my mother-in-law and get her going again.

GERMAINE: She's your problem, not mine! Why didn't you leave her at home?

THERESE: Germaine Lauzon!

GABRIELLE: Well, she's right. You don't go out to parties with a ninety-three year old cripple.

LISETTE: Mme. Jodoin, didn't I just hear you tell your sister to mind her own business?

GABRIELLE: Keep your big nose out of this, you stuck up bitch! Shut your yap and keep pasting or I'll shut it for you.

LISETTE: (getting up) Gabrielle Jodoin!

OLIVINE DUBUC spills the saucer she has been playing with.

THERESE: Mme Dubuc, for Godsake!

GERMAINE: Aw, shit, my tablecloth!

ROSE: She's soaked me, the old bag!

THERESE: That's not true! You weren't even close!

ROSE: Sure, call me a liar right to my face!

THERESE: Rose Ouimet, you are a liar!

GERMAINE: Look out, she's falling out of her chair!

DES-NEIGES: Oh, no, she's on the floor, again!

THERESE: Somebody give me a hand.

ROSE: Not me, no way!

GABRIELLE: Pick her up yourself.

DES-NEIGES: Here, I'll help you, Mme. Dubuc.

THERESE: Thank you, Mlle. Verrette.

GERMAINE: And you, Linda, you watch your step for the rest of the evening.

LINDA: I feel like going back to the restaurant.

GERMAINE: Do that and you won't set foot in this house again, you hear?

LINDA: Sure, I've heard it a thousand times.

LISE: Can it, Linda . . .

THERESE: For Godsake, Mme. Dubuc, make a little effort. You go limp like that on purpose.

MARIE-ANGE: I'll hold the chair.

THERESE: Thank you . . . .

ROSE: If it was me, I'd take that lousy chair and . . .

GABRIELLE: Rose, don't start again!

THERESE: Whew! What I go through . . . .

GABRIELLE: Hey, will you get a load of de Courval, still pasting her stamps . . . The bloody snob. As if nothing had happened! I guess we're not good enough for her.

Blackout. Spotlight on LISETTE DE COURVAL.

LISETTE: It's like living in a barnyard. Léopold told me not to come and he was right. I should have stayed home. We don't belong with these people. Once you've tasted life on an ocean liner and have to return to this, well . . . . It's enough to make you weep . . . I can still see myself, stretched out on the deck chair, a Book-of-the-Month in my lap . . . And that lieutenant who was giving me the eye . . . My husband says he wasn't, but he didn't see what I saw . . . Mmmmm . . . . That was some man. Maybe I should have encouraged him a little more . . . *(She sighs.)* . . . And Europe! Everyone there is so refined! So much more polite than here. You'd never meet a Germaine Lauzon in Europe. Never! Only people of substance. In Paris, you know, everyone speaks so beautifully and there they talk real French . . . Not like here . . . I despise every one of them. I'll never set foot in this place again! Léopold was right about these people. These people are cheap. We shouldn't mix with them. Shouldn't talk about them . . . They should be hidden away somewhere. They don't know how to live! We broke away from this and we must never, ever go back. Dear God, they make me so ashamed!

The lights come back up.

LINDA: I've had it. I'm leaving . . .

GERMAINE: The hell you are! I'm warning you Linda! . . .

LINDA: "I'm warning you, Linda!" Is that all you know how to say?

LISE: Linda, don't be stupid.

GINETTE: Let's stay.

LINDA: No, I'm leaving. I've listened to enough crap for one night.

GERMAINE: Linda, I forbid you to leave!

VOICE OF A NEIGHBOUR: Will you stop screaming up there. We can't hear ourselves think!

ROSE: *(going out on the balcony)* Hey, you! Get back in your house.

NEIGHBOUR: I wasn't talking to you!

ROSE: Oh yes, you were. I'm just as loud as the rest of them!

GABRIELLE: Rose, get in here!

DES-NEIGES: *(referring to the neighbour)* Don't pay any attention to her.

NEIGHBOUR: I'm gonna call the cops!

ROSE: Go right ahead, we need some men up here.

GERMAINE: Rose Ouimet, get back in this house! And you, Linda . . .

LINDA: I'm leaving. See ya! *(She goes out with GINETTE and LISE.)*

GERMAINE: She's gone! Gone! Walked right out! I don't believe it! That kid will be the death of me. I'm gonna smash something. I'm gonna smash something!

ROSE: Germaine, control yourself.

GERMAINE: Making a fool of me in front of everyone! *(She starts sobbing.)* My own daughter . . . I'm so ashamed!

GABRIELLE: Come on, Germaine. It's not that bad . . .

LINDA'S VOICE: Hey, if it isn't Mlle. Sauvé. How are you doing?

ANGELINE'S VOICE: Hello, sweetheart, how are you?

ROSE: Germaine, they're here. Blow your nose and stop crying.

LINDA'S VOICE: Not bad, thanks.

RHEAUNA'S VOICE: Where are you off to?

LINDA'S VOICE: I was gonna go to the restaurant, but now that you're here, I think I'll stay.

LINDA, GINETTE and LISE enter with ANGELINE and RHEAUNA.

ANGELINE: Hello, everybody.

RHEAUNA: Hello.

THE OTHERS: Hello, hello. Come on in, how have you been . . . *etc.*

RHEAUNA: What an awful climb, Mme. Lauzon. I'm all out of breath.

GERMAINE: Well, have a seat . . .

ROSE: You're out of breath? Don't worry, my sister's getting an elevator with her stamps.

They all laugh except RHEAUNA and ANGELINE who don't understand.

GERMAINE: Very funny, Rose! Linda, go get some more chairs . . .

LINDA: Where? There aren't any more.

GERMAINE: Go ask Mme. Bergeron if she'll lend us some . . .

LINDA: *(to the girls)* Come on, guys . . .

GERMAINE: *(low to LINDA)* We make peace for now, but wait till the others have gone . . .

LINDA: I'm not scared of you. If I came back it's because Mlle. Sauvé and Mlle. Bibeau showed up, not because of you. *(LINDA goes out with her friends.)*

DES-NEIGES: Here, take my seat, Mlle. Bibeau . . .

THERESE: Yes, come and sit next to me . . .

MARIE-ANGE: Sit down here, Mlle. Bibeau . . .

ANGELINE and RHEAUNA: Thank you. Thanks very much.

RHEAUNA: I see you're pasting stamps.

GERMAINE: We sure are. A million of 'em!

RHEAUNA: Dear God, a million! How are you getting on?

ROSE: Not bad . . . But my tongue's paralyzed.

RHEAUNA: You've been doing it with your tongue?

GABRIELLE: Of course not, she's just being smart.

ROSE: Good old Bibeau. Sharp as a tack!

ANGELINE: Why don't we give you a hand?

ROSE: Okay. As long as you don't give us some tongue! *(She bursts out laughing.)*

GABRIELLE: Rose, don't be vulgar!

GERMAINE: So, how was the funeral parlour?

Blackout. Spotlight on ANGELINE and RHEAUNA.

RHEAUNA: I tell you, it came as a shock . . .

ANGELINE: But I thought you hardly knew him.

RHEAUNA: I knew his mother. So did you. Remember, we went to school together. I watched that man grow up . . .

ANGELINE: Such a shame. Gone, just like that. And us, we're still here.

RHEAUNA: Ah, but not for long . . .

ANGELINE: Rhéauna, please . . .

RHEAUNA: I know what I'm talking about. You can tell when the end is near. I've suffered. I know.

ANGELINE: Ah, when it comes to that, we've both had our share. I've suffered, too.

RHEAUNA: I've suffered a lot more than you, Angeline. Seventeen operations! A lung, a kidney, one of my breasts . . . Gone! I'm telling you, there's not much left.

ANGELINE: And me with my arthritis that won't let up. But Mme . . . What was her name . . . You know, the wife of the deceased . . . She gave me a recipe . . . She says it works wonders.

RHEAUNA: But you've tried everything. The doctors have all told you, there's nothing you can do. There's no cure for arthritis.

ANGELINE: Doctors, doctors! . . . I've had it with doctors. All they think about is money. They bleed you to death and go to California for the winter. You know, Rhéauna, the doctor said he'd get well, Monsieur . . . What was his name again? The one who died?

RHEAUNA: Monsieur Baril . . .

ANGELINE: That's it. I can never remember it. It's easy enough, too. Anyhow, the doctor told Monsieur Baril that he had nothing to worry about . . . And look what happened . . . Only forty years old . . .

RHEAUNA: Forty years old! That's young to die.

ANGELINE: He sure went fast . . .

RHEAUNA: She told me how it happened. It's so sad . . .

ANGELINE: Really? I wasn't there. How did it happen?

RHEAUNA: When he got home from work on Monday night, she thought he was looking a bit strange. He was white as a sheet, so she asked him how he felt. He said he felt okay and they started supper . . . Well, now, the kids were making a fuss at the table and Monsieur Baril got mad and had to punish Rolande. That's his daughter . . . Of course, after that, he looked like he was ready to drop . . . she didn't take her eyes off him for a second . . . But she told me later that it happened so fast she didn't have time to do a thing. All of a sudden he said he felt funny and over he went . . . His face right in the soup. That was it!

ANGELINE: Lord, have mercy. So sudden! I tell you, Rhéauna, it's frightening. It gives me the shivers.

RHEAUNA: Isn't it the truth? We never know when God's going to come for us. He said it Himself, "I'll come like a thief."

ANGELINE: Don't talk like that, it scares me. I don't want to die that way. I want to die in my bed . . . have time to make my confession . . . .

RHEAUNA: Oh, God forbid that I should die before confessing! Angéline, promise me you'll call the priest the minute I'm feeling weak. Promise me that.

ANGELINE: You know I will. You've asked me a hundred times. Didn't I get him there for your last attack? You had Communion and everything.

RHEAUNA: I'm so afraid to die without the last rites.

ANGELINE: But what do you have to confess, Rhéauna?

RHEAUNA: Don't say that, Angéline. Don't ever say that! We're never too old to sin.

ANGELINE: If you ask me, Rhéauna, you'll go straight to heaven. You've got nothing to worry about. Hey! Did you notice Baril's daughter? The way she's changed! She looks like a corpse.

RHEAUNA: Isn't it the truth. Poor Rolande. She's telling everyone that she killed her father. It's because of her that he got mad, you see, at supper . . . Oh I feel so sorry for her . . . And her mother. What a tragedy! Such a loss for everyone. They'll miss him so . . . .

ANGELINE: You're telling me . . . The father. Mind you, it's not as bad as the mother, but still . . .

RHEAUNA: True. Losing the mother is worse. You can't replace a mother.

ANGELINE: Did you see how nice he looked? . . . Like a young man. He was even smiling . . . . I could have sworn he was asleep. But I still think he's better off where he is . . . You know what they say, it's the ones who stay behind who most deserve the pity. Him, he's fine now . . . Ah, I still can't get over how good he looked. Almost like he was breathing.

RHEAUNA: Yeah! But he wasn't.

ANGELINE: But I can't imagine why they put him in that suit . . .

RHEAUNA: What do you mean?

ANGELINE: Didn't you notice? He was wearing a blue suit. You don't do that when you're dead. A blue suit is much too light. Now, navy-blue would be okay, but powder blue . . . Never! When you're dead, you wear a black suit.

RHEAUNA: Maybe he didn't have one. They're not that well off, you know.

ANGELINE: Dear God, you can rent a black suit! And look at Mme. Baril's sister! In green! At a funeral parlour! And did you notice how much she's aged? She looks years older than her sister . . .

RHEAUNA: She is older.

ANGELINE: Don't be silly, Rhéauna, she's younger.

RHEAUNA: No, she isn't.

ANGELINE: Why sure, Rhéauna, listen! Mme Baril is at least thirty-seven, but her sister . . .

RHEAUNA: She's well over forty!

ANGELINE: Rhéauna, she isn't!

RHEAUNA: She's at least forty-five . . .

ANGELINE: That's what I'm telling you. She's aged so much, she looks a lot older than she is . . . Listen, my sister-in-law, Rose-Aimée, is thirty-six and the two of them went to school together . . . .

RHEAUNA: Well, anyway, it doesn't surprise me she's aged so fast . . . What with the life she leads . . .

ANGELINE: I'm not sure they're true, all those stories.

RHEAUNA: They must be! Mme. Baril tries to hide it 'cause it's her sister . . . But the truth always comes out. It's like Mme. Lauzon and her sister, Pierrette. Now, if there's one person I can't stand, it's Pierrette Guérin. A shameless hussy! Nothing but shame to her whole family. I tell you, Angéline, I wouldn't want to see her soul. It must be black as coal.

ANGELINE: You know, Rhéauna, deep down inside, Pierrette isn't all bad.

Spotlight on GERMAINE LAUZON.

GERMAINE: My sister, Pierrette, I've had nothing to do with her for a long time. Not after what she did. When she was young, she was so good, and she did. When she was young, she was so good, and so pretty. But now, she's nothing but a whore. My sisters and I were nuts about her. We spoiled her rotten. And look what it got us . . . I don't understand. I don't understand. Papa used to call her his pepper pot. He was so crazy about his little Pierrette. When he'd put her on his knee, you could tell he was happy. And the rest of us weren't even jealous . . .

ROSE: We'd say, "She's the youngest. It's always that way, it's the youngest who gets the attention." When she started school, we dressed her like a princess. I was already married, but I remember as if it were yesterday. Oh, she was so pretty! Like Shirley Temple! And so quick at school. A lot better than me, that's for sure. I was lousy at school . . . I was the class clown, that's all I was ever good for . . . But her, the little bugger, always coming home with prizes. First in French, first in Arithmetic, first in Religion . . . Yeah, Religion! She was pious as a nun, that kid. I tell you, the Sisters were nuts about her! But to see her today . . . . I almost feel sorry for her. She must need help sometimes . . . She must get so lonely . . . .

GABRIELLE: When she finished school, we asked her what she wanted to do. She wanted to be a teacher. She was all set to begin her training . . . . And then she met her Johnny.

THE THREE SISTERS: Goddamn Johnny! He's a devil out of hell! It's all his fault she turned out the way she did. Goddamn Johnny! Goddamn Johnny!

RHEAUNA: What do you mean, not all bad! You've got to be pretty low to do what she did. Do you know what Mme. Longpré told me about her?

ANGELINE: No, what?

THERESE: Ow!!!

The lights come back up. THERESE DUBUC gives her mother-in-law a sock on the head.

GERMAINE: Beat her brains out if you have to, Thérèse, but do something!

THERESE: Sure, beat her brains out! Look, I'm doing all I can to keep her quiet. I'm not about to kill her just to make you happy.

ROSE: If it was up to me, I'd shove her off the balcony . . .

THERESE: What? Say that again, Rose. I didn't hear you!

ROSE: I was talking to myself.

THERESE: You're scared, eh?

ROSE: Me, scared?

THERESE: Yes, Rose. Scared!

MARIE-ANGE: Don't tell me there's gonna be another fight.

ANGELINE: Has there been a fight?

RHEAUNA: Oh, who was fighting?

ANGELINE: We should have come sooner.

THERESE: I won't stand for that. She insulted my mother-in-law! My husband's mother!

LISETTE: There they go again!

ROSE: She's so old! She's useless!

GERMAINE: Rose!

GABRIELLE: Rose, that's cruel! Aren't you ashamed?

THERESE: Rose Ouimet, I'll never forgive you for those words! Never!

ROSE: Ah, piss off!

ANGELINE: Who had a fight?

ROSE: You want to know everything, eh, Mademoiselle Sauvé? You want all the gory details?

ANGELINE: Mme. Ouimet!

ROSE: So you can blab it all over town, eh? Isn't that it?

RHEAUNA: Rose Ouimet, I don't lose my temper often, but I will not allow you to insult my friend.

MARIE-ANGE: (to herself) I'll just grab a few more while no one's looking.

GABRIELLE: (who has seen her) What are you doing there, Mme. Brouillette?

ROSE: Fine, I've said enough. I'll shut up.

MARIE-ANGE: Shhhh! Take these and keep quiet!

LINDA, GINETTE and LISE arrive with the chairs. There is a great hullabaloo. All the women change places, taking advantage of the occasion to steal more stamps.

MARIE-ANGE: Don't be afraid, take them!

DES-NEIGES: Aren't you overdoing it?

THERESE: Hide these in your pocket, Mme. Dubuc . . . No! Damn it! Hide them!

GERMAINE: You know that guy who runs the meat shop, what a thief!

The door opens suddenly and PIERRETTE GUERIN comes in.

PIERRETTE: Hi, everybody!

THE OTHERS: Pierrette!

LINDA: Great! It's Aunt Pierrette!

ANGELINE: Oh my God, Pierrette!

GERMAINE: What are you doing here? I told you I never wanted to see you again.

PIERRETTE: I heard that my big sister, Germaine, had won a million stamps, so I decided to come over and have a look. (She sees ANGELINE.) Well, I'll be goddamned! Angéline! What are you doing here?

Everyone looks at ANGELINE. Blackout.

ACT TWO

The second act begins with PIERRETTE's entrance. Hence the last six speeches of Act One are repeated now. The door opens suddenly and PIERRETTE GUERIN comes in.

PIERRETTE: Hi, everybody!

THE OTHERS: Pierrette!

LINDA: Great! It's Aunt Pierrette!

ANGELINE: Oh, my God, Pierrette!

GERMAINE: What are you doing here? I told you I never wanted to see you again.

PIERRETTE: I heard that my big sister, Germaine, had won a million stamps, so I decided to come over and have a look. *(She sees ANGELINE.)* Well, I'll be goddamned! Angéline! What are you doing here?

Everyone looks at ANGELINE.

ANGELINE: My God! I'm caught.

GERMAINE: What do you mean, Angéline?

GABRIELLE: How come you're talking to Mlle. Sauvé?

ROSE: You oughta be ashamed!

PIERRETTE: Why? We're real good friends, eh, Géline?

ANGELINE: Oh! I think I'm going to faint! *(She pretends to faint.)*

RHEAUNA: Good heavens, Angéline!

ROSE: She's dead!

RHEAUNA: What?

GABRIELLE: Don't be ridiculous! Rose, you're getting carried away again.

PIERRETTE: She hasn't even fainted. She's only pretending. *(PIERRETTE approaches ANGELINE.)*

GERMAINE: Don't you touch her!

PIERRETTE: Mind your own business! She's my friend.

RHEAUNA: What do you mean, your friend?

GERMAINE: Don't try to tell us Mlle. Sauvé is a friend of yours!

PIERRETTE: Of course she is! She comes to see me at the club almost every Friday night.

ALL THE WOMEN: What!

RHEAUNA: That's impossible.

PIERRETTE: Ask her! Hey, Géline, isn't it true what I'm saying? Come on, stop playing dead and answer me. Angéline, we all know you're faking! Tell them. Isn't it true you come to the club?

ANGELINE: *(after a silence)* Yes, it's true.

RHEAUNA: Oh, Angéline! Angéline!

SOME OF THE WOMEN: Dear God, this is dreadful!

SOME OTHER WOMEN: Dear God, this is horrible!

LINDA, GINETTE and LISE: Holy shit, that's great!

The lights go out.

RHEAUNA: Angéline! Angéline!

Spotlight on ANGELINE and RHEAUNA.

ANGELINE: Rhéauna, you must understand . . .

RHEAUNA: Don't you touch me! Get away!

THE WOMEN: Who would have thought . . . Such a horrible thing!

RHEAUNA: I'd never have thought this of you. You, in a club. And every Friday night! It's not possible. It can't be true.

ANGELINE: I don't do anything wrong, Rhéauna. All I have is a Coke.

THE WOMEN: In a club! In a night club!

GERMAINE: God only knows what she does there.

ROSE: Maybe she tries to get picked up.

ANGELINE: But I tell you, I don't do anything wrong!

PIERRETTE: It's true. She doesn't do anything wrong.

ROSE, GERMAINE, and GABRIELLE: Shut up, you demon. Shut up!

RHEAUNA: You're no longer my friend, Angéline. I don't know you.

ANGELINE: Listen to me, Rhéauna, you must listen! I'll explain everything and then you'll see!

ROSE, GERMAINE and GABRIELLE: A club! the fastest road to hell!

ALL THE WOMEN: *(except the girls)* The road to hell, the road to hell! If you go there, you'll lose your soul! Cursed drink, cursed dancing! That's the place where our men go wrong and spend their money on women of sin!

ROSE, GERMAINE and GABRIELLE: Women of sin like you, Pierrette!

ALL THE WOMEN: (except the girls) Shame on you, Angéline Sauvé, to spend your time in this sinful way!

RHEAUNA: But Angéline, a club! It's worse than hell!

PIERRETTE: (laughing heartily) If hell's anything like the club I work in, I wouldn't mind eternity there!

ROSE, GERMAINE and GABRIELLE: Shut up, Pierrette. The devil has your tongue!

LINDA, GINETTE and LISE: The devil? Come on! Get with the times! The clubs are not the end of the world! They're no worse than any place else. They're fun! They're lots of fun. The clubs are lots of fun.

THE WOMEN: Ah! Youth is blind! Youth is blind! You're gonna lose yourselves and then you'll come crying to us. But it'll be too late! It'll be too late! Watch out! You be careful of these cursed places! We don't always know when we fall, but when we get back up, it's too late!

LISE: Too late! It's too late! Oh my God, it's too late!

GERMAINE: I hope at least you'll go to confession, Angéline Sauvé!

ROSE: And to think that every Sunday I see you at Communion . . . Communion with a sin like that on your conscience!

GABRIELLE: A mortal sin!

ROSE, GERMAINE and GABRIELLE: How many times have we been told . . . It's a mortal sin to set foot in a club!

ANGELINE: That's enough. Shut up and listen to me!

THE WOMEN: Never! You've no excuse!

ANGELINE: Rhéauna, will you listen to me! We're old friends. We've been together for thirty-five years. You mean a lot to me, but there are times when I want to see other people. You know how I am. I like to have fun. I grew up in church basements and I want to see other things. Clubs aren't all bad, you know. I've been going for four years and I never did anything wrong. And the people who work there, they're no worse than us. I want to meet people, Rhéauna! Rhéauna, I've never laughed in my life!

RHEAUNA: There are better places to laugh. Angéline, you're going to lose your soul. Tell me you won't go back.

ANGELINE: Listen, Rhéauna, I can't! I like to go there, don't you understand. I like it!

RHEAUNA: You must promise or I'll never speak to you again. It's up to you. It's me or the club. If you only knew how much that hurts, my best friend sneaking off to a night club. How do you think that looks, Angéline? What will people say when they see you going there? Especially where Pierrette works. It's the lowest of them all! You must never go back, Angéline, you hear? If you do, it's finished between us. Finished! You ought to be ashamed!

ANGELINE: Rhéauna, you can't ask me not to go back . . . Rhéauna, answer me!

RHEAUNA: Until you promise, not another word!

The lights come up. ANGELINE sits in a corner. PIERRETTE joins her.

ANGELINE: Why did you have to come here tonight?

PIERRETTE: Let them talk. They love to get hysterical. They know damn well you don't do anything wrong at the club. In five minutes, they'll forget all about it.

ANGELINE: You think so, eh? Well, what about Rhéauna? You think she'll forgive me just like that? And Mme. de Courval who's in charge of recreation for the parish, also President of the Altar Society at Our Lady of Perpetual Help! You think she'll continue speaking to me? And your sisters who can't stand you because you work in a club! I'm telling you it's hopeless! Hopeless!

GERMAINE: Pierrette!

PIERRETTE: Listen, Germaine, Angéline feels bad enough. So let's not fight, eh? I came here to see you and paste stamps and I want to stay. And I don't have the plague, okay? Just leave us alone. Don't worry. The two of us'll stay out of your way. After tonight, if you want, I'll never come back again. But I can't leave Angéline alone.

ANGELINE: You can leave if you want, Pierrette . . .

PIERRETTE: No, I want to stay.

ANGELINE: Okay, then I'll go.

LISETTE: Why don't they both leave!

ANGELINE gets up.

ANGELINE: *(to RHEAUNA)* Are you coming? *(RHEAUNA doesn't answer.)* Okay. I'll leave the door unlocked . . .

She goes towards the door. The lights go out. Spotlight on ANGELINE SAUVE.

It's easy to judge people. It's easy to judge them, but you have to look at both side of the coin. The people I've met in that club are my best friends. No one has ever treated me so well . . . Not even Rhéauna. I have fun with those people. I can laugh with them. I was brought up by nuns in the parish halls who did the best they could, poor souls, but knew nothing. I was fifty-five years old when I learned to laugh. And it was only by chance. Because Pierrette took me to her club one night. Oh, I didn't want to go. She had to drag me there. But, you know, the minute I got in the door, I knew what it was to go through life without having any fun. I suppose clubs aren't for everyone, but me, I like them. And of course, it's not true that I only have a Coke. Of course, I drink liquor! I don't have much, but still, it makes me happy. I don't do anyone any harm and I buy myself two hours of pleasure every week. But this was bound to happen someday. I knew I'd get caught sooner or later. I knew it. What am I going to do now? Dear God, what am I going to do? *(Pause.)* Damn it all! Everyone deserves to get some fun out of life! *(Pause.)* I always said that if I got caught I'd stop going . . . But I don't know if I can . . . And Rhéauna will never go along with that. *(Pause.)* Ah, well, I suppose Rhéauna is worth more than Pierrette. *(She gives a long sigh.)* I guess the party's over . . . .

She goes off. Spotlight on YVETTE LONGPRE.

YVETTE: Last week, my sister-in-law, Fleur-Ange, had a birthday. They had a real nice party for her. There was a whole gang of us there. First there was her and her family, eh? Oscar David, her husband, Fleur-Ange David, that's her, and their seven kids: Raymonde, Claude, Lisette, Fernand, Réal, Micheline and Yves. Her husband's parents, Aurèle David and his wife, Ozéa David, were there too. Next, there was my sister-in-law's mother, Blanche Tremblay. Her father wasn't there 'cause he's dead . . . Then there were the other guests: Antonio Fournier, his wife Rita, Germaine Gervais, also Wilfred Gervais, Armand Campeau, Daniel Lemoyne and his wife, Rose-Aimée, Roger Joly, Hormidas Guay, Simmone Laflamme, Napoleon Gauvin, Anne-Marie Turgeon, Conrad Joanette, Léa Liasse, Jeanette Landreville, Nona Laplante, Robertine Portelance, Gilbert Morrissette, Lilianne Beaupré, Virginie Latour, Alexandre Thibodeau, Ovila Gariépy, Roméo Bacon and his wife Juliette, Mimi Bleau, Pit Cadieux, Ludger Champagne, Rosaire Rouleau, Roger Chabot, Antonio Simard, Alexandrine Smith, Philemon Langlois, Eliane Meunier, Marcel Morel, Grégoire Cinq-Mars, Théodore Fortier, Hermine Héroux and us, my husband, Euclide, and me. And I think that's just about everyone . . . .

The lights come back up.

GERMAINE: Okay, now let's get back to work, eh?

ROSE: On your toes, girls. Here we go!

DES-NEIGES: We're not doing badly, are we? Look at all I've pasted . . .

MARIE-ANGE: What about all you've stolen . . .

LISETTE: You want to hand me some more stamps, Mme. Lauzon.

GERMAINE: Sure . . . coming right up . . . Here's a whole bunch.

RHEAUNA: Angeline! Angeline! It can't be true!

LINDA: *(to PIERRETTE)* Hi, Aunt Pierrette.

PIERRETTE: Hi! How're you doing?

LINDA: Oh, not too hot. Ma and I are always fighting and I'm really getting sick of it. She's always bitching about nothing, you know? I'd sure like to get out of here.

GERMAINE: The retreats will be starting pretty soon, eh?

ROSE: Yeah! That's what they said last Sunday.

MARIE-ANGE: I hope we won't be getting the same priest as last year . . . .

GERMAINE: Me too! I didn't like him either. What a bore.

PIERRETTE: Well, what's stopping you? You could come and stay with me . . . .

LINDA: Are you kidding? They'd disown me on the spot!

LISETTE: No, we've got a new one coming this year.

DES-NEIGES: Oh yeah? Who's it gonna be?

LISETTE: A certain Abbé Rochon. They say he's excellent. I was talking to l'Abbé Gagné the other day and he tells me he's one of his best friends . . . .

ROSE: *(to GABRIELLE)* There she goes again with her l'Abbé Gagné. We'll be hearing about him all night! You'd think she was in love with him. L'Abbé Gagné this, l'Abbé Gagné that. Well, if you want my opinion, I don't like l'Abbé Gagné.

GABRIELLE: I agree. He's too modern for me. It's okay to take care of parish activities, but he shouldn't forget he's a priest! A man of God!

LISETTE: Oh, but the man is a saint . . . You should get to know him, Mme. Dubuc. I'm sure you'd like him . . . When he speaks, you'd swear it was the Lord himself talking to us.

THERESE: Don't overdo it . . .

LISETTE: And the children! They adore him. Oh, that reminds me, the children in the parish are organizing a variety night for next month. I hope you can all make it because it should be very impressive. They've been practicing for ages . . .

DES-NEIGES: What's on the programme?

LISETTE: Well, it's going to be very good. There'll be all sorts of things. Mme. Gladu's little boy is going to sing . . .

ROSE: Again! I'm getting sick of that kid. Besides, since he went on television, his mother's got her nose in the air. She thinks she's a real star!

LISETTE: But the child has a lovely voice.

ROSE: Oh yeah? Well, he looks like a girl with his mouth all puckered up like a turkey's ass.

GABRIELLE: Rose!

LISETTE: Diane Aubin will give a demonstration of aquatic swimming . . . We'll be holding the event next door to the city pool, it will be wonderful . . .

ROSE: Any door prizes?

LISETTE: Oh yes, lots. And the final event of the evening will be a giant bingo.

THE OTHER WOMEN: *(except the girls)* A bingo!

Blackout. When the lights come back up, the women are all at the edge of the stage.

LISETTE: Ode to Bingo!

While ROSE, GERMAINE, GABRIELLE, THERESE and MARIE-ANGE recite the Ode to Bingo, the four other women call out bingo numbers in counterpoint.

ROSE, GERMAINE, GABRIELLE, THERESE and MARIE-ANGE: Me, there's nothing in the world I like more than bingo. Almost every month we have one in the parish. I get ready two days ahead of time; I'm all wound up, I can't sit still, it's all I can think of. And when the big day arrives, I'm so excited, housework's out of the question. The minute supper's over, I get all dressed up, and a team of wild horses couldn't hold me back. I love playing bingo! I adore playing bingo! There's nothing in the world can beat bingo! When we arrive at the apartment where we're going to play we take off our coats and head straight for the tables. Sometimes it's the living room the lady's cleared, sometimes it's the kitchen. Sometimes it's even the bedroom. We sit at the tables, distribute the cards, set up the chips and the game begins!

The women who are calling the numbers continue alone for a moment.

I'm so excited, I go bananas. I get all mixed up, I sweat like a pig, screw up the numbers, put my chips in the wrong squares, make the caller repeat the numbers, I'm in an awful state! I love playing bingo! I adore playing bingo! There's nothing in the world can beat bingo! The game's almost over. I've got three more tries. Two down and one across. I'm missing the B14! I need the B14! I want the B14! I look at the others. Shit, they're as close as I am. What am I gonna do? I've gotta win! I've gotta win! I've gotta win!

LISETTE: B14!

THE OTHERS: Bingo! Bingo! I've won! I knew it! I knew I couldn't lose! I've won! Hey, what did I win?

LISETTE: Last month we had Chinese dog door stops. But this month, this month, we've got ashtray floor lamps!

THE OTHERS: I love playing bingo! I adore playing bingo! There's nothing in the world beats bingo! What a shame they don't have 'em more often. The more they have, the happier it makes me! Long live the Chinese dogs! Long live the ashtray floor lamps! Long live bingo!

Lights to normal.

ROSE: I'm getting thirsty.

GERMAINE: Oh, God, I forgot the drinks! Linda, get out the Cokes.

OLIVINE: Coke . . . Coke . . . Yeah . . . Yeah, Coke . . .

THERESE: Relax, Mme. Dubuc. You'll get your Coke like everyone else. But drink it properly! No spilling it like last time.

ROSE: She's driving me up the wall with her mother-in-law . . .

GABRIELLE: Forget it, Rose. There's been enough fighting already.

GERMAINE: Yeah! Just keep quiet and paste. You're not doing a thing!

Spotlight on the refrigerator. The following scene takes place by the refrigerator door.

LISE: *(to LINDA)* I've got to talk to you, Linda . . .

LINDA: I know, you told me at the restaurant . . . But it's hardly a good time . . .

LISE: It won't take long and I've got to tell somebody, I can't hide it much longer. I'm too upset. And Linda, you're my best friend . . . Linda, I'm going to have a baby.

LINDA: What! But that's crazy! Are you sure?

LISE: Yes, I'm sure. The doctors told me.

LINDA: What are you gonna do?

LISE: I don't know. I'm so depressed! I haven't told my parents yet. My father'll kill me, I know he will. When the doctor told me, I felt like jumping off the balcony . . .

PIERRETTE: Listen, Lise . . .

LINDA: You heard?

PIERRETTE: Yeah! I know you're in a jam, kid, but . . . I might be able to help you . . .

LISE: Yeah? How?

PIERRETTE: Well, I know a doctor . . .

LINDA: Pierrette, she can't do that!

PIERRETTE: Come on, it's not dangerous . . . He does it twice a week, this guy.

LISE: I've thought about it already, Linda . . . But I didn't know anyone . . . And I'm scared to try it alone.

PIERRETTE: Don't ever do that! It's too dangerous! But with this doctor . . . I can arrange it, if you like. A week from now you'll be all fixed up.

LINDA: Lise, you can't do that!

LISE: What else can I do? It's the only way out. I don't want the thing to be born. Look what happened to Manon Belair. She was in the same boat and now her life's all screwed up because she's got that kid on her hands.

LINDA: What about the father? Can't he marry you?

LISE: Are you kidding! I don't even know where he is. He just took off somewhere. Sure, he promised me the moon. We were gonna be happy. He was raking it in, I thought everything was roses. One present after another. No end to it. It was great while it lasted . . . but Goddamn it, this had to happen. It just had to. Why is it always me who ends up in the shit? All I ever wanted was a proper life for myself. I'm sick of working at Kresges. I want to make something of myself, you know, I want to be somebody. I want a car, a decent place to live, nice clothes. My uniforms for the restaurant are all I own, for Chrissake. I never have any money, I always have to scrounge, but I want that to change. I don't want to be cheap anymore. I came into this world by the back door, but by Christ I'll go out by the front! Nothing's gonna stop me. Nothing. You watch, Linda, you'll see I was right. Give me two or three years and you'll see that Lise Paquette is a somebody. And money, she's gonna have it, okay?

LINDA: You're off to a bad start.

LISE: That's just it! I've made a mistake and I want to correct it. After this I'll start fresh. You understand, don't you, Pierrette?

PIERRETTE: Sure, I do. I know what it is to want to be rich. Look at me. When I was your age, I left home because I wanted to make some money. But I didn't start by working in a dime store. Oh, no! I went straight to the club. Because that's where the money was. And it won't be long now before I hit the jackpot. Johnny's promised me . . .

ROSE, GERMAINE and GABRIELLE: Goddamn Johnny! Goddamn Johnny!

GINETTE: What's going on over here?

LISE: Nothing, nothing. *(to PIERRETTE)* We'll talk about it later . . .

GINETTE: Talk about what?

LISE: Forget it. It's nothing!

GINETTE: Can't you tell me?

LISE: Look, will you leave me alone?

PIERRETTE: Come on, we can talk over here . . .

GERMAINE: What's happening to those Cokes?

LINDA: Coming, coming . . . .

The lights come back up.

GABRIELLE: Hey, Rose, you know that blue suit of yours? How much did you pay for it?

ROSE: Which one?

GABRIELLE: You know, the one with the white lace around the collar?

ROSE: Oh, that one . . . I got it for $9.98.

GABRIELLE: That's what I thought. Imagine, today I saw the same one at Reitman's for $14.98.

ROSE: No kidding! I told you I got it cheap, eh?

GABRIELLE: I don't know how you do it. You always find the bargains.

LISETTE: My daughter Micheline just found a new job. She's started to work with those F.B.I. machines.

MARIE-ANGE: Oh yeah! I hear those things are tough on the nerves. The girls who work them have to change jobs every six months. My sister-in-law, Simonne's daughter, had a nervous breakdown over one. Simonne just called today to tell me about it.

ROSE: Oh my God, I forgot, Linda, you're wanted on the phone!

Linda runs to the phone.

LINDA: "Hello? Robert? How long have you been waiting?"

GINETTE: Tell me.

LISE: No. Beat it, will you? I want to talk to Pierrette . . . Go on, get lost!

GINETTE: Okay, I get the message! You're happy to have me around when there's nobody else, eh? But when someone more interesting comes along . . .

LINDA: "Listen, Robert, how many times do I have to tell you, it's not my fault! I just found out!"

THERESE: Here, Mme. Dubuc, hide these!

ROSE: How are things at your place, Ginette?

GINETTE: Oh, same as usual, they fight all day long . . . Nothing new. My mother still drinks . . . And my father gets mad . . . And they go on fighting . . .

ROSE: Poor kid . . . And your sister?

GINETTE: Suzanne? Oh, she's still the brainy one. She can't do anything wrong, you know? "Now there's a girl who uses her head. You should be more like her, Ginette. She's making something of her life" . . . Nobody else even counts, especially me. But they always did like her best. And, of course, now she's a teacher, you'd think she was a saint or something.

ROSE: Hey, come on, Ginette. Isn't that a bit much?

GINETTE: No, I'm serious . . . My mother's never cared about me. It's always, "Suzanne's the prettiest. Suzanne's the nicest" . . . Day in, day out till I'm sick of it! Even Lise doesn't like me anymore!

LINDA: *(on the phone)* "Oh, go to hell! If you're not gonna listen, why should I talk? Call me back when you're in a better mood!" *(She hangs up.)* For Chrissake, Aunt Rose, why didn't you tell me I was wanted on the phone? Now he's pissed off at me!

ROSE: Isn't she polite! You see how polite she is?

Spotlight on PIERRETTE GUERIN.

PIERRETTE: When I left home, I was head over heels in love, I couldn't even see straight. No one existed for me but Johnny. He made me waste ten years of my life, the bastard. I'm only thirty now and I feel like sixty. The things that guy got me to do! And me, the idiot, I listened to him. Did I ever. Ten years I worked his club for him. I was a looker, I brought in the customers, and that was fine as long as it lasted . . . But now . . . now I'm fucked. I feel like jumping off a bridge. All I got left is the bottle. And that's what I've been doing since Friday. Poor Lise, she thinks she's done for just 'cause she's pregnant. She's young, I'll give her my doctor's name . . . He'll fix her up. It'll be easy for her to start over. But not me. Not me. I'm too old. A girl who's been at it for ten years is washed up. Finished. And try telling that to my sisters. They'll never understand. I don't know what I'm gonna do now. I don't know.

LISE: I don't know what I'm gonna do now. I don't know. An abortion, that's serious. I've heard enough stories to know that. But I guess I'm better off going to see Pierrette's doctor than trying to do it myself. Ah, why do these things always happen to me? Pierrette, she's lucky. Working in the same club for ten years, making a bundle . . . And she's in love! I wouldn't mind being in her shoes. Even if her family can't stand her, at least she's happy on her own.

PIERRETTE: He dumped me, just like that! "It's finished," he said. "I don't need you anymore. You're too old and too ugly. So pack your bags and beat it." That son-of-a-bitch! He didn't leave me a nickel! Not a goddamn nickel! After all I did for him. Ten years! Ten years for nothing. That's enough to make anyone pack it in. What am I gonna do now, eh? What? Become a waitress at Kresge's like Lise? No thanks! Kresge's is fine for kids and old ladies, but not for me. I don't know what I'm gonna do. I just don't know. And here I've gotta pretend everything's great. But I can't tell Linda and Lise I'm washed up. *(Silence.)* Yeah . . . I guess there's nothing left but booze . . . good thing I like that . . .

LISE: *(interspersed throughout PIERRETTE's last speech)* I'm scared, dear God, I'm scared! *(She approaches PIERRETTE.)* Are you sure this'll work, Pierrette? If you only knew how scared I am!

PIERRETTE: *(laughing)* 'Course it will. It'll be fine, kid. You'll see . . .

The lights come back up.

MARIE-ANGE: It's not even safe to go to the show anymore. I went to the Rex the other day to see Belmondo in something, I forget what. I went alone, cause my husband didn't wanna go. Well, all of a sudden, right in the middle of the show this smelly old bum sits down next to me and starts grabbing my knee. You can imagine how embarrassed I was but that didn't stop me. I stood up, took my purse and smashed him right in his ugly face.

DES-NEIGES: Good for you, Mme. Brouillette! I always carry a hat pin when I go to the show. You never know what'll happen. And the first one who tries to get fresh with me . . . But I've never used it yet.

ROSE: Hey, Germaine, these Cokes are pretty warm.

GERMAINE: When are you gonna stop criticizing, eh? When?

LISE: Linda, you got a pencil and paper?

LINDA: I'm telling you, Lise, don't do it!

LISE: I know what I'm doing. I've made up my mind and nothing's gonna make me change it.

RHEAUNA: *(to THERESE)* What are you doing there?

THERESE: Shh! Not so loud! You should take some, too. Two or three books, she'll never know.

RHEAUNA: I'm not a thief!

THERESE: Come on, Mlle. Bibeau, it's not a question of stealing. She got these stamps for nothing and there's a million of 'em. A million!

RHEAUNA: Say what you will, she invited us here to paste her stamps and we've got no right to steal them!

GERMAINE: *(to ROSE)* What are those two talking about? I don't like all this whispering . . .

She goes over to RHEAUNA and THERESE.

THERESE: *(seeing her coming)* Oh . . . Yeah . . . You add two cups of water and stir.

RHEAUNA: What? *(Noticing GERMAINE)* Oh! Yes! She was giving me a recipe.

GERMAINE: A recipe for what?

RHEAUNA: Doughnuts!

THERESE: Chocolate pudding!

GERMAINE: Well, which is it? Doughnuts or chocolate pudding? *(She comes back to ROSE.)* Listen, Rose, there's something fishy going on around here.

ROSE: *(who has just hidden a few books in her purse)* Don't be silly . . . You're imagining things . . . .

GERMAINE: And I think Linda's spending too much time with Pierrette. Linda, get over here!

LINDA: In a minute, Ma . . . .

GERMAINE: I said come here! That means now. Not tomorrow!

LINDA: Okay! Don't get in a flap . . . so, what do you want?

GABRIELLE: Stay with us a bit . . . You've been with your Aunt long enough.

LINDA: So what?

GERMAINE: What's going on between her and Lise there?

LINDA: Oh . . . Nothing . . .

GERMAINE: Answer when you're spoken to!

ROSE: Lise wrote something down a while ago.

LINDA: It was just an address . . .

GERMAINE: Not Pierrette's, I hope! If I ever find out you've been to her place, you're gonna hear from me, got that?

LINDA: Will you lay off! I'm old enough to know what I'm doing! *(She goes back to PIERRETTE.)*

ROSE: Maybe it's none of my business, Germaine, but . . .

GERMAINE: Why, what's the matter now?

ROSE: Your Linda's picking up some pretty bad habits . . .

GERMAINE: You can say that again! But don't worry, Rose, I can handle her. She's gonna straighten out fast. And as for Pierrette, it's the last time she'll set foot in this house. I'll throw her down the goddamn stairs!

MARIE-ANGE: Have you noticed Mme. Bergeron's daughter lately? Wouldn't you say she's been putting on weight?

LISETTE: Yes, I've noticed that . . .

THERESE: *(insinuating)* Strange, isn't it? It's all in her middle.

ROSE: I guess the sap's running a bit early this year.

MARIE-ANGE: She tries to hide it too. It's beginning to show, though.

THERESE: And how! I wonder who could have done it?

LISETTE: It's probably her step-father . . .

GERMAINE: Wouldn't surprise me in the least. He's been after her ever since he married her mother.

THERESE: It must be awful in that house. I feel sorry for Monique. She's so young . . .

ROSE: Maybe so, but you must admit, she's been looking for it, too. Maybe so, but look how she dresses. Last summer, I was embarrassed to look at her! And you know me, I'm no prude. Remember those red shorts she had on, those short shorts? Well, I said it then, and I'll say it again, "Monique Bergeron is gonna turn out bad." She's got the devil in her, that girl, a real demon. Besides, she's a redhead . . . No, you can say what you like, those unwed mothers deserve what they get and I got no sympathy for 'em.

LISE starts to get up.

PIERRETTE: Take it easy, kid!

ROSE: It's true! It's their own damn fault! I'm not talking about the ones who get raped. That's different. But an ordinary girl who gets herself knocked up, uh! uh! . . . She gets no sympathy from me. It's too goddamn bad! I tell you, if my Carmen ever came home like that, she'd go sailing right through the window! Not that I'm worried about her, mind you. She's not that kind of girl . . . Nope, for me unwed mothers are all the same. A bunch of depraved sluts. You know what my husband calls 'em, eh? Cockteasers!

LISE: I'll kill her if she doesn't shut up!

GINETTE: Why? If you ask me, she's right.

LISE: You shut your trap and get out of here!

PIERRETTE: Isn't that a bit much, Rose?

ROSE: Listen, Pierrette, we know you're an expert on these matters. We know you can't be shocked. Maybe you think it's normal, but we don't. There's one way to prevent it . . .

PIERRETTE: *(laughing)* There's lots of ways. Ever heard of the pill?

ROSE: It's no use talking to you! That's not what I meant! I'm against free love! I'm a Catholic! So leave us alone and stay where you belong, filthy whore!

LISETTE: I think perhaps you exaggerate, Mme. Ouimet. There are occasions when girls can get themselves in trouble and it's not entirely their fault.

ROSE: You! You believe everything they tell you in those stupid French movies!

LISETTE: What have you got against French movies?

ROSE: Nothing. I like English ones better, that's all. French movies, they're too realistic, too far-fetched. You shouldn't believe what they say. They always make you feel sorry for the girl who gets pregnant. It's never anyone else's fault. Well, do you feel sorry for tramps like that? I don't! A movie's a movie and life's life!

LISE: I'll kill her, the bitch! Stupid fucking jerk! She goes around judging everyone and she's got the brains of a . . . And as for her Carmen. Well, I happen to know her Carmen and believe me, she does a lot more than tease! She oughta clean her own house before she shits on everyone else.

Spotlight on ROSE OUIMET.

ROSE: That's right. Life is life and no goddamn Frenchman ever made a movie about that! Sure, any old actress can make you feel sorry for her in a movie. Easy as pie! And when she's finished work, she can go home to her big fat mansion and climb into her big fat bed that's twice the size of my bedroom, for Chrissake! But the rest of us, when we get up in the morning . . . when I wake up in the morning he's lying there staring at me . . . Waiting. Every morning, I open my eyes and there he is, waiting! Every night, I get into bed and there he is, waiting! He's always there, always after me, always hanging over me like a vulture. Goddamn sex! It's never that way in the movies, is it? Oh no, in the movies it's always fun! Besides, who cares about a woman who's

gotta spend her life with a pig just 'cause she said yes to him once? Well, I'm telling you, no fucking movie was ever this sad. Because movies don't last a lifetime! *(Silence.)* Why did I ever do it? Why? I should have said no. I should have yelled no at the top of my lungs and stayed an old maid. At least I'd have had some peace. I was so ignorant in those days. Christ, I didn't know what I was in for. All I could think of was "the Holy State of Matrimony!" You gotta be stupid to bring up your kids like that, knowing nothing. My Carmen won't get caught like that. Because I've been telling her for years what men are really worth. She won't be able to say I didn't warn her! *(On the verge of tears)* She won't end up like me, forty-four years old, with a two year old kid and another one on the way, with a stupid slob of a husband who can't understand a thing, who demands his "rights" at least twice a day, three hundred and sixty-five days a year. When you get to be forty and you realize you've got nothing behind you and nothing ahead of you, it makes you want to dump everything and start all over . . . But women . . . women can't do that . . . They get grabbed by the throat, and they stay that way, right to the end!

The lights come back up.

GABRIELLE: Well, I like French movies. They sure know how to make 'em good and sad. They make me cry every time. And you must admit, Frenchmen are a lot better looking than Canadians. They're real men!

GERMAINE: Now wait just a minute! That's not true.

MARIE-ANGE: Come on! The little peckers don't even come up to my shoulder. And they act like girls! Of course, what do you expect? They're all queer!

GABRIELLE: I beg your pardon. Some of them are men! And I don't mean like our husbands.

MARIE-ANGE: After our husbands anything looks good.

LISETTE: You don't mix serviettes with paper napkins.

GERMAINE: Okay, so our husbands are rough, but our actors are just as good and just as good-looking as any one of those French fairies from France.

GABRIELLE: Well, I wouldn't say no to Jean Marais. Now there's a real man!

OLIVINE: Coke . . . Coke . . . More . . . Coke . . .

ROSE: Hey, can't you shut her up? It's impossible to work! Shove a Coke in her mouth, Germaine. That'll keep her quiet.

GERMAINE: I think I've run out.

ROSE: Jesus, you didn't buy much, did you? Talk about cheap!

RHEAUNA: *(as she steals some stamps)* Oh, what the heck. Three more books and I can get my chrome dustpan.

ANGELINE comes in.

ANGELINE: Hello . . . *(to RHEAUNA)* I've come back . . .

THE OTHERS: *(coldly)* Hello . . .

ANGELINE: I went to see Father Castelneau . . .

PIERRETTE: She didn't even look at me!

MARIE-ANGE: What does she want with Mlle. Bibeau?

DES-NEIGES: I'm sure it's to ask forgiveness. After all, Mlle. Sauvé is a good person and she knows what's right. It'll all work out for the best, you'll see.

GERMAINE: While we're waiting, I'm gonna see how many books we've filled.

The women sit up in their chairs. GABRIELLE hesitates, then speaks.

GABRIELLE: Oh, Germaine, I forgot to tell you. I found a corsetmaker. Her name's Angélina Giroux. Come over here, I'll tell you about her.

RHEAUNA: I knew you'd come back to me, Angéline. I'm very happy. You'll see, we'll pray together and the Good Lord will forget all about it. God's not stupid, you know.

LISE: That's it, Pierrette, they've made up.

PIERETTE: I'll be goddamned!

ANGELINE: I'll just say goodbye to Pierrette and explain . . .

RHEAUNA: No, you'd best not say another word to her. Stay with me and leave her alone. That chapter's closed.

ANGELINE: Whatever you say.

PIERRETTE: Well, that's that. She's won. Makes me want to puke. Nothing left for me to do here. I'm getting out of here.

GERMAINE: Gaby, you're terrific. I'd almost given up hope. It's not everyone can make me a corset. I'll go see her next week. *(She goes over to the box that is supposed to hold the completed books. The women follow her with their eyes.)* My God, there isn't much here! Where are all the booklets? There's no more than a dozen in the box. Maybe they're . . . No, the table's empty! *(Silence. GERMAINE looks at all the women.)* What's going on here?

THE OTHERS: Well . . . Ah . . . I don't know . . . Really . . .

They pretend to search for the books. GERMAINE stations herself in front of the door.

GERMAINE: Where are my stamps?

ROSE: I don't know, Germaine. Let's look for them.

GERMAINE: They're not in the box and they're not on the table. I want to know what's happened to my stamps!

OLIVINE: *(pulling stamps out from under her clothes)* Stamps? Stamps . . . . Stamps . . . *(She laughs.)*

THERESE: Mme. Dubuc, hide that . . . Goddamn it, Mme. Dubuc!

MARIE-ANGE: Holy Ste.-Anne!

DES-NEIGES: Pray for us!

GERMAINE: But her clothes are full of them! What the . . . She's got them everywhere! Here . . . And here . . . . Thérèse . . . Don't tell me it's you.

THERESE: Heavens, no! I swear, I had no idea!

GERMAINE: Let me see your purse.

THERESE: Really, Germaine, if that's all the faith you have in me.

ROSE: Germaine, don't be ridiculous!

GERMAINE: You too, Rose. I want to see your purse. I want to see all your purses. Every one of them!

DES-NEIGES: I refuse! I've never been so insulted!

YVETTE: Me neither.

LISETTE: I'll never set foot in here again!

GERMAINE grabs THERESE's bag and opens it. She pulls out several books.

GERMAINE: Ahah! I knew it! I bet it's the same with all of you! You bastards! You won't get out of here alive! I'll knock you to kingdom come!

PIERRETTE: I'll help you, Germaine. Nothing but a pack of thieves! And they look down their noses at me!

GERMAINE: Show me your purses. *(She grabs ROSE's purse.)* Look at that . . . And that! *(She grabs another purse.)* More here. And look, still more! You too, Mlle. Bibeau? There's only three, but even so!

ANGELINE: Oh, Rhéauna, you too!

GERMAINE: All of you, thieves! The whole bunch of you, you hear me? Thieves!

MARIE-ANGE: You don't deserve all those stamps.

DES-NEIGES: Why you more than anyone else?

ROSE: You've made us feel like shit with your million stamps!

GERMAINE: But those stamps are mine!

LISETTE: They ought to be for everyone!

THE OTHERS: Yeah, everyone!

GERMAINE: But they're mine! Give them back to me!

THE OTHERS: No way!

MARIE-ANGE: There's lots more in the boxes. Let's help ourselves.

DES-NEIGES: Good idea.

YVETTE: I'm filling my purse.

GERMAINE: Stop! Keep your hands off!

THERESE: Here, Mme. Dubuc, take these! Here's some more.

MARIE-ANGE: Come on, Mlle. Verrette. There's tons of them. Here. Give me a hand.

PIERRETTE: Let go of that!

GERMAINE: My stamps! My stamps!

ROSE: Help me, Gaby, I've got too many!

GERMAINE: My stamps! My stamps!

A huge battle ensues. The women steal all the stamps they can. PIERRETTE and GERMAINE try to stop them. LINDA and LISE stay seated in the corner and watch without moving. Screams are heard as some of the women begin fighting.

MARIE-ANGE: Give me those, they're mine!

ROSE: That's a lie, they're mine!

LISETTE: *(to GABRIELLE)* Will you let go of me! Let me go!

They start throwing stamps and books at one another. Everybody grabs all they can get their hands on, throwing stamps everywhere, out the door, even out the window. OLIVINE DUBUC starts cruising around in her wheelchair singing "O Canada." A few women go out with their loot of stamps. ROSE and GABRIELLE stay a bit longer than the others.

GERMAINE: My sisters! My own sisters!

GABRIELLE and ROSE go out. The only ones left in the kitchen are GERMAINE, LINDA and PIERRETTE. GERMAINE collapses into a chair.

GERMAINE: My stamps! My stamps!

PIERRETTE puts her arms around GERMAINE's shoulders.

PIERRETTE: Don't cry, Germaine.

GERMAINE: Don't talk to me. Get out! You're no better than the rest of them!

PIERRETTE: But . . .

GERMAINE: Get out! I never want to see you again!

PIERRETTE: But I tried to help you! I'm on your side, Germaine!

GERMAINE: Get out and leave me alone! Don't speak to me. I don't want to see anyone!

PIERRETTE *goes out slowly.* LINDA *also heads towards the door.*

LINDA: It'll be some job cleaning all that up!

GERMAINE: My God! My God! My stamps! There's nothing left! Nothing! Nothing! My beautiful new home! My lovely furniture! Gone! My stamps! My stamps!

She falls to her knees beside the chair, picking up the remaining stamps. She is crying very hard. We hear all the others outside singing "O Canada." As the song continues, GERMAINE *regains her courage. She finishes "O Canada" with the others, standing at attention, with tears in her eyes. A rain of stamps falls slowly from the ceiling . . .*

END

DAVID FREEMAN (b. 1945)

At the age of seventeen David Freeman found himself at a dead end, sanding wooden blocks in Toronto's Adult Interfraternity Workshop, a job for which he was paid seventy-five cents every two weeks. Freeman had been born with cerebral palsy. As a spastic CP who drooled and slurred his speech and lacked coordination in his limbs, he seemed doomed to the circum-scribed world of the severely handicapped. But his whole life had been a series of battles against heavy odds. By his own account, "When I was born, the doctor predicted I wouldn't last the night. When I lasted the night he predicted I wouldn't last the week. When the week was over, I wouldn't last the month. After a year, the doctor realized a CP could be damn stubborn." Before he was thirty Freeman would parlay that stubbornness into a career as one of the most dynamic young playwrights in the Canadian theatre.

Born in Toronto, Freeman spent his childhood in the Sunny View School for handicapped children where he was encouraged by a speech teacher to try writing stories. By sixteen, with the help of a special typewriter, he was able to type up to two pages a day with one finger. But when he left Sunny View in 1962 he was shocked to find that no one took his education or aspirations seriously. Instead he was expected to live off charity, filling his time with such therapeutic exercises as sanding blocks or sorting nuts and bolts all day in a sheltered workshop. Feeling patronized and belittled—"they tend to build a wall of tinsel between us and reality"—Freeman left the workshop after six months to look for work as a journalist. In 1964 *Maclean's* published his first article, "The World of Can't," telling of his frustrations as a CP victim trying to live a normal life in the face of misunderstanding and condescension. In further pursuit of that life, he enrolled at McMaster University in 1966, graduating in 1971 with a B.A. in political science.

Creeps had its genesis in 1964 when a CBC-TV producer asked Freeman to write a dramatic script based on "The World of Can't." But when it was finished the producer rejected it on the grounds that the characters were too unattractive for television. The script didn't re-emerge until 1970 when Freeman's old friend Bill Glassco, looking for Canadian plays to direct at the newly opened Factory Theatre Lab, suggested he rewrite it for the stage. As Freeman recalls in *Stage Voices*, "I found the rewriting of *Creeps* painful primarily because I lived it. I knew every inch of that washroom and every dream and fantasy, depraved or wholesome, that every one of those four characters had. This was because I happened to be every one of those four characters . . . ." *Creeps* became a major success for the Factory early in 1971 and an even bigger hit later that year when Glassco remounted it as the first production of his new Tarragon Theatre. It won the Chalmers Award for best Canadian play in 1972, and when a Washington, D.C. production moved to off-Broadway in 1973 it won Freeman the New York Drama Desk Award for Outstanding New Playwright. Since then the play has been frequently produced, touring Great Britain and running for almost two years in Los Angeles.

Freeman briefly retained a high profile with his subsequent plays *Battering Ram* (1973) and *You're Gonna Be Alright, Jamie Boy* (1974), both first successfully presented by Bill Glassco at the Tarragon, followed by productions across Canada. Neither, however, lived up to the expec-tations raised by *Creeps*. In 1976 Freeman's *Flytrap* was staged in Montreal where he has since made his home. With each successive work Freeman moved further away from the radical physical disabilities of the characters in *Creeps* to explore the emotionally crippled of the "normal" world, a realm of sexual frustration, alcohol and addiction to TV. In *Scar,* as yet unstaged, he imagined a post-holocaust future. But he has yet to recapture the power or three-dimensional humanity that made *Creeps* such a major dramatic achievement.

Freeman can hardly be blamed for his difficulty in writing another *Creeps,* for it is a very special play. Even the usually jaded New York critics found it an unforgettable experience— "like a punch in the mouth," wrote Douglas Watt in the *Daily News*—and their reactions have been typical. For Kevin Sanders on WABC-TV it was "the most harrowing evening I've ever spent in the theater." Edith Oliver of *The New Yorker* was left shaking her head: "There are people on that stage. Watching them is all but unbearable. I wish I could forget them, but I doubt I ever will."

The primary impact of *Creeps* derives from its two-fold naturalism. The play's dramatic conflict unfolds in the sordid washroom setting as the spastics fight among themselves and against the do-gooders whose "pityshit" degrades them and impedes their attempts at self-sufficiency. At the same time, and ultimately even more central to the play's potency, there is the conflict inherent in the characters' own bodies. Every movement involves an enormous physical struggle; every speech is an effort. In his prefatory notes Freeman suggests that *Creeps* not even be attempted unless the actors have access to first-hand observation of CPs' various physical problems. The realism of the presentation must be absolute, and the characters must seem grotesque, embarrassing, and even horrifying. Only in the full light of their disabilities, the ways in which they are not like us, do we in the audience get to experience the ways in which they are.

In contrast to its documentary naturalism are the play's fantasy sequences—the Shriners' visits and the carnival barker's "brain speech"—which not everyone has found effective. Walter Kerr for one, in his *New York Times* review, objected that their superimposed theatricality interfered with the "gut accuracy" of the play and impeded audience involvement. But in fact the black comedy of these scenes reinforces rather than undermines the horror of the characters' situation (in ways similar to the vaudeville routines played out by the parents of the brain-damaged child in Peter Nichols' *A Day in the Death of Joe Egg*). They are a further manifestation of the grim humour and self-mockery of the spastics themselves, the angry laughter that keeps them sane and alive.

Like *The Ecstasy of Rita Joe* and *Fortune and Men's Eyes, Creeps* depicts a repressive system whose agents (flat characters in all three plays) thwart the protaganists' desire for freedom and fulfillment. But the real thematic focus of all three plays is the *self*-imprisonment, the self-condemnation and self-destruction of those who internalize the system's view of them and thus become incapable of freeing themselves from it. The other two plays allow no exit for their protaganists; in *Creeps* at least Tom walks out the door at the end, perhaps echoing the liberating exit of Nora at the end of Ibsen's *A Doll House.* Alternatively, we might be reminded of the ominous final slam of the jail door in *Fortune and Men's Eyes* as the lights fade on an unliberated Jim sitting dejectedly, while the triumphant Mr. Carson stands over him and the offstage voice of Thelma cries for a priest. That impotent cry, the refrain that runs through the play, is for help from outside the self, and on that score David Freeman is unequivocal. "The play was about freedom and having the guts to reach for it," he has written. "No one can give another person freedom."

•

Creeps first opened at the Factory Theatre Lab, Toronto, on February 5, 1971.

PETE	Victor Sutton
JIM	Robert Coltri
SAM	Steven Whistance-Smith
TOM	Frank Moore
MICHAEL	Len Sedun
SAUNDERS	Kay Griffin
CARSON	Bert Adkins
GIRL	Christina Zorro
SHRINERS	Bernard Bomers, Mark Freeborn

Directed by Bill Glassco
Designed by Peter Kolisnyk

This revised version of *Creeps* opened at the Tarragon Theatre, Toronto, on October 5, 1971, with the same principal actors, director and designer. Among the minor cast replacements was John Candy as a Shriner.

CREEPS

CHARACTERS

PETE
JIM
SAM
TOM
MICHAEL
MISS SAUNDERS
MR. CARSON
GIRL, *"Miss Cerebral Palsy"*
2 SHRINERS
THELMA, *an offstage voice*
The actor playing the role of Michael also plays the Chef, Puffo the Clown, and the Carnival Barker in the three Shriners sequences.

SOME NOTES ON THE CHARACTERS' MOVEMENTS

Each actor taking the role of one of the characters with cerebral palsy is faced, as the character, with major physical problems, the practical solution of which is paramount to a successful rendering of the play. It is to be noted that there are many kinds of spasticity, and each actor should base his movements on one of these. There can be no substitute for the first-hand observation of these physical problems, and one might even suggest that the play not be attempted if opportunities for such first-hand observation are not available. These notes indicate the approach taken by the actors in the original production.

PETE: The actor in the original production developed a way of speaking that is common to many spastics. The effort required to speak causes a distortion of the facial muscles. The actor was able to achieve this by thrusting the jaw forward, and letting the lower jaw hang. Whatever speech problem is adopted for this role, no actor should attempt it unless he has an opportunity for first-hand observation. The deformed hand was not held rigid in one position. The actor used the hand for many things, keeping the fist clenched and employing the fingers in a claw-like manner.

JIM: The actor walked with his knees almost touching, feet apart, back bent much of the time, using his arms more than any other part of his body for balance.

SAM: Sam is a diaplegic, his body dead from the waist down (except for his genitals). He is in a wheelchair. The problem for this actor was to find how to make the wheelchair an extension of his body.

TOM: The actor walked with one hip thrust out to the side. Forward motion always began with the foot of the other leg, rising up on the toe, and then thrusting downward with the heel. His arms were held in front of him, his fingers splayed, upper arms and shoulders constantly being employed for balance.

MICHAEL: The actor always staggered, his head lolling, his body very loose, constantly on the edge of falling. He fell, or collapsed, rather than sat, and grinned most of the time. He too had a speech problem, very slurred, not employing the facial muscles like Pete.

SCENE

The play is set in the washroom of a sheltered workshop for cerebral palsy victims. A "sheltered workshop" is a place where disabled people can go and work at their own pace without the pressure of the competitive outside world. Its aim is not to provide a living wage for the C.P., but rather to occupy his idle hours.

SET

A men's washroom in a sheltered workshop. The hall leading to the washroom is visible. In the washroom are two urinals and two stalls. A chair is set against one of the stalls and there is a bench.

When the lights go up one of the stalls is occupied. MICHAEL, a mentally retarded C.P. of about eighteen, comes along the hall, enters the door of the washroom, and starts flushing the toilets, beginning with the urinals. He comes to the occupied stall and knocks on the door.

PETE: Who is it?

THELMA: *(An offstage voice. It is important that this voice be spastic, but that what she is saying always be clear.)* I need a priest!

Michael chuckles to himself, does not answer. Meanwhile TOM has entered, walking in a sway and stagger motion. Having observed the game MICHAEL is playing on PETE, he ushers MICHAEL out, then sits in the chair up against the stall occupied by PETE. PETE drops his pack of cigarettes.

TOM: *(disguising his voice)* Hey, Pete, you dropped your cigarettes.

Pause. A comic book falls.

TOM: Hey, Pete, you dropped your comic book.

Pete's pants drop to the floor.

TOM: *(his own voice)* Hey, Pete, you dropped your pants.

PETE: That you, Tom?

TOM: Course it's me. Who were you expecting, Woody the Pecker?

PETE: Why didn't you answer?

TOM: When?

PETE: Didn't you knock on the door just now?

TOM: No.

PETE: Must have been Michael flushing toilets.

TOM: Doing his thing.

PETE: He wants to be toilet flushing champion of the world.

TOM: Well at least he's not like some lazy bastards who sit on their ass all day reading comic books.

PETE: I'm on strike. They only pay me seventy-five cents a week. I'm worth eighty.

TOM: You're always on strike.

PETE: How many boxes did you fold today, smart ass.

TOM: Oh, about two hundred. How's the rug?

PETE: Fucking rug. I wish to hell she'd put me on something else. At least for a day or two. It's getting to be a real drag.

TOM: Yeah, that's the way I feel about those boxes.

THELMA: I need a priest! Get me a priest!

TOM: *(wearily)* Oh God.

PETE: Old Thelma kind of gets on your nerves, doesn't she?

TOM: Yeah.

THELMA: Someone get me a priest!

TOM: Pete, I gotta talk to you about something.

PETE: Okay, shoot.

TOM: No, I'll wait till you're out of the can.

Knock at the door

SAM: Open up! *(pause)* Who's in there?

TOM moves to open the door.

SAM: Come on, for Chrissake.

TOM: All right, hang on.

With difficulty TOM gets the door open. SAM wheels by him into the washroom.

TOM: Wanna take a leak, Sam?

SAM: No, I wanna join the circle jerk. Where's Pete?

PETE: In here.

SAM: Well, well, Pete is actually using the shithouse to take a shit.

PETE: Okay, Sam, knock it off.

Pause.

TOM: *(to SAM)* How are you making out with the blocks?

SAM: Screw the blocks. You know how many of those fuckin' things I done today? Two. Do you know why? Because that half-ass physical therapist . . .

TOM: Physio.

SAM: Physio, physical, what the fuck's the difference? They're all after my body. She keeps making me do the same damn blocks over again. "That's not good enough," she says. "Get the edges smoother," she says. *(pointing to his crotch)* Take a bite of this.

PETE: *(flushing the toilet)* She can be a pretty miserable old cunt at times.

SAM: All the time. How's the rug, Pete?

PETE: That thing.

TOM: I told him, he's never gonna finish it sitting in the john all day.

PETE: *(emerging from the stall)* I've been weaving that stupid rug beside that hot radiator every day now for three months. And what has it got me? A big fat zero.

SAM: That's because you're a lazy bugger. You know what that stupid idiot who runs this dump says about you.

PETE: Yeah, I know. "Pete, if you worked in my factory, you wouldn't last a day . . . "

TOM: "But since you're a helpless cripple, I'll let you work in my workshop . . . "

SAM: "For free!"

PETE: And the government will give me a pension, just for breathing.

TOM: And the Rotary and the Shriners will provide hot dogs and ice cream.

SAM: And remember, boys, "If they won't do it . . ."

ALL: "Nobody else will!"

Blackout. Circus music and bright lights. Enter two SHRINERS, a GIRL (Miss Cerebral Palsy) in a white bathing suit, and a CHEF. They dance around the boys, posing for pictures, blowing noisemakers, and generally molesting them in the name of charity. The CHEF stuffs hot dogs into their hands. They exit, the music fades, the light returns to normal. The boys throw their hot dogs over the back of the set.

PETE: Sometimes I wonder how I ever got myself into this.

TOM: Good question, Pete. How did you?

PETE: Another time, Tom, another time.

THELMA: I need a priest!

PETE: What's this big piece of news you have to tell me?

TOM: It doesn't matter.

PETE: Come on, Tom, crap it out.

TOM: It's okay, forget it.

PETE: I postponed my shit for this.

TOM: That's your problem.

SAM: Hey, I bet he's gonna get laid and he doesn't know what to do.

PETE: Well the first thing he better learn is how to get undressed faster.

TOM: Very funny.

PETE: What's the matter? This place still getting you down?

TOM: Yeah, I can't hack it much longer.

SAM: Can't hack what?

TOM: Everything. Folding boxes, the Spastic Club, Thelma, the whole bit.

PETE: How's the art coming?

TOM: Didn't you hear me ?

PETE: Sure I heard you. You said you couldn't hack folding boxes. Well I can't hack weaving that goddamn rug. So how's the art?

TOM: Screw the art. I don't want to talk about art.

PETE: Okay.

SAM: Chickentracks.

TOM: What's that?

SAM: Chickentracks. That's what you paint, Tom. Chickentracks.

TOM: I paint abstract. I know to some ignorant assholes it looks like chickentracks . . .

SAM: Listen, Rembrandt, anything you ever tried to paint always looked like shit warmed over, so you try to cover it up by calling it an abstract. But it's chickenshit and you know it.

TOM: You wouldn't know the difference between a tree and a telephone pole, Sam.

SAM: There isn't any difference. A dog'll piss on both of them.

TOM: And you'll piss on anything, won't you?

PETE: Okay, Tom, cool it.

TOM: Why the fuck should I cool it? This prick's attacking my art.

PETE: You shouldn't take yourself so seriously.

TOM: Oh, do forgive me, gentlemen. I took myself seriously. *(getting up)* I shall go to Miss Saunders and insist she castrate me.

He starts for the door.

SAM: Castrate what?

PETE: Where are you going?

TOM: Where does it look like?

PETE: Dammit, Tom, come on back and stop acting like an idiot.

TOM: Why should I? Whenever anyone tries to talk serious around here, you guys turn it into a joke.

PETE: Nobody's making a joke.

SAM: Look, Tom, even if you do have talent, which I seriously doubt, what good is it to you? You know bloody well they're not going to let you use it.

TOM: Who's they, Sam?

SAM: The Rotary, the Shriners, the Kiwanis, the creeps who run this dump. In fact, the whole goddamn world. Look, if we start making it, they won't have anyone to be embarrassed about.

PETE: Come on, Sam, there's always the blacks.

TOM: And the indians.

SAM: Yeah, but we're more of a challenge. You can always throw real shit at a black man or an Indian, but at us you're only allowed to throw pityshit. And pityshit ain't visible.

TOM: I think you're stretching it just a bit.

SAM: The only way you're going to get to use that talent of yours, Tom, is to give someone's ass

an extra big juicy kiss. And you ought to know by now how brilliantly that works for some people round here.

TOM: You mean Harris?

SAM: If the shoe fits.

TOM: You lay off Jim, 'cause if you'd had the same opportunity you'd have done the same thing.

SAM: So now he licks stamps in the office on a weekly salary, and he's president of the Spastic Club. Whoopee!

TOM: *(to PETE)* Are you going to talk to me or not?

JIM enters and goes to the urinal. He is surprised to see TOM. His walk is slow and shaky, almost a drunken stagger.

SAM: Here's Mommy's boy now.

Pause.

PETE: Things slack in the office, Jim?

JIM: Naw, I just thought I might be missing something.

SAM: Oh you're sweet. Isn't he sweet? I love him.

PETE: Cigarette?

JIM: *(flushing the urinal)* No thanks, I'm trying to give them up.

SAM: Shouldn't be difficult. Giving up is what you do best.

JIM: Aren't you guys worried about getting caught? *(to PETE)* You know the you've been in here for over an hour.

SAM: Shit time. Push me into the crapper, will ya, Pete.

PETE: Saunders won't come in here.

JIM: She might, Pete. Remember Rick and Stanley.

PETE: I do, but I'm not Rick or Stanley.

TOM: Jim, that story's horseshit. Those guys weren't queer.

SAM: *(from the stall)* Sure they were queer. Why do you think they always sat together at lunch, for Chrissake?

PETE: I'll never forget the day she caught them in here necking. Screamed her bloody head off. *(to TOM)* Of course the reason she gave for separating them was that they were talking too much and not getting their work done. Right, Jim?

JIM says nothing.

PETE: No, Saunders won't come in here now. Not after a shock like that.

SAM: Maybe not, but she might send Cinderella to check up on us. How 'bout it, Princess?

JIM: Why would I do a thing like that?

PETE: Then why did you come in?

JIM: Is this washroom exclusive or something?

TOM: It's not that, Jim. It's just that you haven't been to one of our bull sessions for a long time. Not since your promotion.

JIM: I already told you. I just wanted to see if I was missing something.

SAM: You are. Your balls.

Knock at the door.

SAUNDERS: Jim! What's happening in there? I haven't got all day.

Silence. PETE and TOM look at JIM.

JIM: Okay so she asked me. But I didn't come in here to spy.

SAM: Well move your ass, Romeo. You heard what the lady said, she can't wait all day.

SAUNDERS: Jim?

SAM: Bye-bye.

SAUNDERS: Jim, are you there?

JIM moves towards the door.

TOM: Wait, Jim, you don't have to go.

SAM: Dammit, let the fucker go. His mommy wants him.

PETE: Shut up, Sam.

SAM: I wasn't talking to you.

TOM: Why don't you stay for a while?

PETE: Yeah, tell old tight-cunt you're on the can or something.

He grabs JIM and pulls him away from the door.

SAUNDERS: Jim Harris! Do you hear me!?

PETE signals to JIM to answer.

JIM: Yes, Miss Saunders, I hear you. But I'm on the toilet at the moment.

SAUNDERS: What are you doing on the toilet?

PETE: *(at the door)* He's taking a shit. What do you do on the toilet?

SAUNDERS: If you boys aren't back to work in five minutes I'm reporting you to Mr. Carson.

She walks back down the hall.

SAM: Once upon a time, boys, there was a boudingy bird, and the cry of the boudingy went like this . . .

TOM and PETE: *(in falsetto, forestalling SAM)* Suck my boudingy!

Silence while PETE listens at the door.

JIM: I could use that cigarette now.

PETE: *(bringing him one)* Thought you were trying to quit.

JIM: I am.

Pause.

TOM: Jim, why did you lie?

JIM: I did not lie. Saunders saw me coming in, and she thought I might remind you that you'd been in here a long time. That's all.

TOM: Then why didn't you say so when Sam asked you?

SAM: Because he's so used to telling lies, if anyone said he was spastic, he'd deny it.

TOM: Will ya shut up, Sam.

JIM: That's okay. Sam didn't care for me when I was sanding blocks with him.

SAM: Pete, push that chair in here, will you?

JIM: Now that he thinks I've gone over to the other side, he's got even less reason to like me.

SAM: Listen, Princess, nobody likes a white nigger.

TOM: What's that mean, Sam?

PETE: (as he holds the chair for SAM) Why don't you use a bedpan?

SAM: Why do you think, dummy? Because my ass begins to look like the other side of the moon. (By now he is off the toilet and back in the chair.) All right, all right.

He wheels backwards out of the stall.

JIM: Well, Sam?

SAM: Well what, stooge?

JIM: What do you mean, white nigger?

SAM: Well since you're so all fired fuckin' dyin' to know, I'll tell you. You finished high school, didn't you.

JIM: Yes.

SAM: And you got a degree?

JIM: So?

SAM: Well, you went to university. You wrote all that crap for the paper about how shitty it was to be handicapped in this country. Then what do you do? You come running down here and kiss the first ass you see. That's what I mean by being a white nigger, and that's what fuckin' well pisses me off.

JIM: All right, Sam, now you listen to me. I still believe everything I wrote, and I intend to act on it. But you can't change things until you're in a position to call the shots. And you don't get there without being nice to people. By the way, what are you doing about it? All I ever get from you is bitch, bitch, bitch!

SAM: I got every fuckin' right to bitch. You expect me to sand blocks and put up with the pityshit routine for ninety-nine years waiting for you to get your ass into a position of power? Fuck you, buddy! You give me a choice and I'll stop bitching.

TOM: Now look who's taking himself seriously.

SAM: (to TOM and PETE) What do you guys know about the bullshit I put up with? My old lady, now get this, my old lady has devoted her entire goddamn life to martyrdom. And my old man, you ever met my old man? Ever seen him give me one of his "Where have I failed?" looks? Wait'll ya hear what happened last night. He invited his boss over for dinner, and you know where the old bugger wanted me to eat? In the kitchen. First I told him to go screw the dog— that's about his style—and then, at the height of the festivities, just when everything was going real nice for Daddy, I puked all over the table.

TOM: Charming.

SAM: It was beautiful. Stuck my finger down my throat and out it all came: roast beef, mashed potatoes, peas, olives. There was a *real* abstract painting, Tom. You should have seen the look on his boss's face. Be a long time before he gives at the office again.

MICHAEL enters. During the ensuing dialogue he attempts to flush the urinals, but is stopped by signals from PETE.

JIM: You know, Sam, you amaze me. You say you don't want to wait ninety-nine years, but you're happy if you can set us back a few. A stunt like that doesn't make Carson's job any easier.

PETE: Okay, Timmy, you're not addressing the Spastic Club.

SAM: Piss on Carson! He doesn't give a shit about us and you know it.

JIM: I don't know it. I don't know what his motives are. But I do know he's trying to help us.

PETE: His motives are to keep the niggers in their place.

SAM: Yeah, by getting Uncle Timmy here to watch over them.

TOM: (to SAM and PETE) What are you guys, the resident hypocrites? Look, no one twists your arm to go to those Spastic Club meetings. No one forces those hot dogs down your throat.

PETE: Sure, we take them. Why not? They're free. Why look a gift horse in the mouth? But at least we don't kiss ass.

JIM: No, you let me do it for you. *(slight pause)* But that's beside the point. The point is that Carson does care about what happens to us.

SAM: He does?

JIM: You're darn right he does.

SAM: You ever been over to his house for dinner?

JIM: Yes.

SAM: Ever been back?

JIM: No.

SAM: In other words, you got your token dinner, and now you only see him at Spastic Club meetings and here at the workshop?

JIM: That's not true. He comes to my place sometimes, doesn't he, Tom?

TOM: Yeah, but what about all those times your mother invited him for dinner and he cancelled out at the last minute?

JIM: So? That doesn't prove anything.

SAM: It proves a helluva lot to me.

MICHAEL pokes PETE on the shoulder.

PETE: What is it, Michael?

MICHAEL: Cigarette, please.

PETE: Okay, Michael, but smoke it this time, don't eat it. Last time everyone accused me of trying to poison you.

Banging at the door.

SAUNDERS: Boys! What's going on in there? If you don't come out this minute I'm coming in.

SAM: We dare you!

TOM: Shut up, Sam.

SAUNDERS: What was that?

PETE: Nothing, Miss Saunders. Sam just said, "We hear you."

SAUNDERS: Oh no he didn't. I know what he said. He said, "We dare you."

PETE: Well Christ, if you already knew, what the fuck did you ask for? *(to himself)* Stupid bitch!

SAUNDERS: Jim. What's happening in there? Are they doing something they shouldn't?

SAM: Yeah, we're pissing through our noses!

JIM: Cut it out, Sam. No, Tom and Pete are on the toilets and I'm holding the bottle for Sam.

SAM: Hey, that hurts! Don't pull so hard, you idiot!

SAUNDERS: *(nonplussed)* Well hurry up, and stop fooling around. I can't wait on you all day.

She starts down the hallway, stops when she hears . . .

SAM: *(to the door)* That's it, Pete, no more blowjobs for cigarettes! Jim, take your hands off me, I've only got one! Michael, don't use your teeth! Christ, I've never seen so many queers in one place. I could open a fruit stand!

SAUNDERS listens, horrified, then runs off down the hall. MICHAEL sits on the floor and begins to eat the cigarette. The laughter subsides.

PETE: I think she left.

Pause.

TOM: Do I finally get to say something?

PETE: Oh yeah, where were we? You couldn't hack folding boxes.

TOM: Or the Spastic Club.

PETE: Or the Spastic Club.

TOM: Or Thelma.

PETE: Or Thelma.

TOM: Pete.

PETE: What's the matter now?

TOM: Cochran, for once in your life, will you be serious.

PETE: I'm fucking serious.

SAM: It's the only way to fuck.

PETE: If I was any more serious, I'd be dead. I wish to hell you'd get on with it, Tom.

Pause.

TOM: You guys ever read a story called "Premature Burial"?

SAM and JIM shake their heads.

PETE: What comic was it in?

TOM: Edgar Allan Poe.

PETE: Oh.

TOM: Anyway, it's about this guy who has this sickness that puts him into a coma every so often. And he's scared as hell someone's going to mistake him for dead and bury him alive. Well, that's the way I feel about this workshop. It's like I'm at the bottom of a grave yelling "I'm alive! I'm alive!" But they don't hear me. They just keep shovelling in the dirt.

THELMA: I need a priest!

JIM: Tom, if you really feel that way, you ought to talk to Carson.

TOM: Oh, fuck off.

JIM: He's not an idiot, you know.

PETE: Tom, you want to know what I think? I think you should stop reading junk like Edgar Allan Poe. You take that stuff too seriously.

SAM: Pete's right. You should stick to your regular diet.

TOM: What's that crack supposed to mean?

SAM: It's sticking out of your back pocket, sexy.

TOM: *(reaching round, removing a book from his pocket, and tossing it to SAM)* Here, Sam, why don't you take it for awhile? Maybe it'll shut you up.

SAM: *(as he flicks through the book)* Hey, he's got the dirty parts underlined in red.

PETE: Read some.

SAM: *(reading)* "Nothing like a nice yellow banana," she said aloud. It touched every sensitive area of her pussy. Tears came to her eyes in shots of violent lust. Then her movements began to increase and she spliced herself repeatedly . . .

TOM: That's enough, Sam.

SAM: The thick banana swirled in her cunt like a battering ram. She grasped it hard and shoved it faster and faster. Then she sat up, still gorged with the banana . . .

TOM: I said, that's enough!

He gets up and moves to take the book away from SAM.

SAM: *(who has not stopped reading)* It hit high up against the walls of her wet cunt. She could move whichever way she liked. "Oh, shit, this is juicy," she said aloud. The reflection she saw in the mirror was ludicrous and made her even more hot. "Oh you big banana, fuck me! . . ."

TOM grabs the book

PETE: Wait. I want to find out about the banana split.

TOM: If you're so hot about the banana, you can have the goddamn book.

He gives it to him.

SAM: It'll only cost you a nickel, Pete, it's underlined.

TOM: Okay. So I get a charge out of dirty books. What does that make me, a creep?

SAM: Well, at least I don't pretend to be something I'm not. I don't work myself up during office hours.

TOM: No, you just do it at picnics.

SAM: What about a goddamn picnic?

JIM: Come on, Sam, you remember the Rotarian's daughter.

SAM: So I remember a Rotarian's daughter. What now?

PETE: She was sitting beside you and you were feeling her up like crazy, that's what now.

SAM: If the silly little fart is stupid enough to let me, why not?

JIM: You were making a bloody spectacle of yourself.

SAM: Love is where you find it.

PETE: Yeah, but with you working her over like that, I could hardly keep my mind on the three-legged race. Didn't she even say anything?

SAM: Nope, she just sat there. Smiled a lot.

THELMA: I need a priest!

Pause.

JIM: There's a girl who isn't smiling, is she, Sam?

SAM: Shut up, Harris.

THELMA: Get me a priest!

TOM: Ever since I've been here, Thelma's always calling for a priest. How come?

PETE: Sam knows.

SAM: Yeah, well mind your own business.

THELMA: Someone get me a priest!

SAM: (screams, overlapping THELMA) Dry up, you stupid fuckin' broad!

PETE: Why don't you go comfort her, Sam? You used to be pretty good at comforting old Thelma.

JIM: Yeah, you couldn't keep your hands off her.

SAM: What's the matter, were ya jealous, princess?

TOM: Hey, I'd like to know what the hell's going on.

PETE: This was before your time, Tom. Thelma was all right then. Cute kid, as a matter of fact. Until old horny here got his hands on her and drove her off her rocker.

SAM: That's a fuckin' lie. The doctors said it wasn't my fault.

JIM: They only told you that to make it easy for you.

SAM: Look, it wasn't my fault.

JIM: What you did sure didn't help any.

SAM: Well why bring it up now?

PETE: Because we're sick and tired of having you put everybody down. It's time someone put you down for a change.

TOM: Well, what did he do? Will you please tell me?

PETE: From the day Thelma got here, Sam was after her like a hot stud. Being so nice to her, and then coming in here and bragging how she was letting him feel her up, and bragging how he was gonna fuck the ass off her soon.

THELMA: I want a priest!

PETE: Maybe you've heard, Tom, that Thelma's parents are religious. I don't just mean they're devout, they're real dingalings about it. Like they believe Thelma's the way she is because of some great sin they've committed. Like that. Anyway, she was home in bed one weekend with a cold, and Sam went over to visit her, and her parents weren't out of the room two seconds when Sam was into her pants.

SAM: That's another goddamn lie. It didn't happen that way.

PETE: Okay, so it took a full minute. Don't quibble over details.

SAM: Look, I didn't mean for anything to happen that day. What do you think I am, stupid? In the first place, she had a cold, and in the second place, her parents were out on the goddamn porch. I just wanted to talk. She started fooling around, trying to grab my cannon and everything. Naturally I get a hard-on. What am I supposed to do? Silly little bitch! We were just going real good when she changed her mind. That's one helluva time to exercise her woman's perogative, isn't it? Anyway, we . . . she fell out of bed. In a few seconds in come Mommy and Daddy. They thought I'd fallen out of my chair or something. Well, there I am in bed with my joint waving merrily in the breeze and Thelma's on the floor minus her PJs, and all hell broke loose. You'd have thought they'd never seen a cock before. The old man, he bounced me out of bed along the floor and into the hallway. The old lady, she dragged Thelma up behind. Then they held us up in front of a little Jesus statue and asked it to forgive us 'cause we didn't know what we were doing. (Pause) The doctors said it wasn't my fault.

JIM: They were only feeling sorry for a horny cripple in a wheelchair.

PETE: Yeah, but we all know the truth, don't we Sam?

SAM: (overlapping) Why don't you shut the fuck up, Cochran!

JIM: Hey, Pete, remember how Thelma used to dress before Sam put his rod to her? So pretty.

TOM: Okay, guys, knock it off.

PETE: Yeah, but that's all over now. She only wears black and brown, and everything's covered, right up to the neck.

JIM: She used to laugh a lot too.

TOM: That's enough!

THELMA: I need a priest!

MICHAEL: (sing-song) Thelma needs a priest. Thelma needs a priest.

SAM: Fuck off! Piece of shit!

SAM goes for MICHAEL, who is sitting on the floor, and hits out at him. MICHAEL is surprised, but hits back. To stop the fight, PETE grabs SAM's chair from behind. SAM then lashes out at PETE. At the same time, JIM and TOM go to rescue MICHAEL. JIM falls while TOM tries to get MICHAEL's attention away from SAM. Throughout the commotion MICHAEL continues to yell, "Thelma needs a priest." Finally, SAM wheels angrily away and PETE helps JIM up.

TOM: (at one of the urinals) Hey, Michael, look, a cockroach. Big fat one.

MICHAEL sees the cockroach and gets very excited. PETE, TOM and JIM gather round him at the urinal.

PETE: Hey, Sam, there's livestock in the pisser.

TOM: (to MICHAEL) Why don't you use your ray gun and disintegrate it?

MICHAEL: What ray gun? I got no ray gun.

SAM: Yes, you have. That thing between your legs. It's a ray gun.

MICHAEL looks down and makes the connection.

MICHAEL: (delighted) I disintegrate it. I disintegrate it all up.

He turns into the urinal.

SAM: You do that.

SAUNDERS returns and knocks at the door.

SAUNDERS: For the last time, are you boys coming out or not?

SAM: Go away, we're busy.

SAUNDERS: Very well then, I'm coming in.

She enters the washroom.

PETE: Have you no sense of decency?

SAUNDERS: All right, I don't know what you boys have been doing in here, but I want you back to work immediately. Pete, you've still that rug. Tom, there's boxes to be folded. Sam, you'd better get busy and sand down the edges of those blocks if you expect to earn anything this week. As for you, Jim, well I'm beginning to have second thoughts.

JIM: Yes, ma'am.

Pause. No one makes a move to go.

SAUNDERS: Well, get moving!

PETE: I have to take a crap.

He heads into one of the stalls.

TOM: Me too.

He goes into the other one.

SAM: I have to use the bottle.

SAUNDERS: And how about you, Jim? Don't you have something to do?

SAM: He has to hold the bottle for me.

SAUNDERS: He has to what, Sam?

SAM: Well, it's like this. I don't have a very good aim, so Princess here is gonna get down on her hands and knees . . .

SAUNDERS: (cutting him off) All right, that's quite enough. When you're through here, I want you back to work. And fast. Michael, you come with me.

MICHAEL turns around from the urinal. His pants are open, his penis exposed.

MICHAEL: *(to SAUNDERS)* I'm gonna disintegrate you.

SAUNDERS: *(screams)* Michael! Oh, you boys, you put him up to this! Didn't you?

PETE: We did not.

SAUNDERS: Right! Mr. Carson will be here any minute. We'll see what he has to say.

She opens the door to leave.

SAM: *(calling after her)* Hey, be careful. He's got one too.

More screams. She exits, and is seen running down the hall. PETE and TOM emerge from the stalls laughing. JIM tidies MICHAEL and sends him out the door.

PETE: Sam, you have a warped sense of humour.

SAM: Yeah, just like the rest of me.

JIM: Proud of that, aren't you Sam? Professional cripple.

SAM: Eat shit, princess.

JIM: And such a sterling vocabulary.

Pause. JIM begins to pick up cigarette butts and matches, which by now litter the floor.

TOM: Hadn't you better go before Carson gets back?

JIM: The office can wait.

TOM: What'll you do when he gets here?

JIM: I'll cross that bridge when I come to it.

TOM: Well, we'll all have to cross that bridge soon. We've been in here for over half an hour.

SAM: Yeah, we do tend to take long craps.

PETE: I don't care how long it takes me to crap.

Pause.

TOM: Did you get your typewriter fixed yet, Jim?

JIM: No, I haven't had time.

TOM: Well, my dad's offer still stands . . . if you'd like him to take a look at it.

JIM: Thanks, I would. How is your father?

TOM: He's okay. Why don't you bring it over Sunday?

JIM: I'll have to see. I'm kind of busy at the club. Christmas is coming.

TOM: It will only take an hour.

JIM: You wouldn't like to give us a hand this year, would you?

TOM: What did you have in mind?

JIM: I thought you might like to do our Christmas mural.

TOM: No, I don't think so.

JIM: Spastic Club's not good enough for chicken-tracks, eh? Seriously, Tom, I could use some help. Not just for the mural, but to paint posters, stuff like that.

TOM: How much is the Spastic Club willing to pay for all this?

JIM: Come on, you know there's no payment. All the work for the club is done on a voluntary basis. Carson's never paid anyone before.

SAM: So why should the old fart break his record of stinginess just for you?

JIM: It may interest you to know, Sam, that Carson doesn't get paid for his services either.

SAM: Bwess his wittle heart.

TOM: In that case, the answer's no. If I get paid for folding boxes, why the hell should I paint a lousy mural for free?

JIM: I just thought it might keep you busy.

TOM: I'm busy enough.

JIM gets up, staggers over to the waste basket and deposits his litter. SAM applauds.

PETE: Jim, what's the Spastic Club planning for us boys and girls this year?

JIM: Oh, we've got a few things up our sleeve. Actually, we'd appreciate it if some of the members were a bit more co-operative. So far the response has been practically nil.

TOM: That's horseshit.

PETE: What about my idea of having that psychologist down from the university?

JIM: Well, since you're so interested, Pete, I'll tell you. Carson didn't think too much of it. He was afraid the members would be bored. I don't happen to agree with him, but that's the way he feels.

SAM: What about my idea for installing ramps in the subway?

JIM: It's a good idea, Sam, but that sort of thing doesn't come under our jurisdiction.

SAM: Who says so?

JIM: It's up to the city. We're not in a position . . .

TOM: Okay, Jim, what does the Spastic Club have up its sleeve for this year?

JIM: There's the trip to the Science Centre. One to the African Lion Safari. We're organizing a finger painting contest, that sorority is throwing a Valentine's Day party for us . . .

PETE: Wheee! A party!

Circus music is heard low in the distance.

TOM: What's the entertainment, Jim?

JIM: Puffo the Clown, Merlin the Magician . . .

PETE: And Cinderella, and Snow White and the Seven Fucking Dwarfs. Jesus Christ, Jim, Puffo the Clown! What do you and Carson think you're dealing with, a bunch of fucking babies?

Blackout, circus music at full and bright lights. PUFFO, in clown suit, has arrived, carrying balloons. Enter also the GIRL and two SHRINERS, the GIRL dressed in circus attire. She is marching and twirling a baton. One of the SHRINERS is wearing a Mickey Mouse mask and white gloves. He follows the GIRL, weaving in and around the boys, dancing in time to the music. The other SHRINER appears on a tricycle (or on roller skates, if preferred) waving to the audience. PUFFO presents SAM, TOM and PETE each with a balloon, and exits following the GIRL and SHRINERS. The music fades.

PETE: Who was that masked man, anyway?

On a signal from PETE, the boys burst their balloons with their lighted cigarettes.

JIM: Wait a minute, Pete, let me finish. We've got other things planned.

PETE: Like what?

JIM: Well, for one, we're planning a trip to a glue factory.

TOM: You're kidding.

JIM: No, I'm not. Carson thinks it might be very educational.

TOM: What do you think, Jim? Do you think it will be very educational?

JIM: I don't know. I've never seen them make glue before.

PETE: Well, you take one old horse, and you stir well . . .

JIM: We're planning other things too, you know.

TOM: What other things?

JIM: Well you know, theatre trips, museum trips. These things take time, Tom. We've written letters and . . .

TOM: What letters? To whom?

JIM: Letters. Lots of letters. They're at home in my briefcase. I'll show them to you tomorrow.

TOM: Any replies?

JIM: What?

TOM: How many replies did you get to the letters?

JIM: Look, am I on trial or something?

TOM: I don't know, Jim. Are you?

JIM: Okay, maybe some of the things we do aren't as exciting as you and I'd like them to be, but I'm doing the job as well as I can, and I can't do it all on my own. You guys bitch about the program, but you won't get off your asses and fight for something better. That idea of Pete's about the psychologist, I really pushed that idea. Pushed it to the hilt . . .

PETE: Bur Carson didn't like it.

JIM: Carson didn't like it, and the more I pushed the firmer he got.

SAM: Why didn't you push it right up his ass?

JIM: (ignoring this) So I told Pete he should go down and talk to Carson himself. I even made him an appointment. But he never showed up, did you, Pete?

PETE: I was busy.

TOM: Why the hell should you or Pete or anyone else have to beg that prick for anything?

JIM: Tom, that's not fair. So he's a little stuffy, at least he's interested. He does give us more than the passing time of day.

PETE: Sure, he was in for a whole hour this morning.

JIM: Pete, you may not like Carson, but just remember. If he, or the Kiwanis, or any of the other service clubs decide to throw in the towel, we're in big trouble.

SAM: "If they won't do it . . . "

JIM: If they won't do it, who will? You?

A long pause.

PETE: I've got nothing against the Rotary or the Kiwanis. If they want to give me a free meal just to look good, that's okay with me.

TOM: You sure of that?

PETE: Tom, the Bible says the Lord provides. Right now He's providing pretty good. Should I get upset if He sends the Kiwanis instead of coming Himself?

JIM: If you feel like getting something, why don't you give something?

PETE: No, sir. I don't jump through hoops for nobody, and certainly not for a bastard like Carson. I might have nothing to say against the groups, but I don't have anything to say for them either.

TOM: You can't stay neutral all the time.

PETE: Tell that to Switzerland. Tom, you're young. You don't realize how tough it is for people like us. Baby, it's cold outside.

SAM: (under his breath) Christ!

PETE: When I came to this dump eleven years ago, I wanted to be a carpenter. That's all I could think about ever since I can remember. But face it, whoever heard of a carpenter with a flipper like that? (holding up his deformed hand) But I had a nice chat with this doc, and he told me I'd find what I'm looking for down here. So I came down here, and one of Saunders' flunkies shoves a bag of blocks in my hand. " What gives?" I said. And then it slowly dawned on me that as far as the doc is concerned, that's the closest I'll ever get to carpentry.

And I was pissed off, sure. But then I think, good old doc, he just doesn't understand me. 'Cause I still have my ideals. So in a few days I bust out of this place and go looking for a job— preferably carpentry. What happens? I get nothing but aching feet and a flat nose from having fucking doors slammed in my face all the fucking time.

And I'm at my wits' end when I get a letter from the Spastic Club. And I said fuck that. I'm about to throw it in the furnace, but I get curious. I've heard of the Spastic Club and I always figured it was a load of shit. But I think one meeting isn't going to kill me.

So I go, and I find out I'm right. It's a load of shit. It's a bunch of fuckheads sitting around saying, "Aren't we just too ducky for these poor unfortunate cripples?" But I get a free turkey dinner.

When I got home I took a good look at myself. I ask myself what am I supposed to be fighting? What do these jokers want me to do? The answer is they want to make life easier for me. Is that so bad? I mean, they don't expect me to keep you guys in your place or nothing. They just want me to enjoy life. And the government even pays me just for doing that. If I got a job, I'd lose the pension. So why have I been breaking my ass all this time looking for a job? And I got no answers to that. So I take the pension, and come back to the workshop. The only price I gotta pay is listening to old lady Saunders giving me hell for not weaving her goddamn rug.

Blackout. Fanfare. Lights up on the far side of the stage. The actor playing MICHAEL enters dressed as a freak show barker. With him is the GIRL, his assistant, dressed in similar carnival attire. The following sequence takes place in a stage area independent of the washroom.

BARKER: (to the audience) Are you bored with your job? Would you like to break out of the rat race? Does early retirement appeal to you? Well, my friends, you're in luck. The Shriners, the Rotary, and the Kiwanis are just begging to wait on you hand and foot.

Charleston music. The BARKER and the GIRL dance. The music continues through the next several speeches until he is handed the brain.

BARKER: To throw you parties, picnics. To take you on field trips. To the flower show, the dog show, and to the Santa Claus Parade.

More dancing.

BARKER: Would you like to learn new skills? Like sanding blocks, folding boxes, separating nuts and bolts? My friends, physiotherapists are standing by eager to teach you.

The GIRL hands the BARKER a wooden block and another block covered with sandpaper. More dancing as he sands the block.

BARKER: Whoopee, is this ever fun.

He hands the block back to the GIRL.

BARKER: Now, I suppose you good people would like to know, how do I get this one-way ticket to paradise? My props, please.

The GIRL hands him a life-size model of a human brain which has the various sections marked off, and a hammer. The music stops. He walks down-stage into a pool of light directly in front of the audience.

BARKER: Now all you do is take a hammer and adjust the motor area of the brain. Like this. Not too hard, now, we wouldn't want to lose you.

He taps the brain gently.

BARKER: Having done that, you will have impaired your muscle co-ordination, and will suddenly find that you now *(speaking with the speech defect of the character MICHAEL)* "talk with an accent." You will then be brought to our attention either by relatives who have no room for you in the attic, or by neighbours who are distressed to see you out in the street, clashing with the landscape. Now, assuming you are successful in locating the proper point of demolition, we guarantee that this very special euphoria will be yours not for a day, not for a week, but for a lifetime. There's no chance of relapse, regression, or rehabilitation because, my friends, it's as permanent as a hair transplant. It's for keeps. Should you, however, become dis-enchanted with this state, there is one recourse available to you, which while we ourselves do not recommend it, is popular with many, and does provide a final solution to a very complex problem. All you do is take the hammer and simply tap a little harder.

He smashes the brain. At the moment of impact, he becomes spastic, and slowly crumbles to the floor. Blackout.

The lights come up on the four boys.

SAM: Guys like you really bug me. You got two good legs and one good hand. So the other's deformed. Big Fuckin' Deal. By the way, who the hell said you couldn't be a carpenter? You had your loom fixed up in five minutes last week while that old fart of a handyman was running around town looking for something to fix it with.

PETE: That was just lucky.

TOM: You know what I think, Cochran? I think you're lazy. I think eleven years ago you were looking for a grave to fall into, and you found it in the Spastic Club.

PETE: Don't be self-righteous about things you don't understand.

TOM: I understand laziness.

PETE: You don't understand. I tried.

TOM: Aw, c'mon Pete, you didn't try very hard.

PETE: There's no place in the outside world for a guy who talks funny.

SAM: Aw, you poor wittle boy. Did the big bad mans hurt your wittle feelings?

PETE goes for SAM, is about to hit him, but is restrained by TOM.

TOM: That's not funny, Sam. *(to PETE)* But it is a bit ridiculous. And here you are, thirty-seven years old, and you're still worried about some-thing as small as that.

PETE: It may be a small thing to you, Tom. It's not to me.

JIM: Howdya like to have kids following you down the street calling you drunk? I get that all the time, but you learn to live with it.

SAM: Sure you learn to live with it. You learn to rub their noses in it too. Last week I was at this show and I had to be bounced about twenty steps in the chair just to get to the lobby. Well, you know what that does to my bladder, eh? So naturally I make for the washroom. The stalls are two inches too narrow, of course. As for the urinals, I never claimed to be Annie Oakley. They don't have urinal bottles 'cause they'd fuck up the interior decoration. But then I did spy this little Dixie cup dispenser . . .

JIM: Sam, you didn't!

SAM: Yeah, sweetie, I did. I was just doing up my fly when the usher walked in, saw the cup sitting on the edge of the sink. He thought it was lemonade. Told me patrons weren't allowed to bring refreshments into the washroom. Then he moved closer and got a whiff.

PETE: What happened?

SAM: Another United Appeal supporter had his dreams all crushed to ratshit.

JIM: And Sam set us back another twenty years.

SAM: What do you expect me to do, Harris? Piss my pants waiting for everything to come under your jurisdiction?

PETE: Sam's right. It's like you said, Jim. You do the best with what you got.

TOM: Come on, Pete, that's a cop-out and you know it. Sam should have got rid of that cup as soon as he took his leak. Putting it on the sink in plain view of everyone, for Chrissake!

PETE: Don't be so smug. A guy survives the best way he knows how. You wait, you'll find out. They don't want us creeps messing up their world. They just don't want us.

TOM: Tough! They're going to get me whether they want me or not. I'm a man, and I've got a right to live like other men.

PETE: You're the only man I know who can make a sermon out of saying hello.

He goes into one of the stalls, slamming the door behind him.

TOM: Yeah and pretty soon I'm gonna say good-bye. You expect me to spend the rest of my life folding boxes?

PETE: *(over the top of the stall)* Look, Rembrandt, we know you're a great artist, and all that shit. But if you paint like you fold, forget it.

JIM: Wait a minute, Pete. I've seen some of Tom's paintings. I'm no expert on abstract, but I think they're pretty good. They're colourful and . . .

SAM: Colourful chickentracks?

TOM: Fuck off!

JIM: Still, I'm not other people. I might like them, but folks on the outside might not. People get pretty funny when they find out something's been done by a handicapped person. Besides, we both know you can't draw.

TOM: That doesn't make any difference. I paint abstract.

SAM: So you'll win the finger painting contest.

JIM: Tom, we've been over this I don't know how many times. Name me one good abstract painter who isn't a good draftsman.

SAM: Name me one good writer who'd be caught dead in a glue factory.

JIM: Seriously, can you think of one famous artist who was spastic?

TOM: Jim, if you're sure I can't make it, what about the letter?

PETE: What letter?

JIM: *(shrugs)* Oh, a letter he got from an art critic.

PETE: *(emerging from the stall)* What did it say?

TOM: Here, you can read it yourself.

He hands the letter to PETE who begins to read it to himself.

SAM: Out loud.

PETE starts to read it, gives up, hands the letter to JIM.

JIM: *(reading)* Dear Mr. March, I was fascinated by the portfolio you submitted. I cannot recall an artist in whose work such a strong sense of struggle was manifest. You positively stab the canvas with bold colour, and your sure grasp of the palette lends a native primitivism to your work. I am at once drawn to the crude simplicity of your figures and repulsed by the naive grotesqueries which grope for recognition in your tortured world. While I cannot hail you as a mature artist, I would be interested in seeing your work in progress this time next year.

SAM: Which one of your father's friends wrote it?

TOM: None of them.

SAM: One of your mother's friends?

TOM: The letter's authentic. I'll bring the guy's magazine column if you don't believe me.

PETE: Oh, we believe you, Tom. Critics are so compassionate.

TOM; You shit all over everything, don't you?

PETE: *(handing Tom the letter)* It's a good letter, I guess.

TOM: You guess?

PETE: Well, what the hell am I supposed to say? You're the artist. I don't even like the Mona Lisa. To me she's just a fat ugly broad. But I can't help wondering, Tom . . .

TOM: What?

PETE: If he wouldn't have said the same thing if you sent him one of your boxes. *(TOM starts to protest but PETE goes on.)* Like when I'm weaving that goddamn rug and we have visitors. Now I'm no master weaver. Matter of fact, I've woven some pretty shitty rugs in my time. But whenever we have visitors, there are always one or two clowns who come over and practically have an orgasm over my rug, no matter how shitty we both know it is.

SAM: It's the same with the blocks. They pick one up, tell me how great it is, and then walk away with a handful of splinters.

TOM: It's not the same. This guy happens to be one of the toughest art critics around.

JIM: Even tough art critics give to the United Appeal.

TOM: Yes, and sometimes writers write for it.

JIM: Well, it keeps me off the streets.

SAM: Yeah, Jim peddles his ass indoors where it's warm.

PETE: And Carson has an exclusive contract on it. Right Jim?

JIM: I work because I want to work. It's a challenge, I enjoy it, and I can see the results.

PETE: Sure. So can we. Hot dogs, ice cream, balloons, confetti . . .

JIM: Well at least I don't have illusions of grandeur.

TOM: What illusions have you got, Jim?

JIM: Tom, you've got to come down to earth sooner or later. For someone in my situation the workshop makes sense. I can be more useful in a place like this.

TOM: Useful to Carson?

JIM: No, to people like Michael and Thelma.

TOM: What about Carson? Are you going to go on kissing his ass?

JIM: Call it what you like. In dealing with people, I have to be diplomatic.

TOM: Fine, Jim. *(getting up)* You be diplomatic for both of us.

PETE: Where are you going?

TOM: I'm bored. I'm leaving.

PETE: What's the matter?

TOM: Nothing, Cochran, go back and finish your shit.

JIM: Tom, what is it?

TOM: I'm quitting.

JIM: You're not serious?

TOM: Getting more serious by the minute.

JIM: You're building a lot on a few kind words, aren't you?

TOM: The man doesn't know I'm spastic.

JIM: He's going to find out. And you know what'll happen when he does. You'll be his golden boy for a few weeks, but as soon as the novelty wears off, he'll go out of his way to avoid you.

TOM: What if the novelty doesn't wear off?

JIM: Tom, I don't think you should rush into this.

TOM: How long do I have to stay, Jim?

JIM: Stay until Christmas. Stay and do the mural.

TOM: No.

JIM: But you like painting. It won't hurt you.

TOM: I said no!

JIM: Why not?

TOM moves toward the door.

JIM: Won't you at least talk about it?

TOM: *(turning and looking at JIM)* That's all you know how to do now, isn't it? No writing, no thinking, just talking. Well get this straight. I don't want any part of the Spastic Club or the workshop. It's finished, okay?

JIM: I know this place isn't perfect. I agree. It's even pretty rotten at times. But, Tom, out there, you'll be lost. You're not wanted out there, you're not welcome. None of us are. If you stay here we can work together. We can build something.

SAM: Yeah, a monument to Carson. For the pigeons to shit on.

TOM: How long are *you* going to stay here?

JIM: How long?

TOM: Are you going to spend the rest of your life being Carson's private secretary?

JIM: Well, nothing's permanent. Even I know that.

TOM: Stop bullshitting and give me a straight answer.

JIM: Okay, I'll move on. Sure.

TOM: And do what?

JIM: Maybe I'll go back to my writing.

TOM: When? *(No reply.)* When was the last time you wrote anything?

JIM: Last month I wrote an article for "The Sunshine Friend."

PETE: *(joined by SAM)* " You are my sunshine, my only sunshine . . . "

TOM: Shut up! I mean when was the last time you wrote something you wanted to write?

JIM: Well, you know, my typewriter's bust . . .

TOM: Don't give me that crap about your typewriter. You don't want to get it fixed.

JIM: That's not true . . .

TOM: Do you know what you're doing here? You're throwing away your talent for a lousy bit of security.

JIM: Tom, you don't understand . . .

TOM: You're wasting your time doing a patch up job at something you don't really believe in.

JIM does not reply. TOM moves toward him.

TOM: Jim, there are stacks of guys in this world who haven't the intelligence to know where they're at. But you have. You *know*. And if you don't *do* something with that knowledge, you'll end up hating yourself.

JIM: What the hell could I do?

TOM: You could go into journalism, write a book. Listen, in this job, who can you tell it to? Spastics. Now think. Think of all the millions of jerks on the outside who have no idea of what it's really like in here. Hell, you could write a best-seller.

JIM: I thought about it.

TOM: Well, *do* something about it.

JIM: Don't you think I want to?

TOM: Jim, I know you're scared. I'm scared. But if I don't take this chance, I won't have a hope in hell of making it. And if you keep on doing something you don't want to do, soon you won't even have a mind. Do you think if Michael had a mind like yours he'd be content to hang around here all day flushing toilets?

PETE: He's right, Jim. You don't belong here. Why don't you and Tom go together?

TOM: Look, I'll help you. We can go, we can get a place, we can do it together. Come on, what do you say?

SAUNDERS and CARSON enter the hallway.

SAUNDERS: They've been in here all afternoon. I tried to reason with them, but they refused to come out. I know you're busy, and I hate to bring you down here, but I'm really afraid this Rick and Stanley business is repeating itself . . .

CARSON: Miss Saunders.

SAUNDERS: Yes?

CARSON: Thanks, I can take it from here.

SAUNDERS exits. CARSON opens the door and stands in the doorway.

CARSON: Okay, guys out.

Brief pause, then JIM moves to go.

TOM: Jim, how about it?

JIM: Later, Tom.

CARSON: Much later. It's time to get back to work.

TOM: I'm quitting, Carson.

CARSON: First things first. We can discuss that in the morning. *(He waits.)* Let's go.

JIM: I'm quitting too, sir.

CARSON: Right now I've got a good mind to fire you. Go to my office and wait for me.

SAM: He's making it real easy for you, Jim. He just fired you.

CARSON: You too, Sam. Out.

SAM: I need the bottle. Hand me the bottle, Carson.

CARSON: You've had all afternoon to use the bottle. Now, out!

SAM: I need the fucking bottle!

TOM goes to get the bottle, is stopped by CARSON.

CARSON: You leave that bottle alone. I want you all out of here.

PETE gets the bottle, gives it to SAM.

CARSON: Pete! Goddamn it, what's wrong with you guys?

SAM now has the bottle in his lap.

CARSON: Give me that bottle! *(He takes it away from SAM.)* Now get out of here, all of you.

Nothing happens, so he starts to wheel SAM's chair.

SAM: Take your fuckin' hands off my chair!

JIM: Listen! You never listen to me!

CARSON: For god's sake, Jim, I'll listen, but in my office.

JIM: No, here. Now!

CARSON: What's eating you?

SAM: Give me the goddamn bottle.

He tries to get it, but CARSON holds it out of his reach.

CARSON: Get out of here, Sam!

He pushes the chair away.

SAM: Fucking prick!

CARSON: *(shaken)* All right, what is it?

TOM: Jim, he's listening.

JIM: I don't want to spend the rest of my life here.

CARSON: Fine. You probably won't. Now can we all get back to work?

SAM: I need the fucking bottle!

TOM: Didn't you hear what he said? He said he doesn't want to spend his whole life in this dump.

CARSON: Look, March, you've been in here all afternoon. You've got Miss Saunders all upset because of Michael, and . . .

SAM: *I need the bottle!*

CARSON: Shut up, Sam!

TOM: Do you know why we've been in here all afternoon? Did you ever think of that?

SAM: Son of a bitch! Do you want me to piss my pants?

CARSON shoves the bottle at him. SAM wheels into the doorway of one of the stalls.

TOM: Did it ever enter your head that we might think of something besides the workshop, the club, and making you look good?

CARSON: Look, I don't know what you think, and right now I really don't care. All I'm concerned with is that you get out of this washroom. If you've got a complaint, you can come and talk to me.

TOM: I won't be there. Neither will Jim.

CARSON: I said, we can discuss that in the morning. *(He turns to SAM and PETE.)* Come on Sam, Pete, let's go.

PETE: He can't find it, Carson.

JIM: I want to be a writer.

CARSON: *(to SAM and PETE)* Quit fooling around, and hurry up.

JIM: I want to be a writer!

CARSON: You are a writer.

JIM: You don't understand. I want to make my living from it.

CARSON: Maybe you will, some day. But it's not going to happen overnight, is it?

TOM: If you stay here, Jim, it won't happen at all.

CARSON: It sure as hell won't if he runs off on some half-assed adventure with you.

TOM: Come on, Jim, the man's deaf.

CARSON: And what is it this time, Rembrandt? Poverty in a garret somewhere?

TOM: Better than poverty at the workshop.

CARSON: What are you going to paint, nude women?

TOM: You son of a bitch!

CARSON: Okay, Tom. Let's go.

He moves to usher TOM out.

TOM: You fucking son of a bitch!

In pushing him off, TOM loses his balance and falls. CARSON tries to help him up.

TOM: Get the fuck off me, Carson!

Slowly JIM and PETE help him to his feet.

TOM: Jim, you can stay and fart around as much as you like, but I'm going. Now are you with me or not?

CARSON: No, he's not. Now beat it.

TOM: Is that your answer, Jim?

JIM: Tom, wait . . .

TOM: I'm tired of waiting.

JIM: Maybe if I had just a little more time.

TOM: There's no time left.

JIM: Couldn't we wait till the end of the week?

CARSON: No, Jim. If you're serious about going, go now.

JIM: What about the Christmas program?

CARSON: I can find someone else.

JIM: But Christmas is the busiest time.

PETE: Go, Jim! Go with Tom!

SAM: *(overlapping)* Don't let him do it to you, baby. Go!

JIM: But Tom, it's Christmas!

TOM: Jim, please!

JIM: I can't let him down now. Maybe after Christmas . . .

SAM: Fuck Christmas! What about Tom?

JIM: I've written all these letters, made all the arrangements . . .

TOM turns and moves towards the door.

SAM: Piss on the arrangements! Are you going to let him walk out that door alone?

PETE: If you don't go now, Tom will be alone, but you'll be more alone. Believe me, I know.

JIM: I can't go! I can't go, Tom, because, if you fall, I'll be the only one there to pick you up. And I can hardly stand up myself.

TOM has gone.

SAM: How did you get around on campus, princess? Crawl on your belly? *(He wheels angrily to the door.)* Fuckin' door! Hey, Carson, how about one cripple helping another?

CARSON: Get him out, Pete.

SAM and PETE exit. They wait outside the door, listening. JIM staggers over to the bench and sits.

CARSON: Why don't we talk about this over dinner? At my place, if you like.

THELMA: I need a priest! Get me a priest! Someone get me a priest!

Slow fade to the sound of THELMA's sobbing. PETE wheels SAM down the hallway. SAM is laughing.

END

DAVID FRENCH (b. 1939)

If a single playwright can be said to epitomize the success of modern Canadian drama, it would be David French. From his apprenticeship with the CBC and his early identification with alternate theatre in Toronto to the current status of his plays as a mainstay of the regional theatres and a cultural export, his career has coincided with the growth and maturation of Canadian theatrical art. French has written broadly popular, commercially appealing plays while remaining true to his roots and his craft. His Mercer family saga and the phenomenally successful *Jitters* are painful, funny, and affectionate examinations of conditions that are widely recognizable, yet at the same time distinctively local and emphatically Canadian.

French was born in Coley's Point, Newfoundland, but moved to Toronto with his parents and four brothers when he was six. After finishing high school in 1958 he studied acting for two years in Toronto and Pasadena, California, and from 1960-65 worked as an actor, mostly for CBC-TV. Meanwhile he was also writing. In 1962 CBC bought his first play, "Behold the Dark River," and over the next decade broadcast seven more of his half-hour television scripts. Through the late '60s French supported his writing by working at a variety of jobs including a two-year stint in the Regina Post Office.

While summering on Prince Edward Island in 1971, he decided to try writing a stage play about his family's experience of adjusting to life outside Newfoundland in the late 1950s. By autumn he had a one-act called "Behold This House" which he offered to Bill Glassco after seeing Glassco's production of *Creeps* at the Tarragon. Retitled and expanded to full length, *Leaving Home* opened in May 1972 and immediately made French a star. The play has since enjoyed nearly a hundred productions. It also marked the start of a rich collaboration that has seen every one of French's plays premiere under Glassco's direction, all but the two most recent at the Tarragon.

At the end of *Leaving Home*, young Ben Mercer sets out on his own after a terrible row with his father, Jacob, leaving the rift between them as unresolved as Jacob's own sense of manhood and feelings of cultural alienation. *Of the Fields, Lately* (1973) picks up two years later with Ben's temporary return to his parents' home in Toronto, ending with Jacob's death. The play is gentler and more elegiac, but also slighter than its predecessor. It won the Chalmers Award for 1973 and has been very successful in its own right with productions across Canada and the United States.

After a number of abortive attempts to write a third Mercer play, French altered his focus to the sleazy underworld of cheap hoods, hookers and con men, but *One Crack Out* (1975) was a disappointment. Glassco then suggested that he try translating Chekhov. French's version of *The Seagull* (1977) seemed to get him creatively on track again. (In 1992-93 it ran for two months on Broadway.) Now inspired to write a full-out comedy, he returned to a subject he knew well, this time the wonderful world of Canadian theatre itself. *Jitters* (1979), a self-referential backstage comedy set in a small, low-budget Toronto theatre, is both a conventional genre play—"an almost perfect comedy of its kind," the *New York Times* called it— and a hilarious rendering of Canadian cultural schizophrenia. To the standard insecurities and insanities common to show biz people everywhere are added those peculiar to a culture which continually looks across its border for approval and in which, at the same time, "success is like stepping out of line." *Jitters* was a smash hit in Toronto, then had productions in nearly every regional theatre across Canada and a successful run in New Haven prior to a planned Broadway opening in 1981. Ironically, like the play-within-the-play itself, *Jitters* never made it to that Promised Land. (*Of the Fields, Lately* did have a brief Broadway run in 1980.) Nevertheless, *Jitters* has been French's most popular play with well over a hundred productions.

The Riddle of the World (1981), a comedy of ideas about the sexual and spiritual lives of urban sophisticates, is probably French's least notable play. But he found his way once again by returning to the Mercer family. *Salt-Water Moon* (1984), a "prequel" to his two earlier Mercer plays, chronicles the courtship of young Jacob and Mary in rural Newfoundland in 1926. A lyrical romantic comedy featuring only the two characters, it has proven as substantial a success as its predecessors. A Los Angeles production in 1985 earned it the Hollywood-Drama-Logue Critics Award for best play, and the published text won the Canadian Authors Association Literary Award for drama the following year.

In 1989 the Mercer trilogy became a tetralogy with what French insists is the last play in the series, *1949*. For three days before Newfoundland officially joins Canada, Jacob and Mary host in their Toronto home a politically divided extended family of mostly expatriate Newfoundlanders whose personal dramas unfold against the larger issue of cultural survival. By turns comedy and melodrama, *1949* brings onstage for the first time important out-characters from the earlier Mercer plays, and provides rich subtext for the events, a decade later, of *Leaving Home*. In 1993 French shifted gears again with a mystery thriller, *The Silver Dagger*, produced in Toronto by Canadian Stage, the company that premiered *1949*.

The Mercer plays are driven by archetypal energies: the difficult passage into manhood, the fierce protective love of one sister for another, the tangled dynamics of the family. What make the plays special are the cultural circumstances that shape those energies, especially the conflict between the characters who remain bound by the powerful pull of Newfoundland and those who make the perilous choice of "leaving home." Understood in the context of all four plays, that phrase resonates with emotional, psychological, political and cultural complexities in addition to its generational and geographical meanings. In *Leaving Home* Jacob asks Minnie about her boyfriend Harold: "What is he, Minnie? Newfie?" "No, boy—" she answers. "Canadian." After ten years of Confederation and even longer living in Toronto, Jacob and his expatriate contemporaries still think in terms of us and them.

Harold is a brilliant comic symbol of the "Canadian" Other as the Newfies see him: the gray, humourless undertaker who speaks not at all but carries a very big stick. Harold's comic potency serves as foil for Jacob's sense of impotence, of patriarchal failure. His own sons, after all, are colourless, fully assimilated Canadians for whom Newfoundland exists not even in memory but only in their father's embarrassing prejudices and oft-told tall tales. As Chris Johnson has argued, Jacob's cultural identity is closely tied to his patriarchal self-image. In order to sustain the legend on which his own sense of self is based ("I was out fishing on the Labrador when I was ten years old"), he must perpetuate it in his sons. So he tests Ben's manhood by demanding that Ben drink not Canadian whiskey but Newfie "screech." He tries desperately to keep Ben from going by showing him photos of the family back "home." Leaving home literally as they already have figuratively, the sons shatter Jacob's hope of sustaining and defending his cultural heritage within the garrison of the family.

Lacking the colourful language and theatrical vitality of Jacob, Mary and Minnie, the younger characters seem somewhat pale and conventional by comparison. French himself loses interest in the Bill-Kathy subplot, abruptly resolving it in a single stage direction. Ben's story is more compelling in its oedipal twists and turns and dramatic conclusion. In the context of the youth culture's ongoing generational battles and the nationalist impulse driving the new Canadian theatre, Ben's thrust for independence made a powerful statement. But in the end the play's focus is fixed firmly on Jacob and on Mary, who gets the last word and makes the final adjustment to our emotional allegiance.

•

Leaving Home was first performed May 16, 1972 at the Tarragon Theatre, Toronto, with the following cast:

MARY MERCER	Maureen Fitzgerald
BEN MERCER	Frank Moore
BILLY MERCER	Mel Tuck
JACOB MERCER	Sean Sullivan
KATHY JACKSON	Lyn Griffin
MINNIE JACKSON	Liza Creighton
HAROLD	Les Carlson

Directed by Bill Glassco
Designed by Dan Yarhi and Stephen Katz
Costumes by Vicky Manthorpe

LEAVING HOME

CHARACTERS

MARY MERCER
JACOB MERCER
BEN MERCER ⎱
BILLY MERCER ⎰ *their sons*
KATHY JACKSON, *BILLY's fiancée*
MINNIE JACKSON, *her mother*
HAROLD, *MINNIE's boyfriend*

SCENE

The play is set in Toronto on an early November day in the late 1950s.

SET

The lights come up on a working-class house in Toronto. The stage is divided into three playing areas: kitchen, dining room and living room. In addition there is a hallway leading into the living room. Two bedroom doors lead off the hallway, as well as the front door which is offstage.

The kitchen contains a fridge, a stove, cupboards over the sink for everyday dishes, and a small drop-leaf table with two wooden chairs, one at either end. A plastic garbage receptacle stands beside the stove. A hockey calendar hangs on a wall, and a kitchen prayer.

The dining room is furnished simply with an oak table and chairs. There is an oak cabinet containing the good dishes and silverware. Perhaps a family portrait hangs on the wall—a photo taken when the sons were much younger.

The living room contains a chesterfield and an armchair, a TV, a record player and a fireplace. On the mantel rests a photo album and a silver-framed photo of the two sons—then small boys—astride a pinto pony. On one wall hangs a mirror. On another, a seascape. There is also a small table with a telephone on it.

ACT ONE

It is around five-thirty on a Friday afternoon, and MARY MERCER, aged fifty, stands before the mirror in the living room, admiring her brand new dress and fixed hair. As she preens, the front door opens and in walk her two sons, BEN, eighteen, and BILL, seventeen. Each carries a box from a formal rental shop and schoolbooks.

MARY: Did you bump into your father?

BEN: No, we just missed him, Mom. He's already picked up his tux. He's probably at the Oakwood. *(He opens the fridge and helps himself to a beer.)*

MARY: Get your big nose out of the fridge. And put down that beer. You'll spoil your appetite.

BEN: No, I won't. *(He searches for a bottle opener in a drawer.)*

MARY: And don't contradict me. What other bad habits you learned lately?

BEN: *(teasing)* Don't be such a grouch. You sound like Dad. *(He sits at the table and opens his beer.)*

MARY: Yes, well just because you're in university now, don't t'ink you can raid the fridge any time you likes.

BILL crosses the kitchen and throws his black binder and books in the garbage receptacle.

MARY: What's that for? *(BILL exits into his bedroom and she calls after him.)* It's not the end of the world, my son. *(pause)* Tell you the truth, Ben. We always figured you'd be the one to land in trouble, if anyone did. I don't mean that as an insult. You're more . . . I don't know . . . like your father.

BEN: I am?

Music from BILL's room.

MARY: *(calling, exasperated)* Billy, do you have to have that so loud? *(BILL turns down his record player. To BEN)* I'm glad your graduation went okay last night. How was Billy? Was he glad he went?

BEN: Well, he wasn't upset, if that's what you mean.

MARY: *(slight pause)* Ben, how come you not to ask your father?

BEN: What do you mean?

BILL: *(off)* Mom, will you pack my suitcase? I can't get everything in.

MARY: *(calling)* I can't now, Billy. Later.

BEN: I want to talk to you, Mom. It's important.

MARY: I want to talk to you, too.

BILL: *(comes out of the bedroom, crosses to kitchen)* Mom, here's the deposit on my locker. I cleaned it out and threw away all my old gym clothes. *(He helps himself to an apple from the fridge.)*

MARY: Didn't you just hear me tell your brother to stay out of there? I might as well talk to the sink. Well, you can t'row away your old school clothes—that's your affair—but take those books out of the garbage. Go on. You never knows. They might come in handy sometime.

BILL: How? *(He takes the books out, then sits at the table with BEN.)*

MARY: Well, you can always go to night school and get your senior matric, once the baby arrives and Kathy's back to work . . . . Poor child. I talked to her on the phone this morning. She's still upset, and I don't blame her. I'd be hurt myself if my own mother was too drunk to show up to my shower.

BILL: *(a slight ray of hope)* Maybe she won't show up tonight.

MARY: *(glances anxiously at the kitchen clock and turns to check the fish and potatoes)* Look at the time. I just wish to goodness he had more t'ought, your father. The supper'll dry up if he don't hurry. He might pick up a phone and mention when he'll be home. Not a grain of t'ought in his head. And I wouldn't put it past him to forget his tux in the beer parlour. *(Finally she turns and looks at her two sons, disappointed.)* And look at the two of you. Too busy with your mouths to give your mother a second glance. I could stand here till my legs dropped off before either of you would notice my dress.

BEN: It's beautiful, Mom.

MARY: That the truth?

BILL: Would we lie to you, Mom?

MARY: Just so long as I don't look foolish next to Minnie. She can afford to dress up—Willard left her well off when he died.

BEN: Don't worry about the money. Dad won't mind.

MARY: Well, it's not every day your own son gets married, is it? *(to BILL as she puts on a large apron)* It's just that I don't want Minnie Jackson looking all decked out like the *Queen Mary* and me the tug that dragged her in. You understands, don't you, Ben?

BEN: Sure.

BILL: I understand too, Mom.

MARY: I know you do, Billy. I know you do. *(She opens a tin of peaches and fills five dessert dishes.)* Minnie used to go with your father. Did you know that, Billy? Years and years ago.

BILL: No kidding?

BEN: *(at the same time)* Really?

MARY: True as God is in Heaven. Minnie was awful sweet on Dad, too. She t'ought the world of him.

BILL: *(incredulously)* Dad?

MARY: Don't act so surprised. Your father was quite a one with the girls.

BEN: No kidding?

MARY: He could have had his pick of any number of girls. *(to BILL)* You ask Minnie sometime. Of course, in those days I was going with Jerome McKenzie, who later became a Queen's Counsel in St. John's. I must have mentioned him.

The boys exchange smiles.

BEN: I think you have, Mom.

BILL: A hundred times.

MARY: *(gently indignant—to BILL)* And that I haven't!

BILL: She has too. Hasn't she, Ben?

MARY: Never you mind, Ben. *(to BILL)* And instead of sitting around gabbing so much you'd better go change your clothes. Kathy'll soon be here. *(as BILL crosses to his bedroom)* Is the rehearsal still at eight?

BILL: We're supposed to meet Father Douglas at the church at five to. I just hope Dad's not too drunk. *(He exits.)*

MARY: *(studies BEN a moment)* Look at yourself. A cigarette in one hand, a bottle of beer in the other, at your age! You didn't learn any of your bad habits from me, I can tell you. *(pause)* Ben, don't be in such a hurry to grow up. *(She sits across from him.)* Whatever you do, don't be in such a hurry. Look at your poor young brother. His whole life ruined. Oh, I could weep a bellyful when I t'inks of it. Just seventeen, not old enough to sprout whiskers on his chin, and already the burdens of a man on his t'in little shoulders. Your poor father hasn't slept a full night since this happened. Did you know that? He had such high hopes for Billy. He wanted you both to go to college and not have to work as hard as he's had to all his life. And now look. You have more sense than that, Ben. Don't let life trap you.

BILL enters. He has changed his pants and is buttoning a clean white shirt. MARY goes into the dining room and begins to remove the tablecloth from the dining room table.

BILL: Mom, what about Dad? He won't start picking on the priest, will he? You know how he likes to argue.

MARY: He won't say a word, my son. You needn't worry. Worry more about Minnie showing up.

BILL: What if he's drunk?

MARY: He won't be. Your father knows better than to sound off in church. Oh, and another t'ing—he wants you to polish his shoes for tonight. They're in the bedroom. The polish is on your dresser. You needn't be too fussy.

BEN: I'll do his shoes, Mom. Billy's all dressed.

MARY: No, no, Ben, that's all right. He asked Billy to.

BILL: What did Ben do this time?

MARY: He didn't do anyt'ing.

BILL: He must have.

MARY: Is it too much trouble to polish your father's shoes, after all he does for you? If you won't do it, I'll do it myself.

BILL: *(indignantly)* How come when Dad's mad at Ben, I get all the dirty jobs? Jeez! Will I be glad to get out of here! *(Rolling up his shirt sleeves he exits into his bedroom.)*

MARY takes a clean white linen tablecloth from a drawer in the cabinet and covers the table. During the following scene she sets five places with her good glasses, silverware and plates.

BEN: *(slight pause)* Billy's right, isn't he? What'd I do, Mom?

MARY: Take it up with your father. I'm tired of being the middle man.

BEN: Is it because of last night? *(slight pause)* It is, isn't it?

MARY: He t'inks you didn't want him there, Ben. He t'inks you're ashamed of him.

BEN: He wouldn't have gone, Mom. That's the only reason I never invited him.

MARY: He would have went, last night.

BEN: *(angrily)* He's never even been to one lousy Parents' Night in thirteen years. Not one! And he calls *me* contrary!

MARY: You listen to me. Your father never got past Grade T'ree. He was yanked out of school and made to work. In those days, back home, he was lucky to get that much and don't kid yourself.

BEN: Yeah? So?

MARY: So? So he's afraid to. He's afraid of sticking out. Is that so hard to understand? Is it?

BEN: What're you getting angry about? All I said was—

MARY: You say he don't take an interest, but he was proud enough to show off your report cards all those years. I suppose with you that don't count for much.

BEN: All right. But he never goes anywhere without you, Mom, and last night you were here at the shower.

MARY: Last night was different, Ben, and you ought to know that. It was your high school graduation. He would have went with me or without me. If you'd only asked him. *(A truck horn blasts twice.)* There he is now in the driveway. Whatever happens, don't fall for his old tricks. He'll be looking for a fight, and doing his best to find any excuse. *(calling)* Billy, you hear that? Don't complain about the shoes, once your father comes!

BEN: *(urgently)* Mom, there's something I want to tell you before Dad comes in.

MARY: Sure, my son. Go ahead. I'm listening. What's on your mind?

BEN: Well . . .

MARY: *(smiling)* Come on. It can't be that bad.

BEN: *(slight pause)* I want to move out, Mom.

MARY: *(almost inaudibly)* . . . What?

BEN: I said I want to move out.

MARY: *(softly, as she sets the cutlery)* I heard you. *(pause)* What for?

BEN: I just think it's time. I'll be nineteen soon. *(pause)* I'm moving in with Billy and Kathy and help pay the rent. *(pause)* I won't be far away. I'll see you on weekends. *(MARY nods.)* Mom?

MARY: *(absently)* What?

BEN: Will you tell Dad? *(slight pause)* Mom? Did you hear me?

MARY: I heard you. He'll be upset, I can tell you. By rights you ought to tell him yourself.

BEN: If I do, we'll just get into a big fight and you know it. He'll take it better, coming from you.

The front door opens and JACOB MERCER enters whistling "I's the b'y." He is fifty, though he looks older. He is dressed in a peaked cap, carpenter's overalls, thick-soled workboots and a lumberjack shirt over a T-shirt. Under one arm he carries his black lunchpail.

MARY: Your suit! I knowed it!

JACOB: Don't get in an uproar, now. I left it sitting on the front seat of the truck. *(He looks at BEN, then back to MARY.)* Is Billy home?

MARY: He's in the bedroom, polishing your shoes.

JACOB: *(Crosses to the bedroom door.)* Billy, my son, come out a moment. *(BILL enters, carrying a shoe brush.)* Put down the brush and go out in my truck and bring back the tux on the seat.

BILL: What's wrong with Ben? He's not doing anything.

JACOB: Don't ask questions. That's a good boy. I'd ask your brother, but he always has a good excuse.

BEN: I'll go get it. *(He starts for the front door.)*

JACOB: *(calling after BEN)* Oh, it's too late to make up now. The damage is done.

MARY: Don't talk nonsense, Jacob.

JACOB: *(a last thrust)* And aside from that—I wouldn't want you dirtying your nice clean hands in your father's dirty old truck!

The front door closes on his last words. BILL returns to his room. JACOB sets his lunchpail and his cap on the dining room table.

JACOB: Did he get his diploma?

MARY: Yes. It's in the bedroom.

JACOB: *(breaks into a smile and lifts his cap)* And will you gaze on Mary over there. When I stepped in the door, I t'ought the Queen had dropped in for tea.

MARY: You didn't even notice.

JACOB: Come here, my dear, and give Jacob a kiss.

MARY: *(She darts behind the table, laughing.)* I'll give Jacob a swift boot in the rear end with my pointed toe. *(JACOB grabs her, rubs his rough cheek against hers.)* You'll take the skin off! Jake! You're far too rough! And watch my new dress! Don't rip it.

JACOB: *(releases her and breaks into a little jig as he sings)*

I's the b'y that builds the boat
And I's the b'y that sails her,
I's the b'y that catches the fish
And takes 'em home to Lizer.

Sods and rinds to cover your flake
Cake and tea for supper
Codfish in the spring of the year
Fried in maggoty butter.

I don't want your maggoty fish
Cake and tea for winter
I could buy as good as that
Down in Bona Vista.

I took Lizer to a dance
And faith but she could travel
And every step that she did take
Was up to her ass in gravel.

JACOB ends the song with a little step or flourish.

MARY: There's no mistakin' where you've been to, and it's not to church.

JACOB: All right, now, I had one little glass, and don't you start.

MARY: *(as she re-enters the kitchen)* How many?

JACOB: I can't lie, Mary. *(He puts his hand on his heart.)* As God is my witness—two. Two glasses to celebrate the wedding of my youngest son. *(He follows her into the kitchen.)*

MARY: Half a dozen's more like it, unless you expects God to perjure himself for the likes of you. Well, no odds: you're just in time. Kathy'll soon be here, so get cleaned up.

JACOB: I washed up on the job.

MARY: Well, change your clothes. You're not sitting down with the likes of that on. *(She returns to the dining room with bread and butter for the dining room table.)*

JACOB: I suppose it's fish with Kathy coming and him now a bloody Mick. Next t'ing you knows he'll be expecting me to chant grace in Latin.

MARY: And I'll crown you if you opens your yap like that around Kathy. Don't you dare.

JACOB: *(Following MARY, he sits at the dining room table.)* 'Course we could have the priest drop by and bless the table himself. *(He makes the sign of the cross.)*

MARY: Jacob!

JACOB: Though I doubts he could get his Cadillac in the driveway.

MARY: *(back to kitchen)* If you comes out with the likes of that tonight, I'll never speak to you again. You hear?

JACOB: Ah, go on with you. What do you know? If you had nothing in your pockets but holes, a priest wouldn't give you t'read to sew it with.

BEN: *(enters with the box.)* I put your toolbox down in the basement while I was at it, Dad. And rolled up the windows in your truck, in case it rains tonight.

JACOB: Did you, now? And I'm supposed to forget all about last night, is that it? Pretend it never occurred? Your brother's good enough for you but not your own father. *(As BEN crosses to kitchen)* Well, it would take more time than that to stitch up the hurt, I can assure you. And a long time before it heals. Don't be looking to your mother for support.

BEN: I wasn't. *(He sits at kitchen table.)*

JACOB: Or for sympathy, either.

MARY: Jacob, it don't serve no purpose to look for a fight.

JACOB: *(to MARY)* You keep your two cents worth out of it. Nobody asked you. You got too much to say.

BILL: *(enters, carrying the shined shoes, which he gives to his father)* Hey, Dad, do me a favour? When Kathy gets here, no cracks about the Pope's nose and stuff like that. And just for once don't do that Squid-Jiggin' thing and take your teeth out. Okay? *(He sits at table across from his father and reads the evening paper.)*

JACOB: Well, listen to him, now. *(to MARY)* Who put him up to that? You? Imagine. Telling me what I can say and do in my own house.

MARY: *(returning to dining room)* Billy, my son, I got a feeling you just walked into it. *(She takes a polishing cloth from cabinet and rubs her good silverware, including a large fish-knife.)*

JACOB: *(to BILL)* If you only knowed what my poor father went t'rough with the Catholics. Oh, if you only knowed, you wouldn't be doing this. My own son a turncoat. And back home, when we was growing up, you wouldn't dare go where the Catholics lived after dark. You'd be murdered, and many's the poor boy was. Knocked over the head and drownded, and all they done was let night catch them on a Catholic road. My father's brother was one. Poor Isaac. He was just fifteen, that summer. Tied with his arms behind him and tossed in the pond like a stone. My poor father never forgot that to his dying day. *(The family wait out the harangue.)* And here you is j'ining their ranks! T'ree weeks of instructions. By the jumping Jesus Christ you don't come from my side of the family. I'm glad my poor father never lived to see this day, I can tell you. The loyalest Orangeman that ever marched in a church parade, my father. He'd turn over in his grave if he saw a grandson of his kissing the Pope's ass. Promising to bring up your poor innocent babies Roman Catholics and them as ignorant of Rome as earthworms.

Oh, it's a good t'ing for you, my son, that he ain't around to see it, because sure as you'm there he'd march into that church tomorrow with his belt in his hand, and take that smirk off your face! Billy, my son, I never expected this of you, of all people. No, I didn't. Not you. If it was your brother, now, I could understand it. He'd do it just for spite . . . .

MARY: Hold your tongue, boy. Don't you ever run down? I just hope to goodness Ben don't call on you at the wedding to toast the bride and groom. We'll all be old before it's over. *(slight pause)* Did you try on your tux?

JACOB: No, boy, it was too crowded.

MARY: Then try it on. You're worse than the kids. *(She hands him the box.)* Go on.

JACOB: *(to BILL, referring to the shoes)* T'anks. *(He exits into his bedroom.)*

MARY: Ben, do your mother a favour? Fill up the glasses. I left the jug in the kitchen. *(She sits at the dining room table, checks and folds five linen napkins.)* Look at him, Ben. The little fart. My baby. *(to herself)* How quick it all goes . . . . I can still see us to this day . . . the t'ree of us . . . coming up from Newfoundland . . . July of 1945 . . . the war not yet over . . . . Father gone ahead to look for work on construction . . . that old train packed with soldiers, and do you t'ink a single one would rise off his big fat backside to offer up his seat? Not on your life. There we was, huddled together out on the brakes, a couple, t'ree hours . . . with the wind and the soot from the engine blowing back . . . until a lady come out and saw us. 'Well, the likes of this I've never seen,' she says. 'I've got four sons in the war, and if one of mine was in that carriage, I'd disown 'im!'

We've never had anyt'ing to be ashamed of, my sons. We've been poor . . . but we've always stuck together. *(to BILL)* Is you frightened, my son?

BILL: No. Why should I be?

MARY: Don't be ashamed of it. Tomorrow you'll most likely wish you was back with your mother and father in your own soft bed.

BEN: He's scared shitless, Mom. *(to BILL)* Tell the truth.

MARY: Ben, is that nice talk?

BILL: *(to BEN)* I'll trade places.

MARY: Well, as long as you loves her, that's all that matters. Without that there's nothing, and with it what you don't have can wait. But a word of warning, Billy—don't come running to us with your squabbles, because we won't stick our noses into it. And before I forgets—you'd better not say a word to your father about moving out. I'll tell him myself after the wedding.

JACOB: *(off)* Mary!

MARY: *(calling)* What is it, boy?

JACOB: *(off)* Come here! I can't get this goddamn button fast!

MARY: *(shaking her head)* It's one of those mysteries how he made it t'rough life this far. If he didn't have me, he wouldn't know which leg of his pants was which. *(She exits.)*

BILL: *(slight pause)* You told her, huh? She doesn't seem to mind.

BEN: Keep your voice down. You want Dad to hear?

BILL: What did she say? Is she going to tell him?

BEN: Yeah, but do you think I ought to let her?

BILL: What do you mean?

BEN: Well, maybe I should tell him myself.

BILL: Are you crazy?

BEN: If I don't, you know what'll happen. Mom'll get all the shit.

BILL: *(pause)* Ben, you really want to do this? Are you sure?

BEN: Look—my books and tuition're paid for. All I got to worry about is the rent. I can handle that, waiting on tables. I'll make out. Listen, whose idea was it anyhow? Mine or yours? I wouldn't do it if I didn't want to.

BILL: Okay.

BEN: I need to, Billy. Christ, you know that. Either Dad goes, or I do.

BILL: I wish I felt that way. I don't want to move out. I don't want to get married. I don't know the first thing about girls. I mean, Kathy's the first girl I ever did it with. No kidding. The very first. We've only done it four or five times. The first time was in a cemetery, for Chrissake!

BEN: Well, at least you've been laid, Billy. I never.

BILL: Really? (He laughs. Pause.) I like Kathy. I like her a lot. But I don't know what else. What do you think Dad would do, if he was in my shoes? I think if Kathy was Mom he'd marry her, don't you?

MARY: (enters) Listen to me, you two. I don't want either one of you to say one word or snicker even when your father comes out. Is that understood?

BEN: What's wrong?

MARY: They gave him the wrong coat. I suppose he was in such a rush to get to the Oakwood he didn't bother trying it on.

JACOB enters singing, now dressed in the rental tux and polished shoes. The sleeves are miles too short for him, the back hiked up. He looks like a caricature of discomfort.

Here comes the bride,
All fat and wide,
See how she wobbles
From side to side.

The boys glance at one another and try to keep from breaking up.

JACOB: Well, boys, am I a fit match for your mother?

BEN: Dad, I wish I had a camera.

JACOB: Is you making fun?

MARY: No, he's not. The sleeves are a sight, but— (giving BEN a censorious look) —aside from that it's a perfect fit. Couldn't be better. Could it, Billy?

BILL: Made to measure, Dad.

JACOB: I t'ink I'll kick up my heels. I'm in the right mood. (as he crosses to the record player)

What do you say, Mary? Feel up to it? (He selects a record.)

MARY: I'm willing, if you is, Jake.

JACOB: All right, boys, give us room. (The record starts to play—a rousing tune with lots of fiddles.) Your mother loves to twirl her skirt and shows off her drawers! (He seizes his wife, and they whirl around the room, twirling and stomping with enjoyment and abandon.)

BEN: Go, Mom! (He whistles. BILL and BEN clap their hands to the music.) Give her hell, Dad!

MARY: Not so fast, Jacob, you'll make me dizzy!

JACOB stops after a few turns. He is slightly dizzy. He sits.

JACOB: (to BILL) Dance with your mother. I galled my heel at work. (BILL does.) You ought to have seen your mother in her day, Ben. She'd turn the head of a statue. There wasn't a man from Bareneed to Bay Roberts didn't blink when she passed by.

MARY: Come on, Ben. Before it's over. (She takes BEN, and they dance around the room.)

JACOB: That's one t'ing about Ben, Mary. He won't ever leave you. The day he gets married himself he'll move in next door.

Finally MARY collapses laughing on the chesterfield. The music plays on.

JACOB: (expansively) I t'ink a drink's in order. What do you say, boys? To whet the appetite. (He searches in the bottom of the cabinet. To MARY) Where's all the whiskey to? You didn't t'row it out, did you?

MARY: You t'rowed it down your t'roat, that's where it was t'rowed.

JACOB: Well, boys, looks like there's no whiskey. (He holds up a bottle.) How does a little "screech" sound?

BEN: Not for me, Dad.

JACOB: Why not?

BEN: I just don't like it.

JACOB: (sarcastically) No, you wouldn't. I suppose it's too strong for you. Well, Billy'll have some, won't you, my son? (He turns down the music.)

BILL: *(surprised)* I will?

JACOB: Get two glasses out, then, and let's have a quick drink. *(BILL does and hands a glass to his father.)* Don't suppose you'd have a little drop, Mary, my love? *(He winks at BILL.)*

MARY: Go on with you. You ought to have better sense, teaching the boys all your bad habits. And after you promised your poor mother on her death-bed you'd warn them off alcohol . . .

JACOB: Don't talk foolishness. A drop of this won't harm a soul. Might even do some good, all you know.

MARY: Yes, some good it's done you.

JACOB: At least I'd take a drink with my own father, if he was alive. I'd do that much, my lady.

MARY: *(quickly)* Pay no attention, Ben. *(to JACOB)* And listen, I don't want you getting tight and making a disgrace of yourself at the rehearsal tonight. You hear?

JACOB: Oh, I'll be just as sober as the priest, rest assured of that. And you just study his fingers, if they'm not as brown as a new potato from nicotine. I dare say if he didn't swallow Sen-Sen, you'd know where all that communion wine goes to. *(to BILL)* How many drunks you suppose is wearing Roman collars? More than the Pope would dare admit. And all those t'ousands of babies they keep digging up in the basements of convents. It's shocking.

BEN: That's a lot of bull, Dad.

JACOB: It is, is it? Who told you that? Is that more of the stuff you learns at university? Your trouble is you've been brainwashed.

BEN: You just want to believe all that.

MARY: And you'd better not come out with that tonight, if you knows what's good for you.

JACOB: *(to BILL)* Mind—I'm giving you fair warning. I won't sprinkle my face with holy water or make the sign of the cross. And nothing in this world or the next can persuade me.

BILL: You don't have to, Dad. Relax.

JACOB: Just so you knows.

BEN: All you got to do, Dad, is sit there in the front row and look sweet.

JACOB: All right, there's no need to get saucy. I wasn't talking to you! *(He pours a little "screech" in the two glasses. To BILL)* Here's to you, boy. You got the makings of a man. That's more than I can say for your older brother. *(JACOB downs his drink. BILL glances helplessly at BEN. He doesn't drink.)* Go on. *(BILL hesitates, then downs it, grimacing and coughing.)* You see that, Mary? *(his anger rising)* It's your fault the one's the way he is. It's high time, my lady, you let go and weaned him away from the tit!

MARY: *(angrily)* You shut your mouth. There's no call for that kind of talk!

JACOB: He needs more in his veins than mother's milk, goddamn it!

BEN: *(shouting at JACOB)* What're you screaming at her for? She didn't do anything?

JACOB: *(a semblance of sudden calm)* Well, listen to him, now. Look at the murder in his face. One harsh word to his mother and up comes his fists. I'll bet you wouldn't be so quick to defend your father.

MARY: Be still, Jacob. You don't know what you're saying.

JACOB: He t'inks he's too good to drink with me!

BEN: All right, I will, if it's that important. Only let's not fight.

MARY: He's just taunting you into it, Ben. Don't let him.

JACOB: *(sarcastically)* No, my son, your mother's right. I wouldn't wish for your downfall on my account. To hear her tell it I'm the devil tempting Saul on the road to Damascus.

MARY: Well, the devil better learn his scripture, if he wants to quote it. The devil tempted our Lord in the wilderness, and Saul had a revelation on the road to Damascus.

JACOB: A revelation! *(He turns off the record.)* I'll give you a revelation! I'm just a piece of shit around here! Who is it wears himself out year after year to give him a roof over his head and food in his mouth? Who buys his clothes and keeps him in university?

MARY: He buys his own clothes, and he's got a scholarship.

JACOB: *(furious)* Oh, butt out! You'd stick up for him if it meant your life, and never once put in a good word for me.

MARY: I'm only giving credit where's credit due.

JACOB: Liar.

MARY: Ah, go on. You're a fine one to talk. You'd call the ace of spades white and not bat an eye.

JACOB: *(enraged)* It never fails. I can't get my own son to do the simplest goddamn t'ing without a row. No matter what.

BEN: It's never simple, Dad. You never let it be simple or I might. It's always a *test*.

JACOB: Test!

MARY: Ben, don't get drawn into it.

JACOB: *(to BEN)* The sooner you learns to get along with others, the sooner you'll grow up. Test!

BEN: Do you ever hear yourself? "Ben, get up that ladder. You want people to think you're a sissy?" "Have a drink, Ben. It'll make a man out of you!"

JACOB: I said no such t'ing, now. Liar.

BEN: It's what you meant. "Cut your hair, Ben. You look like a girl." The same shit over and over, and it never stops!

JACOB: Now it all comes out. You listening to this, Mary?

BEN: No, you listen, Dad. You don't really expect me to climb that ladder or take that drink. You want me to refuse, don't you?

JACOB: Well, listen to him. The faster you gets out into the real world the better for you. *(He turns away.)*

BEN: Dad, you don't want me to be a man, you just want to impress me with how much less of a man I am than you. *(He snatches the bottle from his father and takes a swig.)* All right. Look. *(He rips open his shirt.)* I still haven't got hair on my chest, and I'm still not a threat to you.

JACOB: No, and you'm not likely ever to be, either, until you grows up and gets out from under your mother's skirts.

BEN: No, Dad—until I get out from under *yours*.

The doorbell rings.

MARY: That's Kathy. All right, that's more than enough for one night. Let's have no more bickering. Jake, get dressed. And not another word out of anyone. The poor girl will t'ink she's fallen in with a pack of wild savages.

JACOB: *(getting in the last word)* And there's no bloody mistakin' who the wild savage is. *(With that he exits into his bedroom.)*

MARY: Billy, answer the door. *(to BEN)* And you—change your shirt. You look a fright.

BEN exits. BILL opens the front door, and KATHY enters. She is sixteen, very pretty, but at the moment her face is pale and emotionless.

KATHY: Hello, Mrs. Mercer.

MARY: You're just in time, Kathy. *(MARY gives her a kiss.)* Take her coat, Billy. I'll be right out, dear. *(She exits.)*

KATHY: Where is everyone?

BILL: *(taking her coat)* Getting dressed. *(As he tries to kiss her, she pulls away her cheek.)* What's wrong? *(He hangs up her coat.)*

KATHY: Nothing. I don't feel well.

BILL: Why not? Did you drink too much at the party?

KATHY: What party?

BILL: Didn't the girls at work throw a party for you this afternoon?

KATHY: I didn't go to the office this afternoon.

BILL: You didn't go? What do you mean?

KATHY: Just what I said.

BILL: What *did* you say?

KATHY: Will you get off my back!

BILL: What did I say? *(slight pause)* Are you mad at me?

KATHY: *(looks at him)* Billy, do you love me? Do you? I need to know.

BILL: What's happened, Kathy?

KATHY: I'm asking you a simple question.

BILL: And I want to know what's happened.

KATHY: If I hadn't been pregnant, you'd never have wanted to get married, would you?

BILL: So?

KATHY: I hate you.

BILL: For Chrissake, Kathy, what's happened?

KATHY: *(sits on the chesterfield)* I lost the baby . . .

BILL: What?

KATHY: Isn't that good news?

BILL: What the hell happened?

KATHY: I started bleeding in the ladies' room this morning.

BILL: Bleeding? What do you mean?

KATHY: Haemorrhaging. I screamed, and one of the girls rushed me to the hospital. I think the people at work thought I'd done something to myself.

BILL: Had you?

KATHY: Of course not. You know I wouldn't.

BILL: What did the doctor say?

KATHY: I had a miscarriage. *(She looks up at him.)* You're not even sorry, are you?

BILL: I am, really. What else did the doctor say?

KATHY: I lost a lot of blood. I'm supposed to eat lots of liver and milk, to build it up. You should have seen me, Billy. I was white and shaky. I'm a little better now. I've been sleeping all afternoon.

BILL: *(slight pause)* What was it?

KATHY: What was what?

BILL: The baby.

KATHY: Do you really want to know?

BILL doesn't answer.

BILL: What'll we do?

KATHY: Tell our folks, I guess. My mother doesn't know yet. She's been at the track all day with her boyfriend. *(slight pause)* I haven't told anyone else, Billy. Just you.

Enter JACOB and MARY. He is dressed in a pair of slacks and a white shirt. He carries a necktie in his hand. MARY wears a blouse and skirt.

JACOB: Billy, my son, tie me a Windsor knot. That's a good boy. *(He hands BILL the necktie and BILL proceeds to make the knot. Shyly, to KATHY)* Hello, my dear. *(KATHY nods.)* Lovely old day.

MARY: Come on. We may as well sit right down before it colds off. I'll serve up the fish and potatoes. *(She transfers the fish and potatoes into serving dishes.)*

JACOB: *(calling)* Ben! *(to KATHY, referring to the tie)* I'm all t'umbs or I'd do it myself.

BEN: *(enters, his shirt changed)* Hi, Kathy.

KATHY: Hi, Ben. Congratulations.

BEN: For what?

KATHY: Didn't you graduate last night?

BEN: Oh. Yeah.

JACOB: I suppose if Ben ever becomes Prime Minister, I'll be the last to know unless I reads it in the newspapers.

MARY: Kathy, you sit right down there, dear. Billy, you sit next to her. And Ben's right here. *(BILL hands his father the tie. Jacob slips it on as he approaches the table.)* Father, why don't you say grace?

JACOB: Maybe Kathy would like to.

KATHY: We never say grace at our house.

JACOB: Is that a fact? Imagine.

BILL: *(jumping in)* "Bless this food that now we take, and feed our souls for Jesus' sake. Amen."

ALL: Amen. *(They dig in.)*

JACOB: Have an eye to the bones, Kathy. *(slight pause)* You was born in Toronto, wasn't you? Someday you'll have to take a trip home, you and

Billy, and see how they dries the cod on the beaches. He don't remember any more than you. He was just little when he come up here.

MARY: That was a long time ago, Kathy. 1945.

KATHY: *(slight pause)* Have you been home since, Mr. Mercer?

JACOB: No, my dear, and I don't know if I wants to. A different generation growing up now. *(glancing at BEN)* A different brand of Newfie altogether. And once the oldtimers die off, that'll be the end of it. Newfoundland'll never be the same after that, I can tell you. *(slight pause)* Do you know what flakes is?

KATHY: No.

JACOB: Well, they'm spread over the shore— these wooden stages they dries the codfish on. Sometimes—and this is no word of a lie, is it, Mary?—the fishflies'll buzz around that codfish as t'ick as the hairs on your arm. *(slight pause)* T'icker. T'ick as tarpaper.

MARY: Jacob, we're eating. *(to KATHY)* He's just like his poor mother, Jacob is. She'd start on about the tapeworm as you was lifting the pork to your mouth. *(to JACOB)* Let the poor girl eat in peace, Father. *(to KATHY)* You've hardly touched your food, dear. Has he spoiled your appetite? It wouldn't be the first time.

KATHY: I'm just not too hungry, Mrs. Mercer.

MARY: I understands. Big day tomorrow. I was the same way, my wedding day. It's a wonder I didn't faint.

JACOB: *(slight pause—to KATHY)* You notice Ben don't look my way? He's sore. *(KATHY glances at BEN, who goes on eating, oblivious.)* Oh, he knows how to dish it out with the best, but he can't take it. You can joke with Billy, he likes a bit of fun, but with the other one you don't dare open your mouth.

BEN: Will you shut up, Dad?

JACOB: *(to KATHY)* I'll bet you didn't get sore with your poor father and talk back all the time when he was alive, did you, my dear? No, that's what you didn't. You had more respect. And I bet now you don't regret it.

MARY: Don't ask the child to choose sides, Jacob. You've got no right to do that. Anyhow,

Kathy's got more sense than to get mixed up in it. Don't you, Kathy?

JACOB: The Bible says to honour thy father and thy mother . . .

MARY: *(exasperated)* Oh, hold your tongue, for goodness sake. Don't your jaw ever get tired?

JACOB: *(to KATHY)* Well, you can see for yourself what happens, my dear. Anyone in this room is free to say what they likes about the old man, but just let him criticize back and you'd t'ink a fox had burst into the chicken coop, the way Mother Mercer here gathers her first-born under her wing. *(slight pause—to KATHY, but meant for his wife)* I suppose by now you've heard your mother and me once went together? I suppose Minnie's mentioned it often enough? Fine figure of a woman, Minnie. Still looks as good as ever.

BILL: I hear you used to be a real woman's man, Dad.

JACOB: Who told you that?

BILL: Mom.

MARY: *(quickly)* Liar. I told you no such t'ing.

BILL: You did so. Didn't she, Ben?

BEN smiles at his mother.

JACOB: Well, contrary to what your mother tells, that particular year I had only one sweetheart, and that was Minnie Jackson. Wasn't it, Mary?

MARY: *(nodding)* She was still a Fraser then. That was the same year I was going with Jerome McKenzie. Wasn't it, Jacob?

JACOB: Oh, don't forget the most important part, Mary, the Q.C., the Queen's Counsel. Jerome McKenzie, Q.C. *(to KATHY)* Jerome's a well-known barrister in St. John's, and Mrs. Mercer's all the time t'rowing him' up in my face. Ain't you Mary? Never lets me forget it, will you? *(to KATHY)* You see, my dear, she might have married Jerome McKenzie, Q.C., and never had a single worry in the world, if it wasn't for me. Ain't that so, Mary?

MARY: If you insists, Jacob.

BILL and KATHY stare silently at their plates, embarrassed. BEN looks from his father to his mother and then to BILL.

BEN: Did you get the boutonnieres and the cuff links for the ushers?

MARY: It's all taken care of, my son. *(pause)* What kind of flowers did your mother order, Kathy?

KATHY: Red roses.

MARY: How nice.

KATHY: I like yellow roses better, but— *(She stops abruptly.)*

BILL: But what?

KATHY: Nothing.

MARY: Yellow roses mean tears, my son.

KATHY: Did you carry roses, Mrs. Mercer?

MARY: I did. Red butterfly roses. And I wore a gown of white satin, with a lace veil. I even had a crown of orange blossoms.

KATHY: I'll bet you were beautiful.

JACOB: My dear, she lit up that little Anglican church like the Second Coming. I suppose I told you all about the wedding ring?

MARY: No, you didn't, and she don't want to hear tell of it, and neither do the rest of us. Don't listen to his big fibs, Kathy.

JACOB: I still remembers that day. I had on my gaberdine suit, with a white carnation in the lapel. In those days Mary t'ought I was handsome.

MARY: Get to the point, Father.

JACOB: We was that poor I couldn't afford a ring, so when the Reverend Mr. Price got t'rough with the dearly beloveds and asked for the ring, I reached into my pocket and give him all I had— an old bent nail.

MARY: Last time it was cigar band.

JACOB: *(still to KATHY)* And if you was to ask me today, twenty years later, if it's been worth it—my dear, my answer would still be the same, for all her many faults—that old rusty nail has brung me more joy and happiness than you can ever imagine. And I wouldn't trade the old woman here, nor a blessed hair of her head, not for all the gold bullion in the Vatican.

BILL: Dad.

JACOB: And my name's not Jerome McKenzie, Q.C., either. And the likes of Ben here may t'ink me just an old fool, not worth a second t'ought— *(BEN shoves back his plate, holding back his temper.)* —and run me down to my face the first chance he gets—

BEN: Ah, shut up.

JACOB: —and treat me with no more respect and consideration than you would your own worst enemy!—

BEN: Will you grow up! *(He knocks over his chair and exits into his bedroom.)*

JACOB: *(shouting after him)* —but I've always done what I seen fit, and no man can do more! *(The door slams—slight pause.)* I won't say another word.

MARY: You've said enough, brother. *(slight pause)* What Kathy must t'ink of us! *(slight pause)* And then you wonders why he's the way he is, when you sits there brazen-faced and makes him feel like two cents in front of company. You haven't a grain of sense, you haven't!

JACOB: Did I say a word of a lie? Did I?

MARY: No, you always speaks the gospel truth, you do.

JACOB: I never could say two words in a row to that one, without he takes offence. Not two bloody words! *(MARY collects the supper plates. BILL and KATHY remain seated.)* Look. He didn't finish half his plate. *(calling)* Come out and eat the rest of your supper, Ben. There's no food wasted in this house. *(slight pause)* Take it to him, Mary.

MARY: *(picking up BEN's chair)* You—you're the cause of it. You're enough to spoil anyone's appetite.

JACOB: Ah, for Christ's sake, he's too damn soft, and you don't help any. I was out fishing on the Labrador when I was ten years old, six months of the year for ten dollars, and out of that ten dollars had to come my rubber boots. *(to KATHY)* Ten years old, and I had to stand up and take it like a man. *(to MARY)* That's a lot tougher than a few harsh words from his father!

MARY: *(as she serves the dessert)* And you'll make him hard, is that it, Jacob? Hard and tough like yourself? Blame him for all you've suffered. Make him pay for all you never had.

JACOB: Oh, shut up, Mary, you don't understand these matters. He won't have you or me to fall back on once he gets out into the world. He'll need to be strong or— *(He winks at BILL.)* —he'll end up like your cousin Israel.

MARY: And don't tell *that* story, Jacob. You're at the table.

JACOB: *(to KATHY)* Israel Parsons was Mrs. Mercer's first cousin.

MARY: Might as well talk to a log.

JACOB: He was a law student at the time, and he worked summers at the pulp and paper mill at Corner Brook, cleaning the machines. Well, one noon hour he crawled inside to clean the big sharp blades, and someone flicked on the switch. Poor young Israel was ground up into pulp. They didn't find a trace of him, did they Mary? Not even a hair. Mary's poor mother always joked that he was the only one of her relatives ever to make the headlines—if you knows what I mean.

MARY: She knows. And just what has Israel Parsons got to do with Ben, pray tell?

JACOB: Because that's what the world will do to Ben, Mary, if he's not strong. Chew him up alive and swallow him down without a trace. Mark my words. *(He lifts the bowl to his mouth and drinks the peach juice.)*

The front door bursts open.

MINNIE: *(off)* Anybody home?

JACOB: Minnie! *(He glances at MARY, then rises.)*

MINNIE enters. She is in her late forties, boisterous and voluptuous, a little flashily dressed.

MINNIE: Is you still eating?

JACOB: No, come in, come in.

MINNIE: If you is—guess what?—I brung along me new boyfriend to spoil your appetites . . . . Where's he to? Can't keep track of the bugger! *(She returns to the hallway, and shouts offstage.)* For Christ's sake, you dirty t'ing, you! You might have waited till you got inside!

KATHY: *(to BILL)* What's *she* doing here?

MINNIE: *(off)* Come on. There's no need to be shy.

HAROLD enters with MINNIE. He is conservatively dressed but sports a white carnation.

MINNIE: *(to HAROLD)* That's Jacob and Mary. This here's Harold. *(They shake hands.)*

JACOB: Here give me your coats. *(He takes the coats.)*

MINNIE: T'anks, boy. *(to KATHY)* Hello, sister! Still mad at me? *(KATHY doesn't answer. To MARY.)* Harold works in a funeral parlour. He's an embalmer. Imagine. We met when poor Willard died. He worked on his corpse.

MARY: *(incredulously)* You made that up, Minnie. Confess.

MINNIE: As God is my witness, maid!

JACOB: Just as long as you'm not drumming up business, Harold.

HAROLD doesn't crack a smile.

MINNIE: He ain't got an ounce of humour in his body, Harold. *(looking at JACOB)* But he's got two or t'ree pounds of what counts. Don't you, Lazarus?

KATHY: *(sharply)* Mother!

MINNIE: "Mother" yourself. *(sitting on arm of chesterfield next to HAROLD)* I calls him Lazarus because he comes to life at night. And what a resurrection. Ah, I'm so wicked, Mary. To tell you the truth, I haven't been exactly mourning since Willard died, as sister over there can testify. And I'll tell you why. I took a good solid look at Willard—God rest his soul!—stretched out in his casket the t'ree days of his wake, all powdered and rouged and made up like a total stranger, and I says to myself, Minnie, live it up, maid. This is all there is, this life. You're dead a good long time. *(to JACOB)* And I for one wouldn't bet a t'in dime on the hereafter, and God knows I've t'rowed hundreds of dollars away on long shots in my day.

JACOB: Now, Minnie, enough of the religion. Would you both care for a whiskey? *(MARY reacts.)*

MINNIE: *(meaning HAROLD)* Look at his ears pick up. Sure, Jake. That's one of the reasons we come early. *(JACOB crosses to the cabinet during MINNIE's speech and brings out a bottle of whiskey. He pours three drinks.)* And Mary, I got to apologize for last night. I suppose I'll never live it down. I don't know what happened, maid. I laid down with a drink in me hand after supper and the next t'ing I know it's this morning and I'm in the doghouse.

MARY: That's okay, Minnie. *(She sits.)*

JACOB: Billy, my son, bring me the ginger ale. That's a good boy. *(During the dialogue BILL fetches the ginger ale from the fridge and returns to the dining room table.)* How do you like your drink, Minnie?

MINNIE: A little mix in mine, and not'ing in Harold's. The ginger ale tickles his nose and gets him all excited.

JACOB: What is he, Minnie? Newfie?

MINNIE: No, boy—Canadian.

JACOB: Harold, there's only two kinds of people in this world—Newfies and them that wishes they was.

MINNIE: That's what I tells him, boy.

JACOB: Why else would Canada have j'ined us in '49? Right, Minnie? *(JACOB crosses to chesterfield with the drinks.)*

MARY: I t'ought you didn't have no whiskey? I t'ought all you had in the house was "screech"? Do you mean to tell me that was deliberate, what you put Ben t'rough?

JACOB: *(quickly changing the subject)* Minnie, don't you want to see the shower gifts?

MINNIE: Sure, boy. Where's they to?

JACOB: They're in the bedroom. Show her, Mary. Now's a good time.

MARY rises and crosses to the bedroom door. MINNIE follows.

MINNIE: *(indicating HAROLD)* Don't give him any more to drink, Jacob, till I gets back. The bugger likes to get a head start.

They exit.

MINNIE: *(off)* Maid, will you look! A gift shop! Jesus!

JACOB: *(slight pause—to HAROLD, embarrassed)* Well.

HAROLD nods. They drink.

MINNIE: *(off)* Even a rolling pin! *(She pokes out her head.)* My Jesus, Harold, I finally found somet'ing that compares!

JACOB glances at HAROLD. HAROLD glances at JACOB. They drink.

JACOB: *(after a moment)* Grand old day.

HAROLD nods. Silence.

JACOB: *(after a moment)* Couldn't ask for better.

HAROLD nods. Silence.

JACOB: *(after a moment)* Another grand day tomorrow.

HAROLD clears his throat.

JACOB: Pardon?

HAROLD shakes his head. Silence.

JACOB: *(embarrassed)* Well, why don't we see what mischief the women are up to?

HAROLD nods. With visible relief both men exit together.

BILL: Tomorrow's off! We've got to tell them, Kathy! And right now!

KATHY: We don't have to call it off.

BILL: What do you mean?

KATHY: You know what I mean.

BILL: You mean you'd get married without having to?

KATHY: I work, you know. I'll be getting a raise in two months, and another six months after that. I'll be making good money by the time you get into university. I could help put you through. *(slight pause)* I wouldn't be in the way. *(slight pause)* Billy? Don't you even care for me?

BILL: Sure.

KATHY: How much?

Enter HAROLD. During the dialogue he helps himself to another drink from the dining room and crosses to the chesterfield.

BILL: A lot. But I still don't want to get married. I'm not ready. We're too young. Christ, you can't even cook!

KATHY: And you're just a mama's boy!

HAROLD is now seated. KATHY stares at him a moment. Then she smiles.

KATHY: Well, Harold wants me, even if you don't. Don't you, Harold? *(She rises and crosses to the chesterfield, flaunting herself.)*

BILL: Kathy!

KATHY: *(to HAROLD)* I've seen the way you look at me. *(She drops on the chesterfield beside HAROLD.)* You'd like to hop in the sack with me, wouldn't you? Tell the truth.

BILL: Why are you doing this?

KATHY: You think he's any different than you?

BILL: What do you mean?

KATHY: This makes you jealous, Billy? *(She caresses the inside of HAROLD's thigh.)*

BILL: *(grabbing her by the wrist)* I don't understand you, Kathy.

KATHY: I understand you, Billy. Only too well. Poor trapped Billy.

BILL: I'm not trapped.

KATHY: Aren't you?

BILL: No! I'll call it off!

KATHY: Yes! Why don't you?

BILL: I will!

KATHY: I wouldn't want you to waste your life. I'll bet now you wished you'd never met me, don't you? You wish you'd never touched me. All this trouble because you didn't have the nerve to go to the drugstore!

BILL: Well, why did you let me do it if it wasn't a safe time? Answer me that?

Enter MINNIE, JACOB, and MARY.

MINNIE: Well, kids, you're well off now. More than we got when we started out, heh, Mary? Willard and me didn't have a pot to piss in or a window to t'row it out. *(to JACOB, as she sits)* Where's your eldest? I ain't met him yet.

JACOB: Ben? Oh, he's in his bedroom— *(He glances at MARY who is now sitting in the armchair.)* —studying. He's in university, Minnie. *(He calls to BEN's door.)* Ben, come out. *(slight pause)* And bring your diploma. *(He glances sheepishly at MARY and looks away. MARY shakes her head, amused.)*

Enter BEN, dressed in a sport jacket. He carries his rolled-up diploma tied with a ribbon.

JACOB: Graduated from Grade T'irteen last night, Minnie. That's Ben. Ben, this is Mrs. Jackson, and that's Harold.

They all nod hello.

MINNIE: *(appraising BEN with obvious delight)* So this is the best man, heh? Well. Well, well, well. What a fine-looking boy, Jacob. He'll be tall.

JACOB: A little too t'in, Minnie. And not much colour to his face.

MINNIE: What odds? You was a skeleton yourself at his age. Tell you what, Ben. Be over some Saturday night and give you a scrubbing down in the tub. We'll send your father and mother to the pictures. *(to MARY)* Oh, how wicked, maid. Don't mind me, I've got the dirtiest tongue. The t'ings I comes out with. That's what comes of hanging around racetracks and taverns with the likes of the Formaldehyde Kid here. *(slight pause)* You looks like your mother's side of the family, Ben.

JACOB: I kind of t'ought he looked like my side. *(to BEN)* Show Minnie your diploma.

BEN hands the diploma to MINNIE.

MINNIE: *(to BEN)* Proud father.

BEN: *(to JACOB)* I thought you didn't have any whiskey?

JACOB: *(ignoring BEN and glancing over MINNIE's shoulder as she reads the diploma)* He got honours all the way t'rough high school, Minnie. He got a scholarship.

MINNIE: Where'd he get his brains to? *(embarrassed silence—to BEN)* Told you you look like your mother's side. *(She hands back the diploma, rises, and hands her glass to JACOB.)* Next round less ginger ale, Jacob. Gives me gas. *(crossing to the record player)* And I'd hate to start cracking off around Father Douglas. *(She puts on a record—"Moonglow" theme from* Picnic.*)* What a face he's on him, already, the priest. Pinched little mouth. You'd t'ink he just opened the Song of Solomon and found a fart pressed between the pages like a rose. *(She starts to move slowly to the music.)*

KATHY: Mother, do you have to?

MINNIE: Do I have to what, sister?

KATHY: Make a fool of yourself.

MINNIE: Listen to who's talking! *(slight pause)* I'd dance with Harold except the only tune he knows is the Death March. And the only step he knows is the foxtrot. Imagine foxtrotting to the Death March. *(to JACOB)* Jacob, you was a one for dancing years ago. Wasn't he, Mary?

MARY: He still is, Minnie.

MINNIE: Did he ever tell you how I first got to go out with him?

MARY: I don't believe he did.

MINNIE: He didn't? Well, remember Georgie Bishop? He took me out one night—to the Salvation Army dance at Bay Roberts. It was in the wintertime, and cold as a nun's tit. I saw Jacob there, hanging about, and now and then he'd look my way and I'd wink. Oh, I was some brazen.

JACOB: I t'ought you had somet'ing in your eye, Minnie.

MINNIE: Yes, boy, the same as was in yours— the devil! . . . To make a long story short, Mary, when it come time to go home, Georgie and me went outside where his horse and sled was hitched to the post. He'd tied it fast with a knot, and do you know what this bugger had gone and done?

JACOB: Now don't tell that, Minnie.

MINNIE: Pissed on the knot! He had, maid. A ball of ice as big as me fist. And who do you suppose walks up large as life and offers to drive me home in his sled? *(pause)* Poor Georgie. The last I remembers of him he was cursing the dirty son-of-a-bitch that had done it and was stabbing away at the knot with his jack-knife! *(She notices BEN's amused reaction to her story.)* Come dance with me, Ben. Don't be shy. Come on. If I'm not mistaken, you've got the devil in your

eye, too. Just like your father. *(She puts BEN's arm around her waist and they dance.)* Look, Harold. You might learn a t'ing or two. *(She presses close against BEN.)* Mmm. You know, Jacob, this is no longer a little boy. He's coming of age.

KATHY: Mother, you're dirty.

MINNIE: How fast you've grown, Ben. How tall and straight. Do you want to hear a funny one? I could have been your mother. Imagine. But your grandfather—Jacob's father—put his foot down. I was a Catholic, and that was that in no uncertain terms. Wasn't it, Jacob? *(slight pause)* So I married Willard . . . . *(They break apart. To JACOB, as she sits)* Ah, well, boy, I suppose it all worked out for the best. Just t'ink, Jacob—if you had married me it might have been you Harold pumped full of fluids.

JACOB: That it might, Minnie. That it might.

MINNIE: But you can't help marvel at the way t'ings work out. Makes you wonder sometimes.

JACOB: *(turns off music)* What's that, Minnie?

MINNIE: Your son marrying my daughter and turning Catholic in the bargain. Serves you right you old bugger. The last laugh's on you. *And* your poor old father.

JACOB: You'm not still carrying that grudge around inside you, is you? I'm getting a fine girl in the family. That's the way I looks at it.

MINNIE: *(rising to help herself to another drink)* I don't mind telling you, Jacob, I've had my hands full with *that* one. Not a moment's peace since the day poor Willard died. She was kind of stuck on her father, you know. Jesus, boy, she won't even speak to Harold. Won't let him give her away tomorrow, will you, sister? Her uncle's doing that. Oh, she snaps me head off if I as much as makes a suggestion. T'inks she knows it all. And now look. All I can say is I'm glad her father ain't alive, this night.

JACOB: Now, Minnie, you knows you don't mean all that. Own up to it.

MINNIE: Oh, I means it, boy, and more. T'ank God it's only the second month. At least she don't show yet. If she's anyt'ing like me, she'll have a bad time. Well, a little pain'll teach her a good lesson.

KATHY: I wish you wouldn't talk about me like that, Mother.

MINNIE: Like what?

KATHY: Like I was invisible. I don't like it; I've told you before.

JACOB: Now, now, Kathy.

MINNIE: Listen to her, will you? Invisible. Sister, you may soon wish you *was* invisible, when the girls from work start counting back on the office calender.

KATHY: Let them count!

MINNIE: See, Jacob? See what I'm up against? No shame!

JACOB: Minnie, let's not have any hard feelings. It's most time for church. I'll get the coats.

MARY: Yes, do.

JACOB gets MINNIE's and MARY's coats.

MINNIE: *(crossing to BEN)* You don't know, Mary, how fortunate you is having sons. That's the biggest letdown of me life, not having a boy . . . . We couldn't have any but the one . . . *(bitterly)* and that had to be the bitch of the litter. How I curse the day. A boy like this must be a constant joy, Mary.

MARY: And a tribulation, maid.

MINNIE: Yes, but look at all the worry a daughter brings. *(as JACOB helps her into her coat)* This is the kind of fix she can get herself into.

KATHY: Mother, I just asked you not to.

BILL: Tell her, Kathy.

MINNIE: And then to top it off who gets the bill for the wedding? Oh, it's just dandy having a daughter, just dandy. I could wring her neck.

BILL: Kathy.

KATHY: *(to BILL)* You tell her.

MINNIE: If I had my own way I know what I'd do with all the bitches at birth. I'd do with them exactly what we did back home with the kittens—

KATHY: I'm not pregnant!

MINNIE: What?

KATHY: *(bitterly)* You heard me. I'm not pregnant.

MINNIE: What do you mean you're not? You are so, unless you've done somet'ing to yourself . . . .

KATHY: I didn't.

MARY: Kathy.

MINNIE: I took you to the doctor myself. I was in his office. Why in hell do you suppose you're getting married tomorrow, if it's not because you're having a baby?

KATHY: *(turning to MARY)* Mrs. Mercer, I had a miscarriage . . . .

MINNIE: A miscarriage . . .

MARY: When, Kathy? *(She puts her arms around KATHY.)*

KATHY: This morning. I went to the doctor. There's no mistake. And I didn't anything to myself, Mother.

MINNIE: *(quietly)* Did I say you did, sister?

MARY: Sit down, dear. *(She helps KATHY sit— long pause.)* This may not be the right moment to mention it, Minnie, but . . . well, it seems to me t'ings have altered somewhat. *(She looks at BEN.)* T'ings are back to the way they used to be. The youngsters don't need to get married. There's no reason to, now.

Pause. No one moves except HAROLD who raises his glass to drink.

BLACKOUT

ACT TWO

A moment later. As the lights come up, the actors are in the exact positions and attitudes they were in at the end of Act One. The tableau dissolves into action.

JACOB: Sit down, Minnie. We've got to talk this out. *(to KATHY)* Can I get you anyt'ing, my dear?

KATHY shakes her head. MINNIE sits.

MINNIE: *(slight pause)* What time is it getting to be?

BEN: Seven-fifteen.

MINNIE: The priest expects us there sharp at eight. He's got a mass to say at half-past.

MARY: Now wait just a minute. I t'ink you're being hasty, Minnie. The children can please themselves, now, what they wants to do. Maybe they don't want to get married.

JACOB: Mary's right, Minnie. Ask them.

MINNIE: For someone who don't like to butt in, maid, you got a lot to say sometimes. Stay out of it or I might say somet'ing I'm sorry for.

MARY: I can't stay out of it. I wouldn't advise my worst enemy to jump into marriage that young, and neither would you, Minnie. They'd be far better off waiting till Billy finishes university . . . .

MINNIE: Well, maybe *they* can afford to put it off, but *I* sure as hell can't. The invitations are out . . . the cake's bought, and the dress . . . the flowers arranged for . . . the photographer . . . the priest and organist hired . . . the church and banquet hall rented . . . the food—

KATHY: *(jumping up)* I don't want to get married!

MARY: What?

MINNIE: What? Don't believe her, Mary. She do so. She's got a stack of love comics a mile high. *(to KATHY)* Now you shut your mouth, sister, or I'll shut it for you.

KATHY: I won't.

MINNIE: You knows what'll happen if you backs out now? I'll be made a laughing stock. Is that what you wants, you little bitch?

KATHY: Don't call me a bitch, you old slut!

MARY: Kathy.

MINNIE: *(to JACOB)* Did you hear that? Why, I'll slap the face right off her! *(She goes after KATHY.)*

JACOB: *(keeping MINNIE away from her daughter)* All right, now. This is no way to behave. Tonight of all nights!

KATHY: That's what you are, an old cow! He only wants you for your money. *(indicating HAROLD)*

MINNIE: That's a lie.

KATHY: Is it?

MINNIE: That's a lie. Let me at her, Jacob. I'll knock her to kingdom come.

JACOB: Enough, goddamn it! Both of you! *(Silence)* That's better. Let's all ca'm down. We could all learn a lesson from Harold here. He's civilized. *(slight pause)* What we need's a drink.

MINNIE: *(as JACOB refills the glasses)* Imagine. My own flesh and blood, and she's got it in for me. She's never had much use for me, and even less since I took up with Harold here. She'll say anyt'ing to get back at me. Anyt'ing!

JACOB: Kathy's had a bad time of it, Minnie. No doubt she's upset. *(to MARY)* Remember how you was, when we lost our first? Didn't care if she lived or died. Didn't care if she ever laid eyes on me again, she was that down in the dumps. And I'm surprised, Billy. Not once have you come to her defence or spoken a word of comfort. You've got to be more of a man than that.

BEN: Why can't they get married and Billy still go to school?

MARY: *(to BEN)* Mind your business.

MINNIE: You hear that, Jacob? That's the one with all the brains.

BEN: *(to MARY)* I'm just trying to help.

MARY: Who? Yourself?

KATHY: I want him to, Mrs. Mercer. He doesn't have to quit school. I like to work. Honest.

MARY: Well, Billy, you're the only one we haven't heard from. What do you say?

JACOB: Ah, what's it matter if he gets married now or after university? He won't do much better than Kathy.

MINNIE: She's a good girl, in spite of what I said about her. A hard worker. She always pays her board sharp. And clean as a whistle.

JACOB: That's settled, then.

MARY: Is it, Billy?

JACOB: For God's sake, Mary.

MARY: He's got a tongue of his own. Let him answer. The poor child can't get a word in edgewise.

JACOB: Stop smothering him. He's a man now. Let him act like one. *(amused)* Besides, he's just getting cold feet. Ain't you, my son?

BEN: Did you get cold feet, Dad?

JACOB: All men do. *(MARY glances at JACOB who nudges her.)* Even the best of us. He'll be fine after tomorrow.

MINNIE: T'anks, Jacob. I could kiss you. Now, Harold, wait your turn, and don't be jealous. *(She crosses to the record player and selects a record.)* The mother of the bride and the father of the groom will now have the next dance. With your permission, Mary?

MARY: With my blessing, maid.

JACOB: *(glancing at MARY)* I don't know whether I'm up to it, Minnie.

MINNIE: Go on, Jacob. You'll be dancing a jig at your own wake.

Music: "Isle of Newfoundland." JACOB takes MINNIE in his arms and they dance. BILL goes to KATHY, takes her hand and leads her into the darkened kitchen. They make up.

MINNIE: Ah, Jacob, remember when we'd hug and smooch in the darkest places on the dance floor? The way he stuck to the shadows, Mary, you'd swear he was a bat. Dance with her, Harold. *(indicating MARY)* He's some wonderful dancer, boy. Went to Arthur Murray's. He's awful shy, though.

MARY and HAROLD exchange glances. HAROLD clears his throat.

MINNIE: Ah, boy, Jacob, I'd better give Harold a turn. He'd sit there all night looking anxious. He likes a good foxtrot. Fancies himself Valentino. Come on, Lazarus.

MINNIE and HAROLD dance. JACOB crosses to MARY who is sitting behind dining room table.

JACOB: Dance, Mary?

MARY: You'll make a good match, the two of you.

JACOB: Mary, I t'ink you'm jealous.

MARY: Don't be foolish. And don't start showing off. That's the next step.

JACOB: "How beautiful are thy feet with shoes, O prince's daughter! The j'ints of thy t'ighs are like jewels, the work of the hands of a cunning workman.

"Thy navel is like a round goblet, which wanteth not liquor: thy belly is like—"

MARY: *(sharply)* Jacob!

JACOB: "—an heap of wheat set about with lilies.

"Thy two breasts"—

MARY: All right, boy—enough!

JACOB: *(sitting)* Do you remember, Mary, when you was just a piss-tail maid picking blueberries on the cliffs behind your father's house, your poor knees tattooed from kneeling? Did you ever t'ink for a single minute that one day you'd be the mother of grown-up sons and one of 'em about to start a life of his own?

MARY: No, and that I didn't. In those days I couldn't see no further ahead than you charging down Country Road on your old white horse to whisk me away to the mainland.

JACOB: Any regrets?

MARY: What does you t'ink?

JACOB: Ah, go on with you. *(pause)* The old house seems smaller already, don't it?

MARY: Empty.

MINNIE: *(still dancing)* Tomorrow's a landmark for us all, Jacob. I lose me only daughter and you lose your two sons. *(JACOB reacts.)* Somehow I don't envy you, boy. I t'ink it'll be harder on you. If I had sons . . .

JACOB crosses quickly to the record player and switches it off.

JACOB: What was that you just said, Minnie? Did I hear you correct? Whose sons?

MINNIE: Yours.

JACOB: Mine? Only one's going.

MINNIE: Didn't anybody tell you?

JACOB: Tell me what? I'm lucky to get the time of day. *(to MARY)* Tell me what?

MARY: Ben's moving in with Bill and Kathy. Taking their spare room.

JACOB: He is like hell!

BEN: I am!

JACOB: You'm not!

BEN: I am!

JACOB: Don't be foolish!

MINNIE: I t'ought he knowed, Mary. I t'ought the kids had told him.

JACOB: No, Minnie, they neglected to mention it. I'm not surprised!

MINNIE: I wouldn't have put me big foot in me mouth otherwise.

JACOB: Why should I know any more what goes on in my own house than the stranger on the street? I'm only his father. I'm not the one they all confides in around this house, I can tell you. I'm just the goddamn old fool. That's all! The goddamn fool.

BEN: I wanted to tell you after the wedding.

JACOB: Yes, you did so.

BEN: I would have sooner, but this is what happens.

JACOB: Oh, so now it's all my fault?

BEN: I didn't say that. Stop twisting what I say.

JACOB: How quick you is to shift the blame, my son. (to MARY) How come you to know? He was quick enough to run to you with the news, wasn't he?

MARY: I can't help that.

JACOB: Yes, you can. I'm always the last to find out, and you'm the reason, Mary. You'm the ring-leader. The t'ree of you against the one of me.

MARY: And you talks about shifting the blame.

JACOB: Wasn't I the last to find out Billy was getting married? He told you first, but did you come and confide in me? That you didn't. If I hadn't found that bill from Ostranders for Kathy's engagement ring . . . !

BILL: We would have told you . . .

JACOB: A lot of respect you show for your father. A lot of respect. You'm no better than your brother.

MARY: Ca'm down, boy. You're just getting yourself all worked up.

JACOB: I won't ca'm down. Ca'm down. All I ever does is break my back for their good and comfort, and how is it they repays me? A slap in the face! (to BEN) What did you have in mind to do, my son? Sneak off with all your belongings, like a t'ief, while your father was at work?

BEN: Go to hell.

JACOB: What did you say?

BEN: You heard me. I don't have to take shit like that from anyone. And I don't care who's here!

JACOB takes a threatening step toward his son. MARY steps between.

JACOB: I'll knock your goddamn block off!

MARY: Now just stop it, the both of you! Stop it!

MINNIE: I'd never have gotten away with that from my father. He'd have tanned me good.

MARY: And Minnie—mind your own business. This is none of your concern.

JACOB: Talking like that to his own father . . .

BEN: And if you ever hit me again . . . !

JACOB: I'll hit you in two seconds flat, if you carries on. Just keep it up. Don't t'ink for one minute you'm too old yet!

BEN: Come on. Hit me. I'm not scared. Hit me. You'd never see me again!

MARY: (slapping BEN) Shut right up. You're just as bad as he is!

MINNIE: Two of a kind, maid. Two peas in a pod. That's why they don't get on.

JACOB: Why the hell do you suppose we slaved to buy this house, if it wasn't for you two? And now you won't stick around long enough to help pay back a red cent. You'd rather pay rent to a stranger!

BILL: Dad, I'm leaving to get married, in case you forgot.

JACOB: You don't need to. Put it off. Listen to your mother!

BILL: A minute ago you said—

JACOB: Forget a minute ago! This is now!

BEN: He'll have converted for nothing, if he does!

JACOB: You shut your bloody mouth! *(to BILL)* Put it off, my son. There's no hurry. Don't be swayed by Minnie. She's just t'inking of herself. Getting revenge for old hurts.

MINNIE: And you're full of shit, Jacob.

JACOB: You goddamn Catholics, you don't even believe in birth control. Holy Jumping Jesus Christ. The poor young boy'll be saddled with a gang of little ones before he knows it! And all because my poor father hated the Micks!

MINNIE: Come on, sister, we don't need that. Get your coat. You, too, Harold. Let's go, Billy. The priest can't wait on the likes of us.

BILL and KATHY move to go.

JACOB: Don't go, Billy. There's no need!

BILL: First you say one thing, Dad, and then you say something else. Will you please make up your mind! *(to BEN)* Ben, what should I do? Tell me.

BEN: I can't help you, Billy.

KATHY looks at BILL, then runs out, slamming the door.

MARY: *(to BILL)* Go after her, my son. Now's the time she needs you. We'll see you in church. Go on, now.

BILL: Ben?

BEN: In a minute. I'll see you there.

BILL: Dad? *(JACOB turns away. BILL runs out.)*

MINNIE: I'll take the two kids with me, Mary. See you in a few minutes.

JACOB: You won't see me there tonight, Minnie, and you can count on that. And not tomorrow, either.

MINNIE: That's up to you, Jacob, though I hope you changes your mind for Billy's sake. *(slight pause)* We oughtn't to let our differences interfere with the children. *(slight pause)* Come along, Lazarus. It's time we dragged our backsides to the church.

They exit. Silence. MARY removes her coat, then slowly begins to clear the table. BEN looks over at his father. Finally he speaks.

BEN: Dad . . .

JACOB: What?

BEN: I want to explain. Will you let me?

JACOB: I should t'ink you'd be ashamed to even look at me, let alone open your mouth. *(slight pause)* Well? What is it? I suppose we'm not good enough for you?

BEN: Oh, come on.

JACOB: *(to MARY)* If you's going to the church, you'd better be off.

BEN: We still have a few minutes.

JACOB: *(to MARY)* And no odds what, I won't go to church. They can do without me.

MARY: Suit yourself. But I'm going. Just don't come back on me afterwards for not coaxing you to.

JACOB: You can walk in that church tonight, feeling the way you does? Oh, you'm some two-faced, Mary.

MARY: Don't you talk. You was quite willing to see Billy go, till it slipped out that Ben was going, too.

JACOB: That's a lie!

MARY: Is it?

JACOB: That's a damn lie!

MARY: I'll call a cab. *(She crosses to the phone, picks up the receiver. To JACOB.)* We can't always have it our way. *(She dials and ad libs softly while dialogue continues between father and son.)*

JACOB: A lifetime spent in this house, and he gives us less notice than you would a landlord! And me about to wallpaper his room like a god-damn fool! *(slight pause)* And don't come back broke and starving in a week or two and expect a handout, 'cause the only way you'll get t'rough that door is to break it in! *(slight pause)* You'll never last on your own. You never had to provide for yourself.

BEN: I'll learn.

JACOB: You'll starve.

BEN: All right, I'll starve. And then you can have the satisfaction of being right. *(slight pause)* You're always telling me it's time I got out on my own and grew up.

JACOB: Sure, t'row up in my face what I said in the past!

BEN: Dad, will you listen to me for once? It's not because home's bad, or because I hate you. It's not that. I just want to be independent, that's all. Can't you understand that? *(slight pause)* I had to move out sometime.

JACOB: Was it somet'ing I said? What was it? Tell me. I must have said somet'ing!

BEN: No, it was nothing you said. Will you come off it?

JACOB: Can you imagine what our relatives will say, once they hears? They'll say you left home on account of me.

BEN: Well, who the hell cares?

JACOB: And you any idea what this'll do to your mother? You'm her favourite. *(The last syllable rhymes with "night.")*

MARY: Jacob! That's not fair!

JACOB: What odds? It's true, and don't deny it. *(to BEN)* Your mother's always been most fond of you. She even delivered you herself. Did you know that?

MARY: There's no time for family history, Father.

JACOB moves quickly to the mantel and takes the photo album. He is slightly desperate now. He flicks open the album.

JACOB: *(intimately, to BEN)* Look. Look at that one. You could scarcely walk. Clinging for dear life to your mother's knee. *(turning the page)* And look at this. The four of us. Harry Saunders took that of us with my old box camera the day the Germans marched into Paris. *(Turns the photo over)* There. You'm good with dates. June 14, 1940. Look how lovely your mother looks, my son. No more than ninety pounds when she had you.

MARY: Ninety-one.

JACOB: She was that t'in, you'd swear the wind would carry her off. We never believed we'd have another, after the first died. He was premature. Seven months, and he only lived a few hours.

MARY: Enough of the past, boy.

JACOB: That was some night, the night you was born. Blizzarding to beat hell. The doctor lived in Bay Roberts, and I had to hitch up the sled—

MARY: He's heard all that.

JACOB: Some woman, your mother. Cut and tied the cord herself. Had you scrubbed to a shine and was washed herself and back in bed, sound asleep, before we showed up.

MARY: Took all the good out of me, too.

JACOB: And wasn't she a picture? She could have passed for her namesake in the stained glass of a Catholic window, she was that radiant.

MARY: Get on with you.

JACOB: Your mother'd never let on, but you can imagine the state she'll be in if you goes. You'm all that's left now, Ben. The last son. *(a whisper)* I t'ink she wishes you'd stay.

MARY: I heard that. Look, you speak for yourself. I've interfered enough for one night.

JACOB: Your mother has always lived just for the two of you.

MARY: *(pained)* Oh, Jacob.

JACOB: Always.

BEN: Come on, Dad, that's not true.

JACOB: It is so, now. It is so.

MARY: Well, it's not, and don't you say it is. The likes of that!

JACOB: Confess, Mary. I don't count, I've never counted. Not since the day they was born.

BEN: If that's true, Dad, you should be glad to get rid of both of us. Have Mom all to yourself again.

JACOB: Don't be smart.

MARY: Who's the one making all the fuss? Me or you? Answer me that.

JACOB: No, you'd sit by silent and let me do it for you and take all the shit that comes with it. I'm wise to your little games.

MARY: I can't stop him, if he wants to go. I don't like it any more than you do. I can't imagine this house without our two sons. But if what Ben wants is to go, he's got my blessing. I won't stand in his way because I'm scared. And if you can't speak for yourself, don't speak for me. I'm out of it.

JACOB: If he's so dead set on going, he can march out the door this very minute.

MARY: He will not! Don't be foolish!

JACOB: He will so, if I say so! *(He charges into BEN's bedroom and returns with a suitcase which he sets on the floor.)* There! Pack your belongings right this second, if we'm not good enough for you.

MARY: Ben, don't pay him no mind.

JACOB: I don't want you in this house another minute, if you'm that anxious to be elsewhere. Ingrate!

MARY: If you don't shut your big yap, he just might, and then you'd be in some state.

JACOB: Oh, I would, would I? Well, we'll just see about that. I'll help him pack, if he likes! *(He charges into BEN's bedroom.)*

MARY: Ben, don't talk back to him when he's mad. It only makes it worse, you knows that.

JACOB: *(comes out with a stack of record albums which he hurls violently to the floor)* There. Enough of that goddamn squealing and squawking. Now I can get some peace and quiet after a hard day's work.

BEN: Dad, I think I ought to . . .

JACOB: Don't open your mouth. I don't want to hear another word!

BEN: All right, make a fool of yourself!

JACOB: *(to MARY)* And that goes for you too! *(He charges back into the bedroom.)*

BEN: What'll we do, Mom? We got to get out of here. Can't you stop him?

MARY: All you can do, when he gets like this, is let him run down and tire himself out. His poor father was the same. He'd hurl you t'rough the window one minute and brush the glass off you the next.

JACOB: *(comes out with a stack of new shirts still in the cellophane)* And look at this, will you? Talk about a sin. I walks around with my ass out, and here's six new shirts never even opened. *(He hurls the shirts on the pile of records.)*

BEN: I don't want to spoil your fun, Dad, but so far all that stuff belongs to Billy. *(JACOB stares at the scattered records and shirts, alarmed.)*

MARY: Now you've done it, boy. Will you sit down now? You're just making a bigger fool of yourself the longer you stands.

JACOB: *(Her reproach is all he needs to get back in stride.)* Sure, mock me when I'm down. Well, I'll show you who the fool is. We'll just see who has the last laugh! *(He charges into his own bedroom. MARY picks up the records and shirts.)*

BEN: *(pause)* I wanted to tell him, Mom, a week ago. I kept putting it off.

MARY: I wish you had, Ben. This mightn't have happened.

BEN: It's all our fault, anyhow.

MARY: What do you mean?

BEN: We've made him feel like an outsider all these years. The three of us. You, me, Billy. It's always been him and us. Always. As long as I can remember.

MARY: Blame your father's temper. He's always had a bad temper. All we done was try our best to avoid it.

BEN: Yeah, but we make it worse. We feed it. We shouldn't shut him out the way we do.

MARY: And what is it you're not saying, that's it's my fault somehow? Is that what you t'inks? Say it.

BEN: I didn't say that.

MARY: Your father believes it. He calls me the ringleader.

BEN: Well, you set the example, Mom, a long time ago. When we were little.

MARY: Don't you talk, Ben. You're some one to point fingers. *(slight pause)* Perhaps I did.

Perhaps your father's right all along. But you're no little child any longer, and you haven't been for years. You're a man now, and you never followed anyone's example for too long unless you had a mind to. So don't use that excuse.

BEN: I'm not. I'm just as much to blame as anybody. I know that.

MARY: I always tried to keep the peace. And that wasn't always easy in this family, with you and your father at each other's t'roats night and day. And to keep the peace I had to sometimes keep a good many unpleasant facts from your father. Small, simple t'ings, mostly.

BEN: You were just sparing yourself.

MARY: I was doing what I considered the most good! And don't tell me I wasn't. Oh, Ben, you knows yourself what he's like. If you lost five dollars down the sewer, you didn't dare let on. If you did, he'd dance around the room like one leg was on fire and the other had a bee up it. It was just easier that way, not to tell him. Easier on the whole family. Yes, and easier on myself.

BEN: But it wasn't easier when he found out. On him *or* us.

MARY: He didn't always, Ben.

BEN: No, but when he does, like tonight—it's worse!

JACOB enters the room from the bedroom, slowly, carrying a small cardboard box. He removes the contents of the box—a neatly folded silk dressing gown—and throws the box to one side.

JACOB: I won't be needing the likes of this. Take it with you. I've got enough old junk cluttering up my closet.

BEN: I don't want it, either.

MARY: He gave you that for your birthday. You've never even worn it.

JACOB: Take it! *(He hurls it violently in BEN's face. Then he notices the diploma lying on the table. He grabs it.)*

MARY: Not the diploma, Jacob! No!

BEN says nothing. He just stares at his father, who stares back the whole time he removes the ribbon, unfolds the diploma, and tears it into two

pieces, then four, then eight. He drops the pieces to the floor.

MARY: God help you. This time you've gone too far.

Pause. Then BEN crosses to the suitcase. He picks it up.

BEN: I'll pack. *(He exits into his bedroom.)*

MARY: All right. You satisfied? You've made me feel deeply ashamed tonight, Jacob, the way you treats Ben. I only hopes he forgives you. I don't know if I would, if it was me.

JACOB: I always knowed it would come to this one day. He's always hated me, and don't say he hasn't. Did you see him tonight? I can't so much as lay a hand on his shoulder. He pulls away. His own father, and I can't touch him. All his life long he's done nothing but mock and defy me, and now he's made me turn him out in anger, my own son. *(to MARY, angrily)* And you can bugger off, too, if you don't like it. Don't let me keep you. Just pack your bag and take him with you. Dare say you'd be happier off. I don't give a good goddamn if the whole lot of you deserts me.

MARY: You don't know when to stop, do you? You just don't know when to call a halt. What must I do? Knock you senseless? You'd go on and on until you brought your whole house tumbling down. I suppose it's late in the day to be expecting miracles, but for God's sake, Jacob, control yourself. For once in your life would you just t'ink before you speaks? *Please!* *(slight pause)* I have no sympathy for you. You brought this all on yourself. You wouldn't listen. Well, listen now. Have you ever in your whole life took two minutes out to try and understand him? Have you? Instead of galloping off in all directions? Dredging up old hurts? Why, not five minutes ago he stood on that exact spot and stuck up for you!

JACOB: *(surprised, slightly incredulous)* Ben did . . . ?

MARY: Yes, Ben did, and don't look so surprised. Now it may be too late, but there are some t'ings that just have to be said, right now, in the open. Sit down and listen. Sit down. *(JACOB sits.)* For twenty years now I've handled the purse strings in this family, and only because you shoved it off on me. I don't like to do it any more than you do. I'm just as bad at it, except you're better with the excuses. *(JACOB rises.)* I'm not finished. Sit down. *(He does—slight pause.)* Last fall you tumbled off our garage roof and sprained your back. You was laid up for six months all told—November to May—without a red cent of Workmen's Compensation, because the accident didn't happen on the job. And I made all the payments as usual—the mortgages, your truck, the groceries, life insurance, the hydro and oilman, your union dues. All that, and more. I took care of it all. And where, Jacob, do you suppose the money came from? You never once asked. Did you ever wonder?

JACOB: Where? From the bank.

MARY: The bank! We didn't have a nickel in the bank. Not after the second month.

JACOB: What is you getting at, Mary?

MARY: Just this. (She lowers her voice.) If Ben hadn't got a scholarship, he wouldn't have went to college this fall. He couldn't have afforded to. It was his money that took us over the winter. All those years of working part-time and summers. All of it gone.

JACOB: Ben did that?

MARY: And you says he hates you!

JACOB: I don't want no handouts from him. I'll pay him back every cent of it.

MARY: Shut up. He'll hear you! He never wanted you to know, so don't you dare let on that I told you, you hear? He knowed how proud you is, and he knowed you wouldn't want to t'ink you wasn't supporting your family. (slight pause) Now, boy, who's got the last laugh? (MARY takes her coat and puts it on as she crosses to BEN's door.) Hurry up, Ben. The taxi ought to be here any second. (She turns and looks at JACOB. There is anguish in her face. When she speaks her voice is drained.) I'm tired, Jacob. And you ought to be, too, by all rights. It's time to quit it. A lifetime of this is enough, you and Ben. Declare it an even match for your own sake, boy, if for nothing else. I don't want to see you keep getting the worst of it. You always did and you still do.

Enter BEN, carrying his suitcase.

BEN: (to MARY) Isn't the cab here yet? It's almost eight.

MARY: He'll beep his horn. (slight pause) You don't need to take that now, my son. Pick it up later.

BEN: That's okay, Mom. I've got all I want. The rest you can throw out. (He sits on his suitcase.)

JACOB: Your mother told me what you done last winter. I—

MARY: (sharply) Jacob!

JACOB: I wants to t'ank you. I'll pay you back.

MARY: You promised you— (She stops, shakes her head in exasperation.)

JACOB: (Slight pause) I'm sorry what happened here tonight. I wants you to know that. I'll make it up to you. I will.

BEN: (meaning it) It's nothing. Forget it.

MARY: Let him say he's sorry, Ben. He needs to.

JACOB: Maybe I've been wrong. I suppose I ain't been the best of fathers. I couldn't give you all I'd like to. But I've been the best I could under the circumstances.

BEN: Dad.

JACOB: Hear me out, now. We never seen eye to eye in most cases, but we'm still a family. We've got to stick together. All we got in this world is the family— (He rises.) —and it's breaking up, Ben. (slight pause) Stay for a while longer. For a few more years.

BEN: I can't.

JACOB: You can. Why not?

BEN: I just can't.

JACOB: Spite! You'm just doing this out of spite! (BEN shakes his head.) Then reconsider . . . like a good boy. Let your brother rent his room to a stranger, if he's that hard up. Don't let him break us up.

The taxi sounds its horn.

MARY: There's the taxi now.

JACOB: (desperately) You don't have to go, my son. You knows I never meant what I said before. You'm welcome to stay as long as you likes, and you won't have to pay a cent of rent. (even more desperately) Come back afterwards!

BEN: No, Dad.

JACOB: Yes, come back. Like a good boy. I never had a choice in my day, Ben. You do.

BEN: I don't!

JACOB: You do so! Don't contradict me!

BEN: What do you know? You don't know the first thing about me, and you don't want to. You don't know how I feel, and you don't give a shit!

JACOB: In my day we had a duty to—

BEN: In your day! I'm sick of hearing about your fucking day! This is *my* day, and we're strangers. You know the men you work with better than you do me! Isn't that right? Isn't it?

JACOB: And you treats your friends better than you do me! I know *that* much, I can tell you. A whole lot better! And with more respect. Using language like that in front of your mother!

The taxi honks impatiently. BEN moves to go. JACOB grabs the suitcase.

MARY: Jacob! The taxi's waiting!

JACOB: *(to BEN)* You're not taking that suitcase out of this house! Not this blessed day! *(He puts the suitcase down at a distance.)*

MARY: That's okay, Ben. Leave it. You can come back some other time. *(MARY exits.)*

JACOB: He will like hell. Once he goes, that's it. He came with nothing, he'll go with nothing!

BEN: *(slight pause)* Do you know why I want to be on my own? The real reason?

JACOB: To whore around!

BEN: Because you're not going to stop until there's nothing left of me. It's not the world that wants to devour me, Dad—it's you!

JACOB whips off his belt.

JACOB: *(as he brings it down hard on BEN's back)* Then go!

BEN instinctively covers his head, crouching a little, unprotesting.

JACOB: *(sobbing, as he brings the belt down again and again)* Go! Go! Go! Go! Go!

Finally as JACOB swings again for the sixth time, BEN whirls and grabs the belt from his father's hand. Then with a violent motion he flings it aside.

BEN: You shouldn't have done that, Dad. You shouldn't. *(He exits.)*

Silence. JACOB retrieves his belt. A slight pause.

JACOB: *(fiercely striking the chesterfield with his belt)* Holy Jumping Jesus Christ!

Silence. MARY enters from the hallway. JACOB begins to put on his belt. He notices MARY.

JACOB: What's you doing here? Isn't you going? *(He crosses into the dining room and sits at the table.)*

Slowly MARY puts down her purse and enters the dining room, crossing behind JACOB and sitting at the table beside him. She says nothing.

JACOB: *(anguished)* In the name of Jesus, Mary, whatever possessed you to marry the likes of me over Jerome McKenzie? *(MARY says nothing, Pause.)* I've never asked you before, but I've always wondered.

Pause.

MARY: It was that day you, me, and Jerome McKenzie was all sitting around my mother's kitchen and in walked my brother Clifford. He was teaching Grade Six in St. John's that year, and he told of a story that occurred that very morning at school. You've most likely forgotten. A little girl had come into his class with a note from her teacher. She was told to carry the note around to every class in the school and wait till every teacher read it. Clifford did, with the child standing next to him. The note had t'ree words on it: *Don't she smell?* Well, Jacob, boy, when you heard that, you brought your fist down so hard on the tabletop it cracked one of Mother's good saucers, and that's when I knowed Jerome McKenzie hadn't a hope in hell. *(slight pause)* Q.C. or no Q.C.!

Slowly MARY lifts one foot then the other onto the chair in front of her. The lights slowly dim into darkness.

END

RICK SALUTIN and THEATRE PASSE MURAILLE

(b. 1942)

In his production diary of *1837*, the original version of *1837: The Farmers' Revolt*, Rick Salutin remarks how the opening night audience in Toronto laughed at the mention of Bay and Adelaide, a downtown intersection. That reaction brought into sharp focus for Salutin the reasons for having created the play in the first place, the bizarre attitudes typically held by Canadians towards their own history. "We are so imbued with self-denial," he concluded, "so colonized, that the very thought of something historic happening *here*, at Bay and Adelaide, draws laughs." His ongoing project and that of Theatre Passe Muraille under Paul Thompson was to get Canadian audiences to laugh at themselves in the *right* places, presenting the everyday life and history of Canadians in theatrically playful and often brilliantly comical ways while at the same time insisting that they are subjects worthy of serious dramatic treatment.

Ironically, the man *Maclean's* has called "the country's foremost nationalist playwright" was educated almost entirely in the United States. Between 1960 and 1970 Salutin earned a B.A. in Near Eastern and Judaic Studies at Brandeis University, an M.A. in religion from Columbia, and was doing a Ph.D. in philosophy at New York's New School when he decided to return home to Toronto in 1970 after reading Harold Innis' *The Fur Trade in Canada*, an economic history that Salutin says "made sense of the present by making sense of the past." While working as a journalist and trade union organizer, he wrote his first play, *Fanshen*, produced in 1972 by Toronto Workshop Productions. An adaptation of William Hinton's classic study of the effects of the Chinese Revolution on the life of a small village, the play epitomizes Salutin's concern with the way history and politics are enacted in the daily lives of ordinary people. That concern would be at the heart of his next project, *1837*.

While Salutin was studying in the United States, Paul Thompson was getting an eclectic education in Canada and abroad: a B.A. in English and French from the University of Western Ontario in 1963 followed by a year at the Sorbonne; an M.A. in history at the University of Toronto in 1965 followed by two years' theatrical apprenticeship with Roger Planchon in Lyons. Thompson returned to Canada in 1967 and finally planted himself in Toronto with Theatre Passe Muraille just about the time Salutin came home. By the fall of 1972 when Thompson, Salutin and six Passe Muraille actors set to work creating *1837*, Thompson had been artistic director for a year and had already put his strong personal stamp on the company with innovative productions of Carol Bolt's *Buffalo Jump* and the collectively created *Doukhobors* and *The Farm Show*. The essence of Thompson's dramaturgy, as Brian Arnott has pointed out, "was a conscientious effort to give theatrical validity to sounds, rhythms and myths that were distinctively Canadian." The political and theatrical interests of Salutin and Thompson meshed perfectly with the skills of the Passe Muraille company on *1837* and a year later on *1837: The Farmers' Revolt*, which became one of the most popular plays in the Canadian repertoire.

Thompson continued on as artistic director until succeeded by Clarke Rogers in 1982, after which he pursued freelance projects and became director of the National Theatre School in 1987. He returned to Passe Muraille in 1993 to direct a new collective titled *Urban Donnellys*. Theatre Passe Muraille itself underwent a series of artistic and financial crises, and gradually dissociated itself from the collective process, but remained a major force in the development of new Canadian plays throughout the 80s and into the 90s under Rogers and his successors.

Meanwhile, Salutin worked with Passe Muraille again on the collective *Adventures of an Immigrant* (1974) and on his own plays *The False Messiah* (1975) and *Nathan Cohen: A Review* (1981). He also pursued the collective form with two Newfoundland companies in theatrical examinations of that province's history, *I.W.A.* with the Mummers Troupe (1976) and *Joey* with Rising Tide (1982). His play about hockey and nationalism in Quebec, *Les Canadiens*, first produced at the Centaur in 1977, won the Chalmers Award and has been widely performed across Canada. He collaborated with Ian Adams on the stage version of *S: Portrait of a Spy* (1984) for Ottawa's Great Canadian Theatre Company and wrote *Grierson and Gouzenko* (1986), a CBC-TV drama. He also wrote *The Reluctant Patriot* (1987), a ten-part radio drama for CBC's *Morningside*, commemorating the 150th anniversary of the 1837 rebellion.

In addition to playwriting, Salutin has written books on Canadian trade unionism (*Kent Rowley: The Organizer*, 1980) and the federal election and free trade debate of 1988 (*Waiting for Democracy: A Citizen's Journal*, 1989). *Marginal Notes* (1984) and *Living in a Dark Age* (1991) are lively collections of his award-winning journalism for a variety of newspapers and magazines, including *This Magazine* for which he has been a long-time editor. His novel *A Man of Little Faith* won the *Books in Canada* First Novel Award for 1988.

The politics of *1837: The Farmers' Revolt* are very much Salutin's own. The play presents a Canada lacking independence and subservient to British imperialism, finding its revolutionary impulse in the ordinary people of the time. Created during the heyday of Canadian nationalism, it was meant to speak to the contemporary sense of American imperial domination and economic, political and cultural colonialism many Canadians still feel. Salutin also intended the play as a corrective to what he called "The Great Canadian History Robbery" in a 1973 *Maclean's* article: the textbook view of Canadian history in which "we learned that all our problems were resolved 'peaceably' long ago; that there is nothing in our history to get excited over; that Canadians don't *get* excited; that they never fight back against things as they've always been."

Ideology, however, was probably less crucial to the play's success that its theatricality, a product of the unique collective chemistry brought to bear in its creation. Salutin's diary reveals how he would bring in Mackenzie's newspaper article on the Family Compact or Robert Davis' book *The Canadian Farmer's Travels in the U.S.A.*, and Thompson would lead the actors on improvisational forays through it. The wittiest scenes in Act One, including "The Head" and "The Lady in the Coach," grew out of improvisations based on documentary material. The actors were also asked to improvise 1837 objects and do 1837 "anger exercises," the latter shaped by Salutin into the final scene of Act One. When necessary Salutin would script a scene (like "Doel's Brewery" opening Act Two), but as much as possible the emphasis was on the actors' imaginative reconstructions of the 1837 world, coaxed out of them by Thompson's sympathetic direction.

Salutin's final role was to shape the resulting material into a coherent, dramatically effective whole, and his success in that regard can be seen most clearly in Act One. Its non-linear arrangement of scenes masks a clever and deceptively rigorous dialectical structure. The farmers' struggle with the stump in "Clearing" and Mackenzie's with the mud in "Hat" are both amplified and clarified in "The Tavern" where the people learn that the system itself is the obstacle: the swamp that can only be cleared through collective action. The ensuing scene, "The Family Compact," further illuminates the system by individualizing the forces of oppression. Then the lovely "Mary Macdonald" introduces a wholly different kind of family compact, what Mackenzie will later call "the real nobility of Upper Canada." As Edward exits with Mary he warns, "there's ruts," and "The Lady in the Coach" bogs down in them. That scene provides a wonderful comic illustration of the imperialist approach to problem-solving— let the colonials pull us out of the mud while we give the orders—a view reaffirmed by Sir

Francis' speech in "The Head" promising "paternal care" of his subjects. The self-fulfilling nature of such colonialist attitudes is vividly shown in "The Election of '36." Obviously the farmers *haven't* learned how to take care of themselves politically. Their only solution will be to develop a revolutionary consciousness.

The play's imaginative energy flags a little in the second act. Both Salutin and Thompson have acknowledged feeling "handcuffed by history" into presenting a more or less chronological narrative of the events of the rebellion ending with its defeat. Still, the historical narrative is leavened and humanized by the reintroduction of the non-historical characters we've met in Act One. The farmers, the collective hero, become almost as individualized as their catalyst, Mackenzie himself. And while history dictates that they must fail in the end, Salutin has taken mild dramatic license to ensure that defeat doesn't mean despair; we haven't really lost, we just haven't won . . . yet. Salutin's preface, which follows, illuminates this distinction along with many of the other agonies and ecstasies involved in the making of the play.

•

1837: The Farmers' Revolt opened June 7, 1974, on tour in southwestern Ontario with the following cast:

Doris Cowan
David Fox
Eric Peterson
Miles Potter
Terry Tweed

Directed by Paul Thompson
Designed by Paul Williams

1837: THE FARMERS' REVOLT

PREFACE

1837 was first produced at Theatre Passe Muraille in Toronto in January, 1973. Here is a "diary" of that production.

Fall, 1972

Last year, while I was in rehearsal with a play called *Fanshen*, about the Chinese Revolution, the director said, "Now what we ought to do *next* year is—Quebec!"

Oh no, I thought. No more getting off on these exotic foreign revolutions. Next year if we do a revolution it will be right here in Ontario.

Sunday, Dec. 3

Drove out to the Niagara Peninsula with Paul (director) and Williams (designer). On a winding narrow road that once was the thoroughfare between Hamilton and the frontier we found a neglected monument, high as my waist and shaped like a gravestone. Divided into crescents, it read:

Up the hill 50 feet stood the home of Samuel Chandler Patriot
He guided Mackenzie to Buffalo
And here they had supper
Dec. 10, 1837

It is encouraging. With all the denigration spattered on the rebellion during our schooldays and since, I was beginning to ponder whether we were the first who had ever thought to treat it as a serious national event.

Wednesday, Dec. 6

Rehearsals begin tomorrow, the 7th, the anniversary of the Battle of Montgomery's Tavern. The 7th was also a Thursday in 1837. Odd how those things fuel you. We have no script yet, only general ideas of why and how we want to do it. I've tried too. In September, I sketched out scenes, then showed it to L. "Looks just the way we learned it in school," she said. Back to the drawing board. Paul is delighted. He said all along we're better off without a script, that it makes the actors lazy. Even if we had one, he'd be for hiding it. Fine—but what do they need me for?

Thursday, Dec. 7

We have six actors. Three men and three women. Two I know from *Fanshen*. The rest are strangers. I brought in a few goodies: maps and pictures of Old Toronto. Great stir at finding the *history* of places we've all lived around. We're starting very far back: other countries may have to relive or reinterpret their past, but they know they *have* a past. In Quebec they may hate it, but it's sure as hell there. English Canadians, at least around here, must be convinced there *is* a past that is all their own.

We paraded to Mackenzie House on Bond St. in midafternoon where little Wasp women in period dress served us tea and apple butter. I nearly choked on it, and the rest of what they've wreaked on our only militant independantiste. Our work is cut out.

Before splitting up, we asked each of the actors to present an 1837 object. The best was Clare. She set herself before us and said:

I'm William Lyon Mackenzie's house. My feet are spread wide apart and are firmly planted. My hands are on my hips and I look straight ahead. I have *lots* of windows and any questions you ask me, I'm not afraid to answer.

It's already apparent that Paul is right. The absence of a script is drawing material out of the actors. After all, they have more theatre experience than anyone, and they're almost never asked to draw on it.

Friday, Dec. 8

We gave the actors anger exercises today. Each had to simulate anger around 1837. For some it was agony—or constipation. Neil was superb. "Nobody," he roared, "is going to make me speak with an English accent." That is a true Canadian actor's anti-imperialism. Theatre is one of the few areas left in Canada where the main imperial oppressor remains England and not the U.S. They run every regional theatre in the country; Englishmen waft over and drown in role offers. Stratford—our *national* theatre—gobbling public money to become an acknowledged *second* best in *another* country's national playwright. Neil was one of Stratford's golden boys—an apprentice—in its early years. Then he rebelled by going to act for twelve years in New York, instead of London. He's been back about two years now.

Last spring, when Paul and I first talked about this play, I said it was to be an anti-imperialist piece. He leaped joyfully and cried, "Right—we'll really smash the Brits"—making me wince, but in theatre he was right.

Monday, Dec. 11

First resistance. From Clare. She looked to me and said, "*There's* all the research—bottled up in your head—and we can't get at it."

Actors have been so infantilized. Writers tell them what to say and directors tell them where to stand and no one asks them to think for themselves. They come to work with Paul because they want to break that pattern, but then they freeze up. I remember my first horrified encounter with actors, during *Fanshen*. They were treating this play exactly as they would any other; it might have been *Barefoot in the Park*. Like the mailman, they'd deliver anything. It shocked me that they were like any other group in the country, politically, that is. But the actors are also the real pro- letariat of the theatre; that too was clear from the first rehearsal. They are the bottom rung. They take shit from everyone else, and *their* labour holds it all up: reproduces it all, night after night.

This matter of research: the material on 1837 is endless, to my surprise. The collective method takes the pressure off me for digesting all of it. Everyone reads like crazy. Mornings, before we start, the rehearsal room looks like a library.

Tuesday, Dec. 12

We're still concentrating on texture, and haven't begun to build scenes.

The woman problem remains completely unsolved, although we are ignoring it at this point. Paul originally wanted only one woman. I insisted on at least two and claimed we could show the class conflict through two women. He went along, and since Suzette became available, we now have three, in addition to the three men. But what will we do with them, given the paucity of the sources on women? I've ransacked the records, talked with historians, writers, feminists. All we find are interminable journals by the *gentle*women of the time, who complain of their hard life in the Bush, and how tough it is to get servants. Women didn't fight, and they didn't legislate. Clearly they worked. But what they did, and how they felt, in specifics . . . ? Every time I go back over it, I end up nowhere. In *Fanshen*, the woman issue was so *clear*.

Wednesday, Dec. 13

Williams brought in the set—that is, a mockup in a shoebox. What a triumph. A series of four platforms ranging from 2 to 8 feet off the floor connected by ramps which will be corduroyed. Plus five enormous trees set throughout the theatre that will tower up through the roof.

The effect of the platforms will be to give us the possibility of isolation and concentration— *plus* the possibility of movement (between the platforms); it is the best of all possible worlds, in terms of design. Instantly all our thinking about the play is transformed. I keep wandering by it and conjuring miniature people on the ramps.

Thursday, Dec. 14

We tried Mackenzie's newspaper piece on the Family Compact today. It's a fine hatchet job. He numbers them from one to thirty, and cross references them by number. We did it with five people taking all the roles—switching—and Neil reading. It will, I hope, become the definitive version of the Family Compact. I suppose I like it because I have been writing political satire for radio three years now and see Mackenzie's piece as the start of a Canadian tradition.

I gave Miles *The Canadian Farmer's Travels in the U.S.A.* to read. Written by an Upper Canadian farmer named Davis in 1836. I discovered it in the rare book room of the public library. Heartsick at the election of '36, he went travelling to the U.S., was thrilled by the abundance he saw everywhere and the efficacy of the democratic system, and resolved to return home and struggle for improvement here. He published the book, and died in the fighting in 1838. It's a very naive book—he's so overwhelmed by what he saw, that he loves *everything*—slavery, Indians—all of it. It's a trip scene and should work well, especially with the kind of energy Miles can give it.

More texturing: we've given everyone a minor character to do from the time. Someone who's barely mentioned in the records. Sally Jordan, who worked for Anne Langton, who wrote a journal. Ira Anderson, innkeeper, who's on the arrest record. A name mentioned in Mackenzie's paper as seconding a motion at a meeting. They must build their character according to what they know of the time. We'll quiz the actors in coming days on what may come out of it, but more important is the *thickness*—to pour into and onto whatever and whoever we end up using. We have to build the reality of the ordinary people of the time. They are the core of our past we have to get through to; they must be the centre of the play—not any of the "great" individuals who hog most of the records.

Friday, Dec. 15

Blizzard. After the break Janet said, "Can I go home?" and Paul said, "If you walk all the way up Yonge St. and do it in character." Upshot was we bundled up and trekked through Old Toronto. Down to the site of the hangings on King St., along King to Berkeley, up Parliament and over to the cemetery where Mackenzie, Lount and Matthews are buried. It was locked when we arrived. One thing we concluded: December was a hell of a time to make a revolution here.

Monday, Dec. 18

A row at the end of the day. "I'm sick of our Canadian politeness," Paul complained. We'd been doing break-ins by loyalists at the homes of rebels after the battle. The traditional Canadian knock at the door. Our intruders had tied themselves in knots trying not to be too, too nasty.

It is a crux: the ability to *really* identify with the main struggles and passions of the people at the time; else it will be just play-acting, better or worse. Clare dealt it back the strongest. "One of the nicest things about Canadians is that they *don't* get angry," she yelled.

I argued—academically I fear—that this "typical" Canadian reserve is not genetically rooted; that Canadians did fight and shout in 1837; and that our esteemed diffidence is the result of the failure and repression of such moments of resistance and assertion. If it is that historically based, we're not going to shake it loose by doing a passionate play; still, we may gain an inch or two.

Wednesday, Dec. 30

Pictures: we give the actors five minutes to rummage through books, choose an image, and give it back.

David plunged: "Now sir, when we moved onto that plot, there was nothing there. All I'm asking is . . ." Suzette hauled a table and chair in front of him, and leaned back like a contemptuous land agent. As he stammered on, about how he and his family had worked, the others filled in behind, chopping and clearing. Hewers of wood and drawers of water. Very strong. David is our staunchest, in a way. Our oak—(and we have Miles chop him down in a scene). He grew up in Kirkland Lake, taught high school ten years in Brantford, and did his first professional acting this past summer.

Janet did a brilliant picture. Back to us, passed her palm above her head, saying, "A smooth broad forehead." Then she stood Suzette and Neil side by side facing us as, "Two piercing eyes." Drew their inner arms forward together as, "A classic nose." Got Clare in to make a mouth; and announced it was John Beverley Robinson, one of the leading members of the Compact. Now to find a way of integrating it into the production so that it becomes more than a *tour de force* of theatricality.

(The "Head" developed this way: Paul felt we had to make it the head of Lieutenant Governor Francis Bond Head, not Robinson, since Mackenzie had been so fond of punning on Head's name. Neil found a speech by Bond Head that was the quintessence of the Imperial attitude; as one of the eyes he also delivered it. It fit perfectly as the prelude to the Canadian Farmer's Travels to the U.S. The whole didn't come together until weeks after Janet had given us the original image.)

Friday, Dec. 22

There was no point trying to rehearse today. Everyone is gripped with job insecurity, because Actors' Equity is about to shut down Factory Theatre Lab, and is preparing an offensive against the other small Canadian theatres like ourselves. Ostensibly the issue is kickbacks. Equity actors who work at the small theatres must sign contracts at Equity rates, but since these are unrealistic for the small theatres, they often return a part of what they are paid. We have four Equity actors and they've all received threatening letters from *their* union. (They can't seem to get the incongruity of this through their heads.) They fear they'll be expelled. We talked all day, mostly about American unions and how typical this is of the way they operate in Canada—and about other forms of imperialism, especially American. I am the only one with a thoroughly paranoid interpretation: that Equity's real purpose is to shut down the small Canadian theatres because they provide increasing competition and audience drain from the downtown mausoleums that house touring Broadway shows, American-mounted productions, to which Equity gives its main allegiance. I was alone in deeming it a conspiracy, but various forms of fear and indignation reign among the rest. They're tired of yearly questionnaires from Equity asking how many hours they've worked on-Broadway, off-Broadway, etc. There is certainly no way of avoiding this discussion in the context of the play we are making.

Boxing Day

Finally tried Ventriloquism. Inspired by a handbill for an 1830's travelling show (". . . and featuring—VENTRILOQUISM"). It's a perfect metaphor for colonialism—maybe too perfect? Divided our actors into teams of dummy and master; David and Clare were far the best technically. Now to work on the problem of what they're to say.

Thursday, Dec. 28

We had our good day today, as Janet said.

For his anger homework, David came in with a team stuck in the mud. Got off his wagon, stuffed his shoulder against a wheel, shoved and cursed. Others moved in as horses etc., and Janet sang God Save the Queen. *Finally* we got behind the academicism of the "roads" issue. Each time someone uses it, it sounds plucked from the section of the textbook called Causes of the Rebellion. We've taken to barking "Cause Three" when they mention roads, and "Cause Four" to the Clergy Reserves. But this was real and *felt*.

Neil began musing about the secret meeting at Doel's Brewery in Toronto before the rebellion—the night when the city was unguarded and Mackenzie urged his fellow reformers to seize it and the four thousand arms that were there. I've yearned to do it from the start. It was the time to act, but they stalled till they could bring down the farmers to take the risks for them. Had they acted there is no doubt our history would have been different. The British would have been forced to return half their forces from Quebec, where fighting had already begun; the French just might then have succeeded; in Ontario there'd have been arms and impetus . . . . Still, dreams aside, the point of the scene is not to show what might have been, but the unreliability and timidity of bourgeois leadership in a struggle for Canadian independence. Then as now, Paul felt it was too programmatic to get out of the actors, but Neil was so keen on it that we both gulped, "Let's try it." It went not badly, broad lines emerged, and in this one case, I am going to write it up as a scene, based on the improvised work. My first chance to be a playwright. Now they get a chance to judge my work.

We finally got the Davis scene, the Canadian farmer travelling in the U.S. Miles had had an anxiety attack each time he moved into it. Today we literally sat on him, holding him down, and by the time he finally escaped he'd gathered so much energy it carried him right through the trip. The key is to satirize the farmer's enthusiasm for all things American. To put through our eyes what we saw through his. On one side lethargic Windsor (yawns) and then—Industrious Detroit—everyone pumping and rushing and HAPPY. He adores it all; Neil ran up and said, "Excuse me sir, I'm a runaway slave, which way is Canada?" and he said—"No, don't go, it'll get better here." Got quite wild, snatches of Aquarius, etc. Very exciting. I'm still excited about it.

Friday, Dec. 29

I've got a last line. Talking with Suzette about Canadian plays and what downers they are—always about losers. Yet what to do? Our past is negative. The country has remained a colony; the struggle in 1837 did not succeed. I've thought of changing the ending, having the rebels win (Stop that Hanging!); or cutting off before the battle and the defeat, at, say, the high point in October '37. But finally we have to wrestle with what actually happened and wring something positive out of that. Losing, I argued, does not have to make you a "Loser"; there are winners who lose. It is the difference between saying, "We lost," and saying, "No, we just haven't won yet." There it is.

Saturday, Dec. 30

The Family Compact is turning into a hell, more demoralizing each time we run it. The novelty of the numbering has worn off, they are reaching for ever more corn to cover their changes. We're down to staging number 21-25 as a bloody cricket match. Paul can't get it. Damn. Paul's strength—his genius—is working with people and eliciting their creativity. I try to help—but I'm no director. Christ what a loss it would be—it's right there!

Sunday, Dec. 31

They showed me a scene Suzette had improvised yesterday while I was out. An English gentlewoman doing the tour of the colonies gets stuck in her coach on the road from Toronto to Niagara, blusters at the driver, fidgets about her manservant, yammers endlessly, but together they push free and suddenly she is ecstatic about the "adventure" they've just had. ("My cousin Stephanie was one experience up on me, you know.") I loathed her—extolling "Nature's cathedral" which only she and not the gruff coachman could appreciate, bidding "Goodbye Brave Bush," before she'd climb back in the coach. I grabbed for one of our stage rifles and would gladly have plugged her through her "jaded, civilized eyes." But she is so right and brilliant and hilarious—I suppose there will be no way of keeping it out of the play.

We are starting to think about how to shape these things. About time. It is New Year's Eve. We open on the 17th.

Tuesday, Jan. 2

Working with Mackenzie's newspaper again. Divided them, as usual, into an upper class and a dirt poor family, each reacting to the same articles differently. Today though, they fell into interrupting each other's readings and emerged in fullblown battle. All the good arguments were with the reactionaries. And all the articulateness. "My dear man, you can't expect illiterate farmers to actually *govern*?" "What do *you* know about economics?" "Are you admitting then that you are *disloyal*?" On and on, Neil and his gathering steam; David and his, being ground down. Miles (for the rich) made some patronizing analogy, to which David tried pathetically to respond. Janet got closer to the class reality, barging in with, "That's a stupid argument!" Suzette cooed, "Why can't we all get *along*?" in a perfect Rosedale tone. Janet tore through the paper looking for counterarguments, looking to us—what she really felt was—If only Mac was here, *he'd* tell them. We suddenly saw Mackenzie's real importance for these people. The oppressed never control the ideological apparatus; it is always used by the ruling classes to confuse and demoralize them. Mackenzie took the ideological skills he possessed and put them at the disposal of the oppressed instead of the oppressors, doing for them what they had not been given the resources to do for themselves. He really served the people. What nonsense the way we learned it—as if it was Mackenzie against the Family Compact in personal combat. It was the working people against the Empire. They were the centre, but they needed him.

Wednesday, Jan 3.

I distributed the script for the brewery scene today; reaction was astounding. They blinked and wouldn't believe—a real script—went berserk with gratitude and joy. Much feigned, of course, but it came from somewhere. The pressure and demands on them in this method of work are vast. That we knew; but not quite how *much*.

Most striking was how the presence of a script shot everyone into an instant role. They became actors, underlining their speeches and saying bitchy things like, "Let me feel my way into this, will you?" Paul became a director urging interpretations and line readings on them ("Let me coach you"). And I became a writer, skulking in back, gritting my teeth at what they were doing to "my" lines, nodding when they "got it," and not intervening except to occasionally whisper to Paul. Till now, roles have been loose; everyone was writing, directing and acting, though of course not all to the same extent. With the script, compartmentalization sets in like terminal cancer. I'm glad we did it—just this one scene—to watch it happen.

Toward the end of the day, with everyone tired and loath to take on a bummer like the Compact, Paul spied a length of rope in the corner, looped it six times, put it over their heads and told them they were prisoners being returned to Toronto after the rebellion. They trudged and told us what they felt and saw. Too much self-pity at the moment, but a strong image and one that will work on our set. Where did that come from? I asked Paul. Desperation, he said.

Friday, Jan 5.

Last night I read through seven or eight accounts of the Siege of Toronto between Dec. 4 and 7, culminating with the Battle, and typed a composite account, very long and detailed. Then I cut it up with scissors into thirty different pieces, numbered, and this morning gave five pieces to each actor. Each has to say his section as they come up in sequence, though everyone acts out the events. It will take lots of choreography and coordination, and we will be at it once a day till we open—like taking vitamins, says Paul. I think our audiences will be captivated—all those warlike events up and down Yonge St.

I feel less guilt about my contribution, now that I've done some scripting. And I think I can see the shape of Act II. From Doel's, through the Battle, the march of the prisoners, the hangings. We'll be leaping right into the maw of the defeat, and see what kind of victory we can bring from it. But as for Act I, God only knows . . . .

Monday, Jan 8.

Awful. Just awful. I can't say how bad. There is nothing there. And they will not work, will not give. The Family Compact is a horror; we haven't dared touch it in five days. Miles is stumped on his Farmer's Travels. We all see what a good scene it is; we've seen him do it brilliantly; but he's clogged up, he makes excuses and accuses Paul of not directing him. Paul fires back that Miles won't commit himself. I stalk around the theatre—we moved in today out of the rehearsal room—wanting to rip Miles into bits for his stingy withholding. I know that's false, but it's what I feel. Paul and I confer hostilely, and they pick it up and sulk or fling back angry glares—Janet is doing that more and more. We are at a dead halt—no, we are careening backwards. There is no giving, no expansiveness—and no script to fall back on!

Christ, I said to Paul, is it this way every time?

I don't know, he sighed. I can't remember. I guess so.

How do you stand it?

I must forget. If I remembered, I would never do it again.

Tuesday, Jan. 9

Today it was Clare. She has no lines in the Doel's scene, but is a brewery hand who sets it up and works away in the background while the leaders of the rebellion are conspiring below. She is the lurking presence of the ordinary working people who will have to take all the chances while most of their "leaders" sit tight. But she's been a lump. I challenged her on it and she maintained that since she knows nothing about brewing beer, she can't act it. I said she should figure out something that seemed to her like brewing and do that. She pouted that she'd take off the rest of the day and go research brewing in the library. More tight-assed withholding—I stormed off. Paul? I don't know where he gets the patience. Like a shrink fighting through layers of resistance, he patiently counters argument after argument of hers till she admits she just doesn't want to take a chance. Then she went ahead and did it—beautifully. I don't know what the hell *she* thought she was doing, but at the least it didn't look like *not* brewing beer.

Wednesday, Jan. 10

The Ventriloquism is in trouble. We haven't figured out how to use it—is it metaphor, is it to the audience, is it within the play itself? David and Clare are balking, say it's no fun, no point. I'll try and script it as a two minute skit—as if I were writing for radio.

We did get the Family Compact. We'd written it off regretfully but I was looking at the set today—ramps running down from platform to platform—and said, Why don't we try it on the ramps, unwinding the Compact from top to bottom? So we did, and we have a scene.

Thursday, Jan. 11

Came up with an Act I closing. Our anger exercises. Spread our people over the set, doing bursts of anger one after another. They made them up on the spot; some were extraordinary.

MILES: *(climbing off the floor onto the set)* I don't care who you are and what your name is. From now on you can clean the muck out from under your own damned English footbridge.

NEIL: See this cabinet. Took me six months. Know why I can't sell it? Because it was made in *(an awful angry whine)* Torrrrooonnnttoooo—

JANET: So I sez to her—Milk your *own* cow!

And finally a chance to use Suzette's Quebec half: Moé-la, j'aimais plus je'n chant'rai pour les Anglais!

It is the boiling point of 1837, where grievances and resentments are irrepressible and have to burst into the action of the rebellion itself—in Act II.

Friday, Jan. 12

Just what we'd considered our strongest suit—the pictures—just won't work down here in the theatre. They were grand in the little rehearsal room with the low ceiling but—ah well, they served their purpose: got us into the texture of the time.

Saturday, Jan. 13

Worked with David on his (Lount's) gallows speech. He's been to the provincial archives mornings this week, reading accounts of the trial of Lount and Matthews.

Finally found a use for those lists I like so much—the names of those arrested or charged in the aftermath of the rebellion. 885 men, their homes, and occupations. Fine names—Caleb Kipp, Josiah Dent, Joshua Doan: yeoman, labourer, tanner, etc. When I have been stymied by this work both before and then during rehearsals, I've taken to reading through those names. I've wanted to employ them as a sort of litany. They work well into the rope scene, the march of the prisoners. Each gives his name and when they've gone round once, they go round again, and then again, creating with the six an endless line of captured revolutionaries. I gave a page of name to each actor; they can choose the ones they'll use each night.

The final form is now clear. Act I will be fairly diffuse, a view of the life of the times—our blessed texture—though building to the inevitability of the outbreak. It should end high, with the feeling, This Can't Miss. After intermission we change pace completely.

Act II drives right through with the line of the rebellion, defeat and aftermath. It will have the guts of our politics, what we make of this event and why we are returning to it now.

Monday, Jan. 15

We hit the crunch today with the Farmer's Travels. Miles capsized again midway. He tried to get Paul to call it off, cut the scene, give it to someone else—do *something*. I could see Paul struggling with the offer; then he leapt up on the set and refused. Said he would not become the paternalistic director at this point. If Miles really wanted to do the scene, Paul would stand by him no matter how much it seemed to lack—and he was sure the audience would accept it. Or—if Miles really didn't want to do it, *he* would have to say so. It was a trap for Paul and he was magnificent in avoiding it. Suzette, bless her, said, "I vote to have it in," not pressing but making the point that, if not Miles, then someone else should do it. Miles wrestled with it, started the trip again, stalled, slumped down, and said, "I don't want to do it like this." "O.K.," said Paul, "Janet—will you try it?"

Janet looked to Miles, he nodded generously, she launched it, and was fine. When we tried it again later, Miles came in as the wife, urging the farmer not to leave for the States. It works, and I think it also means we've solved the women problem as far as we can. Clare argued with me the other day that one of the men on the scaffold should be played by a woman, and I argued back that it would be so obtrusive that we would end up with a scene about the equality of women, not about 1837. It might be right politically, but if it doesn't work as theatre there is no point in doing it in a play. Janet plays a man because it has become dramatically necessary in the travel scene. We have women playing men in the battle and the brewery scene for the same reason and it is unobtrusive there. We've failed to find a centrality for women in 1837 terms. But we are *doing* the play in *our* terms—with an equal cast, fair distribution of parts, etc. It is an attempt to portray an oppressive reality in a liberated way.

Tuesday, Jan. 16

We've put the Ventriloquism unit as the introduction to the meeting Mackenzie addresses before the rebellion. As a skit presented by two farmers for their friends at the rally. Agitprop of '37. Allows the other actors to react to it as *its* audience, drains off the heavy symbolism, and clarifies that Clare is playing a real person who is *playing* a dummy.

Great consternation about the newspaper scene with which we'd wanted to open. It is important for me 1) to open a play about Canadian history with a scene of class conflict, and 2) to show the centrality of Mackenzie's paper—its propaganda and education—for the movement. Paul's retort was—it's not doing either of those things as it is now. I had to agree. We put it to them and—wonder of wonders—they say they want to do it as we have it and are sure they can pull it off tomorrow night, though they'd like me to settle on four or five articles and choose an order for them. Instead of suggesting another cut, they propose an inclusion—a good, good sign.

The programs came today, and I like them. They are of a piece with the rest of this work: single sheets with a map of Old Toronto and an alphabetical list of the people who made the play.

I think I see now Paul's vision of theatre and the value he places on improvisation. Without a script, there is real tension and the possibility of creative breakthrough on stage at any moment. It is not *set*. People come to plays thinking of them as movies or TV gone live, perfect realizations of a script or theme, and frozen at that point of perfect realization. But a play is made live each night, and its possibility is not frozen perfection but ongoing re-creation. The edge for an audience should not be awe at a perfect performance, but anxiety about something new and possibly better at any moment.

Opening Night

Two instructive things happened. When Clare started Act II with "Bay and Adelaide, the northwest corner," the audience laughed. If an actor said, "Montmartre, 4 a.m.," or "Piccadilly Circus, twelve noon," no audience anywhere would laugh. But we are so imbued with self-denial, so colonized, that the very thought of something historic happening *here*, at Bay and Adelaide, draws laughs.

Again, during the Battle, in the nighttime skirmish when both inexperienced sides broke ranks and fled, Miles lost his line for a moment, and the audience laughed. Miles—American Miles—said that moment made clear to him for the first time what I'd been saying about the problem of Canadian history for a Canadian audience. There was nothing funny about the moment. It was terrifying or should have been.

Three Weeks Later

The actors have come to take it as a challenge to deliver those lines so that the audience cannot laugh at them. At the same time, Janet says the response to *1837* is different from any play she's ever appeared in. It's not just appreciation. It's something warmer.

It is, I think, identification. Beyond the identification you get in any good theatre. It is a meeting with ourselves.

Over a year later, the play was reworked. The result—amounting to a new play—was called *1837: The Farmers' Revolt*. It was produced in the spring, summer and fall of 1974—first in the auction barns of southwestern Ontario, then in Victoria Playhouse in Petrolia, Ontario, and then in Toronto. It has since had many productions throughout the country. It is the script of this latter production which is included below.

1837: The Farmers' Revolt was developed in exactly the same way as the first version of the play. But it was meant for a tour of farming communities instead of an urban theatre audience and it differed from the earlier play in the following ways.

It was not Toronto-centred. In the first *1837* we had made hay of the events and locales of early Toronto. We de-emphasized these in the country, and looked for elements that reflected what had happened out there, where we were planning to tour the show.

So, for instance, we cleared a larger space for Anthony van Egmond, the old colonel who led the revolutionary force at Montgomery's Tavern. Van Egmond had lived just outside Seaforth—in the village now called Egmondville. The family home is still standing, and local people are restoring it.

Instead of showing the entire four days of fighting around Toronto, we showed only the final battle there. For the first three days, we went out to the country, and followed Van Egmond, as he marched from his home down to Toronto, to take command of the forces there.

Numerous such changes in the script occurred. Another change which took place was, in a way, political.

The earlier play—beamed into the Toronto milieu—could assume a somewhat left-of-liberal politics on the part of the audience; more or less of a sympathy, or at least tolerance, for the revolutionary sentiments of the play. But the farming community is, at least in its explicit attitudes, far more conservative. So some of the rhetoric—what Miles called the "bombast"— came out. And more justification of the movement for change went in. For instance, we had *two* scenes, instead of one, depicting the bitterness of the farmers over the land policies of the 1830s.

The play also changed dramatically, or artistically.

It became much tighter than the earlier version. In the first version, for example, we served the battle up whole. In the second, by concentrating on the experience of Van Egmond, we gave the scene a dramatic focus it had lacked. In the end, I would say version two (the one included here) is a far better play.

This is largely so because on the first time round we were intent on getting clear *what* we were going to say about 1837. By round two, that most crucial of matters was basically settled; we could concentrate on *how* to say it more effectively, refining scenes, characters, etc. The resulting script proves, I think, that the collective process can produce a play as dramatically tight as the more typical scripting approach.

In some ways though, I preferred the earlier version. It would not make as good reading, and it did not play as well. Yet it had a rawness and a timeliness. It felt to me, when we first put this show up in January of 1973, that we were expressing something of what was happening in the country at the time: a determination to throw off colonial submissiveness in all areas. *1837* was a theatrical expression of that feeling, making it more of a political event, and not just, or even primarily, a theatrical one.

By the second time round, a mere year and a half later, things seemed to have changed, have slowed. The movement for Canadianization of trade unions had *not* yet taken off; the universities were more dominated than ever by Americans; the Waffle had been expelled from the NDP, largely for its nationalism; the cries for economic control had muted. The nationalist, anti-imperialist impetus was still present, and *more* necessary than ever; but it was less fresh, was in a bit of a withdrawal.

And so the play became more of a theatrical, and less of a political, event. That is why I preferred version one, though version two is no doubt superior "theatre."

1837: The Farmers' Revolt had an original cast of five: three men and two women. Men played women, and women played men, or animals or objects or parts of the body—depending on the needs of the scene. There were very few props. I mention this because anyone reading the script will be tempted to imagine a well-equipped cast of thousands.

The actors who worked on the various productions were Janet Amos, Clare Coulter, Suzette Couture, Doris Cowan, David Fox, Eric Peterson, Miles Potter, Terry Tweed, and Neil Vipond. I had a notion of including a list with this script indicating which actors were primarily responsible for which scenes—but when it comes to the doing it is terrifically difficult to assign such credit. So I will just reiterate that the play is *entirely* a creation of the company in rehearsals and performance. The present script is an after-the-fact, somewhat composite, effort, assembled *following* the close of the fall 1974 run.

The director of *1837* was Paul Thompson. The designer was Paul Williams. I was the writer on—but not of—*1837*.

Rick Salutin

1837: THE FARMERS' REVOLT

ACT ONE

Walking

A man is walking on the set. He carries an axe and a sack. He walks and walks, seeing the forests and the occasional cleared farm of Upper Canada pass by him as he goes. The audience are still entering. They are asking each other, Who is he? Where's he going? What's he got with him? He keeps walking. This is a play about a time when people in Canada walked to get anywhere and do anything. Eventually two FARMERS enter, one stage left and one stage right. They are taking a rest. They watch him go by their field.

FIRST FARMER: Who is that fellow?

SECOND: Name's Thomas Campbell.

FIRST: Where's he from?

SECOND: Glasgow.

He walks. Enter two more FARMERS.

THIRD FARMER: Where's he going?

FOURTH: He's bought a plot of land near Coldwater.

They watch him awhile. They are all tired from hard work.

SECOND: How much did it cost him?

FIRST: Twenty dollars down—he'll work the rest out.

FOURTH: How long has he been walking?

THIRD: Four and a half days.

FIRST: *(feeling his own feet)* Ouch.

SECOND: Does he have any family?

FOURTH: Wife. Son. Three daughters. Younger brother. All back in Scotland. They'll be over later.

THIRD: What's he got with him?

FIRST: Everything he owns.

SECOND: Think he knows how to use that axe?

THIRD: If he doesn't, he'll learn.

FIRST: What does he see?

THIRD: Trees.

SECOND: Trees.

FOURTH: Trees.

FIRST: Trees and trees and trees and trees—

They all fill in the word "trees" as he speaks. They are planting a forest of trees with their voices. It mounts, then recedes and dies.

THIRD: What's he going to do when he gets there?

He gets there. He puts down his load, very weary. Looks around at the trees, up at the trees, tries to see through to the sky. He decides not to rest, raises his axe, and begins clearing his land.

Blackout.

Clearing

Grunts and sounds of straining in the dark. Lights up slowly. Four people working around a great (imaginary) stump, hacking it and hauling it. With one mighty heave it comes loose and they fall away from it, spent.

VOICE: *(offstage)* Halloooo—

STEADMAN: *(panting)* Hallooo—

VOICE: *(offstage)* is there a Peter Steadman there?

They lie there, too exhausted to respond. Enter MAGISTRATE THOMPSON, obviously an official. He approaches one of them.

MAGISTRATE: Peter Steadman?

He is motioned toward STEADMAN.

MAGISTRATE: Magistrate Thompson, from Richmond Hill.

STEADMAN: Magistrate, how do you do? *(With distaste, the MAGISTRATE shakes STEADMAN's sweaty hand.)* It's a long ride from Richmond Hill. Will you take something to drink? Sit down?

MAGISTRATE: Thank you, no.

STEADMAN'S WIFE: Can I get you anything?

MAGISTRATE: No. I was told I would find you here.

STEADMAN: We've been here a long time.

MAGISTRATE: How long, exactly?

STEADMAN: Close to two years.

MAGISTRATE: This is fine land. How much have you cleared?

STEADMAN: Eighteen acres.

STEADMAN'S BROTHER: Eighteen acres in two years!

STEADMAN'S WIFE: We've been working hard.

MAGISTRATE: Yes. Congratulations. That's a fine home.

STEADMAN'S WIFE: First one I've ever had that was my own.

STEADMAN: We were going to come up to Toronto to see you people pretty soon.

MAGISTRATE: Good, black, fertile soil.

STEADMAN: Yes, it's a good farm.

MAGISTRATE: Could I see your deed please, Mr. Steadman?

STEADMAN: I don't have a deed.

MAGISTRATE: Then your letter of license.

STEADMAN: Now I wouldn't have one of those without a deed, would I?

MAGISTRATE: Mr. Steadman, don't presume to tell me my business. *(He unrolls a survey map, which looks like to us a Union Jack.)* Your lot is number seventeen. On this government survey map, lot seventeen, here in the corner—I see no record whatever of the name Steadman. But it *is* part of a parcel of one thousand acres which was granted three weeks ago to Colonel Sparling of the Forty-Eighth Highlanders.

STEADMAN: Granted!

MAGISTRATE: By the Lieutenant-Governor.

STEADMAN'S SISTER-IN-LAW: This farm is not for sale!

STEADMAN'S BROTHER: You listen—we homesteaded this land.

MAGISTRATE: I choose to call it squatting.

STEADMAN'S BROTHER: Call it what you want. It's what everybody does when they don't have any money to start.

MAGISTRATE: And everybody who does it accepts the risk that something of this sort will happen.

STEADMAN: *(trying to be reasonable)* I'll be glad to go down to Toronto and talk to this Colonel and buy the land from him.

MAGISTRATE: Mr. Steadman, I know with certainty that he simply does not want you on his land. He is not however an ungenerous man, and if you approach him on the right footing, he might be willing to recompense you for your labour on his land.

STEADMAN'S BROTHER: How's he going to pay us for two years of clearing?

MAGISTRATE: He wants you off the land. You have one week, Steadman.

STEADMAN: *(burning)* You have one minute, Magistrate—to get off my farm.

STEADMAN'S BROTHER picks up his axe. The MAGISTRATE beats a retreat.

MAGISTRATE: *(as he goes)* One week, Steadman—

STEADMAN: *(calling after him)* We'll be here a week from now, Magistrate. We'll be here long after you're dead—

Now that they are left alone again, the anger quickly drops away and doubt sets in.

STEADMAN'S WIFE: What do we do now?

STEADMAN: *(ponders, then—)* Go back to work. Come on—

They set in around the stump again, straining and grunting. Lights down slowly to black.

Hat

Lights up on MACKENZIE.

MACKENZIE: My name is William Lyon Mackenzie. I run a small newspaper here in Toronto—it's called *The Advocate*. Used to be *The Colonial Advocate*, but I decided it was high time to get rid of the "Colonial" part. It's a good paper, pick one up if you get the chance. Now I was on my way down King Street to the office the other day—and it had rained just the night before. Well any time it rains here the roads turn into quagmires, and the only way you can use them is to pick your way from one high, dry spot to another. So I was picking my way along King— just outside here—when I noticed this hat lying in the mud in the middle of the road. Well it looked like a good hat and I decided it was worth muddying my boots to get it, so I picked my way over . . . *(He is doing it.)* . . . best I could, and I picked up the hat.

As he lifts the hat he uncovers a MAN's head. The MAN spits out a mouthful of mud.

MACKENZIE: There was a man under it! *(to MAN)* It looks like you're in trouble.

MAN: Yes, I certainly am.

MACKENZIE: *(bending down to hoist him)* Here, let me give you a hand.

MAN: You're quite a little fellow. I think you'd better go for some help.

MACKENZIE: Oh I'm pretty tough. I think I can pull you out myself.

MAN: But it's not just me I'm worrying about. It's the wagon and the two oxen!

Blackout.

The Tavern

Onstage right: ISAAC CASSELMAN, Tavern-keeper; EMMA, his wife; RUTH, a friend and customer; and JAMEY, local drunk and part-time help at the tavern.

ISAAC: *(singing)*
When I got up in the morning,
My heart did give a wrench,
For lying on the table
Was the captain and a wench—

Freeze. Enter FRED BENCH, stage left. Addresses audience.

FRED: That's why you cut your roots and come thousands of miles across the ocean—to buy your own land, be your own boss. I just got back from Toronto about that very thing—

Tavern action resumes.

ISAAC: *(singing)*
And then one fine spring morning,
I did a dancing jig—

Freeze.

FRED: This is Isaac Casselman's Inn. When I'm not working in the bush I spend most of my time right here.

Tavern resumes.

ISAAC: For lying on the table was the captain and—

Enter FRED.

ISAAC: Fred Bench! You're back—

EMMA: Fred—welcome home.

FRED: Hello Emma. Jamey! Hasn't Isaac fired you yet?

JAMEY: He can't fire me Fred.

FRED: Why not?

JAMEY: *(tottering into cellar)* I'm the only one who knows the inventory—

FRED: Ruth—

They embrace. RUTH is so excited she can't talk. Enter JAMEY, carrying a keg.

JAMEY: In your honour Fred. The best keg of rum in Isaac's cellar.

FRED: How do you know that Jamey?

JAMEY: Because I tested four others before I found it. It's the best.

EMMA: Fred—come on and tell us some good stories about Toronto.

RUTH: And show us what you've got!

ISAAC: Now first things first. In honour of the traveller's return—a toast!

ALL: Hear hear; a toast; *etc.*

They all take mugs.

ISAAC: To Fred Bench—and his new land.

ALL BUT FRED: To Fred Bench and—

FRED: Hold it. That's not quite right. To Fred Bench—and his *almost* land.

ISAAC: Wha—?

EMMA: Have you been drinking Fred?

JAMEY: *(undaunted)* To Fred Bench and the almost land. *(Down the hatch)*

RUTH: What do you mean?

FRED: Haven't touched a drop Emma. At least not yet. But now I'll tell you that story. Do you want to hear it?

ALL: Yes; *etc.*

FRED: It's a story about Toronto. What a city! For three days I walked through the bush. It was dark. Trees blocking out almost all the light. But when you get to the top of Yonge St., that bush just sweeps away. And there's Toronto. Morning fog coming in off the lake. Spires poking through here and there. It was like a dream. And I knew that day the city belonged to Fred Bench! Down into it I went—why, do you know they've got it built up all the way to Queen St.? *(disbelief)* I walked right in alongside the gentlemen and ladies. Isaac—you should see the taverns they've got now. And the traffic. Right along the flagstone sidewalks of King Street to the Courthouse—that's where the Land Office is. Up the steps—just a whiff of fish coming in from the wharf—inside are pillars that lay the fear of God in you. And *there's* the Land Office. And behind its thick oak door sits the Commissioner of Crown Lands. *(He is seized with an idea.)* Jamey—c'mere. You want to help me show these fine people some of the facts of life?

JAMEY: *(stumbling to FRED's side)* Facts of life? You've come to the right man for the facts of life.

FRED: Stand over here Jamey. Peter Robinson, Commissioner of Crown Lands. *(JAMEY looks around.)* No. That's you. Straight and tall. Fine satin shirt. Stiff collar. *(JAMEY begins to assume the role.)* Velvet trousers. And boots that you can see your face in.

JAMEY: *(He has become the Lands Commissioner.)* Shine my boots Fred!

FRED: Oh yes sir! Because you see, you control all the government land in the province.

JAMEY: All the land in the province? Mine?

FRED: Lord Jamey!

JAMEY: That's me—Lord Jamey!

FRED moves away from JAMEY.

FRED: Now on the other side of this oak door is the waiting room, three times the size of your tavern Isaac. And it's packed with people like me—all wanting land.

RUTH: Come on, let's help him out.

They all join FRED in the waiting room.

FRED: And we're packed in so tight—fifty or sixty of us—that we can't even sit down. Hey, Jamey, we got no land, you got it all. What do you think of us?

JAMEY: *(swaggering)* I think you're all—pieces of dirt!

FRED: We just couldn't get past the door. We waited one, two, three, four days, and never saw the Commissioner. Then, on the fifth day, in walks a private land agent—a Mr. Bronlyn. *(ISAAC assumes the role as FRED talks.)* A rich man, in a grey suit, with a bit of a paunch and cold grey eyes that look right through anything and anyone they—

BRONLYN barges right through the waiting room, slapping people out of his way. The COMMISSIONER opens the door to him.

ISAAC: *(as BRONLYN)* Ah, Mr. Commissioner—

JAMEY: Mr. Bronlyn, come in. *(to the others)* Slam!

EMMA: Fred—you mean he just walked in there—nice as you please!

FRED: Just like that.

EMMA: What'd you do?

FRED: What would you do?

EMMA stalks up to the door and knocks.

EMMA: Mr. Commissioner! I want to talk to you. We were promised land. We've been waiting here for five days. Some of us are hungry. You've got to—

JAMEY: *(without opening door)* My dear woman—who do you think you're talking to? The Commissioner of Crown Lands—that's who you're talking to. Now can't you see I'm busy? Go away. I've got important business to discuss with my friend, Mr. Bronlyn. If you want, you can leave your names with my clerk.

FRED: So we left our names with the clerk, walked out of the waiting room, and stood around Toronto for another two days. And then, in comes Mr. Bronlyn.

ISAAC: Is there a Mr. Bench here? A Mr. Fred Bench?

FRED: Yeah?

ISAAC: Mr. Bench, I understand that you wish to purchase some land.

FRED: Oh yes, yes sir—you bet I do.

ISAAC: Well I have just the land for you. One hundred acres of good, fertile—

FRED: And I have the twenty dollars here to buy it.

ISAAC: You don't understand Mr. Bench. This land sells for two hundred dollars an acre.

RUTH: What?

EMMA: But that's two hundred dollars—

ISAAC: That's correct, Madam. Well Mr. Bench—

FRED: Now hold on. I got the newspaper that says I can get one hundred acres of government land for twenty dollars.

ISAAC: That might be, Mr. Bench—though I rather doubt it. But I do not represent the government. I am a private land agent. I sell land for a profit.

FRED: *(to EMMA and RUTH)* Now where did he get my name?

JAMEY: *(still in his "office")* I gave it to him, Fred. I gave him all your names—for a little . . . consideration.

FRED: A little consideration. You see, they're in it together. Two crooks working hand in glove.

ISAAC: Well Mr. Bench? Do you or do you not want to buy the land? *(reverting to himself)* What'd you do, Fred?

FRED: I laughed in his face, grabbed him by his fancy shirt, and threw him out—because nobody makes a fool of Fred Bench!

EMMA: Good for you, Fred!

JAMEY: You really did, did you Fred?

RUTH: You mean . . . you didn't get the land . . . there's nothing . . . .

FRED: *(keeping up the bravado)* Well—no. But I've still got twenty dollars, and if it's not going for land, it's going for the biggest party we've ever had around here! Jamey—come on—

JAMEY: I'm with you Fred—

FRED: Isaac, more drinks—

All but RUTH cheer and raise their glasses. Freeze. Lights down on them. RUTH, alone on the other side of the stage, wails her disappointment.

Blackout.

The Family Compact

MACKENZIE: Ladies and gentlemen, this evening for your entertainment, and with the help of my charming assistant . . . *(enter charming ASSISTANT)* . . . I would like to demonstrate for you a magical trick. Now the thing that interests me about magic is not so much the phenomenon of the trick itself, as how it is actually accomplished, and I shall try to perform this trick in such a way that you can share its secret with me. *(to ASSISTANT)* We need the volunteers onstage. *(to audience)* I would have got volunteers from the audience, but you're all far too respectable for that.

Enter the three VOLUNTEERS. They are a sullen, brutish lot.

MACKENZIE: Now this trick will go down in the annals of conjuring history as one of the most remarkable ever performed anywhere in the world, for you are about to see this gang of thieves, rogues, villains and fools transformed before your very eyes into the ruling class of this province. Yes indeed—this band of criminals, by magical transformation, will become the government of Upper Canada. Now I've said I was going to do this trick slowly, so that you'll be able to see the positions they hold in the government, as well as the bonds that tie them together: bonds of blood, marriage, or greed—and in most cases it's all three. Anyway, on with the trick. Number one—

The ASSISTANT covers up the first VOLUNTEER with her cape.

MACKENZIE: Presto—Darcy Boulton Sr.

The cape is whisked away, revealing VOLUNTEER transformed into member of the Family Compact.

MACKENZIE: Retired pensioner, at a pension of five hundred pounds a year, paid by the people of Upper Canada. Number two—Presto—Henry Boulton, son to number one. *(So on with the cape. After three she begins again with one.)* Now Henry is the Attorney General for Upper Canada as well as being bank solicitor. Number three—Presto!—Darcy Boulton Jr., Auditor-General for Upper Canada as well as being Master in Chancery and a commissioner in the police. Numbers four and five—William and George Boulton—Presto!—also sons to number one, brothers to two and three, and holding various positions in the government. Number six—Presto!—John Beverley Robinson. Now Robinson is a brother-in-law to the Boultons there. He is the Chief Justice for Upper Canada. He's a member of the Legislative Council and the Speaker of the Legislative Council. Number seven—Peter Robinson, brother to number six. He's a member of the Executive Council, he's a member of the Legislative Council, he's the Commissioner of Crown Lands and Commissioner of the Clergy Reserves, as well as being the Surveyor-General of Woods. Number eight—William Robinson, brother to number six and seven. He's the Postmaster for Newmarket, he's a member of the Assembly for Simcoe, he's a government contractor, a colonel in the militia, and a Justice of the Peace.

MACKENZIE claps his hands twice. This brings the VOLUNTEERS out of their trance. They are dumbfounded.

MACKENZIE: We'll skip over nine, ten, eleven, twelve, thirteen, fourteen, and fifteen. They're just more of the same: they're all related to each other and they all hold various positions in the government. Which brings us to sixteen.

He claps again, thrusting VOLUNTEERS back into character. The ASSISTANT can barely keep the blistering pace.

MACKENZIE: —James B. Macaulay. Macaulay is a justice of the court of King's Bench. Number seventeen—Christopher Alexander Hagerman—presto!—Now Hagerman is a brother-in-law to Macaulay—

The cape is still in place, and a struggle is evidently taking place behind it. MACKENZIE rushes across, and snatches it away to reveal HAGERMAN in an unseemly clinch with the ASSISTANT.

MACKENZIE: This man is the Solicitor-General of Upper Canada! Now we won't do eighteen to twenty-two for the same reason we skipped the earlier batch, which brings us to twenty-three, twenty-four and twenty-five—the Jarvis family: Samuel Peter Jarvis, Grant Jarvis—his son—and William Jarvis, his brother. They hold such varied positions between them as clerk of the Crown in Chancery, Secretary of the Province, bank solicitor, clerk of the Legislative Council, police justice, judge, Commissioner of Customs, and two high sheriffs. And that brings us to twenty-six, the biggest fish in this small pond of Upper Canada—Archdeacon John Strachan, family tutor and political schoolmaster to this mob. This man is the archdeacon and rector of York. He's a member of the Executive Council, he's a member of the Legislative Council, he's President of the University, President of the Board of Education, and twenty other situations. *(MACKENZIE and STRACHAN glare at each other.)* Oh I almost forgot—twenty-seven—Thomas Mercer Jones. He's the son-in-law to Strachan and he's the agent and director for the Canada Company land monopoly here in Upper Canada. And there you have it—the government of this fair colony. *(They take a bow.)*

Now this family connection rules Upper Canada according to its own good pleasure. It has no effective check from the country to guard the people against its acts of tyranny and oppression. It includes the whole of the judges of the supreme civil and criminal tribunals; it includes the agents and directors for the Canada Company land monopoly; it includes the president and solicitor and members of the board of the Bank of Upper

Canada; it includes half of the Executive Council and all of the Legislative Council. *(They are chortling with self-satisfaction.)* Now this is pretty impressive, I'd say—criminals into government. But there's one piece of magic even more mind-boggling than that you've already seen—and that is how this Family Compact of villainy stays in power in Upper Canada!

They laugh him off the stage.

Mary MacDonald

EDWARD PETERS, a farmer, is stage left. He is waiting for someone to arrive. Enter MARY MACDONALD, stage right. She is expecting to be met. She does not notice him. He approaches her nervously.

EDWARD: Excuse me, are you Miss Mary Macdonald?

MARY: I am. *(She is very Scottish.)*

EDWARD: Oh. I'm Edward Peters.

They are both horribly awkward.

MARY: I'm very pleased to make your acquaintance Mr. Peters.

EDWARD: I'm very pleased to meet you. *(A painful silence.)* You must be tired after such a long trip.

MARY: Yes, I am—a bit.

EDWARD: They have benches here for people if you'd care to—um—

MARY: Oh, thank you.

They cross and sit down.

EDWARD: *(plunging)* I wrote you a letter, Miss Macdonald. I don't know if you received it, proposing a date for the—um—for our wedding.

MARY: *(nearly choking with nervousness)* Yes. I got it.

EDWARD: Ah. Well. Would two weeks be satisfactory then?

MARY: Yes. That would be just fine. I wouldn't want to put you to any trouble.

EDWARD: No. It's no trouble.

They sit in awful silence. He leans over and away from her, to spit. He notices her watching him and swallows it instead.

MARY: Oh feel free.

EDWARD: Ah, no. I didn't really feel like it.

MARY: It's quite hot, is it not?

EDWARD: Yes. It's usually quite hot here in August. It's going to get a lot colder though.

MARY: What kind of farm do you have Mr. Peters?

EDWARD: It's a *good* farm. I raise wheat, built most of a barn, got a good frame house. I think you'll be very comfortable there. Nice furniture. Rough, but it's usable. I built it myself. I'm good with my hands.

MARY: *(trying hopelessly to relax him and herself)* Yes—

EDWARD: And I don't drink.

MARY: *(not really happy about it)* Oh.

EDWARD: I bought a cow.

MARY: You did—

EDWARD: Yes. I thought you'd be used to fresh milk so I went and bought a cow.

MARY: *(pleased)* And what's her name?

EDWARD: *(embarrassed again)* Cow.

MARY: Cow?

EDWARD: Well when you only have one, you just . . . call it . . . cow . . . .

MARY: *(feeling their lack of success in communicating)* Oh—

EDWARD: But you could go ahead and give her a nice name.

MARY: I could?

EDWARD: Sure. You'll be milking her and looking after her. You could go ahead and name her.

MARY: Thank you.

EDWARD: You're welcome.

With great relief he spots someone coming up the street.

That's George. See that big fellow on the wagon there? That's my brother George. He's come down to take us back to the farm.

MARY: Now?

EDWARD: Yes.

They start across the stage. MARY is in front of EDWARD. MARY stumbles and almost falls. EDWARD catches her by the arm. It is the first time they've touched. They smile.

EDWARD: You've got to watch where you're walking, Mary. There's ruts.

MARY: Yes.

They go off together.

The Lady in the Coach

Enter LADY BACKWASH, an English gentle-woman of the memoir-writing ilk. (Note: This role has been played by both male and female actors.)

LADY B.: Ladies, I should like to talk to you this evening about my adventures in Upper Canada. I call this lecture—Roughing It In The Bush. The Bush is a term which these quaint Canadians use when describing the vast trackless forests which cover nine-tenths of the colony; dark impenetrable woods much like a jungle, complete with insects, but not the heat. I was on my way to visit a very old and dear friend, Colonel Stockton, in Niagara-on-the Lake.

As she speaks, the COACH DRIVER appears, brings in and harnesses his horse to the coach and settles in for the ride.

LADY B.: We were to have a sumptuous meal and then witness the spectacular beauty of Niagara Falls by moonlight, which I shall describe later in this evening's talk. Our transportation from Toronto to Niagara was to be accomplished by coach. Now I use this word in the broadest sense of the term, for the vehicle which was produced for our conveyance, if 'twere in England, would not be called a coach. It would be called a great many things, but certainly not a coach. However, despite this hardship, it was with the greatest anticipation that I set out, with my man Johnson . . . *(Enter JOHNSON,*

with a discreet bow toward the audience. JOHNSON is a young lad, notably Cockney.) . . . to travel from Toronto to Niagara.

They enter and are seated in the coach. The DRIVER lets out a "hyaaah" to his horse and they are off with much bumping.

DRIVER: Giddup Winnifred—whoa—hyaah—giddup . . . .

LADY B.: Johnson, have they never heard of springs in this country?

JOHNSON: I don't believe so madam—

They hit an enormous bump, they bounce, stop, and the coach rocks from side to side. The LADY and her man are discomfitted. The DRIVER has leapt from his seat down to the side of the coach and is straining to push it out of the hole in which it is stuck.

LADY B.: Johnson—the driver has jumped off!

JOHNSON: I don't blame him. I'd get off too if I could.

LADY B.: Driver. *(The DRIVER does not respond.)* Driver! We've stopped.

DRIVER: *(hoping she'll go away)* That's right, ma'am.

LADY B.: Why have we stopped?

DRIVER: Well ma'am—it's the mud.

LADY B.: Mud? You hear that Johnson—mud! My dear man, I have a very important dinner engagement in Niagara-on-the-Lake this evening, and with some candor I might tell you that if I am forced to go without my dinner tonight, you shall be obliged to do without your job tomorrow. Mud or no mud!

DRIVER: Ma'am—if you think this is bad, why we've got bogs up the way ahead of us that'll make this look like a puddle. Now we'll be able to get on our way in a minute if you'll just step out of the coach.

LADY B.: Out? Get out? My dear man, your impertinence is only matched by your incompetence as a driver. It is my duty to ride in this coach from Toronto to Niagara. It is yours to get me there. Now I am doing my duty. Kindly do yours.

DRIVER: *(patience, patience)* Ma'am—if you won't get out of the coach, to lighten the load, so that I can push her out of this hole, we'll never get to Niagara.

JOHNSON: *(aping his mistress' tone)* Absolutely not. We paid good money to ride in this coach and we're not getting out of it. *(turning to LADY B., pleased with himself)* Got to be firm with his type.

LADY B.: *(interrupting)* Johnson, you and I shall get out of this coach.

JOHNSON: *(stung)* Wot—

LADY B.: *(firmly)* —thereby lightening the load, thereby facilitating this nincompoop in getting us out of here.

DRIVER: Thank you ma'am. There's a dry spot here—

JOHNSON: I don't see a dry spot—

The DRIVER tries to help JOHNSON down. JOHNSON tries to avoid being dropped in the mud. The upshot is, the DRIVER is holding JOHNSON aloft. LADY B. stands up grandly and strides out of the other door of the coach onto the side of the road. She notices the confusion with JOHNSON and upbraids him.

LADY B.: Johnson, come over here. Don't worry about a little mud. Where would the glorious Empire be today if it weren't above mud?

JOHNSON crosses here and stands beside her. The DRIVER puts his shoulder to the wheel.

DRIVER: Now pull Winnifred. Pull girl—

LADY B.: *(to DRIVER)* Oh you'll not do it that way. You're not strong enough.

DRIVER: *(straining)* Hyaah, hyaah—

JOHNSON: He's not smart enough either.

LADY B.: He's not smart enough to know he's not strong enough.

DRIVER: *(giving up)* Whoa Winnifred—

LADY B.: Told you so. No, Johnson shall have to help you push from behind.

JOHNSON: *(stung)* Wot?

LADY B.: Yes, Johnson shall have to get in the mud and help you push from behind.

JOHNSON: Wot—me get in the mud and push that thing. Not likely—

LADY B.: *(cutting him off with great master-servant authority)* Johnson!

JOHNSON breaks off his tirade and assumes instant humility. He has remembered his place.

LADY B.: This colony is having a most disturbing effect on your personality. Now into the mud and push! (JOHNSON jumps obediently into the mud.) That's British pluck.

DRIVER: Alright Mr. Johnson. You just put your back into it, right about there, and give it what you've got—

JOHNSON wrinkles his nose at the DRIVER.

LADY B.: Johnson, push with a will—the eyes of England are upon you.

DRIVER: Alright, Winnifred, pull girl, hyaah—

They strain away. Enter, rear of LADY BACKWASH, an INDIAN carrying an axe. He is amused by the sight and wanders up. LADY B. hears his laughs, turns to see him and emits a shriek.

LADY B.: Eeek. Johnson, I'm being attacked by a savage!

JOHNSON: *(springing to the rescue)* Savage is it? That's my job. *(running up to confront the savage)* Alright Savage—put 'em up. I studied with the Marquess of Queensbury, I did—Omygawd, he's got an axe!

He flees to the other side of the stage and climbs a tree.

DRIVER: *(to INDIAN)* Hello Bart. How are you today?

INDIAN: *(moving over to Lady B.)* Fine. Hello ma'am, Wells is the name.

He offers his hand which she shakes, her mind already grinding away about how she can use this new arrival.

INDIAN: *(moving on to DRIVER)* Where did you find that one?

LADY B.: Johnson, come down from that tree. You're not a monkey. *(JOHNSON obeys.)* Johnson, it *(referring to the INDIAN)* speaks English. And if it speaks English, it can take orders. Johnson, you shall take the savage in hand and push from behind. Driver—Johnson and the savage shall push from behind. While they push, you shall lift from the middle, and I myself shall take Winnifred by the head, and encourage her to greater effort. Right Winnifred?

WINNIFRED whinnies. They assume their appointed positions.

LADY B.: Altogether now—push, pull, come on Winnifred, it's coming—

They are straining, pushing, lifting. Suddenly, with a lurch, the coach comes free. They are all— except for LADY B.—panting from the effort. She is babbling more than ever.

LADY B.: *(elated)* There! We did it! What did I tell you? Just needed a little leadership. Johnson— you were superb. Driver—you were tremendous. Savage—you were alright. And Winnifred—you pulled with a will.

INDIAN: *(to DRIVER)* You sure it's safe for me to leave you alone with her?

LADY B.: Johnson, I haven't felt so good since I arrived at this wretched colony. *(a sudden inspiration)* Johnson—quickly, my diary.

JOHNSON fetches it and takes down her dictation. She addresses posterity.

LADY B.: We had fought the good fight and won. We had been faced with insurmountable obstacles and we had overcome them. And now we took the rest of the victorious, and what better place than here, in Nature's Cathedral.

JOHNSON: *(copying)* Oh, I like that.

LADY B.: I looked up at the tall trees, like giant columns supporting the vast infinite blue of the sky above. The birds sang, the bees—um, the bees— *(She searches.)*

JOHNSON: Might I suggest "buzzed"?

LADY B.: *(accepting with alacrity)* Buzzed. Of course—buzzed. Very good, Johnson. And everywhere was peace, tranquillity and beauty.

WINNIFRED whinnies impatiently.

DRIVER: Ma'am can I suggest you get back into the coach. Once Winnifred gets us out of one bog, she just can't wait to get us into the next one.

JOHNSON: Huh?

LADY B.: An example of Canadian humour, I believe, Johnson. *(They chuckle.)* That's enough, Johnson.

They get back into the coach. The DRIVER is about to crack the whip. LADY BACKWASH takes one final look at the site of this enchanted event.

LADY B.: Farewell, brave bush!

DRIVER: Hyaah!

The coach bounces into motion. They are bouncing with it.

Blackout.

The Head

Note: Sir Francis Bond Head was Lieutenant-Governor of Upper Canada in 1837. Mackenzie could rarely resist punning on his name. In this scene four actors comprise themselves as Head's head. Two of their heads are his eyes, two arms his arching eyebrows, two other arms his nose. So on for his mouth, dimple, etc. The scene begins with the narrated, piece by piece construction of the head, after which the "head" talks.

VOICE: Two piercing blue eyes . . . *(Enter the eyes.)* . . . arching eyebrows, a long aristocratic nose, a firm mouth—and a dimple on the chin. Sir Francis Bond Head, Lieutenant-Governor of Upper Canada, addresses an assembly of voters before the election of 1836.

HEAD: *(sniffing, scowling, smiling, etc., as the speech proceeds)* Gentlemen, as your district now has the important duty to perform of electing representatives for the new Parliament, I think it might practically assist if I clearly lay before you the conduct I intend inflexibly to pursue. If you choose to dispute with me and live on bad terms with the Mother Country, you will—to use a homely phrase—only quarrel with your own bread and butter. If you choose to try this experiment by again electing members who will oppose me, do so. On the other hand, if you choose to embark your interests with my character, I will take paternal care of them both. Men—women and money are what you want. And if you send to Parliament members who will assist me, you can depend upon it, you will gain far more than you possibly can by trying to insult me. But—let your conduct be what it may—I am quite determined, so long as I occupy this station, neither to give offense, nor to take it. Gentlemen, you may now cast your ballots.

Blackout.

Further note: The above is a quotation from an actual speech by Sir Francis at the time.

The Election of '36

A TORY and a REFORMER

TORY: Hey!

REFORMER: Yeah?

TORY: How're you voting?

REFORMER: Me? Reform.

TORY: Oh Yeah? *(Ploughs him one.)*

ANOTHER REFORMER: Well—you're obviously voting Tory.

TORY: That's right.

REFORMER: Uh-huh. *(Ploughs the TORY. Then loudly proclaims:)* Reform!

ANOTHER TORY: Didn't hear that. All votes have to be heard to be recorded.

REFORMER: I said—Reform!

TORY: That's what I thought you said. *(Wham.)*

ROBERT DAVIS: *(This character has, for some reason, been played by a woman in all productions of 1837 so far.)* Hey don't hit him like that. This is no way to carry on an election—

All then turn on this poor peacemaker and attack him, screaming their political slogans as they flail away at each other and particularly at ROBERT DAVIS. The cry of "Tory" rings above the others. The Tories are obviously most proficient at this political bullying. The mayhem concludes with the brutal cry, "God—Save—The—Queen!" Freeze.

The Canadian Farmer's Travels in the U.S.A.

ROBERT DAVIS, Upper Canadian farmer, drags himself out from the bottom of the brawl during the election of 1836.

DAVIS: Would you believe that was an election? I would! Lost two teeth in it—and that proves it's an election around here. My name's Robert Davis. I have a small farm here in Nissouri Township. Lived here all my life. Got two fine kids. Taught myself to read and write. But this election was just about the end for me. Why we've been working for reform for fifteen years—and now things in Upper Canada are worse than ever. I'd about lost hope. And I needed to get my hope back somehow. So I decided I'd take a trip to the United States. I'd heard things were different down there, and I thought—if I can see that someone else has succeeded, maybe I can keep on trying myself. So I started out.

He walks.

DAVIS: Now the first place I came to on my way to the border was the little town of Chatham. Beautiful little place for a town, but very sleepy . . . .

The Town Council of Chatham comes to order.

MAYOR: My friends, as members of the Town Council of Chatham I think we should establish what is going to be happening here for the next twenty years.

DAVIS: Good. I'd like to see that. What have you got in mind?

The members of the Council yawn, fall flat on their backs, and snore.

DAVIS: See that! That's despair—I'm not going to stay around here. *(Walks.)* So I kept on, till I came to the town of Sandwich, that's right across the river from Detroit. Look around. There's nothing happening here.

BOATMAN: All aboard for Detroit.

DAVIS: Can you take me to Detroit?

BOATMAN: Yup. Get aboard fast. Miss the boat and there isn't another one for a week.

DAVIS: That's ridiculous—one boat a week!

They start across the river.

DAVIS: And as we left Sandwich snoozing in the sunshine, I could see a kind of stir on the other side of the river. And sounds—sounds like I'd never heard before—

The bustling sounds of Detroit begin to come up.

DAVIS: And suddenly we were surrounded by boats, big and little, carrying grain, and goods, and *people* —

BOATMAN: *(yelling)* Detroit! Gateway to the American Dream—

The sounds of industry and trade explode around poor DAVIS. People rush back and forth past him, happy, productive—

AMERICAN: Howdy stranger, I'd like to stay and shoot the breeze, but I'm too busy getting rich.

DAVIS: Look at all these people—and this *industry*, and—and—two thousand immigrants a day—most of them from Upper Canada!

IMMIGRANT: *(kissing the ground)* America! America!

RUNAWAY SLAVE: *(to DAVIS)* Excuse me sir, I'm a runaway slave. Which way is Canada?

DAVIS: No, no. Don't go there. It's terrible. Stay here. I'm sure things will get better for you. *(turning)* Oh—look. A four-storey brick building! *(Someone plays it.)* Isn't it wonderful?

WRECKER: 'Scuse me fella. Gotta tear down this four-storey building.

DAVIS: *(horrified)* Why?

WRECKER: *(knocking it down)* 'Cause we're gonna put up a six-storey one in its place! There— *(Whoosht—up it goes.)*

DAVIS: Oh—and look at what it says on it— Museum!

MUSEUM: Sure. Come on in—

DAVIS enters, sees statues of American heroes— "We got more than we know what to do with"— Whistler's Mother, or some such nonsense. (By the way, this scene has never been "set." DAVIS has seen different things nearly every time he has taken his trip.)

DAVIS: This is all fine, but you know I'm a farmer, and I'll really know what to make of your country when I see what's happening outside the cities. So can you tell me how I can get to the country?

AMERICAN: Sure. How'd you like to go?

DAVIS: How? I thought I'd walk—

AMERICAN: Pshaw—nobody walks down here. Now you can go by coach, or canal—

DAVIS: Don't talk to me about canals! Did you ever hear of the Welland Canal? They've been building it for twelve years! It's only twelve miles long. It's cost us millions of dollars and you *still* have to dig your way through!

AMERICAN: No kidding. Well we've got the Erie Canal. Five hundred miles and clear straight through—

DAVIS: *(stunned)* Five hundred miles . . . .

AMERICAN: But if you don't like that, you can always take the train.

DAVIS: Train? What was that word you just said?

Zip. He is suddenly in the country.

DAVIS: So I went to the country. Acre after acre of cleared, fertile land—

FARMER: Excuse me friend, would you mind moving your foot?

DAVIS: My foot? Why?

FARMER: Well, do you feel something moving under it?

DAVIS: Moving? Why yes—I do!

FARMER: Just move it aside—there.

They both watch as a crop of wheat grows from the floor to the ceiling.

FARMER: Crop of wheat I planted this morning. A little small this year. Well, watch yourself while I harvest it. *(with his axe)* Timber!

DAVIS: Wheat—and apple orchards—and thousands of head of cattle—and sixty pound cheeses!

These appear—or fail to do so—at the whim of the other actors onstage. The most fun occurs when someone introduces into the scene something DAVIS and the others have not expected.

DAVIS: And then I went to one of the hundreds of thriving country towns—

SCHOOLHOUSE: Bong! Bong! Come on kiddies—everybody into school for your free universal education.

DAVIS: Free? Universal? You mean your schools aren't just for your aristocracy?

SCHOOLHOUSE: You watch your language down here. We don't use words like that!

DAVIS: Everyone can go to school! Does it work?

SCHOOLHOUSE: Hah! Where's that dumb kid. C'mere kid, get inside.

The DUMB KID walks through one door of the schoolhouse and emerges from the other.

FORMERLY DUMB KID: E=mc^2.

CHURCH: Ding Dong—Methodist.

ANOTHER: Ding Dong—Lutheran.

ANOTHER: Ding Dong—Quaker.

Somebody has not declared himself.

DAVIS: What are you?

TOWNSMAN: I'm an atheist.

DAVIS: You allow atheists down here too?

CHURCH: We don't like them but we allow them.

DAVIS: But which one is your established church, you know, the official church?

They all laugh.

TOWNSMAN: Say—you must be a Canadian.

DAVIS: *(delighted)* I am. How'd you know?

TOWNSMAN: Say house.

DAVIS: House.

TOWNSMAN: Say about.

DAVIS: About.

TOWNSMAN: I knew it. Now excuse us, we're going to have an election.

DAVIS: *(panicking)* An election? Let me out of here—I'm going to hide—I've lost enough teeth.

He watches from a distance.

FIRST VOTER: Having searched my conscience, I have decided to cast my vote as a Democrat.

The next VOTER steps up. DAVIS winces in expectation of the clash.

SECOND VOTER: Well, in that case, I'm going to vote Republican.

THIRD VOTER: Then I vote Democrat.

FOURTH VOTER: Let's see—the Republicans won last time, so I'll vote Democrat too.

ALL: Hurray!

They all commiserate with the lone Republican.

DAVIS: Hey—wait a minute. When does the fight start?

VOTER: Fight? What do you mean? This is an election. Now come here, uh, what's your name?

DAVIS: Davis.

VOTER: No, I mean your first name. We all use first names here.

DAVIS: Bob.

VOTER: Well Bob, I'd like you to meet the new governor of our state. This is Ole. Ole, this is Bob, from Canada—

OLE: *(a very slow speaking farmer)* Well, how do you do. You wouldn't like to buy a pig would you?

DAVIS: Pig? You mean you're the governor of this state and you still work as a farmer.

OLE: Well, gotta make some money somehow—

DAVIS: You know, you've all given me new hope. You've proven to me it can be done. This is what we've been working for for years, and I can go home now and—

VOTER: Home? Wait a minute Bob. Why don't you stay right here with us and make this your new home?

DAVIS: Here? But why should I?

ANOTHER VOTER: Because it's the best darned country in the world. That's why.

DAVIS: But—but I've got my family back there.

ANOTHER: Bring 'em down here. Bring your whole country.

DAVIS: But—but there's my farm.

ANOTHER: Tell you what we'll do Bob. We'll give you a four hundred acre cleared farm right here. Just for you.

DAVIS: (getting excited) Cleared? (suspicious) How much?

ANOTHER: Nothing. Just take good care of it.

DAVIS: I can have that farm?

ANOTHER: Sure. We'll just sweep those Indians off it and—

DAVIS: Why that's wonderful! You're all so generous! This must be the finest—

ANOTHER: See. He's starting to act like an American already. Being happy and talking loud—

DAVIS: No. No, I can't do it.

ANOTHER: Those words don't exist in America.

DAVIS: I can't stay. You see—it's not my home. I can't just leave Canada. It's up to us to do there what you've done here. But you've given me hope. Now I know it can be done— (He is leaving.) So I went home.

Lethargic, snoring, apathetic Canadians surround him.

DAVIS: And I said—Don't lie around. Get up. Help each other. You can do it.

He drags them to their feet. They are rubbery-legged. They cling to each other and anything they can find.

DAVIS: I've seen it now. I know it can be done. We can do it too, if we stay together. Now is not the time for Reformers to fawn and crouch. Now is the time to unite and fight!

Blackout.

The Dummy

A political rally in rural Upper Canada attended by angry Reform farmers.

FARMER: He's here, he's here alright. The great man is here. I saw him just out back.

They cheer.

FARMER: He's come down here to talk to all of us—now you put that jug away, this is a dry meeting—but before the great man talks to us, a couple of the folks have worked up one of their little skits to do for us. So come on up here and get it over with, so we can all get on with hearing the great man's speech. (Two farmers come up front.) And don't forget your lines this time.

The two stand in front of the rally. One assumes the role of the VENTRILOQUIST. The other plays his DUMMY.

VENTRILOQUIST: Ladies and gentlemen. Presenting for your enjoyment, straight from England, John Bull—your Imperial ventriloquist—and his companion, Peter Stump—the Canadian axeman. Say hello to the people, Peter.

PETER: (The VENTRILOQUIST is throwing his voice.) Hello.

JOHN: Aren't you forgetting to add something, Peter?

PETER: God Save The Queen.

JOHN: Good, Peter. Very loyal. I say—what is that in your hand?

PETER: My axe.

JOHN: What do you do with your axe, Peter?

PETER: Chop down trees. (He chops.) Timber!

JOHN: And what do you do with the wood you cut?

PETER: Send it to you in England, John.

JOHN: Very fine Peter. Say, what else do you have there?

PETER: My rifle.

JOHN: Aha—and who are you going to shoot?

PETER: Yankees.

JOHN: Good. And quickly too— (*He hides behind PETER.*)

PETER: Bang, bang, bang, bang—

JOHN: (*emerging*) Whew! Well done, lad. Now could you loan me twenty of your dollars?

PETER: (*protesting*) John, I'm short myself—

JOHN: (*picking his pocket*) There. I knew you wouldn't mind. Now is there anything else I can do for you?

PETER: Yes.

JOHN: What's that?

PETER: Please take your hand away from my neck.

JOHN: (*surprised*) I beg your pardon?

PETER: Take your hand away from me.

JOHN: If I do that, you will be helpless. Do you understand?

PETER: I want to try.

CROWD: Let him go. Give him a chance.

JOHN: Very well, Peter—

He yanks his hand out. PETER stands stock still. JOHN moves away from him.

JOHN: Now Peter, now let's hear you speak. Ha! Chop down trees Peter! Shoot Yankees! Can't do a thing can you?

CROWD: Come on, Peter. You can do it.

JOHN: Without me, John Bull, you are nothing. Pathetic isn't he, ladies and gentlemen? A pitiable, colonial—

PETER: (*with his own voice, for the first time*) Mm—

JOHN: (*stunned*) What? What was that?

PETER: (*louder*) Mm—mm—I—I—

JOHN: Peter, Peter—what are you up to?

PETER: (*slowly finding his voice*) I want to say: (*more confidently*) Thank God for the man who is giving me a voice— (*shouting, no longer a dummy at all*) William Lyon Mackenzie!

The CROWD cheers. Enter MACKENZIE and bounds onto the rostrum.

The Speech

MACKENZIE: Thank you, ladies and gentlemen, thank you. Now let's start off this meeting by giving three cheers for the men who made it possible, or rather I should say necessary. Let's have three cheers for Archdeacon John Strachan. Hip hip hurray! Hip hip hurray!—

CROWD: Booo—

MACKENZIE: Come now my friends, you won't cheer John Strachan? I didn't realize feelings ran that high. Now I was talking to someone the other day who said about Strachan—if that man's godliness were gunpowder, he couldn't blow his own nose. Alright then, if you won't cheer Strachan, let's have three cheers for Christopher Alexander Hagerman. Hip hip hurray—

CROWD: Booo—

MACKENZIE: My friends, these people tell us over and over that they are the nobility of this colony so we should cheer them. Come on now—

CROWD: No!

MACKENZIE: Alright then, let's give three cheers for the real nobility of Upper Canada. Three cheers for the farmers!

CROWD: Hip hip hurray! Hip hip hurray! Hip hip hurray!

MACKENZIE: Alright now, I'm going to tell you a story. It's an old story, but there's no stories like old stories. It concerns a little Reformer who goes to the Assembly to see what he can do to rectify the wrongs in this colony. So he puts forward all those bills he feels are for the general good and he opposes all those bills he feels are against the general good, please or offend whom it might. And it seemed to offend some people. For Bolton called him a reptile and Hagerman called him a spaniel dog. Now that shows you one thing about Hagerman, and that is—that his knowledge of dogs is only equalled by his knowledge of decent government. For anybody who knew anything about dogs could tell you that this Reformer was not a spaniel dog—but a Scots terrier hot on the trail of a rat!

The CROWD cheers.

MACKENZIE: But these men didn't stop at calling him names. They thought that more forceful action was necessary. So they grabbed him by the seat of the pants and the collar of the coat, and they threw him out of the Assembly! *(MACKENZIE leaps into the CROWD.)* But what did the people do?

CROWD: We put you back. *(They hoist him back onto the platform.)*

MACKENZIE: And they threw him out again! *(He leaps out.)*

CROWD: And we put you back—

MACKENZIE: And out again—

CROWD: And back again—

MACKENZIE: And a fourth time—

CROWD: And back a fourth time—

MACKENZIE: Yes, four times they threw him out, and four times the people sent him back. And that's round one for the people. For try as they might, these men cannot oppose the will of the people to send to the Assembly who they want. So the little Reformer finds himself securely in the Assembly. But what can he do? His hands are tied. So he says to himself, I've got to go above the heads of these people, above Strachan and Bolton, and Hagerman. I've got to go to the top—to the King of England! So the little Reformer goes to England, and he's armed with a petition of grievances that's half a mile long. And the signatures on that petition aren't one, two, three, or four names. Oh no no no—there's twenty-five thousand names on that petition. And the King of England looks at it, and he goes— Oh my my my my! And he calls for the Colonial Secretary, and the Colonial Secretary gets the Colonial Office moving, and the Colonial Office gets our government over here moving, so everybody's moving hither-thither, helter-skelter, but out of all this government activity what real good comes? What happens here in this colony?

CROWD: Nothing!

MACKENZIE: Nothing? Not quite. For the Pharaoh of England in his wisdom sends us a saviour—a new Lieutenant-Governor, Sir Francis *Bone* Head. Now what are Sir Francis' credentials for holding this very important office?

CROWD: None! He hasn't got any!

MACKENZIE: Oh yes he does. It's a long and impressive list and I'm going to tell you what they are, Number one. He's a damn fool. Number two. He's English. Number three. He's arrogant. And number four. He's very good with a lasso.

CROWD: What?

MACKENZIE: The lasso. Sir Francis' specialty is the lasso—a skill he picked up in Argentina, used there for herding cattle. So the first thing Sir Francis does when he gets to our colony is he gets out his lasso, and he circles it above his head once, twice, three times—and he lets it go! And who does he catch? You! He catches the people of Upper Canada, and there we all are in Sir Francis' lasso. And he pulls it a little tighter and he says—alright, now it's time for an election; all those in favour of Reform, stand up! And he pulls very hard and he pulls all of us off our feet. Now how did one man pull all of us off our feet? I'll tell you how he did it. We're all in that lasso and we're pushing this way and pulling that way in our frustration and despair. But I tell you that, if as one man we took hold of that rope and turned to Sir Francis, then with one mighty tug, we could pull him off his high horse and send him back to England on his ass!

The CROWD cheers.

MACKENZIE: And that's what I want to talk to you about today. Pulling as one man— Union! For the power of the people is as nothing without union and union is nothing without confidence and discipline. Now the Tories have been following me around to these various meetings, taking what I say back to Toronto, and I'm flattered by the attention. But I don't want to get in trouble with the authorities—treason or anything of that sort, so I'm going to talk to you now in a roundabout manner. Now first of all I think we have to form ourselves into small groups—say fourteen to forty people—just to talk. There's no law against talking. And each of those groups is in contact with other such groups around the province, so we know who our friends are in case of an emergency. But I think the time for talking is past. It's gone by. And I think now it's time for us to work on our muscle power, develop our strength—and I think the best way to do that is through turkey shoots.

CROWD: Turkey shoots?

MACKENZIE: Yes—

CROWD: We know how to shoot turkeys!

MACKENZIE: But don't you think a turkey shoot would be more fun if there was a little drilling beforehand? And don't you think you could shoot turkeys a bit better if everyone shot at once—bang bang bang bang. Because you see, the thing about a Tory—I mean a turkey—the thing about a turkey is you can shoot it with a rifle, you can cut its head off with an axe, a pike is an excellent tool for getting turkeys out of high places—and if worse comes to worst, you can always grab a turkey in your own bare hands and wring its bloody neck!

The CROWD cheers.

MACKENZIE: Now once we get very good at killing turkeys, we go down to that turkey parliament, and we say—this is what we want! And this is what we intend to get! And if they refuse—

CROWD: Yes! What then?

MACKENZIE: We declare open season on turkeys and you'll all have one on your plate this year for Christmas!

The CROWD cheers.

MACKENZIE: Now who's going to be the first to come up here and sign the paper and pledge themselves to shooting turkeys?

CROWD: Me! I will!

MACKENZIE: That's the spirit!

Freeze. Blackout.

Lount's Forge

SAMUEL LOUNT's blacksmith shop at Holland Landing. LOUNT is at stage centre, hammer in hand, standing over his anvil. Around him are various voices of discontent. All lines are spoken to the audience.

LOUNT: Oh yes! I'm back—doing what I know how to do. I've been a farmer, a surveyor, mostly a blacksmith—but the most useless job I ever tried was politics!

MAN: It took me twelve years to drain the swamp off my land. Then, last summer, the Canada Company dams up the river and floods all the low lands. You look now—you've never seen such a bog!

LOUNT: Samuel Lount for the Assembly! Sam—you've got to run. Sam—we need you.

WOMAN: I can work in her kitchen, but she doesn't want me in the rest of her house. Well I know all about it anyway—because my husband built it!

LOUNT: So off I go to the Assembly. Every man's vote behind me. And went to sleep for two years.

WOMAN: Sure it's a nice farm. And the town's over there, two miles. But there's no road between our farm and the town—because all the land in between belongs to John Strachan and his accursed Church of England!

LOUNT: I'd no sooner stand up to propose a bill, than some Tory would call for a recess.

MAN: Here's a road. Fine road too. Except for the river that runs across it. Now they won't build the bridge. Now what the hell good is a road without a bridge?

LOUNT: Tories got you scared Sam? That why you're not going back? Yes I'm scared. Scared if we waste two more years with this government, there won't be anything left in this country worth saving!

MAN: Now I don't know anything about politics. But there must be *something* wrong in this province. Because there ain't no women!

LOUNT: So Mackenzie comes to me. "Sam, it's time. We need you." I've heard that one before.

MAN: See this cabinet? Took me four months to make. Know why I can't sell it? Because it was made in Toronto!

WOMAN: Yes, I took in travellers for the night. And maybe I did a few favours for men in return for money. But what else can a woman alone with six children do? So they put me in jail and took away my children. Well watch out Mister—because your turn in coming and it's coming soon!

LOUNT: Mac—I said—I'm a blacksmith, not a politician. "Fine, Sam—that's just what we need. A blacksmith."

MAN: I voted Reform in the last election so the Colonel foreclosed on my mortgage. Now that's four years work all gone. But that's all right. Because now I've got nothing to lose!

LOUNT: So I'm back. But I'm not making horseshoes. And I'm not making laws. I'm making pikes—

He raises the redhot pike he has had on the anvil and lowers it into a bucket of water.

ALL: Sssssssss—

Blackout.

ACT TWO

Doel's Brewery

MACKENZIE sets the scene. Onstage with him are three of his Reform associates, and a BREWERY WORKER.

MACKENZIE: November 11, 1837. Doel's Brewery, at the corner of Bay and Adelaide Streets, in Toronto. I've called an emergency meeting of the leading Reformers of this city: John Doel—he owns this brewery; lawyer Parsons; Dr. Rolph. These gentlemen are all leading and respected citizens. And this man over here—he's one of Doel's workers—and a good man he is too. We don't seem to have any influence with the government of this country. We have none at all with the King of England. But to my surprise and delight, I find we have some influence with someone up there *(skyward)* for the opportunity which has been presented to us can only be described as heaven-sent. The brave French patriots under Papineau in Lower Canada have struck for their own freedom. Now that means two things to us. First—it indicates to us in Upper Canada the route we too must take to achieve our ends. Second—and even more important—it means there isn't one English soldier left here in Toronto tonight. They've all marched off to Lower Canada. But our blessings don't stop there. No no no no—for in City Hall are four thousand muskets, still in their crates, not even unpacked yet. Guarded by only two men! Now anyone who would leave four thousand muskets guarded by only two men cannot be averse to them being used. At Government House, Sir Francis Bond Head has just come in

from his ride; he sits before his fire, feet up on the fender, sipping a glass of expensive French brandy, and imagines he presides over the most contented colony in the entire Empire. He is guarded by only one sentry. At Kingston, Fort Henry lies open and deserted. A steamer only has to sail up to the wharf and it's ours. *(turning to his colleagues)* Now here's the plan—we seize Sir Francis, we take him to City Hall and seize the arms, which we distribute to our friends here and in the country. We then declare a Provisional Government and demand of Sir Francis a Legislative Council responsible to a new and fairly elected Assembly. If he refuses—

DOEL: Yes? If he refuses?

MACKENZIE: We go at once for Independence and take whatever steps are necessary to secure it! *(He grabs DOEL and pilots him across the stage.)* Doel, it's so easy, all you have to do is come along here, pick up those muskets, and we've won!

DOEL: *(pulling away)* Shhh. Now we all want the same things Mac—but we *don't* want to cause trouble.

MACKENZIE: Right! And if we do it this way it'll be no trouble at all—

PARSONS: *(trying to settle him down)* Now Mackenzie—you're our leader, we all agree to that. But why don't you just sit down for a moment and—

MACKENZIE: *(springing back up)* This is no time to sit down! It's time to rise up and act!

ROLPH: *(authoritatively)* Mackenzie! What if we fail?

MACKENZIE: Rolph, with this much nerve—this much courage—we cannot fail.

DOEL: Now Mac—don't rush like this. We've put four months of careful organization and preparation into this.

MACKENZIE: Doel, what in God's name have we been organizing *for*?

PARSONS: Mac, I want to go with you, but I just don't know how to make the jump— *(He mimes it.)*

MACKENZIE: If you want to jump—you jump. *(He leaps across the stage.)*

ROLPH: We don't have the men.

MACKENZIE: We do! We've got Doel's own workers. We've got Armstrong's axemakers. Dutcher's foundrymen—they're strong, dependable, and they're ready to *act*—

The WORKER starts moving determinedly toward the stand of muskets (indicated by one or two guns). The three REFORMERS scurry to interpose themselves before the weapons actually are seized. They head off the WORKER by a whisker.

ROLPH: Mackenzie—we have pledged ourselves to Reform—not Revolution.

MACKENZIE: It doesn't matter what you call it Rolph. The question is, what are you going to do about it?

DOEL: Well, if it's force we want, I move we bring down our friends from the country.

MACKENZIE: That's the way is it, Doel? Bring down the farmers to do your dirty work? Besides—it will take four weeks to get the farmers down here.

PARSONS: Well alright then—four weeks. That makes it what?—December seventh.

DOEL: Yes. Agreed. December seventh.

ROLPH: December seventh.

DOEL: Mackenzie?

MACKENZIE: *(with a helpless look at the WORKER, and a gesture of disgust toward his colleagues)* Alright—December seventh!

Blackout.

Drilling

A FARMER is alone onstage, with a pitchfork, drilling with it as one would with a rifle.

FARMER: Present . . . . Attack! Present . . . . Attack! Present . . . . Attack!

Enter another FARMER, who sees the drill and starts to chuckle about it. FIRST continues drilling, but is irked by the derision.

SECOND: Come on. Come on now.

FIRST: Present . . . . Attack! . . .

SECOND: You're not going to march to Toronto with that?

FIRST: Present . . .

SECOND: What are you going to do with it? Feed hay to the British?

FIRST wheels on SECOND and presses the very menacing point of the pitchfork against his throat. (In fact, this scene has always been played by two women.)

SECOND: Wait—what're you doing?

FIRST: Go on. Laugh some more.

SECOND: Alright. Stop.

FIRST continues pressing. It is quite ominous. That is a real pitchfork up there onstage.

FIRST: Say it—

SECOND: Alright, alright—

FIRST: *Say* It!

SECOND: Say what?

FIRST: Present—

SECOND: *(practically a whimper)* Present—

FIRST: *(whirling and stabbing the fork directly out toward the audience)* Attack!

Tiger Dunlop

DUNLOP: The date is November 19. The place—Gairbraid, near Goderich, home of William "Tiger" Dunlop—raconteur, wit, doctor of medicine, and arch-Tory.

Enter MACKENZIE and COLONEL ANTHONY VAN EGMOND, an older man. They join DUNLOP and all three participate in a hearty after-dinner laugh.

DUNLOP: Yes—I believe that was the same evening we were dining at your home, Van Egmond, and your housekeeper said to me—*(imitating the housekeeper)* Doctor, why is it sir, we never see you in church? And I said, Because, Madam, I have an abiding distrust of any place where one man does all the talking, you're liable to meet your wife, and people sing without drinking!

They all laugh.

VAN EGMOND: An amazing likeness, Tiger, and I must tell you that she still anxiously awaits your return. Tiger here is one of the most eligible bachelors in the tract.

DUNLOP: And intending to remain so. But—that was a long time ago. Strange, isn't it, what time does—to men like Van Egmond and myself, who spent so much time in the same camp in the bush—yet now find ourselves in such separate camps.

VAN EGMOND: Perhaps.

DUNLOP: But, times being what they are, I'm sure you gentlemen haven't come here to hear my old stories. Not with having brought this screaming Reformer with you. I imagine you've come for something—so tell me—What can Tiger Dunlop do for you?

MACKENZIE: Tiger Dunlop can let us help him.

DUNLOP: I beg your pardon.

MACKENZIE: Let us help you.

DUNLOP: What could you possibly do to help me?

MACKENZIE: What do you think of John Strachan?

DUNLOP: I hate the bastard.

MACKENZIE: And Thomas Mercer Jones?

DUNLOP: Jones. Well, anyone who would marry Strachan's daughter can't be all good.

MACKENZIE: Dunlop, you and I seem to concur in our opinions of these people.

DUNLOP: Yes. I believe we do.

MACKENZIE: Every time we turn around in this colony, we see its wealth being carted off someplace else. And what about the honest, hard-working people—the farmers and the labourers? The fruits of their effort are being scooped up to support the idle dandies in Toronto or London—

DUNLOP: Just a moment, Mr. Mackenzie. When you start in about the honest, hardworking people, it's obvious you're about to launch one of your famous political speeches. Now don't let my reputation fool you. I'm still a man who likes plain speaking. I beg you—speak to me plainly.

MACKENZIE: Alright. I'll speak to you plainly. There's going to be some changes in this colony, Dunlop. Big changes. It's going to be out with the old and in with the new. Now the question is, Tiger—are you going to be part of the new or are you going out with the old?

DUNLOP: You talk about changes. Now I have always stood for change in this colony. Isn't that true, Colonel?

VAN EGMOND: Yes. Yes, Tiger—that's the man I remember. Long ago, before this part of the country was even opened up, Tiger here, John Galt—remember him, Tiger?—and myself, we used to go up on a rise by the lake, look about us and talk of the tremendous potential of the country. And Tiger had the most vivid dreams of all. Eighty thousand families, I believe you said, could be supported by the Huron Tract alone. And we set about to make that a reality. We built roads—remember, Tiger?—pushing the roads through the bush to bring in the settlers—built mills, provided for schools, and churches, shipped in supplies—anything that would bring in the settlers. And the towns. That you founded.

But look about you, Tiger. Where are the eighty thousand? For every one settler there should be a hundred more. The roads that were built to bring people in are leading them out. By the thousands. Land value is where it was five, ten years ago. Why? What has happened? I think you have let go of your dream, Tiger. Given it up to men like Jones, Strachan, Hagerman. Fops and dandies. Mushroom aristocrats. Bladders of pride and arrogance—who care not a damn for the country—but only for their own fiefdoms—filling their pockets. I don't think you are the kind of man to let this abuse continue. John Galt could not tolerate such leadership and he resigned his post with the Canada Company. I rather think you are cast in the same mould as Galt.

DUNLOP: Time brings changes, Colonel, and might I say—compromise?

MACKENZIE: Compromise! Dunlop, I've been from one end of this colony to the other. Now there is discontent, vengeance, rage—in men's minds. But not compromise! I've seen it at over two hundred public meetings. Thousands of signatures, names of men pledging themselves to use force of arms if necessary to alleviate their suffering. This colony wants cheap, efficient responsible government and it's going to have it, and there's nothing that the Lieutenant-Governor, or the King of England, or the whole British army can do to stop it.

VAN EGMOND: Tiger, you know what the people want, what they think. You talk to them, high and low alike. They admire you. You are a brilliant man—I don't flatter—you have ideas, and you have the energy to put those ideas into effect.

MACKENZIE: An independent country. A new nation. Think of it, Tiger. Think what this country could be with its natural bounty, under the leadership which men like yourself could provide—it could be one of the greatest in the world. It's a tremendous responsibility staring you right in the face. Now are you man enough to meet that responsibility, Dunlop?

DUNLOP: (He deliberates a long while then chuckles.) Excuse me, gentlemen, but you remind me of a couple of Yankee schoolboys who just read the Declaration of Independence. Now I'm a political realist. Change is one thing, but I call what you're talking about rebellion.

MACKENZIE: Call it revolution if you want, Tiger.

DUNLOP: Well, I don't think you're the man to lead it. My God, man, you can't even buy a cow without offending the herdsman. Colonel, you're a dear and old friend, but it is the truth sir—you are old. Waterloo was long ago. Now if you gentlemen will permit me, I believe I have a responsibility to history. Dr. William Dunlop does not join in insurrection against the rightful government of—

MACKENZIE: I take it all this pomposity is leading up to a "no."

DUNLOP: Yes—I mean, no.

MACKENZIE: Well, it's a long ride back to Toronto, Dunlop. Goodbye.

He exits.

VAN EGMOND: Tiger, do you know that you are twice as old as I am?

VAN EGMOND starts out. DUNLOP calls to him as he is almost out the door.

DUNLOP: Van Egmond—

VAN EGMOND: Goodnight.

He exits. Light on TIGER alone. Fade to black.

Leaving

The following six scenes concern people leaving for the battle. Each is introduced by a verse from the song "Across Toronto Bay."

ALL:
Up now and shoulder arms, and join this free men's march boys,
It's time to show the Tories that this country's no man's toy.
So it's march, march, march to Toronto town today,
And we'll use that fork to pitch Bond Head— across Toronto Bay.

A MERCHANT and the man who does his chores. The EMPLOYEE is carrying an armful of wood. He drops it with a crash.

MERCHANT: Rather sloppy of you Thomas.

THOMAS: That's just my way of saying goodbye sir.

MERCHANT: Goodbye?

THOMAS: Yes sir. I'm going to be leaving your employ.

MERCHANT: You've never mentioned anything of this before.

THOMAS: Well, you see the way I figure it sir, I think there's going to be a fight and I have just the merest suspicion that you and me are going to be on different sides.

MERCHANT: Thomas, I would not become embroiled in this if I were you.

THOMAS: I just don't think it would be fair, sir, for me to keep taking your wages, in case we met on the battlefield—and I had to shoot you dead. (chortling) So I'll just be off now sir. Goodbye— and good luck. (A hearty laugh as he goes out.)

ALL:
It's time to do a different job and take a different stand,
They said we're good for chopping wood and clearing off the land.
So it's march, march, march to Toronto town today,
And we'll use that fork to pitch Bond Head— across Toronto Bay.

HAROLD, a farmer, holding a pistol.

HAROLD: I just can't do it. I never thought I'd have to really shoot somebody when we were drilling. I—I'll tell them I can't go. No that's no good. I know—I'll say I can't go tonight. I'll meet them tomorrow.

Enter his friend TOM.

TOM: Ready, Harold?

HAROLD: Tom—uh, yeah, I'm ready.

TOM: Good!

HAROLD: Uh, look—I even stole a pistol.

TOM: A pistol! Well then—you're in charge!

They exit together.

ALL:
So let those Tories have their fun and slop up all that tea.
I'd just as soon I killed myself a Tory as a tree.
So it's march, march, march to Toronto town today,
And we'll use that fork to pitch Bond Head— across Toronto Bay.

FRED BENCH and his new wife RUTH, both of whom we met in the tavern scene in Act One. They are in bed.

RUTH: Fred—I heard awful stories in town today. People were talking about the Rebels. They say that they're going to burn Toronto.

FRED: Some people have just cause Ruth.

RUTH: Fred Bench, don't you talk that way. Oh Fred! You wouldn't yourself—don't tell me that you'd—

FRED: Now Ruth—I'll do what I think is best for you.

RUTH: Well that's better. Don't let me even think that you'd . . . oh well, I'm sure the Governor will soon put a stop to all this.

FRED: Uh-huh.

RUTH: Goodnight.

FRED: Goodnight Ruth.

She falls asleep. He feigns sleep, then rolls out of bed, grabs his boots and rifle, and steals toward the door.

ALL:
A war will bring some death, boys, it's sure to bring you sorrow.
But if we stand back to back today, we'll own this land tomorrow.
So it's march, march, march to Toronto town today,
And we'll use that fork to pitch Bond Head— across Toronto Bay.

A BOY sneaking through the woods. His younger BROTHER and SISTER intercept him.

BOY: How'd you two get in front of me?

SISTER: We followed you.

BOY: Well, you're not supposed to. Go home.

BROTHER: You're supposed to be looking after us.

BOY: I can't for now. So get on home.

SISTER: We know where you're going.

BOY: I don't care if you know. You're not coming with me.

BROTHER: We'll tell.

BOY: Don't you dare tell! Just take your sister and get on home.

They whine.

BOY: Get going. I'll be back.

He exits. His BROTHER darts after him. The SISTER looks around, lost, and cries.

ALL:
Now Old Mac says we've got a cause to load our rifles for,
So leave that stove and woman home and march right out the door.
For it's march, march, march to Toronto town today,
And we'll use that fork to pitch Bond Head— across Toronto Bay.

ISAAC CASSELMAN's Tavern, as in Act One. EMMA and JAMEY are cleaning around. Enter ISAAC, carrying his rifle and pistol.

ISAAC: Emma, put out the fire. Jamey, you lock the tavern. This tavern is closed.

EMMA: What's going on?

ISAAC: There's a war on, by God, and Isaac Casselman is going off to fight.

JAMEY: Isaac—gimme your pistol.

He grabs it and points it into his mouth.

ISAAC: Jamey—what're you doing?

JAMEY: I'm going to kill myself.

ISAAC: *(grabbing the pistol back)* Why?

JAMEY: Well if you're closing the tavern, I've got no reason to go on living.

ISAAC: Jamey—why don't you come along?

JAMEY: *(scornful)* Naaa—

ISAAC: Maybe there'll be a rum ration.

JAMEY: Rum? *(He grabs the pistol and leads the way.)* Forward—

ALL:
Now all across the country, you can hear the Rebel yell,
We'll follow you Mackenzie, to Toronto or to hell.
So it's march, march, march to Toronto town today,
And we'll use that fork to pitch Bond Head—across Toronto Bay.

MARY MACDONALD, whom we met in Act One, fresh from Scotland, is sitting in her farmhouse doing some chore. She is singing to herself.

MARY: Speed, bonnie boat, like a bird on the wing. Onward the sailors cry—

Enter her husband EDWARD.

MARY: Edward, you're home early.

EDWARD: *(kissing her)* Mary—

MARY: Is anything wrong? *(EDWARD sits down uncomfortably.)* What is it, Edward?

EDWARD: You remember when we first met— and we didn't know each other at all—and we were afraid things wouldn't work out—

MARY: Yes, I remember—

EDWARD: I know I've never said very much. That's just my way. But I want you to know that it's been . . . . Hell—I've got to go fight.

MARY: *(accepting it with difficulty)* Yes. Of course.

EDWARD: *(relieved)* Of course? Do you think it's wrong—us being married such a short time?

MARY: No. I don't. Of course you must go.

EDWARD is immensely grateful that she accepts it.

MARY: When do you have to go?

EDWARD: They said they'd come by about daybreak.

MARY: Oh. We have some time then.

EDWARD: Yes. *(getting her drift)* Oh. You mean . . .

He takes her hand and leads her upstairs. There is a knock at the door.

EDWARD: Who's there?

FLETCHER: *(outside)* It's Fletcher, Edward. There's been a change in plans. We have to go meet Lount at the crossroads right now.

EDWARD: But they said tomorrow—

FLETCHER: I don't care what they said. We have to leave right away.

EDWARD: I'll be right out.

FLETCHER: Right now!

EDWARD: *(angrily)* I *said* I was coming!

MARY: I'll get your things.

She hands him his coat and his rifle. They embrace. He starts toward the door, stops, returns to her.

EDWARD: I love you. By God I do. I love you.

He rushes out.

MARY: *(sobbing)* Oh no. No. He never said that to me before. No. No—

Fade to black.

Van Egmond's March

During this scene, the focus is on COLONEL ANTHONY VAN EGMOND as he travels toward Toronto. But around him many things take place: the daily work of the people he passes; events occurring in Toronto; encounters with people on the road. A small table serves as VAN EGMOND's horse.

VAN EGMOND: Colonel Anthony Van Egmond— age sixty-seven, veteran of the Napoleonic Wars, owner of a parcel of fourteen thousand acres in the Huron Tract near Goderich—is appointed commander-in-chief of the Patriot forces. December 3, 1837, he sets out from his farm on horseback, to meet with his troops at Montgomery's Tavern, north of Toronto, on December 7—the date set for the advance on the city.

He mounts his horse and begins his march.

VAN EGMOND: Day one. There is a light snow falling, muffling the sound. I shall travel alone to avoid suspicion. If we are to get the advantage of the enemy, we must take them by surprise. *(Notes as he goes:)* St. Columban—

MESSENGER: *(rushing from the opposite direction)* Colonel! Colonel!—I'm glad I caught you sir. There's been a change—

VAN EGMOND: Change?

MESSENGER: Yes sir—they've changed the date. From the seventh to the fourth.

VAN EGMOND: Who issued this change?

MESSENGER: It's a message sir—from that Dr. Rolph.

VAN EGMOND: Dr. Rolph does not have the power to make such changes. Only Mackenzie does.

MESSENGER: Yes he does. He said—

VAN EGMOND: There has been no change! December 7 is the date for the advance on the city!

MESSENGER: Yes sir. No change.

He exits.

VAN EGMOND: *(continuing his march)* We could not possibly muster enough men before December 7. *(Noting his progress:)* Mitchell.

Ah—another homesteader. He shall see such changes made!

A TORY PICKET IN TORONTO: Anderson!

He fires a shot. ANTHONY ANDERSON, a rebel, is hit, lurches across the stage, and falls dead at the feet of VAN EGMOND.

A FARMER: *(to VAN EGMOND)* You—you hear the news?

VAN EGMOND: News?

FARMER: Yup. Seems a man named Anderson— Anthony Anderson—and another fellow named Moodie—both shot outside of Toronto. Don't know any more about it.

VAN EGMOND: *(dismounting for the night)* Seebach's Inn. Sebringville. *(to the INNKEEPER)* What do you know of events in Toronto?

INNKEEPER: I heard that a government man named Moodie'd been shot. And a Rebel name of Anderson.

VAN EGMOND: Confirmed.

INNKEEPER: No, no—that's just talk as far as I know.

VAN EGMOND: Anthony Anderson was the only other Rebel leader with military experience.

Freeze.

VAN EGMOND: Day two. *(He remounts his horse.)* Stratford. There's much more activity on the roads today.

A TRAVELLER: Where are you going sir?

VAN EGMOND: Toronto.

TRAVELLER: You can't go there. The Americans have attacked. They're going to burn the city—

VAN EGMOND: The Americans have not attacked.

TRAVELLER: Yes they have. I heard it from somebody who heard it from someone who was there—

VAN EGMOND: Nonsense.

TRAVELLER: I'm warning you. I wouldn't go on—

He exits, blathering.

VAN EGMOND: Mackenzie, you must hold fast for more forces!

A MOUNTED HORSEMAN enters, dismounts and posts a handbill advertising a reward for MACKENZIE. (This was done using the actor who played MACKENZIE and, as it were, nailing him to the wall as though he were the poster.)

HORSEMAN: By authority of the Lieutenant-Governor, a reward of one thousand pounds is hereby offered to anyone who will apprehend and deliver up to justice William Lyon Mackenzie. God Save the Queen.

VAN EGMOND: *(dismounting)* Helmer's Inn. Waterloo.

He approaches the "handbill" and addresses it, with MACKENZIE's own call to arms.

VAN EGMOND: Canadians, do you love freedom?

MACKENZIE: *(i.e., the MACKENZIE in the handbill)* I know you do. Do you hate oppression? Who would deny it. Then buckle on your armour and drive out these villains who enslave and oppress our country.

VAN EGMOND: *(responding)* Long after we are dead, free men shall salute us.

They embrace. Freeze. VAN EGMOND remounts.

VAN EGMOND: Day three. Breslau.

OLD MAN: Sir—have you heard the news from Toronto?

As he tells this news to VAN EGMOND, someone else recounts it directly to the audience.

A REBEL: Well I can tell you exactly how it happened because I was there. It was a hell of a battle and it was right there at the corner of Yonge and College. You see, Sheriff Jarvis stationed his men behind a fence, just waiting for the Rebels to come marching down. Well, we came alright—in the dead of night. We moved out of the tavern, formed up at the tollgate at Bloor Street and then marched down Yonge, proud as peacocks, five abreast. They waited till we got really close, and then they let loose. Well they cut some of us down, but we fired back. And then we dropped down to let the men behind us fire. But the men behind—they were green—they

thought we'd dropped because we were all dead. So they turned around and ran back to the tavern. Sheriff Jarvis' men—they were even greener than that—they threw their guns and ran back to Toronto.

Great confusion onstage. People milling and fleeing. VAN EGMOND tries to stem the tide.

VAN EGMOND: Wait! If you want something you stay and fight for it!

They push past him, leaving him alone and dejected. He dismounts and sits down despairingly.

VAN EGMOND: What is happening in Toronto? Why didn't they wait? Fools—so much at stake— if only I *knew!* I am an old man; there is still honour in retreat. I shall return home—

Enter a REBEL, overhears VAN EGMOND.

REBEL: Yah, you go home, go back to your farm. Whatever you do, don't go to Toronto.

VAN EGMOND: Have you come from Toronto?

REBEL: I *ran* from Toronto. I'm going home.

VAN EGMOND: What is happening there?

REBEL: Macnab's in the city. He's brought four hundred armed militiamen. They're barricading the city. They're going to shoot us like rats—

VAN EGMOND: Macnab? I'd like to fight Macnab.

REBEL: You're welcome to him.

VAN EGMOND: What is the condition of the patriot forces?

REBEL: Bad.

VAN EGMOND: Are they still coming in?

REBEL: Yah, they're coming in—

VAN EGMOND: They are—

REBEL: But they're leaving just as fast as they come in.

VAN EGMOND: Why?

REBEL: Because there's no leadership there. Nobody knows what they're doing. Someone orders this. Another one orders that—

VAN EGMOND: If there had been a leader there—whom you trusted—would you have fled?

REBEL: I'm no coward. I'd have stayed.

VAN EGMOND: *(extending his hand)* Colonel Anthony Van Egmond, son—

REBEL: Colonel—

VAN EGMOND: Will you march back to Toronto with me?

REBEL: Yes sir.

A chorus of "yes sir" begins to build in the background.

VAN EGMOND: You see Macnab is no solider. He is a bully but he has no strategy. Help me up. *(He mounts.)* Have you ever been in a real battle, boy?

REBEL: Only on Yonge Street, sir.

VAN EGMOND: That was no battle. It was a skirmish. Do you know—I was fifteen years in the Napoleonic Wars. Wounded fourteen times and never once in the back.

The chorus of "yes sir" builds and transforms into the "Marseillaise."

A REBEL: Remember Moscow!

VAN EGMOND: Macnab, you'll rue the day—

REBEL: Remember Waterloo!

VAN EGMOND: Mackenzie, hold fast now—

REBEL: Think of Montgomery's Tavern!

VAN EGMOND: Lancers ho—

A SENTRY: Halt!

Silence

A SENTRY: Who goes there?

VAN EGMOND: Colonel Van Egmond.

SENTRY: Hot damn general—are we glad to see you!

VAN EGMOND: Where is Mackenzie?

SENTRY: He's inside, sir. I'll show you. We didn't know if you were coming at all. Some said you weren't.

VAN EGMOND: Well I'm here aren't I?

SENTRY: Yes sir. You are. He's right in there. Don't tell him I forgot to salute—

VAN EGMOND: Mackenzie—

He storms in.

The Battle

This scene continues directly from the previous scene.

VAN EGMOND: Mackenzie, what in hell is going on here?

MACKENZIE: Colonel, thank God you're here. Rolph changed the date. Everything's in a mess. Macnab's in the city with four hundred men.

VAN EGMOND: How many do we have?

MACKENZIE: Two hundred and fifty.

VAN EGMOND: Not enough. When do we expect more?

MACKENZIE: Tonight. December 7. They'll be down tonight.

VAN EGMOND: Then we wait till they arrive.

MACKENZIE: Colonel, we can't wait to be attacked.

VAN EGMOND: You cannot go against Macnab with a handful of men.

MACKENZIE: We've got to do something—

REBEL SOLDIER: *(to audience)* It is finally decided to send a diversionary force under Peter Matthews to the east to burn the Don Valley Bridge and draw off the main Loyalist force. The rest wait at Montgomery's for reinforcements. Meanwhile, back in Toronto, the Loyalist army is drawn up in front of Archdeacon Strachan's residence—known as The Palace—on Front Street.

The Loyalist army form up.

BOND HEAD: I am Sir Francis Bond Head. I have a double-barrelled pistol in my bandolier, a rifle leaning against my thigh, and a brace of pistols in my belt. So good to see so many respected citizens standing in the ranks today.

THE RANKS: Pip pip—Hear hear—

BOND HEAD: We march at noon. Forward—march!

They set out.

REBEL SOLDIER: Meanwhile to the east, Matthews and his men have crossed the bridge and moved west on King Street. They meet a contingent of militia and retreat back across the bridge, attempting to burn it as they go. In the exchange of fire, one man is fatally shot through the throat. *(This all is acted out.)* The bridge itself is saved.

A LOYALIST: But the main Loyalist force is already moving north toward Montgomery's. *(Shouts)* Bugler—strike up a tune!

The Loyalist army marches to "Yankee Doodle"— an old British parody of Americans and Americanizers.

LOYALIST: Six hundred men remain in the centre with Bond Head. One hundred fifty off to the right flank. Two hundred on the left.

A REBEL SENTRY: Hey wake up—

HIS FRIEND: What? *(looking out at the approaching army)* Good God!

SENTRY: There must be thousands of them—

FRIEND: I'll stay and watch them. You go tell Mackenzie—

SENTRY: *(riding off)* Mackenzie! They're coming this way—you'd better go see—

MACKENZIE: Form up the men! *(The rebels form up.)* There is the enemy! They outnumber us. They are better armed. And they have artillery—but they are the men we came to fight. Will you fight them?

A hearty Rebel cheer.

MACKENZIE: Forward—

A REBEL: A force of two hundred and fifty under Van Egmond and Samuel Lount advance into the woods to the south of the tavern. Another sixty position themselves behind rail fences on the other side of the road. Two hundred yet unarmed men remain in the tavern.

The battle is staged. The Rebel soldiers talk frantically among themselves as they watch the overwhelming force of the Loyalists moving toward them. The battle itself is bitter and very brief. The two nine-pound cannons of the Loyalists decimate the Rebel formations. The Rebels are crushed. In the end the Loyalists are totally triumphant. The bodies and weapons of the Rebels litter the field. The Loyalists clean up. All of this with much screaming, swearing and writhing.

MACKENZIE: *(as he escapes)* Mackenzie is the last man to leave the field. Together with Van Egmond he goes to a nearby farmhouse. The farmer's wife diverts soldiers while Mackenzie escapes, but Van Egmond, exhausted, is captured. Mackenzie heads west toward the Niagara border. Rewards are offered for him everywhere, but not a soul who sees him reports him. Within days he has established the provisional government of the State of Upper Canada on Navy Island in the Niagara River. He arrives with twenty-six men but soon has hundreds more. Macnab encamps on the opposite shore with a government force of five thousand. Mackenzie gathers the arms and provisions which will enable him to return and join Dr. Charles Duncombe, who has raised a Rebel army near London. He waits for his chance to move. *(stepping into character)* And while I wait, I fire my four cannons here at Macnab across the river—just to let him know I'm still here!

Boom. Boom. Boom. Boom.

Blackout.

Knock on the Door

An old Canadian tradition. The following three scenes depict break-ins by government forces at the homes of suspected Rebels. Knock, knock, knock in the dark. Lights up as a SOLDIER breaks through the door and in on a WOMAN alone.

SOLDIER: Get the hell out of here. We're burning this house down!

She screams. He shoves her out. Blackout.

Knock, knock, knock in the dark.

SOLDIER: Open up in the name of the Queen!

Lights up. A WOMAN opens. He barges in.

SOLDIER: Where's your husband, Mrs. Polk?

WOMAN: I have no husband.

SOLDIER: No? Then who's that ugly man you've been living with for the last seven years.

WOMAN: Go away—

SOLDIER: *(searching)* Where is he?

WOMAN: He's dead. There's nothing here for you, so please leave my house—

SOLDIER: He's been seen Mrs. Polk. He's gone too far this time—

He is bashing away at her belongings with his rifle butt. She leaps on him furiously from behind. He wrestles her to the ground, pins her there. She struggles futilely.

SOLDIER: We're going to get him, and we're going to hang him, but before we do, I'm going to punch his face off. And then, Mrs. Polk, what're you going to do for a man—

She spits in his face. He raises a fist.

ANOTHER SOLDIER: *(from outside)* Come on George. There's no one here.

SOLDIER: I'll be back.

He exits.

Blackout.

Knock, knock, knock in the dark.

Lights up. Enter HAROLD, the fellow from the earlier scene who was afraid to go off to fight. He rushes in and hides under a stair, floorboard or the like. Enter TOM, the friend with whom he'd left to fight the rebellion. TOM is carrying a rifle and clearly searching for Rebels. (Because of all the doubling in this play, it is not immediately evident to the audience that these are HAROLD and TOM from an earlier scene. This works to the advantage of this brief scene as it develops.)

TOM: *(nervously)* Now I seen you come in here. So come on out.

HAROLD coughs.

TOM: If you don't come out by the time I count three, I'll shoot— *(He aims at the place*

HAROLD is hiding.) One, two, three— *(He shoots, but his gun misfires.)* Goldarn gun—

HAROLD leaps out of his hiding place and jumps on TOM; the two struggle for several seconds before they recognize each other.

TOM: Harold!

HAROLD: Tom!

TOM: What're you doing here?

HAROLD: I'm hiding! What're you doing? You were with me at Montgomery's Tavern!

TOM: I doubled back through the woods and joined up. Otherwise they'd have arrested me. They're making everyone search. Harold, they know who you are—

HAROLD: I know. They nearly got me twice today. Tom, you gotta help me. I haven't even got a—gimme your gun.

TOM: I can't do that. They'll ask me where it went.

HAROLD: *(grabbing it)* Tell them—tell them you were searching down a well and it fell in. Thanks Tom—

He rushes off.

TOM: *(calling after)* You hide good next time, Harold— *(looking down at his hands, realizing he's stuck without a gun)* What in hell am I—

Blackout.

The Rope

Captured Rebels being led to jail in Toronto. A rope is looped over each of their necks. Their hands are tied behind their backs. They march single file. They state their names in turn. When they have gone round once, they go round again.

REBELS: Jacob Beemer, farmer. Taken January 3, 1838, near Stratford.
Richard Thorpe, labourer. Taken December 7, at Montgomery's Tavern.
Caleb Kipp, yeoman. Taken on the road to Buffalo.
John Bradley, teacher. I'm no Rebel. I voted Reform but I'm no Rebel.
Absalom Slade, farmer.
Elijah Rowe, tinker. Taken December 7, at Montgomery's. But it took six of them.
They're burning. Look at that smoke—

I can't feel my toes.
William Stockdale, farmer.
Jonathan Grimes, ropemaker.
Damn the Tories! What're you looking at, lady?

They reach their destination

Hey, lookit who's here!
There's thousands of us!
Hey, anybody here from Newmarket?
Hell, the whole country's in here—
Newmarket?—

A rising babble of greetings etc.

Blackout.

Emigrating

A REBEL WOMAN. She is packing, and talking to a neighbour.

REBEL WOMAN: Now the coach is coming at four, got to be ready. And my brother is picking that up, and this is for you. You always admired it and I want you to have it now. We won't need no winter coats where we're going. Yes, I finally convinced my Dan, I just sat down the other day, had the kids all around—they've been getting an awful time from the other kids—and I said, Now Dan, we've tried. We voted Reform, we did what we thought was best, we lost, it's time to face facts. And I just got this letter from my sister. She's got a farm and a fine husband and she said we could go down and stay with them as long as we want, and oh the kids were yelling and screaming and—well what can he say? So we're going.

You know, this place, it's my home, the kids were both born here, but times have changed and we're going to change with them. I wouldn't stay in Stouffville one more day, I'll tell you. But I want you to know you're welcome to come down and visit us any time you want. Oh, it's going to be so fine down there, we'll have a big house, and the kids will go to school— *(calling out the window)* Hey, Mrs. Phipps, you know those two plates you borrowed from me two years ago? You can keep them. She never did like me. What are you people staring at? Anything else in here you can come and take when we're gone. We're leaving it behind. We're going to have five times better. You know why? Because we're going to the Yew-Nited States!

Blackout.

The Hangings

Toronto City Jail.

VAN EGMOND: April 12, 1838. Government forces have scattered Dr. Duncombe's army in the west. Mackenzie himself has fled Navy Island for the United States. Toronto City Jail. Near King and Church Streets. The cells are cold, dark, wet, filled for the most part with patriots awaiting trial and sentencing on charges of high treason. Today they press against the bars of their cells to witness the executions of two of the patriot leaders, Peter Matthews and Samuel Lount. It is the laws, and not their crimes, that condemn them. Anthony Van Egmond might also have been witness to this spectacle but he died, untried, in his cell, December 30, 1837.

MATTHEWS and LOUNT advance to the gallows.

LOUNT: My friends, I address as friends all those in the jail behind me, in all the jails across this province, in the ships bound for Van Diemen's Land, in exile in the United States—there are over eight hundred of us. I am proud to be one of you. John Beverley Robinson—Chief Justice Robinson—you seem to fear we will become martyrs to our countrymen. Well still your fears. This country will not have time to mourn a farmer and a blacksmith. It will be free, I am certain, long before our deaths have time to become symbols. It cannot remain long under the hell of such merciless wretches that they murder its inhabitants for their love of liberty.

As for us, I do not know exactly how we came to this. Except by a series of steps, each of which seemed to require the next. But if I were to leave my home in Holland Landing again, and march down Yonge Street, I would go by the same route, only hoping that the journey's end would differ. And there will be others coming down that road you know, and others after them, until it does end differently. But for us, the only way on now is by the rope.

MATTHEWS laughs bitterly.

LOUNT: What Peter? What?

MATTHEWS: Sam, we lost—

LOUNT: No! We haven't won yet.

The trap falls. They dangle by the ropes.

Blackout.

END

SHARON POLLOCK (b. 1936)

In the preface to her play *The Komagata Maru Incident*, Sharon Pollock writes, "As a Canadian, I feel that much of our history has been misrepresented and even hidden from us. Until we recognize our past, we cannot change our future." The sentiments are similar to those of Rick Salutin, and like him, Pollock delivered to the stage in 1973 a dramatization of nineteenth-century Canadian history meant to change irrevocably the way we view ourselves. *Walsh* was the prototype of a playwriting career that has persisted in bringing to light injustices done in the name of a higher good, past and present, in both formal "history plays" and family histories, utilizing multiple levels of chronology and perspective, and usually featuring a man or woman caught in the squeeze between personal inclination and political or familial pressures. With *Walsh* Sharon Pollock first revealed herself to a national audience as one of the major dramatists of the modern Canadian theatre.

Pollock was born Sharon Chalmers in Frederiction, N.B., where she first became involved in the theatre at university. Later, with the Prairie Players she toured B.C. and Alberta in 1966, and was voted Best Actress at the Dominion Drama Festival. Pollock settled in Calgary the next year, and while pregnant with her sixth child she began writing her first play. The absurdist farce *A Compulsory Option* won the 1971 Alberta Playwriting Competition and was produced in 1972 by the New Play Centre in Vancouver, where Pollock and family were now living. *Walsh* was her next project, followed by a productive association with the Vancouver Playhouse between 1973 and 1976 that resulted in six plays for children as well as *And Out Goes You?* (1975), a political comedy about eviction, expropriation and urban redevelopment, and *The Komagata Maru Incident* (1976), which powerfully dissects the politics of racism behind the refusal to admit Sikh immigrants into Vancouver in 1914. Pollock herself played the title role of Lizzie Borden in a local college production of her next play, *My Name is Lisbeth* (1976), which would go on to become her most popular success, *Blood Relations*, first staged professionally in 1980 by Edmonton's Theatre Three. Her volume *Blood Relations and Other Plays* won the inaugural Governor General's Literary Award for Drama in 1981.

Pollock moved to Edmonton in 1976 to teach playwriting at the University of Alberta, but except for a few brief periods since 1977 she has made her home in Calgary. From 1977-79 she ran the summer Playwrights' Colony at Banff and was playwright-in-residence for Alberta Theatre Projects which produced her fine study of a family of prairie farmers, *Generations*, in 1980. In the same year the Citadel mounted *One Tiger to a Hill*, her dramatization of a notorious hostage-taking at the B.C. Pen. She spent 1981-82 as artist-in-residence at the National Arts Centre, then returned to Theatre Calgary to present *Whiskey Six Cadenza* (1983) and *Doc* (1984), and serve briefly as artistic director in 1984. The former play is a tale of rum-running, coal mining and sexual abuse in 1920s Alberta; the latter an autobiographical treatment of a ravaged New Brunswick family which won Pollock her second Governor General's Award. Major productions of *Doc* include one directed by Pollock herself at Theatre New Brunswick where she worked as artistic director from 1988-90.

She returned to performing in 1989, premiering her one-woman play *Getting It Straight* at the International Women's Festival in Winnipeg. A lyrical feminist monologue about male aggression and abuses of power spoken by an apparent madwoman beneath a rodeo grandstand ("I am not mad I am getting it straight"), the play was remounted at Toronto's Factory Theatre in 1990. The Stratford Festival premiered *Fair Liberty's Call* (1993), the tale of a Loyalist family's travails in late eighteenth-century Canada. Pollock's ongoing concern with both feminist and Native issues was reflected in *The Making of Warriors* (1990), one in a long line of her radio plays that includes the 1980 ACTRA Best Radio Drama Award winner, *Sweet Land of Liberty.*

Walsh had its genesis in Vancouver in 1972-73. While Pollock was researching and writing the play, the artistic director of Theatre Calgary, Harold Baldridge, was reading Dee Brown's *Bury My Heart at Wounded Knee* and becoming interested in the story of Sitting Bull's stay in Canada. He contacted Pollock when he heard about *Walsh*, and after substantial revisions in a New Play Centre workshop the play opened at Theatre Calgary in November 1973. Further revised, *Walsh* was done again the next summer at Stratford's Third Stage with the addition of the Prologue and the characters Mary and Pretty Plume, but minus the recorded readings from documents of the day that preceded each scene in the original production. A new scene involving the American General Terry was added for the play's 1983 revival at the National Arts Centre (the version reprinted here). Theatre Calgary's 1988 Olympic Arts Festival production of the play was dogged by controversy after Pollock removed her name from all publicity material because of a dispute with the theatre's management, and in a life-imitating-art-imitating-history scenario, the Native actor playing Sitting Bull had a run-in with the Calgary police.

Walsh is grounded very firmly in historical fact. Major James Walsh did command the North West Mounted Police detachment that was charged with keeping order in the area that is now the southern Alberta-Saskatchewan border during the period (1877-81) that Sitting Bull and his Sioux spent there in exile. Two histories published the same year as *Walsh*, Grant MacEwan's *Sitting Bull* and C. Frank Turner's *Across the Medicine Line*, also confirm the basic accuracy of Pollock's presentation: the exemplary behaviour of the Sioux while in Canada, the great respect they developed for Walsh, and the political machinations that eventually drove the survivors back across the line. Only at the end does Pollock take liberty with historical fact, telescoping the time between Sitting Bull's return to the U.S. in 1881 and his assassination in 1890 so it appears one followed hard upon the other.

But like British playwright Peter Shaffer, whose *The Royal Hunt of the Sun* shares numerous similarities with *Walsh*, Pollock is less interested in documentary on an epic scale than in history as personal drama. Assuming the real sources of political power to be distant, faceless and bureaucratic, Pollock focuses instead on an intermediary, a well-intentioned local functionary who acts as the instrument of authority and oppression—the prison warden and social worker of *One Tiger to a Hill*, the immigration officer in *The Komagata Maru Incident*, and the good soldier Walsh. Walsh's drama is particularly compelling because he is so fundamentally humane and so ambivalent. As his admiration for Sitting Bull and the Sioux grows, Walsh's loyalty to the Force is stretched to its breaking point until, like Shaffer's Pizarro, he is forced to make the choice that destroys himself as surely as it does the Indians.

Walsh's dilemma is that he cannot ultimately be both a private person and an officer at the service of his political masters. At first he is confident he can juggle the two roles, telling Sitting Bull, "I am a soldier, and I must follow orders, but I am a friend also." "White Forehead" is the friend, "Major Walsh" the soldier. But such a split is both unnatural and unsustainable. Eventually he *must* choose. And when he can no longer avoid committing himself, he chooses duty over friendship, Major Walsh over White Forehead. In the climactic scene where Sitting Bull makes his last appeal to Walsh's sense of charity and justice, Walsh literally buttons himself up in the red tunic that symbolizes his official self. Once having denied his humanity he becomes a broken man, a travesty of the brave soldier he once was and, eventually, the wreck we meet in the Yukon at the beginning of the play, years after his betrayal of Sitting Bull.

Walsh isn't the only character torn between two loyalties. Sitting Bull himself must make the painful choice to protect his own people's status in Canada rather than help the Nez Percés. Louis, the Métis scout, has a foot in both the white and Indian worlds and sees the contradictions with terrible clarity. And Clarence, the naive recruit who grows in sympathy and understanding through the play, idolizes Walsh yet comes to love Sitting Bull and Crowfoot like his own family. His enduring faith in the fundamental goodness and rationality of the Canadian government whose policies effectively condemn the Sioux to extinction prompts Walsh to remark, "That young man should never make the Force his life"—a sad self-commentary on the bitter fate of a professional soldier who would also be a good man.

•

Walsh premiered at Theatre Calgary on November 7, 1973, with the following cast:

HARRY	Frank J. Adamson
CLARENCE	Hardee T. Lineham
LOUIS	Jean Archambault
WALSH	Michael Fletcher
MRS. ANDERSON	Margaret Barton
CROW EAGLE	Stephen Russell
McCUTCHEON	Ron Chudley
GALL	Denis Lacroix
SITTING BULL	August Schellenberg
WHITE DOG	Nolan Jennings
CROWFOOT	Frank Turningrobe, Jr.
COLONEL MacLEOD	Hutchinson Shandro

Directed by Harold Baldridge
Set and Lighting Design by Richard Roberts
Costume Design by Jane Grose

WALSH

CHARACTERS

HARRY, *a wagon master*
CLARENCE, *a new recruit to the NWMP*
LOUIS, *a Métis scout*
WALSH, *a superintendent of the NWMP in charge of Fort Walsh*
MRS. ANDERSON, *a settler*
CROW EAGLE, *a Cree*
McCUTCHEON, *a sergeant in the NWMP*
MARY, *wife of Major Walsh*
SITTING BULL, *a chief of the Hunkpapa Sioux*
PRETTY PLUME, *wife of Sitting Bull*
CROWFOOT, *son of Sitting Bull*
GALL, *a chief of the Hunkpapa Sioux*
WHITE DOG, *an Assiniboine*
TERRY, *a general in the U.S. Army*
COLONEL MacLEOD, *commissioner of the NWMP*

PROLOGUE

The characters in the prologue become the characters in the play proper. McCUTCHEON plays IAN, the bartender. SITTING BULL is the PROSPECTOR; CROW EAGLE is BILLY, the harmonica player in the saloon. LOUIS and MacLEOD are a couple of poker players. CROWFOOT is JOEIE, the newspaper boy. JENNIE is MRS. ANDERSON. WALSH and HARRY play themselves. WALSH is in civvies, impeccably dressed, in contrast to the other characters who look dirty and disreputable. The atmosphere in the prologue is smoky, as if the scene were lit by a coal-oil lamp with a dirty chimney.

The scene is from WALSH's point of view, and the freezes are momentary arrests in the action and are broken by the character's speech or action following. The impression given is similar to that experienced when one is drunk or under great mental stress. CLARENCE stands outside of the prologue scene, never taking his eyes off WALSH. He has on his red tunic and he exists only in WALSH's mind. He is not part of the prologue scene and his scream is heard only by WALSH.

There is no break in staging between the prologue and Act One.

The sound of wind is heard—a mournful sound. In a very dim light, the characters suddenly appear on the periphery of the playing area. WALSH is not among them. They freeze there for a moment, and then, quickly and silently, like ghosts, take their positions onstage, with the exception of HARRY, JOEIE and CLARENCE, who remain in the shadows.

The characters freeze on stage, all facing WALSH's entrance. There is an increase in the howling of the wind and WALSH appears in a spotlight somewhat brighter than the general dim lighting. The wind fades as WALSH enters. He is walking very slowly and carefully, as if he were the tiniest bit drunk. As he enters, JENNIE pulls out a chair at a table and IAN pours a drink into a glass on the table. The PROSPECTOR is blocking WALSH's way and WALSH stops. The PROSPECTOR steps aside and WALSH continues toward the table. All the characters watch him. WALSH stops at the chair, looks out at CLARENCE and turns the chair so that he no longer faces CLARENCE. He sits. There is a momentary freeze, then WALSH reaches for his drink, breaking the freeze. BILLY begins playing the harmonica; JENNIE begins to sing and move among the characters, tipping a hat here and rubbing an arm there as she passes. The characters come alive and the light brightens a bit so that WALSH's spotlight is gone—although the light is still not full.

JENNIE: *(singing)*
George Carmack on Bonanza Creek
Went out to look for gold,
I wonder why, I wonder why.
Oldtimers said it was no use,
The water was too cold.
I wonder why, I wonder why.

PROSPECTOR: Another verse, Jennie!

JENNIE: Is there somethin' else you'd have me do, Mr. Walsh?

WALSH: Do you know . . . "Break the News to Mother?"

JENNIE: There's not much I don't know. How the hell did you think I ended up in Dawson?

Laughs and guffaws are heard from the boys.

WALSH: I always liked "Break the News to Mother."

JENNIE: *(singing)* I wonder why, I wonder why.

HARRY: *(entering from the shadows)* Jeeeesus Chriiiist! It's colder than a witch's diddy.

All the characters turn and look at him, with the exception of WALSH.

HARRY: How about some eats here?

JENNIE: Girls, upstairs to the left: a drink, we can give you here.

BILLY: But you can't buy what there ain't none of . . . .

PROSPECTOR: Which is grub.

There is a momentary freeze, which affects everyone but WALSH, who looks at HARRY.

JENNIE: *(singing as BILLY plays the harmonica)*
They said that he might search the creek
Until the world did end,
But not enough of gold he'd find
A postage stamp to send—

JENNIE stops singing abruptly as HARRY pulls out his poke. There is a momentary freeze. It affects everyone but WALSH. The freeze is broken by hoarse whispers.

BILLY: Better put away that poke, mister.

PROSPECTOR: We got a grafter in the room. *(He indicates WALSH.)* Ain't you noticed?

JENNIE: He'd as soon take ten percent off the top of that as look at you.

WALSH: *(raising his glass to them)* Gentlemen—and sweet Jennie.

BILLY: *(in a low voice)* To hell with Mr. Walsh.

There is a momentary freeze as they all watch WALSH drink. The freeze is broken by WALSH when he puts down his glass. IAN moves to fill it. BILLY begins playing "Garryowen" on his harmonica.

HARRY: Where'd you learn that song? You a Yankee fella? You a cavalry man?

BILLY: Don't have to be a cavalry man to know a song, mister.

He resumes playing his harmonica.

JENNIE: Here's a lady done a lot of ridin' and she don't know that song.

PROSPECTOR: "Garryowen."

WALSH knocks over his drink. There is a momentary freeze as they all look at WALSH and he stares at his spilled drink.

JENNIE: Ah, Mr. Walsh, you've spilled your drink. A drink for Mr. Walsh.

IAN rights his glass and pours him another drink.

BILLY: To hell with Mr. Walsh.

He resumes playing his harmonica and "Garryowen" builds with the sound of a military band creeping in and growing in volume.

HARRY: "Garryowen." Marching song of the 7th Cavalry. Custer's outfit.

JENNIE: Who's that?

HARRY: A long hair killed with long knives at the Greasy Grass.

JENNIE: We speak English here, mister.

"Garryowen" stops abruptly. WALSH bangs down his glass. There is another freeze as he looks around slowly and speaks clearly, carefully, announcing it, giving the impression once again of perhaps being drunk, but really being completely under control.

WALSH: General George Armstrong Custer . . . killed with 261 men of the 7th Cavalry of the United States Army . . . at the Little Big Horn, Montana, June 25th, 1876.

There is a pause. The freeze is broken as he picks up his drink. BILLY begins playing a ragtime tune on his harmonica. The lights brighten. The characters resume their talk.

HARRY: Who's your grafter?

IAN: That's Major Walsh—but he's not with the force. He's Commissioner of the Yukon now.

JENNIE: Did you see me front? Not a bit of snow to the street. Walsh may not be with the force, but he gets a good day's work out of 'em. *(She laughs.)* I must be the only whorehouse in the north whose front is shovelled clear by the North

West Mounted on the orders of the Commissioner of the Yukon. *(They all look at WALSH.)* He knows what those boys are good for.

JOEIE: *(moving out of the shadows)* Anyone want to buy a paper?

JENNIE: Hey, Joeie's here with the Nugget . . . Pass the hat round for Joeie! Isn't he a dear?

The PROSPECTOR starts around with the hat. JENNIE puts her arm around JOEIE.

JENNIE: His Da froze and his Mum takes in washin'. He's sweet Jennie's dear, aren't you, Joeie? You're sweet Jennie's sweetheart, aren't you?

The PROSPECTOR approaches WALSH after collecting some money from the others.

PROSPECTOR: *(holding out the hat)* For Joeie.

WALSH looks at him. There is a look of incomprehension in his gaze.

PROSPECTOR: I'm askin' for somethin' for the little boy.

WALSH: I can give you nothing.

PROSPECTOR: You and your kind have taken enough off us. You kin spare somethin' for the little boy.

WALSH: I can give you nothing!

PROSPECTOR: It ain't enough you're a son-of-a-bitch, you gotta be a cheap son-of-a-bitch!

WALSH hits him in the face, knocking him down. As he goes to get up, WALSH plants a foot in his back, sending him sprawling.

CLARENCE: *(screaming from the shadows)* Noooooooo!

There is a freeze with WALSH with his hand upraised to hit the PROSPECTOR; IAN with the bottle raised as a club; JENNIE drawing JOEIE to her. All of the characters in the saloon are in positions of action, except for HARRY who is a spectator. There is a pause, then HARRY sets forward, moving among the frozen characters.

HARRY: *(addressing the audience)* The Klondike! 1898! And the end for Major James A. Walsh, formerly of the North West Mounted Police, an original member of the first contingent of that force, formed in 1873 by Sir John A. MacDonald to police the Canadian West!

He smashes his fist on the table. The freeze ends. HARRY continues as the actors leave.

Major Walsh never met General Custer, which was kinda a pity, 'cause the day Custer met Sittin' Bull was the beginning of the end for Major Walsh . . . . Old Glory Hound Custer—now he had a fail-proof plan for killin' off Injuns. First off, you found yourself some friendlies. You was forced to kill friendlies 'cause it was too difficult findin' hostiles, but friendlies camped near the forts, to show their goodwill kinda like, and it weren't too hard to come across a bunch of 'em set up in some cozy little hollow, flyin' the 'merican flag for good measure.

He laughs a dry chuckle.

Well now, once you picked yourself some Injuns, you gotta pick yourself a time. Custer thought winter was the best, for the Injun had always figured fightin' in winter wasn't sportin' like, and avoided it if he could . . . Custer was an early riser—and if you team up a winter date with a 4 a.m. charge, when the Injuns was all asleep, you pretty well had it made . . . . Course, tactics comes into it. Custer did all right there too. 'Member that cozy little hollow I mentioned? Sorta a tube-like hollow was best, 'cause what you did was send a bunch of men in one end of the tube and, of course, all hell broke loose there, what with kids screamin', women runnin' and men lookin' for somethin' to hit back with, and the whole works naked as the day they was born, it bein' the middle of the night as far as they was concerned. Anyway, as their attention was somewhat di-verted by this here attack at one end of the tube, Custer, with a bunch of the boys, would sneak round t'other end and ride through, hell-bent for whoop-up, killin' off the strays, and generally gettin' a lot of 'em in the back while they was lookin' t'other way . . . . It were a pretty efficient way to fight a war . . . . The flag did its bit too, for the Injuns was prone to rally under it, thinkin' maybe the fact they was friendly had been missed; occasionally one of 'em even had time to run up a white flag.

He reminisces.

There was almost a kinda festive at-mos-phere to a Custer attack, what with his marchin' band playing "Garryowen." Custer liked to charge to music, and "Garryowen" was his favourite, although he was fond of "The Girl I Left Behind" too . . . . Still, generally, it was "Garryowen."

He whistles a few bars of "Garryowen." The tune begins brightly, but becomes slower and slower, then stops. There is silence for a second. He continues speaking—not as lightly as in the first part of his monologue.

The Little Big Horn . . . June 25th . . . 1876 . . . . First off, wrong time! June ain't December—and that's a fact. Just shows how success kin go to your head. And the Injuns at the Little Big Horn weren't friendly. They was hostile. They was hostile as hell. Sittin' Bull and the Sioux had listened to the 'merican government say, "The utmost good faith shall always be observed towards the Indians, and their land and property shall never be taken from them without their consent." They had taken the government at its word—bein' savages, they weren't too familiar with governments and all, so it was an understandable mistake . . . . So, we got wrong month, and wrong bunch of Injuns. These Sioux weren't sittin' under no flag waitin' to be popped off like passenger pigeons . . . . On June 25th, Custer was up at 4 a.m. all right. Trouble was he never found no Injuns till noon time. His fail-proof plan for killin' off Injuns was goin' to hell in a hand basket. On top of everythin' else, the marchin' band had a prior engagement with General Terry.

So here's Custer . . . at noon time . . . in late June . . . with no marchin' band . . . comin' upon a camp of hostiles. Well now, it weren't hardly a camp either. It was a gathering together, under Sittin' Bull, of the last of those Injuns who weren't willin' to swap their huntin' grounds and freedom for a small corner of a reservation, 'bout 4,000 warriors, plus women and children. And what they was camped in wasn't, by no stretch of the imagination, a tube-like hollow. It was a gentle rollin' sweep of Montana prairie.

Custer, seein' it was gettin' later in the day by the minute, and probably wantin' to avoid that early afternoon slump most early risers suffer from, decided to attack without sendin' out a scout to see how far this here camp of Injuns extended. He had 'bout 500 men, and he figured that would be enough with some left over . . . "Take no prisoners" was the order . . . . Major Reno, who, incidentally, had never fought Injuns before, only other 'mericans in the Civil War . . . this here Reno was given the honour of ridin' with 'bout half the men into one end of the non-tube. Which he did. And got the bejesus beat out of him. He made a hasty retreat to a bluff where he sat with his men for two days, cursin' Custer for runnin' off and leavin' them to the mercy of the Injuns and the sun. Forgot to mention that Custer did have this unfortunate habit of cuttin' his losses and ridin' off.

This time, Custer hadn't ridden off. He wasn't goin' nowhere. He had taken his half of the 7th, ridden a couple of miles, and cut down to what he figured was the outskirts of the camp. Two miles. His figurin' was 'bout eight miles out. He found Injuns aplenty—and none of them was facin' the other way.

On June 28th, General Terry came on a yellow-brown slope dotted with dead horses and pale white bodies—the dead—stripped of arms, ammunition, equipment . . . and clothin' . . . . At the summit of the slope stood a horse. The sole survivor of Custer's Last Stand was a clay-coloured horse—Comanche—still on his feet with ten bullet holes in him. The bullet holes eventually healed and on April 10th, 1878, the horse was commissioned "second commandin' officer" of the 7th Cavalry . . . and, on all occasions of ceremony, saddled, bridled, draped in mournin' and led by a mounted trooper, Comanche paraded with the regiment . . . . I hear tell, that when Terry looked on Custer's dead body, he wept, and said, "The flower of the American Army is gone."

Well now, the rest of the 'merican Army was out to avenge the "Custer Massacre." Sittin' Bull and the Sioux were hard to lay hands on, but there was always the friendlies.

ACT ONE

The action continues without a break.

HARRY: *(beginning to move treaty goods)* Across the line, in the country of the Great White Mother, Major James A. Walsh of the North West Mounted was enforcin' law and order as decreed by Her Majesty's Government.

CLARENCE: *(offstage)* Hey, Harry!

HARRY: I had . . . what you might call, vacated the U-nited States and had myself a job as wagon master . . . .

CLARENCE: *(offstage)* Harry! What're you doin'? Come on!

HARRY: I'm comin'! I was running treaty goods for Canadian Injuns into Fort Walsh.

CLARENCE: *(offstage)* Jesus Christ, Harry! Would you give me a hand!

HARRY: *(without moving to go)* I said, I'm comin'!

CLARENCE: Never mind, you lazy bastard! *(Grunts and groans of effort are heard.)* I'll do it myself!

HARRY: Be right with you.

CLARENCE enters, bent double under a packing case. HARRY sits and watches him.

HARRY: Hey, you better watch out for . . .

CLARENCE trips over a ploughshare. He falls flat on his face, spilling the packing case which is full of shovels.

HARRY: . . . the ploughshare.

CLARENCE sits ups, looking around at the shovels, the packing case.

CLARENCE: *(speaking plaintively)* What the hell are they goin' to do with these?

HARRY: *(matter-of-factly)* Nothin'.

CLARENCE: What do you mean, nothin'?

HARRY: *(explaining a fact of life)* They're gonna do nothin' with these. We're gonna haul 'em over here, your Major's gonna pass 'em all out and they're gonna haul 'em all away. And they ain't gonna do nothin' with 'em. The seed's gonna rot, the 'shares gonna rust and them goddamn shovels is just gonna lie where they flung 'em.

CLARENCE: If they aren't gonna use 'em, why're we luggin' them around?

HARRY: I'll tell you somethin', your Major's gonna be madder than a wet hen when he sees this lot. Second lot I brung in this month. First lot, the Major, he threw a real fit, said he was gonna write the Prime Minister, tell 'im to stuff his farm utensils.

CLARENCE: Hey, did you hear the talk over at the fort?

HARRY: *(biting off a chaw of tobacco and looking at CLARENCE disdainfully)* That talk's everywhere, Clarence.

CLARENCE: Do you believe it?

HARRY: Don't see why it couldn't be true.

CLARENCE: Aren't you scared?

HARRY: Now, why'd I be scared, Clarence?

CLARENCE: We're gonna have ourselves an Injun War, just like the States, that's why!

HARRY gives him a dry look.

CLARENCE: The Sioux are headed north . . . . An Injun War! . . . I could get to kill the man who killed Custer!

HARRY: And who might that be?

CLARENCE: Why, Sittin' Bull, of course.

HARRY: How'd you know it was him personally killed Custer?

CLARENCE: *(defensively)* Well . . . everybody says so! It was Sittin' Bull himself killed Custer at the Little Big Horn—with his huntin' knife! *(He thinks about it and backs down a bit.)* I guess the only ones know for sure are the men who died with Custer, eh?

HARRY: *(politely)* Ain't you forgettin' somethin'?

CLARENCE: What?

HARRY: I seem to recollect there was some other people present at the event.

CLARENCE: Who?

HARRY: Jesus Christ, Clarence! The Indians, that's who! You think a white man's the only person kin know anythin' for sure! Whyn't you try askin' an Injun who killed Custer? You bleedin' redcoats don't know nothin'.

CLARENCE: *(insulted)* You wanna fight?

HARRY looks at CLARENCE and directs a spittle of tobacco juice at CLARENCE's feet. CLARENCE hauls back his fist.

LOUIS: *(from the shadows, speaking to CLARENCE)* 'Ey!

WALSH enters, his attention fixed on the crates.

WALSH: What the hell's this?

HARRY: *(clearing his throat)* Well, sir, I 'spect you'd say . . . it was more . . . .

WALSH: And this . . . and this . . . and this!

He slaps each item with his riding crop.

LOUIS: *(attempting to be helpful)* 'Dat's plough-share. We got 'em last time.

WALSH: I know we got them last time. Why're we getting them this time?

LOUIS shrugs. WALSH's glance falls on CLARENCE. He notices him for the first time. CLARENCE feels obliged to say something.

CLARENCE: I . . . I don't know, sir.

WALSH's irritation seems to go and his manner changes.

WALSH: A new recruit, aren't you?

CLARENCE: Yes, sir.

WALSH: Name?

CLARENCE: Constable Clarence Underhill, sir!

WALSH: Welcome to the fort, Constable. Keep you eyes, ears and mind open . . .

CLARENCE: Yes, s . . . .

WALSH: . . . and your mouth shut. *(He turns to HARRY and speaks real friendly.)* All right, HARRY. *(He leans on a crate beside HARRY and indicates the implements with his riding crop.)* What is all this?

HARRY: Well, sir . . . .

WALSH: *exceedingly friendly* Some immigrant family ordered it, I suppose . . . .

HARRY: Ah . . . I can't rightly say that, sir.

WALSH: Aha . . . . Then you're taking it up to Calgary, are you, for some poor witless farmer there?

HARRY: No sir . . . . Not that either.

WALSH: Mmmmm . . . . Planning on home-steading yourself, are you?

HARRY smiles. The idea amuses him.

HARRY: Not very likely, sir.

WALSH stares at HARRY for a second. He lowers his voice and his speech builds.

WALSH: Are you telling me, man, that once again the government has seen fit to burden me and the natives of these parts with another load of seed and equipment to rot and rust when they know goddamn well, because I've told them time and again, that these Indians are not, and will never be, farmers!

There is a pause as WALSH stares at HARRY.

HARRY: *(answering weakly)* That's it, sir.

WALSH: Right! *His anger seems to subside.* Well . . . can't be helped, can it?

He walks around one of the crates, tapping it with his riding crop, then, extending his hand, he barks.

WALSH: Bill of lading!

CLARENCE: *(startled)* Ah! Yes, sir!

He feels in his pocket as WALSH watches him expressionlessly. He finds the bill, presents it to WALSH—but not quite in his hand. The bill begins to float to the ground. He retrieves it and places it in WALSH's hand.

WALSH: *(dryly)* Thank you, Constable.

CLARENCE: Yes, sir!

WALSH looks at CLARENCE, then moves away with HARRY.

WALSH: What have you got there, Harry?

He and HARRY begin to check the number of crates. LOUIS looks over to CLARENCE.

LOUIS: 'Ey . . . 'ey dere . . . .

He beckons him with his finger. CLARENCE moves over to him, although he's still more or less at attention and focused on WALSH in case he should suddenly want something.

Dis . . . a . . . first time you meet da . . . *(nodding towards WALSH)* . . . commandin' officer up close, eh?

CLARENCE nods and looks at LOUIS warily. LOUIS looks somewhat disreputable in his scout outfit.

What you think of 'im?

CLARENCE: He seems a little . . . .

He casts a nervous glance at WALSH.

WALSH: *(to HARRY)* Read it yourself! *(thrusting the bill at HARRY)* What does that look like to you?

CLARENCE smiles weakly at LOUIS, who smiles back.

HARRY: It . . . ah . . . looks like we're missin' one crate, Major.

WALSH: I trust you'll find it.

HARRY: I'll do that . . . yes, I will, Major. First thing I hit Fort MacLeod.

WALSH: Right.

He takes the bill and begins to check it against the goods listed on the outside of the crates.

WALSH: So . . . contents . . . .

HARRY assists him.

LOUIS: *(indicating himself)* Louis Leveille. *(shaking hands with CLARENCE)* Fort Walsh scout . . . . Mother red, father white . . . but not so white as da Major dere . . . . Louis' father, French.

He laughs. CLARENCE realizes it's a joke and smiles back.

WALSH: Mark it off! Mark if off!

HARRY does so. CLARENCE glances at them nervously.

LOUIS: Ah . . . don't worry . . . mean nothin' . . . . Just 'is way. He care a lot and so he yell a lot, eh?

CLARENCE: Yeah. I guess you gotta know a lot to be an officer.

LOUIS: Louis tell yuh somethin' . . . . Take all da books, da news dat da white man prints, take all dat Bible book, take all dose things you learn from . . . lay dem on da prairie . . . and da sun . . . da rain . . . da snow . . . pouf! You wanna learn, you study inside here . . . *(He taps his head.)* . . . and here . . . *(He taps his chest.)* . . . and how it is wit' you and me . . . *(He indicates the two of them.)* . . . and how it is wit' you and all . . . *(He indicates the surroundings.)* Travel 'round da Medicine Wheel. Den you know somethin'.

WALSH: *(approaching LOUIS and CLARENCE)* Well, Louis, there's another lot, courtesy of those fools in Ottawa.

LOUIS: Dose fools dat're sittin' dere ain't such fools as da people dat sent dem dere, eh, Major?

WALSH chuckles. HARRY begins to clear away the treaty goods.

MRS. ANDERSON: *(offstage)* Major Walsh! Oh, Major!

Walsh sighs. MRS. ANDERSON enters almost hysterical.

MRS. ANDERSON: Major Walsh!

WALSH: *(smiling at MRS. ANDERSON)* Yes, Mrs. Anderson.

MRS. ANDERSON: *(almost in tears)* Major Walsh, the most terrible thing has happened.

CROW EAGLE enters with great dignity. He walks a bit ahead of Sergeant McCUTCHEON. He is in custody, although there is no hand on him.

WALSH: Now, it's all right, Mrs. Anderson. Just tell us what this is all about.

MRS. ANDERSON: Ah, Major . . . this savage . . . this heathen . . . this . . . Indian has stolen my washtub!

A pained expression passes over WALSH's face. He shakes his head and makes an almost inaudible tut-tut sound.

MRS. ANDERSON: Yes! It was right outside the door and these heathens snuck up and stole it! I'm counting on you, Major, to return that tub! I mean, what am I to rinse in otherwise?

WALSH: Well, Crow Eagle, did you take this white lady's tub?

CROW EAGLE: That is so.

MRS. ANDERSON: What did I tell you? *(circling CROW EAGLE in a rage)* Mark my words, they'll be killing us in our sleep next!

WALSH: *(placating her)* Mrs. Anderson . . . . *(turning to CROW EAGLE)* Why'd you take the tub?

CROW EAGLE: We needed a drum.

WALSH: The Great White Mother'd be very angry if she discovered you'd taken this white lady's washtub.

CROW EAGLE: I am sure if the Great White Mother knew how much we needed that drum, she would be glad to let us keep it.

MRS. ANDERSON: As if the Queen cared about them!

CROW EAGLE: We have cut the bottom out of that tub and covered it with buffalo skin. It makes a very good drum.

LOUIS: Da white lady has 'nother tub . . . why does she not use dat?

MRS. ANDERSON: (going to seize CROW EAGLE's arm) What's mine's my own! You'll not take . . . .

WALSH: (taking her arm and drawing her aside) Mrs. Anderson!

MRS. ANDERSON: Whose side are you on, Jim?

WALSH: I was unaware we were choosing sides. My job is to keep the peace and see that justice is done.

MRS. ANDERSON: Then get me my tub!

WALSH: (a trifle tired) Louis, explain it to him.

LOUIS: (explaining to CROW EAGLE in Cree) Na-mo-ya ta-ki otin-a-man ki-kwhy a-ka a-tipay-hitaman (It is not lawful to take what is not your own) . . . .

CROW EAGLE: (dismissing LOUIS and speaking directly to WALSH) White Forehead Chief! Why we should not keep it?

WALSH: (after a pause) You must not take articles from the whites again. They need even what they appear not to need . . . . And you must bring skins in payment for the . . . drum . . . . Make sure he understands, Louis.

LOUIS draws CROW EAGLE aside and speaks to him in muffled conversation while WALSH continues with MRS. ANDERSON.

LOUIS: Wapi-ka-tik-oki-maw it-o-wew-may-scootch ata-yuk ta-pa-so-wa-chik to tippo-what misti-kwa-shihk-asa kotin-nut (The White Forehead Chief says you must bring skins in payment for the drum you have taken.)

CROW EAGLE: Ni-ka-to-tayn namaya-ni-nisto-tayn ma-ka ni-ka-to-tayn keespin wapi-ka-tik ekosi it-o-wen-ni-ka-to-tayn (I will do it. I do not understand it, but I will do it. If the White Forehead Chief says it . . . I will do it.)

LOUIS: Pi-ko ta-na-hi-ta-wat Okimaskoew Kwa-yask ta-pa-mi-hayew ki-ta-yes-si-ni-ma apo tchi ke-yom ta-wan-kiski-sew kiya (You must obey the Great White Mother's law. She will look after your people if you do. Otherwise, she will forget you.)

CROW EAGLE: Wapi-ka-tik chee pa-taw aso-ta-ma-to-aina paski-si-gana, mosiniya nin-ta wahitay-nan paskowaw mastosak aya-wak sa-ka-staynok (Has she sent the White Forehead Chief the goods that I asked for my people? We need ammunition, we have seen buffalo to the south.)

WALSH: (steering MRS. ANDERSON away) Now, look, Emma . . . .

MRS. ANDERSON: What about my tub?

WALSH: Emma . . . the Indians, they see two tubs in your yard . . . . You have to remember they've a different background from us . . . .

MRS. ANDERSON: Background? They don't have any background.

WALSH: Well, as I was saying . . . .

MRS. ANDERSON: Are you telling me I'm not getting my tub back?

WALSH: That's right, Emma.

MRS. ANDERSON: What will you do when they murder us in our beds? You're nothing but a . . .

WALSH: Would you have me throw him in chains? To hell with your damned old tub! We're not going to start an Indian War over it!

MRS. ANDERSON: No! You'll sit by and let the Sioux do that!

She whirls around and exits. WALSH stands stiff and tense as she exits, then he relaxes and turns to McCUTCHEON. He smiles, sighs and shakes his head.

WALSH: The Sioux? . . . Well, McCutcheon . . . hell hath no fury like a woman deprived of her washtub. (He walks around the equipment, looking at it casually.) You'd think it was her very existence.

McCUTCHEON: Aye, sir. You're right there. I tell ye, I'd rather face a hostile in a fit of pique than Mrs. Anderson with her dander up . . . .

LOUIS: Crow Eagle asks for ammunition to hunt da buffalo. His scouts have seen a small herd to da south.

WALSH: Every year there're fewer buffalo and soon there will be no more. His people must think of next year and the year after.

LOUIS: (almost gently) Ever since he was born, he has eaten wild meat. His father and his grandfather ate wild meat. He cannot give up quickly the customs of his fathers.

WALSH speaks directly to CROW EAGLE.

WALSH: (speaking formally) When the white man comes, the buffalo goes . . . . And with the buffalo goes the life you have known. You cannot stop this happening any more than you can stop the sun or the moon. You must find a new life . . . . That is why the Great White Mother sends you these . . . *(He indicates the implements)* . . . so you can start a new life.

CROW EAGLE: I do not wish to be servant to a cow.

HARRY: (laughing) He's got somethin' there . . . .

WALSH: Yes, well . . . McCutcheon, take him over to the post and see he gets ammunition for the hunt.

McCUTCHEON: Aye, sir.

He and CROW EAGLE go to leave.

WALSH: Crow Eagle, you must think of the time when there are no more buffalo.

CROW EAGLE: When there are no more buffalo . . . there are no more Indians.

He and McCUTCHEON exit. WALSH watches them leave.

WALSH: (to himself) I ask you, can you see that man bent double over a hoe?

HARRY: Don't appear likely they'll ever be farmers, that's a fact.

WALSH: Farmers? Not farmers! If they're to grow anything in this dust bowl, the government'll have to turn them into magicians!

CLARENCE: (standing at attention) Excuse me, sir . . . permission to speak, sir.

WALSH appears lost in his thoughts as he stares after CROW EAGLE.

WALSH: Yes . . . . what is it?

CLARENCE: There's been some talk, sir, among the men at the post . . . about the hostiles from the States.

WALSH: (still not particularly attentive) Go on . . .

CLARENCE: (encouraged) About them comin' up into Canada . . . . Sittin' Bull and the whole Sioux nation comin' up into Canada to get away from the U.S. Army . . . .

Sometime during CLARENCE's speech, WALSH becomes alert and is listening.

WALSH: Yes?

CLARENCE: Well . . . . I was just wonderin', sir, if that was true . . . I mean, the whole Sioux nation, sir? And we only got 'bout 60 men here . . .

WALSH: Yes.

CLARENCE: . . . and you know . . . I'm not askin' for myself, sir, it's just that I'd like to write a last letter home to me Mum if we . . . if we were on the verge of war, sir, or anything like that . . . sir.

WALSH: (speaking quietly) What have the Sioux done?

CLARENCE: (blurting it out) They killed Custer!

WALSH: And Custer killed them.

CLARENCE: Yes, sir.

WALSH: What have the Sioux done to us?

CLARENCE: (looking nervously at HARRY, then back to WALSH) Nothin', sir?

WALSH: In which case, I don't believe we're on the verge of war with them. (to LOUIS, lightly) What do you say, Louis?

LOUIS: (smiling) I think our redcoats too damn busy chasin' 'merican whiskey traders. Dey much worse trouble dan any Sioux I run across.

WALSH: (smiling) My sentiments exactly.

He and LOUIS start off. The sound of the arrival of the Sioux creeps in very softly—muted voices, horses, faint drums and singing. It can barely be heard.

CLARENCE: Sir!

WALSH: *(turning back to him)* Yes, Constable?

CLARENCE: *(speaking quickly)* Request permission to accompany the Major when he rides out to meet Sittin' Bull and the Sioux, sir!

WALSH: What about that letter to your mother?

CLARENCE: I'll write it tonight, sir.

WALSH has a hard time keeping a smile off his face.

WALSH: Permission granted.

WALSH exits as CLARENCE and HARRY watch him. CLARENCE is tense and HARRY is casual, then CLARENCE looks at HARRY, relaxes, grins and leaps into the air, throwing his hat off. There is a certain similarity to an Indian youth after his first coup.

CLARENCE: Yip yip yip yip yipeeeeeeeeeeeeee-eee! Whahooo!

CLARENCE and HARRY exit. The lights dim as LOUIS crouches, listening to the sound of the Sioux arriving. As it builds, LOUIS moves about as if he were watching the arrival of the Sioux. The sound is well established before he speaks.

LOUIS: Tabernacle! *(casting a glance over his shoulder)* Major! Dis way!

WALSH and McCUTCHEON enter. They stand on a slight rise.

LOUIS: See . . . da village is dere. *(pointing)* Dat dust, dat is more joinin' dose already camped.

WALSH hands his binoculars to McCUTCHEON. He gazes at the village, using only his naked eye, as the scout does.

WALSH: Must be . . . what . . . two miles away? What would you say, Louis?

LOUIS: *(smiling)* Louis say you damn good pupil.

WALSH: *(smiling)* Louis damn good teacher.

McCUTCHEON: *(looking through the binoculars, then lowering them)* Must be 2,000 people there.

LOUIS: Maybe so . . . 5,000.

CLARENCE enters.

CLARENCE: The horses're picketed, sir.

WALSH turns to CLARENCE and speaks to him with an intensity that indicates he is taut as a bow string and ready for anything.

WALSH: You wanted to see the Sioux, Constable . . . all right, here they come. I want you to remember something . . . . You do not draw your gun unless you see me draw mine. You will follow orders exactly, precisely and immediately. If you do one thing that precipitates trouble between us and the Sioux, you need not worry about a redskin taking your scalp. I myself will place a bullet between your eyes faster than you can say write-a-letter-home.

It is a threat he means.

Do you understand?

For the first time, CLARENCE is aware of the potential explosiveness of the situation.

CLARENCE: I do, sir.

The sound is building.

WALSH: Louis, beside me . . . . McCutcheon and Underhill, behind . . . .

They take up their positions. WALSH gives a quick look to CLARENCE.

I rely on you to uphold the honour of the force.

The sound is at its crescendo—all around the audience—for several seconds. The sound stops. There is a pause.

GALL enters. He is followed by SITTING BULL, who looks austere. He has one feather in his hair. They stop a short distance from WALSH. WALSH raises his hand, palm outward. GALL returns the gesture. There is silence for a second.

WALSH: Louis, tell them . . . .

GALL: We speak as men—to each other.

He means that they do not need an interpreter.

I am Gall of the Hunkpapa Lakota.

WALSH: You've crossed the line into the country of the Great White Mother.

GALL stares at WALSH impassively. SITTING BULL follows their conversation. His movements, if any, are slow and deliberate. He is a man of great presence and personal magnetism. It is not necessary for him to speak or to draw attention to himself in any way for one to be aware of his strength of character. It is his custom to carefully size up a situation before committing himself to a course of action.

WALSH: I am a soldier of the Great White Mother. You may know me, and others like me, by my red coat. *(He indicates his tunic.)*

GALL: *(offering WALSH a George III medal)* My grandfather was a soldier for the grandfather of Queen Victoria. At that time, your people told him that the Sioux nation belonged to that grandfather of the Queen. My people fought against the Longknives for your people then. We were told that you would always look after your red children. Now the Longknives have stolen our land. We have no place to go. We come home to you asking for that protection you promised.

WALSH takes the medal from GALL and examines it. He looks at GALL. He is not actually prepared for this specific argument about Canada's obligation to the Sioux.

McCUTCHEON: *(speaking quietly)* What is it, sir?

WALSH: *(passing the medal to McCUTCHEON)* It's a George III medal. The Sioux fought for the British in 1776 against the Americans.

He looks at GALL and speaks carefully. His orders from Ottawa have not covered this exigency.

We are your friends, that is true . . . .

GALL: The Lakota has need of friends. I want you to know this trouble was not begun by us. The Longknives have come out of the night and for campfires they have lit our lodges. Our women weep and the nostrils of our babies must be pinched lest they cry out and give us away. At the Greasy Grass, the Long Hair attacked our camp and we rose up like the buffalo bull when the cows are attacked and we rubbed him out. Now we are hunted as we hunt animals . . . and we have crossed the line.

LOUIS: *(nudging WALSH)* 'Ey . . . on the ridge . . . is dat not da horse of Père de Corbay?

WALSH: *(looking, frowning towards the hills)* Whose horses graze there?

GALL: *(looking at the hills)* White Dog's, our Assiniboine brother.

WALSH: I wish to speak to him.

The sound of rattles and drums is heard. GALL exits. CLARENCE shifts from side to side nervously. McCUTCHEON gives him a look.

McCUTCHEON: *(in a low voice)* Easy, laddie.

CLARENCE: *(taking a slow look over his shoulder)* We're bloody well surrounded, Sergeant.

McCUTCHEON: Never ye mind, laddie. Just keep your eye on the Major.

WALSH takes a slow walk. He whistles, then he stops, looking directly at SITTING BULL.

WALSH: Gall! *(GALL turns toward him.)* I ask the name of the man who stands with us.

GALL: A wise man . . . .

WHITE DOG enters. He carries a rifle in one hand.

WALSH: *(speaking quickly)* McCutcheon!

WHITE DOG: *(belligerently)* White Dog.

WALSH: The horses on the ridge, are they yours?

WHITE DOG: *(antagonistically)* You say!

WALSH: *(snapping)* McCutcheon!

McCUTCHEON moves quickly and seizes WHITE DOG's arms. WHITE DOG resists, but McCUTCHEON holds him immobile. WALSH's hand rests easily, almost casually, on his holstered gun. As McCUTCHEON seizes WHITE DOG, he cries out. There is a swelling of sound from the surrounding Sioux. WALSH raises his voice and announces as the sound continues in the background.

WALSH: Those are the horses of Père de Corbay! His brand can be seen from here! White Dog is under arrest for stealing!

WHITE DOG: I find loose! It is custom, horses taken! No law!

WALSH: *(after a pause)* Release him!

McCUTCHEON releases him.

WALSH: Next time, you find horses not belonging to you, they must be left alone!

WHITE DOG: *(as he turns to leave, calling back threateningly)* Meet again, Wichitas!

WALSH: White Dog! *(He walks up to WHITE DOG, oblivious of his rifle.)* Repeat your words.

WHITE DOG: *(a coward)* Meet again sometime.

WALSH: *(speaking quietly but now without menace)* Take back those words.

WHITE DOG hesitates a minute, then looks to SITTING BULL and back at WALSH.

WHITE DOG: White Dog not threaten.

WALSH: *(inclining his head slightly)* Then go. I have no grudge against White Dog.

WHITE DOG hurries off. The background sound swells. WALSH walks over to SITTING BULL, who raises his hand. The noise stops.

SITTING BULL: These people are my people. I am Sitting Bull.

WALSH: Major James Walsh of the North West Mounted Police.

He extends his hand and after a second's hesitation, SITTING BULL takes it.

SITTING BULL: My people need ammunition.

WALSH: *(beginning his "government" statement)* The Queen will not tolerate raiding from her soil, nor does she . . .

SITTING BULL: Hard times have come to us. My warriors use the lasso to bring down meat.

WALSH stares at him for a split second and decides to trust him.

WALSH: Ammunition will be issued sufficient for hunting purposes. McCutcheon, take the Constable and see to it.

McCUTCHEON: Aye, sir!

McCUTCHEON and CLARENCE exit. The lights begin to dim.

SITTING BULL: We shall meet again.

WALSH: *(smiling)* I look forward to it.

GALL, WALSH and SITTING BULL exit. PRETTY PLUME enters, unrolls a buffalo skin for the floor of the tent, as LOUIS, singing softly, removes his pack and sits a distance from the tent.

LOUIS: En roulant ma boule roulant, enroulant ma boule.
En roulant ma boule roulant, enroulant ma boule.
Derrier' chez nous, 'y a-t'un e-tang, enroulant ma boule,
Trois beaux canards s'en vont baignant, roulant ma boule, roulant.

The lights brighten as McCUTCHEON and CLARENCE enter, carrying bowls of food. McCUTCHEON passes a bowl of food to LOUIS.

McCUTCHEON: Here y'are, Louis.

McCUTCHEON and CLARENCE sit. All three of them begin to eat. LOUIS eats with relish; McCUTCHEON eats simply; CLARENCE sloshes his bowl around, peering into it with apprehension. He is reassured by LOUIS' appreciation of the contents. He dips his fingers into the bowl and comes up with something unpleasant. He quickly drops it back into the bowl and grimaces. He looks at McCUTCHEON, who tilts his bowl a bit and drains it. CLARENCE swallows and looks down at his bowl. LOUIS glances over at him.

LOUIS: *(teasing CLARENCE)* Dat some good, eh?

CLARENCE smiles weakly and nods half-heartedly. LOUIS gets up.

LOUIS: 'Nother one?

McCUTCHEON: *(putting his empty bowl down)* Not for me, Louis.

LOUIS looks at CLARENCE.

CLARENCE: I still got some. Thanks anyway.

LOUIS exits to get some more.

McCUTCHEON: *(calling after him)* My compliments to the chef, Louis!

CLARENCE stares at McCUTCHEON, then down at his own bowl. McCUTCHEON suppresses a smile.

McCUTCHEON: Laddie, ye better be eatin' that up, if ye want to keep your forelock.

CLARENCE: What do you mean?

McCUTCHEON: *(whispering to him)* It's a great insult not to eat what's put before ye when y're visitin' the Sioux . . . . Men have been known to lose their scalps over such an insult.

CLARENCE: *(sickly)* That so?

He dips his fingers into his bowl again, comes in contact with something unpleasant, drops it back into the bowl, sits for a second, then makes up his mind.

CLARENCE: Well, I don't give a damn! I'd sooner be scalped than eat any more of this stuff! Here, you take it!

McCUTCHEON: *(laughing and pushing the bowl away)* I've done my duty, laddie. Now it's up to you.

LOUIS returns, dejected.

LOUIS: Merde, McCutch. Dey eat it all up. Dere's none left.

CLARENCE: *(looking up, brightening)* Say, Louis, I think . . . *(He feels his forehead.)* . . . I think I overdid it a bit today . . . don't really feel too much like eatin' tonight . . . . If you want mine, well, no sense seein' it wasted.

He offers his bowl hopefully to LOUIS. LOUIS smiles, recognizing his ploy.

LOUIS: Dat so? Weeeellllll . . . .

He takes his bowl, squats and eats. CLARENCE smiles at McCUTCHEON.

McCUTCHEON: Now I wonder how the Major's makin' out.

LOUIS: *(looking up)* Da Major and Sittin' Bull over in da big tipi dere. Dey send Louis away, but he keep an eye out all da same.

He goes back to his food. McCUTCHEON gets out his pipe and stretches his legs, but remains sitting.

McCUTCHEON: The Sioux have behaved themselves, there's no denyin' that. Six months it's been, and they're as good as gold.

LOUIS: *(putting down his bowl and looking at McCUTCHEON)* Dese Sioux, dey not stupid, you know. Make trouble and dey know what

happens. 'Mericans send Longknives up here. Dey kill every Indian dey see—little ones, big ones, mama with bébé—dey don't give a good goddamn, friendly or hostile . . . . You got red skin . . . *(He points his finger.)* . . . bang-bang! . . . Louis' skin got reddish tinge.

There is an awkward silence. The lights dim a bit. McCUTCHEON and CLARENCE look down. LOUIS shrugs and gets out his pipe.

McCUTCHEON: *(passing LOUIS his pouch of tobacco)* Try mine.

LOUIS: *(taking the pouch and fingering it)* You buy new one, eh?

McCUTCHEON: I got it at the post before we left. Feel that leather . . . soft, isn't it?

LOUIS: Dat's nice . . . *(He gazes off into space.)* But not so nice as 'nother pouch I see once . . . many year ago, before the redcoats come . . . I see white man at Fort Whoop-Up, a Longknife . . . . He show everybody mighty nice tobacco pouch he have . . . made from breast of Indian woman he killed at Sand Creek.

He looks in the direction of SITTING BULL's tipi. McCUTCHEON and CLARENCE follow suit. As the lights dim on them, they begin to come up on the tipi. There is a soft background sound of Indian rattles and bells, which continues until the scene with SITTING BULL is established. WALSH and SITTING BULL are eating. WALSH looks up from his bowl after a moment.

WALSH: Louis tells me you've been visiting the Blackfoot and the Cree.

SITTING BULL: They tell me that Major Walsh is the White Forehead Chief . . . and the White Forehead Chief is the Indian's friend. If trouble strikes your camp, they say, send for the White Forehead Chief.

WALSH: The Blackfoot . . .

SITTING BULL: Do you ride out to speak only of the Blackfoot and the Cree . . . . Have you no news for the Sioux?

WALSH: Yes, I have news . . . and it's not good news . . . . My chief says the Queen is not responsible for you. *(He holds up the George III medal.)* This happened a long time ago. The Great White Mother has made peace with the Americans.

SITTING BULL: *(with a hint of sarcasm)* Whose red children are we then?

WALSH: It was decided the Sioux belonged to the President in Washington.

SITTING BULL: It was decided . . . . You are few and we are many. Will you try to drive us back across the line?

WALSH: You're welcome to stay here so long as your young men don't cross the line to raid and so long as the Sioux are self-sufficient . . . . The Queen won't feed or clothe you as she does her own Indians.

SITTING BULL: *(leaning towards WALSH)* My people have never accepted the annuities . . . . We have never touched the pen . . . . We have never sold our land! It has been stolen from us! You need not feed or clothe us. The Hunkpapa Lakota feed and clothe themselves!

WALSH: *(speaking gently)* Soon you won't be able to do that. The buffalo will be gone. You must return to your home before that happens.

SITTING BULL: The Black Hills is our home! And the white man has stolen them! I cannot sign away the Black Hills. They are not mine alone. Before me, they were my father's. After me, they shall be my children's. Do you sign away the birthright of your children?

WALSH: I tell you this because I am a soldier and I must follow orders, but I am a friend also. White Forehead . . . *(indicating himself)* . . . does not say this, Major Walsh says this. *(He speaks officially.)* The President in Washington has requested the Sioux to return . . . and promises fair treatment to all.

SITTING BULL stares at WALSH for a moment, then begins to speak conversationally, casually.

SITTING BULL: Let me tell you what I have heard today . . . . Today, I have news of my good friend Crazy Horse of the Oglala. He was a dreamer, wishing only to serve his people . . . and they loved him well . . . . Brave in battle. Wise in council. He loved the little children and could not bear to see them suffer. The Oglala and the Hunkpapa fought together at the Greasy Grass where Custer died. I brought my people across the line, but Crazy Horse and the Oglala remained behind. Since that time, they've known no peace. General Terry pursued them like a wolf who tears at the soft underbelly of a fleeing doe . . . . There are two reservation chiefs across the line named Red Cloud and Spotted Tail. Some say they are paper chiefs created by the white man to betray their red brothers . . . . Red Cloud and Spotted Tail met Crazy Horse in council and begged him to bring his people in, to touch the pen, to lead a reservation life. They told him, "You will be a great chief!" . . . The Sioux are proud; we love position . . . . My good friend Crazy Horse is dead. He brought his people in and when he stepped into the meeting place, he saw the windows all were barred and 'round about stood soldiers pointing longknives at him . . . and when he turned to run, his arms were pinioned by his red brothers and a white soldier pushed his bayonet into Crazy Horse's stomach! It took one night for him to die. He sang his death song and his mother and father stood outside and sang back, for the white soldiers would not let them enter where he lay dying. And where he stood when he was struck, there is a great gouge gone from the wall, for the soldier's longknife passed through Crazy Horse and lodged there till he withdrew it . . . . I am told that men with skin like yours gaze at that gouge and laugh and joke and say: "There stood a good Indian . . . a dead Indian." . . . My good friend Crazy Horse of the Oglala.

WALSH: Aren't things sometimes done in your name? Things you do not wish? It can be that way with white men too . . . . I am your friend.

SITTING BULL: I have no white friends.

WALSH: For Christ's sake, forget the colour of our skin! If you've got no more to say than that, let's all line up and have it out! To hell with it! Is that what you want?

SITTING BULL: Red men choke and die on white men's words!

WALSH: When have my actions betrayed my words? I came here to speak to you as a man and I expect the same from you! What's past is past! Crazy Horse is dead, but others live and you and I are here to talk of them! . . . People are coming from the White Father in Washington. I ask you to see them. If you don't want to return with them, I will tell them so. I promise you. I'll stand by you.

SITTING BULL: Who do they send?

WALSH: General Terry.

SITTING BULL: You ask me to see this man? The man who burnt my mother earth and killed my friends! You tell me, see this man!

WALSH: If you wish to negotiate a reservation here in Canada, you must make your peace with the Americans first.

There is silence as WALSH and SITTING BULL sit staring at one another.

There's something more I have to say . . . . Last night, two men rode into your camp.

SITTING BULL: With news of Crazy Horse.

WALSH: And news of something more than that, I think.

SITTING BULL: They had a request to make of me.

WALSH: Nez Percés, weren't they?

SITTING BULL: Nez Percés . . . from the valley of the Winding Waters.

WALSH: The Wallowa Valley no longer belongs to them.

SITTING BULL: A thief treaty . . . . Chief Joseph did not sign!

WALSH: Nevertheless, the President has put aside a reservation and the Indians must go onto it.

SITTING BULL: What right has he to tell the Indian where he must go in his own land?

WALSH: Is Chief Joseph trying to bring his people into Canada?

SITTING BULL: I tell you what you already know . . . the Nez Percés are on the run. They have come to me. They request the Sioux to help them fight their way across the line.

WALSH: What I do not know is your decision.

SITTING BULL: I have not made it.

WALSH: Then listen to me. If it can be proven that you've carried out an act of war against the Americans while camping here in Canada, your refuge will be in jeopardy.

SITTING BULL: What could you do?

WALSH: We could open the border and allow the American Army in to drive you out.

SITTING BULL: Even though you know you send us to our death?

WALSH: We don't know that.

SITTING BULL: As we speak, Nez Percés are rotting, their bodies full of bullet holes, their heads smashed in with gunstocks and boot heels. Would you term this a natural death?

WALSH: You see my red coat . . . it represents the Queen and the Canadian government. My duty is to inform you of my government's position . . . and it is this: "Armed excursions across the line . . . for whatever reason . . . will not be tolerated!" *(speaking gently to SITTING BULL)* I'd advise you to deny the Nez Percés.

SITTING BULL: Men, women, children? . . . They have travelled 1,300 miles.

WALSH: Another 60 and they're across the line. My government won't try to stop them, but you must not try to aid them either. They must make it on their own.

SITTING BULL: You ask me to deny them.

WALSH: It's for the good of your people. You can see that.

SITTING BULL: Yes . . . I can see it . . . . Today is a sad day for me . . . . In the past, I have risen, tomahawk in hand. I have done all the hurt to the whites that I could . . . . Now you are here. My arms hang to the ground as if dead . . . . I believe the Blackfoot and the Cree have judged you wisely. I will call you White Sioux and I will trust you. I will speak to General Terry . . . and I will deny the Nez Percés.

As the lights dim on WALSH and SITTING BULL, they come up blue and cold along with a background sound of howling wind. The lights pick out McCUTCHEON and CLARENCE, who are bundled in greatcoats. A winter blizzard is blowing.

McCUTCHEON: *(to CLARENCE who has stopped in front of him)* What is it?

CLARENCE: We've lost the Major.

McCUTCHEON: Keep goin', laddie.

CLARENCE: We've lost the Major.

McCUTCHEON: Here, let me . . . .

He moves ahead of CLARENCE and begins walking, holding his hand up to shield himself from the wind. CLARENCE follows him.

And we've no lost the Major . . . . Come on, laddie, we'll wait for Louis here.

He and CLARENCE huddle together.

CLARENCE: My God, I'm cold!

A blue light picks out WALSH, SITTING BULL and GALL as they enter in single file, leaning against the storm.

McCUTCHEON: *(cupping his hands and calling)* Over here, sir!

WALSH: *(as they approach)* Any sign of Louis?

McCUTCHEON: *(shaking his head)* Are ye sure Sittin' Bull's information is correct?

WALSH looks at SITTING BULL.

SITTING BULL: The Longknives have surrounded the Nez Percés, but some have broken through.

WALSH: Well, if they're out there, Louis'll find them.

CLARENCE: Aren't you worried 'bout him?

McCUTCHEON: Ah, we've got naught to worry about Louis . . . . He can look after himself.

CLARENCE: My God, I'm cold!

They hear a noise. They all turn around and look. A blue light picks out LOUIS. He makes his way toward them. He comes to SITTING BULL and stands before him without speaking. There is a pause for a moment.

WALSH: Well . . . speak up, Louis, have the Nez Percés crossed the border?

LOUIS: *(speaking to SITTING BULL)* I have found da tracks of a small number of people. Dey have few ponies and move slowly. Most are on foot . . . . Dere trail is easy to follow . . . it is marked with frozen blood . . . . Come with me.

SITTING BULL and GALL prepare to follow him. He speaks to WALSH.

Wait here. We speak to dem first. Dey will be frightened. We will bring dem back.

They exit. There is silence. McCUTCHEON moves toward WALSH, who stands at the edge of the light looking out. A wolf howls. There is silence again, then the whinnying of a pony. WALSH points.

McCUTCHEON: Is it them, sir?

SITTING BULL returns without his outer robes. He wears leggings and breeches. He stands outside the circle of light, a silhouette.

WALSH: Sergeant . . . Constable . . . . Help them!

He nods his head briskly in the direction from which SITTING BULL came. He gives them his greatcoat. They exit quickly.

SITTING BULL: *(an honest question)* How does the white man sustain himself beneath the weight of the blood that he has shed?

WALSH looks at SITTING BULL, then off at the muffled sounds of people approaching. The light begins to flicker, as if people were passing in front of it. WALSH turns slowly, looking outside of the light. The sound of people moaning is heard. A blue light picks out CLARENCE as he makes his way toward WALSH.

CLARENCE: Is . . . is it all right, sir? My coat . . . I've . . . I've given it to . . . *(He indicates vaguely outside of the light.)* . . . to . . . to a little girl and her brother. Their feet are frozen, sir . . . . Will the government mind about the coat?

WALSH: *(holding himself erect, military)* I'll speak on your behalf, Constable.

CLARENCE: It's just women and children . . . and a few men . . . . Most of them are . . . got wounds of one kind or another. Chief Joseph, he's not with them. He . . . didn't make it . . . . It's only just people, people that's been hurt! I don't see what they could have done to deserve this . . . . Do you know what they've done?

WALSH: There . . . see there . . . .

He hurriedly removes his tunic. He has on a long underwear top.

Take this . . . take this to the woman on the pony . . . there . . . with the papoose on her back. Take it to her.

CLARENCE: Yes, sir.

He moves toward the figure and freezes a ways from her. The wind howls. LOUIS stands on the rim of the light, watching. CLARENCE returns, moving slowly. He has the tunic with him.

She doesn't need it . . . she's been hit in the chest. The baby's dead. It's got a bit of blood on it.

He gives the tunic an ineffectual wipe, more a touch of the blood, then looks at WALSH.

I didn't notice till I put it 'round her that . . . she didn't need it.

WALSH slowly takes the tunic from him. CLARENCE moves away as WALSH stands there holding the tunic. He extends one arm slowly, deliberately. He drops the tunic and looks out. LOUIS steps forward, picks up the tunic and hands it to WALSH.

LOUIS: You can't just throw it away, sir. Dat's too easy.

WALSH looks at him, takes the tunic and slowly exits with it. LOUIS goes down on one knee. SITTING BULL steps forward slightly. The many voices of the Nez Percés are heard in the background saying "Ay Ay" as LOUIS speaks.

LOUIS: My father has given me this nation.
In protecting it,
A hard time I have.

Friends, hardships pursue me,
Fearless of them,
I live.
My chiefs of old are gone.
Myself, I shall take courage.

The voices grow in volume. They stop simultaneously. There is a second of blackout, then the light comes up on PRETTY PLUME AND CROWFOOT who are with SITTING BULL, who is in his former position.

PRETTY PLUME: Tatanka Yotanka!

CROWFOOT runs toward SITTING BULL and SITTING BULL picks him up, laughing. As he swings him in the air, PRETTY PLUME approaches him and holds out a rawhide bag which contains sacred stones.

SITTING BULL: Aha, Little One! Get to work, your mother says. Clear a spot.

CROWFOOT: Now?

SITTING BULL: Now.

He sits. CROWFOOT kneels, smoothing a spot to lay out the sacred stones, then he sits beside SITTING BULL. PRETTY PLUME sits watching from a distance.

SITTING BULL: So . . . . *(He arranges the stones in the shape of a Medicine Wheel.)* To the Great

Spirit belongs all things. The four-legged and the two-legged . . . but to the two-legged he gives the power to make live and to destroy . . . . To you, he gives the cup of living water . . . . Now . . . see? *(He indicates the circle of stones.)* It makes the sacred hoop. Here is the cross within the circle dividing it in four.

CLARENCE appears and stops before intruding. He draws near during the following speeches as he becomes interested.

The Great Spirit caused everything to be in fours and four is a sacred number. Four directions—north, east, south, west; four divisions of time—the day, the night, the month, the year; four parts of everything that grows—the root, the stem, the leaves, the fruit . . . . What else?

CROWFOOT: Ahhhhh . . . .

SITTING BULL holds out his hands, palms, downward, his thumbs concealed. CROWFOOT thrusts out his hands likewise.

SITTING BULL: Four fingers on each hand . . . and . . . two arms, two legs . . . .

He thrusts his limbs out, laughing.

Four in all!

CLARENCE casts a furtive look at his own hands.

SITTING BULL: *(urging CROWFOOT on)* Four things above the earth—the sun . . . the moon . . .

CROWFOOT: The sky, the stars!

SITTING BULL: *(smiling and nodding at CROWFOOT)* Good . . . . All of the universe is enclosed and revealed in the sacred circle. *(He traces the circle.)* Do you see how the sundance is a sacred hoop . . . and the sundance pole, the sacred centre? What else?

CLARENCE: *(caught up in it all, breaking in)* The tipi!

SITTING BULL looks at him.

Like, it's a circle too and . . . the fire . . . that's the centre.

He shifts nervously, bumping one of the stones. He picks it up, then isn't sure where it goes. He hands it to SITTING BULL.

SITTING BULL: *(holding up the stone)* This is a sacred stone. See how round it is. Everything the Great Spirit does is done in a circle. The sun and moon are round; they come and go forth in a circle. The white man says the earth is round . . . and so are all the stars. What else?

CROWFOOT: Birds make their nests round!

WALSH enters quietly.

SITTING BULL: The winds whirl; the seasons form a great circle . . . and when we, the Sioux, meet as a nation, we set our tipis so . . . . *(He describes an arc with the hand holding the stone.)* The nation's hoop!

He puts the stone back in position, then looks at WALSH.

WALSH: It's time.

CLARENCE: *(scrambling to his feet)* I'm sorry, sir. *(to SITTING BULL)* The Major has asked me to inform you that they're ready. Everything's ready.

SITTING BULL inclines his head acknowledging CLARENCE.

A light comes up on GENERAL TERRY in uniform.

SITTING BULL places a hand on his son's shoulder. They make their way to the meeting place with GENERAL TERRY. GALL appears and joins them as well. PRETTY PLUME goes to leave.

SITTING BULL: Come . . . come.

PRETTY PLUME joins them. Eventually, GALL, SITTING BULL, CROWFOOT and PRETTY PLUME will range themselves for the meeting.

WALSH, LOUIS, CLARENCE and McCUTCHEON attend the meeting as well, CLARENCE almost sneaking in to observe. LOUIS, McCUTCHEON and WALSH are there in a more formal sense. McCUTCHEON joins GENERAL TERRY, acting as a temporary aide de camp for him.

CLARENCE: *(to WALSH, as they make their way to the meeting place)* I got detained, sir. I got caught up.

WALSH places a hand on his shoulder and gives it a reassuring clasp.

When they enter, GENERAL TERRY ignores SITTING BULL's entrance. It is as if the Indians are not present.

WALSH: General Terry.

TERRY: Ah, Walsh. Wonderful man you got here. Been looking after me like I was one of his own.

WALSH: And so he does for me.

TERRY: Great country you have here. *(WALSH nods.)* I'm impressed. Empty as yet; but a course that'll change. My God, man, the wagon trains never cease across the line, and it's settlers that'll open it up . . . economic base, possibilities endless. You follow me? *(WALSH nods.)* Heavy responsibility on you and me, of course. And what's imperative . . . safety, progress . . . is the elimination of the savage.

WALSH: Sir?

TERRY Control of the savage, elimination of the savage aspects of the Indian's character . . . . Do you follow me? Though what you'd have left, be goddamned if I know. *(He chuckles.)* However, governments decree and we, poor bastards that we are, must deliver . . . .

He looks toward the Sioux and sighs, then looks back at WALSH.

You ever met George?

WALSH: General Custer?

TERRY: Great tragedy that . . . and there are the very devils themselves. Savage they must be, but I'll tell you this, Major, they are kittens compared to the Eastern press. I'll take a Sioux sittin' on my chest anyday to a scribe peerin' over my shoulder. You follow me? You know where you are with a Sioux. Headlines coast to coast lauding George . . . and between you and me, he was a man had his faults . . . . Same goddamn papers up for court-martialing him over that Wichitas business, and now up on a pedestal, and bring the villains to justice, wipe them out . . . and of course the government's got to act . . . . Do you follow me? And it's yours and my head on the block . . . . That's the way of it. That's what we live with. So . . . .

He looks at the Sioux and sniffs. He whispers to WALSH confidently.

And I'll tell you this . . . whatever we do, by the time we're finished, they'll have flip-flopped to the other side of the fence. You follow me?

WALSH does not follow him.

The papers, man, the Eastern press.

WALSH: Yes, sir.

TERRY: Not a man among them I'd have at my back in a fight. *(He whispers.)* Nor a position I'd give to George, if the truth be known. *(He chuckles, stops, clears his throat.)* Still, a wonderful soldier, one of the best.

He gets out a pair of wire-rimmed glasses, studies a document and looks up.

TERRY: I am empowered to speak to you on behalf of the American government.

PRETTY PLUME: We are listening.

TERRY: *(looking at her, then continuing)* The Great White Father in Washington is a generous father.

PRETTY PLUME: We are listening.

TERRY: Who the hell is she? . . . Your deeds against the whites have been grievous. The mighty arm and righteous anger of the Great White Father has been raised against you. It is within his power to wipe you out. He has stayed that anger and that might. He has forgiven you.

PRETTY PLUME: We are listening.

TERRY They got a goddamn woman speaking for them . . . . Who speaks for the Sioux?

SITTING BULL: The bearer of our children.

TERRY: I'm here to speak to you!

PRETTY PLUME: We are listening.

TERRY: The Great White Father holds your lives in his hands. The Indian is his . . . to do with as he pleases. You will return across the line. A reservation has been provided for you and you will go on it. Goods will be provided sufficient for your needs. Should you heed my words, you will be safe in the hand of the Great White Father. Should you not . . . .

He closes his hand tightly and makes a gesture of throwing away.

PRETTY PLUME: We have heard you.

TERRY: Get her out of here. *(McCUTCHEON looks at WALSH.)* Get her out! I'm here to talk to you! *(The Sioux start to leave.)* Who the hell do they think they are? Stop them!

The Sioux exit, except for SITTING BULL.

WALSH: Do you realize what he's promised? A reservation, food and supplies for your people, an amnesty. No one will be punished or go to jail for acts of war committed against the government. All that will be forgiven and forgotten!

SITTING BULL: Forgotten? . . . When I was a boy, the Sioux owned the world. The sun rose and set on our land. We sent 10,000 men to battle. Where are those warriors now? Where are our lands? Who owns them? Tell me . . . what law have I broken? Is it because my skin is red? Because I am Sioux, because I was born where my fathers lived, because I would die for my people and my country? . . . This white man would forgive me . . . and while he speaks to me of forgiveness, what do his people say in secret? "Seize their guns and horses Drive them back across the line. The more we kill this year, the less we have to kill next year." Is it not true?

TERRY: Goddamn waste of time.

He thrusts his fist towards SITTING BULL, then makes a throwing away gesture, and leaves. McCUTCHEON follows. LOUIS remains as SITTING BULL and WALSH speak. There is a pause. Eventually, SITTING BULL turns to WALSH and begins intimately.

SITTING BULL: You are a white man. The God whose son you killed must love you and your people well, for he has rewarded you with many gifts . . . and tools . . . and . . . *(indicating their uniforms, their guns, etc.)* . . . all this . . . I am told wisdom is yours as well. Advise me now, White Sioux. Tell me what is best for my people. I will follow your advice . . . and the burden of it will be on your shoulders . . . .

WALSH does not answer him.

SITTING BULL: Shall I lead my people into the arms of the Longknives? Will they protect us as "feathers do a bird"? Look inside your heart . . . You have a heart. I saw it the night the Nez Percés crossed the line. What does your heart say?

WALSH: *(agitated)* You know, if you refuse this offer, there'll be nothing for you here. My government says they won't feed you or give you reservations.

SITTING BULL: Is your advice then to return with the Americans?

WALSH: My advice . . . is . . . to consider . . . to consider the consequences of your actions. That is my advice.

SITTING BULL: What does that mean?

WALSH: It means . . . if you stay . . . you're dependent on the buffalo . . . and when they go, as they are surely going, we won't care for you as we do our own Indians . . . . Now if you go with General Terry, he has given his word that you won't be mistreated or . . . .

He stops himself from saying the word "killed."

You will be fed and clothed.

SITTING BULL: Would you choose to live as you advise me to do?

WALSH: I don't advise you to do this. I . . . merely state your choices.

SITTING BULL: I know many who took the white man's promise . . . Bear Ribs, White Antelope, Iron Shield, Black Kettle, Stirring Bear . . . Crazy Horse. I would ask their guidance, but all of them are dead.

WALSH: You . . . make your point.

SITTING BULL: *(dropping all pretence of asking for advice)* Let us speak clearly to each other . . . . If the President in Washington can say: "Come, you are safe here" and then change his mind and let the Longknives kill us . . . can it not work the other way too? *(looking intently at WALSH)* Cannot the Great White Mother say: "No food or reservations," but then reconsider? Our brothers, the Santee Sioux, from across the line . . .

WALSH: . . . have been given a reservation in Manitoba. Quite right!

SITTING BULL: *(opening up to WALSH, stating his secret fear)* I believe the Americans are only waiting to get us all together . . . and then they will slaughter us. That is what I believe.

WALSH: *(thinking, then deciding)* Right . . . Well now, I've delivered my government's message, to which your reply is . . . .

SITTING BULL: The Sioux are self-sufficient

WALSH: Mmmmm . . . and I shall give your final decision to General Terry, that is . . . .

SITTING BULL: *(joking)* Tell him he can take it easy on the way back. The Sioux only fight with men.

WALSH: *(smiling)* I was thinking of something a bit more formal.

SITTING BULL: *(begins by playing the role a bit)* He came here to tell us lies, but we don't want to hear them . . . . I intend to stay here . . . and to raise my people in this country.

SITTING BULL leaves. The lights begin to fade. WALSH looks after him for a moment, then begins to leave.

LOUIS: *(speaking from the shadows)* Major!

WALSH stops and looks at LOUIS.

Does da Major know what month dis is?

WALSH: The month when the green grass comes up.

LOUIS: *(without humour)* Major damn good pupil.

WALSH: *(almost abruptly)* Louis damn good teacher.

He turns to go.

LOUIS: *(moving toward WALSH)* Louis "request" permission to speak to da Major.

WALSH: *(with a trace of irritation)* Here and now?

LOUIS: Last fall, crossin' da Milk River, da Major's horse step in dat sink hole . . . and Louis, he grab da Major and pull 'im out . . . *(WALSH nods.)* Da other year, when Louis hear all kind of story 'bout da 'ssiniboine makin' trouble . . . Louis tell da Major . . . even t'ough dat 'ssiniboine is son of good friend of Louis' mother . . . .

WALSH: The Major is in your debt.

LOUIS: And some of Louis' mother's people don't speak to him no more, but dis don't matter, for Louis trust da Major to do da right thing . . . . Dis is da month when da green grass come up, da moon of makin' fat: dis is spring . . . . Can da Major make da spring come for da Sioux? What can you do for Sittin' Bull?

WALSH: Everything within my power.

LOUIS: How much is dat?

WALSH: Say what you mean, Louis.

LOUIS: Louis choose to trust, but da Indian can do nothin' else but trust . . . . Trust . . . or die . . . . Sometime, trust *and* die . . . . Can da Major make da spring come for da Sioux?

WALSH: You trust in me . . . and I trust in those above me . . . . Quite simple, eh? . . . Now, let's get on . . . .

He goes to leave.

LOUIS: Da Indian say he would trust da Great White Mother more if she did not have so many bald-headed thieves workin' for her

WALSH: *(stopping and turning, angrily)* The Sioux have a case . . . a strong case . . . and I shall present it!

LOUIS: *(softly)* Who stands behind you dere?

WALSH: Honourable men!

LOUIS spits.

Blackout.

ACT TWO

The lights come up on HARRY, CLARENCE, LOUIS and McCUTCHEON. The lights are punctuated by LOUIS throwing his knife into the floor of the stage. A dull thud is heard. LOUIS sits with his rifle unslung; McCUTCHEON sits cleaning his saddle. CLARENCE is attempting to thread a needle. As HARRY watches the three of them, McCUTCHEON leans over, picks up the needle from CLARENCE, threads it efficiently and passes it back. CLARENCE looks up at McCUTCHEON.

CLARENCE: Thanks . . . .

He begins to mend a sock. HARRY and McCUTCHEON exchange a look of amusement.

HARRY: Sewin' detail, eh?

He begins to roll a cigarette as he watches CLARENCE.

CLARENCE: *(intent on his sewing)* Yeah . . . . I wish me Mum were here.

McCUTCHEON tosses HARRY a match for his cigarette.

CLARENCE: This ain't my idea of police work.

McCUTCHEON: Ah, laddie, your poor wee face would have been wet with tears for your Mum if ye'd been with the force on our march west in '73. I don't know what ye'd have called that.

HARRY: *(settling down to watch everyone work)* It weren't the Mounted Police then, Clarence, it were the Dismounted Police . . . . Lost practically every horse they had. *(He laughs.)*

McCUTCHEON: Aye, a man with the best will in the world couldn't call it the force's finest hour.

LOUIS: Dey didn't have Louis with dem. Dey need a good scout.

McCUTCHEON: I never saw so many bugs . . . blackflies so thick they clogged your nose so ye couldn't draw breath . . . and every man from the Colonel down infected with fleas. It's a lovely time y're havin', laddie. Ye don't appreciate it.

CLARENCE: Yeah . . . well . . . me Mum always mended my things at home.

HARRY: Jesus Christ, Clarence, you had a good thing there, boy, your Mum waitin' on you hand an' foot. What'd you want to go and join up for? You could have had it easy in the East.

CLARENCE: My dad was a soldier.

HARRY: You don't say.

CLARENCE: Yup. Half-pay officer, served in the Crimean, he did . . . . And, after that, he and me Mum, they come out to Upper Canada in '60. First winter out, my Dad, he died . . . . I can't hardly remember him . . . . But, me Mum, she used to tell me 'bout him bein' a soldier and all . . . . It was hard goin' for us . . . . I think me Mum was the real soldier . . . .

McCUTCHEON: No brothers or sisters, laddie?

CLARENCE: Nope . . . . Mum's all alone back East.

HARRY: You ain't told us why you joined?

CLARENCE: Well . . . me Mum, she said I was a man like my Dad . . . and I had to find my own place . . . . Couldn't sit in Glengarry growin' potatoes and tendin' to her. And she was right . . . . I got to thinking . . .

HARRY: Yeah?

CLARENCE: You all'd laugh.

HARRY: No, we wouldn't.

CLARENCE: Well, I got to thinkin', out here in the territories, that was where everything was happenin' . . . the Indian Wars . . . and openin' the West . . . and Wild Bill Hickock sittin' on the biggest, blackest horse you ever saw!

He looks at HARRY, McCUTCHEON and LOUIS, who regard him seriously.

CLARENCE: I wanted to do what was right . . . and excitin' and . . . and make me Mum proud of me.

McCUTCHEON looks out at the horizon and sniffs.

HARRY: How do you figure it's turned out?

CLARENCE: I guess she's proud of me . . . . Not so excitin' as I thought it'd be . . . and as far as what's right goes . . . that don't seem to come into it . . . .

McCUTCHEON: What's that in the air, Louis? Smoke?

LOUIS: Lotta smoke . . . . Dere goin' be more.

CLARENCE: I don't smell nothin'.

HARRY: Hell, Clarence, you won't smell it till tomorrow or next day . . . . The Sergeant here, he smells it today . . . and Louis . . . *(smiling at LOUIS)* When'd you smell it, Louis?

LOUIS: *(holding up two fingers)* Two days ago.

CLARENCE: What's it from?

LOUIS: Da 'mericans fire da border.

CLARENCE: *(curious)* What?

LOUIS: 'Merican soldiers, da Longknives, dey set fires all 'long da border, two or three hundred miles long, every ten mile or so.

CLARENCE: *(to McCUTCHEON)* What's he sayin'? That don't make sense, Louis.

LOUIS: Make a lotta sense.

HARRY: It's this way, Clarence . . . . The buffalo across the line start movin' north, so the soldiers burn all along the border. The buffalo turn back

and then the American government don't have to feed the reservation Indians.

CLARENCE looks at him blankly.

HARRY: They're supposed to hunt and feed themselves!

CLARENCE: Well, what about *our* Indians?

LOUIS: *(surprised)* You got some Indians?

CLARENCE: You know what I mean.

LOUIS ignores him and looks at his gun.

CLARENCE: Okay . . . What about *the* Indians livin' on the Canadian side of the line?

LOUIS: What about dem?

CLARENCE: What're they supposed to do?

HARRY: Eat grass.

CLARENCE: *(angrily)* I don't believe you. Besides, I don't smell nothin'. It's all a lie. There's no smoke in the air! Do you smell smoke, Sergeant?

McCUTCHEON: Look at that haze over the hills, laddie.

CLARENCE: That's a heat haze . . . from the sun.

HARRY: You think so, eh?

CLARENCE: Well, I don't believe it! It ain't fair! And even if it was true . . . and there weren't no buffalo . . . and nothin' for them to eat, well then, the Canadian government, it'd send out food for them. It's got a responsibility!

LOUIS: *(shrugging)* Maybe so.

HARRY: So the Canadian government feeds its own Indians . . . . Who's gonna feed the Sioux?

CLARENCE: They're people, aren't they?

McCUTCHEON, HARRY and LOUIS look at him.

You don't let people starve to death, do you? Just 'cause you wish they'd move someplace else, you don't let people starve! You can't do things like that. You can't do things like that!

He stares at HARRY, McCUTCHEON and LOUIS. They all freeze. HARRY pulls a document out and reads from it. The lights slowly dim.

HARRY: MacDonald reports that though the Sioux have behaved themselves remarkably well since crossing into Canada, their presence in the North West Territories has been attended by serious consequences. The buffalo are rapidly diminishing and the advent of so large a body of foreign Indians has precipitated their diminution. The Sioux are already feeling the hardship and are hard pressed to avert danger and suffering from famine.

The lights black out. About four bars of calliope music are heard. The lights come back up. MARY is sitting there embroidering. WALSH is a distance away from her. The music fades as WALSH speaks.

WALSH: My . . . dearest . . . Mary . . . . My dearest Mary.

MARY: Jim

WALSH: Two letters came in today . . . along with a load of winter supplies. I don't know which I was happier to see.

MARY: The girls are fine . . . . It's been a long time since they've seen you.

WALSH: You'll think I've got a touch of prairie fever, but the solitude here, the emptiness of these Great Plains, fills me with a sense of timelessness.

MARY: Both send their love.

WALSH: Remember the day we picnicked on the river? Cora, plump and placid on the blanket; little Mary showing me her hands stained with the juice of flowers . . . and you bent over the basket, your hair hanging loose and laughing . . . . You looked eighteen.

MARY: I hope you're looking after yourself. *(laughing)* How often do I say that?

WALSH: You're not to worry about my health. McCutcheon's like a mother hen.

MARY: Here in the East, we're always hearing grand tales of Major Walsh . . . how he's subdued the Sioux and Sitting Bull.

WALSH: The Sioux . . . . Common sense, honesty and humanity.

MARY: The treachery.

WALSH: Ah, Mary, we call our actions strategy or tactics; we call theirs treachery . . . . My God,

if I could only show you what I see every day . . . . The buffalo are gone, vanished . . . like frost at dawn . . . one minute here, the next . . . nowhere. In the fall, the Sioux were hungry. Now, it's winter . . . and they starve.

MARY: After church supper, the choir sang.

WALSH: Sickness, plain suffering kills them like flies. Most of their ponies are dead . . . and their rotting carcasses are cut up for food . . . . Yes, they're starving and destitute, yet they endure. They share what little they have . . . and they observe the law. Goddamnit, they'd be a credit to any community . . . . Ottawa has not acknowledged my recommendations . . . .

MARY: *(smiling)* You always say don't worry.

WALSH: I wonder if Dewdney has even forwarded them.

MARY: But, of course, I worry. It's natural to worry. *(laughing)* Yesterday I found another grey hair. You won't know me when you return.

WALSH: I try to understand the government's viewpoint . . . . Jesus Christ, I'm no raw recruit! One thing I know, across the line there's been gross and continual mismanagement of the Sioux. An able and brilliant people have been crushed, held down, moved from place to place, cheated and lied to . . . . And now, they hold on here in Canada, the remnants of a proud race, and they ask for some sort of justice . . . which is what I thought I swore on oath to serve!

The lights begin to fade.

MARY: *(distant)* Your "little" Mary's soon to be thirteen . . . . Don't forget her birthday, will you?

WALSH: We carried great bouquets of flowers home that day . . . *(looking down at his hands)* She's not thirteen . . . .

MARY: Cora's getting thin.

WALSH: Cora, red and bawling; and you with your hair spread on the pillow, smiling and offering me your hand . . . .

The lights go out on MARY. There is a spotlight on the figure of WALSH.

The girls still babies; you eighteen, in the East . . . suspended in amber . . . while I grow old in the West . . . .

McCUTCHEON: Colonel MacLeod to see you, sir.

WALSH: MacLeod? Send him on in.

MacLEOD enters. WALSH springs up to greet him sincerely. Both are original members of the force and are friends.

Welcome to the fort, Colonel. Pleasant journey, I trust?

MacLEOD: Not bad, Major, not bad . . . . You're looking well.

McCUTCHEON: Is there anything else, sir?

WALSH: No, McCutcheon. Stand down.

McCUTCHEON leaves.

MacLEOD: To tell the truth, Jim, you look like death. What the hell have you been up to?

WALSH: If you think I look bad, you should see the horses.

MacLEOD: That so?

WALSH: It's been a hard winter.

MacLEOD: *(clipping the end of a cigar)* Seems to be the case right across the West.

WALSH gets out a flask and looks at MacLEOD who nods, "yes" to a drink.

WALSH: Are you doing the tour early? The boys at Fort Walsh are always on their toes. It'll be a . . .

MacLEOD: Nothing like that.

WALSH: *(stiffening somewhat)* Do you bring news for the Sioux?

MacLEOD: Sit down, Jim. I'd like a wee informal talk with you.

WALSH: Well now, you've caught my interest. *(sitting down)* What is it?

There is a pause as MacLEOD examines the end of his cigar. He looks up at WALSH and pauses again.

MacLEOD: Soooo . . . horses had a bad winter, eh?

WALSH: What the hell are you here for?

MacLEOD: *(putting a letter on the desk)* Recognize that?

WALSH: *(looking at the letter and dropping it back on the desk)* I usually recognize my own correspondence. It's a letter I sent Frank Mills at Fort Benton across the line. Why're you dropping it on my desk like a hot potato?

MacLEOD: I'd be most surprised to hear that you're unaware of the proper channels one must go through when making a suggestion of the nature contained in this letter.

WALSH: My note to Frank Mills suggests an exchange of stolen horses. American horses stolen by Canadian Indians to be exchanged for Canadian horses stolen by American Indians . . . . Hardly an international incident.

MacLEOD: And what is the proper channel through which we should negotiate an arrangement like this?

WALSH: The proper channel? Yes, sir. I should send a recommendation to my commanding officer, Colonel MacLeod. If he decides to act on it, he will send a recommendation to Ottawa. If it ever reaches the Prime Minister's office and he decides to act on it, he will send a recommendation to London. It is possible that London will send it to Washington, and Washington to Mills' commanding officer, and, God willing and the mails providing, Mills will receive a recommendation concerning the exchange of stolen horses. Jesus Christ, man! That's 6,000 miles and the Lord knows how many bureaucratic bunglers. Frank Mills is 60 miles south of me. Are you trying to tell me that you object to my simplifying matters?

MacLEOD: It's not my objecting to it . . . . Mills, apparently, objects to it.

WALSH: What the hell do you mean by that?

MacLEOD: He forwarded your "note" to Fort Robson. To make a long story short, the President has sent a formal protest to the Queen regarding the high-handed methods of a certain officer of the force serving the Canadian West . . . .

WALSH: Son-of-a-bitch! *(to himself)* The next goddamn American horse the boys bring in, I'll have it shot.

MacLEOD: You realize as well as I do that this is only the tip of the iceberg.

WALSH: *(back to MacLEOD)* Where are you now, Colonel . . . back on the cold winter again?

MacLEOD: I'm talking about the real reason for the American protest against your behaviour. I'm talking about Sitting Bull and the Sioux.

WALSH: *(stiffening and becoming more formal)* I'm afraid I don't follow you, sir.

MacLEOD: Jim, the Americans believe . . . and they have convinced the Prime Minister . . . that you are privately urging Sitting Bull to remain in Canada while publically stating that he must leave.

WALSH: Which indicates how little they know of Sitting Bull. When his mind's made up, no man can sway him.

MacLEOD: Not even his friends?

WALSH: He has no white friends.

MacLEOD: He calls you White Sioux. What is that supposed to mean?

WALSH: We have an understanding.

MacLEOD: Oh? . . . Which means?

WALSH: We understand each other.

MacLEOD: *(tapping the letter on the desk)* The protest over this is an attempt to discredit you and it all leads back to the Sioux. You're close to that old war horse. Persuade him to return across the line. Goddamn it, he's a thorn in our flesh. We can't discuss a bloody thing with the Americans without they bring it up!

WALSH: What up?

MacLEOD: Our giving sanctuary to those responsible for the Custer Massacre. They talk of nothing else.

WALSH: Custer was responsible for the death of himself and his men! For Christ's sake, speak the truth!

MacLEOD: I'm not here to argue with you. I'm here as a friend.

WALSH: I've had my orders and I've followed them.

MacLEOD: I'm asking you to do more than that . . . . He trusts you.

WALSH: Because he knows I won't deceive him.

MacLEOD: He'll listen to you.

WALSH: Because he trusts me and he knows I won't deceive him.

MacLEOD: *(softly)* How am I asking you to deceive him? *(pause)* The Sioux have no future here in Canada.

WALSH: Tell me something . . . . It was you, as Commissioner of the North West Mounted Police, who impressed upon me that a part of my duty, no less important than the policing of this area, was the accurate observation and recording of events, no matter how minute . . . . Such a report, to be sent monthly, along with my recommendations for government policy.

MacLEOD: Quite correct.

WALSH: Then, why the hell is nothing acted upon?

MacLEOD: Did you not receive two stallions, come in with Harry, to sire your mares? Are you not now in the act of digging a new well?

WALSH: I'm not talking about domestic trivia! I don't need a statement from the goddamn Prime Minister to undertake a new well!

MacLEOD: Ah, but you do, Jim.

WALSH: My men are not in the act of digging a new well . . . . My men *dug* a new well two months before permission was granted! The entire fort would have been down with typhoid or dead of thirst had I waited for word from Ottawa.

MacLEOD sighs and shakes his head.

WALSH: What about my recommendations concerning the Indians?

MacLEOD: What about them?

WALSH: The Sioux have as much legal right to a reservation here as the Santee Sioux had in Manitoba.

MacLEOD: The Santee Sioux did not kill Custer.

WALSH: They killed over 600 white settlers in Minnesota who were not engaged in an act of war against them. Why are my recommendations not acted upon?

MacLEOD: Out here, you don't see the whole picture. There're other considerations.

WALSH: My recommendations are ignored! I may as well post them in the privy!

MacLEOD: You play chess . . . . Sometimes a pawn is sacrificed on one side of the board to gain an advantage on the other.

WALSH: (in disbelief) I am a pawn?

MacLEOD: No, no, Jim . . . not you . . . . It might be possible to consider Sitting Bull and the Sioux as pawns.

WALSH: What are the advantages to be gained from this . . . this sacrifice?

MacLEOD: We can't know that, can we? That's the kind of weighty decision the Prime Minister and London must contend with.

WALSH: I demand to know what advantage is to be gained.

MacLEOD: The Prime Minister is not responsible to you, Jim!

WALSH: Goddamn it, he is! If I carry out his orders, he is responsible to me.

MacLEOD: You're talking nonsense. An army that operated like that couldn't navigate its way across a playing field! And you know it!

WALSH: What do you think happens when I take off this tunic? At night, in my quarters, what do you think happens to me?

MacLEOD: Jim . . .

WALSH: Do you think McCutcheon hangs me up from some goddamn wooden peg with all my strings dangling? Is that what you think happens? Do you think I'm a puppet? Manipulate me right and anything is possible . . . . I'm a person. I exist. I think and feel! And I will not allow you to do this to me!

MacLEOD: (softly) To do what to you? I merely ask you to use your position with Sitting Bull to convince him to leave the country in the best interests of his people.

WALSH: I've had my orders and I've followed them . . . .

MacLEOD: You're tired, Jim.

WALSH: Ask my men if I'm tired. No one at this post rises earlier or is to bed later. Fatigue is unknown to me.

MacLEOD: You work yourself too hard.

WALSH: I have a job and I do it.

MacLEOD: It's a long time since you've been home.

WALSH: Home? I don't request a leave of absence, Colonel . . . . Shall we get on with the business at hand?

MacLEOD: I have two dispatches from the Prime Minister. The first concerns the Sioux.

WALSH: What is it?

MacLEOD: You are to see that no food stuffs, clothing, ammunition or supplies are given them . . . if they do not possess the money to pay for them.

WALSH: They have no money.

MacLEOD: It has been brought to the attention of the Prime Minister that certain settlers as well as members of the force itself have been supplying the Sioux with various odds and ends of food and clothing. This must stop at once.

WALSH: Yes, sir.

MacLEOD: The Prime Minister feels that, whereas common sense has not prevailed upon the Sioux, hunger will.

He looks at WALSH for a moment, then back at his dispatch.

My second dispatch concerns your ill-advised note to Major Mills.

WALSH: Yes, sir.

MacLEOD: An apology is to be written, couched in the appropriate words, stating that you humbly beg the American government's pardon for over-stepping the limits of your authority. (pause) Is that understood?

WALSH: I . . .

MacLEOD: If you find yourself unable to do this, it is my sad duty to ask you for your resignation.

WALSH: How well you know your men.

MacLEOD: I pride myself on that.

WALSH: They say one's strongest instinct is self-preservation . . . and I've made the force my life . . . . To whom do I send this letter?

MacLEOD: To your commanding officer, myself, naturally.

WALSH: Ah, yes.

MacLEOD: I'll see that it's forwarded to Ottawa . . . . Well, Jim, how about a walk around the post before bed? . . . Bit of pleasure after a surfeit of business.

WALSH: McCutcheon! . . . Sorry, Colonel, I've a few things to attend to. McCutcheon will see you to your quarters. (McCUTCHEON enters.) Goodnight, sir.

MacLEOD: Goodnight, Jim.

WALSH stands rigid until McCUTCHEON and McLEOD exit. When they have gone, he pours himself another drink. He walks outside of his office and stands looking at the prairies, flask in hand. We hear someone whistling "Garryowen." He listens to the whistling, then speaks.

WALSH: That you, Harry?

HARRY: You give me a start there, Major. I didn't expect to see nobody up at this time of night.

WALSH takes a drink and extends the flask to HARRY.

HARRY: Don't mind if I do. (He takes a drink and keeps the flask.) I've been up visitin' with Sittin' Bull . . . . Always a dry night when you visit with the old man . . . . Lots of tobacco, but no booze.

WALSH: Fraternizing, eh?

HARRY: Oh, no, nothin' like that . . . . Just chewin' the fat. (pause) Hear MacLeod come in today . . . . Bit early, ain't he? (pause) Is he here for the tour?

WALSH: (bringing his attention back to HARRY) No, no . . . he isn't.

HARRY: O-fficial business, eh? O-fficial business.

WALSH: Do you know Brockville, Harry?

HARRY: Can't say as I do.

WALSH: Pretty town . . . . Trees. Shade in the summertime . . . cool and green.

HARRY: Hell of a change from this place, I reckon.

WALSH: My wife lives in Brockville . . . and my two girls.

HARRY: Ain't got a son?

WALSH: No . . . . No son . . . just as well . . . no son. Pretty place, though.

HARRY: What the hell! (passing the flask to him) Have another drink, Major!

WALSH: (taking a drink and passing the flask back to HARRY) I've always thought of myself as a man of principle . . . . Honour, truth, the lot . . . . They're just words, Harry. They don't exist. I gave my life to them and they don't exist.

HARRY: (staring at WALSH, uneasy) You should get to bed, Major. It ain't night, it's mornin'.

WALSH: (smiling) Fatigue is unknown to me.

HARRY: (smiling back, feeling he's back on more familiar ground) That's a fact, sir. That's a fact. Ain't never knowed you to be tired.

WALSH: (reaching for the flask, taking a drink and handing it back to HARRY) You were up visiting the Sioux, were you?

HARRY: Yessireee. Course, they knowed MacLeod's come in. Naturally, they's wonderin' if it means anythin' for them.

WALSH: Oh yes, I should say it does.

HARRY: Good news?

WALSH: The Sioux have no future here in Canada.

HARRY: They sure as hell don't have none south of the line.

WALSH: The government's concern stops at the border.

HARRY: Major, you get yourself too het up.

WALSH: I see . . . larger issues at stake.

HARRY: Don't see what's a larger issue than a man's life . . . . No Injun agent's gonna put up with Sittin' Bull.

WALSH: You think not?

HARRY: They'll kill him off . . . . Only smart thing to do, ain't it?

WALSH: And how do you feel about that?

HARRY: Ain't nothin' I can do . . . . Goodnight, Major.

WALSH stares at HARRY as he exits, then WALSH exits. PRETTY PLUME enters, carrying a pipe. She is followed by CROWFOOT.

PRETTY PLUME: *(singing)*
Little One, Little One,
Loved by everyone.
Little One speaks sweet words to everyone.
That is why, that is why,
Little One is loved by everyone.

CROWFOOT puts his head in her lap in the semidarkness outside of the scene. CLARENCE sneaks furtively into the light, carrying a small knapsack.

CLARENCE: *(whispering)* Pssssttttt! . . . Little One! . . . Little One!

SITTING BULL: *(from the shadows)* Is it my son you seek?

CLARENCE: *(frightened)* Oh . . . Ah . . . yes, sir. I was just . . . a . . .

He tries to conceal the knapsack behind him.

CLARENCE: . . . I was just . . . lookin' for your little boy.

SITTING BULL comes into the light. He looks older, his face is drawn.

SITTING BULL: You are the young man who rides out with White Sioux . . . . Is he with you?

CLARENCE: Ah, well, no sir . . . . I . . . come by myself . . . . I brought . . . *(He quickly thrusts the knapsack at SITTING BULL.)* Ah . . . *(nodding at the knapsack)* . . . some things from the mess, sir. I'd like the little boy to have them.

SITTING BULL: *(taking the knapsack and nodding his thanks)* You have a good heart . . . . I have little to offer you in return . . . .

He sees the pipe that PRETTY PLUME has brought on. He checks his tobacco pouch and smiles.

Come! Have a pipe with me!

He sits and motions CLARENCE to sit.

CLARENCE: Well, I . . . don't know if I should.

SITTING BULL: Sit!

CLARENCE sits in silence as SITTING BULL prepares the pipe and passes it to him. There is silence as they smoke for a bit.

SITTING BULL: Times are bad . . . . They say there are still buffalo south of the line, but if we go to hunt them, the bluecoats will kill us. *(laughing dryly)* It hardly matters, as our ponies are too weak to carry us there in the first place. But my heart grows weak and trembles when I hear the little children cry for food . . . . It is a hard thing. *(smiling at CLARENCE)* And you feel that way too. See? We are not so different.

CLARENCE: Don't you think, maybe, you could think about goin' back? Everybody hungry and everythin'. Is it worth it?

SITTING BULL: Across the line, on the reservations, they are starving too. We hear these things and so must your people. *(CLARENCE nods.)* The white man is afraid to kill us outright, but he knows if he kills the buffalo, we must soon follow . . . . I myself do not understand why you should wish this on us.

CLARENCE: I don't wish nothin' like that.

SITTING BULL: And I think . . . if you give me nothing and you will not let me go where I can get something for myself, what is there? I would rather die fighting than die of starvation.

CLARENCE: *(uneasy)* You'd just all get killed that way.

SITTING BULL: Yes. That is the warrior's way out . . . but I am not only a warrior. I must think of all my people. I must think of the ones here now and the ones that come after . . . what is best for them . . . . I know we must change.

CLARENCE: Yeah. I guess that's it.

SITTING BULL: Sometimes one has something of value. Dogs come and spoil it for you, yet you do not wish to see it destroyed . . . . I am of the Hunkpapa Sioux of the prairie and the prairie will provide for me. When the buffalo are gone, my children will hunt mice. When my horse falls, I shall chase gopher. And when there is nothing else, we shall dig and eat roots . . . . And I pray to the Great Spirit that the White Mother gives the thought to her children that I give to mine.

We hear WALSH laughing harshly. The lights dim on SITTING BULL and CLARENCE and come up on WALSH, who is seated, looking at a letter. He rips the letter in half. McCUTCHEON is going through some papers. He concentrates on his business. He knows what's coming and he is preparing himself for it.

WALSH: Why is nothing simple in this life? It all seems perfectly simple to me. Why do people make it complex? The simplest thing . . . complex . . . . McCutcheon! Are you listening to me?

McCUTCHEON: Aye, sir.

WALSH: Well then, why is everything so goddamn complex?

McCUTCHEON: I don't know, sir.

WALSH: *(leaping up and beginning to pace)* I write a report . . . a perfectly simple report . . . in which I state that our Indians as well as the Sioux are suffering severe deprivation because of the extinction of the buffalo. Is that simple or is it not?

McCUTCHEON: Perfectly simple, sir.

WALSH: Right! And if we do not make a sincere and whole-hearted effort to aid these Indians, we can expect trouble, necessitating a build-up in troops, horses and supplies, plus the possibility of loss of life as well as property . . . . And what is the government's reply to this?

McCUTCHEON: I don't know, sir.

WALSH: *(exploding)* The son-of-a-bitch's going to send me more men! And, to top it all off, I'll probably get a recommendation for my foresight!

CLARENCE enters with some papers. WALSH takes the papers.

Were you in court yesterday?

CLARENCE: No, sir.

WALSH: I sat in judgement yesterday. I sat in judgement of a Sioux. His wife and child were starving. He slaughtered a cow belonging to a settler and then . . . .

He laughs. CLARENCE looks nervously, quickly, to McCUTCHEON, then back to WALSH.

Do you know what the damn fool did?

CLARENCE: No, sir, I . . .

WALSH: He took his horse . . . his only horse . . . told the settler what had happened and offered the horse in payment. The settler refused and pressed charges. And yesterday, I sentenced that Sioux to six months imprisonment and fined him twenty dollars, for that is the law! But where's the justice in it?

LOUIS enters. WALSH turns on him and barks.

What is it?

There is a quick look between LOUIS and McCUTCHEON.

For God's sake, man, did you come in here to gape? Speak up!

LOUIS: Sittin' Bull's outside.

WALSH stares at LOUIS for a moment, then he becomes very calm. He sits in a chair, picks up a pencil and begins to examine it.

WALSH: And why is Sitting Bull's geographical location supposed to be of interest to me?

LOUIS: He wants to see you.

WALSH: I'm busy.

LOUIS: *(staring hard at WALSH)* I sent him on in!

He turns to go.

WALSH: Louis!

LOUIS stops.

WALSH: Just . . . give me a minute.

LOUIS exits. WALSH puts his pencil down, looks at McCUTCHEON and CLARENCE, then turns around and does up the top button of his tunic. His shoulders stiffen. SITTING BULL enters. WALSH has his back to him. LOUIS follows SITTING BULL in. SITTING BULL has a ragged blanket wrapped around him. He looks gaunt; not well, although his personal magnetism is still evident. He stops and looks at WALSH's back.

SITTING BULL: White Sioux . . .

WALSH: *(without turning)* Yes.

SITTING BULL: I wish to speak with you.

WALSH: *(turning and looking at him)* I'm listening.

SITTING BULL: Have you had news from the Great White Mother?

WALSH: My news is always the same . . . . No reservations, no food, no clothing, no supplies.

SITTING BULL: I wish you to send the Great White Mother a special message from Sitting Bull.

WALSH: What is it?

SITTING BULL: Tell her . . . once I was strong and brave. My people had hearts of iron . . . . But now, my women are sick, my children are freezing and I have thrown my war paint to the wind. The suffering of my people has made my heart weak and I have placed nothing in the way of those who wish to return across the line. Many have done so. We who remain desire a home. For three years, we have been in the White Mother's land. We have obeyed her laws and we have kept her peace . . . . I beg the White Mother . . . to . . . to . . .

WALSH: Go on.

SITTING BULL: . . . to have . . . pity . . . on us.

WALSH: Right! . . . Well then . . . I'll see that this goes off . . . .

SITTING BULL makes no move to leave.

Is there anything else?

SITTING BULL: *(gazing at WALSH)* White Sioux . . .

WALSH: Yes?

SITTING BULL: *(speaking slowly and with effort)* . . . I find it necessary . . . to make a request . . .

WALSH stares at him.

. . . a request . . . for . . . provisions for my people. We have nothing.

WALSH: *(brusquely)* Your provisions wait for you across the line. If you want provisions, go there for them.

SITTING BULL: We hear you have a quantity of flour and I have come to ask you for it.

WALSH: If you wish to do business, you do it at the trading post.

SITTING BULL takes off his ragged blanket. He holds out the blanket to WALSH. WALSH begins to breathe heavily as he struggles to retain control of himself.

I have appealed to the Great White Mother and the Great White Mother says no.

SITTING BULL: I ask for only a little.

WALSH: *(exploding)* And I can give you nothing! God knows, I've done my damnedest and nothing's changed. Do you hear that? Nothing's changed! Cross the line if you're so hungry, but don't, for Christ's sake, come begging food from me!

SITTING BULL: *(straightening up)* You are speaking to the head of the Sioux nation!

WALSH: I don't give a goddamn who you are! Get the hell out!

SITTING BULL goes for the knife in his belt. WALSH grabs him by the arm, twists it up and throws him to the floor. As SITTING BULL goes to get up, WALSH puts his foot in the middle of his back and shoves him, sending him sprawling. He plants his foot in the middle of his back. CLARENCE and McCUTCHEON enter.

CLARENCE: *(screaming)* Noooooooo!

McCUTCHEON grabs CLARENCE. Everyone freezes for a moment.

WALSH: *(in a strained voice)* McCutcheon, Underhill, go out and alert the boys in case of trouble. Throw a couple of poles across the road.

McCUTCHEON: Yes, sir. *(He starts off.)* Laddie!

CLARENCE looks at him. McCUTCHEON speaks more gently to him.

Come on, laddie. *(He takes CLARENCE off.)* The Major's given an order.

LOUIS steps forward and pushes WALSH aside. He still has his foot in the middle of SITTING BULL's back. LOUIS starts to help SITTING BULL up, but SITTING BULL gets up by himself. LOUIS gets him his blanket. SITTING BULL picks up his knife. He stands there staring at WALSH. There is a pause. SITTING BULL replaces his knife in its sheath. WALSH's hand slowly reaches out to

SITTING BULL as SITTING BULL slowly turns, takes his blanket and exits. LOUIS stares at WALSH.

LOUIS: Is dat all for me, too?

WALSH looks up at him for a moment, then slowly nods his head. LOUIS exits. The sound of "Garryowen" is heard faintly in the background. It builds as WALSH straightens up and walks off. McCUTCHEON and CLARENCE march on, carrying a trunk. They drop it—bang—as the music ends. On the trunk is written: Major James Walsh, NWMP, No. 7 Garden Lane, Brockville, Ontario.

CLARENCE: I've never seen a trunk so roped up. What's he got in it?

McCUTCHEON: When the major says securely fastened, he means securely fastened.

CLARENCE: I'd say that were excessive. You don't need that much rope. It's a waste.

McCUTCHEON: If you want to get on in the force, laddie, know your place. The Major decrees the tying. I oversee the tying . . . and you tie.

CLARENCE: Yes, Sergeant.

McCUTCHEON: Now get on over to the post and saddle up.

CLARENCE: When's the Major leaving?

McCUTCHEON: Later.

CLARENCE: I'd like to speak to him before he goes.

McCUTCHEON: Sorry, Constable.

CLARENCE: I've got to see him!

WALSH approaches the two of them. They do not see him.

McCUTCHEON: Move your ass on over to that post!

CLARENCE: I can't go till I see him!

WALSH coughs.

McCUTCHEON: Constable!

CLARENCE straightens to attention. WALSH glares at McCUTCHEON for not getting rid of CLARENCE, then he looks to the trunk.

WALSH: Ah, good.

CLARENCE: Thank you, sir.

WALSH: Bit too much rope, perhaps.

CLARENCE: *(with a brief look to McCUTCHEON)* Yes, sir.

WALSH: *(tapping one of the lashings of rope with his riding crop)* This, I think, can go.

CLARENCE: *(getting down on his hands and knees)* Yes, sir.

WALSH: You may go, Sergeant . . . .

McCUTCHEON exits.

A thing worth doing is worth doing well . . . . May take more time, but that's not the point, is it?

CLARENCE: No, sir.

WALSH: You wanted to speak to me?

CLARENCE: Yes, sir, I did . . . . Me and the men . . . a lot of us is upset, sir, about your leaving . . . .

WALSH: A simple leave of absence, Constable. I have a wife and children. It's been several years since I've seen them. Colonel MacLeod, upon my request, has kindly arranged several months off for me.

CLARENCE: It all seemed kinda sudden.

WALSH: I need the rest, Constable.

He regrets his statement. He moves around the trunk.

The lettering's not quite right . . . . Had to have it redone . . . . Been a long time since it's been in transit.

CLARENCE: There's something else.

WALSH: Yes?

CLARENCE: It's about Sitting Bull.

WALSH: You see a lot of him . . . . The little boy, rather.

CLARENCE: Yes, sir, I do. He's a very smart little boy and I have a lot of hope for the Sioux when I talk to him, sir.

WALSH: Do you?

CLARENCE: Sitting Bull still considers you his friend.

WALSH: I would have to deny that. I have my men and my wife and children . . . but I have no friends. Friends are a danger. You may not comprehend that statement, Constable, but Sitting Bull would.

CLARENCE: Maybe what I should have said was I still considered you his friend. I know you've seen me out with food and stuff, sir . . . and you haven't hauled me up . . . . I'm not much good at sneaking.

WALSH: That's true. *(laughing)* I would never send you out on reconnaissance.

CLARENCE: No, sir.

WALSH: What do you want to see me about, Constable?

CLARENCE: You're goin' East to Brockville, sir. That's not too far from Ottawa. I know you've been doin' all you can from this end, but I just wondered if maybe you couldn't go up to Ottawa and tell the Prime Minister how things are. It'd make a difference. You'd make him do something.

WALSH: Oh yes.

CLARENCE: Will you try and help Sittin' Bull?

WALSH: I shall give your proposition every consideration.

McCUTCHEON: Sorry to interrupt sir, but . . . .

WALSH: Quite right. I must get on, Constable.

CLARENCE: Can I tell Sittin' Bull that?

WALSH: Our chat has been most informative, Constable. No doubt I'll see you on my return.

CLARENCE exits.

WALSH: Your timing is impeccable, McCutcheon.

McCUTCHEON: I know, sir.

WALSH: The trunk looks solid, don't you think?

McCUTCHEON: Aye, sir.

WALSH: *(looking after CLARENCE)* That young man should never make the force his life.

He looks at McCUTCHEON and exits. The lights dim. SITTING BULL enters. He rolls up his buffalo robe and looks at PRETTY PLUME and CROWFOOT. The lights come up on HARRY, who has a bottle and is singing.

HARRY: Oh, life in a prairie shack, when the rain begins to pour.
Drip, drip, it comes through the roof and I want to go home to my Ma—Maw.
Maw, Maw, I want to go home to my Maw.
This bloomin' country's a fraud and I want to go home to my Maw.

CLARENCE enters from one direction, carrying a cup; LOUIS and McCUTCHEON enter from the other direction.

LOUIS: Alors, je lui dirais, mange la merde!

McCUTCHEON: It's the pay, mostly . . . very poor pay, ye could say . . . .

LOUIS: Mange la merde!

McCUTCHEON: And nobody gives a damn!

CLARENCE: Shut up! This bloody bastard's talkin' French and you're talkin' at the same goddamn time. You make me dizzy!

They fall silent—and drink. There is a pause, then CLARENCE speaks quietly.

Where's the Major?

LOUIS: Eh?

McCUTCHEON: Never mind him, Louis.

CLARENCE: *(louder)* Where the hell's the goddamn Major?

McCUTCHEON: He's not here.

CLARENCE: I know he's not here. What kind of a fool do you take me for? I know he's not here.

McCUTCHEON: Give me another, Louis.

CLARENCE: What kind of a leave of absence is eighteen months? That's what I want to know.

LOUIS pours McCUTCHEON another drink. He looks at CLARENCE.

McCUTCHEON: He's had enough. *(leaning toward CLARENCE)* You've had enough, Clarence!

HARRY: *(singing)* This bloomin' country's a fraud and I want to go home to my Maw.

McCUTCHEON: Come on, y'old buzzard. Sit down and shut up!

HARRY: *(coming over)* I want to go home to my Maw . . . . You boy's been celebratin'?

CLARENCE: What?

McCUTCHEON: When did ye get in?

HARRY: *(filling CLARENCE's cup)* Done and over with . . . . Signed, sealed and delivered. I seen the last of Sittin' Bull.

CLARENCE: How'd it go?

HARRY: Me and five or six of the boys from C Troop, we escorted him down to the border with nary an incident . . . . The boys signed him over and then they came back up.

CLARENCE: Where was you?

HARRY: Sittin' Bull, he asked me to go on down to Fort Robson with him. That's where they was gonna be picked up and taken over to the reservation.

CLARENCE: Yeah?

HARRY: So I did!

CLARENCE: Everythin' go all right?

HARRY: You know that old horse he was ridin'? Bluecoats took that and everythin' else . . . . Said they wouldn't be needing guns or horses where they was goin'.

CLARENCE: I never seen a Sioux without some kind of horse standin' by.

He is insinuating that HARRY is a liar.

HARRY: Yeah . . . well, they sure looked a sight. Real ragtag bunch, I'm tellin' you.

There is a pause as they drink.

CLARENCE: How was they takin' them to the reservation with no horses?

HARRY: Walkin' them . . . 'cept Sittin' Bull.

CLARENCE: What about Sittin' Bull?

HARRY: They put him on some boat. Gonna take him down to Fort Randall.

CLARENCE: Fort Randall.

LOUIS: Dat's da military prison.

CLARENCE: Why's he goin' there?

HARRY: Why'd you think?

CLARENCE: The agreement was nobody'd be punished. *(pause)* Ain't that right?

HARRY: I don't know nothin' 'bout what's right . . . . All's I know is that Sittin' Bull's in Fort Randall for killin' Custer.

CLARENCE: What . . . what'd he do when they told him?

HARRY: He said somethin' 'bout not goin' . . . not havin' to . . . . One of them bluecoats just give him a good clip on the side of the head with his rifle butt and they carried him aboard . . . . Weren't nothin' to it. Yessiree, I seen a historical sight . . . . I seen the end of the Sioux nation.

CLARENCE: That's not true!

HARRY: Was you there? . . . The boat moved off down the river and all them Injuns lined up along the bank makin' this terrible moanin' sound. I'm telling you, it was somethin' to see. What's the matter with you bastards? Me, Harry, is gonna propose a toast!

He holds up the bottle. LOUIS and McCUTCHEON hold up their glasses.

Here's to the Sioux! They won the battle, but they lost the war!

CLARENCE throws his drink in HARRY's face. HARRY stands up and throws one punch at CLARENCE which knocks him cold. McCUTCHEON and LOUIS carry CLARENCE off.

HARRY: *(looking at the audience and proposing a toast)* Bottoms up!

He drinks.

Sir John A.'s policy for dealin' with the Sioux was an all round winner . . . beats Custer all to hell! Not half so messy as ridin' into tube-like hollows at ungodly hours of the mornin' . . . and no need for a marchin' band . . . . Quiet, simple and effective . . . . Do not delay in returning to the United States, for that course is the only alternative to death by starvation . . . . So Sittin' Bull left the Canadian West . . .

WALSH enters and stands behind his desk.

. . . and Major Walsh returned to it. Yessireee, beats Custer all to hell!

McCUTCHEON formally carries on a large board with a map on it; toy soldiers, a train engine, trees. HARRY looks at the board as McCUTCHEON puts it on WALSH's desk. HARRY laughs.

HARRY: Je-sus!

He exits, shaking his head.

WALSH: The railway track is here . . . . There is a slight curve here around a grove of trees . . . . Do you see that, McCutcheon?

McCUTCHEON: Aye, sir.

WALSH: I think possibly twenty men could be concealed amongst those trees . . . twenty men . . . . Do we have twenty men we can rely on? Top notch fellows?

McCUTCHEON: Aye, sir.

WALSH: Good. In an operation like this, there is no room for error . . . . Image of the force and all that . . . . So . . . the men are concealed here. *(tapping the map)* At 2:10 precisely the train should round this curve . . . . You follow me?

McCUTCHEON: Aye, sir.

WALSH: All right . . . . Now, as the train reaches this point, Harry pulls out with a full load across the tracks . . . .

McCUTCHEON: Isn't that a bit dangerous, sir?

WALSH looks at him sharply.

I mean, sir . . . will the train have ample time to stop, sir?

WALSH: All that is calculated. *(speaking coldly)* Would you care to check my figures?

McCUTCHEON: No, sir . . . just wondering.

WALSH: *(staring at him)* Good. *(turning his attention back to the map)* Now, as the train pulls up, the men, myself at the head . . . . There'll be a dress parade before . . . I told you that, didn't I?

McCUTCHEON: Aye, sir.

WALSH: Right . . . I will ride out from the woods, my men behind me, and all of us in full dress . . . . Tell the men to practice war whoops. I want good full-blooded Indian yells, you hear?

McCUTCHEON: Aye, sir.

WALSH: So, out we come . . . yelling bloody murder . . . . I'll swing aboard the train and ride it into Calgary. Well, what do you think? Is that a stirring sight or not?

McCUTCHEON: Very stirring, sir.

WALSH: When you open a railroad, you do it in style, I say! Bloody train will be full of Easterners and we'll scare the pants off every one of them! I want a good show!

CLARENCE enters, followed by LOUIS.

CLARENCE: Major.

WALSH: *(stopping him)* Underhill! You have interrupted an important conference!

CLARENCE: Beggin' your pardon, sir . . . . Request permission to speak, sir.

WALSH: *(long suffering)* What is it?

CLARENCE: A rider's come in from Standin' Rock . . . . Been in the saddle all night.

WALSH: And?

LOUIS: He's dead . . . . Da white man have da Indian Police kill 'im . . . . Sittin' Bull is dead . . . Da rider say he see his face bleed empty and death come starin' in its place.

CLARENCE: They shot him twice and put the boots to him . . . and Little Crow says the soldiers dropped him in a pit of lime, so's his people couldn't bury him proper.

WALSH stands there frozen, staring at CLARENCE.

And Crowfoot? . . . Do you remember Crowfoot, sir? He used to come up to the fort, sir, and us men, we used to play with him 'cause he was just a kid, and ain't none of us got kids here . . . and he was a real good boy . . . and I liked him, sir . . . . And they drug him out from under the bed where he was hidin' and they threw him down and they shot him and he's dead too!

His anger is spent.

I come in to tell you, sir . . . 'cause . . . 'cause . . . I didn't know what else to do.

WALSH stands so still he seems to be a statue. There is a long pause. At last, he speaks.

WALSH: Dis-missed . . . .

McCUTCHEON, LOUIS and CLARENCE make no move to leave.

DIS-MISSED!

They exit. WALSH watches them leave. He moves to his desk and looks at it. He undoes his leather holster and takes out his gun. As he does this, we hear the sound of the Nez Percés from the end of Act One. That sound continues as he lays the gun on the desk and slowly, carefully, takes off his tunic, putting it on the desk as well. We hear SITTING BULL's voice as WALSH slowly lifts both hands over his head. SITTING BULL speaks softly, reminiscent of his speech to CROWFOOT early in Act Two.

SITTING BULL: In the beginning . . . was given . . . to everyone a cup . . . . A cup of clay. And from this cup, we drink our life. We all dip in the water . . . but the cups are different . . . . My cup is broken. It has passed away.

WALSH slams his hands down on his desk.

Blackout.

END

JAMES REANEY   (b. 1926)

Observing how "life reflected art" in Stratford, Ontario, near where he was born and grew up, James Reaney wrote in a 1962 poem, "Let us make a form out of this: documentary on one side and myth on the other." Perhaps no other Canadian dramatist or poet has so successfully transmuted the local into the universal, the stuff of documentary into the stuff of myth. Avoiding for the most part the political edge that Salutin and Pollock give to their work, Reaney makes of the life and history of Souwesto—the small towns and farms of southwestern Ontario—a rich poetic brew stepped in Blake and the Brontës, Walt Disney and the Bible, and leavened with a childlike propensity to treat everything as creative play. In his hands the story of the Donnellys, local history and legend, emerges as an experience of extraordinary theatrical scope and complexity, a trilogy of plays that many consider the finest achievement of the Canadian theatre to date.

Reaney was well established as a poet and academic before attempting to write for the stage. He enrolled at the University of Toronto in 1944, and in 1949 earned an M.A. in English and a Governor General's Award for his first book of poetry, *The Red Heart*. After teaching at the University of Manitoba for seven years, he returned to Toronto to pick up his Ph.D. in 1958 along with another Governor General's Award for his second book of verse, *A Suit of Nettles*. In 1960 Reaney began teaching English at the University of Western Ontario, a position he held for thirty years, and founded the innovative journal *Alphabet* which he published and edited until 1971. He also made his remarkable debut in the theatre that year with *The Killdeer*. Mavor Moore hailed it as "the first Canadian play of real consequence, and the first demonstration of genius among us." It won five awards at the 1960 Dominion Drama Festival and a third Governor General's Award for Reaney on its publication in 1962. The play's eclectic symbolist style, melodramatic plot and archetypal struggle between the forces of innocence and corruption signalled the shape of much of Reaney's work to come, including *The Donnellys*.

Reaney kept writing poetry—*Twelve Letters to a Small Town* (1962) and *The Dance of Death at London, Ontario* (1963)—but from now on most of his work would be in the theatre. *The Killdeer* was followed by *Night-blooming Cereus* and *One-man Masque* (1960), *The Easter Egg* (1962) and a series of fantastical plays for children commencing with the Manitoba Theatre Centre's 1963 production of *Names and Nicknames*.

With *The Sun and the Moon* (1965) at the London Summer Theatre, Reaney began his long association with Keith Turnbull, a key development in the evolution of his stagecraft. In *Listen to the Wind* (1966), produced by Keith Turnbull and directed by Reaney himself, the young protagonist "dreams out" a play-within-a-play from his sickbed. The complex action unfolds on a bare stage with a props table, a few actors, and a chorus of children providing visual metaphors and sound effects. The presentational style reminds us that acting is merely formalized play, a revelation of the power of imagination to transform reality. Out of *Listen to the Wind* developed the Listeners' Workshop. Once a week for two years Reaney led groups of twenty-five or more local children and adults through elaborate play exercises designed to stretch their imaginations by, for example, improvising the Book of Genesis. From these workshops grew what he called the "embryonics" of *Colours in the Dark*, commissioned by the Stratford Festival in 1967. A Joycean epic revealing the macrocosm of all human history in the microcosm of an individual life, the play is described by Reaney as a theatrical experience "designed to give you that mosaic—that all-things-happening-at-the-same-time-higgledy-piggledy feeling that rummaging through a play box can give you."

The embryonics of *The Donnellys* also arose out of the Listeners' Workshop, though Reaney had been fascinated since childhood by this story that had occurred only twenty miles from where he was born. He began researching the project in 1967; and except for a major revision of *The Killdeer* in 1968, *The Donnellys* remained his sole dramatic concern for the next eight years. In 1973 Reaney took what was by then a massive script to Halifax where Keith Turnbull and a group of actors that included Jerry Franken and Patricia Ludwick (the future Mr. and Mrs. Donnelly) put it through a series of workshops from which three separate plays emerged. Bill Glassco agreed to produce them at the Tarragon with Turnbull directing, and in November 1973, *Sticks and Stones: The Donnellys, Part One* opened in Toronto. Part Two, *The St Nicholas Hotel, Wm Donnelly Prop.,* premiered in November 1974 and won the Chalmers Award. *Handcuffs: The Donnellys, Part Three* opened in March 1975. Later that year the newly christened NDWT Company—Reaney, Turnbull, et al.—toured all three plays across Canada. *Fourteen Barrels from Sea to Sea* (1977) is Reaney's highly personal account of the tour.

Reaney continued to use the workshop-preparation method with the NDWT Company for his next series of plays, all based on local Ontario history or pseudo-history: *Baldoon* (1976), written with C.H. Gervais; *The Dismissal* (1977), featuring Mackenzie King as a scheming undergraduate; *Wacousta!* (1978) and its sequel *The Canadian Brothers* (1983), products of nearly two years' intensive workshops (a number of them led by Tomson Highway); *King Whistle* (1979); and *Antler River* (1980). In *Gyroscope* (1981) Reaney returned to more personal dramatic material. With his libretto for John Beckwith's opera *The Shivaree*, first performed in 1982, he was reunited with the composer for whose music he had written *Night-blooming Cereus* twenty years earlier. In 1989 Reaney and Beckwith collaborated on another opera, *Crazy To Kill*, for the Guelph Spring Festival, and the following year Reaney's historical opera *Serinette* (music by Harry Somers) premiered at the Sharon (Ont.) Music Festival. A performance poem for two voices, *Imprecations* (1984), celebrates the arts of cursing and name-calling, a fitting celebration for a writer who has always held names to be as tangible as sticks and stones, only much more powerful.

The Donnelly story as Reaney tells it is very much about the power of names. To carry the Donnelly name is both a curse and a blessing, a sacrament and a doom. In *The St Nicholas Hotel*, Will Donnelly looks into the future and sees how his enemies "smeared our name for all time so that when children are naughty their mothers still say to them be quiet, or the Black Donnellys will get you." Historically, the Donnellys were Irish Catholic immigrants who settled in Biddulph Township near Lucan, Ontario, in 1844. James and Johanna and their seven sons and a daughter almost immediately became embroiled in conflict with their neighbours, and much of the violence that wracked the region—barn burnings, assaults, mutilations of farm animals—was attributed to the Donnellys. In 1857 James Donnelly killed a man in a fight and went to prison for seven years. In 1879 Mike Donnelly was stabbed to death in a hotel bar-room, his assailant imprisoned for only two years. Finally, on the night of February 3, 1880, a mob of vigilantes burst into the Donnelly home and murdered Mr. and Mrs. Donnelly, son Tom and niece Bridget, and later that night son John. Though an eyewitness identified many of the killers, no one ever went to prison for the crimes.

In researching the plays, Reaney discovered that his source material embodied two opposing views of the principals. First there were the evil Donnellys of popular history and local lore, incarnated in Thomas P. Kelley's 1954 best-seller, *The Black Donnellys*, a potboiler that presented the family as "the most vicious and heartless bunch of devils that ever drew the breath of human life." In Kelley's version, the depraved family, led by the monstrous Johannah, terrorize the district for the sheer malicious joy of it and get only what they deserve in the end. A more objective and sympathetic treatment was Orlo Miller's book *The Donnellys Must Die* (1962). Miller argued that the Donnellys were essentially victims of a nasty feud that had carried over from Ireland where they had refused to join the secret anti-Protestant society of Whiteboys (or Whitefeet). As a result, in the largely Irish settlement of Biddulph they were branded with the hated name "Blackfeet," persecuted and made scapegoats for a great deal of local violence which was not of their doing. Reaney ultimately followed Miller's lead, but he went further than just exonerating the Donnellys. He celebrates them.

Part One, *Sticks and Stones*, covers the period 1857-67, opening with an expository flashback showing the Donnellys' stubborn refusal to bend to Whitefoot pressures in Ireland. We see them struggling to make a place for themselves in Biddulph, caught between the Roman (Catholic) and Protestant Lines of settlers, uncomfortable with both. They lose half their farm in a bitter dispute with the Fat Woman and her husband, and Mr. Donnelly is goaded into fighting with the Fat Woman's brother, Pat Farl, who won't stop calling him "Blackfoot." When Mr. Donnelly kills Farl, only a heroic effort by Mrs. Donnelly gets her husband's sentence commuted to seven years in prison. At the end the Biddulph Whitefeet burn the Donnellys' barn and try to intimidate them into leaving the township, but Mr. Donnelly refuses, reiterating what he told them in Ireland: "Donnellys don't kneel." "It was at this time," Reaney writes, "that the Donnellys decided to be Donnellys."

To be a Donnelly in Reaney's portrayal is to be strong, proud, heroic, stubborn, forthright. It is to choose to be true to your own values no matter how much pain that may cause you. It is to stand up against the mob, the community, the church, even the law if they pressure you to be what you are not. It is to be intensely loyal to your own family and to be generous *as a family* to others whose own have rejected or betrayed them. To be a Donnelly, in short, is to have an integrity lacking in almost every character or institution that opposes them throughout the trilogy, from the corrupt magistrates George Stub and Tom Cassleigh in Part One to the churchmen who organize the vigilantes in Part Three, *Handcuffs*, and the jury that finds mob leader Jim Carroll not guilty of their murder. *Handcuffs*, focusing on the massacre itself and the few months in 1879-80 immediately preceding and following it, really just fills in the details of what Parts One and Two have already told us will happen. The Donnellys *must* die; their pride and stubborness cannot be endured. They are tragic.

Whereas *Sticks and Stones* introduces the circumstances of the Donnellys' tragedy and *Handcuffs* presents its dénouement, the second play, *The St Nicholas Hotel*, poses the trilogy's key question: "Why did they all hate you so much?" Rev. Donaldson asks it of Will Donnelly in 1891 on the twelfth anniversary of Mike's murder, and Reaney gives us the events of 1873-79 as an answer. Superficially it is Mike's story. The play opens with intimations of his death and closes with his murder, his ghost, and his bloodstain that will never come out. But Mike doesn't die for anything that he as an individual has done; he dies because he is a Donnelly. The events that build inexorably to his death are part of the larger conspiracy that will culminate in the 1880 massacre.

One reason the Donnellys are so hated is their sheer zest for life which makes *The St Nicholas Hotel*, despite its tragic undertones, the most joyful and exhilarating of the three plays, full of stagecoach races, whirling tops, rousing music and dancing. Brimming with positive energy, the Donnellys provide a constant, unwelcome challenge to the negativity and complacency of their neighbours. Will and Maggie's romantic courtship in Act One is set against the calculated bargaining of Stub and Miss Maguire, and the loveless marriage bed of Bill and Mary Donovan. In Act Two young Tom Ryan tells how he ran away from his own brutal home to the Donnellys—making his humiliated father another of their lifelong enemies— "because they're brave" and "they're handsome," and because "there's love there." The Donnellys themselves understand the double-edged nature of their condition. Mr. Donnelly acknowledges that they deserve the way they are treated: "for we're Donnellys." Like the spinning tops that symbolize their vitality, they are caught up in a momentum over which they have little control. They can't help being what they are. "Yes. It would be nice to stop, but we can't oh no we must keep on spinning and spinning," Mrs. Donnelly says. The context is Stub's proposal that they compromise their support of the Liberal candidate and back his Conservative opponent in exchange for a cessation of hostilities. Their rejection of this deal and the subsequent defeat of the Tory candidate add significantly to the enemies who will destroy them in Part Three.

The St Nicholas Hotel is by no means simply a whitewash of the Donnellys. Having exploded the myth of "the Black Donnellys" in Part One, Reaney seems willing in this play to admit to shades of grey. In Acts One and Two we see at times how pride and strength can turn to arrogance and bullying, playfulness to maliciousness, and energy to destruction. Will and Mike never hesitate to employ unfair business practices in running their Opposition Stage Line, even to the point of putting the competition's drivers in danger. Reaney intentionally leaves ambiguous their role in Ned Brooks' fatal accident, but there is little doubt about the responsibility of James Jr. for a variety of atrocities. By the third act, though, the balance of sympathy has swung back wholly in the Donnelly's favour as a result of the pettiness and cowardice of their enemies in the mob scene as well as in Mike's murder. When Will, Norah and Mrs. Donnelly face down the mob, we understand both the awe and the blind hatred this family could inspire. As Reaney's stage direction notes, "We should feel ashamed ourselves that we did not make a better showing against a lame man & two women."

The lame man, and really the central figure in the play, is Will, often called "Cripple" because of his club foot. He and Mrs. Donnelly are the two strongest characters in the trilogy and the ones at whom the most venom is directed. Will is also the most sensitive Donnelly, an artist of sorts, riding a horse called Lord Byron and opposing Jim Carroll with his handwriting and the music of his fiddle. But most of all he is a function of his name, very much the offspring of his father who is described in Part One as "a small square chunk of will"—the essence of Donnelly. The title of the play, *The St Nicholas Hotel, Wm Donnelly Prop.*, locates Will outside Biddulph in a future beyond the massacre, a survivor, proprietor of his own fate and chief prop of a family name that endures as a curse, a legend, a stain on a bar-room floor, and now as a classic of Canadian theatre.

•

The St Nicholas Hotel, Wm Donnelly Prop.: The Donnellys, Part II was first performed at the Tarragon Theatre on November 16, 1974, with the following cast:

Ken Anderson Miriam Greene
Nancy Beatty Michael Hogan
Jay Bowen Patricia Ludwick
Tom Carew Don MacQuarrie
Peter Elliott Keith McNair
David Ferry Gord Stobbe
Jerry Franken Suzanne Turnbull
Rick Gorrie

Directed by Keith Turnbull
Designed by Rosalyn Mina

Note: The punctuation of *The St Nicholas Hotel*—eccentric, inconsistent and often technically incorrect—has been left as Reaney intended it, to reflect the rhythms of his characters' speech. "Publishers beware: you rob the performers when you change Reaney's punctuation." (Patricia Ludwick, "One Actor's Journey with James Reaney," in *Approaches to the Work of James Reaney* [1983])—Ed.

THE ST NICHOLAS HOTEL, WM DONNELLY PROP. THE DONNELLYS, PART II

CHARACTERS

MR DONNELLY (James)
MRS DONNELLY (Johannah)
MIKE
WILL
JAMES JR
TOM } *their sons*
JOHN
BOB
PATRICK
JENNY, *their daughter*
BRIDGET, *their niece*
NELLIE, *Mike's wife*
NORAH (née Macdonald), *Will's wife*

JOHN MACDONALD, *Norah's brother*
MOTHER

BARTENDER (Frank Walker)
NED BROOKS, *a stage driver*
PATRICK FINNEGAN, *a stageowner*

REV. DONALDSON, *a traveller*

MISS MERCILLA MAGUIRE
   (later Mrs George Stub)
REV. DR MAGUIRE, *her father*
GEORGE STUB, *a merchant*

FAT LADY
JIM CARROLL, *her son*
BRIDGET, *her daughter (the Stubs' parlourmaid)*
WILL FARL, *her nephew*

MAGGIE DONOVAN, *her niece*
FATHER
AUNT THERESA
BILL DONOVAN, *Maggie's brother*
MARY DONOVAN, *his wife*
MOTHER SUPERIOR
NUNS

TOM RYAN
NED RYAN, *his father*
MRS RYAN

BAKER
BAKER'S APPRENTICE
McKELLAR, *a stage driver*
MR SCANDRETT, *a tollman*

MRS SCANDRETT
CHILD
CESSMAN

SQUIRE FERGUSON, *a Justice of the Peace*
CONSTABLE BERRYHILL
HUGH McCRIMMON, *a detective*
BAILIFFS
CONSTABLES
PRIEST
FIDDLER

TIMOTHY CORCORAN, *a Tory candidate*
ELECTIONS CLERK

CHAIRMAN (of the "Peace Society")
O'HALLORAN
DAN QUIGLEY, *a farmer*
SCHOOLMASTER

SID SKINNER (aka "Bill Lewis")
BILL LEWIS, *a trainer*
GREENWOOD
JIM MORRISON, *Mike Donnelly's workmate*

2 MAIDS

STAGE DRIVERS
STAGE PASSENGERS
TOLLGATE KEEPERS
TRAVELLERS
FARMERS
BOYS AND GIRLS
MOB
CHORUS

AUTHOR'S NOTE

The story of this play concerns a race, a race between the Donnelly boys and their enemies. The road the race takes place on has tollgates with signs on them saying: NO DONNELLYS ARE TO . . . run a stage line, marry my daughter, & c., & c. 'Helped' by their brothers, William & Michael Donnelly smash through most of the tollgates, but their victories only drive their enemies to build stronger & stronger barriers until, at last, Michael is suddenly & brutally murdered.

It is a tale of barrooms, wheels, horses, nuns, tops, convent yards, derailed trains, homeless boys, tavern brawls, refinements, squalors, wedding cakes, drunkards—and ghosts. In a certain hotel deserted for thirty years there is a stain on the floor no ordinary scrubbing brush can ever wash away.

James Reaney

ACT ONE

The barroom of the City Hotel, London; later on it will be the barroom of the Royal Hotel in Exeter, the St Nicholas Hotel (Wm Donnelly, prop.) in Appin, and Slaght's Hotel in Waterford. The barman seems always there; his somewhat skullish face and presence will remind us later on before we go to sleep that—this is the man who eventually killed Mike Donnelly. Behind the bar is a picture of Wm Donnelly's black stallion, Lord Byron. Passengers to the stages to the north slowly fill the benches at the sides of the room we too are waiting in; we see actors spinning tops (each one seems to have one) and hear them singing songs from the play. Like a cloud shadow the stage picture is slowly invaded now by the story of a road; the actors stop being actors and become fighters for the ownership of that road, a map of which goes all around the walls of the theatre from Crediton to Exeter to Clandeboye down to Lucan to Elginfield to London to St Thomas to Waterford, and advancing towards us comes the

STAGEDRIVER (NED BROOKS): *(belching)* Are there any passengers for Masonville, St John's, Bobtown, Ryan's Corners, Lucan, Flanagan's Corners, Mooretown, Exeter? Now loading at the front door please.

MIKE DONNELLY: Are there any more ladies and gentlemen for Calamity Corners as tis sometimes called, St John's, Birr—my old friend Ned here calls it Bobtown, the more elegant name is Birr. Elginfield known to some as Ryan's Corners, Lucan that classic spot if it's not all burnt down, Clandeboye, Mooretown, Exeter *and* Crediton. If Ned here hasn't sawn it to pieces the coach is waiting for you at the front door and it pleases you.

STAGEDRIVER: What does it matter if it's Bobtown or Birr; elegance be damned, Mike Donnelly, it's my team will get you there faster.

LADY: *(coming back in)* Which stage is yours then? Louisa, there are no less than four stages out there all with different names. Sir wh—

STAGEDRIVER:
The Favourite Line
Hawkshaw's Stage
Good Horses, Comfortable Stages & Fast Time.
Leaves the City Hotel for all points north at two o'clock p.m.

WILLIAM & MIKE DONNELLY pass out announcement cards.

ANCIENT STAGEDRIVER: *(entering & flourishing a ragged whip)* Come on everybody, Ho! for the North Uriah Jennings here, fifty years on the road, *(coughing)*

YET ANOTHER STAGEDRIVER: Anybody here want a lift up north. You'll have to share the accommodation a little with

LADY TWO: Martha, he's got six young pigs, two geese and a sack of flour in there already.

CHORUS: *(reading cards)*
Notice
Exeter, Lucan & London Daily Stage: Change of Time.

WILL: Leaves City Hotel at 2 p.m. and arrives Maclean's Hotel, Lucan at half past four

MIKE: Twenty minutes ahead of all other stages.

Both halves begin together, but the first half pauses so the names are spoken after the second half has completed its speech:

HALF CHORUS	HALF CHORUS
Drivers	calling all places along the route for passengers
William and Michael Donnelly	

Into the bar comes a hard-driving Irishman who has as much force as the Donnellys but all as hard as grindstone.

FINNEGAN: Just a minute there, Donnelly—whoa!! You boys aren't going to Lucan today.

WILL: *(with whip)* It's Patrick Finnegan says we won't get to Lucan?

FINNEGAN: Ah, yes, Will, because *(to audience)* good evening—don't you know my brother John Finnegan and myself, Pat, have bought out your boss and all his horses and wagons now, so it's the Finnegan Stage now. Come along now, these passengers are mine, the road is mine, and the wheels. Give your whip to my driver, Will. Mr. Brooks, here's—he's driving for me, Will. I don't need you Donnelly boys. *(trying to take whip)*

MIKE: Give that whip back to my brother. *(grabbing it)* No one ever lent us a whip.

WILL: No, my father bought me that whip with the very first money I ever earned, on St Nicholas day—five years ago and that's how long we've been driving our stage.

FINNEGAN: There you go, Will, it was never your stage. It belonged to Hugh McPhee and now it belongs to Pat Finnegan. We leave at two p.m. sharp, ladies and gentlemen, passengers to reach Lucan safely to connect with east and west trains to St Mary's and Sarnia.

MIKE: Do you want to know, Mr. Pat Finnegan, how Will and Mike Donnelly will still beat you to Lucan today by a good half hour?

FINNEGAN: It's my brother and myself here run a store and tavern up the road north of here— why the place is called after our father Finnegan's Corners, for God's sake, there were three hundred buggies at his funeral. Sure our father built the Proof Line Road these fellows say is theirs. So step up into my stage wagon and see whose road it is. Mike Donnelly, we'll run yous off it. Are there anymore passengers— *(exit)*

MIKE: Look, we're starting our own line with our own equipment. Mr. Jennings, how much do you want for your vehicle that's been fifty years on the road. Will, just take a look at his beasts.

WILL: We'll have to get new horses, fast ones, where we can get—

CHORUS: William Donnelly, Groom.

The actors "melt" into a scene at the London races. They are held back from the track by a long rope. The BARTENDER jumps up on the bar and interprets the race through a megaphone. We only hear the drumming of invisible hooves and see on human faces the effect of the race.

MIKE:
The horses for our stage line were bred from the winner of this race. We had the rights to a mare called Irish Girl whose mother you may recall was Billet Doux, grandmother to Sir Walter Scott. So, Will, is it let this race decide who'll sire the foal that is the nighhorse of our team on—what'll we call it.

Get a pool of extra silence around the naming of the line

WILL:
The Opposition Stage

BARTENDER:
The second day's meeting of The London Turf Club on the Newmarket race course attracted a large crowd yesterday afternoon. The weather was delightful and the track in good condition, except that it was a trifle dusty.

CHORUS:
(over & under) Words blown away by the wind, dust & words in the stream of the time we all lie dreaming in

CHORUS:
dreaming of horses and wagons going up the hill

This speech and the ones below go on simultaneously with WILL's "Opposition Stage" coming in just after the CHORUS's "dreaming in." The BARTENDER should blur his voice under and over the other levels so that we get the effect of a real racetrack where wind & distance play tricks with announcements; also it is a remembered racetrack where MIKE DONNELLY not only saw the horse they needed but also the first omen of his own death.

BARTENDER: Dash of 1 1/2 miles. Entries. Sleepy Jim, bay stallion & his colours are blue & yellow owned by Messrs Bookless & Thomas, Guelph. Florence Nightingale, grey mare. Scarlet & white.

CHORUS: Down the hill

BARTENDER: Lord Byron, full brother to Clear Grit out of Fleetwood the Second. He thus comes of good stock & will be heard of further.

CHORUS: Long white road

BARTENDER: Black & red, and *(an actor runs around as Lord Byron—sometimes disappearing from view, then reappearing and followed avidly by all of the spectators' eyes)* they're off! Although the delay in starting caused a good deal of impatience this, ladies and gentlemen, is an ex—citing dash. From the first it lies between Sleepy Jim, Nigger Baby & Lord Byron and, ladies & gents, as they first pass the string they are well abreast. On the turn, however, they're breaking up & now it's an open question. It's an open question, ladies & knights, which is going to win. It's Sleepy Jim, no it's Lord Byron—past the string slightly ahead of Finnegan who flashed up from behind with Nigger Baby third. Lord Byron, ran, ladies & gentlemen, without his regular *(gasp from the crowd who see the jockey's death before the barman does)* trainer & his victory here today is therefore a greater tribute to his speed. Sorry to report. There seems to have been an accident there to Lord Byron's jockey among the oak trees there at the edge of the grove. A low branch.

CHORUS: Words blown away by the wind, dust & words in the stream of

BARTENDER: Time. Two minutes forty-nine & a half seconds.

Two human runners in singlets appear—one of them is DETECTIVE McCRIMMON whom Finnegan will one day hire to pursue the Donnellys.

BARTENDER: Next ladies & gentlemen, it is calculated to have a foot race in addition, 100 yards, for a shake-purse. BANG!

The runners sweep toward us and then—whistles! and the actors all turn into a herd of horses in a Biddulph pasture; the Donnellys with their father have come to take out a team for evening training. Umbrella, fiddle.

MIKE: Our father and another old man helped us to train the horses. Ploughboy! Pilot!

MIKE & CHORUS: Farmer. Indian.

MIKE: You see our horses came running to their names!

MIKE & CHORUS: Manilla. Ginger.

A team comes up for training, umbrella thrown at them, horses shy, then calm. Slowly, all the horses grow used to umbrella & fiddle.

MR DONNELLY: Throw the frightening old floppy thing at him again, Mike. And again. There my beauty. Again. There. Whisper to you. The fiddle, Will. *(excruciating notes)* There my beauty, my dove.

We return from the horse pasture to the tavern; crowd is a crowd once more.

MIKE: Our brother Patrick had been apprenticed to a Carriage Works in town here. As a black-smith. He helped turn the rusty old vehicle we bought from Jennings into a pretty smart, smooth road bird with new wheels for wings.

anvil in distance

FINNEGAN: Are there any more passengers for London? Sure you'll want to see Mr. Barnum's Circus that's in town today, and we've put on an extra stage just to accommodate the crowd.

WILL & MIKE: On the sides of our stage what did we have painted?

CHORUS: *(with varying strength and texture)*
The Opposition Stage.
Between London & Crediton
Through Exeter daily at 4 a.m.
First Rate Accommodation Prices Moderate
Proprietor, William Donnelly,
Driver, Michael Donnelly.
William Donnelly, Gentleman.

LADY: Prices moderate, Mr. Donnelly? How much is a ticket to Lucan on your conveyance?

WILL: Seventy cents, m'am.

TWO GIRLS: Mr Finnegan, does your stage go into Crediton?

FINNEGAN: Shure, and it can be induced to.

TWO GIRLS: Are you entirely sure because your advertisement notes your destination as Exeter which is just four miles short of where Uncle Dan Philip lives.

FINNEGAN: Girls, I'll get you there if I have to take yous on my back. *(to LADY)* Sixty cents.

A rountine where she wavers between FINNEGAN & DONNELLY, running back & forth.

WILL: Fifty

FINNEGAN: Forty it is.

WILL & MIKE: Thirty it is.

FINNEGAN: Donnelly! Twenty, Madam.

WILL: Sure that's nothing at all. We'll take you for a kiss and a penny. Michael, take the fare.

LADY: *(held on MIKE's arms and another's as in a cart, after being kissed)* I prefer the Opposition Stage. A smooth ride with fast, evenly matched horses. Polite & skillful drivers. One hardly knows where the time has gone when—the diligence stops, the driver jumps down . . .

But cows are faintly mooing, as if we had reached her farm, and the actors giggling under her effusiveness have crept around to confront her as embarrassing cows . . .

with firm hand takes yours and helps you across to your very gate.

CHORUS: Her father's cows have come to meet her. *(laughter)*

FINNEGAN: Allaboard for the circus excursion. *(He or his driver blows a horn.)* Here comes Finnegan. Here comes Finnegan.

WILL DONNELLY walks behind the bar and lights a candle as we slide into the next scene. Most of the tavern crowd depart. We hear them getting into the stage & driving off. More horns blast & "Here comes Finnegan." "The Favourite Stage." Behind WILL DONNELLY there is a picture of a black horse. His wife NORAH brings in a tray of glasses and sets them behind the bar. The light changes. Fiddle. Wind.

CHORUS: *(a drifting voice)* Yes, Bill Donnelly ran the St Nicholas Hotel down here at Appin. Was still running it when he died in the nineties. My father bought me some ice cream there in 1924.

And now we are at the St Nicholas Hotel, years after what we have just been watching.

NORAH: Well, so our visitor will not stay the night, is that

WILL: He'll come back. I put something in his cutter

NORAH: It's too stormy a night for anyone to come out save the odd traveller like this reverend gentleman. But perhaps he's right. He should push on to Glencoe now rather than in the morning.

WILL: No. He's going to stay here tonight. You'll see.

NORAH: Are you that lonely, Will?

WILL: Well, if he does not come back maybe we should call up the children and have a game of dominoes. *(pause)* Norah, you know the sort of travellers we get at the St Nicholas Hotel— grainbuyers and sewing machine agents, but— and neighbours into the bar here, but —it's seldom anyone comes down this road from the past, from up there.

The candle wavers.

NORAH: Hsst! That blast came from Biddulph for sure. Sure there's water from there flows by here, in the river doesn't there. But the reverend gentleman did not seem Biddulphian to me, Will.

WILL: We'll find out. I've met him somewhere in the seventies when Mike and me drove stage.

NORAH: So that's why you've lit the candle. I'd forgotten, forgive me, tonight's

WILL: Tonight's the night they murdered Mike, Norah. In a bar not unlike this one

Enter MINISTER with a block of ice in his hands.

NORAH: Sir, you've come back to us out of the storm?

DONALDSON: Who put this block of ice to my feet in my cutter?

WILL: I did, now I'll ask my son to put up your horse. *(through a door)* Jack, we've a customer after all.

DONALDSON: I had to come back to find out why—

WILL: To keep your feet warm, you might as well stay with us, sir. What time is your appointment tomorrow in Glencoe?

DONALDSON: Sabbath School starts at nine. But how would that keep me warm?

WILL: By bringing you back to my St Nicholas Hotel instead of you driving seven miles on through a blizzard. It's warmer here than that.

He takes the ice block and puts it in a pail; all through the evening we watch it slowly melt till it is used by the scrubwomen at the end of the play to wipe MIKE DONNELLY's blood off the floor.

DONALDSON: Now, sir, I've met you some-where before. The name of the hotel you are running is the St Nicholas Hotel, proprietor is—

WILL: My name is William Donnelly *(pause)* Perhaps you'll want to hitch up your cutter again.

DONALDSON: Now why would you say that, Mr Donnelly?

WILL: Aren't you afraid of me?

DONALDSON: No. Quite the contrary. I remember you and your brother when you ran the stage between London and Lucan, excuse me *one* of the stages. The Opposition Stage.

NORAH: That must be a good many years ago, sir. Twenty years?

DONALDSON: More than that. I started visiting the Presbyterian Church in Lucan on appointments which I would receive, oh let me see now—the fall of 1875. I preferred your stage although people at the church wanted me not to patronize your line. *(to us)* Once I happened to come down to Lucan from Parkhill by train—hence to Irishtown by your rival's stage—The Finnegan Line. The Finnegan Line. I asked the driver how the new railway had affected the stage route between London and Lucan. What has become of the Donnellys?

STAGEDRIVER: *(belching)* Ugh, the Donnellys've been run off the line at last.

DONALDSON: And what do they do now then?

STAGEDRIVER: Yes, what don't they do, sir. They're a bad lot and we're bound to get rid of them.

DONALDSON: Yes, Mr Donnelly. A small glass of wine would not go amiss. Thank you. Then I said *(to him)* It's strange that young men so good looking and so polite as I've always found the Donnelly boys to be, should be so much run down and set on by all parties, Romanists, Protestants and Secretists, when they are so very polite and strive so hard to live down all this opposition, by attention to business and kind treatment of all who favour them. He replied:

STAGEDRIVER: You do not know them, sir. They just put on appearances to deceive strangers. I once thrashed Mike and I will thrash him again.

DONALDSON: *(pause)* Which son is Mike?

STAGEDRIVER: The second from the youngest. No sir, the people are bound to get rid of that family some way or another and that too before too long.

DONALDSON: We had reached the railway station and I told him what I thought as a teacher of the Gospel. I said: "You surely do not mean what you say, or you would not speak so to a stranger: there's room enough for the Donnellys and their opponents also in the world. Why, man, competition is the life of trade; we are all the better of the opposition lines."

STAGEDRIVER: *(laughing)* You're too good yourself, sir, to understand what this family is like. *We* are bound to snuff out that family and we shall do it, so that it shall never be known how it was done.

DONALDSON: He turned on his heel and left. So, yes, I was never afraid of the Donnellys. William Donnelly. Mike Donnelly.

WILL: And when would that conversation be?

DONALDSON: In January of 1879. As early as that

WILL: As early as that then we were marked out for slaughter.

DONALDSON: Mike, what happened to Michael Donnelly?

WILL: Oh, they got him first at the end of that year—just before Christmas, December the 9th, 1879.

DONALDSON: This is the 12th Anniversary of his death then? *(pause)* I find it very pleasant to be sitting by such a warm fire after travelling through such a storm this afternoon. *(They listen to the gale outside for a few moments.)* You have settled here, Mr Donnelly, in this peaceful place after a stormy journey far worse. Far worse.

WILL: Yes, I keep the inn here, I travel about in the spring with my stallion—True Grit out of Lord Byron and this may astonish you, but people are saying that I am the best constable this village ever had.

NORAH: Sir, I am going upstairs with a warm brick for your bed. I promise you no more ice blocks. How soon do you wish to retire?

DONALDSON: I may never drive this way again. Midnight. Until then Mrs. Donnelly, I should like your husband to explain what lay behind the bloody statement of that young man at the railway station. Why did they all hate you so much?

NORAH: Oh sir, that would take till the dawn itself. *(passing out of the room)*

WILL: I'll tell you why the stage drivers for the other lines hated us so much. *(taking a scissors from Norah's sewing basket)* They blamed us for cutting the tongues out of their horses. Like this. *(laughing & illustrating!)* But at first it was something not quite so Sodom & Gomorrah we were blamed for.

Screams & curses offstage; some monumental collapse of Mr FINNEGAN's stage. Yes, a wheel has come off, for into the barroom it rolls. Passengers enter, shaken & muttering.

FINNEGAN: Who in the mother of Hell's name loosened the bolts and cut the nuts off my wheels. Oh funny it is, Cripple, and one of my wheels skated right into your hands, and funny it is, Mike. Well it wouldn't be so funny if I'd been going down Mother Brown's Hill and they'd come off; we'd been all killed. *(pause)* Ladies & gentlemen, be patient for the twenty-minute delay there'll be while we fix up the wheels. You see what they done, don't go in his stage, you see what they done to me. Oh, Alec *(to bartender)* give me anything you got, oh

MIKE: Now, are there any more passengers for St John's, Birr, Elginfield, Lucan, Finnegan's Corners, Mooretown, Exeter, and even Crediton.

He has been outside for a quarter of this; we hear his voice again outside and nearly the whole chorus eventually decide to follow the hypnotic elegance. Left now are only a maidservant (MAGGIE) and the FAT LADY.

MIKE: Now leaving the City Hotel—the Opposition Stage.

MAGGIE: Cousin Patrick, do me a pleasant thing and allow me to take the Opposition Stage out of town. They'll be put out with me I'm late to serve dinner.

In a necessary manoeuvre we can't see, the Donnelly Stage goes around the hotel, so that it circles the barroom and MAGGIE follows it inside in a circular, birdlike, trapped motion.

FINNEGAN: Your father says, Maggie, you're to have no truck with the Donnellys, shun them and if you get on with them I'll drag you off of—I'll tell your father, miss.

MAGGIE: No need to, Patrick Finnegan. I'll do that myself *(pause, wavering)* Some day. Well

how long do I have to wait then, for the sake of heaven?

FINNEGAN: How do I know, the blacksmith made no—but I swear I'll get them, for it's only them would do a trick like that, loosen my wheels *(runs outside)* I'll snuff them . . .

FAT LADY: Maggie Donovan I'd wait a week, a year not to have to take that blackguard Donnelly's wagon. I'd walk up to Biddulph on my bare knees rather than use their coach.

MAGGIE: Would you now.

FAT LADY: Why girl, it's them and their mother cheated us out of half the farm that should've been ours. Don't you know how their old woman put a spell on my cows so they bear freemartens and my daughter is barren. Have you no ears?

FINNEGAN: The wheels are back on, Maggie. We'll catch up to them. At Holy Corners. Why yes, why won't we. He's got the weight of all my passengers—

MAGGIE: And you've got the weight of only one of his—Here comes Finnegan! Tootletee too!

FINNEGAN: Onto the stage, girl. Don't you dare make mock of me.

MAGGIE: I won't go. *(FAT LADY & FINNEGAN chase her all over the barroom until he picks her up in his arms and carries her out.)*

FINNEGAN: Well, you will. You will even if I have to hitch you to the wagon and drag you to Lucan. *(horn)* The stage for Lucan, the Favourite Line. Here comes Finnegan. Aroint thee, ye jades, I'm after you, Donnelly.

Whip sounds &c., but also MAGGIE laughing. In the fading light the BARTENDER with his skullish face listens & thinks. He comes towards us and actors with tollgates mime the flow of the road against him.

BARTENDER: Finnegan's stage and Donnelly's stage goes north on the road that goes north from here through crossroads and tollgates and Lucan until the road is outside the parsonage of the English priest.

The barroom clock strikes six. A decisive lady at the top of her youth, MISS MAGUIRE enters & rings a servant bell. She has managed the parsonage for her father ever since her mother's death ten years ago.

MAGGIE: You rang, m'am.

MISS MAGUIRE: That chamberpot needs emptying. Yes, I did ring and I have been ringing to no avail until now why?

MAGGIE: Oh, Miss Maguire, the wheels fell off my cousin Patrick's stage.

MISS MAGUIRE: Very nice that must have been, was anybody hurt, were you?

MAGGIE: Not enough to mention, m'am.

MISS MAGUIRE: Your being so late puts me in half a mind to say you cannot go to vespers, but I suppose the priest would denounce me from the pulpit if I did so, could you finish up this room and be at the door till Mr Stub calls.

MAGGIE: Yes m'am.

MISS MAGUIRE: And did you leave the silk thread in your basket?

MAGGIE: Oh thank you, Miss Maguire, I was so afraid you'd keep me in for being late, just dump the basket out and you'll find the thread, never mind my things.

She goes out with the chamberpot; MISS MAGUIRE looks into the basket. Offstage we hear: "Good evening, Mr Stub. The upstairs drawing room, if you please sir." The REVEREND MAGUIRE enters first; an old, snowy vicar.

DR MAGUIRE: Daughter?

MISS MAGUIRE: Father? Mr Stub is coming to see me tonight.

DR MAGUIRE: Then I shall drop in later, Mercilla I've no intention of ruining your tête à tête with the foremost merchant of Main Street.

MISS MAGUIRE: Are you composing your sermon? I shall tell him that is why you are absent. I suppose you are wondering what I am doing in the maidservant's basket.

DR MAGUIRE: Did she give you permission to rumple it out like that?

MISS MAGUIRE: Oh yes. You're always worrying about the servants, Father.

DR MAGUIRE: We are servants too, you know. Mercilla. *(He fades away.)*

MAGGIE: *(still with chamberpot)* Mr Stub to see you, m'am.

GEORGE STUB: *(with nosegay for MERCILLA)* Good evening, Mercilla.

MISS MAGUIRE: Thank you, Mr Stub. I'd ask Maggie here to put these in some water in a vase, but I'm terrified what she might do. So. Do please be seated, Father is busy in his study with next Sunday's sermon, I'm finding the silk thread for the banner you're having me mend and so—what else?

GEORGE: I've bought the land for a house on what the villagers call Quality Hill.

MISS MAGUIRE: Is it going to be what size of a house, George Stub?

GEORGE: I want you to decide how big it should be, Mercilla.

MISS MAGUIRE: Because I'm to be the mistress of it, is that it?

GEORGE: *(sweating)* Yes.

MISS MAGUIRE: And you're not married to someone else already?

GEORGE: I've been alone in my bed for a year & a half now, Mercilla.

MISS MAGUIRE: What a way you have of putting things. Why I've been alone in my bed ever since I was born. Well, seeing it's your second marriage and I'm older too than is usual, I feel that I ought to put some things in your way.

GEORGE: In my way?

MISS MAGUIRE: Yes, because I needn't get married. So—make it worth my while.

GEORGE: I've already mentioned the house I'm building.

MISS MAGUIRE: Glad you did because I'd not come to live above an old hardware store. Now, here are the rules. After all I'm mending your silly old Masonic banner for you, you do some promising for me.

GEORGE: Mercilla.

MISS MAGUIRE: Who are you anyway?

GEORGE: I've been a self made man. You know what a great thing I've made of the store, and I'm—

MISS MAGUIRE: One of the rules I might make tonight is that I expect the man I marry to be somebody, really somebody, like a Member of Parliament. What about that George?

GEORGE: It'll never come to pass. I'm far better behind the scenes. I get too excited in public.

MISS MAGUIRE: Didn't I hear you say once that you'd been promised a senatorship if you could get a Conservative candidate in this riding?

GEORGE: Yes.

MISS MAGUIRE: Then that's the rules. It's some day to be Senator Stub, or else. I have depths of meanness, George. Don't ruffle them.

GEORGE: If I promise to obey the rules, I want things to be clearer.

MISS MAGUIRE: You mean when? I'll think it over tonight after you'll be gone.

GEORGE: I'd like something on—all this.

MISS MAGUIRE: Something on account. Here take my hand.

GEORGE: No.

MISS MAGUIRE: Oh, my mouth. Here, stop me from talking so much.

Her father enters.

MISS MAGUIRE: Remember, sir, I am no widow. You may be a hot blooded widower, but my father has kept me in his parsonage, a chaste spinster, for many more years than Jacob served Laban for both Leah and Rachel. And I haven't minded that a bit.

GEORGE: Good evening, Doctor Maguire. It is a pleasure to see you looking so well.

DR MAGUIRE: Mr George Stub. How many faces of the poor did you grind in the main street of Lucan today?

GEORGE: Business is business, Doctor Maguire. I have to foreclose and get my money back sometimes twice in a month.

MISS MAGUIRE: Look what treasures I'm finding in the girl's basket. What are these strange lumps of metal, George, and here's a locket. *(a small bell rings)* Father, Maggie said I could "dump the basket out."

DR MAGUIRE: I don't think she meant you to open her locket.

MISS MAGUIRE: *(tempted and walking about the room)* It's the one she's always wearing and she's had the catch fixed by a jeweller in town, why not here in Lucan, ah—George, open it for me.

GEORGE: These are the nuts off the axles of a wagon. Her father must have given her a list of things to bring him home on the farm out there. And this—I hate to tell tales on your servant girl, Doctor Maguire, but this is a picture of William Donnelly, William Donnelly Cripple.

DR MAGUIRE: Is there no other name you can call him them?

GEORGE: No, sir. I'll never call him anything else but that. He and his gang of cutthroats are one of the reasons that this riding often does not return a Conservative candidate.

MISS MAGUIRE: But George, he's devilishly handsome.

DR MAGUIRE: Mr George Stub, if I may venture an opinion in the face of your prejudice, I think he has a very sharp intelligent face. So that is Maggie's secret. Do you know I was asked to officiate at his brother Patrick's wedding not so long ago.

GEORGE: You would have met the whole monstrous family then.

DR MAGUIRE: Monstrous, not at all. They were a very handsome, unusual family with a—as if there was something there they weren't telling you. I disagree with you totally, Mr. Stub, and here's the text for my sermon. Four wheels! *(picking up the nuts)* Now as I behold the living creatures, behold one wheel upon the earth by the living creatures, with his four faces. The appearance of the wheels and their work was like unto the colour of a beryl . . . .

GEORGE: Mercilla, I must leave. Please show me down.

MISS MAGUIRE: Follow me, Mr Stub. Father, George Stub is leaving, oh it is no use when he starts quoting scripture, no use at all.

They leave. As he goes on quoting from the Bible (Ezekiel I) he juggles the four nuts.

DR MAGUIRE: And they four had one likeness; and their appearance & their work was as it were upon a wheel in the middle of a wheel. When they went, they went upon their four sides; and they turned not when they went.

MAGGIE enters with a cup of tea. She collects the nuts, the locket, and begins to work at the banner with the coloured thread.

MAGGIE: Miss Maguire suggests, sir, that you take a drink of this camomile tea to calm your nerves. I have lit the lamp in your bedroom and changed your pillow case.

DR MAGUIRE: Ah, I have frightened him away. The Bible is a great help in getting me rid of people I don't like.

MAGGIE: Mr Stub is no angel of mercy, sir, but your daughter has to have some sort of life. Surely you don't expect her to be cooped up here in the parsonage by the river on this lonely stretch of the road all her livelong days.

DR MAGUIRE: I know what I know. He's the worst of a whole set of flinty hearted shopkeepers, just because my daughter comes from what he knows as an old family he wants her to be the lady in his new big house. You mark my words he'll call it Castle Stub—

MERCILLA enters and calmly slides into her father's flow.

MISS MAGUIRE: George Stub is not going to call his new place Castle Stub, Father. He's going to call if after me—Castle Mercilla, that is, if I marry him. Take heart, Father, I've put so many obstacles in his way.

DR MAGUIRE: The best obstacle is a firm "No." You've no idea what his set, the five families that consider themselves the aristocracy of the village, look like from the pulpit. I once dreamt their pale marble faces turned into sheep and I walked around with my crook— *(on his way to bed)* — until this exquisite pain around my ankles made me look down. There was George Stub, the biggest ram of them all, gnawing away at my leg. Blood.

MISS MAGUIRE: *(also retiring)* Good night, Father. Maggie, clear up the teacups. Goodnight, I shan't get up for breakfast, nervous exhaustion, nervous *(repeat this last phrase ad libato)*

CHORUS: *(singing)*
Oh St Patrick was a gentleman
Who came of decent people
He built a church in Dublin town
And on it put a steeple . . .
No wonder that those Irish Lads
Should be so gay and frisky
For sure St Pat he taught them that
As well as making whiskey . . .

MAGGIE clears the chairs of the previous scene, but leaves the Masonic banner MERCILLA has been mending in the centre of the floor; as members of the CHORUS light candles and kneel by their chairs we are changing from MAGGIE as a servant with a cap to MAGGIE remembering a world of power and love that might have been hers forever.

MAGGIE: As I go to my bed over the kitchen of the parsonage I think I see in the moonlight on the floor—a letter, an envelope coming up through the floor, but it is my sleepy brain remembering what many people would regard as a—the strange thing that happened to me in the church tonight at vespers. *(The Vespers service in the background. There are other kneelers.)* Will Donnelly crawls under the floor of the church, the old wooden frame church, and he as I kneel is pushing the letter up to me through the cracks in the floor. My father and brother are so against me seeing him that it is only by letter or accident we can meet.

WILL: *(lying down)* I sent her my picture which she had cut out to be placed in a locket.

MAGGIE: And I in turn pushed a letter down through the crack in the floor. *(A letter comes down from above into WILLIAM's hand.)* I address you with these few lines hoping they will find you in good health as they leave me enjoying the same blessing at present. I thank you for your picture. Until my next birthday you will understand why I cannot wear it in public. Dear William, I was a long time about getting this picture for you. You can keep it now in hopes you think as much of me as I do of you.

WILL: In my next letter which she burnt to save it from their attention I proposed marriage and on April the 30th, 1873, my girl replied

MAGGIE: I now wish to inform you that I have made up my mind to accept your kind offer, as there is no person in this world I sincerely love but you. This is my first & only secret, so I hope you will let no person know about it. But I cannot mention any certain time yet.

They start rolling on the floor towards each other; this ends up with their standing back to back or kneeling back to back or with the banner veil between them. The rolling might be right over each other, but never so that their bodies coincide.

WILL: In our dreams we did this & wore the lockets although she was afraid to wear hers in the daylight.

MAGGIE: At night I am your wife; in the daytime I drudge for a woman who does not know whether she wants to be married or no. But although my hair is bound up for you and you alone to let down, Will, make no mistake, there was always something between us that summer— a fence, a veil, a muzzle on him, a wall about me, a floor between us. But I cannot mention any certain time yet. You can acquaint my parents about it any time you wish after the first of November next.

WILL fiddles. Since his letters are lost, we hear him play chords & enharmonics instead.

MAGGIE: Do not think that I would say you are soft for writing so often, for there is nothing would give me greater pleasure than to hear from you, but no matter now. I think soft turns is very scarce about you.

WILL fiddles.

MAGGIE: No, Will. Those who told you that I said I could never marry a lame boy are liars. If you have ever heard anything of the kind after me and it has given you pain, ask yourself if I have ever wanted that for you. If it does not suit you to wait so long, let me know about it, and I will make it all right.

WILL: You'll never know, Maggie, how much it's not like me to talk to a woman about that. Because my foot's deformed they think he's not a man. They'd laugh if they knew I write you a letter every day. But, Maggie, they'll come at you about the foot and what can you tell them? Why that he's not a cripple when he's on horseback, nor is he a thing soft when he has a pistol in his hand which makes all men equally tall; *(fiddles)* nor am I a Cripple when I'm driving or writing or riding I'm—our stage is a bird with wheels for wings and I'm free.

And the scene changes to early morning in Lucan with the two rival stages getting ready for the daily race to London. The convention for the stage wagons should involve at least one wheel each and a solid block of actors "inside" the coach; other actors are the sides of the road and move against the coaches to give the illusion of a journey; a sleepy TOLLGATE MAN with his gate is the first of a series of such gates which will keep stopping the stages as they gallop down to London. The drivers hitch up horses and check wheels and parcels; passengers.

CHORUS: The Opposition Stage

NED BROOKS: The Finnegan Stage. My name is Ed Brooks from Exeter. First carefully checking the wheels of my stage with a wrench I climb up determined to beat Donnelly this day, to beat him in the race to London even if it kills me.

A red haired boy makes his first appearance: TOM RYAN.

MIKE: Tom Ryan, you can't come with us today. You should be home in your father's house. Why you've been sleeping all night in Pilot's manger lad, are you stage struck?

TOM: Mike Donnelly, ask your brother if I can go with yous again today. My old man won't let any of us come near the place right now and I watched the stable for you all night, Mike?

WILL: Mike, where's the bridle for the off-horse— Ploughboy. Tom Ryan, they sneaked that away on you when you were sleeping—sure you can come, but go up the street and get us a new bridle. Knock on the shutters till they open up. You don't want him along, do you Mike, is that it?

MIKE: It's his father I'm thinking of. "The Donnellys've stolen my only son away from me, work him to death on their stage line."

WILL: Pilot's shoe is loose, Manilla then. I'll let you drive her then, see if you can control her, my arms were out of their sockets the last time she's such a puller. *(Horn sounds. TOM runs up with the new bridle.)*

MIKE: Ah, but we're having a race today I see so maybe I won't hold him in. *(The Finnegan horn blows.)* Here comes Finnegan. Put those packages with me, Will. Haw, Ploughboy. Easy does it, Manilla, there girl, there . . .

CHORUS:
Out from the yard of Levitt's Hotel
The Main Street of Lucan all quiet and still
Down the road between Goderich & London

The TOLLGATE KEEPER reaches up a cup on a stick; we hear seven pennies.

WILL: Down with that tollgate, Let us out of Lucan
Thank you, Mr. Kelly.

MIKE: Yes, we hope to surpass him
We'll win your wager,

CHORUS:
a spark in each window
people getting up

TOM: Mike Donnelly, I think the coach is a boat.

MIKE: Tom Ryan, it has wheels. Sit into the seat and you can feel the road coming up against our wheels. It's no boat you truant. Where's the sails?

TOM: I've heard Will call it a boat once and I see the sea all around us. Somehow I feel like jumping off into the water.

MIKE: Did you hear that, Will? On the way back we're putting you in a trunk for safety's sake and our own peace of mind. Where'd you buy the bridle, Tom?

TOM: At Mr Stub's store.

MIKE: Well, Will, do we turn back?

WILL: For a penny I would. That was a foolish thing to do, Tom. Don't you know who our enemies are yet? We'll take it off at Birr, the blacksmith will have one there and, Tom, tonight you must take it back to Mr Stub and tell him it was a mistake.

TOM: Why was it a mistake?

MIKE: Because we never buy anything from Mr Stub and as you charged the bridle that means he'll be after us for a debt.

CHORUS:
So early in the morning, shadows aren't yet and stars still out.
The big elm, St Patrick's, the taverns at Elginfield.

MIKE: Open up Mr. Scandrett, Let us out of Biddulph.

This chorus has several "tracks" and ribbons of sound and imagery rippling through it; there's an old doggerel song about the road; there's also a quiet voice naming the concession roads whose numbers get smaller as we get closer to London.

CHORUS:
concession 16
Proof Line Road straight down to London
Down the hill, whizzing down, down into the hollow
Rain in our faces, up the hill.

Two stages converge on one passenger.

FINNEGAN COACH: That's our passenger.

DONNELLY COACH: No, she's ours.

WOMAN: But I'm a Finnegan customer

MIKE: Too late now, ma'm, and we can't stop for we're in competition and—whree whurrah!! we're ahead of you now, Finnegan!

CHORUS:
concession 15
Proof Line Road straight down to London!
Sun's up. Travellers to where we come from
Gallop up to meet us. Up the hill down the hill
The four tavern corners. Holy Corners! *(singing)*
The taverns they lined each side of the way.
As thick as the milestones in Ireland today.
And then the farmers all thought it was fine
If they once got as far as the London Proof Line.
concession 14
Up to then any man that went for a load
concession 13
Generally spent two days on the road;
concession 12
And I hear that Sam Berryhill says to this day
That some took three—when he kept the Bluejay!
concession 11

MIKE: Gate, Mr. Walden, why so slow. Wait a minute, how'd he get through the check gate so fast

WILL: If he gets a pass, we get a pass. That's not fair.

CHORUS:
concession 8
Montgomery House, there, the bar goes east and west!
concession 6
Monoghan's, Talbot's—both bakes bread and brews beer.
concession 5
Up the hill, cross the creek, down the hill to the concession 4
River valley: McMartin's and the last tollgate

TOM: Let us into London, Mr Murrow

CHORUS:

                   & over the river
           concession 2
Past the mill, tree branch shadow, up Mount
    Hope
The Convent of the Sacred Heart

DONNELLY COACH:
            concession 1
We're turning out to pass him, he's going faster,
watch yourself, Brooks, your front wheel. He's
    fallen down on his head. Horses run away.
On his head.
The front wheel came off.
At one end of our journey, we'll stop for a while
Watch your step, sir. Take my hand, m'am.
At the City Hotel. No, the Dead House for him.

*In the conventions worked out for this accident,
BROOKS should be held upside down so that his
words come from an overturned face. CHORUS
might try some upside down speech too.*

MIKE: Oh, for God's sake, Will, he's dying.
Don't try to talk, Ned, we'll put you in our stage
and take you to a physician. *(pause)* He wants to
talk to you, Will.

BROOKS: I got the other one to come over just
when life comes to the edge-place where you
can see for ever and ever because you're neither
alive nor are you dead. I said, Bill Donnelly,
you done this to me and my wife and little
ones will curse you and I'll tell you how your
brother Mike's going to die. Fair play, neighbour.
They'll never finish scrubbing up his blood. My
God, neighbour. I'm gone. They'll never finish
scrubbing up his blood.

His body is carried away and laid on the bar.

MIKE: What did he tell you, Will.

WILL: Nothing. Nothing that matters, Mike.

MIKE: Look at them looking at us. They all think
we killed him.

WILL: Yes, Mike. Now how did we kill him?
He tightened his wheel at Lucan, but still we
managed. Maybe at Swartz's Hotel, or maybe at
the Montogomery House at the eighth concession?

MIKE: Will. I don't want to drive stage anymore.

WILL: Why?

MIKE: Odd how there is always something
happening when we're by. *(pause)* So how did
his wheel come off then?

WILL: Get your head up, my brother. My brother
what does it matter whether we killed him or
Fortune did. We might just as well have, for they
blame us anyhow. Get your head up and we'll
turn and face them.

MIKE: The boy, did you get him to do it?

WILL: *(with irony)* Oh Yes! And Mike. I also got
our father to train our horses so well that when
Brooks' passenger that was riding beside him fell
directly in front of us you were able to stop those
horses on a penny, or he'd been cut to pieces
instead of standing over there gawping at the
Donnelly brothers whose same father failed to
train one of his sons still to hold up his head
though all the world is thinking you should crawl.

*MIKE's face clears; he holds up his head and they
turn to face a crowd that is growling at them.*

CHORUS: We the undersigned jurymen
summoned upon the inquest held upon the body
of Edward Brooks do hereby agree that deceased
came to his death from injuries received by being
thrown from the Exeter Stage which was caused
by the forewheel of said stage coming off and that
the deceased came by his death

                          accidentally

*This scene dissolves into a bakeshop where a
BAKER proudly shows off a wedding cake to an
APPRENTICE.*

BAKER: Isn't that the lovely object now?

APPRENTICE: Who ordered this cake, Pa?

BAKER: Why it's for John Finnegan owns the
store up at Irishtown, he sent down for it as there
is some farmer getting his daughter married in
the vicinity. Now what did you find out about
delivery?

APPRENTICE: Went to the Western Hotel. They
say there'll be no Finnegan Stage today, the driver
fell off this morning and got himself killed. So
they said to send it with the Donnelly Line—it's
the best anyhow for moving a cake and they
leave the City Hotel at 2 o'clock.

BAKER: By golly, we'll start packing it right away
then. Get me some straw. You know I sort of hate
to see it get wrapped up in a mere brown paper
box.

A city bell rings twelve; a street fiddler plays "Buffalo Gals"; distant sounds. A penny in his cup. The CHORUS illustrate the shadows changing of the buildings near the City Hotel.

CHORUS:
Shadows of the building and the trees along the white road
Disappear at noon.
Sun, you golden stage, make our shadows
Passengers again to night, now longer and longer in
the stream
We all lie dreaming in

BAKER: What can I do for you, sir.

McKELLAR: I'm the new stage driver for Finnegan's stage and I've come to collect the cake his brother ordered here.

BAKER: Well, golly, now, we were led to believe that The Finnegan Stage wasn't running today. But we found a way to send the cake.

McKELLAR: What way?

BAKER: The Opposition Stage. They're real good at carrying cakes. I've had good reports from customers whereas you people seem to sit on them or—it's too late. They'll have left town by now. With the cake.

McKELLAR: Look you old gossoon, do you not know there's a war on between them and us? I'll catch up to them and I'll get that cake back. *(The BAKER and his BOY run out of the shop after the STAGE DRIVER in protest.)*

Already simply set up: MAGGIE'S FATHER washing feet in the coal scuttle containing the block of ice; his sister & MAGGIE. Plus another aunt waiting to take MAGGIE away.

FAT LADY: Ever since you came home, Maggie, from service at the English priest's you're so slow in doing things. You was two hours I swear looking for these eggs. Take this switch and keep the flies off your father while I finish packing your trunk.

MAGGIE: Packing my trunk, is it. Where am I going then?

AUNT THERESA: Maggie, you're welcome to come back with me to Limerick and stay as long as you like where that fellow won't be bothering you.

MAGGIE: What fellow won't be bothering me?

FATHER: Cripple. Whoever was playing that fiddle under your window last night till all hours, whoever wrote me a lawyer's letter asking for your hand, who came to my door and took me by the beard to tell me how old you are.

MAGGIE: And how old am I? Am I not of age All Souls' Day, Father?

FATHER: I don't know, maybe you'd better call Father Brennan to look it up, in the baptismal register, have you? *(pause)* But All Souls' Day doesn't change the spots on Cripple, he's a Donnelly and no girl of mine's of age who's thinking of marrying that Cripple. I'd rather see you going to your grave.

MAGGIE: Father, if only you'd speak a little faster. Faster! What have you got against Will Donnelly, tell me now, Father, you've never told me. Is it the father killing the man at the bee?

FATHER: Keep switching the flies off of me, will you? It's evidence not fit for the ears of either a young girl or an old one. He's been the mastermind of a gang in this neighbourhood and fleeces of wool, post offices, derailing a train have been some of that gang's amusements for the last four years until now high and mighty he starts his own stage line.

FAT LADY: Brother, this girl'll never understand I'm afraid and it's a secret place we'll have to put such a girl. Her brother is getting married to the proper sort, but no she has to cross battle lines. Have you no gratitude for your upbringing, girl?

MAGGIE: All the money I've ever earned as a servant girl you've received, Father. I emptied chamberpots so you could buy two new cows. Yes, look at what my brother's marrying. All Mary Egan talks about is cows. Will Donnelly's the only young man around here with brains in his head who didn't go into the priesthood, and no girl is to take a look at him, is it?

AUNT THERESA: A fine priest that lame devil would have made.

FATHER: Theresa, see if Martin's got the cart hitched up. Maggie, you're right. Will is a clever boy. Clever at getting the forewheel of a stage to roll off so the driver gets killed. Yes. But he is a Donnelly and they are to be left alone. They don't dig with the right foot. They always are digging with the wrong foot. Since Cripple's threatening to come and kidnap her—yes Maggie—Theresa, tell Martin to drive over to Finnegan's Corners, but when it gets dark to turn & take her down to Gallagher's. That's right by the Donnellys and they'll never think of looking there.

MAGGIE: I'll run to him now. Will! Will! Come and rescue me, take me away.

She is pursued; there is a struggle and we see her next taken away tied in a net. We are now moving closer to FINNEGAN's store at Irishtown; first to a tollgate house where a bag of pennies is poured out for counting. The counting of the money into a tin box goes under the dialogue like the road itself.

MOTHER: Come, children, help your father count the take at the tollgate today. The shadows are getting so long they're joining together anymore travellers up or down the road, Sam?

The privy cleaner or CESSMAN comes towards us; he is whistling "Buffalo Gals."

TOLLMAN: Just foot travellers. There's that old fellow makes a living cleaning out privies. Good night there, you look dusty.

CESSMAN: Oh I doesn't mind the dust, thank thee, Mr. Scandrett.

CHILD: He always whistles the same tune doesn't he.

MOTHER: Heading north down into Biddulph. What was all that racket today with the second stage that went through.

The tollgate scene begins to move forward and dissolve.

TOLLMAN: They were chasing the Donnelly Stage. The Donnellys got away on them with something. A cake. A wedding cake.

We are in FINNEGAN's store up at Finnegan's Corners.

FINNEGAN: No Donnellys are allowed on Finnegan premises ever again no, neither his store nor his tavern nor his very privy.

MIKE: Even so, Mr. Finnegan, an express parcel from the Forest City Confectionery on Horton Street. Where shall I set it down?

FINNEGAN: I said get out, Mike Donnelly.

MIKE: Now, now, Mr. Finnegan, I do believe it is a cake. I'll just set it down on the floor here and

that will be Cash on Delivery two dollars, twenty-seven and a half cents.

FINNEGAN: Don't you dare tell me it had to be by your line that cake come, when I've got my own stage line, now get that bloody parcel out of here.

MIKE: Well, it is a puzzle but the upshot of it was that our Opposition Stage was preferred. Twenty-seven a half cents plus two dollars. Careful, Finnegan, it's a cake.

FINNEGAN: Is it now, well it's a *(He kicks it around the shop.)*

MIKE: I see how it is, Mr Finnegan. We have to pay for the cake, do we. You should know all about that, you're the bailiff of the Division Court up here, and another thing before I say Goodnight—don't take any more passengers to Crediton. We bought the rights there, you have not got them. Good evening, Mr. Finnegan.

FINNEGAN backs him out of the store with a gun. BILL & MARY DONOVAN come forward behind the dissolving FINNEGAN with a quilt which is their wedding bed.

BILL: Come to bed, Mary. I'm told it's our wedding night.

MARY: Well, you're the boss now, but it did just cross my mind.

BILL: What crossed your mind?

MAGGIE's FATHER is quietly washing his feet in the tub WILLIAM DONNELLY put the ice block in.

MARY: Did you never hear of the custom of leaving the bride alone for three nights.

BILL: Yes, I have, now why don't you get into the bed?

MARY: It did just cross my mind that—they'll come looking here for Maggie.

BILL: *(yawning)* Who'll come looking—

MARY: Bill Donnelly and his gang.

BILL: Well, they won't find her. She was in the cellar during the wedding, but she's crying in the garret at Gallagher's now. Father keeps moving her, and Will Donnelly just keeps missing her. You should of seen the letter he wrote Pa.

WILL: Dear friend, my sole business last night (yes, I was in the crowd myself) was to have satisfaction for some of your mean low talk to your daughter that never deserved it. I want you to understand, dear sir, that I will have my revenge. You or your son will be prepared to receive me and my Adventurers before long again, and if old friend I want it impressed on your mind that if the business must be done on the way to church I can get any amount of men to do it so you may just as well stop getting yourself into trouble first or last.

MARY: Sending his gang of scoundrels into your father's house and pretending it was a tavern and them constables was searching for a horse-thief when all the time it's Maggie they want.

BILL: So come on then.

MARY: Is she never to be married off then, or what is to be done with her?

BILL: She'll either marry one of the Gallagher boys who's soft on her by next Saturday, or then it's Lent and it's too late to get married so I think Father plans to let the Sisters take care of her. If I were her—

MARY: (getting into bed) Good, then this nonsense will be over. Galloping around the countryside trying to kidnap your lovely sister because he loves her. She doesn't really love that Cripple, does she?

BILL: Mary, she does love him, and I don't blame her for it. I do blame her for not making a run for it, but I suppose she can't.

MARY: Oh a woman can never do that. The man would never marry her then. How can you say she could really love him?

BILL: Mary, she does. If ever I saw love. Not like us. Your mother and my father put us together like a pair of cattle.

Shivaree serenaders gather in the shadows.

MARY: Speaking of cows, Bill Donovan, what sort is your cows?

BILL: Don't you like my cows?

MARY: I never saw such miserable calves as them two you had in the yard today. Maybe it's late they were

---

shivaree—a raucous mock-welcome for newlyweds.

BILL: Cows, Mary, always cows.

MARY: That's how the Egans and the Trehys got where they are now. Cows

BILL: And where might that be now?

MARY: Why I think one of them's in bed with a young bull, or is that not what you think you are sir?

BILL: Ah, Mary

MARY: Take it back then that your sister really loves Will Donnelly, that cripple and devil.

BILL: She never loves him, I was wrong, it's a lie.

MARY: That's better now— (knocking) Hark! There's somebody going to shivaree us.

VOICES: Shivaree!

MARY: Get them to go away. Give them some whiskey, Mother of God, it is the Donnellys, Bill.

MIKE: Tell us where Maggie is and we'll go away.

BILL: (at window) Boys, she's not here now and if she were she'd say to leave her alone.

MIKE: Oh no you don't. We got a letter here from Maggie. She says she's being held against her will and to come and get her.

BILL: Mary, shall I tell them she's at Gallagher's and get them off our backs?

MARY: (running and stopping his mouth at the window) You tell them where your sister's hidden & I'll withhold bed privileges. I'll ask for my dower third of the farm back and my red cow with the white ear back.

BILL: She's not here you blackguards. Off with you, Bill Donnelly.

Silence. Husband & wife return to bed. Then a blast of sound. Choose from buzzsaw sounds, guns firing, drums, horns, fiddles, maskers, circle of dancers around a bonfire, maskers entering bridal chamber and lifting up MARY.

MASKER: We found Maggie, Bill. She was under her brother's bed all the time. Is this her, Bill? Quick, for God's sakes, we can hardly lift her off the floor.

WILL'S VOICE: No, that's not Maggie, that's too fat for Maggie. That's probably Mary.

BILL & MARY crouch as the sounds melt into the newspaper's account.

MARY: Mother of God, there goes the chimney.

CHORUS:
RURAL ROUGHS ON RAMPAGE
ATTEMPTED ABDUCTION IN BIDDULPH

MAGGIE: *(in lay sister's working costume, with attendant nun)* I wasn't there of course. I was too much in love to unravel their cunning, and so— we lost sight of each other.

CHORUS:
THE BIDDULPH   DISGRACEFUL
KU KLUX   CONDUCT OF
                              LOVE-SICK SWAIN

Newspaper boy, "extra, read all about it," bulletin readers in front of newspaper office, &c.

CHORUS:
HOW HE WENT ABOUT IT
AND HOW HE FAILED TO SUCCEED

MAGGIE: And a needless enemy was my brother who before had been our ally as much as he dared, but after the serenade

BILL: Except to say hello I don't speak to that man. Speak to Will Donnelly—no, and Mary and me have the very next farm to the Donnelly place now, no, William Donnelly, no. No.

CHORUS:
THE MIDDLE AGES REVIVED
LOVE'S LABOUR LOST EVIDENTLY

WILL: *(with whip)* Read that cheap newspaper heading again.

CHORUS: THE MIDDLE AGES REVIVED

WILL: That's enough, thank you. Middle Ages Revived by whom? Me or them? We were hauled up in court, but I got off I suppose because Maggie had asked us to take her away. My God, I was never to see her again. And I'm not in the least sorry I tried to steal her away if that's what you call a life for a woman. *(to MAGGIE'S FATHER who is in bare feet at the tub)* And I'm not in the least sorry for any thing that happens from now on in that happens to those who try the same trick on me as you pulled on that girl that was once my sweetheart. I'll switch the flies off you you old fool.

He has taken MAGGIE'S FATHER up & is about to whip him, but then throws him down & chases him out of the theatre or attacks his feet with a toy whip & spins him out of the room.

HALF CHORUS: Question. The Convent of the Sacred Heart *(Sung: "incense" music as before)* At Mount Hope on Richmond Street, why does the Opposition Stage always slow down?

HALF CHORUS: Answer. Oh I can answer that. When Will Donnelly is the driver.

MAGGIE: He senses that I am drudging here in the kitchen of the Sisters' house. And when he is not the driver he has told the others to slow down at the chestnut tree because he knows that I wait each day for the sound. In the morning, in the evening—down the hill, past the mill and over Brough's Bridge until you can't hear the wheels or the hooves anymore. You hear the other stage. You hear your own heart. I scrub the stones of the convent yard as close to the gate as I can, but it is no use—the gate is locked. Someday, in the middle of the night, there will come such a knocking at that gate and it will be smashed open, and the nuns will run hither and thither screeching because my husband has come for me and in my wedding dress I will enter his coach to drive up his road forever. I love William Donnelly.

As MAGGIE lies dead before them, the MOTHER SUPERIOR confers with the sisters as to where she should be buried.

NUN: Mother Superior Finnegan, Maggie Donovan is dead. What shall we do with her? *(They kneel.)*

MOTHER: What were the last words she said, Sister Feeny?

NUN: Her last words were

MAGGIE & NUN: I love William Donnelly.

MOTHER: Sister Feeny, where do you think she should be buried.

NUN: *(pause, then crisply and swiftly)* By William Donnelly's grave up in Biddulph.

MOTHER: Sister Gallagher?

NUN: In the convent yard where the rest of us lie.

MOTHER: Sister Egan?

NUN: In the convent yard, Mother Superior, but close by the gate.

MOTHER: And that is where Maggie Donovan lies buried.

MAGGIE: I love William Donnelly.

WILLIAM DONNELLY sings a verse of "Buffalo Gals."

WILL:
I asked her if she'd be my wife
Be my wife, be my wife
She'd make me happy all my life
If she stood by my side.

CHORUS: End of Act One.

ACT TWO

Actors spin tops, dance, recite poems until this recitation of poems slowly fades into TOM RYAN standing up on the bar and letting us see the story from a new angle.

TOM RYAN: And I'll recite you a poem I learnt once at school while we're waiting for the two o'clock stage to Lucan which I may have the honour of driving, young though I am, since the Donnelly boys have to put in a appearance in court.

Waiting for Pa

Three little forms in the twilight grey
Scanning the shadows across the way:
Six little eyes, four black, two blue,
Brimful of love and happiness too,
Watching for Pa

Soon joyous shouts from the window-seat
And eager patter of childish feet
Gay musical chimes ring through the hall
A manly voice responds to the call
"Welcome papa!"

The actor playing NED RYAN, TOM's father, now proceeds to growl drunkenly.

TOM RYAN: Well ladies and gentlemen, my home life wasn't like that quite, and since I'm said to be one of the reasons for the Donnelly Tragedy, you don't understand me unless you understand what waiting for my Pa was like. Tom Ryan is my name, this is my Pa, here's my Ma and a couple of my sisters. What are we doing?

We are all waiting one cold winter morning for Pa—to get his rump off a chest that contains bread, cheese, tea and other necessaries of life which he refuses to let us have

TOM RYAN starts to saw a rail.

NED RYAN: They might cook it and poison me.

TOM RYAN: It's a cold day outside, but there's no fire in the stove because—

NED: You're ruining me with all this wasting of my substance. Stop the sawing, Tom stop sawing that rail! or I'll take this ax to you.

MRS RYAN: It isn't enough to be starving but we must freeze to death as well.

NED: Tell your son to stop sawing that rail and to clear out of here. *(starting to give chase)*

TOM: Oh I admit I was pert and I should have stopped sawing, but I couldn't sit there and see my sisters and my mother shivering much longer.

NED: Get out of the house you bastard brat, talking back to your pa.

TOM: Don't hit me Pa. I was only. I will go and I will never come back, and I stepped out onto the road and looked in the snow for somebody to take me in: Who will take in the barefoot Ryan Boy?

The actors set up the Roman Line gamut of Part One as the road he will run up and down.

Barry?	Trehy?	
Feeny?	O'Halloran?	*He is rejected*
Cahill?	Cassleigh?	*by everyone in*
McCann?	Flynn?	*various ways:*
Egan?	Marksy?	*backs turned,*
Quinn?	Farl?	*clubs, kicks &c.*
Gallagher?	Duffy?	
Clancy?	Donovan?	

Bell and jug sound for the tavern and the church; then MRS DONNELLY comes towards the rejected boy and accepts him.

MRS DONNELLY: Donnelly.

---

*the Roman Line gamut of Part One—in Sticks & Stones Reaney frequently shows the Donnellys caught between the lines of their Catholic neighbours, two parallel rows of actors "like the line-up of a reel."

We see her at the end of a corridor of people. We renew her acquaintance now.

CHORUS: Yes, the Donnellys took him in.

JAMES DONNELLY, the Younger, sitting invalid in a chair by the stove should also register here. His mother has just finished giving him medicine.

MRS DONNELLY: Tom Ryan, climb up on the stove there and stop your shivering till I get these dry feet on you; here's a pair of Tom's pants to put on those you got on are drenched, what devil has your father got into that he drives you out barefoot in this weather or was there a reason, Tom?

TOM: I was only sawing a rail, Mrs Donnelly, to get a fire on so we would be warm.

MRS DONNELLY: Get behind the stove now and hide in the woodbox, your father I can see in the lid of my tea kettle coming in our gate. Can you not get the key to the pantry away from him while he's asleep?

TOM: He sleeps with it tied round his leg, Mrs Donnelly.

MRS DONNELLY: Well there are four of you and one of him, he's no giant, give him clout and get the key some fine day Good day to you, Ned Ryan?

TOM: But he's always got the ax.

NED: Good morning, Mrs Donnelly. Have you seen my madcap, scapegrace harum scarum son Tom about?

MRS DONNELLY: No madcap, scapegrace, harum scarum son of yours has run in here, Ned Ryan.

NED: Then I just heard your stove say something about an ax.

MRS DONNELLY: My stove talks a lot to itself, Ned Ryan, what with the kettle getting up steam and the wood crackling inside and the wind in the chimney. Do you not see my stove has a name? She's called Princess and she just saw the ax you're holding in your hand. I'd have said something myself at the strangeness of a father with an ax in his hand.

He backs up and slides off; MRS DONNELLY returns to sewing. TOM gets up on top of the stove (bar) and continues.

TOM: Pretty soon, he'd drag me back home again and say he'd try to be decent to us, but it didn't last and as I grew older if I could I helped the Donnelly boys with their stage, and if I couldn't I stayed home and caused trouble. Like—I set fire to the barn once with him—Pa—in it, he barely got out in time and he thought it was lightning, and I pissed in his whiskey after drinking half of it, oh my God was he mad at me. *(Violin screech—a poltergeist bottle flies through the air, disappears and we hear it smash.)* Yes, I can make things like that happen if I don't abuse myself for a month. It's like having a fit and I can will it that I'm going to have a fit. One day I asked my mother if it was true I had been born. And she said

MOTHER: Yes, Tom Ryan, you were born.

He starts to pack a carpet bag.

NED: And where might you be going, great high and mighty one with your clothes barely covering your thin little parsnip of a rump and your hair like a snipe's nest on fire, oh little runt of mine.

TOM: My mother here tells me it's St Bridget's Eve and tomorrow I'm old enough so I'm leaving forever.

MRS RYAN: Oh son, where will you stay?

TOM: *(pause)* Donnellys.

MRS RYAN: Could you not pick a better place than that den of everything wicked.

TOM: If you want to know Mother, there's love there.

NED: Your poor father over here, Tom. Will you not give him a look, will you shame him before all our neighbours?

TOM: I'm not going to hang around here anymore and hear you say mean low things to my mother.

MRS RYAN: Would you live with people whose sons tried to carry a poor girl off, Tom?

TOM: Yes, because she wanted to be carried off from a house that was worse than this.

MRS RYAN: Could you not get a job in the town building the new lunatic hospital they're putting up?

TOM starts his speech now and walks into the GEORGE STUB scene.

NED: It's into the lunatic hospital he should be going. *(growling)*

TOM: But of course the first thing I did to the Donnellys was to bring them trouble in the shape of the bridle I bought for them on tick at Mr Stub's store.

STUB: Tom Ryan, lad, just ask your boss William Donnelly, gentleman, when in the name of Heaven is he going to pay for the bridle you tapped on my shutters for last summer?

TOM: Mr Stub, it was a mistake, and we brought it back.

STUB: I know that, lad, but I didn't accept the return, it's used and I want my money.

TOM: We paid for the use.

STUB: Not by agreement, that's not the way I do business but I tell you, lad, I'm suing William Donnelly, gentleman, in Division Court next Tuesday so be warned.

TOM: Aw, sue away. We'll never pay you for it, you old skinflint. But he kept summoning Mr Donnelly, sending summonses and we just wiped our ass with them. I used to ride up and down on the stage, they gave me a cap to wear. There was another lad hung around the Donnellys a lot—Will Farl. Some of the people were shocked that he got on with the Donnellys so well.

The two boys crouch by the Donnelly stove; MRS DONNELLY is sewing while JAMES DONNELLY JR sleeps in a rocking chair.

WILL FARL: Why aren't you sitting still, Tom, does your shirt itch you?

TOM: Old man beat me last night, my back's all welted up.

MRS DONNELLY: Tommy Ryan and Will Farl, what were we talking about just now—yes, you say that you'll help my sons against their enemies, what kind of help do my sons need against what kind of enemies?

TOM: Oh—help.

MRS DONNELLY: Wouldn't it be wise to consult us first before you go helping. *(train whistle)* What is the latest sample of your helping my sons, please tell their mother?

WILL FARL: We've just put a log across the railway down at Granton.

MRS DONNELLY: Now, just how does that help Will & Mike?

TOM: Why don't you know George Stub, your Will's arch enemy, is coming back from the fair at St Mary's tonight. Most women would have screamed here but

MRS DONNELLY: Is he coming back from the fair at St Mary's now, why Tom and Will Farl, my husband Mr Donnelly's at the fair too. You wouldn't want him to be train-wrecked, would you?

TOM: There's lots of time, we'll take the logs off, Mrs Donnelly. See the welts, Will Farl?

WILL FARL: You know I remember my father whaling me like that. And people ask me why I like to stay the Donnellys' so much.

TOM: *(train whistle)* We'd better get a move on. Will Farl there's the train. So why is it you like to stay at the Donnellys' so much then?

WILL FARL: They killed my father.

They run off; train whistle; MRS DONNELLY turns to her patient and says:

MRS DONNELLY: Were you listening, James Donnelly the Younger, or are you still asleep from the medicine the doctor gave you.

JAMES JR: Oh mother, I'm still asleep from the medicine the doctor gave me.

MRS DONNELLY: Good, because it's time you had another dose of it.

JAMES: Mother, I won't take it. *(pause)* I won't take it unless

MRS DONNELLY: Unless what, high and mighty.

JAMES: Where's the saw? Let me hold it in my hand here. And I'll *(She gets the saw. Gives him medicine. Sleepily he continues)* I'll pull his beard out.

An actor sitting on the side benches with his fingers drumming on wood suggests the rain pouring down outside.

MRS DONNELLY: Hsst. There's a whirlwind outside and the sky is dark. Your father's late home from the fair. Maybe he'll bring you something James though you're a trifle big and old for a bauble and did you pull his beard out in this big fight you had with him.

JAMES: Ah, *(in his sleep)* it fell out of him. By God, I'll knock your brains out, there's no constable in Lucan able to take me.

MRS DONNELLY: When I get you on your feet, my son, it's off to the priest and you're taking the pledge. It's either the water wagon or smash and when the smash comes your father and I won't be able to help you one little bit.

JAMES: Where's Will and where's Mike?

MRS DONNELLY: Where else would they be, but driving their stage up and down in this rain.

JAMES: Where's John and Bob and Tom?

MRS DONNELLY: Out plowing. Tom went up to the blacksmith's.

JAMES: Why isn't Pat home helping us fight Finnegan?

MRS DONNELLY: Why isn't he? Have you asked him sure enough and get him into trouble. Is that why you came back from Michigan to get us all into trouble?

JAMES: No. No. I came to help Will and Mike smash Finnegan. Where's Father

MRS DONNELLY: He's just coming into the yard this very minute and if you're not quiet and good I'll tell him on you. Mr Donnelly I'm surprised to see you home from the fair at all.

MR DONNELLY: I am myself. There was a log across the rails. How'd you know about that? *(pause)* How's our first one?

MRS DONNELLY: Mr Donnelly, Doctor Quarry says—and he knows this himself for he was told—that even if we get him to stop the drink he's got only two more years to live.

MR DONNELLY: It's his lungs. And they're bad. How is he now then?

JAMES: Never felt better in my life. I'm going into Lucan.

MR & MRS DONNELLY: No, you're not. *(They hold him down till he falls asleep.)*

MRS DONNELLY: And what's that you've brought us home from the fair to give to a little

one perhaps some time. *(He gives her a top and she spins it. There is a whipstick that comes with it which she uses.)* I wonder how much longer they can all keep going, Jim?

MR DONNELLY: Stub was on the train.

MRS DONNELLY: And I knew that too. The things I've heard this afternoon, Mr Donnelly, and I was at no fair.

MR DONNELLY: Jim, says Stub, Jim—

STUB: *(train whistle)* Jim, thought I saw you back here coming back to see what in hell's holding up this train. Jim—if you and your boys get me Ward Three next election *(pause)* and you alone can do it—I don't care how, tell them not to vote or vote for my man who's going to be an Irish Catholic, Jim, yes—if you can promise me that, Finnegan will stop running his stage wagons tomorrow.

MRS DONNELLY: Yes, and my husband said—

MR DONNELLY: Nothing. We're promised long ago to Mr Scatcherd.

MRS DONNELLY: And you are so promised

MR DONNELLY: And yet

MRS DONNELLY: *(whipping the top)* Yes. It would be nice to stop, but we can't oh no we must keep on spinning and spinning, Mr Donnelly, because if we stop spinning we'll fall down and over and we hit them and they hit us and we—one day—our whip-arm's broke off. Go back to him and say yes!

MR DONNELLY: Never!

TOM: Mother and Father, wake Jim up will you? There's a fight up town and Will and Mike can't get the stage past Levitt's.

MRS DONNELLY: Your brother's not fit to go out anymore, Tom. Hush . . .

JAMES: No, Mother. The medicine worked. I'm well. Father . . . . Get my horse Tom.

MR & MRS DONNELLY: Get back in that chair.

JAMES: *(escaping them)* You heard what Tom said. Every man's needed, my brother's in a fight!

MR DONNELLY: Take your coat, Jim. At least put something on your back.

MRS DONNELLY: Take your hat, it's rain—he took the saw.

MR DONNELLY: Come back here, Tom and Jim. What's he got the saw for? *(Exit)*

FINNEGAN: Now I can explain the saw. Exactly a year ago, Thursday, September the 20th, 1874, someone took my stage wagon after dark and sawed it to hundreds of small pieces. I built a new stage. 1875. Today, Friday, September 20th—someone took that new stage out of my stable, dragged it up the road a piece and sawed it into even more pieces. There are to be no stages on the road, but Donnelly stages, are there? The Donnelly tribe is getting to be a terror to the neighbourhood.

JOHN MACDONALD approaches the bartender and buys a stage ticket. His MOTHER and sister, NORAH, approach for the same reason.

MACDONALD: A ticket, one way to Lucan please.

BARTENDER: Which line will you go on . . .

NORAH: Two tickets the same to Lucan please, for myself, sir, and my mother here. The Donnelly Line.

MACDONALD: Not the Donnelly Line for your brother, Norah, nor for your son, Mother, but the Finnegan Line, please.

NORAH: Please yourself, brother John, if you want your bones shaken to a jelly by Mr Finnegan's drivers. We'll be in Lucan before you.

MACDONALD: I want the two of you to get your money back and come on the same coach as your brother and son is going on. The wagon you're going on carries away more than my mother and my sister, for it bears away sister's reputation and any love for her son my old mother has ever had.

MOTHER: Will you lower your voice in a public place, my son John Macdonald. Why you've palled around with Donnellys ever since you can remember, what have you suddenly determined against them?

MACDONALD: Mother, you know and I know what Norah's up to with their Cripple now he's lost the Thompson girl.

MOTHER: Don't you dare call him a cripple, or there's people here standing'll see me haul off and give you the clout you so long for. Let Norah decide the man she'll marry, one thing, it can't be you, you get such rages into yourself about your sisters, it's the land you're worried about isn't it, that father likes William Donnelly a lot, not just that Norah does, is that not so?

MACDONALD: Your husband and my father make me wonder sometimes if I am his wife's husband's son.

As the quarreling Macdonalds leave the barroom, the other actors form two coaches indicating that we have dissolved into the street outside the City Hotel, but just before this happens MRS MACDONALD raises her arms and says:

MOTHER: No wonder he likes Will Donnelly. At least Will Donnelly can talk straight when it comes to naming his relatives. I've even heard him call his mother his mother and his father his father, but with you John, your mother, why your mother is liable to be your grandfather's daughter and your sister, she's not your sister, she's your unborn grandchild's great aunt.

And out the Macdonalds go to immediately return as if we then saw them step out of the hotel and go to their respective coaches. We are getting ready for a decisive journey up the road, this time to some startling new developments.

MACDONALD: Mother, I'm sorry, but this wouldn't happen if Donnelly would just leave us and Norah alone.

They shout at each other through the windows of the stages, then the Finnegan horn, the tollgate and penny convention, the slight up and down movement of the two stages' passengers indicate that they're off!

NORAH: Brother, who's been at you? I'll tell you I'm proud he's in love with me, can you not remember the love you once felt for himself when you were always over there . . .

MOTHER: Mrs Donnelly had more to do with bringing you up than I did, now look at you. Sure, Father's given you one hundred acres already, he's not made of gold, leave him alone about his property.

MACDONALD: When I get home, Norah, I'm going to dig up all the potatoes in the front field you've been planting and I'll cut down the orchard mark my words if I see you talking to him when we get to Lucan, it's lucky it is there's no Cripple driving today I suppose I'd see you both up on the driver's seat with him. There go the Cripple lovers, folks, my mother and my sister.

NORAH: Oh, Mother, give me the parcels, which one is the iron we bought I'll crack him one on his skull.

MOTHER: Pay no heed to him, darling, I just hope and pray he doesn't get up his courage at the taverns and try to drag us off at a tollgate, but we're outdistancing him I see, here we are shut up in a box with four wheels and the window blinds down for the heat and you can hear the drivers cursing each other through the roof. You have to pretend not to hear.

NORAH: A ride to Lucan is a sentimental education I can tell you. You'd hear Finnegan's driver say— *(trumpet)* hold your ears. I guess only men would understand why they'd have to get down and fight about that, once a Donnelly said, "And your father wasn't married either, McKellar." To which came the reply: *(trumpet)* to which Mike Donnelly said:

NORAH & MIKE: "You'll not drive the stage another morning with your life, McKellar."

MOTHER: I don't mind hearing a good bout of swearing if they're really good at it, but it does slow up the journey which is somewhat more important, and that last remark by my future son-in-law.

NORAH: I think it was Mike said that, Mother.

MOTHER: Well, whoever it was, that would lead to both stage drivers putting in an appearance at a local Justice of the Peace along the road called Squire Ferguson.

WILL: Squire Ferguson, I wish to lay a complaint against Peter McKellar re perjury in the information he laid against me and Mike last July the third, 1875.

SQUIRE: Mr Donnelly, I don't think you can do that.

WILL: Oh yes you can. Victoria, 1859, Chapter 1, subsection 6. Give me your manual, sir, and I'll show

NORAH: When Finnegan's witnesses would try to go down to the courthouse, Will Donnelly would get them arrested somehow at Birr for disorderly conduct. I bought him a couple of old law books for a Christmas box, and it was what we called the game of information and complaint

or Legal Amusements. And if two of the Donnelly boys got arrested why their mother had had the foresight to have seven sons, so it would be Tom or Bob or John would drive if they'd snared my Will or Mike into their clutches.

MOTHER: And they'd be at it again.

A brief horn and fiddle contest. Finnegan's horn taunts are returned with interest by Donnelly fiddle sounds.

MAN ON FINNEGAN'S STAGE: I used to ride both lines and turn about and you could see what was going to happen, sooner or later . . . oh, there were happy times too I observed in my going back and forth. I can remember the whole Donnelly family going down the road on their way to Bothwell to get Jennie married off. Or the day Mike all dressed up went down to London to get married to Ellen Haines, her father kept the City Hotel there. Mike didn't show up for a week after that, too tired, still abed at two in the afternoon his brothers said, stage drivers make good husbands, all the jouncing up and down. God knows, but sooner or later . . .

NORAH: Yes stage drivers do make good husbands. I was so proud of the way William drove and acted to his customers and I knew then that my life with him was like this journey. Through it all we would eventually come to the St Nicholas Hotel here off the road and out of the storm. My old mother's fallen asleep. Where does she dream she is?

LADY ON THE OTHER STAGE: Asleep! Not me, I keep thinking when the wheels will they come off, when will the wheels come off, oh Mother, when will the wheels come have those Donnellys loosened the wheels?

CHORUS: fur hats in winter, straw hats in summer

MAN: our collar limp, our hat crushed, our watch stopped, our brain dizzy with vertigo, the elastic band of our wig snapped, our false teeth displaced in their setting, curses not loud but deep,

MIKE: Gee Ploughboy Gee Pilot

CHORUS: were carriers of passengers upon a stage or covered wagon from the City of London to the Village of Lucan

FINNEGAN: Hrup hrup there you slow beasts, don't try to beat me at the bridge, Donnelly, there's not room for the both of us.

MIKE: There's two sides to a road, Finnegan.

CHORUS: the defendant, William Donnelly, did not safely & securely carried upon the said on the said

MIKE: Oil your wheels, Finnegan.

The "coaches" are getting closer to each other & are blurring in outline just as things do before they collide.

FINNEGAN: Your half of the road's the ditch, Donnelly, *(horn & fiddle)*

CHORUS:
August the 31st, 1875
maliciously ran races with other stage coaches

MAN: I think that Finnegan kept as close as he could to the Hotel side to keep Donnelly from getting to the Hotel before him.

MIKE: The ladies wanted a drink of water at the hotel. He made a quick turn as quick a turn as ever I seen. I had ten passengers three in the driver's seat besides myself   seven inside

Using the whole team of actors, suggest the collision.

CHORUS: plaintiff was thereby wounded & injured in consequence on the said road and suffered great pain and expense in and about the cure of her wounds and injuries. And the plaintiffs—Mrs Louisa Lindsay & Miss Jennie Lindsay—claim five hundred dollars *(groaning)* damages.

MIKE: What did you do that for, Finnegan? *(whip)*

FINNEGAN: *(whip)* Mike Donnelly, I'd do it again like as not until and again till I've run you off this road.

The two stage drivers confront each other among a pile of coach fragments and accident victims slowly re-assembling themselves; but the scene is darkening, a bell rings, MIKE DONNELLY's face grows red from some fire he is looking at.

FINNEGAN: I said to myself under my breath why in God's name is Mike Donnelly's face turning so red. *(turning around)* He's thinking he's looking at my stables going up in flames with five horses alive in them.

FINNEGAN runs out into a blazing stable door as the tollgate between Birr & Elginfield is set up

with the money pouring out for counting of the day's take.

FINNEGAN: Mother of God help me save my poor beasts from Donnelly's fire.

TOLLGATER: Guess that's all for today, let's count her up, sunset's hanging on there quite a while. Good night to you, sir. You're our last traveller for the day.

TRAVELLER: That's not the sunset by the way.

As this scene develops there should be well-spaced red glares that build till the Donnelly Boys in a photograph scene are surrounded by Hell with a mob of farmers in front of them with sharp hayrakes.

SOLO: *(sings)* Patrick Finnegan's stables burning

CHORUS: Dies irae dies illa *(ecclesiastical)*

SOLO: Solvet Finnegan in favilla

WIFE: Sam and me's been seeing quite a few red glows in the sky north of here lately every night.

TRAVELLER: Oh it's them Donnellys, another barn they've set fire to if it's a friend of Finnegan, burned down Pat Finnegan's stable last week with six horses in it burnt up alive.

TOLLGATER: That's one step up from loosening wheels and having you up in court for assault and battery, isn't it.

TRAVELLER: A considerable step indeed. I guess you see the Donnelly boys every day?

TOLLGATER: Twice a day regular as clock-work—their coach, Finnegan's coach down to town; except one day last week when both the stages were awful late and then part of the Finnegan wagon limped by, and then two thirds of the Donnelly conveyance and then the rest of the Finnegan and then the handwheels of the it was a Armageddon of a road catastrophe I can tell you.

WIFE: That night we saw our first red glow.

Three or more FARMERS come up to listen with hayrakes, big wooden spikes on them: lanterns.

TOLLGATER: And I can tell you ladies and gentlemen, when the other Finnegan stable got burnt up in Clandeboye why there was people said—what next?

WIFE:
What next indeed, Sam. The Maclean's Hotel where Finnegan ties up his stage, someone got into their kitchen and broke every dish and cup and teapot and soup tureen Mrs Maclean had to her name.

SOLO:
William Donnelly's stables burn too

CHORUS:
Tuba Finnegan spargens sonum
Per sepulchram regionum
Coget Biddulph ante thronum

CHORUS:
Oh them Donnellys

FARMER ONE: Is it all the members of the family, the mother and the father?

TOLLGATER: There's some say as that they called the oldest of the boys back from where he's been hiding out in Michigan—James Donnelly the Younger—and he drinks you see, and they just sort of let him loose at night

FARMER TWO: There's others say after the outrage at Walker's Hotel where they cut the tongues out of the stage horses there . . .

ALL: Cut the tongues out of the horses!

FARMER TWO: God yes, have you not heard— Finnegan went to hitch up on Monday morning and his horses were all—hacked open, dying or dead, and they had to be shot; the farrier said— put them out of their misery and there was a whole bunch in the village said—lynch Tom Donnelly or Will or Mike or Jim, yes, Jim he's the one and it's Bob who sets the fires and it's Will who plans it all.

WILL & MIKE drive up to the gate.

TOLLGATER: Toll there, travellers. Oh—it's you

WILL: Good evening, Mr Scandrett. Mrs Scandrett. *(pause)* I said Mr Scandrett—Good evening. *(pause)* Mr Scandrett, there's a lady passenger felt under the weather at Swartz's Hotel coming up from London today and she asked us if we could come and pick her up down there later in the evening.

WIFE: Sam, don't let them through, Sam. They're lying. They're out for night mischief.

FARMERS: Sam, we'll help you keep the firebugs out of our township. Nobody's going to cut our horses' throats.

MIKE:
Gate, Mr Scandrett.

SOLO: *(sung)*
Donnelly's new stage sawn to pieces

A suspended moment in which we look at the Donnelly boys held back at the gate. They look at us still as a photograph. Who are they? What are they?

CHORUS: Confutatis maledictis

SOLO: Sawn to pieces Watson's horses

CHORUS: Flammis acribus addictis

The penny slides into the TOLLGATER's cup, a Donnelly penny.

WIFE: I saw blood on his sleeve I could swear. I was going to be sick then—

ANOTHER TRAVELLER: *(from our side of the gate)* Good night, Scandrett. Whoa. Guess we don't need to go any farther, Lila. There's Will and Mike waiting for you and I'm glad you feel more like completing your journey than you did at three o'clock there. *(The gate finally comes down to let Mrs Shoebottom through.)* Good night, Bill, Mike. *(He turns around and goes back towards us.)*

LADY: Thank you, Will Donnelly. Thank you, Mike. You're kind gentlemen both of you to put yourselves out so for an old woman like me. *(They depart with her.)*

WIFE: But when their hands came down to help her up into their buggy the blood on their sleeves was gone.

Bar noise & scene. MIKE going through with trunk.

MIKE: I heard what you said, sir. If you ever say again that my brother Tom robbed Ned Ryan of eighty dollars I'll kill you. *(Exit)*

Voice of man who enters as MIKE leaves with trunk.

SOLO VOICE: The Donnellys are coming, they're walking over from Levitt's.

A knocking, then a door-rending.

Lock up your doors, close the bar; hide everybody.

JIM, TOM & BOB enter to face a lone bartender, FRANK.

FRANK: No Donnelly gets a drink at this bar; I'll not serve you, James.

JAMES: I see. And it's a good bar you used to have too, Frank Walker.

FRANK: Used to have!

JAMES: Because you'll get a scorching inside of six weeks as it's laid out for you now, but I don't intend to have anything to do with it.

FRANK: What'll it be, Jim Donnelly, what'll it be?

JIM: Three gingerbeers for us lads here and a big bowl of porridge.

FRANK: Don't you mean three bowls?

JAMES: No, it's not for us. One big bowl of porridge and hustle it.

CONSTABLE BERRYHILL enters swaggering with his warrants in pocket.

BERRYHILL: *(with beard)* I can lick any man in this tavern, I can lick any man in Biddulph. *(He backs away from JIM DONNELLY.)* Jim Donnelly I've got twelve warrants for your arrest.

Out of range we hear a scream from BERRYHILL & he returns in the power of JAMES DONNELLY, JR.

MIKE: He had followed my brothers to Walker's Hotel.

BERRYHILL: They tore half my beard out.

JAMES: Oh—the beard fell out of him

MIKE: By the time I got there my brothers and their pals were throwing stones at home.

BERRYHILL: Several of the stones weighed five pounds each.

MIKE: That's a lie. Frank, how much does that one weigh?

FRANK: Got a bit afraid when I saw the stones flying through the air. *(weighing a stone in a balanced scale on bar)* It's three pounds? *(MIKE smiles.)*

WILL: My brother Mike then hauled James and the others off and parted them.

BERRYHILL: But left me with them and you know what they made me do, that James Donnelly the Younger took the warrants out of my pocket and

They tear up the warrants, sprinkle them over the porridge and feed it to BERRYHILL.

FRANK: You're probably going to hit me, Jim, for asking you this, but why?

JAMES: I'm only feeding him the ones we didn't do, Frank. This one here—I'll eat myself, yes I did beat that grocer up and I couldn't stand the way he whined and whoever is doing all those terrible things on these warrants will stop doing them, Frank, when the powers that be let my brothers have half of the road again. I started eating the paper and then it tasted bitter, I took it out of my mouth and saw Dr Quarry's signature why it was my death certificate and it was getting time to take the saw back to my mother and father.

Facing us a change comes over him: he dissolves from the bully into someone coughing blood on his sleeve and crawling toward us, towards his mother who waits for him.

MRS DONNELLY:
Yes, my oldest son came home and after the doctor came it was time for the priest to come, but he did not come and we waited and he did not come so that it was I who had to lie down beside this grown man and lead him backwards and forwards through a life he had forgotten the deeds and maps to. As he whispered in my ear, yes, what do you want me to say, I could see life for him again some time. But for the first time I saw my own death. Just before he died I told him what I was to tell another son of mine not many years after.

Ritual walking confession, his back to us, she with her face as his life pours out. They are walking through his brutal life under some of the next scene, then he parts from her forever.

CHORUS:
Nominations for North Middlesex

The CHORUS divide into those watching the

One of the Donnellys
is Dead!

(hilarious reaction)

SOLO:
Solvet Jacobus in favilla

CHORUS:
Another diabolical
outrage—a horse
disemboweled with a
scythe. Flammis
acribus addictus
Fiendish outrage—a
tree across the London,
Huron & Bruce railway
this morning. The
trestles of the Grand
Trunk Railway bridge at
Lucan Crossing sawn
through by some fiend
in human form. There
is work for some clever
detective in Lucan.
Voca me cum
benedictus,
Dies irae, dies illa
Dona eis requiem.
The Detective. Our
serial for the month
of December. "A
Detective's Diary," or

*news bulletin board
where several are
chalking up headlines,
and others reading
newspapers.*

*MRS DONNELLY's
arm cannot keep her
oldest son here
anymore; she lets it
drop to her side and
walks across the
CHORUS gossipers.*

McCRIMMON: *(disguised as an old beggar-woman)* How I brought the Donnelly Gang to heel. Gentlemen, are all the blinds down and the doors to Mr Stub's store room locked? Yes? Then I will resume my civilian garb. *(flinging off his disguise)* Mr Finnegan, I have been for some time engaged in ferreting out at your behest the perpetrators of certain crimes which have been committed in Lucan & its vicinity. Today is—I make this interim report to you Thursday, February the 24th, 1876. Sunday—5th of December, 1875—we met here as you recall in camera.

FINNEGAN: First of all, let me introduce you to Mr George Stub at the back of whose store we are hiding. Mr Stub, this is the private detective the town council gave permission to bring in. He's been here incognito already for about a month and I sure hope to hell he's going to tell us what we can do to prevent all our business affairs going bust. Gentlemen, Hugh McCrimmon.

CHORUS: A giant in size, he was gentle as a child. Shy as a woman, his heart was bold as a

lion's. Modest as a maiden . . . . And in first place in the five mile dash! Hugh McCrimmon!

McCRIMMON: Yes. For my athletic prowess in weight-lifting and foot running alone I have won over a thousand gold medals both here and in Uncle Sam's dominions. You may remember how I asked you each to tell me your story and to tell me *all* of the story. Because there is a great detective up in the sky *(all glance up)* who does know and He'll make it known if you don't so I want all of the truth. My notes. This family— seven of them have done all these terrible things and they've been charged, but the constables can't arrest them. Too bad the one died and got away on us. You say no witnesses will dare to testify for fear of reprisal, in short they're running this town with a reign of terror, you want to run it and I'm here to help you. Chapter One, sirs, is to

STUB: I'm having Will Donnelly arrested today if you must know—he's owed me a bill at the store in there for a bridle for over a year now and I'm having him arrested for that debt.

McCRIMMON: An arrest for a minor debt? Rather small potatoes, don't you think?

STUB: He won't pay, his bowels hate me so much he won't pay that debt even though today is his wedding day, he won't pay it to keep out of jail.

CHORUS: May the God of Israel join you together and may He be with you, who was merciful to two only children: and now, O Lord, make them bless Thee more fully. Alleluia, alleluia.

PRIEST: William Donnelly, wilt thou take Norah Macdonald here present for thy lawful wife according to the rite of our holy Mother the Church?

WILL: I will

PRIEST: Norah Macdonald, wilt thou take William Donnelly here present for thy lawful husband, according to the rite of our holy Mother the Church?

NORAH: I will *(They hold right hands.)*

PRIEST: Ego conjungo vos in matrimonium, in nomine Patris, et Filii et Spiritus Sancti, Amen

He sprinkles them with water. Then he blesses the ring, gold & silver coins. BAILIFFS appear at the back of the church with staves.

Let us pray. Bless, O Lord, this ring which we bless in Thy Name, that she who shall wear it, keeping true faith unto her husband may abide in Thy peace and will, and ever live in mutual charity. Through Christ our Lord, Amen.

He sprinkles the ring with holy water in the form of a cross. The bridegroom receives from the PRIEST the ring and places it on the fourth finger of his bride.

WILL: With this ring I thee wed and I plight unto thee my troth. *(silent Lord's Prayer)*

BAILIFF: Are you just about through. Because which one of you is William Donnelly; we've come with writ against him for debt.

PRIEST: Look, O Lord, we beseech Thee, upon these Thy servants, and graciously assist Thine own institutions, whereby Thou hast ordained the propagation of mankind, that they who are joined together by Thy authority may be preserved by Thy help. Through Christ our Lord. Amen. Mr & Mrs William Donnelly, who are these men?

WILL: Father Flannery, they are bailiffs for a debt I refuse to pay to a man you know well. Mother and Father, who used the ignorance of a child six months ago to snare me now on my wedding day. How many days?

BAILIFFS: It says here—ten days in the jug, Bill.

WILL: Norah. Meet me at Tom Ryder's wedding dance which is to be in ten days time at Fitzhenry's Tavern. Promise? We'll recommence there and no, Mother and Father, don't offer to pay, as a man I've decided not to. If George Stub wants me in jail he can have what he wants. And when I want him to lose this election that's coming up then I can have what I want. Got my fiddle there? I'll give you a tune as the bailiffs here march me off. Attention! March! *(He goes off playing "Boney over the Alps." They listen to it dying away and then follow.)*

NORAH: Mrs Donnelly, you gave Will that fiddle didn't you.

MRS DONNELLY: Are you thinking if I hadn't you might have your husband in your arms at this very moment, Norah, instead of his doing such a proud fool thing?

NORAH: No. I've never been so happy in my life to have married such a man.

McCRIMMON: Chapter One. January the twenty second, I wrote to my sweetheart. Chapter Two. I visit the outlaw's nest—in disguise.

Our attention focuses on JOHN washing himself at the Donnelly farmhouse. MIKE drives into the yard.

MIKE: What are we going to do, Jack? There's a detective on the way out here.

JOHN: He's already here. The boys brought him home with them.

MIKE: Do they know who he is?

JOHN: They think he's a pal, he stood up for them in some dispute at the Dublin House and slapped a man down. You should see him, he's all muscle. Should we tell them?

MIKE: No. It'd be too much for their minds to bear. Is he disguised?

MRS DONNELLY enters, kisses MICHAEL, and shows him a baby shawl she has knit.

JOHN: *(whispering)* He's got an eye patch.

McCRIMMON enters & slouches around. BOB & TOM stand behind him.

MRS DONNELLY: Nellie was just showing me the baby, Mike, what shoulders he has already on him, and this is what I've knitted for Jenny's child and your father and me's off to the christening in St Thomas. Bob and Tom are you not going to say goodbye to your mother and father?

They come over to kiss her; she singles out the lounging pirate for a glance.

McCRIMMON: *(vulgar voice)* Well, look at who it is. This must be your mother, boys. Old Johannah Donnelly herself. *(He is hoping to provoke something.)*

MRS DONNELLY: I always thought that gentlemen stood up when a lady came into the room.

McCRIMMON: I'm no gentleman, and this is no room. *(laugh)*

MRS DONNELLY: The yard of any house I live in, sir, has a very high blue ceiling called a sky, and I call it a room particularly if I say so and I step out into it.

McCRIMMON: *(shambling & bowing)* Mrs Donnelly, I'm enchanted to meet you, met your two youngest ones while strolling through the village, and I gather you do not mind if they entertain a stranger at your high ceilinged residence. *(glances up)*

MRS DONNELLY: Strangers are always welcome here and I'm only sorry my husband and myself won't be here this weekend since we're going to St Thomas to visit my daughter and granddaughter there. Tom and Bob, why don't you take your friend to help father catch the driving horse. It seems to me I caught a glimpse of you earlier on looking at one of my son's shirts on the clothesline. *(She comes over to him with a shirt & claps her hands together in front of his face.)* Well, if you're that interested in our laundry and linen out here, you can mend the big tear in that one yourself which was no doubt got in the sort of place my boys would meet you.

TOM: Mother, he stuck up for us. You and Will always do this to our friends.

MRS DONNELLY: Do what, this is the first one I ever caught pawing over my clothesline. Off to help with the horse now. *(They exit.)* Mike and John, who is that man? Of all the orphans and has beens and poor lost souls you've brought home for me to take the edge of hunger off them, this is the only one I cannot seem to stand. How in Heaven's name can Tom and Bob not see that he's a rascal.

JOHN: Mother, you don't know what a dreadful comment this is on your character.

MRS DONNELLY: How so, is he really a good man? *(The boys laugh as she leaves.)*

McCRIMMON: And with that she swept out. I took notes on all they said and done, but she breaks any pencil I have around me to describe. But I put them through their paces, and they never caught on. For instance, *(vulgar voice again)* Bob. Which would you rather see— it burn, or put it out and have it cool in your pocket—a nice green dollar bill?

He sets fire to a dollar bill & floats it. BOB watches in fascination and fails the test utterly, squiggling as it burns and obviously "interested" in fire.

TOM: You know, Jake, you're not the only clever person around here and this is all among friends now. *(He sticks a lead pipe in his trousers & drops a penny from his nose into the pipe.)* Mike?

MIKE: I haven't the skill, Tom, but I bet your new friend can't do it either.

McCRIMMON: *(taking the pipe & sticking it in his trousers)* Bender's the name, Mike, Jake Bender.

JOHN: Ladies are present, Mr. Bender.

After making sure they're not, McCRIMMON balances the penny; TOM pours a dipper of cold water down the pipe. He roars & chases after them.

JOHN: *(with head to ground)* What a runner he is, Mike. You can hear him pounding the earth like a giant. Where is he now?

MIKE: Where the creek runs through. He's caught up to them. He's bringing them back, one under each arm. Look at the front of his pants!

McCRIMMON enters & modestly turns his back to us; STUB, FINNEGAN et al. resume the backroom positions. The wedding party music strikes up.

McCRIMMON: Yes, I was the first man to bring the Donnelly gang to heel. She got a pair of pants I had to leave out there, but I got all the sons save Mike into the jails and prisons they belonged in. Thursday February the 24th, 1876, Gentlemen, my constables are ready. I hear the dance about to start over at Fitzhenry's Hotel over there and we'll soon see some more wildcat action.

STUB: Well, I hope so, the room we used to meet in got burnt down. What kind of a case have you made out against them?

McCRIMMON: *(going over to barrel)* They've got about thirty friends. I'm going to select the weakest and dance him on a rope till he tells us what he knows about the Donnellys' activities, starting right here with this redhaired lad in the barrel. It's Tom Ryan the little sneaking spy it is. Chapter Three!

He closes the barrel & they roll TOM off as the wedding sweeps in. A FIDDLER jumps out over the bar; someone collects money in a hat to pay him; the bar in full flow, someone ladling out the punch, girls sitting on boys' knees.

BOY: What will you dance?

GIRL: Your will is my pleasure, Dan.

FIDDLER: What'll you have?

BOY: Barney, put your wrist in it or Kitty here'll leave us both out of sight in no time. Whoo! Success! Clear the floor. Well done, Barney. That's the go.

The dance: Polka, Schottische, Reel if time. Play WILL's march "Boney over the Alps" when he & JOHN enter, NORAH, Mr & Mrs Tom Ryder—the new bride & groom whose party this is.

CONSTABLE(S): *(with staves)* John Donnelly, we've come to arrest you for assault & battery of Joseph Berryhill. Read the warrant if you like. Come along now, John.

JOHN: But it's dated a month ago, why have you waited till now when I'm at the dance?

CONSTABLE: Come along with us to the lock-up.

WILL: Come back here, John. Don't be dragged away by that fellow.

CONSTABLE: Come back here, Jack Donnelly.

WILL: Stay here, John. You're staying with me at this dance. I'm just out of jail and my brother's not going there and I'm not going back. Bob, where's Tom and Will Farl?

VOICE: Give it to him. Will

CONSTABLE: Hey you! Bring that man back here, he's my prisoner *(grabbing)*

JOHN: What's this about, Bawden? When you arrested me before I went with you like a man.

CONSTABLE: Yes, when you had to

He pulls at John, crowd pulls the other way.

VOICES: *(chanting)* We won't let John go ever from this party oh

WILL: Let him go, you son of a bitch. You couldn't have tried this at a more infuriating time I'll blow your heart out of you or any other man that'll try, just try to take him or any other of the family.

Melee, shots. All out save the hanging scene.

McCRIMMON: Chapter Four! Tom Ryan, the militia are rounding up your friends and herding them into the lock-up so there's no one to gallop by and see you hanging up in this tree, so just tell us the answers please like a good lad.

CONSTABLES enter with JOHN & put him behind a ladder.

CONSTABLE: The Queen versus John Donnelly. Assault and resisting arrest.

CHORUS: Three months in the Central Prison.

STUB: Three months! It should have been three years!

McCRIMMON: You won't tell. No? Pull him up *(pause)* Now will you tell on the Donnellys?

CONSTABLES: The Queen versus Tom Donnelly. Misdemeanor.

CHORUS: Nine months in the Central Prison. The Queen versus Bob Donnelly

Again the two are brought in & placed behind ladders with clanking sounds.

CONSTABLES: Shooting with intent, two years in the penitentiary

McCRIMMON: Do you know anything about the burning & cutting up of those stage wagons? Do you know anything about the meat that's been stolen?

TOM: Listen, mister, if you'd let me see who you are I'd tell you everything. *(McCRIMMON motions to have his eyebandage removed.)* Ready? *(pause)* I done them things. I stole the meat because I was hungry, I broke the dishes in the hotel. The Donnelly boys themselves would like to know who does half the things— *(He is pulled up.)*

McCRIMMON: The young liar. If he wants to go to prison with those he loves so let him go.

CHORUS: The Queen versus William Donnelly.

RYAN comes to his ladder cell about the same time as WILL.

CONSTABLES: Shooting with intent. Nine months in the county jail.

McCRIMMON: Gentlemen, I'm ashamed of the brevity of their sentences, but we could not break the boy. I wish you'd warned me that he was subject to fits. Chapter Five!

TOM: Will, I'm so proud to be in jail with you. I love the jail.

WILL: Oh God, Tom Ryan. I hate the jail. Did Norah send anything along with you when you left Lucan now?

TOM: A bar of soap. Here. *(throws)* Has it got a saw in it, Will, you're eating it?

WILL: I know I am, Tom, and it's going to make me terribly ill.

McCRIMMON: But despite all that, gentlemen, I have rid your township of the vermin for some time and you Finnegan are again the King of the Road and you Squire Stub—can look forward to an election campaign where your candidate will meet only fair opposition, not the shears, clippers and torch he very well might have. Gentlemen, my pay. *(Just as they give him a bag—)*

VOICE: *(lady reading newspaper)* Well it says here that William Donnelly is very sick of a low fever in the jail and is not expected to live much longer—his wife is petitioning the Attorney General to let him off his sentence.

McCRIMMON: Chapter Six! Thank you. Thursday, August 22nd. Today I proposed to my beloved and was accepted. She will marry a man who has just been appointed Chief of Police for Belleville.

He exits into the audience with the quilt that is MIKE & NELLIE's bed held behind him.

CHORUS: Like a flower, Eunice found herself and her pink frilly dress swept into the powerful arms of the brave Detective, winner of many athletic events.

MIKE & NELLIE in bed.

NELLIE: Always seem to wake up before Mike. Listen for the children. Take a look at the newspaper. Think. The village has been quiet since they're all gone off to jail. Didn't get Mike though. In his dreams he's finally got off the stage, you can tell from his breathing. When he first wakes up there's a minute before he tenses up for the day on the road which goes by our window and in that moment you can tell him things that might get him too excited later on, apt to rush off and hit somebody. But there's something I've got to tell him before it's too late. When we first met at the dance—I broke off my engagement with a lad called Sid Skinner because I fell so in love with Mike. Sid and me'd been courting for a year, but I could not help it, Mike was the man for me, but Sid's been coming to my mother's house on Horton Street lately, tipsy from his work at the hotel and saying he's

going to kill you, Mike. Wake up, Mike, so I can put this to you. I've never told you but the man who tends bar at the City Hotel used to be in love with me. Mike?

MIKE: What time is it? Five o'clock by the light. Nellie?

NELLIE: Mike.

MIKE: Do you want to spend the rest of your life here in this house on Main Street of Lucan? Don't be afraid to tell me.

NELLIE: You know how happy I've been with you, Mike, wherever you are and whatever happens.

MIKE: I don't mean that, I know that, but have you ever thought you'd like to live another place?

NELLIE: Yes, oh God yes, Mike. *(Finnegan's stage horn)* Mike, there's Finnegan's stage—it's later than I thought, you'll be late for work.

MIKE: Nellie, I don't know why I've been ashamed to tell you, but yesterday was the last day I'll ever drive the Opposition Stage. They've won. Without my brothers beside me I can't go on. So I've got a job as a brakeman on the Canada Southern and we'll leave today for St Thomas. Do you feel ashamed of me?

NELLIE: God no, Mike. There was something else I wanted to tell you, but it's all right now we're moving so far away, what's the matter.

Stage passes with horn and shout.

MIKE: *(shaking fist out window)* I'll drive over your grave yet, McKellar. Oh God, I loved driving that road. *(pause)* Nellie, there's smoke coming out of our kitchen window downstairs, they've set fire to our house, quick get the babies. Mother of God save us from Finnegan's Fire.

A red glare we have seen before. Viewpoint: roll on floor with baby dolls; scream from wife.

CHORUS:
The Election of 1878
Then shout John A. forever boys,
That is the heading cry;
Every election we will win,
The time is drawing nigh,
The scheming Grits may bag their heads
That is if they've a mind,
Or go and dig up taters
With their shirts hung out behind.

STUB: Gentlemen of Ward Three, it gives me great pleasure to see the Conservative Meeting at the Donnelly Schoolhouse so crowded tonight. As I see some of our Grit friends here I trust and hope that you will give our speaker a fair hearing. May I give a particularly warm welcome to Mr William Donnelly whom the Grit government of our fair province has seen fit to release from his chamber at the Queen's boarding house where he was reportedly deathly ill. Although looking quite recovered from his fever, I would ask as a special favour that he not overtax himself or it might bring on another—attack. As you all know the Conservative Candidate for this riding is an Irish Catholic nominated by his Irish Protestant brothers. Gentlemen, I have been requested to perform a very pleasing duty this evening and it is to introduce to you the next member for the riding of North Middlesex—Mr Timothy Corcoran. *(applause)*

CORCORAN: *(manipulating a puppet version of himself)* Gintlemen farmers of Biddulph, yees are ruined by Mr McKinsey and his free trade. Ivery market in the country is filled with Yankee horses, cattle and hogs. Yees are losing fifteen cints on ivery bushell of barley ye sell, and yees can't get over half price for yees pays and oats, bekase millions uv bushels uv Yankee corn comes into the country not paying a cint of duty. You farmers have to pay tin cints more for yare tay and two cints more for yare sugar—Mr Chairman, I see a hand up at the back of the room.

MRS DONNELLY: *(who has been following the speech in a newspaper and has been reading along with the speaker for a bit)* This is the same speech as he gave in Ailsa Craig a week ago. It's all printed down here in the *Advertiser.*

STUB: Don't heed that hand, on and louder, Tim.

COCORAN: —two cints more for yare sugar, yes, Will Donnelly what did you want to ask?

WILL: If, Mr Corcoran, you were elected to parliament next Tuesday and say in a year's time—say your party got in, Macdonald's party—and again there was a scandal about money and there came up a vote of confidence in the government how, Mr Corcoran, would you vote?

CORCORAN: I don't know. When the time comes, Bill, I'd know by that time because I'd have studied it up you see.

WILL: Although you are a Catholic the Orange Lodge supports your candidacy, Mr Corcoran.

What is your vote likely to be when their Grand Master tries to ram a bill through Parliament for the incorporation of the Orange Lodge?

CORCORAN: Oh, Will Donnelly, never fear I'd vote for such a thing.

WILL: But Mr Corcoran, you would have to as a member of the Conservative Party.

CORCORAN: Yes, I suppose I would. Mr Stub—

VOICE: It's Mr Stub should be telling us instead of Tim

VOICE: Sure, it's well known George Stub here gets a senatorship if Tim gets in

VOICE: Sure, send him to parliament by voting for Tim. I say three cheers for the Grit Candidate Mr Colin Scatcherd who has one face under one hat. Hip Hip Hurrah.

In the cheers, objects fly at the speakers who withdraw. The newsclerk chalks up results on the bulletin board; a feeling of tension, torches, election night fever, close arithmetic.

CLERK: Mr Scatcherd . . . the North Middlesex Riding has been won by the Grit Candidate in a tight race. Mr Scatcherd has won the seat by seven votes. *(Cheers for Scatcherd led by WILL DONNELLY.)*

STUB: *(in the drawing room)* Seven votes. We lost by seven votes. We were supposed to win by four hundred! Where's my wife, Bridget?

BRIDGET: *(parlourmaid)* Master Stub, your wife has gone back to live with your father-in-law. She said to tell you it might look like a Senator's house, but she read about the election results in the paper and you had not kept her promise to her.

STUB: She's nervous and overwrought with the baby coming on. Bridget, what's your family's theory about why we lost. Is it not just the Donnellys?

BRIDGET: Sir, my brother says, sir, it is the Donnellys. Without them and we'd have a Catholic gentleman in parliament this evening and maybe in Sir John A.'s cabinet, but no—it's the Donnellys don't want that.

STUB: Could I speak to your brother some time, Bridget. How long has it been since he's back from the States?

BRIDGET: Please, sir, not very long. He just arrived on the Finnegan Stage from town a good hour ago and sure I'm giving him a bit of supper in your kitchen.

STUB: Tell him to come in here. (pause) What's your name?

CARROLL: (wiping mouth) I told him what my name was.

STUB: James Carroll. Did you leave here for the States because you were in any kind of trouble, Jim?

CARROLL: No, sir. My father married again and I could not get along with my stepmother, after he died, she got his land away from us and I've come back to see about that and—

STUB: Your mother was a Farl, was she not, Jim?

CARROLL: How'd you know that?

STUB: Donnellys killed her brother, didn't they?

CARROLL: Yes. (to audience) What this man was asking me to do was what my mother on her deathbed made me promise to do. To kill the Donnellys. But at first no one had the courage, no one except my poor dead mother, to say that. At first it was drive them out of the township, they were all out of prison more or less and all back on top of us so I was made a constable in Lucan and my aim was to find one victim of the Donnellys brave enough to stick to his story and fight it out in the courts and keep after them again and again until we had these Donnellys behind bars or out of the township or—out!

NED RYAN: (falling flat) I've been robbed! Tom Donnelly robbed me of, he and Jim Feeney, robbed me of 85 dollars!

CARROLL: When did the robbery take place, Mr Ryan?

NED: Wednesday night, whatever night that was. About a year ago.

WILL: Mr Ryan, what did you have to drink at Walker's Hotel?

NED: Well, I do not get drunk often. I treated Tom and Jim to some whiskey, but I myself had some sherry wine and some ginger wine.

WILL: Is it true you were come into town that day for a spree, that you had been at the following hotels first: the Dublin House, the Queen's, the Royal, Fitzhenry's, the Western, Levitt's—

NED: Never at Levitt's, never darken his door, haven't got to Fitzhenry's, still haven't got there!

WILL: Is it true that you have several times lately entered my father's house and my own house in search of your son who has run away from you?

NED: My son! Waiting for his pa to come home with some food for the table and the Donnellys have stolen all his money away from him and I'm at home waiting for my son and he does not come to his pa and you want to know why—because the Donnellys've stolen him away from his dear pa and ma like the fairies used to steal little children away when you weren't watching.

WILL: Is it not true also that although you say that my brother choked you when you fell down, the inmates of the house who took you in could find no marks on your throat?

SQUIRE: I dismiss this case, Ned Ryan. I think one of the constables summed it all up when he said that you were so drunk that night you couldn't have known your mouth from your arsehole.

CARROLL: Your honour, may I as a friend of Ned Ryan's here and as a—may I say that I am not satisfied with the way my friend's case has been handled. We will bring it up before another magistrate.

WILL: Your honour, in view of Mr Carroll's statements, I would like the fact that the charges against my brother, Thomas Donnelly, have been dismissed, I would like a certificate made out to that effect.

CARROLL: Yes, and I could make you out a certificate about the way justice has been administered in this village so that his family and their ruffian friends can bully and terrify a township of three thousand inhabitants. You Donnellys say you're persecuted; ask the horses and cattle and the barns and the stables and the women and the men here like Ned Ryan who's lost his boy to you who is being persecuted. Is there anybody in this room who'll stick up for this gang of mad Donnelly dogs—look at his foot!—whom some of you think of as being so wonderful. And I hear one or two of yous thinking of renting my father's farm from my stepmother and there's some of you stopping at the Donnellys' for a drink of water at their well. There's a whole lot of you still doing that and if we hear of any such, or of any man or woman offering Mrs Donnelly a ride in their cart on the way to mass or

He menaces the whole theatre; we are afraid of him.

WILL: *(lightly and suddenly entering)* Now is that you, Jim Carroll, sitting on that horse of yours, under the tree talking to yourself about us give me that whip of yours before you hurt yourself with it and come out of the shadow so we can get a look at you. Yes, you won. You smeared our name for all time so that when children are naughty their mothers still say to them

WILL & CHORUS: Be quiet, or the Black Donnellys will get you.

WILL: Isn't that what most of you in this room think of us as being? Because of him my mother was turned into a witch who rode around burning down sheds and barns, because of him . . . but there's one thing, Jim, that some people coming after will remark on. And that is—the difference between our handwritings. There is my signature. There is his. Choose. You can't destroy the way my handwriting looks, just as you can never change the blot that appears in every one of your autographs and the cloud and the smudge and the clot and the fume of your jealousy. There! the living must obey the dead! Dance the handwriting that comes out of your arm. Show us what you're like. Very well, I'll dance mine.

First WILL (fiddle) then CARROLL (trumpet) dance; the latter falls down in a fit. Placards displaying their signatures are held up for us to see.

WILL: Oh now Jim, I didn't mean you were to fall down in one of those fits you have now and again. Is it your heart sometimes, is it your mind sometimes, is it your great big feet sometimes, Jim, is it that you couldn't stand the way the Donnellys dressed, the way they looked right through you, the way my mother looked down at you. So you clubbed her to kneel at your feet, but you forget that our eyes don't kneel at your feet, but you forget that our eyes don't kneel and that her eyes will look down and through you until dies irae and beyond. Down and through the clown with blood on his sleeves they call James Carroll. *(Exit)*

CARROLL: It's true. I couldn't club down their eyes. After it was over I had to leave Biddulph. I never went back there. You people here'd used me like a piece of dirty paper to wipe the Donnellys off your backsides. I died out West alone. Grave whereabouts unknown. I hate William Donnelly. I hate William Donnelly.

CHORUS: End of Act Two.

ACT THREE

A gravel train with MIKE DONNELLY as brakeman backs into the audience. Three whistles for stop after MIKE has signalled this with his lantern. Switch light and the two red lanterns on the back of the train move accordingly. Song over and NELLIE to one side as commentary.

MIKE & CHORUS:
I want to be a brakeman
And with the brakeman stand
A badge upon my forehead
A tail rope in my hand

With links & pins & bell cord
And signals red & white
I'd make a freight train back up
Or slack ahead all right.

When ere a train I shunted
At St Thomas so fair
I'd not forget my darling wife
But keep the crossing clear

NELLIE: My husband, Michael Donnelly, was a brakeman on a gravel train out of Waterford on the Canada Southern Line, division point St Thomas where I live with our children in a house on Mill Street—two nights he spends alone boarding at Waterford; tomorrow is his day off and he'll be home with us for four nights. But this is Wednesday, December 9th 1879. There's no snow yet. About four o'clock it begins to rain. His mate afterwards told me this is the way it went with Michael and the train, I wanted to know every crossing they came to before when their work was over they walked into the barroom at Slaght's Hotel.

Two blasts. The journey establishes itself then goes under her speech.

That means the engineer is ready to go. From the hind end of the train Mike gives him the highball so he whistles two short blasts meaning "I understand." Yes, I understand—that in the months before my husband was murdered in that barroom at Slaght's Hotel—there was a train, there was another sort of train that started out just after that election of 1878 and every crossing it blew its whistle for was a crossing that was closer to my husband's death and I wish I could be clear in my own mind what that First Crossing was but I think I can see you there in cold blood talking about how you'll kill him and I run towards you to stop you but I meet the glass of mystery and time and trickery. I fall down and only know that I must listen for all the other four crossings Mike's train whistled for before the last time he walked out of the rain.

The barroom of the City Hotel fades in: CARROLL, SID SKINNER & a TRAINER (BILL LEWIS).

CARROLL: Well, shall we get started? We've got the job set up for you, Sid.

SID: That's good of you. And then what do I do?

CARROLL: What's the matter?

SID: It's a great thing I'm to do, kill a man and go to prison for God knows how long. All today, all tonight at this bar I've been thinking about it and I have to pinch myself to wake up—this is happening to me, this is happening to you, Sid. Sid is getting out of here.

CARROLL: Suit yourself, Sid Skinner. Maybe, and Bill here would agree with me, it'd just prove what Mike Donnelly said about you as he boasted about the girl he took away from you.

SID: I don't want to know what he said. Just the last few days I realized what a duck I was going to her mother and saying I was going to kill Mike Donnelly. I'm not a fighting man.

CARROLL: Then what kind of man was it who handled the bar in here tonight, eh Bill? That was a fighting man, but a fighting man that's not all just fight, but some brains in his head as well, eh? If Mike had seen you tonight he'd have had to eat his words—

SID: What words?

CARROLL: That you were a man of no prick. Yes, them's the dirty words he used about you, auh, he's a little fellow with no prick on him at all—*that* little fellow.

SID: Teach me how to kill him then. What dirt do I have to go through to wipe that off his mouth, yes, what's the false name you're giving me?

CARROLL: After the lesson tonight, Sid, if you learn it well, you'll have a new name. Now, you're lucky you don't have to deal with the whole tribe the way I have to up in Biddulph. I wish I just had the one desperate character to clean up, but I've got six or seven of Mike's relatives to deal with every day and do you know who's the worst?

SID: You're afraid of them?

CARROLL: The mother, she's the one I'm

SID: You're afraid of an old woman?

CARROLL: Well, what would you have done? If you can do it, maybe I can Sid, I don't know. On Monday morning last, Bill here saw me just after in Gallagher's yard and I was shaking like a leaf, for not an hour ago, I'd took my life in my hands and dared to walk down the road past the Donnellys' place—was going to get some notes from a man I'd sold a fanning mill, Jack Donnelly was out plowing. Mrs Donnelly was milking a cow by the gate and Tom had just cursed me—Jack said—

JOHN: Now there's that fighting man, Mr Jim Carroll. Jim—I want to talk to you. What were you saying about Bob and our family at the sale last night?

CARROLL: I don't want to talk to you, Jack Donnelly. I've got too much respect for myself. Meet me this afternoon at Whalen's Corners.

JOHN: Let's have no mobbing at Whalen's Corners, Jim. I'll fight you, right now, I'll make your big head soft right there on that road. What business is it of yours how light a sentence Bob got?

CARROLL: Don't want much to fight, but if you'll meet me at Whalen's Corners I'll fight you. I'll lick all the Donnellys. Well, Jack drops his plow and he strode at me. I'm an inoffensive man. You come at me and I'll shoot you. Keep off

TOM throws a stone.

JOHN: Tom—get out on the road and thrash him—the coward, the thief.

CARROLL: Now listen to what she said.

MRS DONNELLY: You son of a bitch, you thief, you rogue. Give it to him, Tom, on his big head. Point a gun at an old woman milking a cow, would you, you bastard, you should be arrested,

Jim Carroll, and when they arrest you they should put you back down into the devil with thirty tails you belong to.

CARROLL: Oh—the dirty names she called, calling my mother a dog and saying my father never married her, she made me feel so jumpy I just walked on, oh—I need someone to show me the way, I wouldn't dare shoot any of them now or ever. It's her, Sid, do you understand me, she's a witch and we'll never get rid of any of them unless there's someone brave enough to just—But there isn't. The mad dogs have won.

SID: No, they haven't.

CARROLL: Oh, well then, Bill to the bar please and just let on that you're Michael Donnelly taking a drink. Now, Sid—

SID goes up to the TRAINER, hauls him around by the shoulder; they fight, but the TRAINER soon pins SID to the ground.

BILL: It's no use, Jim, all we've taught him doesn't put the weight on him Donnelly has and I'm doing just the things Donnelly does.

CARROLL: Let's add something. Sid, watch me. Bill. Stop shooting off your big mouth, Mike Donnelly.

BILL is stationed by the bar again. CARROLL draws a jackknife which he holds in his left hand; he hits BILL from behind and draws BILL into chasing him behind the bar. In the clinch, BILL has hold of CARROLL's shoulders but CARROLL holds him by the vest and with the other knife hand stabs him below the belt.

BILL: Do you want something from me. Holy name of God, Jim Carroll, go easy with that open knife. Do you want to try that now, Sid? And I think, Jim, the first few times with Sid here we'll have the knife closed.

SID: Stop shooting off your big mouth, Mike Donnelly.

BILL: Do you want something from me?

SID & BILL go through the new business. Exhausted but livened up & confident once more, SID leans back against the bar while CARROLL unlocks the bar and pours them all a drink . . . even for the privy cleaner who now comes forward with shaving mug & lather.

CARROLL: The mad dogs have lost.

SID: Who's he? He's been watching all this.

CARROLL: He's Mr Nobody, Sid, a retired barber, well semi-retired, he'd like to start shaving you just to rearrange your face whiskers a bit as well as your topknot.

SID: He smells!

CARROLL: Well, when you enter the world where you have two faces under the one hat, Sid, you can't be too choosy about your barber any more. Cleans out privies for a living now because the razor hand got rather unsteady there one famous time, oh nothing to fear, Sid, by the way we've got to start calling you by your new name.

SID: What's my new name.

CARROLL: You've got a new name with the new job you're going to take tonight—you'll be a navvy for the Canada Southern near Waterford where your friend from Biddulph is a brakeman on their gravel train right now and everything is fixed up, don't worry, remember borrow the jackknife a few days before from some chum at your rooming house, let's go back in here to shave him.

SID: What's my name.

BILL: Same as my name, Bill Lewis.

SID: But that's your name. I'm not a bit like you

BILL: Sure it is. Sure you're not, but look here don't start wanting some other name. Jim, he doesn't like my name. I'm getting sore.

CARROLL: Ah, darling, you like his name really don't you at heart. It's a stout little plain name for a stout little plain little—you'll be like St Patrick, "Bill Lewis."

Laughing they both sing the St Patrick song as they escort him out behind the bar.

BOTH:
When blind worms crawling in the grass
Disgusted all the nation,
He gave them a rise which opened their eyes
To a sense of their situation.

So, success attend St Patrick's fist
For he's a saint so clever;
Oh! he gave the snakes and toads a twist
And bothered them forever . . .

The toads went pop, the frogs went hop,
Slap-dash into the water;
And the snakes committed suicide
To save themselves from slaughter.

So, success &c.

The clock in the St Nicholas Hotel strikes eleven: wind—establish this well before the other scene quite fades and we are back with the MINISTER & WILL.

WILL: Mr Donaldson, the next time the clock strikes, I know that I will have come to that part in my story I promised you—my brother Michael's death.

DONALDSON: You were telling me, Mr Donnelly, that the new priest formed a society against your family from among your fellow parishioners.

WILL: Oh he turned them against us. But the man who really worked at turning people against us, and you see we were not to be trusted because we had led the parish in not voting the way that Bishop and Sir John A would have had us vote—the man who really worked at it was a drifter named James Carroll. I'll show you, sir, how our family first met him. We became an obsession with him, I think he was hungry for land, our land, our eyes, our clothes, our mother. They'd just lost the election, we'd won and down the road he came and my mother was milking a cow by the gate.

JOHN: Oh I was on speaking terms with him. But he was a queer fellow.

CARROLL: Jack, what's this you were saying about me.

JOHN: Nothing yesterday, Jim Carroll, but what I could say today.

CARROLL: I wish you'd come out of that field and do it. You meet me at Whalen's Corners at two o'clock and we'll fight there.

JOHN: There's none here but the two of us. We'll have it out here, Jim Carroll, and have no mobbing about it.

CARROLL: *(drawing a revolver)* You son of a bitch. If you come one foot further, I'll blow your brains out.

TOM comes with stones.

WILL: Tom—throw the stones down, he wants law, not fight.

MRS DONNELLY: Go back, John, don't mind the blackguard or he'll shoot you.

CARROLL: I'd as leave shoot you as him.

MRS DONNELLY: *(She rises, looks at him & turns her back on him.)* Go away and mind your own business. I don't want anything to do with you.

CHORUS: The Queen against Julia Donnelly

CARROLL: Using abusive and insulting, grossly insulting language.

MRS DONNELLY: And I was convicted of doing so and fined one dollar and costs. He dragged me into court and into one of the newspapers where it was printed that I had thrown stones at him. Why, sir, are you hunting me down. Yes, I must be a beast if you can draw a revolver and aim it at me and no one says no

CHORUS: The Queen against James Carroll

MRS DONNELLY: Making threats to use revolver with intent. *(pause)* Well, I see that we get nowhere with that charge so that next time he walks by our house it may be with a mob who will—Jim Carroll, when I looked into your eyes I could see your mother's eyes *(FAT LADY's ghost crosses to her chair.)* and I could see you hating me long ago because you were fat and we'd killed your brother, on your deathbed you must have sharpened his teeth for me. And if you have got some mud on the mother, the next crossing is to bring a mob to their father and mother's door, but first we have come to the *(train journey up with crossing signal)*

CHORUS: Third Crossing.

Actors form Roman Line leaving their chairs unguarded. TOM RYAN, TOM DONNELLY, JAMES CARROLL with cheesecloth over their faces play tricks, steal props from chairs, spin tops illegally, pick pockets, gallop up & down the road after they've gone asleep, snoring—whole Puck episode, ladies on their bums from chamberpots sort of thing.

WILL: *(after a silent build)* Soon after this there began in the neighbourhood a whole parade of little mischievous things—Little, they began to get bigger and bigger and they told stories that my brother Tom took out horses, their horses at night and rode them up and down.

CHORUS: From tollgate to tollgate.

FARMER: Until they're nigh dead and you know what Tom Donnelly's tied to her tail.

He holds up a placard saying "Vote Grit & Vote Right."

FAT LADY: *(a scream of rage at this)* That's Cripple's beautiful handwriting.

WILL: There were stories that Tom Ryan in the middle of the night let people's cattle out of their fields and drove them up into Blanshard township.

VOICES IN SUCCESSION: Who stole my disk? Who stole my pig? My tea chest is gone. Who done that? I know who done that. Who shaved my horses' tails? Who put stones in my threshing machine and iron pins? We know who done that

WILL: Do you now and who done that?

CHORUS:
Who? stole my disk and stole my pig
rode my horses and drove my cows
cut out their tongues and cut off their ears?
                                            (repeat softly)

The three mystery faces whip them like tops humming: Donnelly!

WILL: Until my father said one day: If a stone fell from heaven they'd say

WILL & CHORUS: Donnelly done it.

WILL: We were blamed for everything and people shunned us, *would* not talk to us. Three times Carroll arrested my brother Tom on the charge of stealing

NED: One hundred dollars from me—Ned Ryan—and three times the case fell through

WILL: But one fall night Carroll got a new warrant from the Grand Jury and he was out at our house at dawn to serve it.

MRS DONNELLY: Yes, you should look behind the stove, Mr Carroll, and why not look right in the stove while you're at it.

CARROLL: I could not find him. I went over as far as Skinner's in Usborne and where Will lived at Whalen's Corners before I turned back.

MARY DONOVAN: I was spinning opposite the doorway in the house that day—could see the concession from where I was working. Saw Thomas Donnelly in his father's potato field picking potatoes. I went upstairs for yarn rolls and I saw William Donnelly drive into his father's place and signal to Tom in the field

CARROLL: I went over the fence into Mr Donnelly's field—went across a fall wheat field expecting to get in his tracks to follow him

MARY: When I saw Carroll & Thomas Donnelly running they were both near the stable. Saw John Donnelly come out with a horse. Tom Donnelly came up running, got on the horse and ran away.

CARROLL: If you'll stay away out of the country it's not particular if I catch you, Tom Donnelly. *(To JOHN)* I'll make it hot for you when I get to Lucan, John Donnelly. You'd no business giving him that horse to escape with.

JOHN: Jim, you never told me you had a new warrant for Tom.

CARROLL: What do you think I was running all over that wheat field for?

JOHN: Jim, Tom's not running away on you, sure he hardly seen you, he's going up to Kenny's blacksmith shop to get us some

CARROLL: I went over to Quigley's and stopped the thrashing. They got their horses and we chased Tom Donnelly into the bush all around the township from tollgate to tollgate all that night, but by the holy name of God could we *(helter skelter pursuit OF TOM DONNELLY)*

CHORUS:
We've got him who stole my disk and stole my
    pig
rode my horses and drove my cows
cut out their tongues and cut off their ears

NED RYAN: It's my son, Tom, dressed up in Tom Donnelly's clothes. Tom, why would you play such a trick on us? Why would you side with the family that won't let the thrashing machine come to thrash at your father's farm and the crops are rotting in the field, why

TOM: You old ruffian—I'll tell you why I side with the Donnellys. And you clodhoppers and you drifter—trying to pull them down. Three reasons. Because they're brave. They're not afraid. They're so little afraid of living here among you that this morning they started sowing their fall wheat. Two. They're handsome. Look at your faces—your faces'd fit into the hoofprints of forty old cows hopelessly lost in a bog. Yes, high & mighty one with your dirty linen scarce covering your hippopotamus rump and your hair like— Third. When pa here took the ax to mother and Bridget and Sarah & me who was the only family on the whole road with enough sand to take us in? *(pause)* So that's why I side with them, Pa, and if you want to know who's doing all the mischief on this road it's him over there— Jim Carroll.

CARROLL: Is it Jim Carroll for sure now, Tom Ryan?

NED RYAN: Stand back from him all of you, let a father deal with his begetting. Come here my darling. I want you to be my boy again and not the Donnelly's boy.

TOM: You're going to beat me, aren't you, Pa.

NED: No. *(pulling open his shirt)* Look at my heart in my chest now beating with love for you. Come to my heart—don't the rest of you lay a hand on him. Tom.

His arms are extended although we do see the club in his back pocket ready. TOM pauses, then runs at his belly with his head down and knocks him down, escapes. Everyone feels out of fuel; gawk listlessly, even CARROLL. All at wits' end then cowbell and spinning sound before it, leading up to

MARY: *(ear-shattering)* My cow! The Donnellys have stolen my cow. On Sunday evening my cattle were all at my gate when I came home. On Monday morning I went to look for her. I cannot get a trace of her. Who's man enough here to come and help me look for my cow? My cow! They're skinning and eating and cooking my cow right this very minute now and you just sit on your backsides and gawp at me, you gomerils. My cow's hidden somewhere at the Donleys.

CHAIRMAN: Mary Donovan, Magistrate Stub says we can't have a warrant now because it's night time, but we are to keep watch and at dawn we can search. Will all members of the Peace Society who plan to visit the Donnelly homestead tomorrow come into the schoolhouse and take turns watching for dawn?

MARY: *(whispering as she exits with the others)* It'll be too late by daybreak, they'll have eaten my cow all up, my cow! I had good reason to suspect the Donleys of taking my cow. The reason I suspected the Donleys is I had heard things spoke against them.

Silence as the night passes; crickets of early September, a bell rings matins, a wagon passes, train whistle, a clock strikes an early hour in the Donnelly house.

MRS DONNELLY: The air was hollow so that you could hear things far away that night. Or did I dream it that first I was on a coach and then a train and I was taking an empty coffin to a tavern where they were going to kill one of my sons. Their leaving the school and tramping down the roads towards our place must have wakened me, but as I lit the stove and went to wake up my niece Bridget they were quiet enough.

CHORUS: There's smoke coming up now from their chimney.

Whispers offstage under the audience. We are part of the mob.

MRS DONNELLY: The sun comes up, there's my shadow line—getting shorter already, turn earth another morning and noon and night I wish I could stop it Bridget take out the pail and pump us a fresh pail of water, yesterday I could hear Mary Donovan spinning in her doorway, watching us, I wonder

BRIDGET screams and runs in.

BRIDGET: Aunt Judith, where shall we hide, there's a mob in the yard with sticks in their hands.

JOHN sleeps behind the stove.

MRS DONNELLY: Augh! what has possessed them now. Go tell Mr Donnelly. John, get dressed. I stood behind the door and looked through the crack at them. Why is it getting so dark in our house. Because the light of each window is shut out by the people there.

BRIDGET: Uncle Jim, the yard is full of men with clubs. Johnny, you'd best get up.

MR DONNELLY, hitching up trousers, goes to the door and addresses a mob whose presence we feel rather than see.

MR DONNELLY: Good morning, boys, what's up with you?

CARROLL: We want nothing but to tell you Donnellys that we're not afraid of you

MRS DONNELLY: Look at the dark bunch of them and he alone, what is it, it's

VOICE: We're not afraid of you anymore, Donnelly.

MARY: I have lost a cow

MRS DONNELLY: A cow they say has been stolen from Mary Donovan's farm and we are suspected

VOICE: We're through being scared of the Donnellys.

MRS DONNELLY: Why 'tis only right the cow should be found. If you think the cow is here, Jim Carroll, don't leave one straw on top of another

JOHN: Turn the strawstack upside down. There's no stolen cow here, but I see the man who stole your cow in your crowd

Searching sounds, pails getting kicked, doors slammed &c.

VOICE: We'll make you keep quiet, Jack Donnelly.

JOHN: If you go up to the priest he'll curse the man who stole the cow and you'll find the cow before night.

CARROLL: How'd you like a good stiff kick in the ribs?

MR DONNELLY: And you can all kiss my backside. And I was a man, Jim Carroll, when you were not able to wipe your backside.

CARROLL: We could break your bones at your door and you won't be able to help yourself.

MR DONNELLY: I'll be here if the devil would burn the whole of you. I'm not in the least afraid of you. *(He comes into the house.)*

MRS DONNELLY: They're kicking over hencoops and looking down the well, yes, fall down if you can, John Macdonald, what is it I hear him begging them to do, they're putting forks through the strawstacks we thrashed yesterday, he's saying—

MRS DONNELLY: I wish John would stay in closer to the house, do you see that?

MRS DONNELLY: Yes, they've circled him and they're saying things like

CHORUS: Who stole my disk

JOHN: I don't know who stole your disk

CHORUS: Who stole my pig

JOHN: How the hell would I know

CHORUS:
who stole my disk and stole my pig
rode my horses and drove my cows
cut out their tongues and cut off their ears
who shaved off my horses' tails

JOHN: I don't know anything at all about your horses' tails, all I know is that you're trespassing and my father's farm has a fence, my father's land is enclosed, by the way you're acting you'd think it was a public path

MARY: I have lost a cow.

CHORUS: Don't you tell us to get out Jack Donnelly. We're not afraid of you I'll get satisfaction if it's for twenty years. This work'll be put down and it'll be put down by us.

A roar as they find TOM RYAN. They rush on stage with him & now we & the Donnellys look out at the mob.

CHORUS: Here's one thing found.

CARROLL: Sit up there in the wagon and don't you move

CHORUS: Harbouring this young horserider and cattle driver, eh Donnelly.

MR DONNELLY: I'd harbour your father's son, O'Halloran, if all the world said no

O'HALLORAN: Little do you care Donnelly for my father's sons. Tie his hands, it's off to jail with this one.

TOM RYAN: Mr Donnelly wasn't harbouring me, I slept in their strawstack last night, they didn't know I was there. *(pause)* And I sat up there on the wagon. She came out. I was handcuffed. She came out and looked across at me. Between me and her was them with their clubs. What have I brought down on you, or would it have happened anyhow? Mrs Donnelly she was tall. If I could have I would have died for her. The wagon took me off to jail. I never saw her again.

Carrying TOM RYAN on their shoulders the mob circle and depart.

MRS DONNELLY: Yes, I stood there and I watched them tie up that lad and cuff him and knock him about. They were leaving, they hadn't found Mary Donovan's cow, but I was so glad they were leaving that I didn't dare try to help the boy because for the first time in my life I felt old and small & afraid. There were so many of them. Is this not a pretty way we are treated Mr Donnelly?

MR DONNELLY: But we deserve it, Mrs Donnelly.

MRS DONNELLY: In the name of Heaven how?

MR DONNELLY: For we're Donnellys.

MRS DONNELLY: Yes, and I also heard Will's brother-in-law say they were going to his place at Whalen's Corners next. John, hitch up the driving horse for me, please.

There is a slight tug of war over the whip with MR DONNELLY.

Haven't they gone up the road by Keefe's, Mr Donnelly?

MR DONNELLY: Yes. If you must go, Mrs Donnelly, then you can cut over on the sideroad.

MRS DONNELLY: *(pause)* I *must* go.

What we have now is a bare stage with the bar as a place where MRS DONNELLY can coast up & down & around. A blacksmith should enter and stand near the bar which is going to be WILL DONNELLY's house. MARY DONOVAN should be sitting getting ready to spin & we need a girl who can simply fill in the choral replies to MRS DONNELLY, spin about perhaps supported by offstage voices. I'm in favour of a "Listen to the Wind" wheel & horse with MRS DONNELLY running behind. Simple & light.

JOHN: Mother, what are you listening for? *(triangle sounds)*

MRS DONNELLY:
I can hear the blacksmith who lives over at the village where Will & Norah live
Closer and louder the sound of his hammer
Wheels take me   Hooves draw me
Out of the yard of his father's house

GIRL:
In the stream that I lie dreaming in I hear
A humming sound that fills me up with fear

MRS DONNELLY:
My neighbour, Mary Donovan, cow lady,
I leave you behind me.

And MRS DONNELLY has done one circuit of the stage & vanished.

MARY: I heard a cow bawling over on Donley's place that sounded like my cow. I honestly believed the Donleys had my cow. The Donleys had my cow shut up. A great deal of pork & cattle stealing has been taking place in our neighbourhood. *(A FARMER enters with two pails, which he sets down.)* Dan Quigley, did you hear I've lost my cow? The Donleys've stolen my cow.

FARMER: Mary Donovan, I just seen your cow.

MARY: Seen my cow? Impossible. Where?

FARMER: She's in our yard. I keep telling you the fence is down by McLaughlin's bush there and she strayed up to our yard with our cattle last night.

MARY kicks the pails & hits him off with either stick or spinning wheel or spindle.

MARY: Who the hell's side do you think you're on, Dan Quigley. Are you telling me I didn't hear her bawling over at Donley's?

anvil

MRS DONNELLY:
Closer and louder the sound of his hammer
Wheels take me
Hooves draw me
Gee Pilot! round the corner of Marksey's farm
Down this road grown over with grass

Mob humming the tune of the St Patrick song & just about to burst out from beneath bar crossing down to us & meet SCHOOLMASTER.

GIRL:
In the spinning I lie dreaming in I hear
A humming sound that fills me up with fear

MRS DONNELLY:
Look not this way, Jim Carroll, my enemy.
I leave you behind me

Circuit ends & she disappears.

MOB:
When blind worms crawling in the grass
Disgusted all the nation
He gave them a rise which opened their eyes
To a sense of their situation

SCHOOLMASTER: I was the schoolmaster at the Donnelly School. On the morning of September 3rd, 1879, I met 40 to 50 men at half past eight in the morning. They had clubs and bludgeons in their hands in the name of God, where are you all going to?

CHORUS: We are going away for a heifer that was lost.

SCHOOLMASTER: Did every one of you lose a heifer?

CHORUS: No, no.

SCHOOLMASTER: Then it's time to bid the devil good morning when you meet him.

CHORUS: Oh, we're a long time seeking him.

SCHOOLMASTER: Would you know the old lad when you meet him?

CHORUS: Would we know him, sure he's a cripple and lives near a forge. *(anvil)*

MRS DONNELLY:
Closer and louder the sound of his hammer
Wheels take me   Hooves draw me
Haw Pilot! turn north on the Cedar Swamp Line!
What is the matter with that field of grain?

GIRL: In the humming I lie dreaming in I wake and hear

MRS RYAN: Mrs Donnelly, have mercy on my children, tell your sons to please let the thrashing machine come harvest our wheat and barley. We'll starve this year if it rots away.

MRS DONNELLY: *(The anvil gets louder & louder)* No! There's no time for the wife of Ned Ryan *(and louder as she enters Whalen's Corners)*
The first house, a shed, the second
A ditch, picket fence, gateway, a path, my
     journey is over
Will, Norah *(she knocks)* at my son's door.

But she has no sooner entered WILL's house than we hear the mob already at the blacksmith's; the anvil stops and there are sounds of hammers and forges being tossed down.

MOB: *(offstage)* We'll visit you at all hours of the night when you least expect it.

Now WILL, NORAH & MRS DONNELLY come out. WILL can use either a fiddle or a gun—both are hanging behind the bar that represents his house.

WILL: Mother, Norah—I'll ask them for their authority to search either my house or its premises. Did they show Father any warrant to search?

MRS DONNELLY: Nothing but their shadows

WILL: Well then, if they can't show me a warrant, I'll shoot the first man who comes in the gate.

MOB:
Nine hundred thousand reptiles blue
He charmed with sweet discourses,
And dined on them at Killaloe
In soups and second courses

The mob now slowly come towards the backs of the Donnellys. They are afraid. It's not the same as at the other house. WILL's hand reaches up for his fiddle, he turns, tunes & then plays "Boney over the Alps" laughing at them. Some of them get into the audience by mistake. We should feel ashamed of ourselves that we did not make a better showing against a lame man & two women.

MRS DONNELLY: Are you looking for your mother Dennis Trehy? That you left to starve in the workhouse at Ballysheenan though you're rich here in Canada?

WILL: My mother's taken the hunger off a great many of you days gone by when your parents sent you to our school with no lunch.

MRS DONNELLY: And I wonder at Martin O'Halloran being with such a gang as his father's the decentest man in Biddulph.

WILL: Give them another, they're in full flight down the road. *(She turns sharply away.)* James Carroll fell down and there's others tripping about the proud Napoleons they are. Mother, Norah, do you remember I told you how mother gave me this fiddle? *(sings)*

Then they sold me to the brewer
And he brewed me on the pan,
But when I got into the jug
I was the strongest man.*

And it's right what you told me then. If you're afraid you should be. If you're not you'll live. Today I thank you. One fiddle you gave me, a

---

*Then they sold me to the brewer . . . I was the strongest man—a verse from the Barley Corn Ballad which opens and closes *Sticks & Stones* and runs through the play as the Donnellys' theme.

lame boy of twelve, has been worth forty men with rifles and clubs.

MRS DONNELLY: Yes, I've marked you with all my foolish words

WILL: Not foolish. You've been dreaming of a train. This fiddle stopped that train.

MRS DONNELLY: Yes. But only in the daylight. The night, Will and Norah, may have—the dark has shoulders they can stand upon. To reach our eyes and our minds at last. Hush!

They stand again with their backs to the vigilantes who enter with a sick CARROLL. It is as if MRS DONNELLY can hear them for she half turns. They stagger about as before. CARROLL is stretched on floor.

VOICE: What's the matter with him?

NED RYAN: They've made him ill. *(tends him with some restorative)*

VOICE: He's having a fit if you ask me and I don't want to have anything more to do with this. I'm leaving.

They are all sitting down on their haunches.

CARROLL: How's your old mother, Dennis, back in the workhouse at Ballysheenan?

NED RYAN: How'd she get there ahead of us so fast?

CARROLL: She's a witch, that's why. And she shall be burnt for a witch. *(relapses)*

VOICE: Ned Ryan, I think he wants something. Bend over him and—

NED RYAN: *(pause)* He wants you to bring him the Holy Bible out of the school cupboard.

It is brought & CARROLL uses it for a pillow.

CARROLL: Yes, Dennis, I ran like the rest of you. Now that's better. I ran like the rest of you—but there wasn't one of you behind me and there wasn't one of you I could keep up to—tell me, how many of yous are willing to draw lots— *(They all shy away.)* to see who will sue Jack Donnelly for perjuring himself when he says that we trespassed on his father's farm today. Because, you'll note the old man did tell us "If you think the cow is here, Jim Carroll, don't leave one straw on top of another."

They raise hands & come closer.

Well, who wouldn't dare to do that, but here's one more thing, and we'll just see who's man enough to raise their hands to this proposition. In this Bible someone has placed eight slips of paper each with the name of a Donnelly written thereon. Who is brave enough to come up and draw one of those slips of paper out?

VOICE: Jim, what does it mean if we do draw the piece of paper out?

CARROLL: It means that that Donnelly will be executed before the year is out. If it can be shown that one can be killed and the executioner get away with it how many of you are then willing to go on with me at your head against the rest of the family and I promise you there will be no risk involved.

VOICE: Sure if this one is killed and no one is punished, sure.

CARROLL: Let's take a vote then. Ned, take the vote will you?

NED: Yeas? *(hands are raised)* Nays? *(some hands go up)* Forty-one to seven, Jim.

CARROLL: The seven nays are to leave this room forever, and I dare them to speak. When the execution takes place remember—you must help or join the Blackfeets. Come up and swear.

VOICE: But, Jim, nobody's drawn the lot yet and I'm not.

NED: I'll draw it. She took away my son, I'll take back one of hers.

CARROLL: Remember what you're about to promise because yes a brave man has been found, not afraid of them, and he'll show us the way, the way I could not show you this shameful morning.

VOICE: Who's he going to kill then?

NED RYAN: Michael Donnelly.

MRS DONNELLY says the name too, screams "My son," train whistle, the train proceeds to the

CHORUS: Fourth crossing!

The BARTENDER at Slaght's Hotel slides a glass down the bar as MIKE & MORRISON, his mate, enter. "WILLIAM LEWIS" is waiting; an old man

named GREENWOOD is standing at the bar, sometimes bending down to spin a top.

BARTENDER: Mike, Jim. You're off early tonight. Still raining outside?

MIKE: We both ordered hot whiskeys because we were cold & wet still. I could feel the heat of the drink coming through the glass into the flesh of my hand. There's that old fellow always in here spinning his top and going to make the same joke he always does about fighting dogs. My top against your top, Greenwood. You've been waiting for this all day, haven't you?

They both spin tops which fight each other.

GREENWOOD: How's your big bulldog you got, Mike Donnelly.

MIKE: Back home in St Thomas I've got a bulldog that can lick anything its weight in Ontario

GREENWOOD: I ain't got no dog, just this top, but I can whip any dog myself, I'll strip off my clothes and commence anytime.

MIKE: Ah, you couldn't beat my bulldog, you can't even beat my top with your old top it's got more than a few holes gnawed out of it, where do you keep it, old fellow, there's been rats biting away at this one.

GREENWOOD: Here, don't you insult my top. Those holes are for balance.

LEWIS: You don't want to hop on that man, Donnelly.

MIKE: No one is touching him, and it's none of your business if there was.

LEWIS: You are always shooting off your mouth, aren't you Donnelly. (taking off his coat)

MIKE: Do you want anything of me.

MORRISON: Now look, you two, quit it. All he said, Bill Lewis, was that his top had holes in it. Turn around away from each other. Greenwood if that's your name, see if Mike'll do you a favour and have a return match with his top meanwhile where's the washroom around here?

A clock strikes six.

MIKE: You do want something from me.

"LEWIS" strikes DONNELLY from behind; as MIKE tries to pin him he leads him back behind the bar with the knife open & ready. Just as MORRISON returns from the washroom, MIKE is stabbed below the belt. LEWIS glides away; MORRISON catches MIKE just as he falls. Train whistle.

MIKE: My God, Neighbour, I'm gone   stabbed. Jim, that's our train!

The CHORUS comes—at the wake for MICHAEL at the Donnelly farm—with four poles which represent the fourposter bed he was laid on. Candles. People kneel by the bier, then retire to the sides of the room.

MRS DONNELLY: Yes, his bed is ready. Bring Michael in here boys. Bridget, bring me the clean shirt I've got ready for him.

She takes off his old shirt, washes him & puts on a white shirt.

MORRISON: We carried Mike to the washroom. I held his head for a while and saw him die.

CHORUS: He was under bonds to keep the peace, and he was considered a desperate character.

MORRISON: We were brakemen on that train together. I think he would fight if he was set upon, but as a bully I never saw him have a row.

CHORUS: The first named testified that the deceased was a quarrelsome bully and started the row, but the others testified that he was not a disorderly character—

MORRISON: I caught hold of Donnelly for the purpose of assisting him. I never heard anybody say anything against Donnelly, and I never saw him engaged in a row.

MRS DONNELLY: I then read in the newspaper that the respective lawyers and the judge then addressed the jury, after which they retired and returned in a short time with a verdict of manslaughter. Since there was no defence offered at all, one supposes that if the lawyer for this William Lewis had offered a defence why my son's murderer might have got off completely scot free, but as it was the judge sentenced this man whom Michael had never even met before that night, whom none of us knows—two years in prison. In this forest there is now a proclamation that the hunting season on my sons is open now. There are only five of them left, the breed is rare, but do not let that limit your greed for their hearts' blood.

Michael. I wish that as I spoke with your oldest brother as he lay dying last summer I could have been there with you this winter. I told him what I tell you now—to look straight ahead past this stupid life and death they've fastened on you— just as long ago your father and me and our firstborn walked up over the last hill in Ireland and saw, what you will see now—for the first time in our lives we saw freedom, we saw the sea.

MR DONNELLY: Mrs Donnelly, the sleighs have come to take our son to the church.

Candles, fourposter, all sweep out of the room. We are in a barroom again. Slaght's years after; two CHAMBERMAIDS have just been assigned to clean out the barroom; outside the sun is just getting up. The old tramp is whistling "Buffalo Gals" as he walks up the empty Main Street of Waterford; train whistle. The one MAID throws the pail of water over the floor and starts scrubbing. A clock strikes twelve. The ghost of MIKE DONNELLY stands behind the bar.

MAID ONE: Ugh, clean the hotel from top to bottom would you. We won't be done in here till midnight, the old muck from their feet and mouths. What're you looking so pale for, it's only an old barroom, been closed up for thirty years till this fool thinks he can run it for a profit again.

MAID TWO: I thought I saw someone standing by the end of the bar over there.

MAID ONE: There's no one there I can see, Mary.

MAID TWO: You don't know Waterford, this place, too well do you.

MAID ONE: What's there to know? There's that old man sloping off into the dawn, I wish I were free to walk the roads, not tied down like this to a scrubbing brush.

MAID TWO: I wish you wouldn't pick that place by the bar to scrub so, Sarah.

MAID ONE: There you go with your ghosts again. I don't believe them.

MAID TWO: Would you please stop your damn scrubbing at the same spot, Sarah.

MAID ONE: Are you against clean floors or something? There's something on the floor here that won't come out.

MAID TWO: He's looking right down at you

MAID ONE: I'll wet his feet for him then. Give me that soap, I'll . . .

MAID TWO: Don't you know there was a murder in this barroom about thirty years ago, one of the brakemen on the Canada Southern, was stabbed right there where you're scrubbing. That's the blood from his wound you're trying to wash out and my mother says . . .

MAID ONE: Mary, go up and start the sitting room if this is too . . . what did your mother say?

MAID TWO: That's the blood of Michael Donnelly on the floor there. No matter how hard you try it never comes out.

A top spins across the floor. Scrubbing of the remaining woman; Ghost still there. Whistling dies away. "Buffalo Gals."

CHORUS:
The St Nicholas Hotel
     William Donnelly Proprietor
         The Donnellys, Part Two

END

THREE SONGS USED IN THE PLAY

ST PATRICK
(to the tune of *Pop Goes the Weasel*)

Oh! St Patrick was a gentleman,
    Who came of decent people;
He built a church in Dublin town,
    And on it put a steeple.
His father was a Gallagher;
    His mother was a Brady;
His aunt was an O'Shaughnessy,
    His uncle an O'Grady.

CHORUS
So, success attend St Patrick's fist,
    For he's a saint so clever;
Oh! he gave the snakes and toads a twist,
    And bothered them forever.

The Wicklow hills are very high
    And so's the Hill of Howth, sir;
But there's a hill much bigger still,
    Much higher nor them both, sir.
'Twas on the top of this high hill
    St Patrick preached his sarmint
That drove the frogs into the bogs,
    And banished all the varmint.

So, success attend St Patrick's fist, &c.

There's not a mile in Ireland's isle
    Where dirty varmin musters
But there he put his dear fore-foot,
    And murdered them in clusters.
The toads went pop, the frogs went hop,
    Slap-dash into the water;
And the snakes committed suicide
    To save themselves from slaughter.

So, success attend St Patrick's fist, &c.

Nine hundred thousand reptiles blue
    He charmed with sweet discourses,
And dined on them at Killaloe
    In soups and second courses.
When blind worms crawling in the grass
    Disgusted all the nation,
He gave them a rise which opened their eyes
    To a sense of their situation.

So, success attend St Patrick's fist, &c.

No wonder that those Irish lads
    Should be so gay and frisky,
For sure St Pat he taught them that,
    As well as making whiskey;
No wonder that the saint himself
    Should understand distilling,
Since his mother kept a shebeen shop
    In the town of Enniskillen.

So, success attend St Patrick's fist, &c.

Oh! was I but so fortunate
    As to be back in Munster,
'Tis I'd be bound that from the ground
    I never more would once stir.
For there St Patrick planted turf,
    And plenty of the praties,
With pigs galore, ma gramma's store,
    And cabbages . . . and ladies!

Then my blessings on St Patrick's fist,
    For he's a darling saint, oh!
Oh! he gave the snakes and toads a twist;
    He's a beauty without paint, oh!

HECTOR O'HARA'S JUBILEE SONG
(to the tune of *Perhaps She's on the Railway*)

Hark! the trumpets sounding
Proclaim this is the day,
With hearts so bright and bounding,
Thousands haste away;
To have a look on Salter's Grove,
The lads and lasses true
All thro' the day will shout hurrah,
For the Dominion's bonny blue.

CHORUS
Perhaps you've come to London
Upon this glorious day,
To Salter's Grove to have a lark,
You're sure to take your way.
The blues so true will stick to you,
So boldly they will stand,
The Grittish crew will never do,
No longer in the land.

The lads and lasses in their best,
Will ramble thro' the grounds—
The bands will play throughout the day,
In music's sweetest sounds;
The pleasant strains goes thro' the brains
Of each unhappy Grit,
It gives them all the belly ache,
And sends them home to—

From here and there and everywhere,
The folks have come today,
Darby and Joan have come from home
To see the grand display.
From east and west from north and south
There's people without end,
With frills and bows and furbelows,
They'll do the Grecian Bend.

Elgin girls and Biddulph swells,
Each other try to please,
By doing the lardy dardy dum,
All among the trees,
From Westminster the pretty girls
Are rolling in the hay.
Their mothers say they mustn't,
But their fathers say they may.

There's little Popsy Wopsy here,
From Ingersoll she has come—
She's doing the double shuffle
With the chap that beats the drum;
There's Bob and Jack, Sal and Pat
And Polly coming on,
Upon her head she carries a bed
And calls it her chignon.

Strathroy girls are here today,
So nicely dress'd in blue—
With chaps that come from Exeter,
The grand they mean to do.
Polly Strong, couldn't come on
For a nasty old tom cat,
Has got a lot of kittens in
Her Dolly Varden bat.

Then shout John A. forever boys,
That is the heading cry;
Every election we will win,
The time is drawing nigh,
The scheming Grits may bag their heads
That is if they've a mind,
Or go and dig up taters
With their shirts hung out behind.

BUFFALO GALS

CHORUS
Buffalo gals won't you come out tonight
Come out tonight, come out tonight
Buffalo gals won't you come out tonight
And dance by the light of the moon.

1.
As I was tramping down the street
Down the street, down the street
I chanced a pretty girl to meet
Oh, she was fair to view

2.
I asked her if she'd have some talk
Have some talk, have some talk
Her feet covered the whole sidewalk
As she stood close to me

3.
I asked her if she'd be my wife
Be my wife, be my wife
She'd make me happy all my life
If she stood by my side.

MICHAEL COOK (b. 1933)

The particular power of Michael Cook's plays is the result of a fortunate congruence of writer and subject. Cook is not, like James Reaney, a poet by trade, but like Reaney he is a connoisseur of the spoken word. Raised on a diet of BBC radio in its Golden Age and gifted with the ability to articulate both the English and Irish traditions which are his heritage, Cook found in Newfoundland a culture bursting with linguistic vitality. The rich verbal flavour of his plays, redolent of Arden and O'Casey, is one result. At the same time he brought with him a Jesuit background and existential outlook in sympathy with what he calls the island's "obviously threatened ceremony of a way of life in which individuals struggle with the timeless questions of worth and identity against an environment which would kill them if it could." He sees himself as the chronicler of a traditional culture, language and spirit doomed to extinction, a situation rendered in *Jacob's Wake* with mixed feelings of sympathy and savage humour.

Cook was born in London, England, of Anglo-Irish parents. After a round of Catholic schools he joined the Army in 1949 and spent the next twelve years posted in Europe and the Far East. In addition to his regular duties Cook wrote, directed and acted in numerous troop entertainments. In 1962 he enrolled in a teacher-training course at Nottingham University, graduating three years later with a specialty in drama and a desire to emigrate. He began a new life in St. John's, Newfoundland, in 1966, at first directing plays for Memorial University. By 1970 he had been appointed Lecturer in English at Memorial and artistic director of the St. John's Summer Festival. Meanwhile he was writing a theatre column for the St. John's *Evening Telegram* and an average of two radio plays a year for the CBC.

All of Cook's first stage plays were performed by The Open Group, a local amateur company, before being professionally produced. *Colour the Flesh the Colour of Dust* was his debut, presented by The Open Group in 1971 under his own direction, then at the Neptune in Halifax in 1972. A Brechtian-style history play set in St. John's in 1762, *Colour the Flesh* was a preview of one direction Cook's drama would take. The other direction was established by *The Head, Guts and Soundbone Dance*, first staged in 1973. The play combined the naturalistic detail of a Newfoundland fisherman's "splitting room" with a Beckettian sense of absurdist isolation and futility as two old men play out their endgame, indulging in mad dreams of a romanticized past and an unlikely future while ignoring at great cost the realities of the present. Despite their obvious differences, Cook conceived of these plays as the first two parts of a "Newfoundland trilogy." The third part was *Jacob's Wake*, performed by The Open Group in summer 1974 and premiered professionally at Festival Lennoxville the following summer.

Cook moved from St. John's to the isolation of Random Island in 1975. The influence of that outport environment along with the continued pertinence of Beckett to Cook's view of the Newfoundland experience is evident in the two long monologues, "Quiller" and "Therese's Creed," presented as a double bill at the Centaur in 1977. He reached back again to historical material for *On the Rim of the Curve* (1977), a play about the extinction of Newfoundland's Beothuk Indians, and *The Gayden Chronicles*, his ambitious tale of a British seaman whipped through the fleet and hanged at St. John's in 1812 for revolutionary activities. Workshopped at Lennoxville and the O'Neill Centre in Connecticut, *Gayden* was first produced in Los Angeles in 1980. Cook has continued to write radio plays, including a 1993 adaptation of *King Lear* for CBC. He has served as an editor of *Canadian Theatre Review* and Chairman of Playwrights Canada. Since 1982 he has divided his time between Newfoundland and Stratford where he was playwright-in-residence in 1987.

Jacob's Wake is Cook's richest play, and the one generally acknowledged by academic critics to be his best, despite being critically panned by reviewers when it opened in Lennoxville. Perhaps that production failed to achieve the difficult balances *Jacob's Wake* demands. Like a wake it is both celebration and dirge, a mixture of moods and styles: by turns raucously funny, bitter, maudlin; intensely naturalistic for the most part but with a spooky, surreal quality that increases with the strength of the storm until it moves beyond realism altogether at the end. Taking his cue from that ending, director Neil Munro painted his 1986 National Arts Centre production of the play in stark expressionist shades, his actors caked in gray makeup, moving like zombies in and out of slashes in the iceberg-painted set to the accompaniment of screeching electronic sound. Reviewers were left radically divided in its wake, their responses ranging from "a chilling dance of death" to "a cross between *The Rocky Horror Picture Show* and *I'se the B'y*, with a little bit of *Lost in Space* and *Night of the Living Dead* thrown in for good measure."

The play itself invites comparison with various dramatic texts, integrating elements of *Long Day's Journey into Night* and *Heartbreak House* with an overlay of *Endgame* and echoes of *The Homecoming*. At one level a domestic drama contained within the Blackburn family home, at another it adduces the spiritual malaise of an entire culture. Beyond that it mixes biblical allusions with a stark existentialism to climax in an apocalypse without salvation or resurrection. It is a play about Newfoundland battered by difficult social transformations and unrelenting Nature, and haunted by ghosts.

Maundy Thursday and Good Friday provide an ironic setting for the failed communion and multiple betrayals that mark the gathering of the Blackburn clan. Against the background of the hymn "Eternal Father Strong to Save" we see measure after measure of patriarchal failure. The Skipper has sent his son Jacob to his death, left his other son Winston a drunken welfare bum and his daughter Mary an embittered old maid. Winston's legacy has been the cynicism, madness and treachery of his own three sons. The women have done little better. Mary despises her father, her brother and the children she teaches. Even Rose, the family glue and the ultimate nurturer, probably does more harm than good in her excessive mothering of Winston. Despite all attempts of the aptly named Rosie to put the best face on it, this family is a disaster. Its rituals, as Cook notes in a stage direction, have degenerated into "killing games."

Behind the bitterness hover the family's unexorcised ghosts. Cook has been criticized for bringing a literal ghost on stage at the end of the play, but he gives us ample warning. All three generations of Blackburns are haunted. For more than thirty years the Skipper has lain in bed crippled by guilt and remorse, holding his wake for Jacob and for the demise of the seal hunt that killed him. Winston is doubly haunted, living in the wake of his dead brother and unable to bury the memory of his own lost daughter Sarah. Brad is obsessed and finally destroyed by his ghosts, Mildred Tobin and her infant boy. Given the play's Easter Week setting we might expect the characters to discover meaning or redemption in these deaths. But ironically they see only emptiness and a future without hope.

The condition of the Blackburns reflects in extreme form Cook's view of contemporary Newfoundland itself: "somewhere in the transition between rural and industrial man they left behind a portion of their souls." In the old Skipper, relic of pre-Confederation days, the authority and self-sufficiency of the ship's captain and seal hunter are reduced to impotent ravings and an unhealthy fixation on the past. Winston's generation, the most painfully conscious of changing times, is unable to cope, caught "like rats in a trap, with the Welfare as bait." The future, such as it is, rests with Winston's sons, and their ascendancy marks the final overthrow of traditional values. The times of the seal are gone, Alonzo says. "It's the day of the dogfish now." If government, business and religion are represented by Wayne, Alonzo and Brad, they are in bad shape. Education is no better off with Mary.

Though Cook's prognosis is exceedingly gloomy, *Jacob's Wake* itself is not. The Blackburns don't just go blindly to their doom. Their Day of Judgement is tempered by significant moments of recognition and a pretty good showing when they are forced finally "to steer into the starm and face up to what ye are." Theirs may be a sinking ship capsized by their own turpitude and neglect, but they go down with the sort of theatrical élan that ought to keep us from judging them too harshly.

•

Jacob's Wake was first produced by the Open Group at the Arts and Culture Centre in St. John's, Newfoundland, on July 22, 1974, directed by Tony Chadwick. The play had its first professional performance on July 11, 1975, at Festival Lennoxville in Lennoxville, Quebec, with the following cast:

MARY	Rita Howell
ROSIE	Candy Kane
SKIPPER	Griffith Brewer
BRAD	R.H. Thomson
ALONZO	David Calderisi
WINSTON	Roland Hewgill
WAYNE	August Schellenberg

Directed by William Davis
Set and Costume Design by Michael Eagan
Lighting Design by Douglas Buchanan
Sound Design by William Skolnik

JACOB'S WAKE

CHARACTERS

SKIPPER ELIJAH BLACKBURN
MARY, *his daughter*
WINSTON, *his son*
ROSIE, *Winston's wife*
ALONZO ⎫
BRAD ⎬ *their sons*
WAYNE ⎭

THE DIALECT

I have taken a certain amount of dramatic licence in the presentation of dialect as spoken by the principals. Rose, of all the characters, has been untouched by the wider world and her dialect is, as accurately as I am able to determine, authentic. Winston is a man of considerable experience and education, both of which he seeks to suppress. In consequence, whereas he retains most of the rich verbal inversions which are one of the great strengths of the Newfoundland dialect, I have resisted the temptation to localize his speech, i.e., the substitution of 'd' for 'th' and the dazzling varieties of the use of the aspirant which change from locale to locale about the Coast. As with both the Skipper and Alonzo, Winston occasionally broadens his dialect under stress or when the sound of the sentence requires it. Brad, Wayne and Mary have successfully suppressed their native speech and of the three only Mary, under pressure, sometimes reverts to the older and more satisfying use of the personal pronoun.

THE SOUND

It is essential if we are to believe and participate in the tragedy of the Blackburn family and, indirectly, the world that they inhabit, that the storm becomes a living thing, a character whose presence is always felt, if not actually heard, on the stage. Whereas this might make remarkable demands upon sound technicians, it is not so remarkable in reality. The fury of the North Atlantic is well known. Perhaps what is less well known is the elemental fury of that ocean in the early spring when snow and ice and hurricane combine to create a world in which nothing can live, save the creatures of the sea itself. The history of the early sealing tragedies has been well documented and the conditions that men struggled against, notably in Cassie Brown's epic account of one such disaster in *Death on the Ice* and Farley Mowat's moving testament, matched with David Blackwood's remarkable etchings, The Lost Party Series, in *Wake of the Great Sealers*.

I have, however, extended the known reality to encompass the possibility of an environment no longer responsive to the timeless bonding between itself and man which makes communion upon this earth possible, an environment with the will for destruction to match our own and a greater capacity to ensure that destruction, an environment which bred E.J. Pratt's *Titanic*-sinking iceberg, a vast neolithic structure created for just such a time when man's hubris had made him blind to nature, his own matching nature and that harmony which alone makes survival possible.

The storm then has a voice and a presence complementary to the voices and presences on the stage, but one which ultimately outstrips them, engulfs them, destroys them.

THE SET

The play can be staged in a variety of ways. The most obvious representation is one of total realism corresponding to the two levels of a typical Newfoundland outport house. The downstairs area is divided into two areas, although the room itself is one kitchen. The centrepiece is a large wood and oil stove, which must be totally functional. To the left is the eating area. A simple wooden table, with corresponding chairs will suffice, or a rather hideous chrome set. The sink is on the left wall. Water is piped in from a well during the summer. During the time of the play, however, it can be assumed that the ground is still frozen and that water is being brought in ten gallon plastic buckets. One or two full may be seen between the sink and the stove. There is a window behind the sink.

The area centre and left contains a rocking chair by the fire and at extreme left, beneath the second matching window, a rather lumpy day bed stretches against the wall. Cupboards line the wall between the sink and the stove. One of these may be open to display various items of kitchen ware. There would be, on the walls, an oval picture of the SKIPPER and his wife in the heyday of their youth. One of those incredibly stiff, formal pictures in which the woman, often a sad-faced and beautiful wooden doll, is dominated by the glaring light eyes and the walrus moustache of the male. An illuminated prayer with a sorrowing Christ would confirm the family's Catholic origins, and perhaps a sepia tinted photograph of an old iron ship wallowing in a dead sea. The walls are papered, and should have that bulky consistency that comes from placing layer upon layer over the years upon wooden walls. At backstage centre is the one entrance, leading to the stairs and exterior. We should be aware of a small corridor leading offstage left and the stairs rising, fairly steeply, backstage centre. The dimensions should be contained so that at no time is it possible for anyone on stage not to be aware of, or have to move a great distance to, anybody else. There should be a sense of confining, of a claustrophobic intensity which washes against, and adds to, the emotional tensions built up during the play.

Upstairs, a landing runs centre, with two bedrooms right and left respectively. The rooms are small, low-ceilinged, with barely any room for physical movement other than walking around the beds, getting into them, or getting objects from the wall. In the SKIPPER's bedroom, right, there is a narrow pine highboy or chest of drawers. On it lies the SKIPPER's log book and on the wall behind, a barometer. Beneath the bed is a large chamber pot.

Both beds are old-fashioned, metal-framed. Each room contains a small window, backstage. The boys' room contains one chair, used for clothes; the SKIPPER's room, one chair used by visitors. Both beds are slightly raked and face the audience.

There are obvious small variations on the theme, but if staged for realistic presentation, then they must conform to our expectancy. It is, in fact, minute attention to realistic detail that heightens the progression towards symbolism and abstraction in the action of the play.

An acceptable alternative would be a stark, skeletonized set. The levels would have to remain essentially the same, but a structure as white as bone, stripped of formality, the house equivalent of a stranded hulk of a schooner, only the ribs poking towards an empty sky, would serve the play's purpose, and free the director for an existential interpretation of the play.

ACT ONE
Scene One

The stage is in semi-darkness. Sound of storm. A dawn light filters through the windows.

ROSIE is sitting in the rocking chair, sewing a patchwork quilt. MARY is at the kitchen table left, marking papers. There is no sound for a long minute, save the squeaking of the rocker as ROSIE sews, rocks, sews, rocks. MARY puts down a book and sighs wearily. She stands up, pushing a lock of hair from her eyes, looks at ROSIE, waiting for some comment. None is forthcoming. ROSIE rocks and sews. MARY goes to the stove and checks to see if the kettle is boiling. It is. She crosses to the cupboards left and takes a cup. She rummages again and comes up with a teabag. She crosses to the fridge, pauses and sighs. She turns and puts the cup on the table. She turns back to the refrigerator, opens it and takes out a small bottle of lemon juice. Leaving the door open, she moves to pour a drop of lemon juice into the cup. She moves back and replaces the lemon, and shuts the door. She turns back to the table and sits. She picks up another book, then puts it down. ROSIE sews and rocks.

MARY: I just can't do any more.

ROSIE: What, dear.

MARY: I said . . . I can't do any more of this marking. It's like washing the same dirty dishes over and over again . . . without any results.

She sips delicately at her tea.

ROSIE: *(resting her quilt in her lap)* Ye works hard at the teaching, maid. I knows. I wor talking to Sally Ivany t'other day. She boards dat new teacher, Mr. Farrell.

MARY: That one! She'd better watch herself then. The man has no principles. I don't understand how people like that ever get into the profession.

ROSIE: He got a powerful lot of degrees, Sally said. He's right clever. But he don't play uppity wi' her, she says. He's jest like one of the family. Eats his bit of fish and brewis. Jest loves a salt pork dinner. Sits down an 'as a beer afore dinner wid Rob when 'e's 'ome from the fishing. Right fond of him, she is.

MARY: I can imagine! Degrees don't necessarily make good teachers, Rose. Experience is the only teacher. Experience, common sense and a few good old fashioned virtues. There are too many Farrells about these days, walking into the best jobs, carrying on with their students . . . .

ROSIE: I said as 'ow ye was always at it an' Sally wor surprised. She said he don't ever bring no work 'ome.

MARY: (angrily) Because he doesn't set any homework, that's why. I don't know what things are coming to. They all seem intent upon producing a generation of illiterates and I'm afraid the few of us who are left can hardly stem the tide.

A gust of wind shakes the house. There is a moan from SKIPPER upstairs. ROSIE looks up anxiously.

ROSIE: Skipper's not sleeping well dese days.

MARY: Has he ever? (sipping her tea) I don't suppose I could either, with so much blood on my hands . . . . Some of it my own too. Ink, I suppose, has its advantages.

There is another gust of wind, and again SKIPPER moans.

ROSIE: I should go up to 'n.

She makes no move. MARY finishes her tea, gathers up her books and crosses towards the day bed. She bends down and pulls out a wooden chest from beneath it.

MARY: Rose, I know you do your best, but don't you think Father should be in a place where he can be properly looked after?

ROSIE: In the hospital. In St. John's, ye mean?

MARY: Something like that. Yes.

She bends again and begins to stack the books into the chest. She lowers the lid and pushes it back underneath.

ROSIE: No, maid. I'd never sleep a wink worrying about'n getting his drop o' rum, knowing 'e'd have no one to tend to'n or read from his book. Having no real voices to talk to. (rocking, reflective) Me own fader now, he were different. When his turn come to be took, he sent me mudder out. To spare 'er, he said. Then he begun to say the psalms. I wor young den. I minds me mother sent me in to look at'n. She reckoned he'd tolerate me where the sight of her would only irritate'n. It wor funny really. Me own fader.

Shrivelled face, all yellow it were, an' a black hole for a mout' . . . . He had nar tooth left in his head . . . the words dribbling out. And . . . him wi' that old cap on his head like 'e always wore when 'e read the Book to us. I wanted to laugh, but was too afeard.

MARY: Laugh? And your father dying?

ROSIE: Ah, but he wor allus gone, maid, working at one t'ing or anudder. I nivir knew'n see. He wor jest somebody dying and I wor just a slip of a maid. Strange. I s'pose dat's why I likes to look after yer fader now. It's like he does for the both of'n.

A gust of wind. Another moan from SKIPPER. From inside the house, a clock strikes the half hour. MARY finishes stacking her books.

MARY: There is a difference, Rose. I don't believe Father looked at the Bible once in his life unless it was to mumble a few words over the men he lost at the ice. And only then because the law required it.

ROSIE: Ah well. I must go up to'n.

She puts her work down in the basket at her side, heaves herself up out of the chair and crosses to exit.

MARY: (exasperated) For goodness sake, Rose. Leave him be. He's worse than a child.

ROSIE: Yes, maid. I 'lows that 'e is. But den, I nivir could say no to none o' dem neither.

She goes out. Upstairs, SKIPPER mumbles something indistinct. MARY looks up. An expression of near hatred crosses her face.

MARY: Why don't you just die and leave us alone.

A beam of light spills into SKIPPER's room as ROSIE puts the hall light on. He is sitting upright in bed, crying soundlessly. ROSIE bustles in, lays him back, smooths his forehead, then sits, holding his hand. A door bangs, loudly, off.

MARY: Winston! Back already.

She makes for the door to get out before WINSTON arrives, but just as she reaches it, it is flung open and BRAD stands there carrying a suitcase. He has left his topcoat in the outer hall and is wearing a neat grey suit, surmounted with a clerical collar. Despite the traditional mode of his appearance, there is something wild about his eyes. His hair is dishevelled.

MARY: Brad. Thank goodness, it's only you.

BRAD: Hello, Aunt. *(pushing unceremoniously past her, dropping his suitcase down by the wall)* Where's Mother?

MARY: Upstairs tending to your grandfather.

BRAD: *(moving out into the hallway)* Mother! Mother!

MARY: She's busy. Do you have to announce your arrival?

BRAD: *(coming back in)* Yes. Yes, as a matter of fact, I do.

MARY: Why? She knows you're coming. God knows, we all do. You always come on Maundy Thursday though why I've yet to find out. It's a time when most pastors choose to stay with their flock, isn't it? But then you always did make up your own rules.

BRAD: Not any more, Aunt.

MARY: What do you mean?

BRAD: I . . . have been replaced. Thrown out.

MARY sits as the implications of his words sink in. With purposeful energy, as if laying some claim to the house, asserting his presence, he begins to make himself a cup of tea.

My ministry is ended . . . for the moment. But God's work doesn't end when one servant fails. Does it? Does it, Aunt Mary?

MARY: What have you done now?

BRAD: I challenged corruption. That is what I did, single handed. But what is one man against the Devil? One man against the armies of Cain? I wasn't strong enough, Aunt Mary.

MARY: Still the same old delusions. Why are you wearing that collar?

BRAD: The collar? *(He wrestles with it, takes it off and holds it out.)* The collar is a symbol. A link in the chain of pride. It chokes the soul. *(throwing it to the ground)* I am done with false images.

MARY: What are you going to do now?

She is confused, almost defeated. BRAD is an unbearable complication in an already intolerable situation.

BRAD: Stay here, of course. Wait to be called. Learn to be strong again.

MARY: No. No, Brad. You can't stay here.

BRAD: Why not? This is my house.

MARY: And so it is mine. I . . . your mother and I . . . we can't stand any more disruption, Brad. You know what it's like here.

BRAD meets her challenge without flinching. She turns from him in disgust.

You were always an emotional cripple. Of course you failed, as you put it. What made you think you could use God as a crutch for your fantasies?

There is still no response from BRAD.

Don't you think, at least, that your mother has enough to contend with? Or are you going to be content to just sit and add your weight to the rest pulling her down to an early grave?

BRAD: He was despised and rejected of men.

MARY: How dare you compare yourself to the Lord. You're sick, Brad. Sick. You need help.

BRAD: *(taking her hands with a sudden movement)* You're right, Aunt Mary. I do need help. Will you help me? Show me my faults?

MARY: *(shaking him off)* We don't need you here, Brad. Will you get that into your thick head. Go. Go anywhere but here. There's a world out there waiting to be saved.

BRAD: But this is where I come from. This is where my work must be.

A door bangs off. ALONZO and WINSTON offstage stamp their boots, wheeze and laugh.

MARY: I think I hear your work coming now.

ALONZO and WINSTON appear in the doorway, arms round each other, singing, palpably the worse for wear. Like a travesty of an old music hall duo, they try to get through the door together and get stuck.

ALONZO AND WINSTON: *(singing)*
In Dublin's city where I did dwell
Lived a butcher's boy I loved right well.
He courted me . . .

The crescendo is broken as ALONZO staggers through the door first, nearly falling.

ALONZO: Christ, Father. You're getting as fat as a pig.

He spots BRAD and peers at him. WINSTON follows him in.

ALONZO: Well, well, well. It's the Reverend Blackburn. How are ye, Brad?

ALONZO slaps him on the back and nearly knocks both BRAD and himself over. He clutches BRAD for support. WINSTON crosses to the day bed as MARY rises and crosses to the door to escape.

WINSTON: 'Tis the Prodigal himself, come fer to wish us a Happy Easter. A Happy Easter, son. *(belching loudly)*

MARY: It's Maundy Thursday. A few minutes from now it will be Good Friday.

WINSTON: Oh. 'Tis mauzy* Thursday, is it? I t'ought the weather were a bit queer.

ALONZO finds this very funny. MARY surveys the scene grimly and points to BRAD.

MARY: For once, Winston, your besotted brain has stumbled upon a truth. You should welcome Brad with open arms. That is, if you can open them. Your second mistake has come home. To roost.

She exits. WINSTON sits up, puzzled.

WINSTON: What did she say?

ALONZO: Dunno, boy. Something about a dicky bird.

BRAD: *(crossing to his father and holding out his hand)* Hello, Father. I trust you're well.

WINSTON catches his hand and pulls him down on the day bed.

WINSTON: I think I wor, until I saw ye. Lonz. Lonz, b'y. D'ye hear that. He trusts I'm well.

_____
*mauzy—hazy.

ALONZO: That's what all them religious say when yer dying.

WINSTON: That's right too.

ROSIE enters and goes straight to the stove to fill a jug of hot water from the kettle.

ROSIE: Oh my. Yer all back. I jest bin sitting up wid yer fader, Winston. He's bin right upset tonight.

BRAD, disengaging himself from WINSTON, crosses to ROSIE.

BRAD: Mother . . . . *(He puts out his arms for an embrace.)*

ROSIE: *(turning towards him, holding the kettle)* Why, Brad, I t'ought I heard ye when I wor upstairs . . . . How are ye? . . .

BRAD: Mother . . . I've come home.

ROSIE crosses to the kitchen area. BRAD follows her.

ROSIE: I knows, son. Ye allus comes to see us Easter. Yer a good boy.

BRAD: No, Mother. You don't understand. You see, I've come home for good. I've . . . left the church.

WINSTON: That's what Mary meant! Well be the Lard Jesus, what have I done to deserve that?

ALONZO: I dunno, Father. It might do us all good to have the family conscience restored to the fold.

WINSTON: Family pain in the arse. That's what he is. Always wor, now I comes to think of it.

BRAD: *(trying to maintain a semblance of dignity)* Father . . . I've had a difficult day . . . .

ALONZO has found the collar on the floor and gleefully tries it on.

WINSTON: So have I, son, and ye've made it worse . . . .

BRAD: I don't expect you to understand . . . . I don't expect anyone to share my burdens . . . . But a little welcome . . . .

ALONZO: *(prancing about the kitchen, the collar firmly fastened)* How do I look, Mother?

ROSIE is pouring herself a cup of tea. She turns and laughs, the laughter of shocked delight.

ROSIE: Yer some shocking boy. Have ye no respect? Take it off.

ALONZO: *(in a dreadful imitation of Garner Ted Armstrong)* I'll take your bets now . . . . You're all gamblers . . . . We all gamble with our souls . . . . Yes, our souls . . . . So I'll take your bets now on the second coming. What's that, sir . . . . You haven't had one since you were eighteen . . . .

ROSIE: *(putting down her tea and chasing ALONZO round the room, laughing)* Lonz. Lonz! Now you give me dat.

He dodges round her. She pauses breathless and laughing at the table. WINSTON staggers to the fridge and gets a beer. He raises it and drains half the bottle in one gulp. Sighing with satisfaction, he wipes his face with the back of his hand. He belches loudly and begins to sing.

WINSTON: *(singing)*
Here's a health to ye, Father O'Flynn
Drink it in ginger or drink it in gin . . . .

BRAD: *(anguished)* Mother.

ALONZO: *(sternly to WINSTON)* Today's sermon will, yet again, be on the evils of drink. Last week . . . last week, the collection amounted to two dollars thirteen cents and one Japanese yen. And yet only the previous night many of you . . . yes, women too . . . spent triple, nay, quadruple, in fact, a hell of a lot more than that at that place of sin . . . The Blue Flamingo . . . .

WINSTON collapses on a kitchen chair. ROSIE too laughs.

BRAD: Mother. Stop them.

ROSIE: Oh, don't mind them, b'y. Dey's only having a bit of fun wid ye. Now come on and I'll git ye a lunch. Ye must be starved come all dat way.

He stands uncertain. ALONZO capers round him.

ALONZO
Brad, Brad, wouldn't
Listen to his dad.
Went to be a preacher
Cos his folks they was all bad

Whooooo . . . eeeee.

ROSIE: And so ye are whooping and hollerin' and carryin' on. Set the table, the lot of ye. I'll get ye a cup o' tay.

WINSTON: Who needs tea? Rosie, get Brad a beer.

BRAD: No thank you, Father.

WINSTON: But ye've left the ministry. Ye said so.

BRAD: Yes. I have but . . . .

WINSTON: Then ye've no call not to be normal like the rest of us. Lonz, git a beer into him.

WINSTON hands ALONZO his beer. ALONZO stalks BRAD. ROSIE watches half shocked, half laughing.

ALONZO: Come on, Brad. Here, boy. Here. Ye've dropped yer collar now. It's jest like the ould days.

BRAD: I can't, Alonzo. It's not like that.

WINSTON: What is it like then, son? Ye comes home and tells us yer back wit' the family, so ye must takes what ye gets. Like the rest of us.

ALONZO has forced BRAD back onto the day bed. ROSIE is laughing outright. ALONZO forces the bottle to BRAD's mouth.

ALONZO: Come on, baby. Drink . . . drink . . . .

BRAD wrestles furiously. The beer pours all over him. WINSTON and ROSIE laugh aloud. BRAD, almost hysterical, succeeds in pushing ALONZO back. He falls on all fours. BRAD leaps up frenziedly wiping his mouth.

BRAD: *(close to tears)* Damn you. Damn you.

ROSE Alright, b'ys. 'Tis gone far enough.

WINSTON: Nice words from a man of the cloth.

ALONZO: And assault and battery.

BRAD rushes for the door, but WINSTON, sensing his move, blocks his way. BRAD moves round the room like a trapped animal.

ROSIE: *(alarmed)* Dat's enough now, Winston. Stop it.

BRAD: (screaming) I haven't given up anything. That's a symbol. A collar is just a symbol . . . . I haven't given up on God.

WINSTON: (moving back away from the door) Stay around here long enough and He'll give up on ye.

BRAD: Never. No. Never. He won't desert me.

Unnoticed, WAYNE has appeared in the door. He's immaculately suited and carries an executive overnight case.

WAYNE: Well, well. The same old animal farm, I see.

ALONZO: Welcome home, brother. Ye've missed the sermon, but yer just in time for the collection.

ROSIE: (crossing to welcome him) Wayne. (He kisses her.) Yer father said ye'd not be coming dis year.

She takes his case and puts it behind the day bed. WAYNE comes on in.

WAYNE: Well, Mother, I have to fight through the paper this high to get into the office, but it can wait another day or so. And I've some constituents with a few problems to see up this way . . . . So here I am.

ROSIE: We're right pleased ye could come, aren't we, Winston?

WINSTON: I'm overjoyed, maid.

ALONZO: Who are ye trying to kid, Wayne. Seeing constituents on Good Friday! Ye're not that conscientious. There's something else in the wind. Wouldn't be anything to do with me, would it? A contract or two?

WAYNE: Who knows.

WINSTON: Come to see me, didn't ye, son? Unlike a few I could mention, he's proud of his father. Talks about me all the time in that House of Assembly . . . (chuckling) to the Minister o' Welfare.

WAYNE: (ignoring him) Where's Aunt Mary?

ROSIE: Oh, she's gone. Must've gone to bed while I wor upstairs wid yer grandfader. That wor afore Brad come. Poor Brad. They bin tormentin' 'im somethin' terrible.

BRAD has been standing stiffly by the window, trying to bring himself under control. WAYNE crosses to him and holds out his hand.

WAYNE: Hi, Brad.

BRAD: (turning, ignoring the hand, still dripping slightly) You!

WAYNE: Good God. Have you been drinking?

WINSTON and ALONZO laugh.

BRAD: Devil. You sent them. You did, didn't you?

WAYNE: I don't know what you're talking about.

BRAD: Oh yes, you do. Judas!

He rushes out.

ROSIE: Dat's dem two, see. Nivir did take much to a ribbin', Brad didn't. I'd better go and see'n settled. (She makes for the door and turns.) He'll be sleepin' wid ye, Lonz. Ye don't mind, do ye?

WAYNE: Why should he. Lonz has never been particular about who he slept with.

ALONZO: Watch it, brother. Watch it.

ROSIE exits.

WINSTON: Want a drink, son? (proffering a beer) Oh yis. I'm sorry, sir. (tugging his forelock) Beer's a working man's drink, i'n it?

WAYNE: (mocking) Jesus, Fader. Then what are ye doing drinkin' it.

WINSTON goes to the dresser, opens a drawer, produces a bottle of moonshine, holds it up to the light and eyes it with great satisfaction.

WINSTON: Now . . . that's a good brew. One of the best I ever made, though I says it myself. (He puts the bottle on the table.) Lonz. Get a jug of hot water, boy. Wayne, me son. Git the mugs.

It's a traditional part of the family ritual. WINSTON gets sugar from the dresser and one teaspoon from a drawer. WAYNE gets three mugs. ALONZO pours hot water from the kettle into a substantial aluminum jug. All three deposit their burdens, pause and sit, almost simultaneously. The irony is that whereas the rules of the ritual have evolved into killing games, the unifying structure remains the same. WINSTON pours and mixes a drink.

WINSTON: Now, boys. Let's celebrate the annual family reunion.

WAYNE: What family? What union?

WINSTON eyes him steadily. WAYNE, unmoved, helps himself to a drink.

WINSTON: Now, b'y. I knows ye've gone up in the world. Weren't nowhere else to go from here, was there? But ye still comes back every year. Or nearly every year. They must be something in it.

ALONZO: The thrill of disaster.

WINSTON: A good crack.

ALONZO: No, b'y. Love. That's what it is. Love.

WINSTON: I 'lows I nivir t'ought o' that.

They both laugh. WAYNE allows himself a grin. He knows the game, the rules, and showing emotion isn't one of them. ROSIE re-enters.

ROSIE: Oh. Ye's all settled den. I bin talking to Brad, Winston. He's some upset. Seems like dey t'rew him out. Now, isn't dat shockin'? After all he done for dem too.

ALONZO: About time they come to their senses. I heard stories about him, Mother, that ye wouldn't have been so proud of.

WAYNE: Me too.

WINSTON: Oh. What wor that then? I t'ought he wor incapable of sin.

WAYNE: He was becoming a damned nuisance. Moved one community from a decent fishing ground to a hole in the bog. Pestered us and Ottawa for grants of one kind or another. Even tried a little arson though we couldn't prove it.

ALONZO: So he was right. Ye got rid of him.

WAYNE: Did I say that?

ALONZO: Ye didn't have to. I can see I'll have to watch you, boy. Yer getting dangerous.

WAYNE: Thanks for the compliment.

WINSTON: Jesus. Politics! Let's get off the subject, afore I pukes. Rosie . . . Rosie, maid. Git the cards, will ye?

In the interior, a clock strikes twelve. ROSIE fetches a pack of cards.

ROSIE: Oh my. 'Tis twelve already. *(yawning widely)* Shall I go up and git the bed warm, Winston?

WINSTON: Ye can do what ye likes, maid. I 'lows it'll take more than warmth to dress me leg* tonight.

During the following speech, ROSIE exits and reappears with a handful of splits for lighting the fire in the morning. She lowers the oven door, places the wood in the oven and leaves the door down.

WAYNE: Father. For God's sake.

WINSTON: He allus wor squeamish, Lonz. I suppose that's what they calls sensitivity.

ALONZO: Is it? Jes', Fader. Ye're a walking encyclopedia. I learns something every time I comes here.

ROSIE: Goodnight then, b'ys.

WAYNE: Goodnight, Mother.

ALONZO: 'Night.

ROSIE exits. WINSTON picks up the cards.

WINSTON: First Jack deals?

They nod. He rapidly spins round the cards off the top of the pack. The first Jack falls to WAYNE.

Jesus, if he fell off a skyscraper, he'd land in a pile o' shit.

He throws the pack at WAYNE, who shuffles them and begins to deal. They are playing one hundred and twenties. The cards are dealt, five apiece, in blocks of two and three.

ALONZO: I blames Aunt Mary for Wayne, Father. Shoving all them books and morals into his head when he were young. Unhealthy, I says.

All three examine their cards, WAYNE in particular making sure that no one can catch a glimpse of his hand.

WAYNE: Jealousy will get you nowhere. Anyway, you haven't done too badly out of me, one way or another.

WINSTON: Jealous! Of you! I'll go twenty. I wouldn't change me peace of mind fer all yer House of Assemblies.

---

*dress me leg—have sexual intercourse.

ALONZO: Twenty-five. I make more money than he does anyway.

WAYNE: I'll take your twenty-five. If you want to live by selling watered booze and importing prostitutes as strippers you're welcome to it.

ALONZO: There's more than one way of prostitution.

WINSTON: Make it, son.

ALONZO: And for me.

WAYNE: Diamonds!

WINSTON: I nivir told ye, Lonz, about the time we 'ad to get Wayne circumcised when he wor little. I'll take three.

ALONZO: No. Ye didn't. Two fer me.

WINSTON discards and accepts three cards from WAYNE. ALONZO, likewise. WAYNE goes through the discards, ignores them and takes two cards.

WINSTON: 'Is mother wor some proud of his bird. It wor about t'ree inches long when he wor borned.

WAYNE: *(rattled)* Your down, Father. Your down!

WINSTON: *(playing and continuing unperturbed)* All the neighbours come in to look at'n. It wor the eighth wonder of the world, boy. Even yer Aunt Mary were excited, though she didn't know why.

WAYNE: For God's sake, Alonzo. Play, will you. Or pack it in.

ALONZO: *(plays)* What happened?

WAYNE: *(plays)* Can't you ever get your mind out of the gutter, Father?

WINSTON: It wor keeping yer cock out of the gutter that worried us. An' the doctors said if it wor real, ye'd nivir be no good to no one, 'cept an old ewe maybe. *(He plays.)*

ALONZO: *(chuckling and beginning to sing)*
Ewe take the high road
An' I'll take the low road . . .

WAYNE: Play!

ALONZO plays.

WAYNE: You're just trying to beat this hand. It

won't work . . . *(He takes the trick.)*

WINSTON: Anyways, we took'n to St. John's. Yer mother took a photograph of'n afore we left, just in case they cut'n right off.

WAYNE: Your card, Father. Your card. That's the Jack of trumps.

WINSTON: So it is. Well, I got nar' one. *(He throws away.)*

ALONZO: What happened? The five of trumps, Wayne.

WAYNE: *(shouting)* It can't be. I just played that.

ALONZO: You're mistaken, brother. I wondered why you took my twenty-five in the first place.

WAYNE searches back through his tricks, finds the offending card and throws it in front of ALONZO.

ALONZO: You accusing me of cheating.

WINSTON: Like all politicians, Lonz. They can't bear to lose, even to family and friends.

WAYNE: I say you cheated.

SKIPPER: Jacob! Jacob!

WINSTON: There he goes. Slippin' out through the Narrows agin.

ALONZO: What happened?

WAYNE: You cheated.

SKIPPER: Jacob . . . .

WINSTON: It wor all skin. They was nothing there. Nothing at all. Smallest damn thing ye ever did see.

ALONZO collapses in hysterics. WAYNE, furious, strides round the table. Delves into ALONZO's pocket and comes up with a set of trump cards.

WAYNE: You disgusting, cheating pimp. No more favours, d'you hear. No more contracts. Not from me. Not from anybody in this government.

ALONZO: *(unmoved)* Did it ever grow?

WINSTON: Never, b'y. Never. That's why he'd only let Aunt Mary give'n 'is weekly bath. An' that went right on 'til he wor thirteen or so.

ALONZO shrieks with laughter.

WAYNE: *(shouting)* Stop lying. Stop lying, for Christ's sake.

MARY appears in the door, dressed in a voluminous nightgown.

MARY: What in the name of Christian charity is going on in this house? The noise is enough to wake the dead.

Coming forward, she sees WAYNE.

Wayne.

SKIPPER: I nivir sent the starm, Jacob. Ye can't blame me for that.

WINSTON: The dead arose and appeared to many.

WAYNE: I'm sorry, Aunt.

He attempts to recover composure, moves round the table, putting on his jacket which has been discarded at the beginning of the game. WINSTON watches him carefully, waiting for a further opportunity. ALONZO's chuckles punctuate the brief silence. MARY moves to WAYNE and puts her hand on his arm.

MARY: You shouldn't let them do this to you, Wayne.

WINSTON: That's right, maid. We shouldn't a let 'em do it to'n in the first place, I 'lows.

MARY: Do what? What drunken gibberish are you on with now?

WAYNE: For the love of . . . Shut up. *(to MARY)* Each time I walk into this house, I lose my sanity. You'd think by now I'd know better.

MARY: You shouldn't come.

WINSTON: But he do, maid. He do. And we all knows why, eh, Lonz?

ALONZO: *(sputtering)* For his bath.

WAYNE goes for ALONZO.

MARY: Wayne. Don't. That's just what they want.

WAYNE: *(drawing back)* Don't worry, Aunt. *(to WINSTON and ALONZO)* This is definitely the last time, d'you hear? You've played your last game of cards at my expense, the pair of you.

He crosses to the day bed, picks up his case and walks out into the livingroom with MARY.

ALONZO: God, Father. That were worth coming home for. Father!

WINSTON slumps back on the chair, mouth open, and begins to snore. ALONZO shakes his head, gets up, moves as if to exit, but the old force of habit pulls him back. He closes the bottle, puts it back on the chest of drawers. He picks up the scattered cards and crosses, the cards in his hand, to the stair door.

Mother. Mother.

He goes back to the table, puts the cards in the box, and puts them away. He tries to lift WINSTON and gets him as far as centre, then the pair collapse. ALONZO gets up as ROSIE enters, tying her nightdress about her.

ALONZO: There ya are. Help me to git him upstairs, will ye?

The two manage to raise WINSTON and begin to drag him towards the door.

Jesus. He never used to be this heavy.

ROSIE: I knows, b'y. 'Tis all the beer, I suppose. What wor all the racket about?

ALONZO: *(laughing)* Oh nothing, Mother. Jest a friendly game of cards. Jest like the old days . . . .

They exit. The lights dim, except upstairs on SKIPPER. He is listening intently. There is an ominous gust of wind, the beginnings of a storm. He nods and smiles. He folds his hands and lies back. The light fades.

Scene Two

The following morning. A cold dawn light filters through the windows. A savage gust of wind shakes the house, then subsides to a threatening moan. ROSIE bustles in with a kerchief tied about her head. Her first action is to turn on the radio before she lights the fire. As the radio fades in with a hymn, she hums and part sings along with it, putting in the splits, checking the oil burner, lighting the wood, filling kettles, making general preparations for breakfast. On the radio, John Beverley Shea sings.

VOICE: *(singing)*
There is a green hill
Far away beside a city wall
Where our Dear Lord was crucified
Who died to save us all.

MARY enters.

ROSIE: Good morning, Mary.

MARY: Is it? Have you looked outside?

ROSIE: What's dat, maid?

MARY: I asked, have you looked outside?

ROSIE: No maid. Dis time of year I prefers not to do dat. 'Tis right depressing!

MARY crosses to the window. She looks out. She returns to the rocking chair. The hymn continues.

MARY: We're in for a storm it seems. It's snowing hard already. Just the excuse some people will be looking for, I suppose.

ROSIE: What for? Nobody's working today, girl.

MARY: I know that, dear. I really shouldn't myself. But I have so much to do before term begins.

She crosses and reaches under the day bed for the trunk with the exercise books in it.

ROSIE: Oh, dat's not work in dat way, Mary. Teaching is the Lord's work, dey say.

MARY: *(settling down with some books on the day bed)* You're a good woman, Rose. Where's Winston? Although I should know better than to ask. Still sleeping it off, I suppose.

ROSIE: He'll be down in a minute, maid. Likes to come down to a warm kitchen, Winston do. It sets 'im up fer the day like. And when he's 'appy, we's all happy.

MARY: Are we? Winston's happiness spells disaster for those of us who don't enjoy alcohol or obscenity. Do you know what they did to Wayne last night?

ROSIE: Dey was only having a bit o' fun wid'n, maid. Dey allus done dat.

MARY: Fun is it. *(She corrects some mistakes and sighs.)* Rosie. Wouldn't it be nice, just for once, if you could stay in bed one morning and come down to a nice warm kitchen?

ROSIE: Stay in bed. Me. *(laughing)* I'd be lost in dat big bed all be meself, maid.

MARY: I've got my doubts about that. But you're probably right. Winston would set fire to the woodbox.

The last lines of the last verse of the hymn are heard.

VOICE: *(singing)*
Oh dearly, dearly has He loved,
And we must love Him too,
And trust in His redeeming blood
And try His works to do.

MARY: That's a lovely hymn, even if it is Anglican!

ANNOUNCER: Good morning, Newfoundland, on this Good Friday morning. The sponsors of our Sacred Music Hour would like to remind you that at the time of bereavement, their trained, dignified and sympathetic staff will attend to your personal needs with discretion. And now we continue with the stirring hymn, "Stand Up, Stand Up for Jesus" . . .

There is an enraged roar from SKIPPER's bedroom upstairs.

SKIPPER: Fer Jesus sake, Mary . . . . Turn that damn thing off . . . .

The light goes up slowly to reveal SKIPPER in bed, struggling to prop himself up on the pillows and at the same time to retrieve his stick, a vicious looking piece of polished oak, from the side of the bed. Having done both things, he begins to thump loudly with the stick on the floor. The singing continues.

MARY: *(angrily)* I'll drown him out.

She turns up the radio volume. SKIPPER renews his banging.

SKIPPER: And where's me rum? I wants me rum.

MARY: *(shouting up)* It'll do you no harm to hear a hymn or two on this one day of the year. And Dr. Barr said you were to have no more spirits!

SKIPPER: I don't give a tinker's cuss what the doctor said and if that thing isn't turned off this minute, I'll come downstairs and knock its brains out . . . .

He accompanies this with terrifying blows of the stick.

MARY: Don't be talking such nonsense. Ye haven't been out of that bed for thirty years, and what miracles will occur this day aren't likely to happen in this Godforsaken house.

SKIPPER: *(hammering furiously)* Ye bousy* ol' bitch. I'll . . . .

ROSIE, alarmed, scuttles to the radio and turns it off.

ROSIE: Now, Mary, ye knows how he is. And he's not much longer fer dis world, God rest his soul . . . .

MARY: I've got my doubts about that . . . .

ROSIE: What's dat, maid?

MARY: Whether God will rest his soul.

SKIPPER has been straining to hear this conversation. He leans back on his pillows and laughs, a ravaged, toothless laugh.

SKIPPER: Heh. She's turned it off, anyways. Cantankerous as a starved gannet. Can't believe she ever sprung from these loins. Mustn't have known what I was about then, Mother. A poor substitute for Jacob, so she was.

He lolls back and pauses. The lights fade on the kitchen below. There is the sound of a storm building.

A man should be surrounded with ould friends in his dyin'. Ould shipmates. Not a bunch of harpies. All those brave boys . . . iced down . . . rolling in the Labrador current.

He sits up suddenly, staring straight ahead, and roars.

Over the side, lads. Over the side. Look lively, now. Gaff and sculp.* Gaff and sculp.

---

*bousy—grey-haired.

  gaff—Sealer's saviour, now banned. A stout stick, heavily bound, with a two-pronged iron hook at the end. It was used for clubbing the seal; for drawing pelts across the ice; for surviving when the sealers fell through.

  sculp—skin.

He sits back. The wind howls in his mind.

The ice and the sun and the brave boys.

He sits up roaring.

Git after them, damn ye. East . . . to the East. To hell wi' the starm. Ye can face into it. They must be East.

The sound of the storm increases in intensity.

De yer worst, ye howling black devil. I'm not afraid o' ye, nor me boys neither. Out of my way. I'll git the men. Aye and the swiles* too. I defy ye. I defy ye.

He swings with his stick at the imagined but real enemy, the spirit of death, the spirit of the ice. The storm fades. He stares into the nightmare of the past then sinks back, exhausted. The lights fade on him and come up in the kitchen. WINSTON is warming his hands over the stove. MARY is sitting on the day bed, surrounded with books. ROSIE is laying the table.

MARY: First you and that insolent bar owner last night. And now Father. He does it deliberately. I'm sure of it. Every time there's a storm, roaring and blaspheming, damning us all with his tortured conscience. If I had my way . . . .

WINSTON: Ye'd have him in the Mental, along with the rest o' the family. And have the house to yerself then, eh? Or p'raps ye'd keep Rosie to look after yer ladylike needs. Go on wid ye. Give the old man his rum. It's a holiday.

MARY: Holiday is it. Every day's a holiday for some folk. And this the occasion of The Lord's death. I'll remind you, brother, that the origin of holiday is holy day.

WINSTON: Ye're not at school now, Miss! And I'm not one of yer students, thanks be to God.

MARY: Amen to that.

WINSTON: He's had his rum now every day since the day he wor borned. One drop, more or less, won't affect his chances of salvation.

MARY: And a day's work, more or less, won't affect yours. But that would be more of a miracle than getting old Lazarus up there to leave his room.

---

*swiles—seals.

WINSTON: *(exaggeratedly clutching his heart—on the wrong side)* Now, sister. We've been over all that before. That murmur in my heart . . . I can hear it now.

MARY: If that's all we did hear from you, life might be easier in this house of useless men. I'm no feminist, but I swear to God I know why the movement was started.

WINSTON: Ye'd hardly qualify as a feminist, would you? Aren't they all women in that?

ROSIE: Now don't ye two start at it again. Come and sit down, Mary, whiles I gits yer breakfast . . . .

MARY: I'll be there in a minute.

MARY, glancing at WINSTON, crosses into the eating area and sits. ROSIE pours her a cup of tea, then scurries back to the stove where a variety of pots and pans are bubbling away.

ROSIE: It's some nice having all the family home for the holiday. Just like when dey was growing up!

MARY: Wayne was down at Christmas.

ROSIE: Well, it's different at Christmas. Dere's so much to do. And den dere's all the visiting. Dere's hardly time to see yer own. But dis time, dere's no celebratin' to git in the way. What are ye doin', Winston?

WINSTON has crossed to the fridge. He opens it and rummages for a beer.

WINSTON: Getting meself a beer.

ROSIE: Before yer bit of bologna?

MARY: He's celebrating the family reunion, aren't you, brother?

WINSTON: Right, sister. Life is one long celebration. *(He opens the beer, takes a swig from the bottle and sighs with satisfaction.)* Never ye mind about me, Mary. *(belching loudly and crossing to the day bed)* Ye just get right on with all that marking ye've got to do. What is it this time?

He picks up one of the books, beer in one hand, book in the other.

MARY: *(rising)* Leave those books alone, you savage . . . .

WINSTON: *(declaiming)* "Daffodils," by William Wordsworth. By Mary Freak for Miss

Blackburn, Grade 6. "Daffodils is a poem all about yellow flowers called daffodils. The poet is flying in an aeroplane and looking down through the clouds, he sees . . ."

MARY rushes across to WINSTON and tries to seize the book. They struggle.

MARY: Give me that, you illiterate . . . . Give me that book . . . .

The book is torn in half. WINSTON collapses on the day bed, laughing. MARY falls back centre, clutching the remnants of Mary Freak's book. She is nearly in tears. ROSIE rushes to comfort her.

ROSIE: Winston, ye shouldn't have . . . . Whatever will Mary say to the Principal.

WINSTON: *(unrepentant)* Well, what's she doing bringing all that stuff home? Just does it to make us feel guilty, that's all. Ye can see the words like little balloons at the back of her head every time she picks up one of those poor kids' essays . . . . *(mimicking)* Ye're all lazy and ungrateful and I've spent the best years of my life looking after ye and Father . . . . *(He goes to the stove, lifts the lid, spits expertly into the flames and replaces it.)* Hell, if she'd taken the trouble to roll about in the grass a bit when she wor young, it might've made a difference. Some foolish fella might've married'n. Too late now, I allows.

ROSIE: Winston! Now dat's enough, boy.

WINSTON: Who else would have her now except we?

ROSIE: I swear to God ye'd never know Mary wuz your sister! I'm not going to have the day spoilt afore it's even started. Ye had yer bit o' devilment last night wi' Lonz. Now give over, boy.

MARY has gone across to the day bed and is collecting the remainder of the assignments. She has recovered her composure and is icy.

MARY: It's alright, Rosie. It's all the thanks I can expect from him. He was always destructive of anything he couldn't understand. Even as a small boy. In fact, there was a time when everyone thought he was retarded.

WINSTON: *(laughing)* And ye've nivir changed yer mind, have ye, sister? *(He fills his pipe. MARY stacks her books away.)* That's the one thing we have in common though, Mary. Neither one of us 'as changed a bit and we in't about to.

Take me now . . . born retarded . . . dyin' . . . at least I thinks that's I'm doing . . . still retarded. And Mary . . . born a virgin. Getting ready to be laid out a virgin . . . widout any of the benefits of an Immaculate Conception.

ROSIE: Winston! Dey's no call fer dat kind of talk.

MARY: Don't worry about me, Rose. I can look after myself. It's you I feel sorry for, dear. Plodding along after all these years with a man who's an expert at two things. Making moonshine and cheating the Welfare.

WINSTON: That's right, Mary. Haven't ye heard o' specialization? 'Tis what everyone has to do these days.

ROSIE: 'Tis not as bad as dat, Mary. (wistfully) I wishes sometimes ye wouldn't fight so much. But den the two of ye nivir got on and dat's it, I suppose. An' I'm luckier dan me mother and dey whose men nivir spent a minute at home, traipsin' off to the Labrador or Toronto or such. I allus reckoned it wor his life to do what he would wit', providin' dey was a bit of food in the house and wood fer the stove . . . .

WINSTON crosses to ROSIE and slaps her backside.

WINSTON: That's my Rosie. Fat and comfortable and mindin' her own business. Aye, and warm on a cold night too. (He swings on MARY.) But ye, ye frozen wharf junk. Ye wouldn't know anything about that part of life now, would ye?

MARY crosses to the table and sits down. WINSTON follows her, leans across at her, breathing into her face. She averts it in disgust.

WINSTON: Turn away ye might. I seed ya once. Through the winder of the school house. Strappin' some poor kid across the hand, and it a bitter morning, until he screamed fer ye to stop.

MARY slaps him across the face. For a moment, it looks as if WINSTON is about to spit in her face in reply, but ROSIE hurriedly intervenes.

ROSIE: Winston . . . (pushing him away from the table) Why don't ye take a drop of rum and sugar up to yer fader?

She hurriedly opens a cupboard, takes down a bottle of rum, pours a glass, shoves the glass into WINSTON's hand and hurries across to the stove, where she fills a jug with hot water.

Ye knows how he likes to talk to ye.

WINSTON: Doesn't talk to me. Talks to ghosts.

ROSIE: I know, dear. (She crosses back with the jug and gives it to WINSTON.) But 'tis good company for'n. Go on now. (trying to shoo him out) Go on, afore dere's any more trouble.

WINSTON: Who's good company, Rosie. Me? Or the ghosts?

He drains the glass of rum, collects the bottle and moves to exit.

Alright, alright. I'm going. And mind, woman, that there's a clean cloth on the table for the children when they finally haul their arses out of bed. We must make some effort to keep up appearances, eh, Mary?

MARY: We! You could turn Buckingham Palace into a beer parlour.

WINSTON chuckles and exits up the stairs.

ROSIE: My, my. Dey's always somet'ing in't there? I'd better start the fish. The boys'll be down soon.

MARY: Boys! Rosie, they're all grown men, quite capable of looking after themselves. I'm sure Wayne, at least, wouldn't expect you to put yourself out.

ROSIE: I knows. (with satisfaction) But old habits dies 'ard.

In the boys' room, upstairs left, BRAD suddenly sits bolt upright.

BRAD: (shouting) Fire . . . . Fire . . . . Mother . . . .

WINSTON pauses on the landing outside the room.

ROSIE: That's Brad having one of his dreams agin. The doctor said it wor on account of . . .

BRAD: Alonzo. Wake up. Wake up.

ALONZO: What . . . .

BRAD: I had a dream of fire. Everything burning . . .

ALONZO: (leaping out of bed) Fire . . . . Where? . . .

MARY: On account of what?

ROSIE: H'imagination. Dat's what 'e said.

BRAD: Flames reaching up to the Heavens. And all the souls of the damned crying out. Yes. And you were there, Alonzo. And Father. Burning.

The lights go up in the boys' bedroom, as ALONZO, clad in a scanty pair of boxer shorts, releases the blind. BRAD is sitting stiffly up in the bed. He is wearing thick woolen combinations. WINSTON has stayed to listen at the door.

ALONZO: Oh, is that all? I thought it were something serious. *(shivering back to the bed and climbing in)* Mother. Mother.

MARY: If it's not one, it's the other.

ROSIE: *(calling)* What is it, Lonz?

ALONZO: Would you get me a cup of tea, for the love of God. Brad's burning, but I'm near froze to death.

WINSTON moves into the doorway.

WINSTON: *(disgusted)* Get it yerself. Jesus. I nivir saw the like of it.

ALONZO: Now now, Father. I learnt all me good habits from you, remember?

WINSTON: What I does is between yer mother and meself, and don't ye fergit it. Ye always were too damned saucy.

BRAD suddenly leaps out of bed. He rushes to the window and looks out.

BRAD: Damned. We were all damned.

He stares at WINSTON clutching the rum bottle. He rushes at him.

Father, I beg of you. Throw that evil away.

He wrestles for the bottle. WINSTON easily shakes him back onto the bed, where he is about to fall on ALONZO. ALONZO, as BRAD staggers, pushes him sideways.

ALONZO: Watch it.

BRAD: *(pleading)* Father. Put that away.

WINSTON: *(pointing at BRAD's crotch)* Ye put that away. I nivir knew ye'd got one.

ALONZO: *(laughing)* The sword of the Lord out of its scabbard. A little rusty, but ready for action.

BRAD, embarrassed, discomfited, backs to a chair, covering himself, then turns and begins to dress with great speed. WINSTON and ALONZO watch with interest.

BRAD: Why won't you listen. Why will nobody listen to me. God. *(He drops to his knees.)* God. Is this your will. Give me a sign, Lord. A sign.

ALONZO: Who's he shouting at now?

WINSTON: God knows.

SKIPPER: I wants me rum. Me rum. Goddamn it, what's happenin' in dis house this marnin'.

ROSIE: *(shouting up)* Winston's on his way, Mr. Eli.

WINSTON: Coming, Skipper. Coming.

He crosses to SKIPPER's bedroom, turns on the light and enters. The house is now ablaze. BRAD gets slowly to his feet and turns to face ALONZO.

ALONZO: Nar sigh, eh, Brad? Well, me son. Keep on trying, that's my motto.

BRAD: I feel sometimes as if I'm wrestling with the Devil.

MARY: The goings on in this house. It's disgusting. Rose. What must people think.

ALONZO: *(interested)* What's he like, Brad. I used to think he wor like a long lizard with a spiny tail.

ROSIE: *(moving to the door with some tea)* I 'low it's too late to be t'inking of others now, maid.

BRAD: He's like you, Alonzo. You.

ALONZO: *(shaken by BRAD's intensity)* Jesus. Yer as mad as the Skipper.

ROSIE arrives in the doorway.

ROSIE: *(handing the cup to him)* Here you are, Lonz.

ALONZO: Thanks, Mother. Get me cigarettes, will ye. There . . . in me trousers . . . .

He indicates the place his trousers are hanging. ROSIE obediently fetches them.

ROSIE: Would ye like a cup of tea, Brad?

BRAD: I want nothing, thank you, Mother.

ROSIE: Ye got to eat and drink sometime, boy. Dey's hardly a t'ing to ye now. I got to fatten ye up.

ALONZO: The prodigal goose.

BRAD: Mother, no! I'm too upset. I have to pray. I feed on the Lord.

ROSIE: Well, if ye says so. Anyways I'll light the fire in the front room for ye. I knows how ye likes to be alone . . . . Allus did, even as a youngster. *(to ALONZO)* And ye leave off torementin'n. Dey was quite enough o' dat last night! *(She turns to go.)*

BRAD: Mother.

ROSIE: Yes, Brad.

BRAD: Could you fetch my Bible for me. I think I left it in the front room.

ALONZO: *(echoing WINSTON)* Jesus. Git it yerself. Can't ye see she's run off her feet.

ROSIE: I'll get it the onct.

The lights fade in their bedroom. WINSTON, in SKIPPER's room, is pouring him a drink. SKIPPER takes it, drains it with immense satisfaction and holds the glass out for a refill.

SKIPPER: What were going on down there last night and this marnin'?

WINSTON: Oh nothing, Skipper. Celebratin' Good Friday, that's all.

ROSIE re-emerges at the top of the stairs and takes BRAD's Bible in to him. She comes out and rests wearily in the shadow, listening to SKIPPER and WINSTON, before going on down.

SKIPPER: Ah. That wor it then. I seen lots of 'em. Some good. Some bad. They's places in the world where 'tis jest a normal day.

He pauses and drinks. A gust of wind shakes the house. SKIPPER becomes intent, listening.

Tell me, boy, is the war over yit?

WINSTON: Not yet, Skipper. Not yet. Never will be, I reckon.

SKIPPER: Bloody Germans. Hampering the seal fishery. Lost me best barrelman* last week . . . . All the good hands gone to be soldiers. Foolishness.

WINSTON: Never mind, Skipper. Ye've still got a ship. And a crew.

SKIPPER: Crew. They's wet behind the ears, me son. Frightened o' me. Frightened o' wind and water, sick at the sight of blood. Jump when they hears a swile bark. I 'ad better eleven year old hands when I took me own schooner out of Trinity, conning through the gut,* the church rising and falling behind, the bells ringin' . . . . Women prayin' to God to send we back . . . but not too soon . . . . One-eyed Bugden at the lookout. Tough as gads in them days, boy! Are ye listenin'?

WINSTON: I hear ye, Father.

He pours SKIPPER and himself another drink. The old man drinks, then sighs deeply.

SKIPPER: That Kaiser. He must be some strange feller. Wears a gaff on his head I'm told. *(pause)* I tell ye, a man's enough to do fightin' nature. The rum, boy, the rum. *(WINSTON fills his glass again.)* You nivir did take to the salt water did ye, boy?

WINSTON: No, Father, I can't say as I did. Too much work. Nothing but living gales and fog and no fish.

SKIPPER: Fish. Who cares about fish. Oh, they was necessary. On account o' them, we took to the salt water. An' we shovelled them into our guts till our blood were colder'n theirs. That were schoolin' ye might say, but the hunt, that's different. Every man, once in a lifetime, has to know what it's like. To hunt. To kill. To risk yerself, yer ship. Yer sons. Aye, and to lose sometimes.

WINSTON: Ye can do that at war, Father. And ye can do it at 'ome, too!

SKIPPER: The hell ye can. It's not the same. Fightin' nature and fightin' yer brother . . . . How kin that be the same? How old are ye now, boy?

WINSTON: *(scratching his head)* Fifty-eight, I 'lows. Or is it fifty-nine? Ye should know.

---

barrelman—lookout.

conning through the gut—steering through a narrow passage between two points of land.

SKIPPER: Aye. I remembers. Two years afore yer sister. One afore yer brother, God rest his soul. *(He pauses and drinks.)* What makes a woman dry up like that . . . like an ould cod. *(pause)* Did I do wrong, boy?

WINSTON: Ye didn't do anything, Skipper.

SKIPPER: Aye. That's right. Not fer any o' ye.

He lies back on the pillow with his eyes closed.

Cold seas. Cold land. Nothing growing. Only the harp,* the whitecoat.* Rust and blood and iron. No place fer a daughter. Shouldn't a made one. No place fer me son, neither. Should we a made'n, Rachel? Should we?

Suddenly roaring.

I don't care if the wind has backed sou'east. Send the men over, damn you. Send them out. There's swiles to be killed. Ice to be trod. Out . . . . Out . . . .

He reaches for his stick and swings. WINSTON puts out a restraining hand.

WINSTON: Easy, Skipper. Easy, now.

SKIPPER: *(glaring, then coming back to normal)* Ach. Ye were always a disappointment to me, boy. But ye're human. Ye talk to me. Yer mother now . . . wunnerful fine woman, a comfort in me kitchen, aye, and me bed too. But she never talked. Not after yer brother died that time. Blamed me fer turnin'n out on the ice and steamin' off. But as God is me witness, I couldn't move. When the starm came it wor like the Divil had the ship in his hand. He wor a good man on the water. Better still on the ice. But he's gone now, along wi' the rest. *(pause)* Where's me gran'children? They's in the house. I heerd 'em. Bawlin' and shoutin'.

WINSTON: Aye. They's in the house, Skipper. They'll be schoolin' around like the dogfish by'n by, but I wouldn't expect too much from 'em if I was you. One of 'em pretends ye don't exist and the other wants to save yer black soul. *(chuckling)* And the third waits fer yer will.

SKIPPER: And what do ye want, boy?

---

harp—the harp seal. Generally refers to the mother.

   whitecoat—baby seal.

WINSTON: Nothing, Skipper. Ye knows that. Nothing at all. Jest this. A place to come and have a quiet drink, away from the women, and look out at the sea.

He gets up, takes a barometer from the wall and hands it to the SKIPPER. He moves to the chest of drawers. The top is littered with the SKIPPER's medicine, old charts, a telescope. He picks up the telescope and moves forward, looking out over the sea. The storm sounds rise.

SKIPPER: What does she look like today, boy?

WINSTON: Grey and ugly. Like an ould hag. They's some slob ice* by the look of it. But it's gittin' hard to see. They's a big starm brewing I'd say.

SKIPPER: *(tapping the glass and studying it)* Aye. The bottom's gone out of her. Twenty-eight seven and still fallin'.

WINSTON: They's a small boat runnin' in now. Crazy fools. Nearly too late too, be the look of'n. She's down at the stern and nearly awash. Jesus. . . . She'll nivir get t'rough the Barracks wi' that sea runnin'.

SKIPPER: Ice, boy. Any ice?

WINSTON: I told ye. Some slob . . . . Could be pack out there, but I can't see the sea from the sky now . . . . Christ, boys, what are ye playin' at . . . *(turning)* He's swinging back. *(unbelieving)* He's going back out to sea!

SKIPPER: After the swiles, boy. This is swile weather.

WINSTON: I'd say he's after a quick trip to Hell. . . .

He comes back and pours another drink for himself and SKIPPER.

SKIPPER: Swiles is bred and killed in Hell, boy. Dis is their starm! The starm fer the young swiles! Oh, they'll love it. Swimming up in their t'ousands, looking for the pack ice to breed on. Fierce mothers, boy. Fierce and proud, I tell ye . . . . And the young, helpless, floundering. But we be the same, boy, plunging and stumbling on the floes. *(starting to get excited)* It's their element, boy. Not ours. Our gaffs is their enemy.

---

slob ice—ice formed in harbours by frost, as distinct from pack ice.

The nor'easter and the ice is our enemy. I tell ye, boy . . . I tell ye . . . .

WINSTON: Yes, Skipper . . . ye tells me. All the time.

SKIPPER: (sitting back, quiet) Ah, I thinks it's all gone at times. But ye never had anything to lose. Least, that's what ye thinks. And how could it be different when ye've done nothing but walk the shore all your life. But it isn't true for me, boy. They'll come back. The swiles'll come back in their t'ousands and when they do, I'll go greet 'em just like in the old days . . . .

WINSTON: What about yer legs, Skipper?

SKIPPER: To hell wid 'em. I can crawl, can't I? That's what I did when I lost the use of 'em. When the ice took 'em. Is the house secure?

WINSTON: Aye, Skipper. Mooring fast fore and aft.

SKIPPER: (to himself) But not fer much longer I allows. Let me know when she starts to drag . . . . How's the sea now?

WINSTON: (going through the ritual again, crossing to the telescope and peering out) Worse. Can't see nar thing. Nothin' alive out there . . .

SKIPPER: The boat . . .

WINSTON: She must 'ave gone. Must 'ave.

SKIPPER: Aye, that's the way of it. Let me know when we starts to drift.

He is getting drowsy. He leans back on the pillow, clutching the barometer. WINSTON goes to him and takes the empty rum glass from the bed.

Send Rosie to me, boy. She knows how to comfort an old man.

WINSTON: Knows how to comfort any man.

SKIPPER: Makes ye tolerable, boy. Ye learned something after all. Ye picked a good ship. Steers herself . . . makes no mind o' we and our foolishness.

He dozes. WINSTON begins to leave, quietly.

SKIPPER: (calling from the depths of his bed) Wake me when we gits to the field, boy. Don't ye fergit, mind!

WINSTON: Aye, aye, Skipper.

The sound of a hymn drifts up into the bedroom, "Eternal Father Strong to Save." SKIPPER sings the first two lines. The lights fade in the SKIPPER's room and go up on the kitchen as WINSTON comes down the stairs. MARY is sitting in the rocking chair and ROSIE is at the table, finishing her breakfast. The SKIPPER's voice, keeping broken time with the hymn, drifts down softly. WINSTON enters as the ANNOUNCER breaks in.

ANNOUNCER: We interrupt our broadcast to bring you a storm warning, just issued from Environment Canada in Gander. A disturbance to the east has deepened rapidly in intensity and is expected to bring storm force winds and a heavy snowfall to all parts of the island by midday. Marine interests are advised that severe storm warnings are now in effect for all Newfoundland waters. And now, before returning you . . .

WINSTON: (turning off the radio) According to the Skipper, 'tis the storm fer the young swiles.

He crosses to the day bed, lies down, stretches and yawns.

Rosie, love, fetch me a beer from the fridge, will ye.

MARY: Can't you see that she's having her breakfast. The poor woman hasn't stopped since she got up.

WINSTON: Neither have you. More's the pity.

ROSIE: Here ye are, love . . . . (She hands him a beer and a hot bologna sandwich from the oven.) Now eat up yer baloney, boy. Ye've got to soak up the liquor wid somethin' else ye'll nivir get t'rough the day.

WINSTON: I'll do me best, maid, but it's a kind thought.

With one hand he swigs at the beer and with the other he tries to get up ROSIE's skirt.

ROSIE: Here you. Git your t'ievin' hands out of dat.

She swipes at him, pleased, and goes back to the table.

MARY: Rose, I sometimes believe you encourage him deliberately to keep the peace.

WINSTON: *(exasperated)* Shut up, woman, fer the love of God before I say something I might regret. I've had a hard mornin' . . . *(MARY sniffs.)* Oh yis. Sneer all ye want. Talking to me father is always hard work, like reading hist'ry backwards. Yer own. *(leaning back, subdued)* I wish sometimes that I could have been the son he wanted.

MARY: *(vindictive)* Then you'd have been dead. Like Jacob.

WINSTON: That's right, Mary. *(He tips and drains the bottle.)* That's absolutely goddamn right.

MARY moves as if to speak, thinks better of it, and exits towards the livingroom. WINSTON, visibly upset, crosses to the window and stares out. ROSIE keeps on eating, placidly.

Scene Three

The lights rise on the boys' bedroom. ALONZO is standing in his shirt and underpants looking out of the window, smoking. BRAD is sitting on a chair reading the Bible, his lips moving soundlessly.

ALONZO: Hell of a day out there, Brad.

No response.

Bit like the night Mildred Tobin died.

No response.

I don't suppose ye'd care to remember that though. Always seemed to be able to block out things ye didn't want to remember.

No response. Disgusted, ALONZO comes down, stubs out his cigarette in the teacup and gets his trousers.

D'ye mind when we left ye in the woods that time, fer a joke. Then couldn't find ye. *(laughing)* That were the time of yer first vision, weren't it? Though as I recall it weren't God or the Virgin . . . . The headless horseman, weren't it?

He struggles into his trousers. Annoyed at the indifference to his baiting, he crosses and looks over BRAD's shoulder. He declaims:

"Many times have they afflicted me from my youth, yet they have not prevailed against me." Heavy stuff, Brad.

No response. ALONZO loses his temper.

Brad, for God's sake, put that away and talk to me as a brother should.

BRAD: Are you my brother, Alonzo?

ALONZO: Ah ha. A voice. Out of the depths. More! More!

With a sudden movement he grabs the Bible from BRAD and throws it to the floor. BRAD rises and makes as if to strike him. ALONZO adopts a boxer's stance and prances round him.

That's it, brother. That's it. Do it, fer Christsake. Let's hurt each other like real people.

BRAD: *(sitting slowly, retrieving the Bible and dusting it off)* You're not a real person, Alonzo. There aren't any real people in my family, apart from Mother.

ALONZO: *(crossing to him and willing BRAD into subjection)* Now listen, Brad. I've tolerated you ever since you were a snot-faced brat stealing quarters from me coat pocket. I remember you.

BRAD moves quickly to his feet, pushes past ALONZO with some force, and turns on him.

BRAD: You listen. All my life I've been jeered at. That's all I can remember. By stupid drunken men who were my fathers or my brothers. And when they weren't drunk, they hated me. Just for being alive. And now you jeer at me for saying God is my father. Don't you think that he's better than the one I've got?

ALONZO: You mind yer mouth.

BRAD: *(in an ecstasy of rejection)* And everyone here fearful, afraid to call on Him. Catholic, Protestant, United . . . . They're all the same. Mumbling into prayerbooks. Sleeping in pews with obscenities carved in the back of them. Trying to keep God hidden. Like some dirty secret . . . .

ALONZO: *(shouting)* That's it. And that's all of it. I remember, God help me, when Mildred Tobin gave ye yer first and last piece of tail. That were it, weren't it? Slobberin' and crying on me shoulder, shouting out how ye was damned. Damned foolish, that's what ye was, too stunned to use the French safes I give ye. She, poor bitch, led ye to God, or whatever crazy thing it is ye've got in yer head.

BRAD: You're an open sewer, Alonzo.

ALONZO: Sewers are necessary, Brad. And don't fergit. It's your shit I carry to the landwash, as well as me own.

BRAD: You don't have to lecture me. I'm responsible for myself.

ALONZO: Then keep to yerself and leave us alone to burn or freeze as we wish.

BRAD: I can't Alonzo. I have to learn . . . to love you.

The words are a release, an orgasm. BRAD takes a pace towards ALONZO who backs away, unconsciously wiping his mouth with the back of his hand. BRAD recognizes a victory. He smiles. For a few moments his disintegrating soul is at rest.

ALONZO: You're sick, Brad. Really sick. *(recovering his composure and eyeing BRAD thoughtfully)* Tell me, what really happened up there? To yer flock? What did ye call yourselves . . . . Oh yes, the Church of the Revelations.

BRAD: In the age of the Apocalypse, we are afflicted by many beasts.

ALONZO: Jesus!

BRAD: My congregation were led astray.

ALONZO: They couldn't've been that dumb after all. Must've seen ye were leading 'em to a God of blind alleys. I heard ye burnt out Joel Miller.

BRAD: Miller tried to corrupt my congregation. He was one of them. An agent of the Devil.

ALONZO: He was an agent for Labatt's. Fer Christsake, he ran a bar, that's all. A bar. Even Noah was allowed moonshine on the ark. Give me the book and I'll find the place for ye. *(snatching the Bible)* Father taught me that, years ago.

BRAD: The fire was an act of God.

ALONZO: Ye don't say. Well, 'twas nearly an act of murder. He were lucky to get out with just his face and hands burnt, to say nothing . . .

BRAD: There's no point in continuing this conversation, Alonzo. I've nothing to say to you.

ALONZO: I've noticed. But one thing puzzles me. Ye've been fired from the only job, if I kin call it that, that ye've ever had and ye come running back here. Why? Nobody wants ye.

BRAD: This is my home. This is where I began. Where we all began. That's right, isn't it? You were born in this room. Probably on that bed. And this is where we're going to die. All of us. You too, Alonzo.

ALONZO: Spare yer thoughts for the Skipper. It's his house. He might not like the idea of it being filled wit' corpses.

BRAD: Yes. *(pause)* I must see him. I must pray with him. *(crossing to the door and turning)* Alonzo, as it seems that we can't get on, would you leave me alone for the rest of the day. Please. For the sake of Mother, if no one else.

ALONZO: A pact, is it? Like when we were kids. Alright then. Here.

He holds out his little finger. BRAD, searching his face, slowly holds out his. Just before the fingers touch and hook, ALONZO grabs for BRAD with his free hand with the intention of twisting finger and arm around. BRAD is too quick for him.

ALONZO: Ah, ye little bugger. Ye haven't forgotten, have ye?

BRAD, after a second, leaves to cross the landing. ALONZO shouts after him.

I wouldn't make a pact with you if it were the Day of Judgement.

BRAD: It is, Alonzo. It is!

WAYNE emerges on the landing from the stairs.

WAYNE: Good morning, Brad. At it again, I hear.

BRAD ignores him and goes on into SKIPPER's room. The old man is, or appears to be, asleep. BRAD leans down, listens to his heart and nods.

BRAD: Grandfather. Grandfather . . . .

The old man doesn't stir. BRAD sits down by the side of the bed, opens the Bible and begins to read from the Book of Job. WAYNE has entered the boys' bedroom. ALONZO is at the window. He turns.

ALONZO: D' you think Brad's queer?

WAYNE: I don't know. I never slept with him.

ALONZO: I can see ye're looking for more than a game of cards. I thought ye were finished with us last night.

WAYNE: Look, Alonzo. Let's face it. We don't like each other. Never have.

ALONZO: It's a morning of revelations. Now tell me, ye're learning to love me.

WAYNE: (mocking) I respect your ability.

ALONZO: And I respect your position.

WAYNE: I think you still owe me, Lonz.

ALONZO: (shaking his head) Uh hunh. I deliver this district whenever it's required. That's worth a lot.

WAYNE: And so is my survival.

ALONZO: Check. What do ye want?

WAYNE sits on the bed, the sparring done.

WAYNE: It's about Grandfather.

ALONZO: You getting him committed.

WAYNE: It's possible.

ALONZO: What have I got to do with it?

WAYNE: I need your signature. Well . . . not yours.

ALONZO: Father's?

WAYNE: That's right.

ALONZO: That's dangerous.

WAYNE: You win some. You lose some.

ALONZO: You son of a bitch. Ye want me to forge the old man's signature in return for the motel contract.

WAYNE: I think I could guarantee it.

ALONZO: Think. Ye'd damn well better make sure of it if I'm going to forge the old man's signature. He'd kill the both of us if he ever found out.

WAYNE: He won't know. He'll never know.

ALONZO: (disturbed) Aunt Mary's been at ye, hasn't she? She's behind this.

WAYNE: Look. We're all worried about Mother. How much more of this can she take.

ALONZO: The hell ye are. Christ! (pacing in agitation) Will ye guarantee that contract? No delays. No bits and pieces. The lot.

WAYNE: I will.

ALONZO: Christ! What a bunch of rats we are. Have ye got the forms?

WAYNE gets them from the inside of his coat pocket. ALONZO takes them, scans them quickly, not wanting to read what they contain. He flips to the last page, takes the form to the chair and kneels, using the chair for backing.

Pen.

WAYNE passes him a gold pen.

Shit. Look at this.

He begins to scrawl, then looks up.

It's a long time since I've done this. (scrawling) There . . . .

WAYNE takes the forms and puts them back in his pocket. ALONZO gets up.

WAYNE: Well, I suppose we'd better go and make the regulation visit. Get it over with. Are you coming?

ALONZO: (staring at WAYNE:) I don't believe it.

WAYNE: What?

ALONZO: Doesn't matter. We'll go and pay our last respects. My arm . . .

He proffers his arm to WAYNE. The irony is lost on him. They cross the landing into SKIPPER's room and stay in the doorway. BRAD is intoning softly.

BRAD
Yea the light of the wicked is put out
And the flame of his fire does not shine
The light is dark in his tent
And his lamp above him is put out
His strong steps are shortened . . .

SKIPPER: (sitting bolt upright, roaring) Miserable Comforter. What the hell do ye know about it. Get out. I'm not dead yet. Get out.

BRAD: (getting up a little hastily) How are you feeling, Grandfather?

SKIPPER: How do I look, ye fool. Better than ye do, I hope.

BRAD: You're fading, Grandfather. You should be . . .

SKIPPER: I'm not fading. What do ye think I am? A goddamned flower? I'm dyin', ye pasty-faced pup. And I don't need ye for company. It's hard enough as it is. *(pause)* From the look o' ye, I judge ye to be 'Lonzo.

BRAD: I'm Brad, Grandfather.

SKIPPER: Ye all look and sound alike to me. *(to himself)* What happens to the roots? They isn't what they used to be. So much rotten timber. *(calling out)* Jacob . . . Jacob . . .

ALONZO, who has been delighted at this interchange, comes in.

ALONZO: Well, Grandfather. Still around I see.

SKIPPER: *(coming out of it with a start)* Ye're not Jacob. Get out.

ALONZO: No, I'm not Jacob.

BRAD: Jacob is dead, Grandfather. We must pray that he is with God.

ALONZO: Brad. Who cares? Leave the old man with his nightmares.

SKIPPER: Dead! Jacob, dead. *(lost again)* Eighteen thousand and the decks awash with blood. It's not enough, boys. Get over the side and to hell wid the glass. Gaff and sculp . . . . Gaff and sculp.

There is another great gust of wind and a menace in the silence that follows.

ALONZO: Aren't ye coming in, Wayne? Join the wake!

WAYNE: *(advancing with his best politician's smile)* Grandfather. It's so good to see you.

SKIPPER: Is it?

WAYNE: Indeed it is. And you're looking well too. You'll see the lot of us out, as I've always said.

SKIPPER: *(venomously)* I don't give a damn what ye've always said.

He suddenly snatches up his stick and swings it viciously. ALONZO manages to get out of its path but it catches WAYNE squarely across the forearm.

WAYNE: My God.

He backs away staring at SKIPPER as if he were looking at the Anti-Christ.

Grandfather. You've broken my arm.

SKIPPER: I should have had ye to the ice. Just onct. *(lashing out at the air with his stick)* Living off me. Grandchildren. Crackies* more like. Not one o' ye a man. Not one of ye like Jacob. Ye've no God. And ye've no guts. Ye're nothin', the lot of ye. *(shouting)* Rosie . . . Rosie . . . . Come and git yer whelps out of here. Rosie.

The lights partially rise downstairs. ROSIE is sitting eating, her mouth full of toast. WINSTON is standing looking out the window.

ROSIE: What is it, Fader?

WINSTON: Fer the love of God, woman, leave him be. He's having a chat with the boys, that's all . . .

WAYNE: We're going, Grandfather. We're going. Just came to pay our respects.

SKIPPER: And that's about the only thing ye can pay.

WAYNE: He doesn't know who I . . . who we are obviously.

ALONZO: He knows, brother. He knows too well.

BRAD: I'll pray for you Grandfather . . .

SKIPPER: *(roaring with rage)* Curses, boy. I wants the curses of men. Not the piddlin' prayers of a mewlin' pup. I wants . . .

He glares about him in impotence, then sinks back, exhausted. BRAD leaves, clutching his Bible, and goes downstairs into the livingroom. WAYNE, holding his arm, turns to leave.

ALONZO: You're not thinking of leaving.

WAYNE: No.

---

*crackies—mongrel pups.

ALONZO: Good. I'd hate to be left without me thirty pieces of silver. I'll see ya later then.

WAYNE hesitates, then exits in the direction of his bedroom. ALONZO pokes about in the room, finds the bottle of rum and pours himself a stiff drink. He sits down at SKIPPER's bedside. The old man makes a gurgling sound. ALONZO raises his glass.

ALONZO: I knows ye don't mind, Skipper. Ye nivir did when I were a boy. Used to come up and read to ye. D'ye minds that. An' fer me birthday, ye'd allus give me a gold sovereign from out your chest. I've often wondered who ye'll leave that lot to. Mother, I 'lows. And the old man'll kill himself with the proceeds. Here . . .

He props him up with an arm and holds the glass to his mouth. SKIPPER drinks. ALONZO almost gently lays him back on the bed. He sits staring, eyes open.

ALONZO: Ah, boy. Ye had your day. A good one too I allows if you're any recommendation. The times of the seal. But they've gone, Skipper. Gone, 'cept in your head and a few old log books. It's the day of the dogfish now.

He drains his glass and rises, placing the glass on the bureau. He goes out quietly. The lights fade and go up to full in the kitchen area. ROSIE is sitting having a cup of tea and toast, dipping her toast in the tea. WINSTON is standing downstage left looking out.

ROSIE: *(with her mouth full)* What is it, love? What's the matter? Kin I get ye somethin'?

WINSTON: No, maid. No. Not just yet.

ROSIE: I knewed ye should have stayed in bed dis mornin'. Ye didn't look well . . . and yer stomach was grumblin' something awful . . . *(She dips more toast.)*

WINSTON: *(without turning, half to himself)* How long is it now?

ROSIE: What?

WINSTON: How long is it since we lost Sarah?

ROSIE: Oh my. Ye're t'inkin' o' dat again, are ye?

WINSTON: *(crossing to table)* Every time I gits afflicted with me family I thinks of the one that might have been different. And Skipper don't help much.

ROSIE: *(smiling)* Aye. She wor a bonny thing. Not like me or ye at all. More like Grandfather Penton. Same colour eyes she had . . . and dat cow's lick atop her head. What ever would she have done wid her hair I wonder?

WINSTON hasn't heard.

WINSTON: She might have had a chanct. *(turning to ROSIE)* I asked ye, Rosie. How long is it?

ROSIE: T'irty one years and two months. She'd have 'ad youngsters of her own be now. She wor borned in the February dark. *(She pauses, struggling with memories and affection.)* Ye minds how ye had to rush me to the hospital in the starm?

WINSTON: Aye, bundled ye up in the sled like an old walrus. And Trigger ploughing through drifts up to his chest. Like he knew . . .

ROSIE: I never seed ye like it. Ye were like a wild man. Like yer fader almost. *(proudly)* I believe ye'd 'ave faced the Divil dat night and gone on. *(laughing)* The pains wor comin' every five minutes and the sled were rearin' from side to side, but I still minds ye cussin' . . . trying to drive the snow away, I allow . . .

WINSTON: It wor never the same after she died. I doesn't know why. Once she'd gone, they wor . . . *(struggling painfully with the recollection)* I'd git into the woods and I'd see her, crouching in the snow, under the trees . . . . And the damned foreman coming round charging ye five cents for every stump ye left in t'ree inches above ground. And me hacking away and not thinking, not thinking at all . . . . Jesus!

ROSIE: I had to bind me breasts wit' oakum. I 'ad more milk for her and longer dan fer any of the boys. Still an' all, the Good Lord saw how much we loved'n, and so he got a mite jealous I suppose . . .

WINSTON: The Good Lord! What's he got to do wi' us livin' and dyin'? To hell wid'n.

ROSIE: Winston!

WINSTON: They's nothin', Rosie. Nothin'. They's madness and they's death and they's some who work at it and some who wait for it. *(brutally)* Sarey's out there and they's nothin' left of her save a peck o' dust.

ROSIE: Winston . . . Winston . . . . It wor thirty years ago . . . .

WINSTON: And two months. But it weren't, Rosie. It were today.

He crosses to exit.

ROSIE: *(upset and flustered)* Winston, don't ye be goin' now like dat. I'll get ye a beer . . . . Ye're upset . . . .

WINSTON: No!

ROSIE: I cares for ye, Winston.

WINSTON: *(stopping by the entrance and looking at her)* I suppose ye do, maid. I s'pose ye do.

He laughs without mirth.

SKIPPER: Rosie! Rosie!

WINSTON: And when he thinks I'm Jacob, so do he . . . .

The lights fade.

ACT TWO

ROSIE is attending the SKIPPER, tidying up the bed, rolling him from side to side with great speed and efficiency. Occasional curses spill from him, but they are not serious.

SKIPPER: Dammit, woman . . . . Ye've got hands like a squid. D'ye think I'm a barrel of flour?

ROSIE: Dere now, Skipper . . . all done . . . . How does dat feel?

SKIPPER: Terrible.

ROSIE: I knew ye'd feel better. Now it's time fer yer medicine.

SKIPPER: *(roaring)* I won't take it. I won't take it . . . . I needs to capsize me cock.*

ROSIE: Ye've just done dat. 'Tis jest an excuse. Ye should be ashamed of yerself.

Impervious, she has gone to the chest of drawers, where she pours a liberal dose of evil-looking

fluid into a small glass. SKIPPER struggles to slide down under the bedclothes, but thrashing and cursing is hauled up by ROSIE with one hand. He roars for the third time.

SKIPPER: Woman, I'm in charge of me own ship and she don't need none of that . . .

ROSIE seizes an opportunity when the toothless mouth is wide open and down the medicine goes. Sputtering and grumbling, SKIPPER swings at her with his stick, but she's already back at the cabinet and returns with a glass of rum.

ROSIE: I s'pose ye'll make me force dis down yer stubborn old t'roat too?

He glares, then chuckles and lays down the stick. He clutches the rum and lies back with a deep sigh of contentment.

SKIPPER: Ah, Rosie, Rosie. What a tumble we'd have had sixty years ago . . . .

ROSIE: Ye'd have been tumblin' by yerself, yer badminded ould divil . . . . I weren't t'ought of den.

SKIPPER: Oh yis, maid. Ye wor thought of. We've all got our own courses prepared long afore us gits here . . . . The winds and currents waiting. The ships we meet. And the crews . . . .

ROSIE: Well now, I don't know not'ing about dat and I don't t'ink I wants to . . . . If ye're all settled . . . .

SKIPPER: No, Rosie. No. Don't go. Not yet. I wants ye to read to me.

ROSIE: *(a little distracted)* Ye've chosen a bad day fer dat an' me wit' a houseful downstairs.

SKIPPER: They's old enough to look after theirselves.

ROSIE pauses, irresolute, then she goes back to the chest of drawers. She opens a drawer, pulls out an old logbook, returns to the bed and sits in the rocker by the bedside.

ROSIE: What day d'ye want?

SKIPPER: *(with eyes shut)* Aye, what day shall I have? There were that day in '19? 18th March it wor . . . . Lost the cook. Crew gaffed him. Swore he wor pissin' in the stew. *(He chuckles.)* Tasted like it too. 30th March . . . . No. That's not the day I'm lookin' fer . . . 5th April. Try that . . . .

---
*capsize me cock—urinate.

ROSIE leafs through the ship's log and comes to the date. She begins to read.

ROSIE: Log of the *S.S. Bonavista*. Master, Captain Elijah Blackburn, Trinity, Trinity Bay. Day dawned a bit mauzy. Glass dropping but not'ing to indicate real bad wedder. Big patch of swiles to the sout'east. Barrelman spotted anudder herd to the north. Sent half the men over, wid Jacob Blackburn as Master Watch. We steamed on into the mist. Looked back once to see how dey was doing, a weak sun spilling t'rough a scad* of snow. The way dey was, so far away, dey seemed to form a t'in black cross on the ice. Den the ground drift swallowed dem up . . . .

She stops reading and sits immobile in the chair. SKIPPER is crying great silent sobs that tear him apart. The light dims as we go downstairs to the kitchen. MARY is putting on her hat and coat, gloves, etc. She crosses to the bureau and takes down a Missal, checking herself in the mirror as she does so. Suitably impressed with her appearance before her Maker, she is about to depart when WAYNE comes through the door.

MARY: Wayne!

WAYNE: Good morning, Aunt.

He comes in and kisses her on the cheek.

MARY: Did you sleep well?

WAYNE: Like a baby. It was good of you to give up your bed.

MARY: Oh, that's nothing. It's warmer down-stairs after all. And once your father had been dragged upstairs, it was quiet enough . . . .

The events of the past twelve hours have under-mined her reserves. She sits on the day bed, face averted, close to tears.

WAYNE: Aunt. Something's wrong. *(crossing quickly to her)* What's the matter?

MARY: *(dabbing quickly at her eyes)* Oh, nothing. It's foolish of me to get so upset. Oh dear. I see you so rarely, Wayne. I'm not used to . . . kindness.

WAYNE: Father's been at you this morning?

MARY: He always is these days. *(rising)* I was just on my way to church.

_____

*scad—a light shower.

WAYNE: You can't go like that. Sit down for a moment, come on. *(He leads her, vaguely protesting, to the rocking chair.)* Now. I'll get you a cup of tea and then we'll go together.

MARY: Oh, Wayne. Would you?

WAYNE: We always used to. *(He gets her a cup of tea.)* I still remember those summer mornings. We'd leave early, just the two of us. You stopping to point out the bank swallows, the terns. Steerings, we used to call them. And I'd grab handfuls of wildflowers and grasses from the roadside and you could identify every one.

MARY: Yes. Yes, I remember. There were some happy times then.

WAYNE: I owe a great deal to you, Aunt Mary.

MARY: Oh no, Wayne. You've repaid any debt a thousand times over.

WAYNE: It's not the kind of debt that can be repaid.

MARY: Wayne, I love to see you, you know that. But I wish you wouldn't come here. You don't belong here. That's what we worked for together, you and I, all those growing years. To free you from the cancer of this house, the horror of this place.

WAYNE: I know. But it disturbs me sometimes to think I've gained my freedom at your expense. Why don't you leave? Here am I, a bachelor with a huge apartment I can't run . . .

MARY: No, Wayne. I won't be a burden.

WAYNE: Burden? Aunt . . .

MARY: What could I do? I couldn't sit at home day after day waiting for you to get back. Oh, I know it's tempting. God knows, I lie awake at nights dreaming about it sometimes. But it would spoil, Wayne. I'd get to be like a nagging wife. I'm too old now. And I can teach here until I retire.

WAYNE: I could get you a job in the school system in town. There'd be no difficulty.

MARY: Allow me some pride, Wayne. I'm not qualified. I survive here because I'm something of an institution, I suppose. And no one has the nerve to fire me. You do help me you see, indirectly. Perhaps when Father goes . . . *(pause)* It might seem petty, Wayne. But I'm entitled to something from here. After all these years.

WAYNE: I don't think justice is petty, Aunt. And that's all you're asking.

It is a moment of complete sympathy and bonding between them. She hands WAYNE her cup. He takes it and puts it on the table.

D'you know Grandfather hit me this morning.

MARY: What?

WAYNE: Well. You did warn me in your last letter. I got a bit too close to that stick of his, that's all.

MARY: The old savage. Are you all right?

WAYNE: Oh yes. Just a bruised arm. I think he'd like to have done more damage than he did.

MARY: I'm worried, Wayne. What if he struck your mother one day in one of his fits. He doesn't know where he is or who he's talking to half the time.

WAYNE after a moment checks the entrance to the stairs and pauses a moment at the livingroom door. He comes back to MARY and lowers his voice.

WAYNE: I've good news for you, Aunt. That's the main reason I'm here. I've spoken to the Health and Welfare people. We can get him into a home by making a case for psychiatric treatment.

MARY: Psychiatric treatment! *(Hope flares up in her.)* Wayne, there can't be any doubt. He's been living in the past for so long, I swear sometimes he believes that we're all crew members on his wretched boat. *(pause)* Will it take long?

WAYNE: I think we can get him off your hands within the week.

MARY: A week! Wayne . . . Wayne. I knew you wouldn't let me down. You've never let me down. But are you sure? What do we have to do?

WAYNE: Now don't you bother your head with the details. You've quite enough to worry about.

MARY: Oh, I'm so excited! I should be sorry—or ashamed—but all I can feel is relief. Oh, I do my best to keep up appearances but it's so difficult. And the people have got such a respect for him when it's you they should be proud of. I heard you were in line for a Cabinet post. Is that true?

WAYNE: *(laughing)* So much for Cabinet secrecy.

MARY: Then it is true.

WAYNE: Murdock's retiring next month on the grounds of ill health. He's really being fired for inefficiency. You're looking at the next Minister of the Environment.

MARY: Wayne. I'm delighted for you.

WAYNE: And I am delighted for you. With Grandfather in a place where he can be properly looked after things might change a little round here. Why, you might even be able to finish your marking. *(He crosses to the day bed, picks up a loose book and thumbs through it, laughing at her gently.)* Let's see if you've changed your style. No. No. Nothing has changed. Do you remember how you trusted me to mark the grades beneath mine. Severe but fair. Those were your instructions. I've never forgotten them.

MARY: *(crossing to him taking his hands)* You're right, Wayne. Things will be different. Perhaps I could come down for a weekend or two. Then you wouldn't need to come back here at all. *(pause)* Wayne. Can I ask you something?

WAYNE: Surely.

MARY: You're doing something for Alonzo again, aren't you?

WAYNE: Well . . . it's something of mutual benefit, Aunt.

MARY: Be careful, Wayne. Alonzo has designs upon you, I know it. He's clever. And without scruples.

WAYNE: He's a bit of a crook, I know. But he does organize the party in this district and I have no choice but to work with him on occasions . . .

MARY moves to interject, but he cuts her off.

You're right, Aunt. But don't you worry. I can handle him. Now . . . *(He proffers his arm.)* Shouldn't we be going?

ROSIE bustles in.

ROSIE: My, Wayne. You're the first down! Lord knows what the udders is doing. Have ye' 'ad somet'ing to eat?

WAYNE: No, Mother. As a matter of fact, I'm just on my way to church with Aunt Mary.

ROSIE: Ye can't go out in dis widout a bit o' somet'ing in yer stomach. And jest look at ye, ye're not dressed fer the Divil wettin' his mudder* an' it blowin' a livin' starm out dere. Now, ye sit down here . . . *(She bustles him protesting to the table.)* An' 'ave a nice cup o' tay whiles I gits ye a bit o' fish.

WAYNE clutches his stomach.

Would ye like a drop o' rum in yer tay, das if yer fader's left any?

She scurries rapidly to the stove with a plate, dollops a handsome portion of fish and brewis on it and thrusts it in front of him just as he is trying to rise.

WAYNE: Mother. Really, I couldn't . . .

He turns an appealing face to MARY.

MARY: I'm afraid your mother believes all men to be carbon copies of your father.

ROSIE: Carbon or not, yer not goin' out widout somet'ing and dat's dat. Whatever would dey say in St. John's if ye got sick out here, an important man like ye?

WAYNE: *(desperately)* Mother. Just the look of that makes me feel sick. Now take it away! Please!

MARY: Wayne . . . . *(taking one arm)* We must be going. It will be a hard walk in this weather.

ROSIE: Now, Mary . . . . *(grabbing his other arm)* He's not leaving until he's at least 'ad a cup o' tay.

MARY: *(tugging firmly)* It's time our little church was honoured with the presence of its most famous son. Surely Rosie, you, his mother, would agree to that.

ROSIE: *(tugging him the other way)* And what if he faints wid hunger as dey're taking up the collection . . . . Some proud we'd be den, I 'lows.

WAYNE: *(finally breaking clear of them both)* Please . . . Please . . . . Both of you! *(inspecting his suit for damage)* Look, don't you think it would be better if we went in the car? I have studded snow tires. It shouldn't be too much of a problem.

MARY: *(pleased)* Why, Wayne! How nice of you. It's a long time since I had a ride in a car. Well, in that case, you do have time for something.

WAYNE is about to protest, but MARY puts a restraining hand on his arm.

Rose. Stop fussing. You've got quite enough to take care of. Wayne, you sit down there . . . . *(proferring the rocking chair)* And' here's your tea . . . .

(She deftly evades ROSIE and gets the poured tea from the table.) Now . . . what would you like?

WAYNE: Some lightly scrambled eggs please, with just a little milk. Doctor's orders, I'm afraid . . . . My ulcers.

ROSIE: *(taking the fish and brewis from the table and pouring it splashily back into the pot)* My Wayne, you got ulcers? Uncle Jim Tobin had one o' dem last year. Or wor it two? Just afore 'e died. Terrible pain 'e wor in . . . bleeding like a pig inside.

WAYNE winces.

Leastaways, dat's what Aunt Sadie said, but I always reckoned it wor 'is conscience dat killed'n fer driving poor Mildred out of the house. And her only one hour from borning the baby.

MARY has doffed her hat and gloves and Missal, putting them back on the bureau. She takes off her coat and, laying it on the day bed, starts to prepare WAYNE's scrambled eggs.

MARY: Uncle Jim may have been severe, Rose, but he was morally right. *(to WAYNE)* His own niece now. Everyone knew. Carrying on on the day bed while he was upstairs praying for Winifred, God rest her soul.

ROSIE: *(stubborn)* It were a wicked t'ing she done, I allow, dough God knows the fellers she done it wit' is alive and well enough to sing the Lord's praise on the Sabbath and nobody minds dat.

MARY: It's the girl's responsibility to keep herself pure. Until marriage at least. What do you think, Wayne?

ROSIE: What do he know about it. Men are all alike when it comes to dat an' I suppose dey's no harm in it in the long run.

MARY: That's a matter of opinion. I'm sure if Wayne had spent his college days running

---

Divil wettin' his mudder—a few spots of rain when the sun is shining.

around after every loose girl he wouldn't be where he is now.

ROSIE: Jest the same, I wish I'd a knowed. It blowin' a starm jest like today and cold as a drowned man's breat'. And she desperate and shamed into crawling under Winston's old punt.

MARY: *(grim)* Aye, and because of that bit of stupidity the tongue waggers pointing at Winston for the father as if we didn't have enough trouble already.

ROSIE: *(reliving her emotions, her compassion struggling for expression)* I don't care if Winston wor or worn't. I doubts it dough, the liquor had him slowed down a bit even afore you, Wayne.

MARY: Rose. Does he have to be reminded of those things? *(handing him his scrambled eggs)* There you are, Wayne.

ROSIE: We all needs to be reminded of some t'ings, maid. And t'were a terrible way to die in a place where we're all kin. Baby boy it were. The pair of 'em frozen together until Winston found 'em when the ice cleared in the spring. If only she'd 'ave come 'ere. Ye was in St. John's den, Wayne. At the University. Ye minds dat? I wrote and told ye. Ye was sweet on her one time I remember, used to follow 'er home from school. *(laughing at the memory)* But she were a wild one dat, I remembers . . .

MARY: *(getting irritated by ROSIE's reminiscences)* For goodness sake, Rose. Christian charity is one thing, sloppy sentiment is another. She got her just desserts.

As she speaks, there is a howl of wind, a door opening and slamming at the side entrance left. WINSTON appears carrying a dozen beer, stamping the snow off his boots and shaking himself. He is in by the last line.

WINSTON: Here, Rosie, get me coat, will ye?

She scurries across and helps him off with it. She disappears into the passage left.

Christ! The things a man has to do to get a dozen beer on a public holiday. *(He crosses to the fridge and begins to stack in the beer.)* Who got her just desserts, Mary? What poor soul are ye tormentin' this time?

ROSIE comes back.

ROSIE: Mildred, dear. Mildred Tobin . . . . Ye remember.

WINSTON: I'm not likely to forget, am I?

He uncaps a beer and, still by the fridge door, takes a satisfying swallow.

And I suppose the baby did, too, eh? Breath enough for one cry before the air froze in his throat. I reckon he got his just desserts. Or should we be thankful that God took him back before more harm could befall the little bugger?

He has wandered into the main area and crosses in front of WAYNE.

Good morning, son. I hardly recognized ye. What in the name of God are ye eating?

WAYNE: Oh, good morning, Father. Scrambled eggs.

WINSTON is interested. He swivels around, grabs the plate and looks at the remains.

WINSTON: Scrambled. I thought that only happened with brains. *(handing WAYNE back the plate)* What do ye do? Smash 'em up with a fork and fry 'em? Looks like baby shit to me.

MARY: Do you always have to be so crude?

WINSTON: *(shouting)* Yes, by God. Because I am crude. I drinks because it helps me to fergit where I am and I swears because I like it. It sounds good and it protects me from your kind of literacy. And I likes jokes about natural functions because they're funny and they're particularly funny when aired in front of ye. I suppose ye've never farted in yer life. What is it ladies do, break wind? *(laughing)* I can see ye now, catching it and bending it over yer knee and trying to tan its little arse off . . . *(laughing again)* What do you think of that, son?

MARY: *(taking WAYNE's plate)* If only the child were the father of the man.

WAYNE: Then I could wish my days to be bound each to each by natural piety.

MARY: *(delighted)* You haven't forgotten.

WINSTON: Jesus, I've sired a book of sayings. *(taking a swig)* Well, son . . . . Now that ye've finished yer scrambled eggs I wants to ask you a question. How's the government?

MARY: Wayne . . .

She scurries to the chest of drawers and once again attires herself in her church accessories.

We really should be going now.

WAYNE: Right.

WAYNE rises from the rocker, but is suddenly thrust back as WINSTON turns and forces him down with one hand.

WINSTON: It's not alright. I'm asking ye a question, son, and I wants an answer. Don't see ye very often. Ye can talk to God any day of the week, like the Virgin Mary there, but it's not often ye gets a chance to talk with yer father.

MARY: Thank God for small mercies, Wayne. I don't have such luck.

WAYNE: *(rising again, and managing it, but keeping a wary eye on WINSTON)* I'm sorry, Father, but I promised Aunt Mary I'd run her to church. I'll be right back . . . . We can chat over lunch.

WINSTON: *(staring at him in disbelief)* Chat! Over lunch!

ROSIE: Heard your name on the radio yesterday, Wayne. Just afore ye arrived. It said ye'd sold somet'ing to the Japanese.

WAYNE: *(moving towards MARY)* That's right, Mother. The last fifty thousand acres of standing timber to the Nippon Match and Transistor Company. I don't mind telling you, it was tough going.

WINSTON: What're they going to use it for, matches or transistors?

WAYNE: That's only the name of the parent company. They're global now, oil, shipping, newsprint. This province is the only one in Canada whose economy is on the upswing.

WINSTON: I'm not interested, son.

He suddenly swings up and spins around WAYNE.

Whether you've sold yer arse to the Japanese. I am interested in the Welfare. Now. When is that crowd yer with going to do something about increasing it? Ye don't get my vote until ye do. And that would be a terrible thing, son, for the press to discover.

He reads from an imagined newspaper.

Mother and father vote for son's political opponent. "He's neglected us for years," said pale-faced Mrs. Rosie Blackburn, clutching a five-year-old to her empty dug. "Ever since we put him through college when me husband developed heart trouble from overwork!"

WAYNE: Father, I already send you a considerable allowance on top of your social assistance. And I'm taking a risk doing that.

MARY: Wayne. You know he's only goading you. Come along now. We're going to be late.

WINSTON: *(dodging between WAYNE and MARY)* Ye do send us a piece of yer travelling expenses I know, and yer mother and I are very grateful, aren't we, Rosie?

ROSIE: Oh, yis, I don't know what we'd do widout it, the price of liquor being what it is.

WINSTON: Things is going from bad to worse in this house, son, because yer aunt hides all her money and try as I might, I can't find it. And I haven't got the heart to take any more from me father.

MARY: What I do with my money is none of your business, Winston Blackburn. I earn it, d'you hear. By work. It's mine. Mine! And I'm saving it to keep the rest of us alive when you've drunk yourself into a beery grave.

WAYNE puts a restraining hand on her arm.

I swear, Wayne, that if he could forge my signature at the bank, every penny of it would have been gone long ago.

ALONZO comes downstairs and through the centre door into the scene.

ALONZO: Good morning, all. What a lovely Good Friday this is.

He goes to his mother and gives her a swing which drops her breathless.

My God, Mother. You're getting broad in the bean.

ROSIE: Yis, boy, and ye helped make it dat way. Git on wid ye now.

She pushes him away and, taking a pot from the stove, moves into the pantry area. He follows her.

ALONZO: It's an amazing household ye run, Mother. Brad's been reading the Bible now for the past hour. Skipper's loaded, and the rest of the family's plotting to send each other to the funny farm.

WAYNE: Alonzo!

ALONZO: Easy, brother. Don't strain yer ulcers. Ah Mother, if only I could begin to describe to ye the glow of goodness that fills me breast on this day of days. Ye see in me, Mother, a new man.

MARY: Mph. The Good Lord had better watch the patent.

ALONZO: *(swinging round, advancing on MARY and grabbing her hands)* Aunt Mary, by all that's holy. You look as ravishing as ever. Why has no one ever sought to suck the honey from those sweet lips. Drown in those pools of blue, lay his tired head upon that gentle breast . . .

MARY: *(throwing off his hands)* Wayne. I'm leaving this instant.

WAYNE crosses to MARY and takes her arm.

ALONZO: No ye don't, brother. Not yet. We've business to discuss and time is running out. I've got to be gone be dark.

WAYNE: We'll talk later, Alonzo. When I get back from church.

ALONZO: *(reading his mind)* We'll talk now I think, Wayne. I knows what's on yer mind. Ye're aiming to slip off to church and then barrel off back to town or wherever it is you're going. Aunt Mary kin find her own way to Salvation. Ye stay put.

He grabs WAYNE by the arm, the bruised arm. WAYNE gives a yelp of pain and with a reflex action strikes out at ALONZO. ALONZO prances round him and hits him in the midriff, catching him off balance and knocking him down. He crouches in boxer style, both fists at the ready.

ALONZO: Come on then. If that's the way ye want it. Come on.

MARY: *(almost in tears)* Wayne!

WINSTON: One, two, three, four, five . . . . Rosie, maid, this is better entertainment than TV.

WAYNE rises with murder in his soul. For an instant it looks as if he's about to give battle. ROSIE pushes between them.

ROSIE: Fer the love of God, boys, give over dis foolishness.

WINSTON: Sock it to'em, Rosie.

WAYNE: There'll be no contract, Alonzo. I can promise you that.

ALONZO: Oh yes there will, brother. Haven't ye forgotten something? Father . . . I got something to tell ye.

WAYNE: *(reverting to origins)* By Jesus, 'Lonz. I'll take you with me.

They square off. Again, ROSIE pushes them apart.

ROSIE: Nobody's taking nobody nowhere, 'cepting Wayne. Now, boy, ye take Mary off to church afore dere's any more trouble. And ye. *(turning to ALONZO)* Ye mind yer manners. Dis is still my house and I'm not above giving ye a tanned arse.

ALONZO: What about it, Wayne?

WAYNE: I'll be back.

He and MARY move to exit. ALONZO prances after them.

ALONZO: I've just lost me stripper down to the Blue Flamingo, Aunt Mary. Me and the boys was wonderin' whether ye was any good with a bottle.

MARY: Rose. I won't set foot in this house again until I have an apology from that brothel keeper there.

Mustering the remnants of dignity, she and WAYNE sweep out.

WINSTON: *(calling out)* Is dat a threat or a promise?

A great gust of wind. The door slams. ALONZO, laughing, turns and shuts the door. He is greeted with a stinging slap on the face from ROSIE.

ALONZO: *(startled)* Jesus, Mam. What was that fer?

ROSIE: Ye knows. And ye'll git anudder if ye keeps up like dat. I'm well able fer ye and don't ye ferget it. Yer poor aunt. She's been driven right crazy dis marnin' by yer fader. And ye spoils the one chanct she gits to see Wayne. *(with unconscious irony)* An' she been like a mudder to'n.

ALONZO: *(a little subdued, going down into the pantry area and sitting)* Oh come on, Mother. If Mary hadn't got anything to be disgusted about, she'd commit suicide.

WINSTON: Drive some poor kid in school to suicide more like.

ALONZO: *(beginning to examine the plates on the table)* Mm! What have we here . . . fat back . . . fish and brewis, herring . . . . My God, Mother, you've excelled yourself . . . . I can see I'll have to get married.

WINSTON: I heard ye had . . . widout the benefit of the clergy. Several times . . . .

ALONZO: *(sardonically)* They's not too many women like Mother around any more, Father. They don't seem to want to put up wit' it somehow.

ROSIE: *(sadly)* It'd be so nice if one o' ye would at least. I 'lows if Sarah 'ad been alive we'd a had some grandchildren of our own be now.

SKIPPER: Winston . . . . Winston.

WINSTON: *(impatient)* What is it now? *(under his breath)* Jesus.

SKIPPER: Winston.

WINSTON: *(resigned)* Aye, aye, Skipper.

SKIPPER: She's slipping her moorings, son. Git up on the bridge.

WINSTON: Don't be so foolish, Skipper. She's fine.

BRAD has entered silently.

SKIPPER: Be the Lar' liftin' Jesus. Haul yer arse up on that bridge afore I . . .

WINSTON: Alright, Skipper. Alright.

ALONZO: He's in a bad way this morning.

WINSTON crosses to the fridge for another beer. ROSIE bustles out through the door and leaves it open.

WINSTON: He's been in a bad way every morning this past twenty years.

He turns to go up, pausing to swig from the bottle.

He sees BRAD.

My God! It's the Second Coming. Again!

BRAD: You shouldn't do that, Father.

WINSTON: What?

BRAD: You shouldn't encourage him. It's not good for him.

WINSTON stares at him, amazed. BRAD gains courage.

BRAD: He's living in the past instead of getting ready to meet God. That's not good for anyone. He's dying and you're destroying his soul. With that. *(pointing at the bottle)* As well as your own.

WINSTON: Oh. I am, am I?

BRAD: Yes.

WINSTON: *(advancing to BRAD)* Let me tell you something, son. I encourage him because it's all he's got. Because his dreams mean more to'n than what's left of his children. That's me and yer aunt, son, if you gits me meaning. And they mean a damn sight more to him than his grandchildren do, including ye, with or without yer collar.

He moves away and turns back.

And I'll tell ye something else. I encourage him because beneath that wrinkled old skull and those mad eyes I kin sometimes see a truth about meself which might make some sense out o' dying. D'ye understand. Killing him! Christ!

ROSIE appears in the doorway with an armful of splits. She puts them in the woodbox.

ROSIE: Ye see, Brad, for yer fader, it's a way o' getting out of the house.

WINSTON: *(laughing)* Rosie, Rosie, wiser than us all . . . .

ROSIE: 'E'll need a drop o' water now fer 'is toddy.

She gets a small jug and fills it.

BRAD: You're as bad, Mother. *(restraining her)* Can't you see that? Are you frightened of them? Are you? I'm not. Oh, they can humiliate me. They can laugh at me. But God . . . yes, God has made me strong this morning. He'll help me to make you strong.

ROSIE: (upset) I doesn't know what ye're on about, Brad.

BRAD: What do you think is going to happen when Father and Grandfather, and yes, Alonzo too, stand before God in all His glory, stinking of rum. It is today, Mother. Today. Listen. Listen to the Voice of the Angels.

BRAD has worked himself up into a pitch of fervour. His is not true insanity, but the glorification of a mutilated ego as narrow as it is intense. Clothed in the richness of his fantasy, in the words of revelation, he becomes at this instant radiant, superior, his words imbued with an impact beyond his own fragile identity. He is The Messenger and even WINSTON and ALONZO are spellbound confronted by this immolation of the spirit.

Babylon is fallen, is fallen, that great city, because she made all nations drink of the wine of the wrath of her fornication. If any man worship the beast and his image and receive his mark on his forehead or in his hand, the same shall drink of the wine of the wrath of God which is poured without mixture into the cup of his indignation and he shall be tormented with fire and brimstone in the presence of the Holy Angels and in the presence of the Lamb. And the smoke of their torment ascendeth up forever and ever and they shall have no rest . . . day or night!

Hushed pause.

Mother. Come with me.

WINSTON: She won't be going, Brad.

ROSIE: (sensing an assault) 'Tis alright, Winston. He wor always like dis. Me fader wor much the same. There wor no one like God to his way of t'inking.

WINSTON: (ignoring her) I won't be there neither. In fact, I've no intention of going in front of Him at all if I kin 'elp it. I nivir took to the idea of bein' surrounded by a bunch o' damn fairies singing hymns day and night.

ALONZO: Heave it out o' ye, Father.

BRAD: That's blaspheming, Father. (still riding the power of a few moments ago) Your soul is burning.

WINSTON: Feels like heartburn to me, son. An' what ye calls blasphemy I calls common sense. Nivir could stand that nonsense, 'Lonz, even as a young feller. All them damned fairies bursting their little hearts out blowing the last trump. Like a Billy Graham revival hour. When I goes, I'll go wit' what I knows. An' that's nothing, boy. D'ye hear. Nothing.

BRAD: Ye see, Mother. He's lost. He's doing it deliberately.

WINSTON: You're damn right I'm doing it deliberately. Which is more I kin say fer ye when I spawned ye. Rosie, I half blames ye. Ye nivir fed me enough that night. Jesus. If I started to tell the Good Lord what I t'inks o' ye, 'twould fill the Book o' Judgement.

BRAD with a swift movement takes ROSIE's hands and slowly brings her to her knees.

BRAD: God, in your infinite kindness look down upon this wretched house and see that there is one yet who is pure of heart, whose sins are of omission only, Lord . . . of love. Spare her, Lord. Spare her!

ROSIE, confused and upset, is in tears. She struggles to release BRAD's grip, but WINSTON, outraged, moves swiftly and throws BRAD sprawling.

WINSTON: Ye leave yer mother be. An' if I wor ye, I wouldn't be so anxious to get to them pearly gates, because ye knows who'll be waitin' fer ye.

BRAD: (shouting, frightened at the violent intensity of WINSTON's anger) God. God will be waiting.

WINSTON: God! No, b'y. Mildred Tobin. Wit' that poor little bastard of hers still froze to her tit. And what will ye say to that, ye snivellin' gospeller.

BRAD: (wavering) That's between me and God.

WINSTON: Oh it is, is it?

ROSIE: Now, Winston. Ye don't know that he wor the fader fer sure.

WINSTON: I've allus knowed. I heard a conversation between him an' 'Lonz the night after he done it. Book o' Judgement. (standing over BRAD) Ye might be a true disciple now me son, but don't fergit yer mother and I remember the shape and colour of yer arse.

He half lifts then throws BRAD across the room where he crashes into the wall.

ROSIE: Winston!

WINSTON: Git out. I don't want ye in my house. Git out.

BRAD: God, help me. Help me.

In the brief silence, only the howl of the storm is heard.

ALONZO: *(softly)* They's nobody out there, Brad. They's only us.

BRAD: Mother . . . I've nowhere to go.

WINSTON: Then go to Hell and keep a place fer me.

WINSTON moves as if to assault him again, but ROSIE gets between them.

ROSIE: Don't be mindin' yer fader, Brad. Ye knows what he's like when 'e's 'ad a few. *(wiping her eyes with her apron)* I don't know what's happenin' in dis house dis day. Everyone at it like cats an' dogs. I wish . . . I wish we could all sit down like we used to an' sing a bit an' laugh . . . .

WINSTON: *(savagely)* We nivir laughed, woman. Stop coddin' yerself. And fer the love o' Jesus, will ye stop motherin' that. Let'n go and crawl out under me ould punt. Might be some justice in that.

BRAD: I didn't know! Christ believe me. *(sobbing)* I didn't know.

WINSTON: Well, ye knows now. And it's time ye kept that picture in front of ye, son. Instead of a God ye've invented to please yerself and a book ye don't understand. And when ye learns just what ye are, ye might be more of a man than ye've ever shown yerself to be in this house.

He crosses to the stove and picks up the jug of water where ROSIE has left it.

This water's cold, woman.

He exits upstairs. ROSIE kneels to comfort BRAD. He grabs at her.

ALONZO: That's told ye, boy. Ye should have listened to me this marnin'.

ROSIE: Ye keep yer big mout' out o' dis. Ye've done enough harm fer one day. God knows.

ALONZO: Me?

BRAD: He hates me.

ROSIE: No, b'y. *(comforting him)* Yer fader don't hate nobody. He's a good man. 'E would've liked somet'in' better fer all of us, but dat's it, I suppose.

BRAD: Do you love me, Mother?

ROSIE: Dat's a foolish question.

BRAD: No, it isn't. You never told me.

ROSIE: *(hurt and confused, releasing BRAD and getting up)* Brad. Ye always makes me feel so guilty. I means, ye don't talk about what's dere.

ALONZO: Leave her alone, Brad.

He moves protectively to ROSIE.

They was never any love here, sure. Not the kind o' thing you're looking fer anyways. We was too busy survivin' to put up with any o' that foolishness.

BRAD gets up and for one stricken moment looks from one to the other, then suddenly hurls himself from the room. There is the bang of the outside door.

ROSIE: *(rushing after him)* Brad. Brad . . . . Ye come back 'ere. Brad . . . .

The storm shakes the house. ROSIE re-enters. She is at the breaking point.

'E's gone out now, widout not'in' on, no coat or boots, not'in'. He'll perish sure.

ALONZO: *(crossing to her and putting his arms about her shoulder)* Don't worry about'n, Mother. He'll not do anything foolish.

ROSIE: But it's so bad. It's so bad. *(She crosses and sits in the rocking chair, closing her eyes.)* 'Lonz. Git me a cup o' tay, will yer?

ALONZO: *(surprised)* What . . . are ye sick, Mother?

Nonetheless he rapidly gets her a cup of tea.

ROSIE: I dunno, b'y. Tell ye the trut'. The stomach's left me. Everyt'in' seems to be gone . . . or going . . . somehow. *(She sips her tea and rocks.)* Turn the radio on would ye, 'Lonz. Dere's a good boy. Dere might be a nice hymn or two playing to cheer me up.

ALONZO turns on the radio and the last verse of "Amazing Grace" played by the Pipe Band of the Royal Scots Greys swells out. It has the cadences and the implication of a dirge for the fallen.

ALONZO goes and sits in the pantry area, picking up a paper from the top of the cupboard as he does so. He sits and reads as the lights dim in that area. They remain on ROSIE while the hymn plays. She is sitting back, eyes closed, rocking slightly. The tears fall down her cheeks.

The lights fade to black as the band falls silent. Suddenly, there is a crackle of static and into the blackness a rather panicky ANNOUNCER says . . .

ANNOUNCER: We interrupt our program to advise all listeners that a state of emergency has been declared and . . . *(crackle of static)* All communications with the mainland have been disrupted and difficulty is being . . . *(crackle of static)* RCMP advise that no vehicles may be operated except . . . *(crackle of static)* Power disruptions may be expected and residents are . . . .

There is more static which fades off into a low hum and then out. From this moment on the radio remains on, fading off and on as the power flows intermittently. The lights go up slowly in the SKIPPER's room as WINSTON enters. They are at about half power.

WINSTON: Master Watch reporting for duty, Skipper.

SKIPPER: Master Watch. Jesus, b'y. Ye'd nivir have made second cook on my ship.

WINSTON: I wouldn't a made that on me own neither.

SKIPPER: Listen, boy. Listen.

The storm howls.

WINSTON: 'Tis bad enough alright. Not fit fer man or beast . . . .

SKIPPER: Listen, I tell ye!

Silence. Again, the storm howls. It is very eerie . . . like a voice out of the elemental past.

Did ye hear it that time?

WINSTON: The wind, that's all.

SKIPPER: No, b'y. A swile. They's a swile out there.

WINSTON: Can't say as I heard him, Skipper.

SKIPPER: *(sighing)* Are we fast, boy?

WINSTON: Aye. Fast enough. Couldn't shift her wi' dynamite.

SKIPPER: *(sitting bolt upright)* I said that. Told yer mother, but she never did listen. Every bit of charge we had. Blow the goddamned ice apart, I says. We've got to get back. Oh, they sweated. I'll give 'em that. They laboured till their eyelids was weighed down wid ice and they couldn't see no more. I went down meself, boy, lined up on the ropes wid'n. But what's mortal man when nature sets her face agin him. Black as hell it wor. And the ice buckling and rafting beneath us, laughing, I swear. Laughing . . . . Hell isn't fire, boy. It's ice. Black, bitter, cold. Empty. Filled with the frozen breath of fallen men. Tinkling over their dead hands like spoons in teacups. I saw Jacob in Hell, boy. Out there in the dark.

A great gust of wind seems to shake the whole structure. He grips WINSTON.

She's dragging, boy. Ye're lyin' to me. Lyin'. Like the glass . . . .

WINSTON: Skipper. We'se got to have this out. We're not at sea. We're not in a boat. I'm not Jacob. We might be in Hell, but they's probably better or worse ones. I don't know yit. Ye're at home, Father. Stuck in yer own bed without the use of yer legs just as ye have been for the last thirty years and yer daughter and grandsons are plotting to have ye removed to the Mental. A few more roars from the bridge and I allows ye'll be gone, being pushed in a wheelchair down a long corridor stinking of piss and antiseptic, to yer grave.

The old man clutches at him. He shakes him as if he were a puppy.

SKIPPER: Ye're a damn fool, boy.

WINSTON: Aye, I'm all of that.

SKIPPER: A house is a ship. Lights agin the night . . . some adrift . . . some foundered, some rotting old hulks full of the memories of men . . . . They's no difference.

WINSTON: (surprised) I 'lows that's right enough.

SKIPPER: Then I tell ye boy. This one's adrift.

He sits upright abruptly. He seizes WINSTON's shoulder with one hand and points out at the audience.

Look, b'y. Look. Kin ye see'n.

WINSTON: Can't see in front of me own eyelids, Skipper.

SKIPPER: Mark me. Look. 'Tis the shape of death, boy. I kin see'n jest like that first time, rising out of the drift, moving across the ice widout a sound, a man like a cross growing up into the sky.

WINSTON: Father, they's nothing there. Nothing. (peering into the SKIPPER's eyes) It don't matter. When all's said and done, ye sees plainer than I.

SKIPPER: (relaxing as the vision fades) Ah. It's time. (closing his eyes) Ye'll check her moorings, son.

WINSTON: Aye. I will.

SKIPPER: That's good, Jacob b'y. That's good.

WINSTON draws the blanket about SKIPPER. The storm howls. He goes out softly and stands for a moment on the landing. The light remains on in the SKIPPER's room, but begins to change, narrowing in focus throughout WINSTON's next speech until there is only one white light on the SKIPPER's face giving us the distinct impression that the old man has died. WINSTON looks out of the window.

WINSTON: Jesus. They's something out there. Looks to be blowed agin the fence. 'Tis moving. (pause) 'Tis gone. (rubbing his eyes) Ach, the old man's got me seeing things now.

The storm howls. There is the quality of an inhuman voice in the sound, an intense and savage fury.

But what if he's right? If we is a ship? Then we's as good as gone. She'll nivir ride this one out. And what's to become of you then, Winston Blackburn? Eh?

A door bangs downstairs. WAYNE and MARY are heard. The lights fade up on the kitchen.

WAYNE: (offstage) Here, Aunt. Let me help you off with that coat.

MARY: (offstage) Thank you, Wayne.

They stamp the snow off their boots and enter the kitchen, shivering, making straight for the stove. ROSIE is asleep. WINSTON has remained at the top of the stairs. ALONZO is reading yesterday's newspaper in the pantry area.

MARY: I don't remember ever seeing it as bad. Lord bless us, it's a miracle we got home. You were marvellous, Wayne.

WAYNE: I've driven in storms before, but I'll admit I wouldn't try that again in a hurry. Where d'you think Brad was going.

MARY: He seemed to be heading for the wharf.

ALONZO: (coming out of the kitchen area) Did ye say ye saw Brad? Mother's worried about him.

MARY: She might well be. He was running and stumbling like a wild man, talking to himself.

ALONZO: Didn't ye stop?

WAYNE: Of course I stopped. But I'd hardly wound the window down before the ground drift swallowed him up. You can't see a thing out there.

ALONZO: I suppose he'll dodge in somewhere. Look at this, Wayne. (taking the newspaper up to him) I've just bin reading the Provincial Report for this area. It's pretty bleak. Unemployment is up. Liquor sales is down . . . .

WAYNE moves away, averting his face. ALONZO follows him.

Fer God's sake, boy. What's wrong with you?

WAYNE: To put it bluntly, you stink of fish.

ALONZO: (mildly) Oh, do I? I though the brewis were a bit strong. Must've been some old leggies Father put down last year. Never gives 'em enough pickle, Father don't.

MARY: Wayne, don't forget what I told you. Please.

WAYNE: (slightly irritated) Don't worry, Aunt.

The radio suddenly crackles and blasts on.

ANNOUNCER: And this reading from Psalm 69. "Save me, oh God, for the waters are come in even unto my soul . . . . I am come unto deep waters so that the floods run over me . . . ."

The radio breaks down to static and cuts out. MARY makes herself a cup of tea. ROSIE is still dozing in the rocking chair. WINSTON enters and crosses to the table.

ALONZO: Amen to that. Now, brother.

WAYNE: Alonzo. Can't it wait? From the look of things outside, I'm going to be here for days.

ALONZO: No. It can't wait. Fer me own peace of mind, I'd like to get the business settled once and for all. Where's the tenders.

WAYNE: I don't have them here. D'you think I'm a fool? *(tapping his head)* But I can give you the details.

ALONZO: I don't trust you, Wayne. I want to see it in black and white.

WINSTON: Jesus. What have we here, a meeting of great minds . . . . Hang on to yer trousers, Wayne. Yer no match fer him.

ALONZO: Thanks, Father. Recognition at last.

MARY: I've always known what you were, Alonzo. The sins of the parents come home to roost.

WINSTON: And what sins would they be, Mary. What could Rose an' me have contributed to that. *(pointing at ALONZO)*

MARY: Moral ignorance . . . .

WINSTON: *(enraged)* Moral ignorance. Ye mind yer tongue, woman. Ye can call me what you likes, but ye leave Rosie out of this, d'ye hear? Ye wouldn't recognize holiness if ye tripped in it.

MARY: Holiness. I'd prefer to call it childlike simplicity.

WINSTON hurls a bottle across the room. The glass splinters. The crash wakes ROSIE. WAYNE, who is shocked, hurries to MARY.

ROSIE: My . . . . What is it now? I were having such a strange dream . . . about when we shot Trigger. Do you remember, Winston, and had to push him over the cliff, on account of he wouldn't fall . . . Winston?

He is breathing hard, clutching his chest, and is palpably upset as he tries to suppress tears.

What is it, love? What's the matter?

WAYNE: After all this time, Mother. You still don't know? He's drunk.

WINSTON collapses into a chair.

ROSIE: He's not drunk. And if he was, what business is it of yours to be talking to your father so and shaming him? It's between him and me, so it is. *(bending over him)* What is it, love, eh? Has the ould man upset you?

WINSTON raises a ravaged face and tries to smile, an awful smile.

WINSTON: Tell ye the truth, love. *(gasping)* I hardly knows meself. *(suddenly gripping her hands)* It's me heart . . . it really is. The real one this time. Ould bugger finally going to demand payment for services rendered. *(He pauses, then faces her, anguished.)* What else could I ha' been Rosie? What else could I ha' done?

ROSIE: *(gently)* Nothing, love. Ye was good enough for me.

WINSTON: *(gritting it out)* It weren't good enough, Rosie. Not good enough. Seems as the times was wrong. Everything changed afore I knew what to do. The old ones so damned sure . . . and they . . . *(nodding towards WAYNE and ALONZO)* So certain. Though what about, the Lord knows. And us, Rosie, us . . . . Like rats in a trap, with the Welfare as bait. I didn't know what to do, so I didn't try. There didn't seem any p'int. But Jesus, Rosie . . . Jesus . . . .

His inarticulate cry for meaning in life is wrenched from the gut. It is painful. There is only one antidote. There has only ever been one.

ROSIE: Here, love . . . . Here . . . have a beer . . . . It'll calm ye down.

ALONZO hands ROSIE an open bottle. She pours it in his mouth like a baby. He swigs, then has a clear vision of himself. He takes out the bottle and chokes with laughter.

WINSTON: Epitaph for a Remittance Man

Stranger, watch when ye're walking on this ground,
Fer Winston Blackburn, her wor drowned,
Not at sea, as ye might suppose,
But in a bottle, held by Rose.

He laughs, then drains the bottle and staggering to his feet, crosses to the rocking chair.

WAYNE: Mother of God, Alonzo. Did you see that?

ALONZO: Wayne, I'm impressed. Beneath that tailor's dummy there lurks a heart. You should watch that, brother. It could prove fatal. Now. When do I get that information.

MARY: Don't have anything to do with him, Wayne. Please.

WAYNE: *(crossing to MARY and taking her hands)* It's alright, Aunt. Trust me.

MARY: It's silly of me, but I have a premonition . . . .

WAYNE: Look . . . .

ALONZO: Come on, Wayne. Stop playing footsie with Aunt Mary and get to the point.

WAYNE hesitates a moment, then crosses back to ALONZO.

WAYNE: What point?

ALONZO: I want duplicate copies of those tenders.

WAYNE: You'll get them once I get out of here. Within forty-eight hours.

ALONZO: And how can I guarantee that once you've left here with that piece of paper. I was a little hasty there. The dying pains of conscience.

WAYNE: You have my word.

ALONZO: Oh Jesus! Your word. Come off it, Wayne. You're not talking to the voters now. It's me, remember. We know what we are.

WAYNE: *(annoyed)* What else can I do, man? You're not prepared to accept what I can tell you. I've said you'll get the copies and you'll get them.

ALONZO: Alright. I'll have to be content with that, I suppose. But until I get them, I'll take that document back.

WAYNE: No.

WINSTON: Jesus, Rosie. Turn the radio on, would ye? I preferred 'em fightin' to talking.

ROSIE: 'Tis on, Winston. The power keeps going or somet'ing.

ALONZO: Look, boy. Give me that paper else I'll blow the whole thing wide open.

He makes a grab for WAYNE's pocket, where the top of an envelope can be seen sticking out. WAYNE jumps back, taking the envelope from his pocket.

WAYNE: No. I'll tear the damn thing up first.

WINSTON, who has been watching the inter-change keenly, suddenly bounds from the chair and snatches the envelope from WAYNE's hand.

MARY: Wayne.

ALONZO: Christ. Now we're in fer it.

WINSTON: Now I'll find out what in the name of God ye were muttering about.

WAYNE goes after WINSTON but he pushes him away, pulls out the document and begins to read.

My God. *(turning to WAYNE)* You bastards. You black, scheming bastards.

WAYNE backs across the room.

Rosie, they've forged me signature. They've written me name to git the Skipper into the Mental. I allus knew they'd like to, but . . . . *(The words are ground out.)* My name! 'Tis all I've got left. *(turning on MARY)* You, you bitch. Ye were in on this.

ROSIE: Now, Winston . . .

MARY: Wayne. You should have told me. I didn't want it that way.

WAYNE: *(shouting)* It was the only way!

WINSTON moves at speed into the parlour. WAYNE shouts from the door.

Father. Look. It's for his own good. For the good of everyone in this house. He'd be well cared for, given the best medical. . . . My God.

WINSTON reappears carrying a shotgun and savagely shoves WAYNE out of the way as he proceeds towards the bureau, hauls out a drawer and produces two shells which he runs into the breech.

WAYNE: They could keep him alive for years, Father. Tell him, 'Lonz.

ALONZO: Ye keep me out of this. I jest wrote your name, Father, that's all. I bin doing that one way or another all me life, ye knows that.

ROSIE: Winston. Don't.

He turns and raises the gun. Everybody dives for cover. There's a mighty gust of wind and the lights go off as WINSTON fires.

ALONZO: Christ. Give over, Father.

MARY: *(screaming and trying to pray)* Holy Mother of God, pray for us now and at the hour of our death, amen.

WINSTON curses and fires again.

WAYNE: You're mad, Father.

WINSTON: Yis. And I suppose ye'd like me to commit meself next. And suppose I goes, I'll go fer something worthwhile.

The lights go up. WINSTON looks about him.

Jesus. Nary one.

He throws the gun down in disgust.

First decent thing I ever wanted to do in me life and the power fails. To hell wid'n.

ROSIE hurriedly retrieves the gun and takes it back to the livingroom. There's a different sound added to the storm, as of a house straining at her shores. The radio blares.

ANNOUNCER The Government has resigned. I repeat . . . the Government has resigned . . . .

The radio crackles and fades. WAYNE, forgetful of WINSTON, leaps to his feet and rushes to the radio. He beats at it furiously.

WAYNE: Did ye hear that? For God's sake, come on . . . . Come on . . . .

WINSTON: *(breaking into roaring laughter)* Well, well . . . if that don't beat all.

ROSIE re-emerges and closes the door behind her.

Rosie . . . the Government has resigned. That takes care of 'em better than me old shotgun.

WAYNE: *(still beating the radio)* Come on.

MARY: Wayne . . . don't get so upset. I don't like to see you like this.

WAYNE: Will you stop nagging me.

WINSTON: *(roaring again and clapping his hands)* That's telling ye.

The lights go out again. There's a strange silence, then once again a fearful gust of wind that strains at the very foundations of the house.

WAYNE: Why in the name of God is everything so dark?

ALONZO: We're snowed in, b'y. Where the hell are ye going?

WAYNE: *(making for the door)* I've got to get to a phone.

ALONZO: *(shouting)* Ye won't git ten yards.

In the interior, a clock strikes three.

WINSTON: 'Tis three o'clock. That's the hour, eh, Mary?

ROSIE: Winston. Kin ye get some candles.

WINSTON: I couldn't see afore the power went, maid. 'Tis worse now. 'Lonz. Ye get 'em.

ALONZO: How the hell do I know where the candles is?

ALONZO fumbles out.

ROSIE: *(calling after him)* An' Lonz. Mind ye takes one to yer grandfather.

WINSTON: Rosie, me duck. Rosie. Come here. Come here, maid.

ROSIE finds WINSTON and sits with him on the day bed.

Has turned out to be a good day after all, one way or another. An' I suppose we shouldn't complain too much, eh? Life's bin as good as it could've bin to the likes o' we, I suppose.

ROSIE: *(softly)* I nivir complained, Winston.

WINSTON: I knows, maid. And they was times I suppose ye should've done. *(chuckling)* Does ye mind the time we wor desperate? I wor visiting your folks and we hadn't had it for a week or more.

ROSIE: Ye ould Divil.

She sighs. A light appears on the landing as ALONZO moves upstairs, crosses to SKIPPER's room and puts a lighted candle on the chest of drawers. As before, a light illuminates the SKIPPER's face. What is illuminated now, however, is a Death Mask, the actor playing the SKIPPER having left the room during the blackout and commotion downstairs. It is essential that the audience is left with the illusion that, though the SKIPPER is possibly dead, his corpse remains in the bed and it must be illuminated in the manner described until the end of the play. ALONZO, without checking on the old man, comes back down the stairs.

ROSIE: Ye took me out on the pint, and it cold, the snow hard on the ground. I nivir t'ought me backside'd ever git warm agin.

WINSTON: Ye minds, today I think it wor, when ye said ye cares for me.

ROSIE: Yis.

WINSTON: Well . . . *(struggling)* I cares fer ye too. 'Tis hard to put it into words sometimes. That's all.

ALONZO enters with two candles.

ROSIE: Take one over to yer aunt, 'Lonz, and bring one 'ere.

He does so. WINSTON gets up, crosses to the pantry and gets down the remains of the bottle of moonshine. WAYNE, like a man in a trance, comes slowly back in.

ALONZO: Jesus, b'y. What's the matter with you?

WINSTON: Well. I don't know what's happening boys. Or what's happened even. But as we is all here, we might as well take a little drink together. *(pouring a glass and crossing to WAYNE)* Here, boy. Ye lost after all. More than yer dignity, I allows. Ye've come home. *(proffering the glass)* Jine me in a drink?

WAYNE: *(blankly)* What? What's that?

ALONZO: Don't seem to have any choice, do we?

WINSTON: We nivir did have.

He crosses to MARY, who is sitting numbed and betrayed at the table. WINSTON puts an arm around her.

And ye lost too, maid. 'Twas wrong of me to laugh at yer. I . . . I don't suppose ye'd care to jine me, eh? Fer all the times we went down the road together to that same school ye teaches at now . . . hand in hand . . . *(to himself)* Up over the hill, the bell ringing, the rivers running over our boots in the first thaw.

He holds out the glass to her. MARY looks at it and reaches for the glass slowly. Then, in a swift movement, she snatches the glass and throws the liquor in his face. He doesn't move. The liquid runs down his face.

They's tears, Mary. I'm crying. Ye've made me cry.

He leans sobbing against the wall. There is an upsurge of wind and storm and the sound of timbers straining, cracking. A distant sense of catastrophe pervades the atmosphere. The light remains on the SKIPPER.

Into this mixture of fear and pain and expectancy come three loud, imperative knocks at the door. Everybody, appalled, looks fearfully in that direction. WINSTON raises his head. He looks aloft and, although not seeing, understands. He whispers . . .

'Tis his token.

He moves slowly to the door.

ROSIE: Winston!

He opens the door and falls back. The SKIPPER stands there dressed in his Master's uniform, his brass button coat and hat, seaman's boots. ROSIE crosses herself.

Blessed Virgin.

The SKIPPER strides into the room with the vigour of a man in his prime, inspecting the ship.

SKIPPER: Rosie. Rosie, woman. Git me a glass o' rum.

He pauses in front of WINSTON.

Take the wheel, boy.

WINSTON is confused.

SKIPPER: The wheel.

He roars it out, indicating a position downstage. WINSTON stumbles to the spot.

Hold it steady, boy. Steady.

WINSTON reaches, feels for and then grasps the imaginary wheel. We must be in no doubt that for him it exists. He wrestles with it. ROSIE fearfully tenders the SKIPPER his rum. He drains it and gives her back the glass.

Forty years, it's been. Forty years, waiting to see if any o' ye could steer this ship. I give ye fair warning. Have ye anything to say? Good. Comes a time when things has to be brought together as best they kin. When ye has to steer into the starm and face up to what ye are.

He pauses in front of MARY.

Yer mother nivir did that, Mary. Turned her face to the wall and died like an old ewe. But what's lambs fer if they isn't to be sacrificed sometimes.

MARY: God help us

SKIPPER:
North Nor' East
And South South West
From the Round Head Isles
To Cape Bonavist,
Steer it clear
And steer it true
And the same will take ye
To Baccalieu.*

Did I teach you that, boy?

WINSTON: Aye, Father. Ye did.

SKIPPER: Some damn use ye made of it. *(crossing to WAYNE and ALONZO)* Who are ye?

ALONZO: 'Lonz Blackburn, Skipper.

---

*North Nor East . . . To Baccalieu—The refrain chanted by the Skipper is part of a much longer poem by which schooner men of the East Coast of Newfoundland committed sailing instructions to memory. The Round Head Islands, Bonavista and Baccalieu are all critical landmarks on the voyage round the coast.

WAYNE: Wayne Blackburn, Skipper.

SKIPPER: Fust voyage?

WAYNE and ALONZO: Aye, Skipper.

SKIPPER: Ach. That wor always the way of it. But 'tis a pitiful crew for an old haverbeen on his last voyage. *(roaring)* CREW TO STATIONS. Women, git below.

ROSIE and MARY exit, taking the candles with them. WAYNE runs right and grips an imaginary rope. ALONZO leaps upstairs and goes to the edge of the SKIPPER's room, peering out. The sound and the process of disintegration have been building throughout the foregoing.

SKIPPER: What's the conditions?

ALONZO: *(from aloft)* She's cracking up, Skipper. They's a lead up ahead. Wind East Nor' East . . . .

SKIPPER: A lead. Then we'll blast her out. Are ye ready?

ALL: Aye, Sir. Ready.

SKIPPER: Listen . . . . Listen . . . .

Above the storm sounds, very distantly, comes a seal bark, then another.

Blood and fire and ice. A swile. A swile. I wor right, boys. They've come back. The swiles is back. Newfoundland is alive and well and roaring down the ice pack. A swile. A swile.

There is a moment when all are poised, a tableau, then there is a blackout and the sound of a cosmic disaster, a ripping and rending and smashing, the final release of the insensate fury of nature that has been building throughout the play. There comes a flash that lights up the stage. There is nobody there. Then again, a blackout, the storm dying. The lights go up again, intense, white light that illuminates the threadbare reality of the stage home. Upstairs, the Death Mask is still lit. All fades into the lone quiet crying of a bitter wind.

END

ERIKA RITTER

(b. 1948)

In a very funny essay in her book *Urban Scrawl*, Erika Ritter imagines a group of single women trying to talk their friend Sarah out of getting married. But citing a long catalogue of the indignities singles have to suffer, Sarah goes ahead and does it anyway—even while admitting that Elmer is hardly her ideal man, what with his annoying habits like reading movie credits out loud and keeping his money stapled to his undershirt. The essay ends not long after the wedding with Sarah's friends barely resisting the temptation to say "I told you so."

The characters in Ritter's plays occupy the same precarious comic ground, though their stakes are much higher. Most of her plays feature a marriage in which a woman is victimized by her husband's inadequacies and has to learn to cope with her own. As in the essay, these women are torn by a dual impulse: hang on to the security of marriage—even a bad one— or follow the painful path of independence. The singles life after a separation means guilt, insecurity, and confusing new codes of sexual behaviour. But, like marriage itself in Ritter's cosmology, it has to be faced as one of the rites of passage of the comtemporary urban female. When the woman is a professional writer or performer, her relationship to her work is an additional complication. In *Automatic Pilot* Ritter attacks this material with sizzling wit, creating one of the funniest comedies in the Canadian repertoire.

Born in Regina, Ritter left for Montreal and McGill University in 1965, graduating with a B.A. in drama in 1968. She went on to an M.A. at the University of Toronto Graduate Centre for Drama in 1970, married, and was back in Montreal from 1971-74 teaching at Loyola College. Her first play, *A Visitor from Charleston*, was staged at Loyola in 1974. Eva, its main character, refuses to deal with the emotional wreckage of her life which includes an actor ex-boyfriend and a would-be novelist ex-husband, opting instead for the fantasy of *Gone with the Wind* which she has seen forty-eight times. Though not a good play, *A Visitor from Charleston* provides interesting indications of the better things which were to come.

In 1974 Ritter moved to Toronto where she has lived ever since. For the next few years she wrote articles and stories for magazines such as *Chatelaine*, and in 1976 a writers' workshop at Tarragon Theatre sent her back to playwriting. By now separated herself, she wrote a hard-edged comedy about marital collapse and the need for emotional and artistic integrity. *The Splits* centres on Megan, a script writer who finally finds the strength to get her life together and "split" from all the dependencies that diminish her as a human being: the ex-husband who bleeds her, the producers who want to turn her serious drama into a sitcom, and most of all her own fearful refusal to let things die when their time has come.

After the popular success of *The Splits* at both Toronto Free Theatre and Actors' Theater of Louisville in 1978, *Winter 1671* was produced by Toronto Arts Productions in 1979. An ambitious historical drama set in seventeenth century Quebec, it is also a play about marriage and the still timely problems of three women. The central character, Renée, is a lot like Megan in period dress. But neither the costume-drama style nor the solemn tone of the play really suited Ritter's talents, and for the next project she returned to the sexual follies of our day. In preparation for dramatizing one of her own stories about a female stand-up comic recently estranged from her husband, Ritter spent the summer of 1979 performing stand-up routines at Yuk Yuk's, a Toronto comedy club. The story "You're a Taker" (published in *Saturday Night* in December 1979) became the play *Automatic Pilot*. It opened in January 1980 at Toronto's Adelaide Court, moved to Toronto Free in February and reopened in the summer for an extended run, subsequently playing in seven regional theatres from Thunder Bay to Victoria and eventually in Los Angeles in 1988. When it won the Chalmers Award for 1980, Ritter split the

$5000 cash prize with director William Lane, explaining that "marriage is a comparatively trivial undertaking beside finding a good director."

Since 1980 Ritter has examined the shaky marriage and ethical turmoil of a journalist couple in *The Passing Scene* (Tarragon, 1982), and the relationships of four professional women at an exclusive all-women's club in *Murder at McQueen* (Tarragon, 1986). A new comedy, *The Road to Hell*, premiered at Calgary's Lunchbox Theatre in 1993. Much of her dramatic writing has been for radio, including an adaptation of *Automatic Pilot* that won the 1982 ACTRA Award for radio drama. In addition to *Urban Scrawl* (1984) and *Ritter in Residence* (1991), two collections of comic essays, she continues to publish short fiction and write regular columns for magazines. Ritter has been writer-in-residence at Concordia University, Smith College and the Stratford Festival, and has hosted the shows *Dayshift* and *Aircraft* for CBC radio.

Automatic Pilot is a comedy that explores the potential dangers of a comic approach to life. Charlie is a compulsive comedienne. Onstage and off she responds to nearly everything with a joke, an avoidance mechanism that establishes safety through ironic distance. She uses humour as protective colouration, deflecting real feeling and ultimately impeding her own emotional growth. It is one of the regular manifestations of her "automatic pilot" syndrome, the switch she pulls whenever she can't bear to confront reality head-on.

Charlie has good reason to be a little gun-shy. Her ego has taken a terrible beating in the aftermath of her marriage. To have your husband leave you for another woman is bad enough; to have him leave for another man, as Alan has, can reduce a fragile self-image like Charlie's to mush. Her reactions are characteristically compulsive. She won't let go of Alan, hanging on in the desperate hope that it will all prove just a horrible misunderstanding. She naturally seeks sexual approval from other men, but uses sex "like a drug" as if it might cure her of whatever drove Alan away. On the other hand she denies her sexuality, wearing male clothing to perform a self-deprecating comedy routine that presents her as unfeminine and unattractive. Charlie seems able to operate only at extremes. She is either monogamous or promiscuous, drunk or on the wagon, funny or maudlin. She cleans the fridge either incessantly or not at all. She writes soap opera fantasy or exaggeratedly cynical comedy, but somehow misses the reality in between. The choices she makes available to herself inevitably exclude the middle ground.

Charlie's taste in men shows a similar design. In some ways the fey Alan and the macho Nick couldn't be more different. Yet in other respects they are almost doubles. Both call her "babe" and both are self-serving "seventies people," always keeping their options open. Nick is the more straightforward of the two, a jerk but refreshingly honest about it, and extremely perceptive about Charlie's need to self-destruct. Alan comes off as an unsympathetic manipulator at first. But by the end he faces up to his own identity crisis more honestly than Charlie does to hers. Neither man is particularly good to or for her, but neither is finally to blame for Charlie's condition. In *The Work* Ritter says of her female characters that "their oppression is largely a product of their own mentality and their attitude about themselves . . . . It's not what people are doing to them; it's what they're doing to themselves."

That appears to be Charlie's case, as we see through her relationship with Gene. Ritter has described him as "a man of the Eighties because he combines the kind of commitment of the Sixties with the individualism of the Seventies." He is as naturally funny as Charlie but knows when to be serious. He is a writer like Charlie but uses his writing for genuine self-discovery. His perspective dominates the second act as the emotional centre of the play shifts, along with our sympathies, from Charlie to Gene. Ritter leaves the ending ambiguous, suggesting that rejecting him may be a trade-off necessary for Charlie to pursue her creative life in comedy. Charlie's inability to accept the sanity and stability Gene offers her may be the ultimate measure of her failure. On the other hand, as Rota Herzberg Lister argues, that decision may be the completion of Charlie's redefinition of herself from female into woman and from woman into human being—the new feminist paradigm: "a symbol of woman's intellectual and creative potential actualized." In any case, as Charlie's closing monologue makes clear, it is one of those painful choices of adult life that no amount of wisecracking can make easy.

•

Automatic Pilot was first performed on January 17, 1980, produced by New Theatre at the Court Theatre, Adelaide Court, in Toronto, with the following cast:

CHARLIE	Fiona Reid
GENE	Geoffrey Bowes
NICK	John Evans
ALAN	Patrick Young

Directed by William Lane
Designed by Roderick Hillier

AUTOMATIC PILOT

CHARACTERS

CHARLIE, *30*
GENE, *23*
NICK, *35*
ALAN, *30*

SCENE

Toronto, 1980. The action takes place over approximately two months in the late summer and early fall.

ACT ONE

Scene One

Lights come up on the area of the stage designated as The Canada Goose, a comedy club, suggested by a mike on a stand and a spotlight. CHARLIE, dressed simply in a blouse and jeans, and without her glasses, stands nervously at the mike, speaking awkwardly into it without daring to remove it from the stand.

CHARLIE: *(to the audience)* I decided to try my luck as New Talent tonight, because at my age, it's an accomplishment to appear as new *anything*. This is my first time. You'd never know it, but I'm scared to death. I can't imagine why. What could be more natural than this, standing up in front of a room full of total strangers, attempting to give them the time of their lives? Actually, I'm accustomed to making a fool of myself. In real life, I'm the head writer for a soap opera. Many people ask me exactly what a head writer *is*. The fact is, the head writer is responsible for the characters only from the neck up. We have hand and foot writers, too. Even elbow writers, if the script calls for a lot of nudging. People ask me how I can waste my talent writing for *Land of Dreams*—that's the name of the soap. What I tell them is writing soap opera is a valuable community service. After a few afternoons watching *Land of Dreams*, even the chronically unemployed run out and get jobs. In case you're one of them, and wonder what's new on my show, I'll tell you. Not much. Tommy's cystic fibrosis has flared up again; Sue's abortion didn't take. And Sarah's *still* hoping no one will notice that peculiar smell coming from the basement. . . . Soap opera's what you call sit-down comedy. They told me the difference with stand-up was that the audience would rise if they liked a joke. So? . . . Does this mean I'm bombing? Too bad. I was planning to give up soap and get into this full-time. Not that TV hasn't been good to me. I live in a real classy part of town—the chic Carlton-Sherbourne area? Also known as the Heart of Darkness? You know, Yorkville Avenue has nothing on my neighborhood.

Blackout on CHARLIE. In the black, a tape of her voice takes over and continues the story. The taped voice is surer, brisker, more experienced, and there is audience laughter on the tape.

CHARLIE: *(on the tape)* I mean, my neighbourhood has exclusive high-priced shops, too. They're called variety stores. In variety stores they look at you as though you're out of your mind if you ask for something really exotic—like a lemon. But they're great for staple items . . .*if* your idea of a staple item is a plaster-of-Paris cheetah. And say it's after six, and the other stores are closed and you run out of fluorescent yo-yos . . . .

Lights now come up on the area that is CHARLIE's apartment, as the tape continues to run. CHARLIE, wearing her glasses, is slumped wearily in an armchair, with a cigarette, a drink and a wrist-watch. She also has a notebook and a pen. To suggest that there has been progress in her stage "style" she wears a too-large suit jacket, a long aviator scarf, and a gaudy brooch or artificial flower. Her voice comes from a small cassette recorder on a nearby table.

Still, you gotta watch those stores or they'll rip you off. I bought one of those litre-and-a-half bottles of Coke the other day? Damn thing *refused* to explode. It was a dud—

CHARLIE snaps off the tape, scribbles a note to herself.

(spoken) Fifteen-thirty. Too fucking long.

She looks down at the notations on the pad for a moment, then loses interest, slumps back in the chair, sips her drink. Finally, after some indecision, she reaches for the phone, dials a long-distance number.

(into phone) Hi, sweetheart, I— *(pause, then coldly)* Oh. Is Alan there? *(pause)* That's right, it's Charlie. *(pause)* Yes, I know it's you, Jackie. *(quickly)* Jimmy, I mean. Sorry, Jimmy. *(pause)* Look, I said I was sorry. A simple mistake. Is Alan there? *(pause)* Thank you so much. *(a longer pause, then her tone becomes warmer)* Hi, sweetheart. I just thought I'd call and— *(pause)* Jimmy, right. Okay, okay, I won't get it wrong again. *(pause)* Alan, I don't want to discuss my attitude. I'm lonesome and I need to talk to you. *(pause)* Yeah, I'm still doing it. I was up tonight, in fact. Fifteen triumphant performance at The Canada Goose. But I'm getting better. It would be nice if you'd come up to Toronto sometime and catch me. *(pause, trying for lightness)* That's right, I work without a net. Look, is there any chance of you coming to town? *(pause, then with some asperity)* Uh huh. Well, when you have an audition here then. When it's worth your while to make the trip. *(pause)* I know you didn't mean it that way, Alan. You never mean it that way. Look, I've got to get some sleep here. *(pause)* Yeah, fine. Just fine. Don't worry. Bye, bye, sweetheart. Goodbye, *Jackie.* I can hear you breathing on the extension. *(slamming down the phone)* Fuck it.

She pours herself another drink, ponders for a moment, then her expression relaxes and a sardonic smile crosses her face. She connects the mike to the tape recorder, pushes the record button.

(into the mike) Jackie, Jimmy, what's the difference? I mean, they've all got names basically suitable for embroidering on the front of a pair of coveralls, right? Names they swiped off the Mouseketeers. Aw, but they're great guys, the Jackies and the Jimmies and the Bobbies. I figure God invented gay guys so there'd be people around to remind us of how good the Bette Midler special was. If it weren't for gay guys, who'd buy bean-bag frogs? Or dimmer switches for the chandeliers? Most important, if there were no gay guys, who'd point out the smudged glasses in restaurants and send them back? Gay guys are terrific at sending back smudged glasses. It's weird, though. How they'll pick up some stranger at the baths, no questions asked, and end up on penicillin for six months. But they won't go near a smudged glass at Bemelmans. *(pause, then wearily)* Take my life—please.

Blackout.

Scene Two

Lights come up on GENE, in shirt and jeans, sitting at the desk in the area that serves as his room. He speaks into the mike of a cassette recorder.

GENE: *(improvising)* Deathless Prose, by Eugene Bolton, is simply that. This daring, tough, tender, compassionate, evocative first novel by a breath-taking new talent makes *Crime and Punishment* look like a cakewalk; towers head and shoulders over anything Thomas Pynchon ever dreamed of writing, and would have *killed* Faulkner, were he not already dead. The young Canadian author . . . law student, bon vivant, and sometimes employee of the Hudson's Bay Department Store—

An alarm clock on the desk rings. GENE breaks off, shuts off the alarm and then the tape.

Shit. *(staring at the clock)* Now, what the hell? Oh. *(leaning back, shouting)* Nick? Nick!

No response. GENE puts on his glasses, rises, and leaves the desk area which is then plunged into blackness. As he moves into NICK's bedroom area, lights come up there to reveal an anonymous form asleep alone in a large rumpled bed. GENE approaches the bed without really looking at the contents.

Come on, tiger. You order wake-up, you get wake-up. Ohh, say can you seee, By the—

CHARLIE, startled, sits up, clutching the sheet around her.

CHARLIE: What the fuck??—

She and GENE stare at each other uncomprehendingly.

GENE: Oh. Sorry. *(starting to leave)* As you were. As you were.

CHARLIE: Wait!

She locates her glasses, puts them on, gazes around again, but with no more comprehension. GENE watches as her glance falls on her own clothes, strewn on the floor.

GENE: *(kindly)* What's the matter? Don't you know where you are?

CHARLIE: Of course I do. *(with a hopeful smile)* At your place.

GENE: Lucky shot.

CHARLIE: Don't be silly. I . . . . *(infusion of warmth)* I had a wonderful time.

GENE: Good. You must get it into your diary. Before it fades. *(as she continues to stare at him)* What's wrong?

CHARLIE: You . . . look different, somehow.

GENE: No way. I've looked the same since I was sixteen. I can show you my high school yearbook. *(He sits companionably on the bed.)* Come on, admit it. You don't remember a goddamn thing.

CHARLIE: I wish you wouldn't say that. *(rubbing her temples)* So loudly.

GENE: Oldest story in the world. You have a couple too many, it feels like somebody slipped you a Mickey Finn. Strange guy brings you home, practises a little necrophilia on your comatose body. You wake up with a big headache and a big blank where your memory used to be . . . .

CHARLIE: You've got a great way with words. Have you considered cheap detective fiction?

GENE: *(bleakly)* Right now I'm considering the monastery.

CHARLIE: What?

GENE: I might as well. I mean, usually a night with me is something a woman remembers all her life, tells her grandchildren about when they're old enough to hear . . . . But look at the impression I made on you. El Blanco.

CHARLIE: Bullshit. Total recall. It was great.

GENE: Don't try to spare me. Besides, I wasn't too bowled over either.

CHARLIE: Oh now, look, maybe the earth didn't pitch violently for either of us, but you don't have to be like *that.*

GENE: No, as far as I'm concerned, it never happened.

CHARLIE: Of all the insulting . . . . Look, we both made a mistake, that's all.

GENE: *(grinning)* Uh-uh. *You* made a mistake, honey—

NICK *enters through the doorway, dressed only in slacks and socks, towelling his slightly damp hair.*

GENE: Now, does *this* guy ring a bell?

CHARLIE: *(glancing rapidly from NICK to GENE)* Why, you son of a bitch!

NICK: *(mildly)* Hey, babe . . .

CHARLIE: *(indicating GENE)* I mean him.

GENE: You sure now? We all look alike in the dark.

NICK: I see you two have met. *(kissing CHARLIE)* Hiya, babe.

CHARLIE: *(faintly)* Hi.

GENE: *(to CHARLIE)* His name is Nick.

CHARLIE: *(quickly)* I know. Nick. I *know.*

NICK: *(to CHARLIE)* Gene's my kid brother. But I guess you know that.

CHARLIE: I didn't. But your awful secret's safe with me.

NICK: *(laughing)* That's what you get, Geno. For sneaking in and trying to make time with my chick.

GENE: You set your clock in my room. I assumed you wanted a wake-up.

NICK: I did? Guess I was a little hammered last night.

GENE: *(smiling at CHARLIE)* Lot of that going around.

NICK: Anyway, I woke up early. And went down for a swim.

CHARLIE: Swim?

NICK: Yeah, this building has everything. Pool. Sauna. Squash.

GENE: Elevators. The rent's six-ten a month. *(to NICK)* I thought I'd save you the trouble of telling her.

NICK: Five-twenty. Fuck off, little brother.

GENE: And as a struggling student, I can only afford to give him one-twenty-five. He'll tell you that, too.

CHARLIE: Well, I'll try to act surprised.

NICK: I said fuck off. There's coffee in the kitchen.

GENE exits.

CHARLIE: Is he always like that?

NICK: Just lately. He's working at the Bay for the summer. It gets him down. *(putting a robe around her shoulders)* He's going to make one sharp lawyer, though. Hey . . . *(warmly)* You were really good last night, babe. Did I tell you that?

CHARLIE: *(pleased)* Thank you. You weren't so bad yourself.

NICK: How do you think that stuff up?

CHARLIE: Well . . . I just lie there, and it comes to me . . . .

NICK: Goddamn, that bit about lottery tickets—

CHARLIE: Oh. The *act.*

NICK: I'm telling you, you'd be great in a movie with that stuff.

CHARLIE: Oh, come on, now . . . .

NICK: Seriously. You'd go. I've got an instinct for what goes. Every film I've put money in, I've made back at least double.

CHARLIE: You're involved in movies?

NICK: The financial end. And you'd go. But I told you that. Last night.

CHARLIE: Nick, to tell you the truth, I'm just a little vague about last night. I mean, I guess we met at the club, and—

NICK: You guess. You're cute. Christ, we sat there talking till they cleared all the glasses off the table— *(pause)* You don't remember that? Jesus.

CHARLIE: It's just . . . . After the show, I—check out sometimes. Especially if I drink.

NICK: Well, you certainly can drink. Hey, you were bombed? No shit?

CHARLIE: I wasn't bombed. Did I act bombed?

NICK: No. Believe me, I'm not in the habit of dragging home drunken women.

CHARLIE: And I wasn't drunk. I just have—gaps sometimes. My body keeps going after my mind quits . . . *(softly)* Hey, I remember some things. And I had a wonderful time.

NICK: You sure now? I guess I could tell you it was the greatest sexual experience of your life and you'd have to believe me.

CHARLIE: And how did it rate for you? *(quickly)* Forget it. It was a dumb question.

NICK: Real dumb. *(He kisses her.)*

CHARLIE: You have a certain backhand way with compliments.

NICK: My forehand's pretty good too.

CHARLIE: Well, sure. Squash courts right in the building.

NICK: *(laughing)* You're great. Hey—

He kisses her.

CHARLIE: Hey what?

NICK: Hey, where have you been all my life?

CHARLIE: Waiting under the clock at Grand Central. What kept you?

NICK: You want coffee or something?

CHARLIE: *(seductively)* Something. If I have the choice.

NICK: I'll get you some coffee.

CHARLIE: *(disappointed)* Oh.

NICK: It's just that I have a meeting this morning.

CHARLIE: On Sunday? What are you, a Quaker?

NICK: I have to see a man about a restaurant. That's my main weakness, restaurants. But I told you that.

CHARLIE: This seems to have been a very open relationship. Too bad I missed it.

NICK: What do you take in your coffee?

CHARLIE: Cream and sugar. But I told you that.

NICK: Smartass.

NICK exits. Humming happily, CHARLIE locates her purse among the rubble of her clothing, takes a compact from it, looks at herself and abruptly stops humming. She starts scrubbing the smudged makeup on her face with a kleenex.

CHARLIE: Jesus Christ. Gone for coffee, my ass. He's gone to call a plastic surgeon.

GENE appears at the doorway with a mug of coffee.

GENE: You look ravishing.

CHARLIE: *(turning in surprise)* Where's Nick?

GENE: He's running late. Cream and sugar, right?

CHARLIE: You mean he left?

GENE: You know Nick. He hates emotional goodbyes. *(He puts the coffee in her hand.)* But he wanted you to have this. Don't worry, I'll drive you home.

CHARLIE: You don't have to do that.

GENE: Oh, I'm used to it.

CHARLIE: What kind of crack is that—you're used to driving Nick's girls home?

GENE: I don't want you to feel alone. As though you'd bombed somehow.

CHARLIE: Thanks.

GENE: Actually, I don't usually drive his girls.

CHARLIE: Aha, I did bomb.

GENE: No! It's just that most of them have cars.

CHARLIE: I liked it better when I just felt alone. Gene, if you don't mind, I'd like to get dressed. Before you tell me how many other girls you've seen in this robe.

GENE: Very few. It's mine.

CHARLIE: Oh—I'm sorry.

GENE: No sorrier than me. It looks good on you, though. That'll give me incentive.

CHARLIE: Thank you. If you'll let me get dressed, you can have it back.

GENE: You know, you shouldn't take Nick personally. He's got the manners of a forklift.

CHARLIE: *(brightening)* You mean it was nothing I did?

GENE: Boy, you are really something. You meet the guy—what, last night? And take the blame for the habits of a lifetime. *(as she says nothing)* Do you always assume everything's your fault?

CHARLIE: I suppose this is a course in law school. Badgering the Witness.

GENE: Law school's Nick's idea. Actually, I'm a writer.

CHARLIE: Ah, you writers. Nothing much gets past you, does it? I'd really love to read your work. I think I've got an old sales slip from the Bay. Maybe it's one of yours?

GENE: *(starting for the door)* The car's in the underground garage. Come down to the front door when you're dressed.

CHARLIE: Gene! *(as he turns around)* I'm sorry. I make a lot of crummy jokes. Ask Nick. He saw my act.

GENE: Nick liked your act. He told me.

CHARLIE: Did he—mention anything else?

GENE: *(smiling)* He'll call you. Sometime this evening.

CHARLIE: You wouldn't kid me about that?

GENE: No. I'm sorry I gave you such a hard time, when I woke you up.

CHARLIE: Oh, what the hell . . . . Talk to me when you're my age, sonny. We'll see if *you* get all the names straight in the morning.

GENE: Bullshit. You're the type who puts "Sleep Around" on her Things To Do List.

CHARLIE: Now, what the hell is that supposed to mean?

GENE: I just don't think you've got a lot of experience with this kind of thing. What are you, married or something? Divorced? Or—separated? Yeah, I like separated. Very half-assed. Very seventies.

CHARLIE: Lucky shot.

GENE: Naw, a lot of Nick's ladies are separated.

CHARLIE: *(sinking down dispiritedly on the bed)* Just the ones without cars, I hope. I'd hate to fuck up the demographic profile.

GENE: *(sitting down beside her)* I'm sorry. I really am.

CHARLIE: So am I. About everything. Particularly the invention of alcohol.

GENE: How much do you remember about last night?

CHARLIE: Not much. Pretty funny, eh?

GENE: I'm not laughing.

CHARLIE: Neither am I. Say something hilarious.

GENE: Want to get married?

CHARLIE: *(with a startled laugh)* What?

GENE: See? I knew that would raise a smile.

CHARLIE: I can't marry a man with prospects. It's against my religion.

GENE: I'm thinking of quitting law school.

CHARLIE: Aw, that's what they all say.

GENE: No, seriously, I am.

CHARLIE: Even so, you can't marry me, sonny. I'm old enough to be your mother.

GENE: Bullshit. You're only as old as you feel.

CHARLIE: *(looking into her compact mirror wearily)* I know. Christ, look at me. First runner-up in the René Lévesque Look-Alike Contest.

GENE: Stop that. But I am going to quit. Don't tell Nick.

CHARLIE: When am I going to tell him? I'll probably never see him again.

GENE: Oh, you'll see him. If you want to.

CHARLIE: You make it sound like I shouldn't.

GENE: You make it sound like you want to. Get dressed and I'll drive you home.

CHARLIE: I told you, I can get home myself.

GENE: Okay. Whatever you like.

He moves to the door.

CHARLIE: Gene— *(as he stops)* Thanks—for the use of the robe.

GENE: Anytime. I know—that's what they all say.

He gives her a smile and exits on a blackout.

Scene Three

A couple of weeks later. Lights come up on the area that is CHARLIE's apartment. The room is empty, but there is the sound of someone rattling at the door. The rattling continues until a credit card slides through the lock, then the door opens and ALAN enters, with a small suitcase. He is obviously pleased with himself for pulling off the credit card stunt, shuts the door and tenderly replaces the card in his wallet. He puts down the suitcase, goes immediately to the phone and dials.

ALAN: *(into the phone)* Hello, Deborah? It's Alan. *(pause)* Alan Merrit. The actor? One of your clients? *(laughing)* Right. That explains why you never get me any work. You have no idea who I am. *(pause)* Yeah, slow season, I know. Funny how it's always slow season when I'm in town and Audition City when I'm away . . . . *(pause)* Skip it, Deborah. I'll be in town a couple of days at— *(checking phone dial)* 967-1313. I'll check back with you before I leave. *(pause)* Alan, that's right. Alan Merrit.

He hangs up dispiritedly, lights a cigarette, looks up an address in his book, then dials again, singing quietly, "I really want this job, I really need this job . . . ."

ALAN: *(into the phone)* Hello, Grant Austin, please. It's Alan Merrit calling. *(pause)* Hello, is he in? It's Alan Merrit. *(pause)* Hello, Grant it's— *(pause)* Oh. Well, *could* he come to the phone? It's Alan Merrit. He's expecting my call. *(pause)* Look, I made a special trip into town to see him. Couldn't he—? *(pause)* Thank you. I appreciate it. *(longer pause, then)* Grant! Hi! You said to call Tuesday and it's— *(pause)* Alan Merrit? You said— *(pause)* Alan, right. The actor? We met at the Molière opening and— *(pause)* No, I wasn't exactly *in* it, but we talked at the bar after and— *(pause)* Yeah, I guess I might have been in a red shirt. *(pause)* Thank you, it's one of my favourite colours too . . . . Look, Grant, you said Tuesday would be a good day to call, so I came in from Stratford and— *(pause)* No, I'm not exactly *in* the Stratford company, but— *(pause)* Oh, *next* Tuesday. I guess I misunderstood. But I did come into town to see you, and— *(pause)* Well, how be if I call back in the morning? Just to see if your schedule's cleared? I'd really like five minutes of your— *(pause)* Okay, Grant, fine. I'll call back in the morning.

He hangs up, speaking bitterly to himself.

ALAN: Any special colour you'd like me to wear?

The phone, which is in his lap, rings. He starts violently, picks it up.

(into the phone) Hello? *(pause)* Look, I said not to call here. You know how she is— *(pause)* Yeah, I just got off the phone with Austin. He's delighted I'm here and wants to see me tomorrow. *(pause)* Oh, it's not such a big deal. If you know the right strings to pull. *(pause)* I don't know. Tomorrow night, maybe, or Thursday. Depends.

Unnoticed by ALAN, CHARLIE has come in the open door and stands in the doorway. She has a paper bag of liquor in her arms.

ALAN: *(into the phone)* Yes, I miss you, too. But I—

As CHARLIE rattles the bag angrily, ALAN turns and sees her.

ALAN: *(into the phone)* Look, I've got to go, okay? Call you tomorrow.

He hangs up, turning to CHARLIE with a bright smile.

Hiya, babe!

CHARLIE: Well, surprise, surprise! *(allowing him to kiss her)* Who was that on the phone?

ALAN: Nobody. Casting people.

CHARLIE: Who miss you? Shucks, I bet they say that to *all* the actors. It was him, wasn't it?

ALAN: He's got a name, you know.

CHARLIE: "Casting people." Why do you keep lying? Force of habit?

ALAN: I just got here. Can't we save the cracks for later?

CHARLIE: How'd you get in?

ALAN: Credit card.

CHARLIE: That's amazing.

ALAN: *(self-effacing)* Oh, I wouldn't go that far . . . .

CHARLIE: That *you* were actually issued a credit card? That's nothing short of miraculous.

ALAN: Actually, it's Jimmy's.

CHARLIE: Good old Jimmy. Say it with plastic. So what are you doing in town?

ALAN: You've been after me to come up and see you.

CHARLIE: Uh-huh. And—?

ALAN: And . . . I've got some people to see.

CHARLIE: Yeah, I figured.

ALAN: Grant Austin, for one. I hope that's okay.

CHARLIE: Well, if it's okay with Grant Austin, it's okay with me.

ALAN: I mean, it's all right to stay here.

CHARLIE: Here? In my apartment? It's out of the question.

ALAN: Charlie, I'm your husband. Who's going to object?

CHARLIE: My boyfriend. To name one.

ALAN: I didn't know you had a steady boyfriend.

CHARLIE: I figured if you had one, I should too. Alan, Nick will be here in a minute. We're going to The Canada Goose.

ALAN: You're on tonight? Terrific. Can I join you?

CHARLIE: You want to come along? You won't feel a little weird about Nick?

ALAN: Should I? I mean, is there something organically wrong with him?

CHARLIE: I give up. You can't crash here. That's all there is to it.

ALAN: That's nice. That's very nice. After eight years of marriage, this is what I get?

CHARLIE: *(quiz show voice)* This, Alan, and much much more! During your marriage, you received: four million loads of clean laundry; the keys to a car your wife never got to drive; leftovers no more than twice a week; plus sex available at several convenient locations in your own home! Yes, Alan, these are only some of the prizes you won playing Eight Years of Marriage!

ALAN: Charlie, don't be that way. I thought we'd got past all the bitterness.

CHARLIE: I hope not. I mean, when that's gone, what's left?

ALAN: I don't know. A new start, maybe?

CHARLIE: As what? I admit, I've always *wanted* a sister, but—

ALAN: Knock that off.

CHARLIE: Then *you* knock it off. *(pouring herself a drink)* Oh, Alan, don't tell me you're having doubts about your femininity again.

ALAN: I should know better than to expect to be taken seriously.

CHARLIE: Oh, I took you seriously, all right. The last two years of our marriage when you said you were working all those nights. I took you seriously when you told me I was crazy to think any different. And I took you very seriously indeed when you disappeared into the pages of *Christopher Street*, never to emerge again. Now, I'd say there was a limit to just how long a person can go on taking you seriously. Or any way at all. Wouldn't you?

ALAN: If that's how you feel, why do you keep asking me to come and see you?

CHARLIE: I don't know.

ALAN: Neither do I. Can you pour me one too?

CHARLIE: On one condition. That you refrain from referring to homosexuality as a "phase." You always make it sound like teenage acne. *(She gives him a drink.)*

ALAN: I know what you've been through. But it's not easy on me, either. Especially when you phone me up, late at night—

CHARLIE: There won't be any more calls. Not that kind. I'm feeling much better now.

ALAN: Thanks to Nick?

CHARLIE: What's the matter? Don't you believe someone could be interested in me?

ALAN: Oh, I believe it. Do you?

CHARLIE: I don't have this adverse effect on everybody, you know. I don't drive all men to gay bars.

ALAN: Did I ever say you did?

CHARLIE: Yes.

ALAN: *(after a pause)* I'm sorry. I guess I had to blame somebody.

CHARLIE: I wish you'd picked your mother, like everybody else. She lives six hundred miles away. It wouldn't have fucked *her* up.

ALAN: You're not fucked up. Not any more. Thanks to Nick.

CHARLIE: So it does bother you a little?

ALAN: We've been split up almost a year. I know there've been guys . . . .

CHARLIE: Oh dear, and I thought I was so discreet!

ALAN: Come on. You always made sure I knew.

CHARLIE: *(after a pause)* Most of those guys were clunkers.

ALAN: And Nick isn't a clunker? *(pause)* Okay, it bothers me.

CHARLIE: *(gently)* It's just this phobia you've got. About closed doors. Most people think of the world as their oyster. In your mind, it's one big telephone exchange. With everyone on Hold.

ALAN: Only you, babe. Come here, and let me put you on Hold.

He hugs her. There is a knock on the door.

CHARLIE: That's Nick. I guess he forgot his credit card.

She opens the door. NICK enters and gives her a bottle of champagne.

NICK: Hiya, babe. Bubbly to the bubbly. In honour of your performance.

CHARLIE: I perform twice a week. Champagne is for special.

NICK: Then be specially good. Dom Perignon, kid. Don't give me no domestic-bubbly performance.

He kisses her, then sees ALAN.

Oh. Hi.

CHARLIE: Nick, this is Alan. *(as the men shake hands)* My late husband.

NICK: *(dropping the hand like a hot rock)* Charlie! Je-sus.

ALAN: Charlie's little joke. And it's little.

NICK: *(backing toward the door)* Look, I didn't know you were double-booked here. And if you two have things to straighten out—

CHARLIE: *(quickly)* No, Alan's just dropped in from Stratford.

ALAN: *(also quick)* Just to say hello.

CHARLIE: *(even quicker)* Not even that, practically.

ALAN: Don't mind me.

NICK: *(shrugging sheepishly)* If you'd had as many husbands sprung on you as I have . . . . Now, whenever I hear the word, I automatically check the exits. *(to ALAN)* In from Stratford, eh?

ALAN: Couple of business things.

NICK: Ball bearings?

ALAN: I beg your pardon?

NICK: *(innocently)* That's what they do up in Stratford, isn't it?

CHARLIE: Nick's little joke. He grew up there. He knows goddamn well there's a theatre there.

NICK: She's right. Saturday nights, our idea of a hot old time was driving into town to bash a few faggot actors.

CHARLIE: *(quickly)* Have a drink, Nick. *(producing a bottle from the bag)* I got some Scotch, just for you. Alan?

ALAN: *(campily)* No thanks. I'll stick to Shirley Temples.

NICK: *(laughing)* Hey, that's good. So, you're with the Festival. Watch your ass, that's all I can say.

ALAN: *(very macho)* I'm not with the Festival yet. You think I'm watching my ass *too* closely?

NICK: Could be. What do you think, Charlie? You're the resident expert on the gay scene.

ALAN: *(to CHARLIE)* Do tell.

NICK: Babe, how does that bit go, about the faggots in the restaurant? *(to ALAN)* They're always sending back dirty forks, right, then they pick up some stranger and get the clap.

ALAN: That's very funny, Charlie. Not very insightful, but funny.

CHARLIE: I do a whole bunch of different stuff. You'll see.

ALAN: Some other time, maybe.

CHARLIE: I thought you wanted to come tonight.

ALAN: I've changed my mind. *(picking up his suitcase)* Have a good show. I'll call you tomorrow.

CHARLIE: Alan—

ALAN: *(more conciliatory)* Look, I've got a heavy day tomorrow. I have to be on the phone early to Grant Austin and—

NICK: Grant? You working with him?

ALAN: *(stiffly)* I'd like to.

NICK: *(to CHARLIE)* Grant was on that picture I told you about. Christ, I more than tripled on that one.

ALAN: *(setting down his suitcase)* Lupercal? You had money in that?

NICK: Lucky me. You see the numbers on that fucker?

ALAN: No, but I saw the fucker. It was great.

NICK: Grant's dynamite. Camp as a row of tents, but a hell of a director. You seeing him tomorrow?

ALAN: He's not sure what his time is like.

NICK: Well, he starts casting next week. You better catch him before the big rush.

ALAN: You don't happen to know what the film is?

NICK: Another blockbuster, I hope. I've got money in this one too.

ALAN: *(avidly)* No kidding? You haven't seen a script, by any chance?

NICK: I know where to get one. Why?

ALAN: *(to CHARLIE)* Listen, maybe I *can* join you at the club. Once I dump the suitcase . . . .

CHARLIE: I thought you had such an early day ahead.

ALAN: *(artificially sweet)* I thought you wanted me to see your act.

CHARLIE: *(the same)* A minute ago, my act rated slightly below trench-mouth.

ALAN: I haven't got any idea what you're talking about.

CHARLIE: Haven't you? I mean it's just amazing how the atmosphere in this room has warmed up since Grant Austin dropped in.

ALAN: *(to NICK)* You don't mind if I join you later at The Canada Goose? And maybe talk about this new script?

NICK: I don't mind. I like to talk. Charlie knows that.

ALAN: *(picking up his suitcase)* See you later, then. Bye, babe.

He exits. CHARLIE takes a long sip of her drink.

NICK: Nervous kind of guy. He any good?

CHARLIE: I don't know. He never gives himself a chance to find out. He's too busy making useful contacts.

NICK: You should talk. Soon as you found out I backed movies, you couldn't get your clothes off fast enough.

CHARLIE: Nick! You don't believe that.

NICK: Come on, you're entitled to your self-interest, like everybody else. It doesn't detract from the quality of the sex.

CHARLIE: I'm telling you, I'm not in it for the fringe benefits. I want to get that clear, Nick.

NICK: You people with "pure motives." You make me nervous.

CHARLIE: Oh, I'm not so pure . . . . *(putting her arms around him)* Let's not talk about work. You've already got Alan prepared to lay down his life for you because you might be useful to him. Isn't that enough?

NICK: I don't get it. If I can get him in to see Austin, why shouldn't I? If I can do you a favour too, why not? What is it, you've got your life in ledger columns? "Business." "Romance."

CHARLIE: That's right. Just don't mix me in with business, that's all. This town is one giant office. Casting done in bars. Contracts ratified on waterbeds. People sucking up to power because it might rub off. Those macrobiotic people had it all wrong. Around here, you are *who* you eat.

NICK: You don't know a goddamn thing about it. Work, sex, dinner, dealing—it's all the same. I don't even try keeping them apart. And I like people who do the same. No questions asked.

CHARLIE: *(pouring herself a drink)* That's a tall order.

NICK: *(indicating drink)* Hey, you're working tonight. Were you always such a little lush? Even when you were married to what's-his-name?

CHARLIE: Lush. You make me sound like a golf course. This is only my second. And anyway, what's it got to do with what's-his-name?

NICK: That's what I wonder. What broke you two up? You never told me.

CHARLIE: You never asked. I like that arrangement. *(kissing him)* I don't want to talk about it. I want to fool around.

NICK: You always want to fool around. What did you do, wear the guy out?

CHARLIE: *(sharply)* Will you forget about Alan?

NICK: No, I want to know. What was the problem?

CHARLIE: *(exasperated)* Isn't it obvious? My frigidity!

NICK: Hey, How come you always act like you'll never get laid again?

CHARLIE: Right now, I'd settle for a really decisive kiss.

NICK sighs, then kisses her very decisively. She pulls away finally, hesitates for a moment before speaking.

Nick . . . . Do you think I'm attractive?

NICK: You haven't figured that out?

CHARLIE: I mean—do you like being with me?

NICK: Hell, no. When you stop giving green stamps, I'm gone.

CHARLIE: *(urgently)* Nick—please?

NICK: *(pause, then with slight distaste)* Okay. Of course I like being with you. Very much.

CHARLIE: Yeah, I figured.

She pulls him to her, kisses him.

NICK: Hardcore comes later. It's almost show time.

CHARLIE: How be if I skip the club? We could have a nice evening—just you, me and Dom Perignon.

NICK: You can't just back out.

CHARLIE: Sure I can. There's always someone hanging around who'll take over my spot.

NICK: You expect to get ahead with an attitude like that?

CHARLIE: It was just a thought.

NICK: What's the problem?

CHARLIE: I just don't feel very funny tonight.

NICK: No? Well, you goddamn well better be. Unless you want to sleep alone.

CHARLIE: *(mock terror)* Oh, shit. *(quickly)* Say, did I ever tell you the one about the lady comic, her bullying boyfriend and the vat of cold vichyssoise? Funny? You bet. Seems the comic was walking over the vichyssoise on a tightrope and—

NICK: Okay, okay. You don't sleep alone. Now let's get the fuck out of here.

She picks up her purse and he slaps her on the ass on the way out the door on a blackout.

Scene Four

Later that night. Lights come up on The Canada Goose. CHARLIE wears the now habitual uniform of her performance—her glasses, jacket, scarf and brooch.

CHARLIE: *(bounding down to the mike, removing it from stand, addressing the audience)* Hi, how is everybody tonight? Come on, it's not a trick question. How about you, sir? How are you? *(if the audience doesn't answer)* It's all right, sir. I read lips. *(if audience member does answer)* Who asked you?

Hey, I'm in a great mood tonight. I just got my Mensa card. *(taking a card from her pocket, showing it)* You know what that means? It means I'm insured against ever skipping a period.

So . . . how do you like my hair? Mr Doug did it. That's my hairdresser—Mr Doug. Ever notice what flamboyant names Canadian hairdressers have? Mr Doug. Mr. Glen. Mr Garth of North Bay. Mr Doug told me he was just going to "shape the hair." Notice how they never refer to it as YOUR hair? This is so they can wreck it without either of you feeling personally affected by it.

But I trust Mr Doug. Implicitly. I mean, he doesn't charge an arm and a leg like those trendy uptown places, where you pay for the decor and the cute little cover-up robe. Mr Doug works out of an auto body shop. He keeps his costs down that way. Although I notice the Turtle Wax IS doing strange things to my hair. And there was this mix-up one day where a lady came in for a cut and set and wound up getting a ring job. *(to an audience member who is laughing)* Hey, that's not funny. It's tragic. I suppose you laughed when Ben Hur's mother and sister got leprosy.

You know, I have what people in showbusiness describe as a great RADIO face. Actually, it's not mine. It comes attached to the glasses. It's part of a disguise. See, when you look like Bo Derek, everybody mobs you. Okay, okay . . . so I don't look like Bo Derek. But I am a Ten. I'm what they call a Canadian Ten. Which means they don't even accept me at par in Buffalo. *(indicating audience member)* This man is laughing. He has no idea what I go through. Great shirt, sir. How long do you have to wear it before you win the bet?

Oh, by the way, a note was slipped to me backstage. But I intend to go on with the act anyway. No, seriously . . . I have a note here.

(producing note from her pocket, reading from it) Mrs. D of Erin Mills writes: "Dear Charlie, Where do you get your ideas for the characters on *Land of Dreams*?" Oh, in case you don't know, *Land of Dreams* is the name of this soap opera I write for. Where do I get my ideas for characters, Mrs D? I steal them from American soaps and change their names to Glen and Doug. Any more questions? (without waiting for a reply) Fine.

Hey, you know, I always wanted to be one of those teensy little girls. You know the kind I mean? The kind of girl whose nickname is Bitsy? The kind of girl I lend a bracelet to, and she wears it as a belt. Helpless. That was always my goal in life. To be helpless. Helpless and sweet and quiet. Like Bitsy. Bitsy never has to talk. She's mastered one simple basic sentence—"How was your day, honey?"—and the world's beating a path to her door. I meanwhile am lucky if a guy ventures up my walk to read my meter. See, men just don't come on to big, capable girls—girls who speak English as if it was their native language. Especially when your voice sounds like Full Alert in the London Blitz. I ask a guy if he wants to come to bed, and it sounds like a threat. Now, Bitsy has this tiny, feminine, whispering voice, right? Put her on a phone, man, and she gets results. (imitating) "Hello? Oh, hi, Brad. Dinner? No, thanks. I just ate half a soda biscuit and I couldn't touch another thing."

When Bitsy goes shopping for clothes, the clerks always advise her to try the Petite Section, right? The Petite Section. It even sounds elegant, doesn't it? So what do they call the large section? You guessed it. The Large Section. And I so much as even try walking into the Petite Section and they throw a cordon around the entire department and get on the bullhorns— (imitating) "Attention all staff. Large Person attempting entry. Large person attempting entry." Then they send some little Munchkin over to reason with me, right? (imitating) "Listen, honey, nothing personal, but you're built like a Maytag, all right?"

You notice how tiny all the clerks are in the Petite Section? The manager of the department wears a point-zero-six dress. I'm not kidding. And when I won't go quietly, the entire staff rushes to the barricades. It looks like a convention of jockeys. They all swarm around my kneecaps chanting— (imitating) "Follow the yellow brick road. Follow the yellow brick road . . ."

Hey, you've been a great audience. Thank you and goodnight!

Blackout

Scene Five

Later that night. Lights come up on a table in The Canada Goose where Alan sits alone with a full drink. CHARLIE, dressed as in Scene Four, hurries breathlessly to the table. She stops short, glances around.

ALAN: (rising, kissing her) Babe, that was dynamite.

CHARLIE: Where's Nick?

ALAN: He said he's sorry he missed the act. Something—

CHARLIE: (joining in) "Something came up." Fuck.

She sits down.

ALAN: He went to make a call about that script, and when he came back he said he had to leave.

CHARLIE: You had to have that goddamn script, didn't you?

ALAN: Since you ask, yes. It would be very helpful. (pause) He said he'd try to make it back to your place later.

CHARLIE: White of him. I want a drink.

ALAN: (pushing the drink over to her) Here. I ordered it for you.

CHARLIE: Thanks.

ALAN: Babe, you were wonderful. The fact that Nick missed it doesn't change that.

CHARLIE: You think that's all I care about? Whether he saw the fucking act?

ALAN: I figured you'd care. Nick says he'd like to back a film with you in it.

CHARLIE: I'm not in it to get ahead! I don't quaff cocktails with people I hate just to get a script.

ALAN: Is that how you think I operate?

CHARLIE: I *watched* you operate with Nick.

ALAN: (bitterly) All right, so what? The guy's a redneck, but his money's the same colour as anyone else's. If Grant Austin can put up with Nick's faggot jokes, I guess I can too. (pause) You don't understand, Charlie. You can stand up in front of a roomful of people without anybody's help and run your own show. I can't.

CHARLIE: Oh, I know how to get love from groups of twenty or more, all right. But one to one? You could give me some tips in that area. I mean, at least you've got Jackie—

ALAN: (mechanically) Jimmy—

CHARLIE: —Jimmy, to keep the home fires burning while you're out knocking on doors. I come out of the spotlight, and find the bastard's taken a powder.

ALAN: Charlie, it's not easy. For anybody. But as long as you've got the spotlight, you're way ahead. I wish I could do what you do—dress up in a costume and act out my worst fears about myself.

CHARLIE: It's not a costume!

ALAN: Come on. You look like an out-take from *Annie Hall*. All the years I knew you, you were too vain to wear your glasses, even.

CHARLIE: (snatching off the glasses) There are no glamorous lady comics. It doesn't work.

ALAN: You dress like that because you think it's how you really look. I admire you for that. I wouldn't have the nerve to go up there—or anywhere else—and try to be myself.

CHARLIE: (taking his hand) Sweetheart, what's the matter?

ALAN: It's—confusing, that's all. I think I've got my priorities straight—or bent, or something. Then I see you, and you're telling stories about queers and picking up tricks—

CHARLIE: (quickly) I didn't use any of that stuff tonight.

ALAN: But you tell the stories all the same. And I don't recognize myself in them.

CHARLIE: Of course not. Alan, that isn't *you*.

ALAN: Then what is? What do you see, Charlie?

CHARLIE: I don't know. What do you want me to see? What do you want me to do?

ALAN: I don't know. I had some idea when I decided to come into town that maybe . . . (He shrugs.)

CHARLIE: That maybe what?

ALAN: Of course, I didn't know about Nick. I hadn't counted on that.

CHARLIE: (urgently) Alan, you can't *do* this to me. If you want something, tell me.

ALAN: I guess there's nothing you can do.

CHARLIE: Not if you're going to be so goddamn cryptic.

ALAN: Charlie, what difference does it make now? Nick's in the picture, and all bets are off.

CHARLIE: You mean it's safe to make overtures, now that I'm hooked on someone else?

ALAN: Yeah. I guess maybe that's it. You are hooked, aren't you?

CHARLIE: Yes, I'm afraid so.

ALAN: That's all right, then.

CHARLIE: Not from where I sit. God, I wish I knew how he felt about me.

ALAN: And if the verdict's favourable? You might decide you're fit to live?

CHARLIE: Isn't that what it means when you're hooked?

ALAN: No! There's a big difference between caring about him and building your life around the idea. I mean, when do you stop expecting other people to supply you with self-respect?

CHARLIE: You make me sound like a backward nation. (travelogue voice) "Here in Charlieland, the natives try to find enough self-esteem to power even one generator."

ALAN: That's not funny, babe.

CHARLIE: Neither is venereal disease. But you know, it's a sure-fire laugh?

Blackout.

Scene Six

A few days later. Lights come up in NICK's bedroom. NICK is asleep. GENE comes in, begins stealthily dialing the phone. NICK stirs, raises his head.

NICK: *(annoyed and sleepy)* What? Gene, what the fuck are you doing?

GENE: *(hanging up the phone)* Sorry, but the one in the kitchen is temporarily out of service.

NICK: *(rubbing his eyes)* This is just an extension, you asshole. It won't work either.

GENE: Sure it will. It's out of the war zone. Mustard gas attack in the kitchen. *(German accent)* It's dat Sharlie again, mein Kapitan. She shrikes mitout varning.

NICK: Charlie? *(looking at the empty side of the bed)* What's she doing up?

GENE: Cleaning the fridge.

NICK: Oh fuck. This is too much. Yesterday she made blueberry pancakes.

GENE: Last week she washed the windows.

NICK: Next thing I'll wake up to find my goddamn room re-papered.

GENE: I think you should nip this in the bud. Remember your stewardess? Almost six feet of stunning blonde stooped over the bathtub, scouring away with Spic and Span?

NICK: If that's how you feel, why don't you tell Charlie to knock it off?

GENE: Because it's not *my* fault she thinks the way to your heart is through your stinking refrigerator. Nick, you owe it to her to straighten her out.

NICK: No way. A woman's determined to dig her own grave, I'm not going to hide the shovel.

GENE: Christ. Maybe you should just tell her you don't *have* a heart.

NICK: Come on, it's too early in the morning for that crap.

GENE: It's eleven-thirty, and there's a woman in your kitchen *humming*, if you'll believe it, while she dungs rotted matter out of the fridge whose stench would turn the stomach of a wart hog. Christ, there are carrots covered in blue fuzz and mutated leftovers that the Special Effects Department at Universal should only take a look at. And yet she is out there humming, Nick— I swear it's God's honest truth—because those noxious vapours emanate from *your* fridge, *your* kitchen, *your* apartment, and as far as she's concerned, anything that pertains to *you* is strictly Chanel Number Five. No, I don't think it's at all too early in the morning for that crap. And either you go out there and tell her you love what she's doing or advise her she's spelling out her own destruction in moulded spuds. But either way, wear a gas mask, I'm warning you.

NICK: I don't need advice on women from you. I wrote the book.

GENE: I know. It's the one with the large print and the small words. You won't help her, will you? You won't help her at all.

NICK: All this sudden concern for Charlie. What's the matter, you fumble the ball with that great-looking cocktail waitress? Sure you did, I can tell. I fix you up on Saturday night, and here you are on Sunday morning, all by yourself. Unless Donna is out in the kitchen battling bacteria with good old Charlie.

GENE: Donna would be better off if she *were* into fridges. Something. Anything. What do you talk about to someone whose idea of a moral dilemma is whether hot pink clashes with green?

NICK: You took Donna out to *talk*?

GENE: I had it in mind as an option.

NICK: Christ, what am I going to do with you? I fix you up with a beautiful girl who borders on genius, sexually speaking, and you complain because she isn't a Rhodes scholar in the bargain. What is it, they haven't invented a woman good enough for you?

GENE: Once in my life, I'd like a shot at a woman you haven't slept with first. Although I realize such women are hard to find.

NICK: Too bad you feel that way. Otherwise, you could take Charlie off my hands.

GENE: Oh, sure, we'd both go for that. I mean, her glasses are almost as strong as mine. Lasting relationships have been based on less. *(with distaste)* Nick, Jesus Christ . . . .

NICK: You're right, it's not much of a thought. She's cute, but she's nutty as a fruitcake. And she acts like she's mainlining Spanish Fly.

GENE: That doesn't sound so bad.

NICK: Don't kid yourself. That woman doesn't just *like* to screw. She needs it. Like a drug.

GENE: Like a drug, eh? Wow. Of course, you're in your thirties. I keep forgetting. No longer the ideal . . . drug pusher?

NICK: You know who puts out that crap—about men beginning to decline at age nineteen? Hostile women put it out, that's who. It's all part of a plot to discredit us. *(pause)* Anyway, Charlie's too old for you.

GENE: I'm twenty-three.

NICK: And she's thirty. That's exactly what I mean.

GENE: No, that's exactly what *I* mean. Charlie and I would be the ideal combination.

NICK: Bullshit. Sexual peaks have nothing to do with Charlie.

GENE: I wonder. I mean, here you are, so impressed with Donna's sexual prowess. A younger woman, not yet in her prime, not so difficult to keep up with . . . .

NICK: Good, Geno, you're doing fine. You'll be looking for a new apartment by lunchtime.

GENE: Hey, Nick, for Christ's sake. I'm only kidding.

NICK: *(sulkily)* I'm telling you, that stuff about peaks is crap. I'm as hot as I ever was. With the right woman.

GENE: You mean you really don't want Charlie any more?

NICK: For Christ's sake. I just woke up. How the hell do I know what I want? I want to be a millionaire before I'm forty, I want a cup of coffee. I want a woman for a change who doesn't turn into Betty Crocker on a moment's notice.

GENE: So what are you going to do? Order the perfect one out of the catalogue? Relationships have to be worked on, haven't you heard?

NICK: I work hard all day long. Why should I work when I come home, too? Either it clicks with a woman or it doesn't, and all the heart-to-heart talks in the world never fixed anything. Take it from Nicky. Nicky knows. Gene, on the other hand, knows zip.

GENE: *(quietly)* Poor Charlie.

NICK: Will you cut it out? Anyway, it's not like we're a couple or anything.

GENE: What would you call it? A string quartet?

NICK: It was just for—fun, that's all. But when the fun goes . . . . Well, I just don't have that much enthusiasm for it any more.

GENE: Big brother, you haven't had much enthusiasm for anybody since about 1968. Since then, it's been painting by numbers.

NICK: You know, this interest you take in my relationships is downright unhealthy. Why don't you find a project of your own—like losing your virginity?

GENE: You think anybody whose little black book comes in fewer volumes than the *Britannica* is a virgin. I've been around. But unlike you, I can remember *where*.

NICK: Yeah? When was the last time you got laid? I mean, here you are, so hot to be a writer. What the hell are you going to write about?

GENE: If you're still pissed off about law school, why don't you just admit it?

NICK: Me, pissed off? Hell, no. Why, I've got the First Lady of Show Business into some heavy defrosting out in my kitchen. And in the bedroom, the kid I staked through two years of law school who's decided on a permanent career at the pen counter of the Bay instead. By God, I'm a lucky son of a gun. I think my life would make great musical comedy, don't you?

GENE: I'm sorry, I'm just not cut out for law school. Besides, I won't be at the Bay forever. Look at Charlie. She makes a living writing.

NICK: Charlie! Is *she* the inspiration behind this? God, it was a dark day when I let her and her arsenal of cleaning products in here.

GENE: Don't be so melodramatic. It was my own idea.

NICK: Yeah? Well, at least you're right about one thing. If you're going to be a writer, make a full-time career out of it. I know people who'd be interested in you.

GENE: I don't think I want to write menus.

NICK: Not restaurant people, you asshole. Movie people.

GENE: I've got to do it my way. Me and Sinatra.

NICK: First you let somebody get you in the door. Then you do it your way.

GENE: Nick, it's bad enough I live here at the Club Med with you and pay one-twenty-five in rent. I'm not going to use your connections too.

NICK: You're my brother. I feel responsible.

GENE: *(Italian accent)* Eh, Niccolo, listen to your brother, eh? Alla time, you give, give, give. But never nothing outa yourself. Capisce?

NICK: Jesus, it's as bad as talking to Charlie. Worse.

GENE: All my life—fastest cheque book in the West, favours done while you wait. And champagne always on ice.

NICK: I never bought anybody in my life.

GENE: I've seen you buy a few people *off*. Tell me, when Charlie gets her pink slip, will she get the bouquet of roses that traditionally goes with it?

NICK: Jesus, I wish you'd get off that. Or go after her yourself, if you're so concerned.

GENE: And break Jane Fonda's heart?

NICK: *(grinning)* Don't lie to me, you little fucker. You'd do it, wouldn't you? You'd do it just for spite.

GENE: Not for spite. But maybe to jazz up her sex life a little.

NICK: *(laughing)* Get the fuck out of my room. And don't touch my phone either.

GENE goes.

You little wise-ass, you're twenty-three years old and a law school drop-out. *(wearily)* And I'm a hundred and twelve. Easy.

Blackout.

Scene Seven

Two days later. Lights come up on CHARLIE on the phone in her apartment. There are a couple of empty wine bottles beside her and she has a glass in her hand. She is drunk, but not inarticulate. A bouquet of roses is bundled conspicuously in a wastebasket.

CHARLIE: *(into the phone)* No, I'm not drinking. Alan, you sound like my mother, except your voice is higher. *(quickly)* I'm sorry. I didn't mean that. Don't hang up, please. *(pause)* I know there weren't going to be any more calls, but this is important. Maybe I've been too categorical about things. Maybe we *could* get back together someday. Stranger things have happened, right? And until everything went crazy, we were happy together. *(pause, then firmly)* Goddamn it, we *were*, until you took this notion to emulate the late Oscar Wilde. I think it's a fad, Alan, just a trendy fad. In the sixties, everybody went back to the land. In the seventies, they went gay. *(pause, then wearily)* I know. I still love you, too. But we sure have a funny way of showing it. *(pause)* Yes, okay, I'm drinking. Maybe I'm drunk. *(pause)* I don't know why. See, there was this bottle here and I— *(pause, then bitterly)* No, Nick is not here. *(beginning to cry)* How the hell do I know where Nick is?

She listens into the phone, nods corroboration, and when she can manage it, speaks.

Yes, finished. As far as I knew, everything was going fine. Then today I get the kiss-off, and tonight these roses arrive. He sends roses and a note that Kahlil Gibran must have ghosted. "No regrets. No bitterness. No blame." What the hell does than *mean*? After all this, he buys me off with cryptic platitudes. And a lunch. I knew there was going to be trouble when he asked me to lunch. Never, never go to lunch. It's always the bad-news meal. Everytime I— *(pause)* Nick has nothing to do with this call. I told you, I love you. And you said that you— *(pause, then angrily)* Wait and see? How the hell do you expect me to wait and see? You were a beautiful boy when I met you and now you're nothing but a— goddamn—faggot! *(pause)* I *can't* get past it. Can you get past it? Eight goddamn years, Alan. How the hell do I get that back? There's just nowhere to go from here. *(pause)* I don't *know* what I mean by that!

She slams down the phone and pulls the jack out of the wall on a blackout.

Scene Eight

A few hours later. Lights up in CHARLIE's apartment. The scene is unchanged except for an added empty bottle or two. CHARLIE sits on the bed, more sober, singing into the mike on her tape recorder.

CHARLIE:
"When the tires are humming,
And the engine purrs,
And your car is eager,
And the thought occurs;
It's good to be alive in this land of ours,
It's good to drive in this land of ours—"

Unnoticed by CHARLIE, GENE has entered and as CHARLIE falters, he sings the next line of the song.

GENE:
"What a great, great feeling,
What a wonderful sense—"

CHARLIE with no hint of surprise, turns to him and they continue the song together, building to a strong and zesty finale.

CHARLIE and GENE:
"Of sheer enjoyment,
And of confidence.
There's something you're aware of,
Your car's been taken care of,
At the Esso sign of confidence,
At the Happy Motoring Sign!"

CHARLIE and GENE salute each other simultaneously and bark "Happy Motoring" Murray Westgate-style, then laugh uproariously.

CHARLIE: How do you know that? You weren't even born back then.

GENE: Don't you believe in the collective unconscious?

CHARLIE: Oh sure. It's the collective *conscious* I have doubts about.

GENE: Aren't you going to ask me how I got in?

CHARLIE: Chargex, American Express—what's the difference?

GENE: The door's open, that's how. Charlie, it's late. Don't you ever lock it?

CHARLIE: Is that what brings you here? A survey on the Imprudent Habits of Single Women?

GENE: They missed you down at The Canada Goose tonight.

CHARLIE: What were you doing at the club?

GENE: I knew you were on tonight.

CHARLIE: Yeah? How did I do?

She laughs, but he doesn't join in.

GENE: When I got there, Mel was trying to get you on the phone to find out where the hell you were.

He goes to the phone, examines the disconnected jack.

Out, I see.

CHARLIE: In a manner of speaking.

GENE: Anyway, I was worried.

CHARLIE: And you rushed right over, in the hopes of being the first to say, "I told you so." *(indicating wastebasket)* Congratulations. You made it.

GENE: Roses. Jesus.

CHARLIE: You want to look at the card?

GENE: *(looking her in the eye)* "No regrets. No blame. No bitterness." Something along those lines?

CHARLIE: *(after a pause)* Say, did I ever tell you the one about the dumb broad, the professional bastard and the professional bastard's know-it-all younger brother?

GENE: Let me tell you one. Nick never promised you anything. So you've come out ahead. If you count the flowers as a bonus.

CHARLIE: Don't you stick up for him.

GENE: He's my brother, Charlie. He has his faults, and I'm sorry if he hurt you. But he tried to play it straight with you and you know it.

CHARLIE: Am I supposed to thank you for pointing that out?

GENE: No, but you could offer me a drink.

CHARLIE: Not if you've come here to gloat.

GENE: No.

CHARLIE: In that case, have a drink. *(She unscrews the top from the last bottle of wine.)* Care to smell the cap?

GENE: Where did all these bottles come from?

CHARLIE: The liquor store sends their empties over. I'm too young to drink, of course. But I like my garbage to look adult.

GENE: *(taking a swig of wine)* My favourite. Melted cough drops.

CHARLIE: If you don't like the house wine, don't blame me. I stole it from my neighbour. He's out of town and I'm feeding his cat. Of course, we can always try our luck with the neighbour on the other side. I'm watering her plants. *(shaking a key ring)* The keys to the kingdom, baby.

GENE: How much of this did you drink tonight?

CHARLIE: All of it.

GENE: All of it? Holy shit. Charlie, are you all right?

CHARLIE: Never better. Oh, the day's had its ups and downs, I don't deny it. But I'm feeling better now. I had a good cry, I guess, and a little nap, and now I'm even working on the act.

She switches on the tape, sings into the mike.

"You can trust the products at the Esso sign—"

But as GENE regards her steadily, she switches off the tape.

Oh well, a little later, maybe. *(close to tears)* After a cigarette. You got one, by any chance?

GENE: *(handing her a cigarette)* You're in no mood to work on the act now.

CHARLIE: I know. But maybe that's no excuse.

GENE: Charlie, that doesn't make much sense.

CHARLIE: I don't know. I was thinking tonight, about this comic they brought up from L.A. one time to headline at The Canada Goose. There was this one night, the show hadn't gone very well at all. And he invited three or four of the comics—young guys and me—back to his hotel room. He said he wanted to smoke dope and forget about the way the act had gone. But you know what happened when we got back to the hotel room?

GENE: What?

CHARLIE: The headliner brought out the dope all right, but while the rest of us smoked it and watched the gangsters on the Late Late Show, the comic just sat in a corner, all alone, and played the tapes of his act. The room was a mess—dried up old pizza crusts and coffee cups and cigarette butts. But the comic just sat there in the mess, with a stop-watch and a notepad, and played the tapes.

GENE: So what did the rest of you do?

CHARLIE: What could we do? He *was* the headliner from L.A. So after every line, somebody would say, "That's a funny bit, man. That's very funny." And gradually the headliner began to pay attention to the fact that we were there, and he started throwing out new lines he'd spun off from the stuff on that tape. And after every line, he'd stop and ask, "What about *that?* Could *that* be funny?" Some of it was funny and some of it wasn't, but we told him it was dynamite and he wrote it down. I think that he was afraid that if he stopped, he'd die. You know, the way a shark has to keep moving or die? I think he was afraid that if he stopped, he'd be consumed by the garbage in the hotel room, or the ambition of the young comics coming up behind him, or the brutality of the Late Late Show.

GENE: But he was the one who messed up the room. He was the one who invited you in, and turned on the TV.

CHARLIE: That's right. *(pause)* I wonder. Maybe he actually *needed* the awfulness around him for incentive. Maybe he needed some place like that, that he *had* to be funny in or die.

GENE: Could be.

CHARLIE: So, maybe this is no time for *me* to stop. Maybe I've got to keep going now, or die.

GENE clicks on the tape recorder and speaks into the mike.

GENE: Charlie, you're not going to die. Not tonight, anyway. *(clicking it off)* There. Now you've got it on tape. Play it back whenever you need reassurance.

CHARLIE: That's the worst part of being a comedian. Everybody just laughs at you. *(as GENE laughs)* See what I mean?

GENE: You're priceless. You really are.

CHARLIE: You're not so bad yourself. I've always liked you, Gene.

GENE: Now, there's a case of revisionist history.

CHARLIE: After that first morning, I mean. And you were right. To give me a word of warning.

GENE: It could be worse. You could be in love with him.

CHARLIE: Who says I'm not?

GENE: I do. What do you say?

CHARLIE: *(after a pause)* No. I toyed with the possibility while we were in the restaurant today and I realized he was looking for a way to kiss me off. I came very close to being in love with him, out of pure spite. But I'm not. It's more of a fascination, I guess. How anybody with so many connections can be so unconnected to anything. Women fall for stuff like that.

GENE: Yeah? I'll make a note of it.

CHARLIE: No, don't. Don't you turn into one of those half-assed seventies people. There are enough of them already. I guess we used up our quota of commitment in the sixties. Now we always keep our options open, as my late husband would say.

GENE: And what does he mean by that?

CHARLIE: Someday, sonny, when you're older, you'll understand.

GENE: Do you?

CHARLIE: No.

GENE: Then you're not one of those people either, are you?

CHARLIE: Gene, why did you come here tonight?

GENE: I never miss a chance to sing the Happy Motoring Song.

CHARLIE: Is that all?

GENE: I like you, Charlie. I always have.

CHARLIE: Now, there's a case of revisionist history.

GENE: Seriously, from the first moment I saw you. I said to myself, "Now there's a woman I could quit law school for."

CHARLIE: Bullshit. You quit law school to become the greatest novelist the world has ever know. You told me so yourself.

GENE: Charlie, you've got to learn to take a compliment.

CHARLIE: I want to know why you came here.

GENE: You mean did Nick send me? No.

CHARLIE: You mean he's not in the habit of passing along his old girlfriends? Like hockey skates? I wouldn't put it past him.

GENE: You ought to think a little better of me.

CHARLIE: I'm sorry.

GENE: So am I.

CHARLIE: Are you?

GENE: Sorry. *(He kisses her.)* Sorry. *(He kisses her again.)* Sorry. *(And again.)*

CHARLIE pulls away.

Uh . . . that's not exactly how I planned my move.

CHARLIE: This isn't quite how I saw today shaping up either.

GENE: Charlie, this may come as a surprise to you, but you're not a pair of hockey skates.

CHARLIE: Is that one of those compliments I'm supposed to learn how to take?

GENE: If I'd wanted wisecracks, I'd have stayed at The Canada Goose.

CHARLIE: And if I'd wanted to save my sanity, I'd have stayed away from the Bolton boys.

GENE: I'm not one of the Bolton boys. I'm Gene. And what went wrong with you and Nick has nothing to do with me.

CHARLIE: You mean, don't throw out the baby with the bathwater? *(suddenly laughing)* Oh God, I'm sorry . . . . *(still laughing)* I just realized what I said.

GENE: *(sharply)* Charlie, I said cut the cracks, I'm not a baby and I'm not the relief pitcher, or any other goddamn thing you think. And if you had any kind of decent opinion of yourself, I wouldn't have to tell you that.

CHARLIE: *(staring at him uncertainly)* Gene . . . . Do you want to sleep with me?

GENE: It's crossed my mind. From time to time. To time.

CHARLIE: Why?

GENE: What kind of a question is that?

CHARLIE: I mean, why am I not a pair of hockey skates?

GENE: *(earnestly)* Listen to me. I don't make a habit of chasing around after the recently broken-hearted, knocking on the door—

CHARLIE: You *didn't* knock—

GENE: Knocking on the door and offering myself as the consolation prize. You attract me, all right? You always have. In spit of your neuroses and your bad taste in men and your habit of calling me "sonny." And right now, I can't think of anything nicer than being in bed with you. I can't see how it can fail as a bright idea.

CHARLIE: But?

GENE: I didn't say but.

CHARLIE: You were thinking but. I saw it, in one of those balloons, over your head.

GENE: But I'm not like Nick and all the open-option people. Gene. The name is Gene. I want you to have that straight in the morning. And the morning after. And the morning after that. What do you say, Charlie?

CHARLIE switches on the tape, picks up the mike.

CHARLIE: *(into the mike)* Gene. I have it straight. And I'll have it straight in the morning. *(She clicks off the tape.)* There. Now you've got in on tape. Play it back when you need reassurance.

She takes off her glasses.

Your turn. Fair is fair.

GENE takes off his glasses, then picks up CHARLIE's, looks through them.

GENE: You're as blind as I am.

CHARLIE: This could be the beginning of a beautiful friendship.

She leans towards him, and he kisses her on a blackout.

ACT TWO

Scene One

A day or two later. Lights come up on GENE at his desk, speaking into his tape recorder.

GENE: *Deathless Prose* by Eugene Bolton. Chapter One. It came as a surprise to him to realize that this was what being in love felt like. He'd imagined the feeling many times, of course, and it had been different. Better circumstances, more exotic locations, a different kind of woman. For he wasn't so caught up in emotion that he couldn't admit that to himself. He'd simply never expected to fall, when he fell, for a woman like her. She was taller than what he'd had in mind, she smoked too much, and she was absolutely nothing like Jane Fonda. And she was older than he was. Most of all, she was older. And while it was nice to be around someone imbued with the kind of wisdom that only comes with age—like knowing all the lyrics to old Everly Brothers songs, and understanding more than he would ever know about how to fold a fitted sheet—while it was nice to have a shortcut to that kind of knowledge, it was also true that she'd had more time to accumulate bad memories. They'd talked about that, of course. They'd talked about it exhaustively, until sometimes it seemed to him that was what new relationships mostly consisted of—performing autopsies on relationships from the past. *(breaking off)* Hey, that's not bad. I wonder if it's true? *(back to business)* Anyway, the more they talked, the more often he caught himself wishing that he'd inherited a prize somewhat more intact, emotionally speaking. Because almost from the first moment, a terrible suspicion had begun to form in him that, in the relationship game, you could actually be held accountable for debts run up long before you appeared on the scene. That he would be punished somehow, for having turned up too late.

Blackout.

Scene Two

A day or two later. Lights up on CHARLIE's apartment. An anonymous figure is under the covers of the bed. There is a knock on the door, a pause, another knock. Finally a credit card comes sliding through the lock, the door opens and ALAN enters, carrying his suitcase. He puts down the suitcase and approaches the bed.

ALAN: Charlie. Baby, wake up.

GENE starts, sits up.

GENE: Who the hell are you?

ALAN: *(startled)* I could ask you the same question.

GENE: You don't know who you are? *(coming to)* Oh, right. I see.

ALAN: Look—I'm sorry.

GENE: It's okay. I know the feeling.

ALAN: Where's Charlie? You do know who Charlie is?

GENE: She was here . . . . Holy shit. I have to be at work at twelve!

ALAN: *(consulting his watch)* It's eleven-o-six.

GENE: Oh, lots of time.

He lies back down in the bed, pulling the covers over himself.

ALAN: Look, is she okay?

GENE: Charlie? *(smiling)* She's fantastic.

CHARLIE, fully dressed except for her glasses, appears from the kitchen with two cups of coffee. She stops short when she sees ALAN.

CHARLIE: Alan! What are you doing here?

ALAN: *(indicating GENE with chagrin)* Charlie, for Christ's sake . . . .

CHARLIE: Alan, this is Gene.

GENE: Oh, you're Charlie's late husband. *(shaking hands)* Nice to meet you. Gene Bolton.

ALAN: *(to CHARLIE)* Bolton?

CHARLIE: Nick's brother. You remember Nick.

ALAN: Better than you, evidently. Well, isn't this just jolly?

GENE: We think so. *(indicating the coffee)* Is that mine?

CHARLIE hands him a coffee, proffers the other to ALAN.

CHARLIE: Coffee, sweetheart? Or should I break out the digitalis?

As he takes the coffee, she peers at his suitcase.

Why, Alan, I didn't know you had a dog.

ALAN: Put on your glasses, will you? It's my suitcase.

CHARLIE: My God. I hope you boys have name tags sewn in your clothes. *(as no one laughs)* I wasn't expecting to see you.

ALAN: Evidently.

CHARLIE: Will you stop saying "evidently"? You sound like you've dropped in from Scotland Yard.

ALAN: I dropped in from Stratford, Charlie. A mere three hours on a very slow train. Because I thought you needed me.

CHARLIE: *(puzzled)* That's very sweet of you. But I'm just fine.

ALAN: You didn't sound fine when you called me the other night.

CHARLIE: The other night?

ALAN: Christ, after that conversation, I rushed down here expecting to find you in a coma, not in flagrante delicto.

CHARLIE: Sorry to disappoint you. Besides, nobody's in flagrante anything. Gene, put your clothes on.

ALAN: I bet you don't remember a goddamn thing about that call, do you?

CHARLIE: Sure I do. I—I guess it was about Nick?

ALAN: You guess. Your heart was broken, I'd let you down too, and when I tried to call you back—

CHARLIE: Oh God. The jack.

She goes to the phone and plugs it in.

ALAN: I've been calling on the hour, and wondering if I could get here before the ambulance.

CHARLIE: Oh, sweetheart. I'm sorry.

GENE: It took you three days to come a hundred miles? Were you really that concerned?

CHARLIE: Gene . . . .

ALAN: Under the circumstances, it's a good thing I didn't run out to the highway and flag down a police car, isn't it?

GENE: But there's no point carrying on as though you had, is there? I mean, I assume you were coming to Toronto anyway.

ALAN: Well, there are people— *(angrily)* Look, what the hell business is this of yours?

GENE: Charlie's business is my business now.

ALAN: Well, good luck. Now that you've checked into the Hotel California, you'll need it.

CHARLIE: Thanks for the glowing reference. I am sorry about the call. But I was drunk and—

ALAN: *(joining in)* —And don't remember a thing about it. Charlie, when is this stuff going to stop?

CHARLIE: I think it's stopped. This time I really think it has.

ALAN: *(glancing at GENE)* I see. That's good, then. *(getting up)* Pardon the intrusion, as we say at Scotland Yard.

CHARLIE: Where are you going?

ALAN: Where do I usually go from here? To see if there are any other inns in Bethlehem. *(pause, then defensively)* I mean, since I came all the way to town, I might as well stay for a day or two.

CHARLIE: *(smiling)* You might as well. If you *do* have people to see, I'd feel a lot less guilty.

ALAN: I can drop in on Grant Austin.

CHARLIE: Good. Don't run away. I'll put on more coffee.

She exits.

ALAN: Anyway, Grant will put me up, probably.

GENE: If not, you could stay here. It's not like I'm moved in officially. I can go back home for a day or two.

ALAN: No thanks.

GENE: I don't mind. I mean, it's not like—

He stops short, busies himself tying his shoes.

ALAN: It's not like what? It's not like having another man staying here?

GENE: I didn't say that.

ALAN: You don't have to. I'm a mind reader. So Charlie's told you all about me?

GENE: The subject's come up. Look, Alan, I only meant everything's in the past with you and Charlie.

ALAN: Everything's in the past? Did she say that?

GENE: No, I'm a mind reader too. I see a couple separated for a year, I'm enjoying a gorgeous relationship with the lady, the guy's living with some other *guy*—I just had a wild hunch.

ALAN: *(after a pause)* Coming out, you know, it's not like having a personality transplant. Some part of me is still her husband.

GENE: *(gently)* That must be confusing.

ALAN: It is. *(smiling ruefully)* As you point out, it takes me three days to show up after one of her calls, but I show up.

GENE: Well . . . . A wife in your past. Maybe it's comforting in a way?

ALAN: Maybe it is. But maybe it's time to stop.

GENE: Maybe it is.

ALAN: Yeah. *(pause)* I'm glad about you and her. I honestly am. It simplifies things a little.

GENE: From the byzantine to the merely baroque?

ALAN: *(smiling)* Something like that.

CHARLIE returns with a coffee pot and her own cup.

CHARLIE: I knew there was more mileage in those grounds. Gene?

GENE: Sounds irresistible, but I have to get to work. A salesclerk's life isn't his own.

CHARLIE: You won't forget to call me on your break?

GENE: Not likely. The one time I forgot, I got calls all afternoon in different accents. From women claiming to be customers I'd seduced and abandoned.

CHARLIE: *(innocently)* No kidding?

GENE: No kidding. You do a lousy Russian, by the way.

CHARLIE: *(Russian)* Pah, ees stinking lie. *(in her own voice)* Smartass.

GENE: Bitch. *(kissing her)* Alan—nice meeting you.

He exits.

CHARLIE: *(pouring ALAN more coffee)* Well.

ALAN: Well, what can I say? You hit the jackpot this time.

CHARLIE: You really think so?

ALAN: Come on, he loves you. Anybody can see that.

CHARLIE: He's very young.

ALAN: Obituaries in advance? It won't work with him.

CHARLIE: You don't think it's a bit silly—working my way through Nick's family?

ALAN: Babe, it has nothing to do with me. It's time we both admitted that.

He rises.

CHARLIE: There's a tone of finality there I don't like. *(quickly)* I poured you more coffee. You can't leave.

ALAN: Someone's got to tell you: your coffee's not worth hanging around for. *(kissing her)* Be happy.

CHARLIE: *(nervously)* There's that tone again.

ALAN: Why are we so stubborn? The sun goes down, and we still won't call it a day.

He picks up his suitcase.

CHARLIE: Alan—

ALAN: Bye, Charlie.

He exits, leaving CHARLIE a little startled on a blackout.

Scene Three

Four weeks later. Lights come up on CHARLIE's apartment, where she sits typing desultorily, and x-ing words out repeatedly. The phone rings.

CHARLIE: Thank God for interruptions. *(picking up the phone)* Hello? *(pause, Italian accent)* Yeah, whatchoo want onna pizza? *(pause)* Yeah. *(pause)* Yeah. *(pause)* No. No anchovies, we no got today. Gino, he still out inna boat. Ciao.

She hangs up. GENE has come in from the kitchen during the conversation, wiping his hands on a dish towel tied around his waist.

GENE: They want Tower of Pizza?

CHARLIE: Who else? Since they opened, nobody ever calls for us. *(unplugging the phone)* This time, I'm leaving it off. Until one of us gets a new number. I wouldn't mind if people didn't get so ugly about the anchovies.

GENE: Guy called earlier, wanted orange sections. On a pizza. It's enough to make you want to get out of the catering business all right.

CHARLIE: Speaking of which, how's dinner coming?

GENE: Later. I'm still working on the fridge. Haven't you ever heard of defrosting?

CHARLIE: You live here too, you know.

GENE: I've only been here a month. I won't say how long it's been since that fridge was touched, but there's a hunk of frozen fish in there wrapped in newspaper. Headline says: "White Sox Throw World Series." *(as CHARLIE laughs)* Anyway, there's no rush on dinner. Nick isn't even coming till eight.

CHARLIE: At this point, I'm ready to start without him. Any excuse to drop this.

She picks up a piece of her writing and reads:

"It's no use, Jerry. We can't get married as long as Alison's ghost stands between us. After all, if she hadn't killed herself because you left her for me, it would be her you'd be taking to the altar Wednesday morning."

GENE: She.

CHARLIE: What?

GENE: It would be *she* you'd be taking to the altar Wednesday morning. There's your problem right there.

CHARLIE: The problem *is*, Alison's suicide has nothing to do with Jerry. Alison was carrying Leonard Casey's child, and somehow, I've got to tip off Ruth and Jerry to that. Otherwise nobody goes to the altar Wednesday morning.

GENE: Well, Wednesday is a stupid day for a wedding anyway.

CHARLIE: It happens to be Jerry's day off. He works Saturdays. At the Bay.

GENE: Yeah? How come the bastard didn't invite *me* to the wedding?

CHARLIE: They're keeping it small. In deference to Alison. And there isn't going to *be* any wedding. Not unless I can get the truth out to somebody.

GENE: Leonard Casey might have a word with Jerry.

CHARLIE: He might—if they hadn't croaked him at the last story conference. On Thursday's show, Leonard's brakes will fail. On Friday, the actor goes into rehearsal in New York.

GENE: It just goes to show. How fleeting is death.

CHARLIE: Look, we can't all be novelists, sonny.

GENE: They called again from The Canada Goose.

CHARLIE: What do they want on their pizza?

GENE: Mel called to find out if he could book you for a night next week.

CHARLIE: What's the point? I haven't got any new stuff.

GENE: There's old stuff, isn't there?

CHARLIE: I have to feel that I want to be there, that's all. Otherwise, it might as well be soap opera.

GENE: Well, wait until you feel like it then.

CHARLIE: Easy for you to say. How many chapters have you knocked out in the last few weeks?

GENE: A couple.

CHARLIE: Only a couple. On top of a full-time job. While I don't know what comes after, "Hi, everybody, and welcome to The Canada Goose."

GENE: Charlie, what's the matter? I thought you were happy.

CHARLIE: It's always hard to cope with the new and bizarre.

GENE: Is that why you asked Nick to dinner? Out of nostalgia for the bad old days?

CHARLIE: Do you think it's a bad idea?

GENE: You, me and Nick? It smacks of such modernity, that's all. "Have Your Ex Over to Dinner to Meet Your Current." It would make a great story for *Toronto Life*.

CHARLIE: Toronto Life is a contradiction in terms.

GENE: Don't change the subject.

CHARLIE: Why should there be hard feelings between you and Nick and me? Everybody's got what they want.

There is a knock on the door.

GENE: Christ. Eight o'clock. I told the asshole. It's five to. Some people have no consideration whatso— *(opening the door to admit NICK)* Nicky! Good to see you. Champagne! You finally off the penicillin?

NICK presents the champagne to CHARLIE along with a kiss.

NICK: Hiya, Charlie. Bubbly to the bubbly.

CHARLIE: The usual bottle of Baby Bear, I see.

NICK: If you don't like Dom Perignon, there are plenty who do.

CHARLIE: It's just that every time you turn up, I feel I should have an unlaunched ship on hand.

NICK: I bought it to launch the new picture. But now it looks like shooting's postponed. So I figured you two could use it.

GENE: Second-hand champagne. How tacky. I'm sorry about the film, Nick.

NICK: *(indicating GENE's dish towel)* I'm sorry I missed the drag show, little brother.

GENE: I was cleaning the fridge.

NICK: Well, no need to ask what brought you two together.

GENE: The screwdrivers I made froze solid. It was time for a little defrosting.

NICK: Okay, but you know what the fridge-cleaning syndrome leads to.

CHARLIE: Nick, we didn't get you over here to reminisce. We're all familiar with the past and presumably none of us is too wild about it. *(taking the champagne)* I'll get you a screwdriver popsicle.

She exits.

GENE: *(firmly)* I'm making the dinner. We might as well have that out in the open too.

He exits. CHARLIE returns momentarily with a frozen pitcher of screwdrivers and two glasses.

CHARLIE: *(prodding at the pitcher)* One lump or two?

NICK: However it comes. I only see two glasses.

CHARLIE: I'm not drinking these days, Nick. And you know something? I thought sobriety would be awful. It's not. It's hideous.

NICK: Then you might as well have a drink.

CHARLIE: Later.

NICK: Later?

CHARLIE: A week Thursday. That'll be a month. I promised myself a month on the wagon.

NICK: But babe, you were always such a fun drunk.

CHARLIE: Such a load of laughs that you dropped me.

NICK: Aw now, don't be that way. I felt rotten that day in the restaurant.

CHARLIE: Your pain showed. As I recall it, you said, "We're through, Charlie. I wonder if the artichokes are any good today?"

NICK: Bullshit, I did not.

CHARLIE: You're right. But I've never let the truth spoil a good story yet.

NICK No brother of Gene's can be that bad. After all, I raised that kid practically single-handed. If he didn't learn decency from me, where did he learn it?

CHARLIE: He probably had to pick it up in the streets. *(There is a knock on the door.)* Are they coming to take *out* pizzas here now?

She opens the door as ALAN, harried, steps in.

Well! The gang's all here.

ALAN: So you *are* home. I've been calling and calling and—

CHARLIE: Oh, right. We get all these wrong numbers, so I've been leaving it off.

NICK: Hi, Alan.

ALAN: Oh, hi, Nick. *(bewildered)* How are you?

CHARLIE: *(plugging the phone in)* There. Now try your call again.

ALAN: I don't know why you bother having a phone, Charlie.

CHARLIE: Who are you? A field worker from the Telephone Appreciation Society?

NICK: What this man needs is a drink. And a glass.

He exits.

ALAN: I don't have time for— *(but NICK is gone)* Charlie, do you still have that metal box we kept all the valuable papers in?

CHARLIE: I've got the box, but you took all your papers out, remember? When we split up.

ALAN: Can you look? I think I must have left my passport. I've got to have it.

CHARLIE: Why? Where are you going?

ALAN: I won't be going anywhere if you don't look in the goddamn box!

CHARLIE doesn't budge.

ALAN: Spain.

CHARLIE: Spain? What with? I mean, I hear it's cheap there, but it can't be free. Or—*who* with? Maybe that's more to the point?

ALAN: Grant Austin.

CHARLIE: You're kidding.

ALAN: Now that I've answered the skill-testing question, can I have my passport?

CHARLIE: You and Grant Austin. So good old Jackie's out in the cold?

ALAN: Charlie, please! Just find my passport, and I'll tell you anything you want to know.

CHARLIE: *(bitterly)* It never stops with you, does it?

ALAN: It has now. This time it's stopped.

CHARLIE stares at him a moment, then exits swiftly. ALAN lights a cigarette. NICK comes back with a glass, pours ALAN a screwdriver from the slightly-melted batch.

NICK: That kid. I never saw him so much as heat up a can of soup, and now he's out there up to his eyebrows in soufflé. Soufflé, for Christ's sake. *(handing ALAN a screwdriver)* Here you go.

ALAN: Thanks.

He gulps it, checks his watch.

NICK: You in a hurry to get somewhere?

ALAN: Yeah. Spain.

NICK: Spain? Lot of that going around. Remember Grant Austin? The fucker's walked off the picture to go to Spain.

ALAN: Is that a fact?

NICK: Jesus, I should have known. The guy may be a cinematic genius, but he goes down the road of life using *True Confessions* as a driving manual. I call him up and ask him what the hell he thinks he's doing to me, and you know what he tells me? He's in love.

ALAN: *(coldly)* It happens.

At this moment CHARLIE comes back to the doorway with the passport, unnoticed for the moment.

NICK: Yeah, Grant's in love with some cute little fruit. And after some little faggot wedding ceremony they're honeymooning in Spain.

CHARLIE: A wedding? *(to ALAN, with deep distaste)* A gay wedding?

ALAN: *(reaching for the passport)* You found it. Great.

CHARLIE: *(slamming it into his hand)* I found it all right.

NICK: Yeah, how about that, Charlie? There's material there for you. Can you see the wedding cake? Two little gays in tuxes under a flowered arch!

ALAN: Why don't you just fuck off?

CHARLIE: Why should he? It's pretty funny at that, Alan. I wish I'd been there to see you go down the aisle. Why wasn't I invited to the wedding? But of course, how *do* you seat the groom's wife? Or is it the bride's wife? I guess Amy Vanderbilt doesn't cover that one.

NICK: Oh Christ, Charlie, I didn't know. Alan . . . .

At this moment GENE enters from the kitchen.

GENE: My soufflé just fell. Who did it?

NICK: *(quietly)* I did it. I put my foot in it.

CHARLIE: My God, if you wanted a divorce, you could have said so. Or would you rather conduct secret ceremonies behind my back? Just to make sure I'm *really* out of the picture?

ALAN: What do you care what I do now? Why should it matter to you? You're living with him, for God's sake— *(indicating GENE)* He drops in for drinks— *(indicating NICK)* You think you can hold onto everybody?

CHARLIE: You do it, don't you? That's always been your stock in trade.

ALAN: Not any more! It's a day, Charlie. Why can't we just call it that?

CHARLIE: Because it isn't. You need me, Alan. If only to trot out for state occasions.

ALAN: Not any more. If anybody wants to think of me as a fruit, or a faggot or a fucking queer, they can go ahead. I've made my peace with it. And I'm not taking the blame any more for the tragedy of poor little Charlie, victim of the Evil Homosexual Conspiracy. There were a hundred things wrong with our marriage and if I'd stayed as straight as Charles Bronson, we'd have fallen apart anyway.

CHARLIE: That's not true.

ALAN: It's true and you know it. But now you've got someone who loves you and so do I. So let's let go. Before we guilt each other to death. Let me go, Charlie.

ALAN touches her arm briefly, pockets the passport and leaves. GENE and NICK stare warily at CHARLIE, as if she were a bomb about to explode.

GENE: *(at last)* Charlie? . . .

CHARLIE: He's going all the way to Spain. And he didn't even say goodbye.

GENE: He said goodbye. You know it.

NICK: Christ, Charlie, I didn't know. You never told me anything about it.

CHARLIE: I know. Look, why don't you guys go ahead with dinner? I'd like to take a walk.

GENE: Now? Come on, why don't you—

CHARLIE: *(snatching up her purse)* I need this walk, Gene. I really do.

She hurries out, slamming the door.

GENE: Oh Christ. *(to NICK)* What the hell did you do?

NICK: I mentioned Austin walked off the picture to marry some little fruit. How did I know it was Alan? Come on, kid. Relax. A week from Thursday has probably come a little early, that's all.

GENE: She was through getting drunk over him. That was all behind her.

NICK: Then you don't have to worry about her, right?

GENE: You don't know a goddamn thing about it.

NICK: You will pardon me, but I do have some experience of the lady. And a few others just like her.

GENE: She's not just "some lady"—some back number in your little black book. She's Charlie, Nick, and you've got no idea. I mean, you didn't even know Alan was gay.

NICK: Maybe not. But I know one thing, Geno, and you'd better deal with it. She just jumped at the chance to go to pieces tonight. And if she's looking for ways to be unhappy, there's nothing you can do about it.

GENE: Stop right there, Nick, because I'm not going to take it. Some underdone theory on another woman you scratched at the gate. I live with her, for Christ's sake. I've taken responsibility. And on that subject, I'm the big brother.

NICK: Listen, you little wise-ass. I'll take a lot from you, but not a lecture. Talk to me about responsibility! I put clothes on your back and a roof over you—

GENE: And you felt virtuous as hell because I needed you! But not anymore. Now I've got someone who needs *me*. And a life of my own. Do you get that, Nick?

NICK: Sure, sure. You're running your own show now—and making a real class job of it. Sitting at the door like a spaniel and whining because she's left you all alone. *(moving to the door)* No, you don't need me. Not much. Because all I ever gave you was cash and connections and everything you're too goddamned good for, right? But when I try to give you anything else—like some sound advice—you tell me to fuck right off. Okay, kid, you've got it. I'm gone.

GENE: Nick! I—don't want you to go.

NICK: Why? Because you're afraid to be here all alone?

GENE: No. I— *(slowly)* I think maybe—I need some—advice.

NICK: Could be. Could be I've considered a few angles you haven't. About having a life of your own.

GENE: She's better off with me, Nick. Better off than she's been in her whole life. And she knows it.

NICK: I don't deny it for a second. Anybody who can't be happy with you ought to have her head read.

GENE: *(laughing weakly)* Yeah. That's what I think, too.

NICK: Okay. But I got to thinking the other day. I was down at The Canada Goose, with some people who want to shoot a film. I asked after Charlie, and what do you know? Seems she hasn't shown up there in almost a month.

GENE: I know. She hasn't felt like working lately.

NICK: Why? Because she's up to her armpits in domestic bliss? Sure, I'll buy that. But it's funny how she only feels like performing when she's got a beef. Inconvenient, too.

GENE: What do you mean?

NICK: Well, she's got nothing to complain about now. With you on the premises—tossing up soufflés and, I trust, keeping her happy in the sack the way only you undergraduates can. I mean, it's the ideal arrangement all down the line. But what can someone like Charlie do with that?

GENE: She can enjoy it, can't she? She's earned it.

NICK: Right. Now she's better off. But does she want to be better off? Does she even know how to be? You're a good kid, Geno, and it's too early in the game to get tied to a losing situation. She wants to be a loser, she can be a loser without you.

GENE: Either it clicks with a woman or it doesn't, is that it? No point in trying to talk about it?

NICK: Oh hell, talk if you want to. But if you're bright, you'll make *her* do the talking. She's the one with the problem. And if you don't like what you're hearing, hit the road.

GENE: Just like that.

NICK: Just like that. There's only one way to go if you're going—fast. *(gently)* Hey, don't look like a house just fell on you. Nothing's happened yet. Relax, and drink your screwdriver before it melts.

He raises his glass to GENE on a blackout.

Scene Four

The next morning. Lights up on CHARLIE's apartment where GENE is listlessly tidying up from the night before. The door unlocks, and CHARLIE, tired and dishevelled, enters. She starts a little when she sees GENE.

GENE: That was some walk.

CHARLIE: It was a little longer than I'd planned.

GENE: Fourteen hours. What did you do, jog out to the airport and back?

CHARLIE: I'm sorry if you were worried. You didn't skip work on account of me?

GENE: It's my day off. Wednesday. Remember? *(pause)* Are you okay?

CHARLIE: I . . . didn't expect to find you here, that's all. I planned to just crawl in and sleep and sleep.

GENE: You can do that. You can do whatever you want.

CHARLIE: You're not mad at me for staying out? I'd be mad. I'd be mad as hell.

GENE: *(after a pause)* The soufflé didn't fall after all, it just buckled at the knees a little. Nick was impressed, in spite of himself.

CHARLIE: What?

GENE: Last night's dinner. You missed it.

CHARLIE: Oh, right . . . .

GENE: I tried to save you some. Except once the fridge got the knack of defrosting, it went hog wild. The butter started melting. A few eggs hatched.

CHARLIE: *(absently)* That's too bad.

GENE: Yeah. I think the fridge is fucked. But Nick said—

CHARLIE: Gene, don't you want to know where I went?

GENE: Not unless you want to discuss it. Anyway, Nick said if we were in the market for a new fridge, he knows some guy—

CHARLIE: I went to a bar and I started drinking. That's the last thing I remember until this morning—

GENE: So you fell off the wagon.

CHARLIE: *(relentlessly)* Until this morning when some guy I'd never seen before shook me awake and told me he'd drive me to the subway because he had to be at work by nine.

GENE: Okay, so now you've told me.

CHARLIE: For Christ's sake, is that all you've got to say?

GENE: What else do you want me to say?

CHARLIE: What the hell kind of question is that? What do you *feel* like saying? I mean, you are entitled to get mad, you know. At the very least you're entitled to raise your voice!

GENE: Why? Because you've got this little trick switch in your mind that allows you to check out whenever you feel like behaving like an asshole? Charlie, it's not worth getting mad about. It's stupid and it's sad, but beyond that it doesn't mean a thing.

CHARLIE: I don't know . . .

GENE: Yes you do, and if you want to tell me, let's get it over with.

CHARLIE: Gene, I wouldn't hurt you, not for the world . . . .

GENE: I know that line. It's what you say just before you hurt someone. *(lightly)* So what's the story? You fell in love with this guy on the way to the subway station?

CHARLIE: No. It was when I saw Alan, Gene. I realized it's not over for me.

GENE: Well, it's over for him. And I love you. Why the hell do you want to louse it up?

CHARLIE: I don't want to louse it up . . .

GENE: But? But what? Come on, I can see it. In a balloon right over your head.

CHARLIE: Sonny, this just isn't working.

GENE: It's working for me. Sorry to be so uncooperative, but there it is.

CHARLIE: *(exasperated)* Look, you're seven years younger than I am, and sooner or later you're going to want to play with girls your own age. Then you'll walk out on me and—

GENE: Oh no you don't. You're the one walking, don't try to pull that switch. I've told you I love you, and you've got no reason to think any different. So if you want to walk, fucking do it. But at least admit it's your own idea.

CHARLIE: *(exploding)* How the hell can you want this? I'm screwed up and I drink too much and you're way too good for me.

GENE: That's not the problem. You want to know what the problem is? The fact that I love you. You just can't deal with that. Because any club that would have you as a member just isn't good enough to join.

CHARLIE: You don't know what you're talking about.

GENE: Don't I? You think you want Alan. It's only because he doesn't want you. That's his entire attraction. All somebody has to do is dump you, and you'll follow them anywhere.

CHARLIE: It has nothing to do with what I *want.*

GENE: It has everything to do with it, because this time *you're* calling the shots. It's not as easy as being the victim, is it? And I have no intention of making it easy for you. Come on—go or stay? What do you want me to do? It's not enough to get loaded and pick up some guy in a bar and hope that'll turn me off.

He snatches up her tape recorder, switches it on and puts the mike in front of her.

You're going to have to tell me. Once and for all.

CHARLIE: *(at last)* Gene, you'll be better off without me.

GENE: *(snapping off the tape)* I asked for an answer, not bullshit! *(more calmly)* But I guess it's an answer all the same.

He reaches under the bed for his suitcase.

CHARLIE: I love you. I don't care if you believe it.

GENE: You know what I believe? That this moment is the closest you've come to it since I first met you. And by the time I go through that door, you'll be there. Now tell me that isn't true.

CHARLIE: I— *(covering her face with her hands)* I never wanted to hurt you, Gene. You're the best man I've ever met.

GENE: I know. I only hope someday you'll find it in your heart to forgive me for it. *(as she touches his arm)* Let go of me. I need two arms to pack. In that respect I'm no better than any of the others.

His perfunctory packing done, he closes the case and moves to the door.

CHARLIE: Gene . . .

GENE: Do me a favour. Don't send roses, okay?

He leaves. Lights hold on CHARLIE for a moment, then blackout.

Scene Five

Some weeks later. Lights go up on The Canada Goose where CHARLIE is on stage in her customary gear plus a feather boa, with the mike in her hand.

CHARLIE: Hey ladies, there's a big vogue now in younger men. You noticed that? I don't know about you, but I don't want to go out to dinner with someone who has to ask the waiter to bring him the Child's Menu. Okay, okay, so the kid CAN come ten times in a single night. So what? It's always over so quickly, right? It's like getting ten episodes of *Leave It to Beaver*—right in a row.

It beats the old guys, though. A session with your average older man is like a screening of *The Sorrow and the Pity*. Only longer and sadder. You nod off two or three times and wake up, and he's STILL at it. "I almost came that time," he says. Eventually, you start trying to outfox him, right? "You came," you tell him. "You definitely came. It's just been so long you've forgotten what it's like. But that was it. Trust me. Now, can we get some sleep?"

But the real bitch about younger men is how goddamn earnest they are. One roll in the hay, and they're ready to move in—provided you're willing to help them with their algebra. And when you say, "Hey, wait a minute, sonny—"

She falters on the name, breaks off for a moment, and then, almost to herself:

Sonny.

Long, baffled pause, then she plunges on, almost desperately.

No, no, I prefer to stick to single guys my own age. Hey, has anybody SEEN any single straight guys lately? You know they're an endangered species. *(gradually regaining composure)* In fact, I heard recently a woman was picketed on Bloor Street by the Greenpeace people for wearing a coat made of the pelts of single straight men.

But I actually met a single guy once, First thing he said to me was, "Babe—" He called all women Babe. I guess it eliminated the problem of learning names he'd only have to forget. "Babe," he said, "I'm not into involvement." And you know something? He wasn't. In fact, if you called him up when he was out, there was this message on his answering machine. "Hi, I'm not home right now. And I'm not into involvement." But I did manage to go out with him—once. And he said to me, "Babe, you chicks are all the same. You're takers." Some taker. We'd been out to dinner, where we split the tab. We split a taxi to the movie—where I paid my own way, plus sprang for his popcorn. Now we're back at my place, doing it in my bed, drinking my Scotch and smoking my cigarettes—and I'm a taker? What do I have to do to be a giver? Donate my kidneys?

Blackout on CHARLIE. Lights up on GENE at his desk speaking into his tape recorder.

GENE: *(into the mike)* In fiction when people split up, they never see each other again. Their farewells are conveniently followed by a blank page or a closing credit roll. In real life, it works a little differently. For a while he avoided anything or any place that reminded him of her, because fiction had taught him that was the right thing to do. But in the end, real life won out, and he went down to the club where she performed and watched her unobtrusively from the back. And while he considered the things that she said to be specious and exaggerated, he did have to concede that she seemed happier up there, telling stories that featured her as the perpetual underdog, perpetually disappointed.

And as he watched her it occurred to him for the first time that perhaps he'd got what he wanted too. That losing not only makes for better prose but is, in the long run, safer than winning. Safe being a relative term, of course. There were, for instance, people who considered it unsafe to set foot in an airplane. And yet he knew for an absolute certainty that it was a hell of a lot more dangerous down on the ground.

Blackout.

END

A SELECTIVE BIBLIOGRAPHY OF SOURCE MATERIAL

I. Backgrounds, Surveys and General Studies

Anthony, Geraldine, ed. *Stage Voices: Twelve Canadian Playwrights Talk about Their Lives and Work.* Toronto: Doubleday, 1978.

Benson, Eugene, and L.W. Conolly. *English-Canadian Theatre.* Toronto: Oxford Univ. Press, 1987.

——, eds. *The Oxford Companion to Canadian Theatre.* Toronto: Oxford Univ. Press, 1989.

Bessai, Diane. "Documentary Theatre in Canada: An Investigation into Questions and Backgrounds." *Canadian Drama,* 6 (Spring 1980): 9-21.

——. *Playwrights of Collective Creation.* Toronto: Simon & Pierre, 1992.

Brissenden, Connie, ed. *Spotlight on Drama: A Teaching and Resource Guide to Canadian Plays.* Toronto: The Writer's Development Trust, 1981.

Brookes, Chris. *A Public Nuisance: A History of the Mummers Troupe.* St. John's: Institute of Social and Economic Research, Memorial Univ. of Newfoundland, 1988.

Canada on Stage: Canadian Theatre Review Yearbook. Ed. Don Rubin. Toronto: CTR Publications, 1974-88.

"Canadian Theatre Before the 60s." Special Issue. *Canadian Theatre Review,* 5 (Winter 1975).

Canadian Writers Since 1960, 1st and 2nd ser. In *Dictionary of Literary Biography.* Ed. W.H. New. Vols. 53 and 60. Detroit: Gale Research, 1986-87.

Conolly, L.W., ed. *Canadian Drama and the Critics.* Vancouver: Talonbooks, 1987.

Contemporary Dramatists. 4th ed. Ed. D.L. Kirkpatrick. London: St. James' Press, 1988.

"Contemporary Dramatists & the Art of the Theatre." Special Issue. *Canadian Literature,* 85 (Summer 1980).

Drainie, Bronwyn. *Living the Part: John Drainie and the Dilemma of Canadian Stardom.* Toronto: Macmillan, 1988.

Filewod, Alan. *Collective Encounters: Documentary Theatre in English Canada.* Toronto: Univ. of Toronto Press, 1987.

Fink, Howard, and John Jackson, eds. *All the Bright Company: Radio Drama Produced by Andrew Allan.* Kingston and Toronto: Quarry/CBC Enterprises, 1987.

Frick, Alice. *Image in the Mind: CBC Radio Drama, 1944-1954.* Toronto: Canadian Stage and Arts Publications, 1987.

Garebian, Keith. *A Well-Bred Muse: Selected Theatre Writings, 1978-1988.* Oakville, Ont.: Mosaic Press, 1991.

Goldie, Terry. *Fear and Temptation: The Image of the Indigene in Canadian, Australian, and New Zealand Literatures,* Chpt. 9. Kingston and Montreal: McGill-Queen's Univ. Press, 1989.

Hendry, Tom. "The Canadian Theatre's Sudden Explosion." *Saturday Night,* 87 (January 1972): 23-28.

Hodkinson, Yvonne. *Female Parts: The Art and Politics of Female Playwrights.* Montreal: Black Rose, 1991.

Johnston, Denis. *Up the Mainstream: The Rise of Toronto's Alternative Theatres.* Toronto: Univ. of Toronto Press, 1991.

Kinch, Martin. "Canadian Theatre: In for the Long Haul." *This Magazine,* 10 (November-December 1976): 3-8.

Miller, Mary Jane. *Turn Up the Contrast: CBC Television Drama Since 1952.* Vancouver: UBC Press, 1987.

Moore, Mavor. *4 Canadian Playwrights.* Toronto: Holt, Rinehart, 1973.

Much, Rita, ed. *Women on the Canadian Stage: The Legacy of Hrotsvit.* Winnipeg: Blizzard, 1992.

Nardocchio, Elaine. *Theatre and Politics in Modern Quebec.* Edmonton: Univ. of Alberta Press, 1986.

New, William H., ed. *Dramatists in Canada: Selected Essays.* Vancouver: UBC Press, 1972.

Parker, Brian. "Is There a Canadian Drama?" In *The Canadian Imagination: Dimensions of a Literary Culture.* Ed. David Staines. Cambridge, Mass.: Harvard Univ. Press, 1977. 152-87.

——, and Cynthia Zimmerman. "Theatre and Drama [1972-84]." In *Literary History of Canada: Canadian Literature in English*. Ed. W.H. New. 2nd ed. Vol. 4. Toronto: Univ. of Toronto Press, 1990. 186-216.

Patterson, Tom, and Allan Gould. *First Stage: The Making of the Stratford Festival*. Toronto: McClelland and Stewart, 1987.

Perkyns, Richard, ed. *Major Plays of the Canadian Theatre, 1934-1984*. Toronto: Irwin,1984.

——. *The Neptune Story: Twenty-Five Years in the Life of a Leading Canadian Theatre*. Hantsport, N.S.: Lancelot, 1989.

Pettigrew, John, and Jamie Portman. *Stratford: The First Thirty Years*. 2 vols. Toronto: Macmillan, 1985.

Profiles in Canadian Literature, ser. 4-8. Ed. Jeffrey M. Heath. Toronto: Dundurn Press, 1982-91.

Ripley, John. "Drama and Theatre,1960-73." In *Literary History of Canada*. Ed. Carl F. Klinck. 2nd ed. Vol. 4. Toronto: Univ. of Toronto Press, 1976. 212-32.

Rubin, Don. "Celebrating the Nation: History and the Canadian Theatre." *Canadian Theatre Review*, 34 (Spring 1982): 12-22.

——. "Creeping Toward a Culture: The Theatre in English Canada since 1945." *Canadian Theatre Review*, 1 (Winter 1974): 6-21.

——, and Alison Cranmer-Byng, eds. *Canada's Playwrights: A Biographical Guide*. Toronto: CTR Publications, 1980.

Rudakoff, Judith, and Rita Much. *Fair Play: 12 Women Speak: Conversations with Canadian Playwrights*. Toronto: Simon & Pierre, 1990.

Ryan, Toby Gordon. *Stage Left: Canadian Theatre in the Thirties*. Toronto: CTR Publications, 1981.

"Stage Canada." Special Section, *The Globe and Mail* (Toronto): 28 November 1983.

Stuart, E. Ross. *The History of the Prairie Theatre*. Toronto: Simon & Pierre, 1984.

Tait, Michael. "Drama and Theatre, 1920-1960." In *Literary History of Canada*. Ed. Carl F. Klinck. 2nd ed. Vol. 2. Toronto: Univ. of Toronto Press, 1976. 143-67.

Usmiani, Renate. *Second Stage: The Alternative Theatre Movement in Canada*. Vancouver: UBC Press, 1983.

Wagner, Anton, ed. *Contemporary Canadian Theatre: New World Visions*. Toronto: Simon & Pierre, 1985.

——. "The Developing Mosaic: English-Canadian Drama to Mid-Century," In *Canada's Lost Plays*. Vol. 3. Toronto: CTR Publications, 1980. 4-39.

Wallace, Robert. *Producing Marginality: Theatre and Criticism in Canada*. Saskatoon: Fifth House, 1990.

——, ed. *Making, Out: Plays by Gay Men*. Toronto: Coach House, 1992.

——, and Cynthia Zimmerman, eds. *The Work: Conversations with English-Canadian Playwrights*. Toronto: Coach House, 1982.

Wasserman, Jerry, ed. *Twenty Years at Play: A New Play Centre Anthology*. Vancouver: Talonbooks, 1990.

Weiss, Jonathan M. *French-Canadian Theater*. Boston: Twayne, 1986.

Whittaker, Herbert. *Whittaker's Theatre: A Critic Looks at Stages in Canada and Thereabouts, 1944-1975*. Ed. Ronald Bryden with Boyd Neil. Greenbank, Ont.: The Whittaker Project, 1985.

II. Individual Plays and Playwrights

Note: Wherever a book in this section has already appeared as an entry in Part I (Backgrounds, Surveys and General Studies), I have used the short form here. *Canadian Theatre Review* is indicated by *CTR*; *Dictionary of Literary Biography* is *DLB*; *English-Canadian Theatre* is *ECT*.

MICHAEL COOK

A. BIOGRAPHY AND CRITICISM

Anthony, Geraldine, ed. *Stage Voices*. 207-32.

Bartlett, Donald R. "Notes Towards Putting Cook into Context." *Newfoundland Quarterly*, 78 (Fall 1982): 12-15.

Benson, Eugene, and L.W. Conolly, eds. *The Oxford Companion to Canadian Theatre*: 113-15.

Brissenden, Connie. "Michael Cook." In *Contemporary Dramatists*. 96-98.

Conolly, L.W., ed. *Canadian Drama and the Critics*. 117-27, 187-94.

Cook, Michael. "Culture as Caricature: Reflections on a Continuing Obsession: Newfoundland." *Canadian Literature*, 100 (Summer 1984): 72-78.

——. "Ignored Again." *CTR*, 10 (Spring 1976): 87-91.

——. "Introduction to *The Head, Guts and Sound Bone Dance*." *CTR*, 1 (Winter 1974): 74-76.

Fishman, Martin. "Michael Cook: A Playwright in His Own Right." *Canadian Drama*, 2 (Fall 1976: 181-87.

Johnson, Chris. "Michael Cook." In *Canadian Writers Since 1960*. 1st ser. *DLB* 53. 147-52.

Lister, Rota."Interview with Michael Cook." *Canadian Drama*, 2 (Fall 1976): 176-80.

Parker, Brian. "On the Edge: Michael Cook's Newfoundland Trilogy." *Canadian Literature*, 85 (Summer 1980): 22-41.

Perkyns, Richard. "*The Head, Guts and Sound Bone Dance:* An Introduction," In *Major Plays of the Canadian Theatre, 1934-1984*. 444-48.

——. "*Jacob's Wake* and the European Tradition." *Canadian Drama*, 15.2 (1989): 159-68.

Wallace, Robert. "Michael Cook." In *Profiles in Canadian Literature*, 4th ser., 109-16.

——, and Cynthia Zimmerman, eds. *The Work*. 156-71.

B. **JACOB'S WAKE:** SELECTED REVIEWS

Ashley, Audrey M. "New Play a Ludicrous Cop-out." *Ottawa Citizen*, 28 July 1975: 50.

Conlogue, Ray. "A Chilling Dance of Death." *The Globe and Mail*, 11 December 1986, A19.

Crook, Barbara. "Ambitious Production of Saga Leaves Confusion in Its Wake." *Ottawa Citizen*, 28 November 1986, F14.

Galloway, Myron. "*Jacob's Wake:* Newfie without a Hint of a Joke." *Montreal Star*, 14 July 1975, E1.

Portman, Jamie. "Bizarre Outpost Saga 'Piece of Nonsense.'" *Vancouver Province*, 13 August 1975, 10.

Usmiani, Renate. "*Jacob's Wake*." *Canadian Book Review Annual, 1976*. Ed. Dean Tudor, et al. Toronto: Peter Martin, 1977: 207.

DAVID FREEMAN

A. BIOGRAPHY AND CRITICISM

Ackerman, Marianne. "Author Turns His Handicap into an Asset." *Montreal Gazette*, 25 January 1984, G4.

Anthony, Geraldine. ed. *Stage Voices*. 251-74.

Benson, Eugene, and L.W. Conolly. *ECT*. 89-91.

——, ed. *The Oxford Companion to Canadian Theatre*. 118-19, 215-16.

Conolly, L.W., ed. *Canadian Drama and the Critics*. 69-81.

Gilbert, S.R. "David Freeman." In *Contemporary Dramatists*. 168-69.

Hendry, Tom. "David Freeman in the Theatre: A Major Surprise." *Saturday Night*, 87 (July 1972): 27-32.

Hofsess, John. "Will Sucess Spoil David Freeman?" *Maclean's*, 87 (February 1974): 35,42.

McKeone, Carolyn A. "*Creeps* Revisited." *Scene Changes*, 8 (May 1980): 19-21.

Smith, Mary Elizabeth. "Freeman's *Creeps* and *Battering Ram*: Variations on a Theme." *Canadian Drama*, 4 (Spring 1978): 25-33.

Spiers, Rosemary. "Loser Turned Winner." *The Canadian Magazine*, 18 February 1978, 4-9.

B. **CREEPS:** SELECTED REVIEWS

Barnes, Clive. "*Creeps*." *New York Times*, 5 December 1973, 52.

Clurman, Harold. "Theater." *The Nation*, 31 December 1973, 734.

Coe, Richard L. "Plight of Body, Flight of Mind: *Creeps*." *Washington Post*, 16 October 1973, B1, 11.

Cohen, Nathan. "A Ferociously Funny Play." *Toronto Star*, 6 February 1971.

Dafoe, Christopher. "Freeman's Play Bares Humanity of Spastics." *Vancouver Sun*, 23 March 1973, 33.

Fraser, John. "Six Years Later, *Creeps* Still Packs a Punch." *The Globe and Mail*, 10 March 1977, 13.

Gartner, Zsuzsi. "*Creeps*: Power with a Twist." *The Globe and Mail*, 30 August 1985, E6.

Kareda, Urjo. "New Theatre's First Production Beyond Praise." *Toronto Star*, 6 October 1971.

Kerr, Walter. "A Ring of Truth But After That?" *New York Times*, 16 December 1973, 11, 5.

Oliver, Edith. "The Theatre—Off Broadway." *The New Yorker*, 49 (17 December 1973): 99-100.

Sullivan, Dan. "An Insider Gives Us the *Creeps*." *Los Angeles Times*, 17 May 1982, VI, 1-2.

Watt, Douglas. "*Creeps* Packs a Terrific Wallop." *New York Daily News*, 5 December 1973.

Whittaker, Herbert. "*Creeps* Excellent Starter for Tarragon Theatre." *The Globe and Mail*, 6 October 1971, 16.

DAVID FRENCH

A. BIOGRAPHY AND CRITICISM

Adams, John Coldwell. "From Coley's Point to Broadway." *Atlantic Advocate*, 70 (July 1980): 59-61.

Anthony, Geraldine, ed. *Stage Voices*, 234-50.

Bemrose, John. "Romancing the Rock." *Maclean's*, 101 (31 October 1988): 58-59.

Benson, Eugene, and L.W. Conolly. *ECT*. 93-95.

Bruhier, Catherine. "Darkness Visible: A Multiracial *Salt-Water Moon*." *Theatrum*, 20 (Sept.-Oct. 1990): 13-15.

Carson, Neil. "Towards a Popular Theatre in English Canada." *Canadian Literature*, 85 (Summer 1980): 62-69.

Conolly, L.W., ed. *Canadian Drama and the Critics*. 87-98, 128-34, 238-45.

French, David. "David French Looks at His 17-Year Love Affair with the Mercer Family." *Toronto Star*, 15 October 1988, F3.

Glaap, Albert-Reiner. "*Noises Off* and *Jitters*: Two Comedies of Backstage Life." *Canadian Drama*, 13.2 (1987): 210-15.

Horenblas, Richard. "*One Crack Out*: Made in His Image." *Canadian Drama* 2 (Spring 1976): 67-72.

Jewinski, Ed. "Jacob Mercer's Lust for Victimization." *Canadian Drama*, 2 (Spring 1976): 67-72.

Johnson, Chris. "David French." In *Canadian Writers Since 1960*. 1st ser. *DLB* 53. 191-94.

———. "Is That Us? Ray Lawler's *Summer of the Seventeenth Doll* and David French's *Leaving Home*." *Canadian Drama*, 6 (Spring 1980): 30-42.

Kareda, Urjo. "Introduction." In *Leaving Home* by David French. Toronto: new press, 1972. v-ix.

Mullaly, Edward. "Canadian Drama: David French and the Great Awakening." *The Fiddlehead*, 100 (Winter 1974): 61-66.

Neary, Peter. "Of Many-Coloured Glass: Peter Neary Interviews David French." *Canadian Forum*, 53 (March 1974): 26-27.

Noonan, James. "The Comedy of David French and the Rocky Road to Broadway." *Thalia*, 3 (Fall/Winter 1980-81): 9-16.

Nothof, Anne. "David French and the Theatre of Speech." *Canadian Drama*, 13.2 (1987): 216-23.

Nunn, Robert. "The Subjects of *Salt-Water Moon*." *Theatre History in Canada*, 12 (Spring 1991): 3-21.

Perkyns, Richard. "*Of the Fields, Lately*: An Introduction." In *Major Plays of the Canadian Theatre, 1934-1984*. 479-83.

Rusted, Brian. "The Plays of David French." *Newfoundland Quarterly*, 82 (Fall 1986): 42-43.

Thalenburg, Eileen, and David McCaughna. "Shaping the Word: Guy Sprung and Bill Glassco." *CTR*, 26 (Spring 1980): 30-43.

Tyson, Bryan F. "'Swallowed Up in Darkness': Vision and Division in *Of the Fields, Lately*." *Canadian Drama*, 16.1 (1990): 23-31.

Wallace, Robert, and Cynthia Zimmerman, eds. *The Work*. 304-16.

Zimmerman, Cynthia. "David French." In *Profiles in Canadian Literature*. 4th ser. 117-23.

B. **LEAVING HOME**: SELECTED REVIEWS

Bevis, R.W. "Sins of the Fathers." *Canadian Literature*, 59 (Winter 1974): 106-08.

Coe, Richard. "Toronto's Theatre Scene." *Washington Post*, 28 June 1972, E5.

Dafoe, Christopher. "*Leaving Home* Will Strike Home." *Vancouver Sun*, 13 November 1973, 35.

Dykk, Lloyd. "Tale of a Family Broken by Father's Heavy Hand." *Vancouver Sun*, 10 July 1985, B11.

Heller, Zelda. "Newfoundland Life Observed." *Montreal Star*, 12 October 1972, C16.

Kareda, Urjo. "Tarragon Theatre's Dynamic Play Quite Exceptional." *Toronto Star*, 17 May 1972.

MacCulloch, Clare. "Neither Out Far Nor in Deep." *Canadian Drama*, 2 (Spring 1976): 115-18.

McKendrick, Coral. "*Leaving Home* a Hit." *Winnipeg Free Press*, 19 March 1980, 42.

Mezei, Stephen. "Toronto Scene." *Performing Arts in Canada*, 9 (Summer 1972): 17.

Pederson, Stephen. "Actors Overcome Flawed Script." *Halifax Chronicle Herald*, 5 November 1990, A11.

Siskind, Jacob. "Leaving Home the Right Way." *Montreal Gazette*, 14 October 1972.

Whittaker, Herbert. "Some Fine Domestic Brawling." *The Globe and Mail*, 17 May 1972, 18.

——. "Kate Reid as Mother Dominates *Leaving Home*." *The Globe and Mail*, 15 November 1973, 14.

JOHN HERBERT

A. BIOGRAPHY AND CRITICISM

Anthony, Geraldine, ed. *Stage Voices*. 165-206.

Benson, Eugene, and L.W. Conolly. *ECT*. 73-75.

——, eds. *The Oxford Companion to Canadian Theatre*. 212-13, 264-65.

Carson, Neil. "Sexuality and Identity in *Fortune and Men's Eyes*." *Twentieth Century Literature*, 18 (July 1972): 207-18.

Conolly, L.W., ed. *Canadian Drama and the Critics*. 45-54.

Fulford, Robert. "A Canadian Play Makes Its Way Around The World." *Saturday Night*, 90 (October 1975): 8,12.

Herbert, John. "My Life and Hard Times in Cold, Bitter, Suspicious Toronto." *Saturday Night*, 86 (December 1971): 21-24.

Hofsess, John. "*Fortune and Men's Eyes*—A Report from the Set in a Quebec City Prison." *Maclean's*, 83 (December 1970): 81-83.

Johnson, Chris. "John Herbert." In *Canadian Writers since 1960*. 1st ser. *DLB* 53. 222-25.

Lister, Rota. "Interview with John Herbert." *Canadian Drama*, 4 (Winter 1973): 173-76.

McLarty, James. "The World According to John Herbert." *Motion*, 1 (March-April 1973): 16-21.

Messenger, Ann P. "Damnation at Christmas: John Herbert's *Fortune and Men's Eyes*." In *Dramatists in Canada*. Ed. W.H. New. 173-78.

Perkyns, Richard. "*Fortune and Men's Eyes*: An Introduction." In *Major Plays of the Canadian Theatre, 1934-1984*. 276-81.

Teague, Francis. "Prisons and Imprisonment in Canadian Drama." *Journal of Canadian Fiction*, 19 (1977): 112-21.

Tyson, Brian F. "'This Man's Art and That Man's Scope': Language and the Critics in *Fortune and Men's Eyes*." *Canadian Drama*, 4 (Spring 1978): 34-39.

B. FORTUNE AND MEN'S EYES: SELECTED REVIEWS

Barnes, Clive. "Question Marks at Stage 73." *New York Times*, 23 October 1969, 55.

Bryden, Ronald. "Theatre." *The Observer* (London), 14 July 1968.

Cohen, Nathan. "When *Fortune and Men's Eyes* Opened." *Toronto Star*, 7 September 1967.

Devin, Susan. "*Fortune and Men's Eyes* Showed a Lot of Foresight." *Toronto Star*, 3 May 1985, D15.

Dykk, Lloyd. "Prison Drama Held Captive by Its Contrived Archetypes." *Vancouver Sun*, 14 October 1992, C5.

Fraser, John. "*Fortune and Men's Eyes* Stands the Test of Time." *The Globe and Mail*, 20 November 1975, 18.

French, Philip. "Serving Time." *New Statesman*, 19 July 1968, 88-89.

Oliver, Edith. "Theater." *The New Yorker*, 43 (4 March 1967): 134.

Pedwell, Susan. "Gripping Plays Offers Slice of Life Behind Bars." *Calgary Herald*, 19 March 1980, B14.

Pritchett, Oliver. "The Power Politics of Homosexual Life." *The Guardian* (London), 21 July 1968.

Sullivan, Dan. "A Distressing *Fortune and Men's Eyes*." *New York Times*, 24 February 1967, 29.

Whittaker, Herbert. "Toronto's Jack Brundage Has a Winner." *The Globe and Mail*, 4 March 1967, 18.

SHARON POLLOCK

A. BIOGRAPHY AND CRITICISM

Baldridge, Harold. "Calgary." *CTR*, 2 (Spring 1974): 118-20.

Bessai, Diane. "Introduction." In Sharon Pollock, *Blood Relations and Other Plays*. Edmonton: NeWest Press, 1981. 7-9.

——. "Sharon Pollock's Women: A Study in Dramatic Process." In *Amazing Space: Writing Canadian Women Writing*. Ed. Shirley Neuman and Smaro Kamboureli. Edmonton: Longspoon/NeWest, 1986. 126-36.

Conolly, L.W., ed. *Canadian Drama and the Critics*. 135-44, 259-76.

Dunn, Margo. "Sharon Pollock: In the Centre Ring." *Makara*, 1 (August-September 1976): 2-6.

Fraser, Matthew. "Doc May Be Tough Pill for New Brunswick." *The Globe and Mail*, 7 March 1986, A12.

Gilbert, Reid. "Sharon Pollock." In *Profiles in Canadian Literature* 6. Ed. Jeffrey M. Heath. Toronto: Dundurn, 1986. 113-20.

Hall, Sharon K., ed. "Sharon Pollock: *Doc.*" In *Contemporary Literary Criticism: Yearbook 1987*. Vol. 50. Detroit: Gale Research, 1988. 222-27.

Hofsess, John. "Families." *Homemaker's*, 15 (March 1980): 41-60.

——. "Sharon Pollock Off-Broadway: Success as a Subtle Form of Failure." *Books in Canada*, 12 (April 1983): 3-4.

Knowles, Richard Paul. "Replaying History: Canadian Historiographic Metadrama." *Dalhousie Review*, 67 (1987): 228-43.

Loiselle, André. "Paradigms of 1980s Québéquois and Canadian Drama: Normand Chaurette's *Provincetown Playhouse, juillet 1919, j'avais 19 ans* and Sharon Pollock's *Blood Relations.*" *Québec Studies*, 14 (1992): 93-104.

Metcalfe, Robin. "Interview with Sharon Pollock." *Books in Canada*, 16 (March 1987): 39-40.

Miner, Madonna. "'Lizzie Borden Took an Ax': Enacting *Blood Relations*." *Literature in Performance*, 6 (April 1986): 10-21.

Nunn, Robert C. "Sharon Pollock's Plays: A Review Article." *Theatre History in Canada*, 5 (Spring 1984): 72-83.

Page, Malcolm. "Sharon Pollock: Committed Playwright." *Canadian Drama*, 5 (Autumn 1979): 104-11.

Perkyns, Richard. "*Generations*: An Introduction." In *Major Plays of the Canadian Theatre, 1934-1984*. 605-08.

Pollock, Sharon. "Dead or Alive? Feeling the Pulse of Canadian Theatre." *Theatrum*, 23 (April/May 1991): 12-13.

——. "Reflections of a Female Artistic Director." In *Women on the Canadian Stage*. Ed. Rita Much. 109-14.

Rudakoff, Judith, and Rita Much, eds. *Fair Play*. 208-20.

Saddlemayer, Ann. "Crime in Literature: Canadian Drama." In *Rough Justice: Essays on Crime in Literature*. Ed. Martin L. Friedman. Toronto: Univ. of Toronto Press, 1991. 214-30.

St. Pierre, Paul Mathew. "Sharon Pollock." In *Canadian Writers Since 1960*. 2nd ser. *DLB* 60. 300-06.

Stone-Blackburn, Susan. "Feminism and Metadrama: Role-Playing in *Blood Relations*." *Canadian Drama*, 15 (1989): 169-78.

Wallace, Robert, and Cynthia Zimmerman, eds. *The Work*. 115-26.

Whittaker, Herbert. "Canadian West at Stratford." *The Globe and Mail*, 22 July 1974, 14.

Zichy, Francis. "Justifying the Ways of Lizzie Borden to Men: The Play Within the Play in *Blood Relations*." *Theatre Annual*, 42 (1987): 61-81.

Zimmerman, Cynthia. "Towards a Better, Fairer World: An Interview with Sharon Pollock." *CTR*, 69 (Winter 1991): 34-38.

B. **WALSH**: SELECTED REVIEWS

Allen, Bob. "Stratford Discovers the West." *Vancouver Province*, 5 April 1974, 3.

Ashley, Audrey M. "Stratford Director, Cast Are Playwright's Delight." *Ottawa Citizen*, 25 July 1974, 50.

Bale, Doug. "Longshot Steals Show at Stratford Festival." *London Free Press*, 25 July 1974.

Brennan, Brian. "Plays Bogs Down in Enigmatic, Historical Difficulties." *Calgary Herald*, 17 January 1988, E2.

Deakin, Basil. "TAG's *Walsh*: Should Be Stuff of Good Theatre." *Halifax Chronicle Herald*, 16 June 1984, 42.

Doolittle, Joyce. "*Walsh*." *NeWest Review*, 13 (April 1988): 13.

Freedman, Adele. "NAC Brings Little to Wild West Yarn." *The Globe and Mail*, 12 May 1983, 25.

Godfrey, Stephen. "Debate Soars Above Earthbound Historical Drama." *The Globe and Mail*, 29 January 1988, A18.

Messenger, Ann P. "More Utile than Dulce." *Canadian Literature*, 65 (Summer 1975): 90-95.

Portman, Jamie. "Calgary II." *CTR*, 2 (Spring 1974): 121-23.

——. "*Walsh* Signals Red-Letter Event for TC." *Calgary Herald*, 9 November 1973.

Whittaker, Herbert. "*Walsh* Beautiful, Tedious Too." *The Globe and Mail*, 13 November 1973, 16.

——. "*Walsh* Serves Up Sad History Straight." *The Globe and Mail*, 25 July 1974, 13.

JAMES REANEY

A. BIOGRAPHY AND CRITICISM

Anthony, Geraldine, ed. *Stage Voices*. 139-64.

Benson, Eugene, and L.W. Conolly. *ECT*. 76-79.

Conolly, L.W., ed. *Canadian Drama and the Critics*. 145-55, 167-86, 302-07.

Day, Moira. "James Reaney," In *Canadian Writers, 1920-1959*. 1st ser. *DLB* 68. 282-90.

Dragland, Stan, ed. *Approaches to the Work of James Reaney*. Downsview, Ont.: ECW Press, 1983; rpt. of James Reaney Special Issue, *Essays on Canadian Writing*, (1982-83): 24-25.

——. "James Reaney's 'Pulsating Dance In and Out of Forms.'" In *The Human Elements*. Ed. David Helwig. Ottawa: Oberon, 1978. 112-33.

Huebert, Ronald. "James Reaney: Poet and Dramatist." *CTR*, 13 (Winter 1977): 125-28.

Johnston, Denis. *Up the Mainstream*. 237-49.

Jones, Manina. "'The collage in Motion': Staging the Documentary in Reaney's *Sticks and Stones*." *Canadian Drama*, 16.1 (1990): 1-22.

Kirk, Heather. "Reaney: After and Before." *Canadian Author and Bookman*, 66 (Summer 1991): 18-20.

Knowles, Richard Paul. "Replaying History: Canadian Historiographic Metadrama." *Dalhousie Review*, 67 (1987): 228-43.

Lee, Alvin. *James Reaney*. New York: Twayne, 1969.

——, and Eleanor R. Goldhar. "James Reaney." In *Profiles in Canadian Literature*. 4th ser. 17-28.

Mayo, John. "Expectations and Compacts in the Beckwith-Reaney Operas: A Case Study." *University of Toronto Quarterly*, 60 (Winter 1990-91): 305-18.

Meyer, Bruce and Brian O'Riordan. "James Reaney: Horses, Buggies and Cadillacs." In *In Their Words: Interviews with Fourteen Canadian Writers*. Toronto: Anansi, 1984. 56-70.

Miller, Mary Jane. "The Use of Stage Metaphor in *The Donnellys*." *Canadian Drama*, 8. 1 (1982): 34-41.

New, W.H., ed. *Dramatists in Canada*. 114-44.

Noonan, James. "The Critics Criticized: An Analysis of Reviews of James Reaney's *The Donnellys* on National Tour." *Canadian Drama*, 3 (Fall 1977): 174-82.

——. "Foreword" and "Concluding Essay." In James Reaney, *The Donnellys*. Victoria: Press Porcépic, 1983. 1-8, 275-88.

Parker, Gerald. "History, Story and Story-Style: James Reaney's *The Donnellys*." *Canadian Drama*, 4 (Spring 1978): 150-59.

——. *How to Play: The Theatre of James Reaney*. Toronto: ECW Press, 1991.

——. "'The Key word . . . is "listen"': James Reaney's 'Sonic Enviroment'." *Mosaic*, 14 (Fall 1981): 1-14.

Perkyns, Richard. "The Innocence of the Donnellys: James Reaney's Three-Ring Circus." *Canadian Drama*, 3 (Spring 1977): 162-73.

Reaney, James. *Fourteen Barrels from Sea to Sea*. Erin, Ont.: Press Porcépic, 1977.

——. "James Reaney Looks Towards a National Repertory." *Theatre History in Canada*, 6 (Fall 1985): 218-26.

——. "A Letter from James Reaney: Halloween." *Black Moss*, 2.1 (Spring 1976): 2-10.

——. "Ten Years at Play." *Canadian Literature*, 41 (Summer 1969): 53-61; rpt. in *Dramatists in Canada*. Ed. W.H. New. 70-78.

——. "Your Plays Are Like Movies—Cinemascope Ones." *Canadian Drama*, 5 (Spring 1979): 32-40.

Reaney, J. Stewart. *James Reaney*. Toronto: Gage, 1977.

Ricou, Laurie. *Everyday Magic: Child Languages in Canadian Literature*. Vancouver: UBC Press, 1987. Chpt. 8.

Roberts, Eric. "*Sticks and Stones*: History, Play, and Myth." *Canadian Drama*, 4 (Fall 1978): 160-72.

Smith, Patricia Keeney. "James Reaney, Playmaker." *Canadian Forum*, 60 (October 1980): 9-12.

Stingle, Richard. "James Reaney and his Works." In *Canadian Writers and Their Works*. Poetry Series, Vol. 7. Ed. Robert Lecker, et al. Toronto: ECW Press, 1990. 191-246.

Woodman, Ross. *James Reaney*. Toronto: McClelland and Stewart, 1972.

B. THE ST. NICHOLAS HOTEL:
SELECTED REVIEWS

Carroll, Michael. "*The Donnellys*: A Canadian Phenomenon in Print and on the Stage." *The Canadian Review*, 3 (September 1976): 34-36.

Kareda, Urjo. "New James Reaney Play Filled with Delights." *Toronto Star*, 18 November 1974, D6.

Leggatt, Alexander. "Letters in Canada 1976: Theatre." *University of Toronto Quarterly*, 46 (Summer 1977): 383-85.

Salter, Denis. "*The Donnellys: Part II. The St. Nicholas Hotel, Wm. Donnelly, Prop.*" *Canadian Drama*, 5 (Spring 1979): 66-68.

Souchotte, Sandra. "Assessing *The Donnellys*." *CTR*, 7 (Summer 1975): 131-35.

Whittaker, Herbert. "More About Those Legendary Donnellys." *The Globe and Mail*, 18 November 1974, 14.

In addition James Reaney has reprinted twenty reviews of *The Donnellys* in *Fourteen Barrels from Sea to Sea*, his account of the Trilogy's national tour in the fall of 1975. The reviews cover performances in London (Ont.), Winnipeg, Vancouver, Edmonton, Calgary, Ottawa, Halifax, Hamilton and Toronto. The following are the most informative:

Beaven, Scott. "*The Donnellys* Production Extraordinary." *The Albertan* (Calgary), 30 October 1975.

Dawson, Eric. "*The Donnellys: St. Nicholas Hotel.*" *The Charlatan* (Ottawa), 14 November 1975.

Fraser, John. "NDWT's Weighty Donnelly Saga Makes a Sterling Return." *The Globe and Mail*, 12 December 1975.

Galloway, Myron. "The Donnellys' Death." *Montreal Star*, 1 December 1975.

Kucherawy, Dennis. "*Donnellys*: Weep for One . . . Not for Four," *The Gazette* (London, Ont.), 10 October 1975.

ERIKA RITTER

A. BIOGRAPHY AND CRITICISM

Benson, Eugene, and L.W. Conolly, eds. *The Oxford Companion to Canadian Theatre*. 37, 470-71.

Brown, Barry. "Interview: Erika Ritter." *Books in Canada*, 11 (April 1982): 26-28.

Conlogue, Ray. "Ritter Stood Up to Research to Keep Her *Pilot* on Course." *The Globe and Mail*, 17 January 1980, 15.

Conolly, L.W., ed. *Canadian Drama and the Critics*. 246-58.

Corbeil, Carole. "Working the Dayshift and Living on Wit." *The Globe and Mail*, 14 December 1985, C3.

Knelman, Martin. "The Playwright as Star of the Play." *Saturday Night*, 93 (April 1978): 59-62.

——. "Urban Lady." *Saturday Night*, 101 (December 1986): 61-63.

Lister, Rota Herzberg. "Erika Ritter and the Comedy of Self-Actualization." In *Gynocritics: Feminist Approaches to Canadian and Quebec Women's Writing*. Ed. Barbara Godard. Toronto: ECW Press, 1987. 143-55.

Milliken, Paul. "Erika Ritter's Search for Integrity on the Stage." *Performing Arts in Canada*, 19 (Summer 1982): 33-37.

Ritter, Erika. "The Woman Playwright in English Canada." *Etudes canadiennes/Canadian Studies*, 15 (1983): 65-70.

Wallace, Robert, and Cynthia Zimmerman, eds. *The Work*. 277-91.

B. **AUTOMATIC PILOT**: SELECTED REVIEWS

Allen, Bob. "*Automatic Pilot* in High Gear." *Vancouver Province*, 17 May 1971, 12.

Ashwell, Keith. "Another Nasty Play Headed for New York." *Edmonton Journal*, 29 January 1981, D15.

Brennan, Brian. "Play is Entertaining, but 'Very Toronto'." *Calgary Herald*, 28 November 1980, C17.

Conlogue, Ray. "This *Pilot* Deserves Automatic Success." *The Globe and Mail*,18 January 1980, 15.

——. "Stand-Up Comic Toned Down." *The Globe and Mail*, 11 September 1980, 19.

Czarnecki, Mark. "Bound for Glory of the Commercial Kind." *Macleans*, 93 (14 July 1980): 54.

Dafoe, Christopher. "A Painfully Amusing Study of Emotions." *Vancouver Sun*, 12 November 1980, H1.

Edmonstone, Wayne. "*Pilot* Flawed but Flying." *Vancouver Sun*, 16 May 1981, B8.

Friedlander, Mira. "*Automatic Pilot*." *Scene Changes*, 8 (March 1980): 35-36.

Johnson, Audrey. "*Automatic Pilot*: It's More than a Comedy." *Victoria Times-Colonist*, 13 November 1980, 48.

Koehler, Robert. "Stage Beat." *Los Angeles Times*, 13 May 1988, Part VI, 7.

Mallet, Gina. "This *Pilot's* a Bit Off Course." *Toronto Star*, 18 January 1980, D1.

——. "*Automatic Pilot* Offers Better Flight." *Toronto Star*, 2 July 1980, D1.

Skene, Reg. "*Automatic Pilot* Covers Old Ground." *Winnipeg Free Press*, 14 February 1985, 39.

GEORGE RYGA

A. BIOGRAPHY AND CRITICISM

Benson, Eugene and L.W. Conolly. *ECT*. 80-83.

——, eds. *The Oxford Companion to Canadian Theatre*. 190-91, 479-81.

Boire, Gary. "Wheels on Fire: The Train of Thought in George Ryga's *The Ecstasy of Rita Joe*." *Canadian Literature*, 113-14 (Summer-Fall 1987): 62-74.

Carson, Neil. "George Ryga and the Lost Country." *Canadian Literature*, 45 (Summer 1970): 33-40; rpt. in *Dramatists in Canada*, ed. W.H. New. 155-62.

Conolly, L.W., ed. *Canadian Drama and the Critics*. 41-44, 55-68.

Gerson, Mark. "The International Acceptance of Playwright George Ryga." *Performing Arts in Canada*, 19 (Fall 1982): 43-46.

Grace, Sherrill. "The Expressionist Legacy in the Canadian Theatre: George Ryga and Robert Gurik." *Canadian Literature*, 118 (Autumn 1988): 47-58.

Hay, Peter. "George Ryga: Beginnings of a Biography." *CTR*, 23 (Summer 1979): 36-44.

——. "The Psychology of Distortion: A Rebuttal of Christopher Innes." *Theatre History in Canada*, 7.1 (Spring 1986): 119-24.

Innes, Christopher. *Politics and the Playwright: George Ryga*. Toronto: Simon & Pierre, 1985.

Johnson, Chris. "Amerindians and Aborigines in English Canadian and Australian Drama, 1606-1975." *Canadian Drama*, 10.2 (1984): 167-87.

Maracle, Lee. "A Question of Voice." *Vancouver Sun*, 6 June 1992, D9.

Martinez, Jill. "An Interview with George Ryga." *Journal of Canadian Fiction*, 35/36 (1986): 106-21.

Moore, Mavor. *4 Canadian Playwrights*. 68-75.

——. "Introduction," In *Two Plays by George Ryga*. Winnipeg: Turnstone Press, 1982. 1-7.

Parker, Brian. "The Ballad-Plays of George Ryga." In *The Ecstasy of Rita Joe and Other Plays*. Toronto: new press, 1971. vii-xx.

——. "Is There a Canadian Drama?" In *The Canadian Imagination*. Ed. David Staines. 152-87.

Parker, Dorothy. "George Ryga." In *Profiles in Canadian Literature*, 4th ser.: 61-68.

Ryga, George. "The Artist in Resistance." *CTR*, 33 (Winter 1982): 86-91.

——. *The Athabasca Ryga*. Ed. E. David Gregory. Vancouver: Talonbooks, 1990.

——. "Contemporary Theatre and Its Language." *CTR*, 14 (Spring 1977): 4-9.

——. "The Need for a Mythology." *CTR*, 16 (Fall 1977): 4-6.

——. *Summerland*. Ed. Ann Kujundzic. Vancouver: Talonbooks, 1992.

——. "Theatre in Canada: A Viewpoint on Its Development and Future." *CTR*, 1 (Winter 1974): 28-32.

Saddlemayer, Ann. "Crime in Literature: Canadian Drama." In *Rough Justice: Essays on Crime in Literature*. Ed. Martin L. Friedland. Toronto: Univ. of Toronto Press, 1991. 214-30.

Teague, Francis. "Prisons and Imprisonment in Canadian Drama." *Journal of Canadian Fiction*, 19 (1977): 112-21.

Wasserman, Jerry. "George Ryga." In *Canadian Writers Since 1960*. 2nd ser. *DLB* 60. 320-24.

Watson, David, and Christopher Innes. "Political Mythologies: An Interview with George Ryga." *Canadian Drama*, 8.2 (1982): 160-72.

Wilson, Peter. "Rita Joe Still Leads to More Anger than Ecstasy." *Vancouver Sun*, 19 March 1992, C1, 5.

Worthington, Bonnie. "Ryga's Women." *Canadian Drama*, 5 (Fall 1979): 139-43.

Zichy, Francis. "Rita Joe in New York: An Interview with Gordon McCall." *NeWest Review*, 10 (Summer 1985): 15-17.

B. THE ECSTASY OF RITA JOE:
SELECTED REVIEWS

Conlogue, Ray. "Long Awaited *Rita Joe* Misses the Mark." *The Globe and Mail*, 11 November 1989, C10.

Crew, Robert. "More Agony Than Ecstasy in *Rita Joe*." *Toronto Star*, 12 November 1989, C10.

Donnelly, Pat. "High Energy Approach in *Rita Joe*." *Montreal Gazette*, 10 March 1989, C6.

Donnelly, Tom. "Theater Journal: Two Views." *Washington Post*, 9 May 1973, F4.

Dykk, Lloyd. "Odd Poetic Touch Fails to Fill Emotional Void." *Vancouver Sun*, 20 March 1992, C5.

Howard, Irene. "Vancouver Theatre Diary: Two Companies and Their Audience." *Canadian Forum*, 47 (February 1968): 252-54.

Kucherawy, Dennis. "Play Stirs New Controversy." *Vancouver Province*, 30 November 1981, B6.

McCracken, Rosemary. "Young Cast Electrifies Play." *Calgary Herald*, 5 April 1984, D1.

Popkin, Henry. "*The Ecstasy of Rita Joe*: A Drama of American Indian Life." *Christian Science Monitor*, 11 June 1973, 12.

Portman, Jamie. "*Ecstasy of Rita Joe* Still Manages to Shock and Scourge." *Vancouver Province*, 12 April 1976, 10.

Richards, Jack. "World Premiere Lays Bare Tragedy of Canadian Society." *Vancouver Sun*, 24 November 1967, 6.

Shales, Tom. "*Ecstasy of Rita Joe*." *Washington Post*, 3 May 1973, B1, 8.

Skene, Reg. "*Ecstasy of Rita Joe* a Powerful Piece of Theatre." *Winnipeg Free Press*, 26 November 1981, 55.

Wardle, Irving. "A Pogrom in Canada." *The Times* (London), 23 September 1975, 12.

RICK SALUTIN and THEATRE PASSE MURAILLE

A. BIOGRAPHY AND CRITICISM

Arnott, Brian. "The Passe Muraille Alternative." In *The Human Elements*. Ed. David Helwig. Ottawa: Oberon, 1978. 97-111.

Bessai, Diane. *Playwrights of Collective Creation*. Toronto: Simon & Pierre, 1992.

Benson, Eugene, and L.W. Conolly, eds. *The Oxford Companion to Canadian Theatre*. 106-08, 486-87, 543-44, 554.

Conolly, L.W., ed. *Canadian Drama and the Critics*. 156-66.

Copeman, Peter. "Rick Salutin and the Popular Dramatic Tradition: Towards a Dialectical Theatre in Canada." *Canadian Drama*, 10 (Spring 1984): 25-34.

——. "Rick Salutin: The Meaning of It All," *CTR*, 34 (Spring 1982): 190-97.

Filewood, Alan. *Collective Encounters*. Chpt. 1-2.

Johns, Ted. "An Interview with Paul Thompson." *Performing Arts in Canada*, 10 (Winter 1973): 30-32.

Johnston, Denis. *Up the Mainstream*. Chpt. 2, 4.

Knowles, Richard Paul. "Replaying History: Canadian Historiographic Metadrama." *Dalhousie Review*, 67 (1987): 228-43.

Miller, Mary Jane. "The Documentary Drama of Paul Thompson." *Saturday Night*, 89 (July 1974): 35-37.

——. "Two Versions of Rick Salutin's *Les Canadiens*." *Theatre History in Canada*, 1 (Spring 1980): 57-69.

Moore, Christopher. "The Return of the Firebrand." *Books in Canada*, 17 (March 1988): 3.

Noonan, James. "Rick Salutin." In *Profiles in Canadian Literature*. 8th ser. 61-68.

Nunn, Robert C. "Performing Fact: Canadian Documentary Theatre." *Canadian Literature*, 103 (Winter 1984): 51-62.

Rudakoff, Judith, ed. *Dangerous Traditions: A Passe Muraille Anthology*. Winnipeg: Blizzard, 1992.

Posesorski, Sherie. "Interview: Rick Salutin." *Books in Canada*, 14 (April 1985): 40-41.

Salutin, Rick. *Marginal Notes: Challenges to the Mainstream*. Toronto: Lester & Orpen Dennys, 1984.

——. *1837: William Lyon Mackenzie and the Canadian Revolution*. Toronto: Lorimer, 1976.

Usmiani, Renate. *Second Stage*. 43-65.

Wallace, Bob. "Paul Thompson at Theatre Passe Muraille: Bits and Pieces." *Open Letter*, 2.7 (Winter 1974): 49-71.

——, and Cynthia Zimmerman, eds. *The Work*. 237-63.

Whittaker, Herbert. "Playwright Rick Salutin: Sniffing Out the Stuff of History." *The Globe and Mail*, 18 January 1973, 11.

Wilson, Paul. "Blyth Spirit [Paul Thompson]." *Books in Canada*, 12 (April 1983): 10-13.

B. **1837: THE FARMERS' REVOLT**: SELECTED REVIEWS

Ashley, Audrey M. "Skimpy Sketches Illustrate Drama." *Ottawa Citizen*, 9 November 1976, 71.

Boru, Brian. "The Spirit of '37: History as Hypothesis." *That's Show Business*, 14 August 1974, 5.

Buttle, Jeff. "*Farmers' Revolt* Disproves Claim Canadian History Dull." *Vancouver Sun*, 20 July 1989, 10.

Conlogue, Ray. "Farmers' Rebellion Stands Test of Time." *The Globe and Mail*, 8 December 1987, D7.

Kareda, Urjo. "History Comes to Life." *Toronto Star*, 18 January 1973.

O'Toole, Lawrence. "*1837*: Dull History Played as Fiercely Involving Anarchy." *The Globe and Mail*, 13 September 1974, 13.

Pappert-Martinello, Margaret. "Revolutionary Parallels." *Essays on Canadian Writing*, 7/8 (Fall 1977): 196-99.

Skene, Reg. "*Farmers' Revolt* Slowed by Stretches of Theatrical Tedium." *Winnipeg Free Press*, 2 April 1981, 27.

Whittaker, Herbert. "*1837* Engrossing Handling of History." *The Globe and Mail*, 19 January 1973, 15.

——. "Passe Muraille Becoming Top Touring Company." *The Globe and Mail*, 29 May 1974, 14.

Wood, Susan. "Found History." *Canadian Literature*, 81 (Summer 1979): 111-12.

Wyman, Max. "An Indisputable Star in a Troupe Not Meant to Have any Stars." *Vancouver Sun*, 29 March 1976, 43.

MICHEL TREMBLAY

Note: Only English-language books, articles and reviews are listed below; a much more substantial body of commentary on Tremblay is available in French. For an annotated bibliography (in French) of both English and French criticism and reviews of Tremblay's work through 1982, see *Voix & Images*, 7.2 (Winter 1982): 225-306.

A. BIOGRAPHY AND CRITICISM

Ackerman, Marianne. "Sweet Jesus! Who's That, Ma?" *Saturday Night*, 103 (June 1988): 40-47.

Anthony, Geraldine, ed. *Stage Voices*. 275-90.

Babington, Doug. "The Shared Voice of Michel Tremblay." *Queen's Quarterly*, 99 (Winter 1992): 1074-81.

Baldassarre, Angie. "The Art Laid Bare." *Performing Arts in Canada*, 26 (Summer 1991): 5-8.

Benson, Eugene, and L.W. Conolly, eds. *The Oxford Companion to Canadian Theatre*. 34-35, 49-50, 59-60, 568-71.

Chadbourne, Richard. "Michel Tremblay's 'Adult Fairy Tales': The Theatre as Realistic Fantasy." *Québec Studies*, 10 (Spring/Summer 1990): 61-68.

Collett, Paulette. "Fennario's *Balconville* and Tremblay's *En Pièces détachées: A Universe of Backyards and Despair*." *Canadian Drama*, 10 (Spring 1984): 35-43.

Dorsinville, Max. "The Changing Landscape of Drama in Quebec." In *Dramatists in Canada*. Ed. W.H. New. 179-95.

Findlay, Bill. "Translating Tremblay into Scots." *Theatre Research International*, 17.2 (Summer 1992): 138-45.

Gerson, Mark. "The Indelible Mark of Michel Tremblay's Theatre." *Performing Arts in Canada*, 18 (Winter 1981): 25-27.

Kapica, Jack. "The Incredible Saga of *Les Belles-Soeurs*, or . . . How a Writer Found Fame Could Be a Costly Gain." *Montreal Gazette*, 27 October 1973, 25.

Knelman, Martin. "The Outlandish *joual* World of Michel Tremblay." *Saturday Night*, 90 (May 1975): 79-83.

Koustas, Jane. "From Gélinas to Carrier: Critical Response to Translated Quebec Theatre in Toronto." *Studies in Canadian Literature*, 17.2 (1992): 109-28.

Loiselle, André. "Film-Mediated Drama: André Brassard's Film *Il était une fois dans l'Est* as a Pivot in Michel Tremblay's Dramaturgy." *Essays in Theatre*, 10.2 (May 1992): 165-80.

McCaughna, David. "Michel Tremblay: No Longer 'That Nasty Boy from Quebec'." *Scene Changes*, 3 (February/March 1975): 9-10.

McQuaid, Catherine. "Michel Tremblay's Seduction of the 'Other Solitude'." *Canadian Drama*, 2 (Fall 1976): 219-23.

"Michel Tremblay Casebook." *CTR*, 24 (Fall 1979): 11-51.

Nunn, Robert C. "Tremblay's *Hosanna* and Pirandello's 'teatro dello specio'." *Canadian Drama*, 6 (Fall 1980): 201-12.

Parker, Brian. "Is There a Canadian Drama?" In *The Canadian Imagination*. Ed. David Staines. 152-87.

Poteet, Susan. "Mind Your Own Language." *Theatrum*, 20 (September/October 1990): 16-19.

Quig, James. "The Joual Revolution: Playwright Michel Tremblay." *The Canadian Magazine*, 14 May 1977, 16-19

Rae, Lisbie. "Tremblay at P'tit Bonheur, 1982-1985." *Canadian Drama*, 13.1 (1987): 1-26.

Ripley, John. "From Alienation to Transcendence: The Quest for Selfhood in Michel Tremblay's Plays." *Canadian Literature*, 85 (Summer 1980): 44-59.

Rudakoff, Judith. "Michel Tremblay." In *Profiles in Canadian Literature*. 6th ser. 65-72.

Sabbath, Lawrence. "Tremblay Ponders His English Prohibition." *Montreal Star*, 11 December 1976, D11.

"*Sainte Carmen of the Main* and the Plays of Michel Tremblay: A Panel Discussion." *Canadian Drama*, 14.2 (1988): 206-23.

Salter, Denis. "Who's Speaking Here? Tremblay's Scots Voice." *CTR*, 74 (Spring 1993): 40-45.

Smith, Donald. *Voices of Deliverance: Interviews*

with Quebec and Acadian Writers. Trans. Larry Shouldice. Toronto: Anansi, 1986. 205-41.

Twigg, Alan. *For Openers: Conversations with 24 Canadian Writers.* Madeira Park, B.C.: Harbour, 1981. 151-61.

Usmiani, Renate. *Michel Tremblay.* Vancouver: Douglas & McIntyre, 1982.

——. "Michel Tremblay." In *Canadian Writers Since 1960,* 2nd ser. *DLB* 60. 342-52.

——. "Michel Tremblay's *Sainte Carmen*: Synthesis and Orchestration." *Canadian Drama,* 2.2 (1976): 206-17.

——. "The Musical Comedies of Michel Tremblay: A Lighter Side of Alienation and Identity Crisis." *Canadian Drama,* 6 (Fall 1980): 192-200.

——. *The Theatre of Frustration: Super Realism in the Dramatic Work of F.X. Kroetz and Michel Tremblay.* N.Y.: Garland, 1990.

Weiss, Jonathan M. *French-Canadian Theatre.* 27-48.

B. **LES BELLES-SOEURS:** SELECTED REVIEWS

Abrams, Tevia. "Theatre du Rideau-Vert Opens New Season with *Les Belles-Soeurs.*" *Montreal Gazette,* 29 August 1988, 24.

Ackerman, Marianne. "*Belles-Soeurs* Stands Test of Time." *Montreal Gazette,* 31 March 1984, C9.

Bolster, Charles. "*Les Belles-Soeurs* a Microcosm of Quebecois Society." *Edmonton Journal,* 17 May 1980, B16.

Chapman, Geoff. "*Soeurs* Cast Lights Up Social Comment." *Toronto Star,* 3 June 1991, B3.

Conlogue, Ray. "A Celebration of Woman's Progress." *The Globe and Mail,* 2 March 1993, A11.

——. "Working-Class Heroines." *The Globe and Mail,* 4 June 1991, A10.

Corbeil, Carole. "The Aging of Tremblay's *Les Belles-Soeurs.*" *The Globe and Mail,* 28 June 1984, E2.

Garebian, Keith. "Liberation in the Rag-and-Bone Shop." *Canadian Literature,* 66 (Autumn 1975): 112-16.

Hawthorn, Maggie. "You'll Feel Guilty But You'll Laugh." *Seattle Post-Intelligencer,* 9 March 1979, 18.

Heller, Zelda. "Tremblay's *Belles-Soeurs* Landmark in Quebec Theatre." *Montreal Star,* 25 May 1971, 64.

Kapica, Jack. "*Les Belles-Soeurs* a Triumph." *Montreal Gazette,* 11 October 1973, 36.

Kareda, Urjo. "*Les Belles-Soeurs* a Breath of Life." *Toronto Star,* 4 April 1973.

Kelly, Brendan. "A Gem in Any Language," *Financial Post,* 5 October 1992, S7.

Malina, Marten. "Rideau Vert Opens New Season with Play by André Brassard." *Montreal Star,* 29 August 1968, 38.

Mezei, Stephen. "Tremblay's Toronto Success." *Performing Arts in Canada,* 10 (Summer 1973): 26.

Monahan, Iona. "Dynamic Quebecers Triumph: Parisians Bow to *Les Belles Soeurs.*" *Montreal Star,* 23 November 1973, B8.

Portman, Jamie. "London's *Belles Soeurs* Bubbles." *Montreal Gazette,* 8 March 1977, 42.

Sabbath, Lawrence. "*Belles-Soeurs*: Canadian Masterpiece." *Montreal Star,* 11 October 1973, C10.

——. "New Run Proves Greatness of *Les Belles-Soeurs.*" *Montreal Star,* 20 June 1974, B15.

Siskind, Jacob. "At the Rideau Vert Tremblay Comedy Revived Brilliantly." *Montreal Gazette,* 31 May 1971, 26.

Whittaker, Herbert. "*Les Belles-Soeurs* Milestone Play." *The Globe and Mail,* 4 April 1973, 13.

——. "*Belles Soeurs* Bright Light for St. Lawrence." *The Globe and Mail,* 7 May 1973, 14.

Wyman, Max. "*Les Belles Soeurs*: A Gem of Comic Commentary." *Vancouver Sun,* 4 March 1976, 37.